Worlds Elsewhere

*Journeys around
Shakespeare's globe*

ANDREW DICKSON

THE BODLEY HEAD
LONDON

1 3 5 7 9 10 8 6 4 2

The Bodley Head, an imprint of Vintage,
20 Vauxhall Bridge Road,
London SW1V 2SA

The Bodley Head is part of the Penguin Random House
group of companies whose addresses can be found at
global.penguinrandomhouse.com

 Penguin
Random House
UK

First published by The Bodley Head in 2015

www.vintage-books.co.uk

Grateful acknowledgement is given to Bob Dylan for permission to reproduce copyright material from 'Stuck
Inside of Mobile with the Memphis Blue Again' © Dwarf Music 1966, renewed 1994

A CIP catalogue record for this book is available from the British Library

ISBN 9781847922458 (Hardback)
ISBN 9781847923424 (Trade Paperback)

Typeset in Dante MT by Palimpsest Book Production Ltd, Falkirk, Stirlingshire

Printed and bound by Clays Ltd, St Ives plc

Penguin Random House is committed to a sustainable future for
our business, our readers and our planet. This book is made from
Forest Stewardship Council® certified paper.

For my parents

Shakespeare one gets acquainted with without knowing how.
It is a part of an Englishman's constitution.

— Jane Austen, *Mansfield Park*

There is a world elsewhere.

— *Coriolanus*

Contents

Prologue

The theatre was packed, people jostling for position. As I watched, three men detached themselves from the crowd and began slowly to climb the steps. A ripple of applause washed over them as they came up on to the stage. Acknowledging it, they glanced around – surprised, bemused to find themselves here in the flat grey light of an English summer afternoon. They were decently dressed, if perhaps a little shabby: long *perahan* tunics in grey and mud-brown, loose trousers, jackets, rubber sandals. Orange security lanyards flapped at their necks. They carried bags; one had a rug slung across his arm. They looked fresh off the plane, and dusty with tiredness.

They settled themselves down, cross-legged, on one side of the stage. Ceremonially, the rug was laid out. The carry-on bags disgorged a series of unlikely objects: a small drum, a case of wooden flutes, a much larger rug. One of the men unzipped what looked like a violin case and produced an Afghan lute, the colour of fresh honey, bristling with pegs and frets. After a few lazy skitterings up the fingerboard, he glanced towards his colleagues. The crowd hushed. Somewhere nearby, there was a brief splash of birdsong. Quietly, insistently, the musicians began to play.

It was June 2012, and I had come to the Globe theatre in London. The company were called Rah-e-Sabz ('Path to Hope'), and they were from Afghanistan; they were about to perform a version of *The Comedy of Errors* translated into Dari Persian. The performance was part of a festival of global Shakespeare, scheduled to coincide with the Olympic Games. Performers from Brazil, Iraq, Tunisia, South Africa, Poland, Turkey, China, Spain, Zimbabwe – nearly fifty countries, all told – had been invited to bring productions to Britain. It was the largest jamboree of its kind in history. Cantonese, Armenian, Bengali, Castilian Spanish, Palestinian Arabic: the plays had been translated into a tumult of languages, many of which had barely been heard on British stages and certainly not in dramas by Shakespeare.

The Comedy of Errors was a brave choice, and not just for a company that had only been in existence a few years and never visited the UK. The text is a notoriously tall order. Two sets of identical twins (two masters, two servants) find themselves separated by a shipwreck. One pair end up in Ephesus (in present-day Turkey) – set up home, settle down. The master marries, the servant gets engaged. Life goes on. Little do they know that their brothers have set off from Syracuse (present-day Sicily) in search of them and have just arrived in town. For the Sicilian twins all hell breaks loose: people they have never met keep recognising them, tradesmen turn up with goods they haven't ordered. Mysterious women sidle up, claiming to share intimate histories. For the Turkish ones, it's nearly as bad: everyone in town suddenly seems to have gone crazy. Not realising they are constantly being mistaken for their twins, all four fear they are bewitched or – worse – going mad.

For most of its history on stage in the west, *The Comedy of Errors* – perhaps one of Shakespeare's first plays, written in the early 1590s – has been dismissed as an apprentice piece, a creaky and mechanistic farce in the mode of the Roman comedian Plautus, on whose work it was based. Even nowadays it is still a rarity, especially compared to more popular comedies such as *A Midsummer Night's Dream* or *As You Like It*. British directors fight shy of its rampant improbabilities, its strenuously Elizabethan wordplay, its corny sight gags (and how does one even go about *casting* two sets of twins?).

But as I watched Rah-e-Sabz perform with their three musicians, notionally setting the play in contemporary Kabul, I saw something quite new. The word 'comedy' was in the title, but it had escaped me how rueful *The Comedy of Errors* was; how much it dwelt on exile, separation. I'd forgotten altogether the character of Egeon, father to two of the twins, who prior to the action has been searching the world for five years, frantic to find his absent sons. He, too, arrives in Ephesus / Kabul and is brusquely arrested for being an illegal immigrant, then placed on death row (here by a female officer in the uniform of the corrupt, western-backed Afghan national police force).

There was farce aplenty, a joyous amount of yelling and chasing around with brooms, but much else seemed fraught. The visiting twins, Antipholus (renamed Arsalan) and Dromio (Bostan), were given an extended Laurel-and-Hardy sequence in which they were required to swap clothes – something that produced hoots in the audience but also had the sinister implication that it was too dangerous to stay as they were. Arsalan was played by the actor Abdul Haq as a lugubrious, haunted-looking character, in flight from something grim in his past. I had to consult the copy of the script on my knee to remind myself what he was saying during a soliloquy in act one, but what I read made me catch my breath:

> He that commends me to mine own content
> Commends me to the thing I cannot get.
> I to the world am like a drop of water
> That in the ocean seeks another drop,
> Who, falling there to find his fellow forth,
> Unseen, inquisitive, confounds himself.
> So I, to find a mother and a brother,
> In quest of them, unhappy, lose myself.

There was laughter as he spoke the lines, but a soft murmur went around a group of Persian-speaking women standing in the yard in front of me; recognition, perhaps.

Rah-e-Sabz's space at the British Council in Kabul had been destroyed in a suicide-bomb attack the previous year; they'd had to rehearse in Bangalore. The actor playing Egeon's wife, Parwin Mushtahel, now lived in Canada, forced into exile after her husband was murdered because she dared perform in public. Nobody here needed reminding what it felt like to lose yourself, thousands of miles away from the people you loved.

The company's work had been held up as a brave example of how theatre could fight back against religious fundamentalism: it was that, certainly. It was also an example of how Shakespeare's plays could take root in places geographically and ideologically remote from those of sixteenth-century England (though, one could argue, not *that* remote: the Taliban had plenty in common with the Puritans who detested Elizabethan theatre).

But as we worked towards the conclusion of *The Comedy of Errors*, as father and mother and brothers, separated for so long, hugged each other disbelievingly, it occurred to me that there was something else, too. This story of journeys, mistakes, confusions, misplaced identities

– being in a strange land, trying to know and comprehend its culture, finding both less and more than you ever imagined – asked a question that lay at the root of global Shakespeare. What does it really feel like to travel?

In Britain, no one really seemed sure what to make of the World Shakespeare Festival. After a brief show of interest, many newspapers tired of the novelty of companies from far-flung countries bringing versions of Shakespeare in languages few journalists could understand. Critics trooped out en masse to see the home-grown highlights – a production of *Timon of Athens* at the National Theatre (an almost unheard-of rarity); the Royal Shakespeare Company's ostensibly 'African' *Julius Caesar* (in fact cast entirely in Britain, with actors from a variety of heritages). News correspondents made sure to be there at the Globe for *The Merchant of Venice* by the Israeli company Habima, briefly interrupted by pro-Palestinian protests. Yet although audiences attended in their thousands, some of the other shows that came – *The Merry Wives of Windsor* in Swahili, *The Winter's Tale* in Yoruba – had barely any reviewers at all.

No doubt logistics were partly responsible: so much else was going on that summer that it was hard to know where to look. But I thought I detected something revealing in the world-weary shrug that greeted much of the World Shakespeare Festival: a very British reluctance to acknowledge that Shakespeare really belongs to anyone else.

It is almost a joke that the British have made our National Poet an integral part of our national identity. More than once, we have voted him one of our Greatest Britons. He is resident deity at the Royal Shakespeare Company and Shakespeare's Globe, and patron saint of the Royal National Theatre, where a plaque with his name graces the foundation stone of the building. His works have been compulsory on the British National Curriculum since its foundation in the 1980s, and a major part of British education for at least 150 years. In pubs called things like the Shakespeare's Head and the Shakespeare, we toast him with pints of lukewarm Flowers bitter (logo: the poet's head), named after the Stratford brewing dynasty that helped build the RSC's predecessor, the Shakespeare Memorial Theatre. (Alas for Little Englanders, Flowers is now owned by the Belgian-Brazilian multinational Anheuser-Busch InBev.)

Shakespeare is a brand as recognisably British as the London Routemaster bus or Queen Elizabeth II's head. Until recently he acted as our financial guarantor: up to 1993, an image of Peter Scheemakers' statue of the poet in Westminster Abbey graced the £20 note, and for many years British cheque-guarantee cards were marked with a hologram of Shakespeare's face. Despite the UK's mistrustful, high-handed attitude to the EU, there is currently a British-led plan to make him European laureate.

Patriotism turns, on occasion, to jingoism. We become defensive when theatre companies from abroad bring their own Shakespeares to these shores. ('We have quite enough gimmicky Shakespeare of our own,' huffed the *Telegraph*'s critic of a Brazilian *Richard III*. 'Do we really need to import it?') Numerous Conservative politicians have cited as their favourite lines in literature the St Crispin's Day speech in *Henry V*, which precedes the glorious trampling of the French at the Battle of Agincourt. Guests on one of the BBC's most-loved interview programmes, *Desert Island Discs*, are – once they have selected the eight pieces of music that would accompany them to a deserted and exotic location – informed that they will also be issued with the complete works of Shakespeare and the Bible by default, for all the world as if they were nineteenth-century missionaries. Simply to get into the BBC studio, they have to pass beneath Eric Gill's sculpture of Prospero and Ariel, which stands on the facade of Broadcasting House in central London.

The cult attains a discomfiting intensity in Stratford-upon-Avon, centre of what the motorway signs call 'Shakespeare's County', Warwickshire – the symbolic as well as literal heart of England. A few months before watching Rah-e-Sabz at the Globe, I went up to Stratford for the annual birthday celebrations, the first time I'd seen them. What I witnessed I found puzzling: a cross between town fete (Morris dancers and decorated floats), militaristic tourist spectacle (cub scouts and the Band of the Royal Engineers) and Bardolatrous seance (volunteers dressed up as Master and Mistress Shakespeare). None of this is especially surprising: the celebrations have their origin in the tub-thumpingly patriotic 'Shakespeare Jubilee' of 1769 masterminded by the great actor-manager David Garrick, which – among many bizarre pieces of pageantry – featured the ritual humiliation of a 'Frenchman' followed by a passionate avowal of Shakespeare's flinty Britishness. What any of it has to do with an early-modern playwright is exceedingly hard to tell.

Even Shakespeare's birthday seems, the closer one looks, like a way of burnishing the patriotic myth. It has become conventional to celebrate it on 23 April. Yet the records are unclear, and no one knows for sure that William Shakespeare *was* born on 23 April – he might just as easily have come into this world on the 21st or the 22nd. But 23 April is St George's Day, the patron saint of England. So 23 April the anointed day has become.

Later that summer I sat down to watch the Olympic opening ceremony, broadcast from the stadium a couple of miles from my home in east London. Its contents had been kept rigorously secret; all I or anyone else knew was that Danny Boyle, a sometime theatre director, had chosen the theme of 'Isles of Wonder', a nod to *The Tempest* and Team GB's very own world-beating Bard.

With an estimated 900 million others, I watched scenes of Maypolers cavorting on the greensward and cricketers running up to bowl. I looked on, a little more apprehensively, as choirs of children from across the British Isles piped their way through 'Jerusalem', 'Danny Boy', 'Flower of Scotland' and 'Guide me, O Thou Great Redeemer'. Where *was* this Shakespearian theme we had all been promised? Was this meant to be it?

Then the actor Kenneth Branagh strode forward, in waistcoat and stovepipe as the nineteenth-century engineer Isambard Kingdom Brunel, and declaimed, to the swelling strains of Elgar's 'Nimrod', a speech many can recite from memory:

> Be not afeard. The isle is full of noises,
> Sounds, and sweet airs, that give delight and hurt not.
> Sometimes a thousand twangling instruments
> Will hum about mine ears, and sometime voices
> That if I then had waked after long sleep
> Will make me sleep again; and then in dreaming
> The clouds methought would open and show riches
> Ready to drop on me, that when I waked
> I cried to dream again.

Words spoken by an oppressed and imprisoned slave, Caliban, in a play, *The Tempest*, that dwells at length on the costs and consequences of colonialism, were being repurposed as a eulogy for the British Empire, placed above music by Edwardian England's most patriotic composer and replayed for the watching world.

As I flicked off the television, I wondered if I would ever discover how Britain had acquired such a curious, conflicted attitude to its National Poet.

Of the numerous things odd about this, the most obvious one is that there was never anything especially British about William Shakespeare.

Granted, if one plots the known facts of his life on a map, the route runs from Warwickshire to London and back again, not far from what is now the M40 motorway corridor. Born in Stratford-upon-Avon, educated at a grammar school a few streets away from his birthplace, Shakespeare married a local girl and had three children with her. By the early 1590s he was in London, a hundred miles south-east. Even the capital seems to have been a temporary halt: Shakespeare never bought a permanent residence there, preferring to acquire property back home in Warwickshire, where he retired (scholars guess) a few years before his death. He was buried in April 1616, in the same town as his forefathers, and the same church where he had been baptised fifty-two years earlier.

A few adventurous biographers have detected glimpses of the playwright in Lancashire (in the so-called 'lost years' between the birth of his twins in 1585 and the first record of him as a playwright in 1592), but the traces are spotty and unconvincing. Even more unconvincing are legends that Shakespeare travelled in continental Europe, perhaps as a soldier: no evidence whatsoever. It is equally feasible that he never went further north than the Midlands, or further south than the London borough of Southwark. In London, one can still pace out his daily commute: from the parish of St Helen's, Bishopsgate, near Liverpool Street station, down through the City and across London Bridge, past Southwark cathedral (then St Mary Overie) to the Globe or the Rose, perhaps with detours via the bookstalls around St Paul's or to Clerkenwell, where scripts were approved by the Master of the Revels. At most, the area covers a few square miles.

But while his physical existence was cramped and confined, Shakespeare's imagination roamed far and free. Taking advantage of the worlds opened up by a grammar-school education and the Elizabethan explosion in publishing (especially travel publishing), he made innumerable voyages of discovery.

Via the historians Halle and Holinshed, he trod the bloody territory of his own country through the Middle Ages and beyond, filling out their chronicle accounts with a cacophony of Welsh, Scottish and French voices. Despite Ben Jonson's gibe about his older colleague's 'smalle Latin and lesse Greeke', Shakespeare raided classical sources with magpie enthusiasm, reading Ovid and Virgil in the original and English translation, and exhibiting an impressive knowledge of Roman comedy and the tragedies of Seneca. He scoured Plutarch's *Lives* – in a version that had been translated via French – for the traces of Caesar, Coriolanus, Cleopatra and Antony on their journeys through the ancient world. The sonnets and narrative poems show the heavy imprint of Dante and Petrarch. On his shelves at various times were copies of Montaigne's *Essais*, collections of Italian and French tales (some read in their original languages) and accounts of journeys around North Africa and the Mediterranean and to the Americas.

Little wonder the plays Shakespeare wrote bestride the world. His characters hail from Tunisia, the Levant, Algeria, India; his dramatic imagination roams restlessly across France, Denmark, Austria, Turkey, Greece, covering a veritable gazetteer of far-flung destinations. He has a particular passion for Italy: Padua (*The Taming of the Shrew*), Venice (*The Merchant of Venice, Othello*), Verona (*The Two Gentlemen of Verona, Romeo and Juliet*), Sicily (*Much Ado About Nothing*); and, behind it, for ancient Rome (*Titus Andronicus, Julius Caesar, Coriolanus*, parts of *Antony and Cleopatra*).

In fact, he seems actively to have avoided writing about the Britain of his own lifetime: the plays Shakespeare does locate in the British Isles are either distanced by time (the English histories) or by theme (the ancient Britain of *King Lear*, feudal Scotland in *Macbeth*, the Roman invasion-era *Cymbeline*). In arresting contrast to born-and-bred Londoners such as Ben Jonson, Thomas Dekker and Thomas Middleton, whose plays place on stage the city in which they lived and breathed, Shakespeare sets only one full script, *The Merry Wives of Windsor*, in anything resembling the Elizabethan world he knew.

On a microscopic level, too, the scripts are littered with tiny but telling references to what Coriolanus calls 'a world elsewhere'. *Macbeth*'s Witches make fleeting mention of the disastrous far-Eastern voyage of the *Tiger*, one of whose shipmates went on to found the East India Company; *Henry V*'s prologue glances at the Earl of Essex's campaign in Ireland; *Love's Labour's Lost* pokes sly fun at the inept diplomacy of Ivan the Terrible. Hamlet frets that his fortunes will 'turn Turk'. In *Measure for Measure* we hear gossip about 'China dishes'. The 'Indies' – in Shakespeare's time America as well as the Indian subcontinent and Indonesia – make a fleeting appearance in several texts, notably *A Midsummer Night's Dream*, where Oberon and Titania wage a fairy-tale war over an enigmatic boy 'stolen from an Indian king'. No fewer than five plays – *Dream, Henry VI Part III, The Merchant of Venice, Much Ado About Nothing* and *Richard II* – mention that remotest location of all from England, the 'Antipodes'.

Shakespeare was not merely indulging his own curiosity about worlds elsewhere (or those of his audiences); as scholars have recently begun to understand, he reflected the world as it was changing around him. Though England lagged far behind colonial powers such as Spain and Portugal, international trade had begun to make its presence felt by the end of the sixteenth century, particularly in London, where the Royal Exchange became a nexus for merchants from across the globe. In 1600, the East India Company was founded to capitalise on the spice routes through Arabia and towards Asia, while other joint-stock companies soon thrust west towards the Americas. In 1603 the Scottish James I took the throne, accompanied by his Danish queen, Anne, ushering in a new, more geopolitically open era after the combative defensiveness of the Elizabethan period.

As well as experiencing this first upsurge in global trade – spices, silks, tobacco, exotic foodstuffs – Shakespeare and other Londoners jostled among a melting pot of immigrants, including people from the Jewish diaspora, Spanish 'blackamoors', former slaves from North and West Africa and religious refugees from the European continent. Simply by strolling down to the docks or around St Paul's, nicknamed 'the whole world's map' by one contemporary writer, the playwright could have heard half the languages of Europe. The expansion of British influence is attested to by the extraordinary fact that in the summer of 1603, around the time Shakespeare was writing *Othello*, a small clutch of Native Americans were shipped across from Chesapeake Bay and ordered to paddle their canoe up the Thames for the amusement of spectators.

Shakespeare (who, as a Warwickshireman, was himself an alien of sorts) seems to have been particularly intimate with the city's expatriates. As well as reading French and Italian, he knew people who could correct his grammar: from around 1602 he lived with the family of a French Huguenot refugee, Christopher Mountjoy, and his wife in Bishopsgate in the City of London, an area known for the diversity of its residents, teeming with Flemish, Dutch and French families. He was apparently on nodding terms with the Italian translator of Montaigne,

John Florio, and perhaps acquainted with the Bassanos, a family of Italian Jewish musicians. One thinks of Bob Dylan's lines in 'Stuck Inside of Mobile with the Memphis Blues Again':

> Well, Shakespeare, he's in the alley
> With his pointed shoes and his bells
> Speaking to some French girl . . .

Footwear notwithstanding, they are accurate enough: not only did Shakespeare know at least one 'French girl', Christopher and Marie Mountjoy's daughter Mary, he acted as a go-between in her marriage to a young apprentice (and later testified in a lawsuit regarding it).

Soon after moving in with the Mountjoys, in 1603, Shakespeare for the first time became a royal servant, putting him into contact with visitors not only from mainland Europe but from far beyond. Ambassadors and tourists from elsewhere in Europe came to see his plays at the public theatres; at court, meanwhile, his newly renamed King's Men played more often than any other company, including for foreign dignitaries.

If Jaques is right to suggest in *As You Like It* that 'all the world's a stage' – the phrase is held to be the motto of the original Globe – then the stage was also a way of reflecting the world back at these increasingly diverse audiences. The Swiss doctor Thomas Platter, who came to London as a tourist in 1599 and witnessed the first-known performance of *Julius Caesar*, claimed that the theatre was the means by which Londoners found out what was happening abroad: 'the English,' Platter remarked, 'for the most part do not travel much, but prefer to learn foreign matters . . . at home.'

There were more literal voyages, too. Rummaging in early production history, I came across a tale frequently repeated in accounts of Shakespeare and the world beyond British shores. It seems almost too good to be true, offering a tantalising connection between the East India Company, the globalising currents beginning to flow through London, and Shakespeare. In March 1607 – the same year the playwright might have begun work on *Pericles* – a vessel called the *Red Dragon* weighed anchor at Tilbury and headed into the North Sea. Commanded by the young captain William Keeling, the *Dragon* was the flagship of the Company's third voyage to the Far East. Keeling's destination was Java in Indonesia; he had orders to buy as many spices as could be squeezed into his hold and open trade negotiations for the English in India and Aden, at the tip of the Arabian peninsula.

Things went badly for the *Dragon* almost from the off. Foul weather split up the convoy of three ships, and a man was swept overboard. Another crew member was found enjoying what a ship's diarist called 'carnall copulation' with a dog, and whipped at the mainmast. A lack of reliable maps created navigational headaches, and despite being bound for the east via the Cape of Good Hope, the *Dragon* and her smaller companion the *Hector* were driven south-west, and ended up crossing the equator near Brazil, the wrong side of the Atlantic altogether, in June. 'Inforced by Gusts, Calmes, Raines, Sicknesses, and other Marine inconveniences', they ended up recrossing it a month later. Water was running low; dysentery and scurvy were rife. Desperate to save his voyage, Keeling hit upon the idea of heading for the coast of Africa, to repair and refuel. They finally reached a Portuguese trading outpost in Sierra Leone in early August.

What they did there was unusual, even by the standards of the voyage so far. While the captain and his colleagues amused themselves by going on an elephant hunt – they managed to wound the creature but not kill it – Keeling's diary records that his crew indulged a taste for more surprising entertainment while moored in Sierra Leone: drama. On the morning of 5 September, he writes, in biscuit-dry, matter-of-fact prose:

> I sent the interpreter, according to his deseir, abord the *Hector*, wear he brooke fast, and after came abord mee [the *Dragon*], where we gave the tragedy of Hamlett.

Three thousand miles and half a world away from Shakespeare's Globe, so it seems, the ship's crew put on a performance of one of Shakespeare's plays. Three weeks later, on 29 September, this devoted cast of amateurs added *Richard II* to their shipboard repertoire. To compound the feat, they gave a repeat performance of *Hamlet* the following March, by then off the east coast of Africa in the Gulf of Aden, near what is now Yemen.

If these accounts are correct, these would be not only the first performances of *Hamlet* and *Richard II* outside Europe, but, in the case of *Hamlet*, also the first public performance it is possible to pinpoint. In other words, the earliest moment anyone would be able to locate this English play about a German-educated, Danish prince (itself a collage of classical learning and Icelandic sagas, translated from French) is when it surfaces in West Africa, in front of a polyglot audience that included a Temne-born, Portuguese-speaking interpreter who had converted to Catholicism and at least three other Sierra Leoneans. For anyone interested in the idea of Shakespeare as a global writer, the story is too tempting to resist.

For as much of the summer of 2012 as I could, I sat in theatres, going on my own voyages of discovery. I watched, awestruck and a little perplexed, as the Ngākau Toa group from Auckland performed an epic, Maori-language *Troilus and Cressida*, complete with strutting *haka* war dance. I saw the great Catalan director Calixto Bieito's desolate reimagining of Shakespeare's pastoral universe, *Forests*, which was acted out on a mound of earth beneath a stricken tree like something out of *Waiting for Godot*. I was overwhelmed by *King Lear* as reinterpreted by the Belarus Free Theatre, who are forced to perform in exile because of their opposition to the Minsk government. Their version of the play was a grim, sardonic folk tale, nonetheless full of heart for a country going to the dogs.

I realised what I had often felt in a decade of watching British performances of Shakespeare: boredom. We had a cosy attitude to Shakespeare in this country, a way of taking him for granted. We regarded him pre-eminently as one of us; no one did him so well. He had helped define the British theatre tradition, and we repaid him by acting as if that tradition was something we had no interest in escaping. We had entrenched ideas not only about our superior grasp of Shakespeare's language, but the way those words should be pronounced – a combination of Mummerset and the emollient Received Pronunciation that has been standard practice in British drama schools since the beginning of the twentieth century.

Yet in translation, so it appeared to me, the plays had a habit of wriggling free. There seemed to be something about being liberated from Shakespeare's own language that allowed theatre-makers to approach his work with quizzical freshness, to unearth themes and ideas that many British companies, drilled in certain modes of thinking and performing, would never have dared to. These companies seemed to have found things in the plays that we rarely glimpsed, even in multicultural, twenty-first-century Britain. The renegade Russian director Dmitry Krymov made *A Midsummer Night's Dream* and *As You Like It* into an anarchic mash-up, complete with teetering, five-metre-high puppets. An Indian company transformed *All's Well That Ends Well*, newly translated into Gujarati, into *bhangwadi*, a popular theatre form that blossomed in Mumbai in the late nineteenth century ('bhang' is hash). Deliciously enjoyable, it bore little relation to the hard-edged interpretations of this 'problem' comedy usually on offer in the west.

Standing in the yard at the Globe or the foyer of the Barbican arts centre, surrounded by people talking many different languages – newly arrived tourists; first-, second- and third-generation immigrants; fluent speakers alongside people who had just a smattering – I realised that this Shakespeare felt thrillingly different. And I, a white, male, Cambridge-educated, English-speaking critic who was supposed to know about Shakespeare, barely knew him at all.

Idling away those summer afternoons and evenings, watching planes on final approach to Heathrow glint through the skies above the Globe, I thought with increasing seriousness about following some of these threads in the opposite direction. Seeing shows was all well and good, but I wanted to go deeper, to examine how Shakespeare had infiltrated literature, education, movies, dance, visual art. What context did the productions I'd been watching, and productions like them, come from? What did Shakespeare actually mean in Seoul, or Bangalore, or Ramallah, or Dar es Salaam? How had he ended up in these places? We were endlessly told that he was the world's most performed playwright, its most translated secular author – but why? Why *was* Shakespeare, a writer who barely travelled, so popular globally? And why had he been not only adapted, but also adopted, in so many countries worldwide?

Global Shakespeare was in the process of becoming a fashionable academic discipline, but the studies I read were in torrid disagreement. Some argued for the universalising force of Shakespeare's writing, its ability to transcend any barrier of colour, class or creed. Others suggested the shadowy postcolonial obverse of this vision – that the reason a dead, white writer was so inescapable was a by-product of the British Empire and its educational factory farms, which turned out dutiful colonial servants who could quote *Hamlet* as readily as recite the Lord's Prayer.

Other scholars knowingly quoted globalisation theory: the Bard as a trans-national brand, or as an example of what the Polish sociologist Zygmunt Bauman has termed 'liquid modernity', part of the free-flowing, ideas-based economy of the global web. More practically, some cited the inexorable global expansion of English, and the remorseless growth of TEFL courses; if one were studying the English language, who better to study than that language's Top Poet? Was it even a *good* thing that – as the British Council claimed – half the world's kids studied Shakespeare in some form or other? Wasn't this cultural imperialism in the guise of cultural relations?

No single explanation seemed satisfactory. I yearned to get away from theorising. I bought a world map, and began to pepper it with dots. Replica Globe theatres in Cedar City, Utah; Neuss, Germany; Jukkasjärvi, Sweden (the globe's northernmost Globe, carved from ice). Kimberley in South Africa, birthplace of the first black Shakespeare translator in Africa. The dacha outside Moscow where Boris Pasternak translated *Hamlet* and *King Lear*. The theatre village near Saitama set up by Japan's most prolific Shakespearian director. The Polish tombstone of Ira Aldridge, the African-American actor who became the nineteenth century's most famous Othello. Points of contact, connection.

I began pestering theatre producers and academic contacts for phone numbers and email addresses; wangling invitations to festivals and conferences, anything that could make a trip worthwhile. I researched flights, and bought the most lightweight copy of the complete works I could find (the venerable Peter Alexander 1951 edition, no notes and recently reprinted in paperback, 1.2 kilogrammes). I kept on reading – books on Asian performance, Zulu adaptations, eighteenth-century French translations, stagings in the post-conflict Balkans: more Shakespeares than I had ever encountered, and rather more than I knew what to do with.

An early plan to track down Rah-e-Sabz to Kabul hit a wall when it transpired that the company, conjoined by Shakespearian comedy, had broken up; one of the actors had claimed asylum in Germany, and others had turned their backs on the group, driven apart by the relentless pressures of touring. After much anguish, I reluctantly laid Russia aside, despite its long and honourable Shakespearian history (which encompassed, impressively, a version of *The Merry Wives of Windsor* supposedly by Catherine the Great). I didn't have the cash for both Japan and China: I plumped for China, persuaded by absorbing stories I'd read about the vexed and illuminating relationship between Shakespeare and communism. I certainly didn't have the cash to visit Sweden, even if the

Ice Globe had still been standing (it turned out to have been a tourist stunt and had lasted only a few months, a decade ago).

Nonetheless, a route began to assemble itself, hewn from the chaos. Not one journey, but a series of journeys; explorations, perhaps, or pilgrimages. I had already seen a fair amount of theatre in Germany, where Shakespeare has been regarded as an honorary citizen since the late eighteenth century, and where English actors visited even earlier. It would be fascinating to return, and trace the trail to its beginning. I could return, too, to the United States, in search of how Shakespeare became a popular household name there in the nineteenth century. Then India, where there were now reckoned to be more cinematic adaptations of the plays than anywhere else in the world, in nearly every Indian language one could name. Then South Africa, where the plays had come head to head with the brute realities of race and racism, perhaps more so than anywhere else on the globe. I would end – if I was still, unlike Rah-e-Sabz, in one piece – in China, where Shakespeare's works had arrived only a century ago, but where he was now so popular (so I read) that there were many times more schoolchildren learning the plays in Mandarin translation than there were in Britain and America studying the English originals.

Five journeys, five acts; the same number, I was pleased to realise, as a play. This expedition into global Shakespeare wouldn't be anywhere completist, even in the countries I visited – such a thing was surely unachievable – but it made incursions into four continents and at least nine languages (none of which I really spoke). It was daunting and, like all daunting things, also wildly exhilarating. From agonising about how much I was having to miss out, I began to get excited by the possibilities, by the collisions and reverberations my route might set up – through places and cultures that wound across and around each other, back to Britain, out again to locations much further afield.

On a brief trip to an arts festival in St Petersburg, a way of salving my conscience for spurning Russia, I told a director what I was planning to do: an impossible quest, I knew, but . . .

Unlike most British people I'd spoken to, who expressed bafflement at the idea of chasing Shakespearian apparitions across the world, he didn't seem remotely fazed. 'There will be many Shakespeares,' he said with the gnomic solemnity special to Russian theatre directors. 'You must let them be unrecognisable.'

There was one conundrum to resolve before I went: the dot on my map next to the coast of Sierra Leone, the site of those supposed performances of *Hamlet* and *Richard II* in 1607. *Had* the plays really been performed on board ship by a company of English sailors in the roiling West African heat, within Shakespeare's lifetime?

I arranged my first expedition, to the British Library in London. It emerged that only a fragment of the hundred-page journal of William Keeling, the 'generall' of the *Dragon*, survives, in the archives of the East India Company. All that exists is a single page, badly torn. It covers an early part of the voyage, March and April, when the ship had still been wallowing across the Atlantic. No mention of Sierra Leone, still less of Shakespeare.

Sections of the Keeling journal had been printed by an editor called Samuel Purchas in 1625, in a huge, five-volume anthology called *Purchas his Pilgrimes*, stuffed with tales of English naval derring-do. Finding the Keeling diaries 'very voluminous', Purchas explained that he had been so bold as to edit them 'to express only the most necessary observations for sea or land affairs'. Again, no Shakespeare. The diary entries relating to *Hamlet* and *Richard II* had only been picked up much later, in the nineteenth century, by an East India Company clerk, one Thomas Rundall, who – not apparently thinking them especially interesting – printed a transcription in the appendix of another compendium of English sea voyages. That was in 1849; it was another two decades before anyone noticed them and realised what they could mean. The story didn't become more widely circulated until the 1920s, when it was taken as stirring proof that British sailors had transported English culture to the furthest ends of civilisation.

The problem was this: by then the evidence itself had long since vanished. The East India Company was notorious for throwing out its early records; indeed, when it became the India Office in 1858, a 'Destruction Committee' had been formed to do exactly that. That single page excepted, the original Keeling diary had disappeared at some point between 1625 and the late nineteenth century. Two journals from the 1607–08 voyage of the *Dragon* are extant, overflowing with colourful detail about the journey – the dates match and the elephant-hunting expedition is there – but neither makes any mention of shipboard theatricals. Neither does an abbreviated contemporaneous copy of Keeling's journal, and there are no other records of English sailors staging drama in this period. Though some scholars have staked reputations on the story of *Hamlet* and *Richard II* on the *Dragon*, the growing consensus is that it simply doesn't add up. In the absence of better evidence, the best guess is that it is a particularly malicious forgery. I asked a curator; was it possible the missing diary could turn up somewhere in the nine miles of shelving that contained India Office records? Her expression told me not to hold my breath.

I sat there in the reading room, working methodically through references and articles, returning every so often to the Keeling manuscript: a single sheet of leathery paper, the colour of silt. It looked unbearably fragile, like a Roman or Etruscan object entombed for thousands of years and only recently prised from the loam. Trying to remember the palaeography lessons I had been forced to do as a postgraduate student, I peered closely at the page, willing it to turn up something new. The tight-knit Jacobean secretary script was cussed and dense, the paper pocked with a shrapnel of holes. I could pick out fragments – 'the Consent sett sayle from Tilbury', 'being bound for London' – but little overall narrative. The text cascaded down and down, before being enveloped by a long, juddering tear. The final letters were identifiable only by their summits, a few scribbled minims and curves in brownish ink. The rest disappeared into oblivion, as if beneath the waves.

It seemed revealing, I thought as I left the library: whether as nineteenth-century colonialists or twenty-first-century postmoderns, we were desperate to find Shakespeare everywhere, even places that bore no trace. It was a useful cautionary tale, one a pilgrim would do well to bear in mind. In any case, the Foreign Office advice on visiting Sierra Leone was none too encouraging because of the bitter aftermath of the long civil war. Whatever the realities of the visit made by the *Dragon*, a visit of my own would have to wait.

Still, it didn't dent my enthusiasm. I'd always been faintly distrustful of travel for its own sake: now, having found a reason to slip away, I could barely wait to be gone. My flights were booked; my diary cleared. I made my excuses to friends and family and put my London life on hold. I was surprised to realise how desperate I'd been for my horizons to be expanded. With the itchy skittishness of all travellers about to embark – somewhere between brittle excitement and plain terror – I suddenly wanted to be on my way.

Hamletomanie

Gdańsk · Weimar · Munich · Berlin

I n the months leading up to 23 April 1864, the 300th anniversary of
Shakespeare's birth, plans in Great Britain are – as is traditional on
such occasions – in almost total disarray.

In Stratford-upon-Avon, a Tercentenary Committee is industriously
attempting to make the Warwickshire town where Shakespeare was
born and bred the focus of worldwide celebrations. Led by the local
brewing magnate Edward Fordham Flower, the committee declares
that 'the eyes of every lover of the Poet will . . . be turned mentally
to Stratford-upon-Avon . . . beyond all question the locality in which
the auspicious day should be specially observed'. A draft programme
centres on a week-long extravaganza of public events; money will go
to two worthy causes. One is King Edward VI school, usually assumed
to be Shakespeare's alma mater. The other is a project to erect an
'enduring monument' to the poet in the town.

Unfortunately, Stratford – and its monument – have competition.
Down in London, a journalist called W. Hepworth Dixon has spotted
an opportunity for that enterprise most beloved of newspaper editors:
a moral campaign. It is obvious to anyone who cares to look that a one-
horse Midlands town, for all that it may have spawned Shakespeare,
is unable to do justice to his supernal genius. It should surely be in
the nation's capital – the great world city where this world-beating
dramatist forged his career – that the National Poet be celebrated on
the tercentenary of his birth.

Only one solution: another committee. Dixon publishes a call to arms
in the magazine he edits, the *Athenaeum*, announcing the formation
of a National Shakespeare Committee to marshal the festivities. 'All
parties would consent to a statue of Shakespeare being the first thing

secured,' Dixon writes – this rival statue to be raised, naturally, in London. 'We do not think,' Dixon adds airily, 'that there would be any great difficulty in either amalgamating the various committees or in harmonising the several projects.'

There are in fact a great many difficulties, and harmony is the last thought on anyone's mind. Determined not to lose face, the Stratford committee announces an impressive line-up including 'Dramatic Readings and Representations,—a déjeûner—A Grand Miscellaneous Concert,—An Oratorio,—Excursions to various places in the neighbourhood in connexion with the Poet's life and history,—A Banquet and Grand Fancy Ball'. In retaliation, Dixon recruits an expeditionary force of dukes, earls and viscounts. Stratford insists that it has numerous backers of its own, and anyway – the town of Shakespeare's birth and death currently lacking a theatre big enough to perform his plays – it will be erecting a tercentenary pavilion by the banks of the Avon seating 5,000 spectators, an engineering marvel of the age.

The arms race escalates. Dixon makes it known that he is masterminding a Shakespeare season across the West End. Flower instructs agents to scout for London actors who will decamp to Stratford.

The press is gorged with material. The mocking verbs 'to tercentenerate' and 'tercentenerise' become current. Every scintilla of gossip is reported with glee. Dixon suffers a public-relations catastrophe when he snubs the novelist William Makepeace Thackeray, who makes the insult incurable by dying. Flower falters when fundraising efforts fail to keep pace with mounting expenses (the pavilion will end up costing £4,500, over four times the projected amount – perhaps £400,000 in today's money).

In January 1864, a coup is mounted to topple Dixon, but he fights back. In the recriminations that follow, *The Times* wearily announces that 'our sympathy, in so far as we have any sympathy with the movement, goes to Stratford'.

By then, however, Stratford is at crisis point. With quite remarkable cack-handedness, Flower's agents have managed to promise the highpoint of the festival, a commemorative production of *Hamlet*, to two actors simultaneously – Samuel Phelps, the most esteemed English thespian of the age, and the dashing Frenchman Charles Fechter. No one appears to have noticed they are deadliest rivals. Grievously affronted, Phelps pulls out. Fechter dithers, then, sensing that a patriotic British public is not on his side, turns tail. In late March, with just a month to go, it looks as though Stratford will have no Shakespearian drama to put inside its luxuriously appointed Shakespearian pavilion.

In everyone's minds is one of the most mortifying episodes in British literary history. Seventeen years earlier, in 1847, Shakespeare's birthplace on Henley Street was on the point – it was reported – of being sold to the American showman P. T. Barnum and shipped brick by brick to New York. Only after a last-minute campaign led by Charles Dickens and the actor William Charles Macready was national pride salved and the Birthplace saved.

With April 1864 just weeks away, history looks set for a farcical repeat. *Punch* publishes a 'tercentenary number' poking sarcastic fun at everything from the *Athenaeum*'s priapic Bardolatry to the saga of the rival memorials. As the big day approaches, an editorial in a London magazine plunges in the knife. '[Shakespeare] has been commentated, expurgated, purified, nullified, annotated, edited, improved, disproved, approved . . . illustrated, painted, drawn and quartered' out of existence, it argues. Why should anyone bother to tercentenarise him too?

When Saturday 23 April finally dawned on the English Midlands, things were not as calamitous as many had feared. The one thing the Stratford Tercentenary Committee had not been responsible for, the weather, turned out beautifully. Crowds came in their thousands, attracted by free fireworks and an exhibition boasting a remarkable twenty-eight different portraits of Shakespeare. Even the pavilion predicament was resolved: at the last minute (and even more expense) performances of *Twelfth Night* and *Romeo and Juliet* were procured from the West End. The grand opening banquet – each dish themed after a play – was accounted a success.

Still, a bitter taste lingered, not least when an anonymous handbill appeared on Stratford's streets pouring scorn on Flower's efforts. Headlined SHAKESPEARE, THE POET OF THE PEOPLE, it criticised the 'profitless swells' clogging up the town and called for a festival less dismissive of Stratford's working-class inhabitants. When the journalist Andrew Halliday paid a visit for Dickens's magazine *All the Year Round*, he, too, scoffed at what he found, accounting the fireworks 'per se, not so very bad', but regretting the fact that the Birthplace ('a general tea-garden aspect') was guarded by 'two huge Warwickshire policemen in full uniform, whose presence was suggestive of a murder, or a robbery'.

Other British cities did the National Poet proud. Liverpool mounted a ball for 1,400 dressed in Shakespearian costume. Unimpressed by the fetish for statues and likenesses, Birmingham's Shakespeare Club outclassed its Midlands neighbour by laying the foundations for a monument much more fitting: a Shakespeare Library 'open freely to all Shakespeare students, from wherever they may come'. (It is still very much going, having reopened inside the new Library of Birmingham in September 2013.)

In London, however, the big day went wrong almost from the off. Dixon's committee produced a so-called official programme, but it was pointed out that nearly everything in it – from revivals of *The Merchant of Venice* at Sadler's Wells to *Henry VI Part II* at the Surrey Theatre in Lambeth – had been organised by other people. More confusion was sown when the Crystal Palace, the vast exhibition space in south London, announced it would hold its own tercentenary celebrations, featuring Shakespeare himself (the actor Arthur Young with bald wig and heavy make-up) rising from the dead from a replica of the Birthplace.

But the nadir came on Primrose Hill in north London, where yet another subcommittee, the Working Men's Shakespeare Committee – hurriedly formed to ensure something actually happened – had arranged to plant an oak sapling in Shakespeare's memory on the anniversary day itself. The planting went to plan, but was swiftly overtaken by a left-wing protest in support of General Garibaldi, then making headlines in Britain. When crowds began to drift on to the hill from the working-class neighbourhood of Chalk Farm, the authorities panicked. Only police intervention prevented a riot.

In a scathing account, *The Times* branded Dixon's event 'ridiculous' and 'pathetic'. 'Notwithstanding this 300th anniversary,' it concluded frostily, 'Shakespeare is not a whit more admired this year than he was last year, or will be next year.' There wasn't even a Shakespeare monument to show for it.

One afternoon, I spent an agreeable few hours in the archives of the Shakespeare Birthplace Trust in Stratford, sifting through the wreckage: newspapers, architectural plans, photographs, printed post-mortems.

The thing that caught me had not often been remarked upon by theatre historians: the tercentenary was an international incident. Britain's grief was all the more humiliating because it was by no means private. In 1864, the world was watching, in fact eager to join in.

In France, Victor Hugo (having turned down an invitation to visit London by the hapless W. Hepworth Dixon), published a sprawling encomium of the poet. Originally intended as an introduction to his son François-Victor's translation of the complete works, it grew into a 300-page meditation on the nature of literary genius. Hugo's 'Comité Shakespeare', formed with George Sand, Alexandre Dumas, Hector Berlioz and nearly every leading writer of the day, achieved a *succès de scandale* when Baudelaire denounced it in *Le Figaro*.

In Prague, meanwhile, the leading lights of Czech culture mounted a celebration that culminated in a performance of Berlioz's choral symphony *Roméo et Juliette* and a pageant of Shakespearian characters two hundred strong, to music specially composed by Bedřich Smetana. Ottawa went in for speechifying and an address. Even the Americans, despite being in the midst of a savage Civil War, put on a decent show: Boston held a ceremony, and after a spirited fundraising effort New York City got what London and Stratford so craved (and would not each get for many years) – a public statue of Shakespeare, the cornerstone of which was laid in Central Park in 1864.

Yet, in the archives that day, I was caught by the prominence of another nation entirely. The *Morning Advertiser* led its report from Stratford with the arrival at the birthday banquet of a 'special deputation from Frankfurt, to present an address on behalf of Germany'. The renowned philologist Professor Max Müller began by stating that 'when honour was to be done to the memory of Shakespeare, Germany could not be absent', and continued in even more rapturous vein:

> Next to Goethe and Schiller there is no poet so truly loved by us, so thoroughly our own, as your Shakespeare. He is no stranger with us, no mere classic, like Homer, or Virgil, or Dante, or Corneille, whom we read and admire and then forget. He has become one of ourselves, holding his own place in the history of our literature, applauded in our theatres, read in our cottages, studied, known, loved, 'as far as sounds the German tongue'.

'[We] will always have in Shakespeare a common teacher,' Müller added, 'a common benefactor, a common friend.'

Müller's compatriot Professor Leitner picked up the baton, affirming the living influence of Shakespeare on German literature. Interestingly, he went further: 'After a century of revolutions in which [Shakespeare's works] were almost forgotten in his own country,' he continued, they 'restored to the mother's strand of Germania old Teutonic strength . . . finish[ing] their conquest by creating that new manhood which forced its way through storms and oppression into light.'

Despite the strangulations of his English, Leitner's message was unambiguous. This was a reminder to his Stratford audience that for all the decades – some would say centuries – Shakespeare had been neglected in Britain, in Germany his influence had only intensified. Speaking in response, the Earl of Carlisle acknowledged that '[Germany's] boast is that she reveres, understands and fathers [Shakespeare] even more throughly than ourselves'.

Leitner was only saying – rather politely – what many of his countrymen held as an article of passionate faith. While London and Stratford had been fiddling and fudging and failing, caught in politicking and money worries and rampant committee-itis, in the German-speaking *Sprachraum* the tercentenary had been nothing less than a phenomenon. Cities from Frankfurt in the west to Königsberg in the east hosted lectures, panegyrics, odes, recitations, *tableaux vivants*. In Düsseldorf, the Goddess of Immortality entered into dialogue with Shakespearian characters before crowning with laurels an image of their creator. In Weimar, a pioneering *Königsdramen* cycle of the English history plays – rarely revived in England itself – was mounted under the patronage of Grand Duchess Sophia of Saxony-Weimar-Eisenach. At the Burgtheater in Vienna, an epic pageant on Shakespeare's life ended with Queen Elizabeth I crowning the poet's bust with a wreath, as angelic spirits frolicked joyously in the air. While Stratford couldn't even get *Hamlet* into production, over ninety performances of Shakespeare plays were mounted across the German states during 1864 – even more impressive when one considers that Germany would not become a unified nation for another seven years.

Reviewing the festivities, an industrialist from Dessau, Wilhelm Oechelhäuser, stated brusquely what Leitner had only hinted: the country that truly honoured Shakespeare was no longer the one in which he was born. Denouncing the British tercentenary as a 'complete fiasco', he wrote that 'even the smallest German university towns honoured the genius with more dignity than did that pompously staged and miserably concluded central festival in Stratford'. 'The English Shakespeare cult' was decayed, he sneered; Germany was now the only country that could do the poet's memory justice.

A new phrase, *unser Shakespeare*, had entered the language. Its translation is simple: 'our Shakespeare'.

ONE HUNDRED AND FORTY-NINE YEARS after the tercentenary, almost to the day, I was scrambling up a hill in northern Poland, trying to see if *unser* Shakespeare went back any further than 1864. It was here, apparently, that Germany had first made Shakespeare's acquaintance.

I had first come to Poland in 2011 to report for the *Guardian* on the building of a new Shakespeare theatre in Gdańsk. When I'd arrived it was to little more than a field of splintered rubble and icy mud. The scheme had been on the cards at least since the millennium, but the contractors had got little further than clearing the site and digging a medium-sized ditch.

Professor Jerzy Limon of Gdańsk University, whose brainchild this new 'Teatr Szekspirowski' was, did his best to entertain the visiting English journalist, crunching around the wind-whipped site in order to show me where the main stage would be – *right here!* – and where the audience would sit – *over there!* Still, it was obvious that the projected opening date, in time for Gdańsk's annual Shakespeare festival in August 2013, was beyond even his considerable powers of invention.

Searching for a story to put in the paper, I realised – far later than I admitted to my editors back in London – that this was not the first Shakespearian theatre to have been built in the city. I was dimly aware that English actors had toured across mainland Europe in the early years of the seventeenth century, but what I hadn't known was that they were said to have constructed a playhouse in Gdańsk some time between 1600 and 1612. This was squarely within Shakespeare's own lifetime, a period covering nearly all his mature plays – *Hamlet*, roughly, up to his final works for the stage, *Henry VIII* (1613) and *The Two Noble Kinsmen* (1613–14). The very site was under our feet, Limon assured me; though long since demolished, evidence of the building had been

found when they excavated foundations for the new theatre. It seemed
to check out. I wrote the article.

Even before my visit was over, I knew I would have to come back: the
idea of English actors tramping through the Baltic states, living on the
hoof, performing at fairs and royal courts, taking Elizabethan drama
out into the world, was too compelling to ignore. If Shakespeare's
plays really had been performed in Gdańsk, it would be the first time
they had definitively been staged outside England, and within the
playwright's lifetime to boot. Forget enticing legends about *Hamlet* and
Richard II in Sierra Leone: here, surely, was where Shakespeare began
to go global.

What I had discovered in the interim about the German adoration
for an English playwright had only sharpened my eagerness to return.
While 1864 may have been the year the concept of *unser* Shakespeare
gained wide circulation, it was here in the far north, two and a half
centuries earlier, that Germany's relationship with Shakespeare first
took root. Though this had been Polish territory since the defeat of the
Nazis, Gdańsk/Danzig had always had a Germanic identity – the city
was German-speaking and for hundreds of years had been as intimate
with powerful German principalities as it was with Warsaw. If my
story began anywhere, I suspected it was here.

Eighteen months after my first visit, I got in touch with Limon and
asked if I could return to Gdańsk and see where his theatre was up to.
He enthusiastically agreed.

So here I was, on top of a hill. Gradually, I gained the summit. Snow
lay in sooty scurfs by the path, and the earth, still half-frozen, was an
unwashed brown. Above me there was a cross: two hulking trusses of
unfinished steel, sixteen metres high. The sky was the blue of raw silk,
scratched with cat's claws of white. Breath clouded in front of my face
in ragged powder-puffs. My lungs felt bruised by the air.

Far below, the town looked dainty, almost too perfect – a confection
of needling spires and steeples, scattered among a forest of sharply
etched triangular roofs. One by one, I ticked off the landmarks: the
double-hatted steeple of Gdańsk's main church; just in front, the
Hanseatic spire of the town hall, scrolled and corbelled, closing to a
sharp point. Its clock was almost legible in the pewtery morning light.
Visible on the horizon was a thin trace of sea.

Wriggling off a glove with my teeth, I yanked a creased paperback
book from my pocket. It contained a black-and-white reproduction of

an engraving of Gdańsk made in 1620, soon after the English actors raised their theatre here. It was a panorama of the city taken from a vantage point somewhere to the south-west, labelled in parallel Latin and German: *Dantiscum*, Danzig.

Holding the book out, I attempted to line up history with reality. Even in blurry miniature, it was a remarkably accurate facsimile. St Mary's church – legendarily the largest brick-built church in the world – was there, its forked steeple unmistakable, as was the town hall. The defensive wall had long gone, and in place of the unpaved road depicted in my engraving there was now a six-lane highway. To the left, there was a whole other city of teetering spires and towers: the cranes of Gdańsk's renowned shipyards, cradle of Poland's anti-communist movement. I could just about see the hulls of ships in dry dock and on them glittering pinpricks of light – welders, I supposed. Every so often a crane moved, a spider-leg patiently adjusting its foothold.

But on the whole, despite the welders and the shipyards and the highway, the image in my hand and the scene beyond slipped into each other surprisingly well: identical, almost. Only the colours – roofs toffee-coloured, a gleam of verdigris – looked new.

They had at least filled in the ditch. In fact Gdańsk's Teatr Szekspirowski had progressed much further: what had been little more than an open site in the centre of town now contained a sleek concrete structure, perhaps a hundred metres long, with a shallow fly tower poking above the roofline. Stark grey, lacking its dark cladding of chocolate-coloured brick, it looked like a naval frigate that had slipped its moorings at the shipyard and drifted up the Motława river.

Limon seemed barely older, still full of boyish enthusiasm. He stood waiting by the perimeter fence, his high-visibility vest harmonising oddly with his bottle-green tweed jacket and gleaming brown leather shoes. Despite the unruly flourish of white hair, he looked as youthful and earnest as ever. But his manner was graver and the lines under his eyes firmly etched. It had been a tough few years, I gathered. He smiled lopsidedly. 'In a way of speaking.'

As we queued for our hard hats, he filled me in: the first firm of builders had run up delays and been removed from the project. There was a running battle to try to recoup expenses. A seven-month pause while new contractors were arranged. And with the weather as unseasonably cold as it was . . .

We looked down into a drainage channel filled with greenish-grey water and broken ice. It was roughly where a corridor in the backstage area should be.

The complex would not now be ready until September 2014. But Limon seemed to take perverse delight in this adversity. 'Bureaucracy, always bureaucracy in Poland. It is our abiding sin.'

As a young English-Literature academic at the University of Gdańsk in the early 1980s, Limon had engaged in modest dissidence against Poland's Soviet puppet government, burrowing in the town archives for evidence of Gdańsk's historic links with the west. He published a book about troupes of actors who visited the city from Germany and beyond. Once communist rule was over, he began to hang around on Gdańsk's punky and burgeoning fringe theatre scene. In 1993 he helped organise the city's first Shakespeare Day, which evolved into a fully fledged international festival, staging performances in improvised spaces across town and the nearby cities of Gdynia and Sopot.

Throughout that time he had a quiet but relentless ambition: to erect a permanent theatre devoted to Shakespeare, as physically proximate to the seventeenth-century playhouse as he could. For some people, the fact that the site had since become the car park of the Gdańsk branch of the Służba Bezpieczeństwa, Poland's KGB, would have been discouraging. For Limon it was a provocation. There would be a nice irony in dispossessing a fleet of government-issue Polski Fiats and Syrenas and erecting a temple to the Bard. Eventually, he got his way: the spooks were forced to park their cars elsewhere.

The first thought had been to raise a replica somewhat like the Globe in London, but Gdańsk's climate – snow on the ground for four months a year – had militated against it. Instead Limon and his architect had opted for a modern space, more flexible, which gestured at Elizabethan amphitheatres. It would have tiers of boxed galleries surrounding a thrust stage on three sides, which could also be adjusted into a proscenium arch as required. A subtle blend of new and old. The secret weapon was a sliding roof, which could be opened during the summer months for the full Globe-like effect.

Impatient to play with his new toy, Limon had already hosted *Hamlet* while work was at a standstill, with a small cast of live performers and video projected on to the exposed concrete walls.

'You should have seen the show,' he said admiringly. 'Transgeneric. Very powerful.'

He was bursting with other plans: summer-long education projects, a new university department teaching arts administration. Not neglecting Gdańsk's links with Britain, he had cajoled the Prince of Wales into being patron.

If I'd met Limon under any other circumstances, I thought, I would have taken him for a dangerous fantasist. But all around us was the evidence of what a little fantasy could achieve.

As I walked back, I turned over Limon's scheme in my mind. Had there genuinely been a theatre built in this city during Shakespeare's lifetime, or was this – like the involvement of the Prince of Wales – merely an astute piece of marketing? What kind of theatre was it? Built by whom? There was talk of the archaeological finds being displayed in the new building, but, with the backstage area still doing a decent impression of the North Pole, that was unlikely any time soon. Limon had offered to accompany me the following day to the town archives, where I hoped to glean more about Gdańsk's Shakespearian past and the strolling actors who braved the Baltic.

Inside a faceless modern complex around the corner from Solidarity headquarters, we were shown into a cramped and drab office. On the table in front were tight beige bundles of documents tied with legal tape. Limon proudly pointed to his signature on the front of one. It was dated 1976. Only three other names were on the list.

Donning white gloves, we creaked the bundles cautiously open. Inside were letters, some in German, some in Latin, some a mixture. I peered at one, done in a businesslike italic hand: late-Elizabethan? early Jacobean? A professional scribe, that was for sure. The ink was clear and dark, the paper looked almost new.

On the reverse was the signature of Elizabeth I, a vaunting construction nearly three inches high, with an extravagant pennant on the summit of the 'b' and more wiggly underlining than would be permitted in a teenage girl's schoolbook. Ploddingly, I worked out the date: December 1566, *Regni vero nostri Nono*, 'the ninth year of our true reign'. Shakespeare would have been two and a half.

At this point, Gdańsk was perhaps the largest city in the Baltic

region and one of the most influential in Europe, home to 75,000
people – modest compared to London, which had a population of
200,000 by 1600, but still significant. Perfectly positioned for ship-borne
trade, it was home to a vigorous mercantile community in contact
with Denmark, Sweden, Flanders, France, Spain, Portugal and much
further beyond. Thousands upon thousands of tons of wood and grain
went out from Gdańsk, and ships from across Europe streamed in for
the access it provided to central European markets.

Gdańsk had never been more cosmopolitan – nor richer – than
during the Renaissance. Długi Targ, the long market in the centre of
town, is still lined by swaggering Hanseatic mansions – fantastical,
many-gabled creations finished in toothsome colours of pink and
marzipan yellow, carefully reconstructed after bomb damage in the
second world war. In the National Museum a few streets away from
my hotel (which had once housed the Dutch consulate) was further
proof of Gdańsk's overseas connections: a vast triptych of the Last
Judgment by the Flemish artist Hans Memling, commissioned for a
Medici church in Florence but seized by a privateer from Gdańsk who
won it after a sea battle with the English.

Despite such conflicts as the Hanseatic War of 1469–74, England
was, on the whole, a valuable ally. Gdańsk had long sat at an oblique
angle from Catholic Poland, an arrangement formalised in 1457 when
the Polish king granted it independent jurisdiction. Lutherans had
brought German translations of the scriptures to Gdańsk as early
as the 1530s, and it became a hotbed of the new faith, home to one
of the few sixteenth-century Protestant gymnasiums to be built on
the Continent (not dissimilar from the grammar school attended by
Shakespeare). In 1577, irked by its semi-detached Lutheran lodger, the
Polish crown attempted to invade. Eventually the rival forces came
to a compromise: fealty and repatriation fees if Gdańsk could have its
old freedoms back. The agreement largely persisted until the Prussian
invasion of 1793.

Little wonder the English found this bullishly independent port
city congenial. In a side street off the main marketplace was Dom
Angielski, the 'English House', built in 1568–70 – three years after
Elizabeth signed that letter – as a centre for the English community
in Gdańsk. It was a towering edifice in louring grey stone that would
have looked more at home on the streets of Manchester than here in
Poland. When it was raised, the English community was one of the

largest outside England, perhaps 1,000 people strong, amplified by a substantial population of Scots.

Limon riffled fast through the documents: communiqués about diplomacy and trade from Elizabeth, a Latin note from James I politely declining to furnish Gdańsk's council with arms.

All at once, we hit the jackpot: letters from the English actors who had visited. I scanned them greedily, trying to decode the German as best I could (which was badly, even with Limon's help). Most were applications to the town council to perform in the city, generally during the annual St Dominic's fair in August. With the brown-nosing formality that is a burdensome feature of Renaissance written communication, they repeatedly protested the players' most excellent skill, and begged humbly to inform the authorities that the drama they performed, comedies and tragedies, was of the highest – and most moral – quality.

They also disclosed more enticing nuggets of information. From a letter of August 1601 by a rival German company one could glean that English actors had begun to visit Gdańsk 'a long time ago', perhaps as early as the late 1580s. By 1600 or so the city had become a regular calling point for actors travelling north through the German states. The English were clearly admired: the same German company begged to inform the authorities, with a tart stab of envy, that 'you may wish to see that we Germans have also learned a thing or two, and just as well as the English'.

This wasn't to say the English had it easy. In 1611, around the time *The Tempest* had its debut in London, one touring company appeared twice in Gdańsk. The players must have wondered why they'd bothered. On the first occasion they were forced to cut short their visit after struggling to drum up spectators; then, on their return, they had the opposite difficulty when an uninvited crowd burst into the theatre without paying, leaving them with no money (their letter lamented piteously) to pay the silk merchants who had made their costumes.

Generally, however, visits went smoothly, implying that the inhabitants of this worldly and wealthy city took visiting performers to their hearts. English companies would come for the next fifty-odd years, through the Thirty Years' War that tore apart Europe, beyond even the English Civil Wars and Cromwell's closure of the theatres in 1642 back in Britain.

At first the actors set up in a civic building at the top of Długi Targ, an undramatic brick hall now heavily restored. But from 1612 references begin to appear in the records to a permanent acting space located in what had been a *Fechtschule* or fencing school. Companies petitioned to play there; one referred to it as a *publicum theatrum*. Limon showed me an image in an engraving: a blocky wooden building, the size and appearance of a large cow barn, with an open roof and galleries just visible inside, perhaps two or three shallow storeys high.

This was the evidence I was after. What made the building properly interesting was its resemblance to designs for the Fortune playhouse back in London, built in 1600 by the same architect-carpenter who had raised the Globe, Peter Street. Instead of the Globe's polygonal, doughnut-like form, the Fortune, raised north of the Thames on the edge of Shoreditch, was, unusually, in a box shape. According to Street's contract – which survives – it was 80 feet square (24.3 square metres) on the outside and 55 feet square (16.7 square metres) on the inside, made of 'good stronge and substancyall timber', with galleries in three storeys, equipped with seats. Its other features were to be constructed 'in the manner and fashion of the saide howse Called the Globe', one of which was the roofed stage that projected out into the middle of the space, around which the groundlings would hustle (though not too closely: Street was also instructed to surround it with iron 'pykes').

No contemporaneous images survive of the London Fortune, once described as 'the fairest playhouse in this town'. But if the information in the archives was accurate, it had a twin right here in Gdańsk, accommodating 1,000 spectators, 1,000 miles from the original. The best guess was that some kind of specification had been brought out from London and constructed locally: not difficult, in a shipbuilding city with skilled craftsmen and plentiful timber. Even the connection with fencing was in character – the same went for many Jacobethan playhouses, where displays of dazzling skill with rapiers and swords were part of the attraction.

The London Fortune's name proved unlucky. The theatre burnt down in 1621 and was replaced by a brick building, itself torn down in the anti-theatrical 1640s; whatever rubble survived the Blitz is now buried somewhere beneath the brutalist concrete of the Barbican (whose 1970s arts centre I had haunted the previous summer, during the World Shakespeare Festival).

But the Fortune's Polish twin flourished. In 1635 a 'lords' room' was installed, after which an Italian architect added complex stage machinery for the avant-garde art form known as opera. In 1695, space was made for an orchestra, and in 1730 the theatre's owners finally gave in to the biting Baltic winters and tacked on a roof. A visiting English merchant described it as 'a large arena for the Baiting of Bulls, Bears and wild Beasts, Amphitheatre-like, capable of containing a vast Number of Spectators, strongly inclosed with Wood, and having convenient Galleries for that Purpose'.

The story was remarkable: a chunk of Elizabethan theatre history that had washed up here on the Baltic coast. The men responsible were assembled in front of me on the page. I turned another leaf: beneath the boldly inscribed names 'John Green' and 'Robert Rainold' were the words *'die Englischen Comedianten'*. Even I could translate that.

But who were the English Comedians? What drew them? What drove them?

In a café opposite St Mary's church, with the photos I had taken at the archive and a jumble of books and notes, I worked through some answers. On the other side of the room a British stag party was clustered limply around a table, surrounding a formidable installation of Żywiec beer bottles. One man, shirt half off despite the temperature outside, was slurringly attempting to chat up the waitress. Another sported a foam hat in the shape of a giant cheese. The waitress gave me a sharp look as she went back to the bar: English comedians, all of us.

The historical variety began to tour continental Europe at the end of the sixteenth century. In Renaissance Europe no less than the present-day G8 it was customary for diplomats to bring substantial entourages, and given that some of these aristocrats had become enthusiastic patrons of the theatre, it was known for actors to travel, too – part entertainment, part political theatre. When one of Elizabeth's showiest nobles, the Earl of Leicester, landed at Flushing in 1585 to support the Dutch in a war against the Spanish, he was accompanied by a group of musicians and fifteen players.

One of Leicester's entourage, a man called Robert Browne, seems to have been bitten by the touring bug. In 1590, Browne crops up in the records at Leiden in the Netherlands, and he led companies that roamed around the northern – generally Protestant – parts of the continent for another thirty years. Usually troupes travelled from town to town, playing at markets and fairs when they could get permission, in addition to being hosted by friendly merchants and nobles, who (assuming they could afford it) were only too delighted to welcome practitioners of this newly chic English art. Indeed, for a certain breed of European noble English Comedians became a must-have accessory: Maurice of Hesse maintained actors at his residence in Kassel for many years, eventually constructing them a theatre, while the Polish royals imported an entire English company wholesale from London to Warsaw in 1617.

The Archduchess Maria Magdalena of Austria seems to have been a devotee, according to a letter she composed to her brother, the Archduke Ferdinand, in February 1608:

> I must tell you, too, about the English players and the plays they gave. Well, after they arrived on the Wednesday after Candlemas, they recovered from the journey on the Thursday, and began on the Friday with *The Prodigal Son*, the same play as they had performed at Passau; this was followed on the Saturday by the *Godly Woman of Antwerp*, truly a very good and proper play. On the Sunday they performed *Doctor Faustus*, and on the Monday a play about a Duke of Florence who fell in love with a nobleman's daughter, on Tuesday they gave *Nobody and Somebody* – that was vastly agreeable. *Fortunatus and his Purse and Wishing-Cap* was also very enjoyable on the Wednesday; on Thursday they gave another of the plays they had performed at Passau, the one about the Jew, and on the Friday they and ourselves all had a good rest . . .

Seven plays in seven days: these actors had more than earned their 'good rest'.

So why did these men – women were not permitted to act professionally in England or this part of the continent, and most wives stayed at home – spend so much time in foreign lands, taking their chances with princes and audiences alike? Wanderlust must have played a part, but to find the rest of the answer one had to look back to Britain.

When we think of the surname Shakespeare, we think of William – a hugely successful royal servant who died in his bed in the second-largest house in Stratford-upon-Avon, having done extraordinarily well in the entertainment business. But William had a brother, Edmund, sixteen years younger – also a performer, also in London. Edmund's shadowy career as a 'player' only grazes the documentary record twice, in the funeral notice for his son (born out of wedlock), followed by his own death four months later in the harsh winter of 1607 at the age of twenty-seven. As far as anyone can tell, Edmund was a failure. I had always found it tantalising that William Shakespeare called the scheming younger son of Gloucester in *King Lear* 'Edmund'; it seemed a gloomy irony that, having failed to make his own mark on stage, Edmund Shakespeare was immortalised (somewhat unflatteringly at that) by his tiresomely successful sibling.

Edmund was, if anything, the norm. The late sixteenth century may have been the great golden age of English drama, but life for all but a lucky few Jacobethan players was desperately precarious (the word 'career' in this period retained its older sense of something a horse does under you when it tries to bolt). A government statute of 1572 branded players as 'rogues, vagabonds and sturdy beggars', and, unless they could acquire the protection of a patron, they were exposed to the whim of the authorities. The Puritan City fathers in London detested theatres and all they stood for, and endlessly, bad-temperedly, angled for them to be closed down: breeding grounds for bubonic plague, incitements to sedition, lewdness, frivolousness, time-wasting. Between 1603 and 1612, London theatres went dark for nearly eighty months, often for long stretches at a time, forcing actors into other work or out on to the road. In the harsh theatre closures of 1592–93 (when even Shakespeare attempted to find another job, as a courtly poet), as many as 200 players were cast out of work.

Some travelled around England and Scotland, hoping that authorities in the provinces would be more forgiving (sometimes they were, often not). A hardy few took their chances in Europe. That same year, 1592, the English traveller Fynes Moryson came across a flabbergasting sight at the annual September fair in Frankfurt:

> I remember that when some of our cast[-out-of-work] despised Stage players came out of England into Germany, and played at Franckford in the tyme of the Mart, having nether a complete number of Actours, nor any good Apparell, nor any ornament of the Stage, yet the Germans, not understanding a worde they sayde, both men and women, flocked wonderfully to see theire gesture and Action, rather than heare them, speaking English which they understand not.

'Germany hath some fewe wandering Comedyians, more deserving pity then prayse,' Moryson went on. 'The serious parts are dully penned, and worse acted, and the mirth they make is ridiculous, and nothing less then witty.'

Yet even the drama-despising Moryson was impressed (or perhaps alarmed) at how successfully his compatriots found an audience. In an era long before theatre surtitles Robert Browne employed a German-speaking clown who could help translate (as well as, presumably, score some extra dirty laughs), but otherwise – as Moryson's account implies – performances were in English, with plentiful 'gesture'. They were also noisy affairs: according to one local who saw them in Frankfurt, Browne's troupe 'have such wonderful, good music, and are so perfect at jumping and dancing that I have never yet heard nor seen their like'.

As the seventeenth century progressed, the English Comedians became both less English and less comical. ('Comedyian' arguably had its older meaning, of a player who could perform any role, comic or tragic.) Naturalised as *Wanderbühnen*, 'travelling companies', they began to introduce German and Dutch performers into their casts, and translate the plays they were performing. In 1605 one company boldly announced it had twenty-four 'comedies, tragedies and pastorals' to offer; another boasted 'chronicles, histories and comedies'. A playlist from 1608 includes such scripts as *The Proud Woman of Antwerp*, *The Jew*, *Doctor Faustus*, *Fortunatus*, *The Turkish Mahomet and Hiren the Fair Greek*. A later list from the same company, under the leadership of John Green, includes plays called *Romeo and Juliet*, *Julius Caesar*, *Nobody and Somebody*, *Orlando Furioso*, *The Spanish Tragedy*, *Doctor Faustus*, *Fortunatus*, *The Jew of Malta*, *King Lear*, *The Prodigal Son* and *Hamlet*.

It was Green's signature I had seen in the archives earlier. A rambunctious comedian who started out playing biddable young women, he had graduated to male parts, one of which was a clownish, two-faced vagabond known as 'Pickleherring' who bore a resemblance to the trickster Autolycus in *The Winter's Tale* and became a stock character in English plays. (Pickled herring was associated with gluttony and lechery, hence Sir Toby Belch's dyspeptic complaint in *Twelfth Night*, 'a plague on this pickleherring'.) Green had joined Browne around 1603 in Lille, and four years later struck out with his own troupe, which visited Graz, Wolfenbüttel, Warsaw, Vienna, Prague and a number of other cities as well as Gdańsk – many hundreds of square miles of territory. It was Green's troupe who had played the newly erected Gdańsk Fencing School in 1612, and perhaps at whose behest it had been built.

The titles he and his colleagues offered were what made my ears prick up. These were dramas by Christopher Marlowe, George Peele, Thomas Dekker, Thomas Kyd, William Shakespeare and a panoply of other Elizabethan dramatists besides – a fair spread of what had been available to audiences back in late Elizabethan London.

Were they actually the same plays? No one was sure: few of these early touring scripts had survived. It was almost impossible to tell whether the *Spanish Tragedies* or *Faustuses* delighting the burghers of Frankfurt or Warsaw bore any relation to the versions written by Kyd or Marlowe, still less whether the Archduchess's reference to 'the one about the Jew' was Marlowe's *The Jew of Malta*, Shakespeare's *The Merchant of Venice* or another play entirely (or some kind of unholy amalgam, in a medley of languages).

The question on which Limon had bet the farm came next: was Shakespeare ever actually acted in Gdańsk? Again, it was tantalisingly difficult to say. *King Lear, Romeo and Juliet, The Taming of the Shrew, A Midsummer Night's Dream* and *Julius Caesar* were among the plays – or the plots – that were doing the rounds in the German states in the early seventeenth century. *The Merchant of Venice* flits vaporously through the archives: in addition to that play 'about the Jew' theatre historians have identified a *Jud von Venedig* given at Halle in 1611 and another in 1626 in Dresden, called *Die Comödia von Josepho Juden von Venedig*. A version of *Titus Andronicus* made its way into the first collection of plays by the English Comedians published in 1620 – the first occasion many of these titles appeared in print.

Whether Shakespeare would have recognised these adaptations, daubed with plentiful splashes of local colour, is debatable. A surviving manuscript of *Romeo and Juliet* dating from later in the seventeenth century refers to towns in south Bohemia and northern Austria, and the Thirty Years' War; it also makes a sizeable part for Pickleherring, who cracks jokes over Juliet's body. In the 1611 *Jud von Venedig* he was given an even lengthier part, abounding in anti-Semitic gags. He was almost the star of the play.

Perhaps this was the point. Generations of critics have dismissed the work of the English Comedians as Fynes Moryson saw it – trivial, crowd-pleasing tinsel, hacked-down texts for audiences who didn't know any better. But I wondered if another way of looking at their achievement was to see it as the truest distillation of theatre, as an adaptive, responsive art that was different every time – every place – it was played.

British writers have often depicted the English Comedians as hardy adventurers exporting Elizabethan drama into the uncivilised wilderness of mainland Europe (much as the crew of the *Red Dragon* were supposed to have brought *Hamlet* to the natives of Sierra Leone).

Myself, I saw something more subtle going on: a process of translation and re-localisation, which helped bring Shakespeare's work – and work like it – alive in unfamiliar environments and in front of new audiences. The comedians weren't really 'English' at all. These trans-cultural, multilingual conglomerates made theatre that was starting to be global.

One other play hovers over the records like a ghost: *Hamlet*. It seems likely that John Green's company performed a script of that name at Dresden in 1626, but no one is sure which *Hamlet* this was. Altogether more fascinating, if more spectral still, is the playtext known as *Der Bestrafte Brudermord* ('Brother-Murder Punished'), printed in 1781 but almost certainly derived from early seventeenth-century performances by the English Comedians.

I had brought the script of *Der Bestrafte Brudermord* with me. It made for a lively travelling companion. Just one fifth the length of *Hamlet*, shorn of soliloquies and bristling with comic business nowhere to be found in Shakespeare's text, the play was exactly as everything I had read about the English Comedians had led me to expect. Ophelia fell in love with a preposterous courtier called Phantasmo before running mad, and there was a perplexing subplot to do with a peasant and his unpaid tax bill. Even the Ghost got in on the laughs, beating one sentry about the head.

In place of Rosencrantz and Guildenstern are two buffoonish ruffians, who are outwitted by the Zorro-like hero while attempting to shoot him:

RUFFIAN 2 Quickly to work; it must be so! You fire from this side, I from the other.

HAMLET Listen to one word more from me. Since even the wickedest evildoer is not executed without being given time to repent, I, an innocent prince, beg you to let me first address a fervent prayer to my Creator; after which I shall willingly die. But I shall give you a sign: I shall raise my hands to heaven, and as soon as I spread out my arms, fire! Level both pistols at my sides, and when I say shoot, give me as much as I need, and be sure and hit me, that I may not suffer long.

RUFFIAN 2 Well, we may do that much to please him; so go right ahead.

HAMLET [*Spreads out his hands*] Shoot! [*Meanwhile he falls down forward between the two servants, who shoot each other.*]

Scholars hotly disagree on what *Der Bestrafte Brudermord* really is – a distillation of the text we know? A translation of the elusive *ur-Hamlet* that supposedly predates Shakespeare's? Another version of the story altogether?

When the pioneering English director William Poel staged a translation of *Brudermord* in London in 1925, the audience fell about laughing; one critic called it 'funnier than any burlesque on *Hamlet* than one can recall'. Poel was horrified, but it is tempting to say that spectators got the point: this is a play that released the comedy latent in Shakespeare's. It plays this longest and most ponderous of tragedies almost entirely for laughs, casting the Prince as the biggest clown of all.

There was one moment in particular that seized my attention, the scene in which the Players arrive at Hamlet's residence to perform for the King, enabling Hamlet to smoke out his villainous uncle (the use of the play-within-the-play remains intact):

CHARLES [FIRST ACTOR] May the gods bestow on your Highness many blessings, happiness, and health!

HAMLET I thank you, my friend. What do you desire?

CHARLES Pardon, your Highness, but we are strangers, High-German actors, and we wanted the honour of acting at his Majesty's wedding. But Fortune turned her back on us, and contrary winds their face towards us. We therefore beseech your Highness to allow us to act a story, that our long journey be not all in vain.

HAMLET Were you not some few years ago at the University of Wittenberg? It seems to me I have seen you act before.

It seems to me I have seen you act before . . . It was a neat meta-dramatic doubling: a touring company of players playing a touring company of players, and a hero half aware he's seen them somewhere else. The reference to 'Wittenberg' – for Shakespeare's audience a faint reference to a town closely associated with Martin Luther, if at all – became, in Germany, much more precise. As an actorly in-joke, it was worthy of Shakespeare himself.

As I read, I found my mind drifting to another Shakespearian connection, an old theory about *Hamlet*, wildly unfashionable now. It was this. After the Earl of Leicester had landed in the Netherlands in 1585, he appears to have recommended his players to King Frederick II of Denmark, who had recently rebuilt an old medieval fortress, Kronborg, as a sumptuous Renaissance palace. The palace's location was Helsingør, on a narrow peninsula looking out on to the Øresund strait towards Sweden.

The actors travelled there to play for the Danish king later in 1585, and were so popular that locals broke down a wall to see them. The following year, a small troupe of English 'instrumentalists and tumblers' came back, and stayed for three months at Helsingør. Will Kempe, the leading figure in Leicester's Men and the greatest comedian of the age, was among their number, as were the actors George Bryan and Thomas Pope. All three would go on to be members of the Lord Chamberlain's Men alongside Shakespeare, so important that they were later named as 'Principall Actors' in the 1623 First Folio, the earliest collected edition of Shakespeare's works, published seven years after his death.

It seems improbable that Shakespeare was there with Kempe, Bryan and Pope in 1586 – this was only a year after the birth of his twins, Hamnet and Judith, and he had yet to make a name for himself on the London stage – but it was surely likely he heard the stories long afterwards. Did dewy-eyed actors' tales about that visit to the Danish royal castle – a wild reception by a Danish crowd, munificent royal fees – prompt him to begin writing a tragedy set in Denmark, a compendium of Icelandic sagas populated by Danes, Norwegians and 'Polacks'? Did Helsingør feed into the Elsinore he imagined in *Hamlet*? Did the English Comedians come alive once again as the travelling 'tragedians of the city' whom the Prince greets so warmly like old companions, almost his only true friends in the play?

You're welcome, masters, welcome all.—I am glad to see thee well.—
Welcome, good friends.—O, my old friend! Thy face is valanced since I
saw thee last. Com'st thou to beard me in Denmark?

It is an enticing idea, particularly as no previous version of the *Hamlet*
story features professional travelling actors: they seem to be wholly
Shakespeare's invention. *The Taming of the Shrew* likewise features a
cast of 'players', who perform the play-within-the-play that forms the
majority of the action; and there is a theory – even less fashionable
these days – that Shakespeare got a start in acting when he joined yet
another touring troupe, the Queen's Men, who visited Stratford. Were
memories of life on the road behind the various strolling players he
put on stage?

Maybe. Yet for all Shakespeare's apparent affection for the players
in *Hamlet*, he makes them isolated, somehow out of joint, with their
lumbering verse forms and their quaint tragedies about Priam and
Hecuba. They are never permitted a bow: sent packing, they are
forced to flee the moment King Claudius takes offence. If this is a
recollection of life in the gilded cage of a glittering European court,
Shakespeare treats the subject coldly. In *Hamlet* he allows his actors
nothing approaching a home.

Still, it was a theory. Even if Shakespeare's plays had never been
performed in Poland during his lifetime, I liked the idea of him paying
a typically cryptic tribute to the kind of drama toured by his colleagues
through northern Europe. And the town that Pope and Bryan visited
next, after their stint in Helsingør? The sources said it was Gdańsk.

THERE IS ONE WHOLLY STARTLING FACT about these early versions of
Shakespeare in mainland Europe: Shakespeare's name remained
unknown. The scripts were altered and adapted in any number of
ways, but the identity of the man who had penned them was regarded
as blithely inconsequential. In 1682, Daniel Georg Morhof, a renowned
polymath, made a brief reference to Shakespeare in an encyclopedia but
confessed, 'I have read nothing,' apparently innocent of the knowledge
that versions of the plays were being performed in the German states
up to the 1660s, if not later.

The connection would not be made until the 1740s. Curiously, information about Britain's most famous playwright travelled via France and – more curiously still – owed a great deal to the leading Enlightenment philosopher Voltaire. Exiled to London in 1726 for daring to quarrel with a nobleman, Voltaire put his two-year banishment to good use, giving himself a crash course in the English language, meeting leading authors such as Pope, Congreve and Swift, and ingratiating himself at court. He also whiled away long hours at the theatre. One of the many playwrights he discovered there was Shakespeare.

It was a fateful encounter. On the one hand, Voltaire was wonderstruck by what he saw on stage, so at odds with rule-bound French drama; on the other, he was appalled. Despite admiring Shakespeare's 'sublime strokes', the Frenchman seems otherwise to have regarded the English playwright with outright horror. More than once, he called Shakespeare 'savage', and lambasted him for ignoring the 'unities' of classical tragedy then de rigueur in France – principles, derived from Aristotle's *Poetics*, which demand that a piece of drama should take place in a single span of action, in a single place, over a single day.

Samuel Johnson's famous appraisal, that Shakespeare's plays exhibited 'the real state of sublunary nature . . . in which, at the same time, the reveller is hastening to his wine, and the mourner burying his friend', was for neoclassicists such as Voltaire a demonstration of everything that was wrong with him: tragedy and comedy and every- thing else clotted together in one undigested, morally questionable lump. In a dissertation on tragedy, Voltaire had particularly stern words for *Hamlet*, a 'rude and barbarous piece':

> Hamlet goes mad in the second act, and his mistress goes mad in the third; the prince slays the father of his mistress, pretending to kill a rat, and the heroine throws herself into the river. They dig her grave on the stage; the gravediggers jest in a way worthy of them, with skulls in their hands; Hamlet answers their odious grossnesses by extravagances no less disgusting. Meanwhile one of the characters conquers Poland.

'One might suppose such a work,' Voltaire added testily, 'to be the fruit of the imagination of a drunken savage.' With a précis like that, it is hard to disagree.

Voltaire spent the next few years penning a series of epic imitations that gave Shakespeare's rough edges a deep French polish and made him acceptable to the European Enlightenment. *Zaïre* (1732, a version of *Hamlet*), *Le Mort de César* (1743) and *Sémiramis* (1748, based on *Othello*) were composed in alexandrines, the taut, inelastic twelve-syllable verse form favoured by Racine and Corneille, and noteworthy for the decorous sobriety of their action.

In Britain, fed by the old enmity with France, the position taken by Voltaire and fellow neoclassicists was caricatured as the last word in Continental foppery. But the German intelligentsia took careful note. Voltaire's criticisms were reproduced almost point for point by the aesthetician Johann Christoph Gottsched, who in the 1720s began to call for a revival of German literature along elegant French lines.

Accordingly, when a German version of a whole play by Shakespeare finally appeared – this time with Shakespeare's name attached – it was in zealously politened and over-restored form. In 1741, the Prussian diplomat Caspar Wilhelm von Borck published a translation of *Julius Caesar*, perhaps the coolest and most classical Shakespearian tragedy of all, making sure to do so – once again – in alexandrines.

Yet, though unfelt by Voltaire, Gottsched or Borck, an earthquake was on its way. The first tremors arrived in the works of Gotthold Ephraim Lessing, twenty-nine years younger than Gottsched and from a different intellectual world. In one of a series of essays on literature written in 1759, Lessing insisted that Germany should abandon any notion of imitating France; instead it must look both inwards and northwards, towards its own *Volksdrama*, and to England, whose 'grand, terrible and melancholic' emotions were akin to those of the Germanic soul. Later in the decade, in an influential collection of writings on modern theatre, 1767–69's *Hamburgische Dramaturgie* ('Hamburg Dramaturgy'), Lessing went further. Inspired by an adaptation of *Richard III* he had seen, he used Shakespeare to attack everything that was wrong with French drama, Voltaire included: too moralising, too stoical, too prissy, too reluctant to examine the dark things inside all of us.

Intoxicated by the philosophy of Lessing's contemporaries Rousseau and Johann Georg Hamann, who urged the primacy of experience and emotion, the young generation growing up in the 1760s and 1770s yearned for something more untamed and Promethean – more *German*. In 1776, the young playwright Friedrich Maximilian von Klinger wrote a play initially called *Der Wirrwarr* ('Confusion'), about the gripping events of the American Revolution, unfolding before his eyes. Following the recommendation of a friend, Maximilian came up with an alternative title, tighter and more dramatic: *Sturm und Drang*, 'storm and stress'. The movement at last had a name.

On the Deutsche Bahn express train heading towards Weimar, 500 miles south-west of Gdańsk, it wasn't just the countryside that was flying past rapidly. I had graduated to the German Romantics. Even in the form of a close-printed Penguin anthology, they were a white-knuckle ride.

My first calling point was Johann Gottfried Herder, thinker and critic, whose explorations into the philosophy of language and history made him one of the most influential figures of the *Sturm und Drang*. Herder's essay 'Shakespeare', published in 1773, places the playwright centre stage, as if in rebuke to the century and a half in which Herder's countrymen had not even bothered to find out his name:

> If there is any man to conjure up in our minds that tremendous image of one 'seated high on the craggy hilltop, storm, tempest, and the roaring sea at his feet, but with the radiance of the heavens above his head', that man is Shakespeare.

In his talk of craggy hilltops and roaring seas Herder was paraphrasing the English poet Mark Akenside, but this could equally have been Shakespeare as painted by the younger Romantic artist Caspar David Friedrich – solitary, unequalled, gazing into untold and possibly undreamed-of distances.

Renouncing the 'masses who explain him, apologise for him, condemn him', Herder declared that his task was to 'make [Shakespeare] alive for us in Germany'. This he proceeded to do by claiming him as a 'northern dramatist', an 'interpreter of Nature', who drew from the landscape all around him. Ideas about Shakespeare as a child of nature had been circulating in England at least since Milton, warbling native woodnotes wild and the rest; but Herder contrived to give the image a bracing new Alpine tang. He made the humdrum act of opening a book sound like a world-shattering event: 'When I read him, it seems to me as if theatre, actors, scenery, all vanish! Single leaves from the book of events, providence, the world, blowing in the storm of history.'

It wasn't hard to work out which 'masses' Herder was turning against, nor which theatre he was trying to obliterate: that of France. Herder had only scorn for neoclassicism, laughingly condemning the 'frivolous Frenchman who arrives in time for Shakespeare's fifth act, expecting it will provide him with the quintessence of the play's touching sentiment'. No – one did not so much watch or read Shakespeare as become consumed by him.

If Herder's feelings were fervent, they were nothing compared to the emotions coursing through his young disciples. A few years earlier, in 1770, a shiftless twenty-one-year-old law student called Johann Wolfgang von Goethe had met Herder in Strasbourg. Goethe was meant to be pursuing his studies, but instead spent much of his time mooning over the soaring Gothic architecture of Strasbourg cathedral and the spectacular landscape of the Alsace (not to mention a pastor's daughter called Friederike Brion, perhaps his first serious romantic relationship). Goethe found his way into the company of a young group of intellectuals led by Herder, and spent the long summer evenings of 1771 debating with them everything that mattered: philosophy, politics, literature, life.

Back home in Frankfurt that October, still reeling from his experiences, Goethe summoned a gathering of friends for a celebration. He had prepared a short speech. His subject wasn't Strasbourg or its cathedral, or even the brief entanglement with Friederike; it was a writer and a poet, a man he called a 'prodigy' and 'the greatest wanderer', someone who 'looms so high, few eyes can reach him, and it is difficult to credit anyone could even take in the entirety of him, let alone surpass him'. That writer was Shakespeare. The day Goethe chose for his address was 14 October, the poet's name day.

Goethe's 'Zum Shakespeares Tag' ('On Shakespeare Day') has become one of the founding texts of German Bardolatry. Even in translation, it is obvious why. Where Herder called Shakespeare 'godlike', Goethe carried the simile to its conclusion:

> The first page of his I read put me in his debt for a lifetime, and once I had read an entire play, I stood there like a blind man, given the gift of sight by some miraculous healing touch. I sensed my own existence

multiplied in a prism – everything was new to me, unfamiliar, and the
unwonted light hurt my eyes.

The simile could barely be more intense: Shakespeare is Christ, Goethe
a halting Saul on the road to Damascus.

After taking a few potshots at neoclassical theatre ('all French
tragedies are parodies of themselves'), Goethe warmed to his theme,
the boundlessness of Shakespeare's vision:

> Shakespeare's theatre is a beautiful curiosity cabinet in which the
> world's history is drawn past our eyes on invisible threads of time. His
> plots are not plots after the common fashion, but his plays all turn on
> the hidden point (yet to be seen or defined in any philosophy) where
> the distinctiveness of Self, the alleged freedom of Will, encounters the
> necessary path of the whole.

'I call out: Nature! Nature!' he went on. 'Where is there anything so
natural as Shakespeare's people?'

Though Goethe had probably read snippets of Shakespeare as
a child, Herder's passion filled him with new depths of awe. While
the older man's essay wouldn't be published until 1773, Goethe read
an early version of it, and to me the two pieces seemed like facing
pages of the same book. They deployed the same arguments, rhyming
phrases: Shakespeare as all-powerful creator, chronicler of humanity
and history, man of destiny, *Weltseele*, 'world soul'.

It is probable that neither Herder nor Goethe had yet seen
Shakespeare performed, and the poet as they imagined him was
certainly beyond the constraints of any mere theatre. Their analogues
were Romantic philosophy and visual art, not drama; their pictorial
equivalent the quixotic pen-and-watercolour extemporisations on
Shakespeare done by William Blake, or the semi-imaginary scenes
from the plays painted by the German-born Henry Fuseli, done in
rushes of ectoplasmic impasto, white on black.

On the cover of my Penguin anthology was a painting by the
Northumbrian artist John Martin, *Macbeth, Banquo and the Three
Witches*, a version of which is now in the National Gallery of Scotland.
It is a tumultuous scene: a churning vortex of blood-clotted cloud and
rock surrounded on all sides by beetling peaks. Just visible in the centre
of the picture, buffeted and helpless, are Banquo and Macbeth, and in

front of them the Witches, cannoned from the sky by a lightning bolt. This, surely, was what Herder's disciples had been imagining on those torrid nights in Strasbourg.

There was an irony here, however: Blake and Fuseli's work wouldn't be done for decades, and Martin's painting would not be complete in its final form until 1820, nearly half a century after Herder and Goethe. It was the Germans who first made Shakespeare Romantic, not the British. When Samuel Taylor Coleridge gave his revolutionary lectures on literature at the Royal Institution in 1808, outlining what he described as Shakespeare's 'organic form' ('it shapes, as it develops, itself from within, and the fulness of its development is one and the same with the perfection of its outward form'), they were taken as a clarion call of Romanticism. Yet remarkably similar arguments had already been made twelve years earlier by August Wilhelm Schlegel, perhaps the foremost Romantic critic in Germany.

Even if Coleridge hadn't actually been cribbing – he claimed not – it would set the tone for what happened next. When it came to the study of Shakespeare in the nineteenth century, Germany led the world.

———◆———

WEIMAR LEFT ONE IN LITTLE DOUBT of its self-image. As the train sighed gently to a halt, I noticed the signs on the platform: 'KulturBahnhof'. It was the first time I had seen a station advertise its cultural credentials. The station itself, an elegant neoclassical edifice with a sweeping red-tiled roof, looked more like the seat of a minor princeling than the mere terminus of the Thuringian railway. At least two people who disembarked with me were carrying cello cases. Presumably they had been forewarned.

Outside, shaking out the knots in my legs, I joined a gaggle of tourists milling near a large-scale town map on a noticeboard. German cities weren't reticent about showing off their illustrious connections, but when it came to shameless name-dropping Weimar was surely in another league. Immediately in front of the station was Schopenhauerstrasse, with Rembrandtweg a few streets to the east. Further south were Schubertstrasse, Hegelstrasse, Kantstrasse, Beethovenplatz, Mozartstrasse.

Goethe and Schiller – who had, unlike nearly all the others, actually lived here – had been granted a *platz* and a *strasse* respectively, not to mention the famous double monument to them outside the Deutsches Nationaltheater. In fact the monument was everywhere: an image of it graced the front of every map of the town at the Weimar station bookshop.

Gutenbergstrasse, Luthergasse, Cranachstrasse, Bachgasse, Hummelstrasse, Lisztstrasse, Wagnergasse, Gropiusstrasse: one could plot a cultural history of Weimar – more, of Germany at large – through its street plan. Nearly everyone who was anyone in German cultural history had passed through the town, from the Reformation to the Bauhaus in 1919, the same year that the terms of the Weimar Republic were signed in the Nationaltheater.

Much of this rich history was down to the generous Duchy of Saxe-Weimar, whose patronage ensured that the arts flourished during Weimar's 'golden age' and long afterwards. Duchess Anna Amalia (1739–1807) founded one of Germany's first public libraries – still open, a marvel of royal-icing Rococo – and coaxed the renowned actor Abel Seyler to play for her, as well as exhibiting talents of her own as a composer. Her son Karl August (1757–1828) continued the family business, inviting Goethe to join him as a privy councillor in 1776 and seeking Herder's advice on redesigning the educational system.

As I rattled my luggage noisily down the hill, Weimar seemed pleasant in a faintly aseptic way: cobbled streets and low-built, red-roofed buildings, their spotless facades coloured handsomely in caramel and mint-white. To the left, I could glimpse the broad green swath of the park that ran through the centre of town. Early on a Monday morning, bar the odd ambling tourist, hardly anyone was around. When the chimes of the town-hall clock in the main square sounded, the sound echoed weirdly. It wasn't just the street plan that put me in mind of a mausoleum.

The town did have a William-Shakespeare-Strasse, but – more interestingly – I had heard that at a house on Carl-August-Allee was a small memorial to the poet.

It didn't take long to find: a plain white villa, now housing local government offices, with a thin terracotta frieze running around it at first-floor level like a band of marzipan. It depicted scenes from Weimar's history. I craned my neck to see the memorial. Eventually I found a podgy-looking cherub, flesh dimpling around thighs and ankles, with a mace in one hand and a bugle in the other, his head garlanded with laurels.

Strange as this was, altogether stranger was the cherub's backpack, which was in the shape of a miniature castle tower, crenellations and all. Stuffed into it was a bald head that was impossible to mistake – Shakespeare, like a gap-year memento brought home to show off to the neighbours. The memorial had been completed in 1864, to commemorate the tercentenary. Weimar's trophy cabinet of premier-league intellects was now complete.

On 20 September 1776, a troupe under the direction of Friedrich Ludwig Schröder, the most acclaimed actor of his day, gave a performance at the Hamburg National Theatre that changed the course of dramatic history. The reports were frenzied: one paper wrote that 'the numerous audience in the playhouse was so attentive, so transported, that it seemed as if there were only one person present, only one pair of eyes, only one pair of hands, because the stillness was so universal, the silence so numbed'.

Such was the demand that Schröder's company acted the same show again and again; the following year they gave it an unprecedented fifteen times, and in Vienna a year later it was performed on another seventy-five occasions. Other troupes, big and small, were soon staging the play. According to one dramaturg, 'royal cities and tiny market towns, splendid halls and wooden booths echo with [the hero's] name, and men and boys, virtuosi and reading teachers, First Heroes and letter-carriers, struggle over him and flaunt their immortality'. That hero was a prince; the play, yet again, was a version of *Hamlet*.

I had an idea that one reason for this abrupt flare of interest was Goethe. Two years earlier, back in Frankfurt and by now determined to be a writer, he had published a book that had been even more of a sensation than Schröder's production. *Die Leiden des jungen Werthers* ('The Sorrows of Young Werther'), printed in 1774, relates the sensational story of a young artist who has fallen helplessly in love with a woman already committed to someone else. Told in the form of letters shared between Werther and a confidant, knowingly named 'Wilhelm', it titillates readers with confession after confession, permitting them to eavesdrop on a world of forbidden passion. Building from Werther's exuberance as he first begins to fall for Lotte, continuing through desperation as he realises the relationship is impossible, the story culminates in suicide, which Werther enacts via the poetic justice of the pistols owned by his lover's fiancé. The book's last line is stark: 'No priest attended.'

Europe went wild for *Werther*. The 1774 edition passed through thirty reprints before the century was out and was translated into English, French and Italian. Young men began to wear clothes like him; women dabbed on 'Eau de Werther'. Napoleon claimed it was a favourite. There was moral panic when a young German woman who drowned herself was found to have a copy in her pocket. The city of Leipzig banned the book entirely. It was partly because of its notoriety that Goethe had been invited by Karl August to Weimar.

Although *Werther* bore striking resemblances to Goethe's own triangular romance with a woman called Lotte Buff – which didn't hurt sales when those facts were revealed – I was more struck by its relationship to the writer he had exalted in '*Zum Shakespeares Tag*'. In October 1771, the very month he had delivered the speech, he had set to work on his first major play, *Götz von Berlichingen*. A rumbustious account in no fewer than fifty-six scenes of the medieval knight and mercenary Gottfried of Berlichingen (famous for having had his hand shot away and replaced by an iron fist), it was a crazily ambitious undertaking. It was also heavily touched by Shakespeare's history plays, which Goethe had perhaps only just read. When Herder saw the manuscript, he exclaimed, 'Shakespeare has quite ruined you.'

Werther, too, was heavily in Shakespeare's debt – but here the resemblance was to one play alone, the text that had so captivated Schröder and German audiences: *Hamlet*.

Young Werther was young Hamlet by another name. Over-intelligent, cripplingly sensitive, tragically ill-equipped to face the realities of the world, he drifts through his luckless love affair without ever managing to take hold of it. He, too, lacks a father; contemplating death, he describes the funeral of a female 'friend' uncannily like the burial of Ophelia.

For sure, there were differences: it is hard to imagine even Shakespeare's Prince botching his death as Werther did, shooting himself above the right eye before haemorrhaging slowly. (Being sliced by an envenomed rapier looks positively wholesome by comparison.) But everywhere there are hints of Goethe's source: in Werther's frenzied soul-searching, his emotional paralysis, his restless drift towards insanity. Early in the book, one of his letters to Wilhelm reads:

> When I consider how narrowly the active and enquiring powers of a human being are confined; when I see that all effective effort has as its end the satisfaction of our needs which themselves have no purpose except to lengthen the duration of our poor existence, and that any contentment on one point or another of our enquiries consists only in a sort of dreaming resignation as we paint the walls within which we sit out our imprisonment . . . All that, Wilhelm, renders me speechless. I go back into myself and find a whole world.

The lines read like an extrapolated version of Hamlet's 'Denmark's a prison' ('I could be bounded in a nutshell and count myself a king of infinite space'), bolted on to a speech from later in the same scene, 'this goodly frame, the earth, seems to me a sterile promontory'. A marvelling statement that follows in Shakespeare's text – 'What a piece of work is a man' – returns to haunt Werther's final letter: 'Who is this thing, the vaunted demigod, a man?'

After *Werther*'s publication and his move to Weimar, Goethe lived in a cottage given to him by the ever-munificent Karl August, but six years later he moved to much grander accommodation on Am Frauenplan here in Weimar, the house where – barring a journey to Italy from 1786 to 1788 and a stint observing the Battle of Valmy – he would remain until his death in 1832.

Dutifully touristic, the morning after I arrived I toured the Goethehaus, aiming my cameraphone at the plank on the threshold painted with the word '*Salve*' ('welcome') and staying right to the end of an alarmingly thorough 3D video presentation about its architecture. Despite its considerable size – more stately home than *Haus*, I thought – the place was harried by school groups and coach parties. At least the thirteen-year-olds sniggering next to the poet's collection of nude classical statuary were having fun; everyone else, drifting around with audio guides clamped to their skulls, looked as if they were waiting on hold. The smell of lilies and furniture polish hung heavy in the air.

Writers' houses have always struck me as the least visitable of visitor attractions, the act of writing so private and undramatic – the creaking of pen across paper, the shuffle of pages – that it leaves almost no imprint on physical space. The Goethehaus, magnificent though it was, felt no different. It was the morbidly tasteful presentation of a life rather than anything more tangible.

After an hour I gave up the house as a poor piece of detective work and retreated with my books to a glowering, wood-lined bar with tobacco-stained walls, filled prettily with beery bric-a-brac.

T. S. Eliot's pursed-lip view, aired in 1921, was that Goethe's borrowings from *Hamlet* were a form of Freudian projection – a way of making up for the deficiency in the poet's own creative powers. (Coleridge came in for the same criticism, that he had simply 'made of Hamlet a Coleridge'.)

I wondered if it were fairer to say that, having encountered Shakespeare at a formative age, Goethe had spent the rest of his life trying to escape his clutches and never quite succeeding. Soon after arriving in Weimar, he had attempted to write a follow-up to *Henry IV Part II* that reversed Shakespeare's cold-blooded decision to banish Falstaff at the end of the play, conjuring prison scenes in which Sir John, Bardolph and Poins lament their plight but live in hope that somehow their fate will be reversed. The script was not to be: Goethe never got further than sketches.

He was more successful with *Egmont*, on which he began working at around the same time. A historical saga on the Dutch struggle for independence against Spanish tyranny, it began as a prequel to *Julius Caesar*. There were numerous mentions made of the '*Cäsar*' project in letters and notes, but at some point Goethe seems to have destroyed the material. The crowd scenes that interspersed the action – obvious echoes of the holidaying, restive cobblers and carpenters in *Julius Caesar*'s opening scenes – were all that remained.

But these early feints with Shakespeare were as nothing to the creative task that occupied Goethe for over twenty years, from the end of the 1770s until late middle age: the composition of the epic, multi-part project that became known as *Wilhelm Meister*. It was while writing *Egmont* that Goethe had first conceived the idea of writing about a young man attempting to find his creative path. In 1777 he began a story he called *Wilhelm Meisters Theatralische Sendung* ('Wilhelm Meister's Theatrical Mission').

Its subject was unorthodox, even by the standards of that nascent, wet-behind-the-ears form known as the novel. Wilhelm Meister, the protagonist, a child when we first meet him, is obsessed by the idea of going on stage. After falling in with a troupe of actors, he becomes involved with a married actress (another doomed romance), all the while attempting to write his own scripts. But when an older man called Jarno introduces him to the work of Shakespeare, Wilhelm is seized by an epiphany. After reading *Hamlet*, he becomes ever more convinced that his purpose in life is to stage the perfect production of that very play.

Goethe had trouble with *Wilhelm Meisters Theatralische Sendung* almost from the off, and only got six books into the projected twelve before abandoning it mid-flow. His ducal responsibilities in Weimar had begun to wear him down, along with an ill-starred relationship a little too close to the fiction he was writing (this time with the wife of Karl August's equerry). It would not be until 1794, seventeen years later, that he returned to the material.

The novel that eventually emerged, now under the title *Wilhelm Meisters Lehrjahre* ('Wilhelm Meister's Apprenticeship'), was recast: the young Wilhelm becomes infatuated by the world of the theatre only, crucially, to grow up and leave it behind, a decisive move that gives it the shape of a classic *Bildungsroman* (roughly translatable as 'coming-of-age story'). Yet even in this revised form, published in 1795–96, the book was saturated by Shakespeare. If *Werther* is haunted by the spirit of *Hamlet*, *Wilhelm Meister* is a full-blown seance – a summoning-up not merely of Shakespeare's text but of Goethe's response all those years before in Strasbourg.

Though viewed with delicate irony from a distance of twenty-five years, the headstrong young Wilhelm was, of course, a version of Goethe himself. The gruff, worldly-wise Jarno resembled Herder, and Wilhelm's revelatory encounter with Shakespeare was tantalisingly like the one Goethe had recorded in '*Zum Shakespeares Tag*'. Having read the plays for the first time, the astonished Wilhelm proclaims:

> They seem as if they were performances of some celestial genius, descending among men . . . They are no fictions! You would think, while reading them, you stood before the unclosed awful Books of Fate, while the whirlwind of most impassioned life was howling through the leaves, and tossing them fiercely to and fro. The strength and tenderness, the power and peacefulness of this man have so astonished and transported me, that I long vehemently for the time when I shall have it in my power to read further.

Books of Fate, a howling wind: the lines were all but stolen from Herder's 'Shakespeare' and Goethe's own 'Zum Shakespeares Tag'.

Wilhelm Meister was the only novel I'd come across that attempted to incorporate live literary criticism into the action, which led to some dubiously undramatic passages (not aided by Thomas Carlyle's puddingy English translation). But there were also moments of brilliance. In Book 4 Wilhelm embarks on an impassioned debate with the actor-manager Serlo (loosely based on the real-life Friedrich Ludwig Schröder) about how Prince Hamlet should properly be played. 'To me it is clear,' Wilhelm declares in words that would ring through German literature:

> that Shakespeare meant, in the present case, to represent the effects of a great action laid upon a soul unfit for the performance of it. In this view the whole piece seems to me to be composed. There is an oak-tree planted in a costly jar, which should have borne only pleasant flowers in its bosom; the roots expand, the jar is shivered.

This most romantic interpretation of Hamlet – the unfit soul, the oak sapling straining against the sides of the vessel that contains it – occupies a good portion of the centre of the book.

As I read on in the café that day, *Wilhelm Meister* struck me as an ungainly hybrid: simultaneously a novelistic reworking and updating of *Hamlet*, a critical commentary, a treatise on the ethics of theatrical adaptation, and an autobiographical account of what it feels like to encounter, then stage, a writer you revere. It was also, perhaps, a kind of exorcism; an attempt to conjure up, and overmatch, the great ghost of Shakespeare.

As the images of the famous monument outside the Nationaltheater plastered across town were forever reminding me, Goethe was only half the story. To appreciate the explosive impact of Shakespeare on German Romantic culture – and his role in forming what became German national drama – one also needed to factor in the role of Johann Christoph Friedrich von Schiller.

Born in 1759, the only son of an overbearing military doctor, Schiller was dominated (revealingly, one feels) in his early life by frustrated struggles with authority. Having abandoned a childhood ambition to become a priest, he had been packed off to military college by his father's equally overbearing patron, Duke Karl Eugen, then instructed to study his father's own subject, medicine. The young Schiller began to read voraciously: first Rousseau and Kant, then avant-garde *Sturm und Drang* writers such as Goethe, Lenz, Klinger and Klopstock. One day, his philosophy tutor introduced him to *Othello*. Despite his hazy English, Schiller was hooked, and filled his medical thesis with lines from Shakespeare. By the time he had taken a job in Stuttgart as a regimental medic in 1780, he had determined what he wanted to be: a playwright.

His debut, *Die Räuber* ('The Robbers') – written at the age of twenty-one while he was ostensibly studying for his finals – made Schiller an overnight sensation. The histrionic story of two sons, the heroic Karl and the calculating Franz, and Franz's attempts to seize his brother's inheritance against the wishes of their father, it could have been purpose-designed for the turbulent new mood then sweeping Germany – something astutely realised by the artistic director of the Mannheim theatre, who put it on as soon as he read it. At its premiere in January 1782, according to one eyewitness, the theatre 'resembled a madhouse: rolling eyes, clenched fists, stamping feet, hoarse screams'.

The echoes of the audience reaction to Schröder's performance of *Hamlet* six years before are hardly surprising – even more obviously than Goethe, Schiller was grappling with Shakespeare. *Die Räuber*'s main theme, brotherly conflict, reprises an abiding Shakespearian motif, drawing from *As You Like It* (where the virtuous Orlando is, like Karl, forced to flee society and join a band of outlaws) and perhaps *The Tempest*, with dashes of Robin Hood, Cain and Abel and Christ's parable of the Prodigal Son lobbed in for good measure.

Some critics detected echoes of *King Lear*'s machiavellian Edmund, or Richard III, in the character of Franz (who goes mad, thinking he is being pursued by devils), but for me the clearest reverberation came in the scene where Karl, alone in the forest, agonises about his position and his conscience:

> Who would be my surety? – All is so dark – labyrinths of confusion – no way out – no star to guide – if it were over with this last-drawn breath, over like a shallow puppet-play – But why this burning hunger for happiness? Why this ideal of unattained perfection? This looking

to another world for what we have failed to achieve in this – when one miserable touch of this miserable object [*holding his pistol to his forehead*] will make a wise man no better than a fool – a brave man no better than a coward – a noble man no better than a rogue?

'To be, or not to be' in a slightly different key – and with a pistol, not a bare bodkin.

In 1787 Schiller came to Weimar and met Goethe, ten years older, who took a sharp interest in this brilliant if volatile young writer. In 1790 Schiller married Charlotte von Lengefeld, a well-connected young woman from Weimar, but he soon began to suffer from ill-health, worsened by overwork. The rest of his mature output – a torrential flood that included seven more plays, poetry, letters, translations, essays and two novels – was produced in a headlong rush against time. Fifteen years later, aged just forty-five, Schiller would be dead.

As well as their shared creative interests and schoolboyish sense of humour, one thing that brought together the two *Dioskuren* (twin sons of Zeus), as this inseparable duo were nicknamed, was their love for Shakespeare. It was largely because of Schiller's encouragement and advice that *Wilhelm Meister* was finished. Soon after its publication, Schiller wrote to Goethe, 'I have noticed that the characters in Greek tragedy are more or less ideal masks and not real individuals such as I find in Shakespeare and in your plays.' Later that year, Schiller commented that he had been working his way through the English histories: 'It was marvellous the way [Shakespeare] could always make the most unpoetic elements yield poetry, and how nimbly he represents the unpresentable.'

In one of the treatises he composed in Weimar, '*Über naive und sentimentalische Dichtung*' ('On Simple and Sentimental Poetry', 1795–96), Schiller attempted to distinguish between the 'simple' or naive poets of antiquity and 'sentimental' writers of modern times, alienated from nature. In the former camp he placed Homer and Shakespeare, commencing with arguments that echoed Voltaire:

When I became first acquainted with Shakespeare at a very early age, I was shocked by his coldness, the lack of feeling which allowed him to joke in the midst of the greatest pathos, to break up the heart-rending scenes in *Hamlet*, *King Lear*, *Macbeth*, etc. by the intro-duction of a Fool, which at times stopped him where my emotions rushed on, at times bore him cold-heartedly on where the heart would gladly have paused. Misled by my acquaintance with more modern poets to look first of all in the work for the author, to encounter his heart, to reflect on his subject matter together with him, in short to look for the subject matter in the person, it was unbearable to me that here the poet could nowhere be grasped, was nowhere answerable to me.

Schiller had since come to regard Shakespeare's elusiveness – that apparently invisible 'heart' – as a measure of his greatness: 'He had already possessed my entire admiration and had been my study for several years before I learned to love his personality.'

Marks of that love were everywhere: in *Kabale und Liebe* (1784), sometimes rendered in English as *Luise Miller*, whose virtuous and courageous heroine has more than a tint of Imogen in *Cymbeline* and Isabella in *Measure for Measure*; and in the triple-decker *Wallenstein* (1798–99), whose panoptic view of the Thirty Years' War is modelled on the English history plays. The source text for *Don Carlos* (1787) is even clearer: written in blank verse in direct Shakespearian imitation, it tells the story of a young and idealistic heir to the Spanish throne, railroaded by his autocratic father and disastrously in love with his stepmother. Schiller wrote that it 'has the soul of *Hamlet* . . . and my own pulse'.

There was one surprising thing, however. So excitable about the raw formlessness of Shakespeare on the page, Goethe and Schiller were notably bashful when it came to staging him. In 1796, Goethe invited Schiller to join him as co-director at Weimar's new court theatre, where the pair worked intimately until Schiller's death in 1805, after which Goethe continued in the role for another decade. Nervous about how audiences might react, Goethe preferred to mount operas, frothy musical comedies and light plays by popular contemporaries such as August Wilhelm Iffland and August Kotzebue, only later broadening the repertoire with his and Schiller's own work. Shakespeare barely figured: only nine of his plays in twenty-six years.

The *Macbeth* they staged in 1800 was a case in point. Goethe directed and designed (his halting, heavy-handed pen sketches are kept in the Goethe-Schiller Archive), while Schiller translated, despite his still-hesitant English. To modern eyes, their version of this darkest and most ethically shady of tragedies is barely recognisable. Anxious that it suffered from a 'superabundance of content' – code for a lack of classical rigour – the pair made the Witches less ethically and sexually ambiguous (they were played by male actors wearing veils and Grecian robes), while the Porter entered with a larksome *Morgenlied* ('morning song') instead of a string of punning obscenities. Macbeth himself was likewise subjected to a moral deep-clean, presented as a '*Heldenmüt'ger Feldherr*' ('valorous general') whose noble nature is overwhelmed by the forces of fate. True evil was distilled into the figure of his wife (a 'superwitch', as Goethe later described her). To further spare the audience's feelings, perhaps the play's most horrific moment, the cold-blooded murder of Lady Macduff and her son by Macbeth's forces, was cut entirely.

Goethe and Schiller were far from alone in cleaning up Shakespeare: 'improved' versions of the plays had been common currency since the 1660s, and were particularly prevalent in England (though *Macbeth*, unusually, had been played more or less in Shakespeare's text from the mid-eighteenth century onwards). But I found it revealing that German critics, so thrilled by the galvanising power of Shakespeare in the comfort of their studies, were so timid about what effect he might have in the theatre. In what became known as Weimar classicism, one could glimpse Voltaire's shadow lingering in the wings.

———•—•———

NEAR THE END OF HERDER'S ESSAY on Shakespeare is a telling section. Addressing his young disciple directly, Herder writes that he has one earnest desire, 'that one day you will raise a monument to [Shakespeare] here in our degenerate country', concluding, 'I envy you that dream.'

Herder's hope was obvious: that Goethe would himself become a new Shakespeare, a Teutonic one. But as the clock ticked towards the tercentenary date of 23 April 1864, many felt that Germany, for all the effect of the *Sturm und Drang* and the eagerness for staging Shakespeare's plays, still lacked an enduring 'monument'. England had a Shakespeare Club, founded in 1824 in Stratford-upon-Avon by enthusiasts who met at a pub called the Falcon Inn. America got in on the act when a group of lawyers in Philadelphia, seeking distraction from statutes and appellate hearings, formed a literary salon in 1852; refounded ten years later as the Shakspere Society of Philadelphia,

its all-male membership still meets regularly for cocktails and
gentlemanly chit-chat (and clings quaintly to the antiquated spelling
of its name).

Like other nineteenth-century Shakespeare societies, these were
amateur affairs – dining and wining clubs with a little light literary
appreciation thrown in. With the 1864 anniversary approaching, there
were calls for Germany to go further. If Goethe and Herder had been
right – that Shakespeare had given birth to a new age in German life
and literature – then surely this should be marked. Was it not time for
Germany to have a professional society in the name of Shakespeare,
made up of the best scholarly minds German-speaking countries could
produce?

Yet another Wilhelm, this time a real one, Wilhelm Oechelhäuser
– the same man who later dismissed the Stratford-upon-Avon
celebrations as 'miserable' and 'pompous' – was a key agitator.
An industrialist from Dessau who had made a fortune in the gas
business, Oechelhäuser had revered Shakespeare since childhood
and had been plotting a *Gesellschaft* or society devoted to him since
at least 1858. Hearing of English plans to celebrate the tercentenary
– though not, one suspects, of their shortcomings – he circulated
a memorandum insisting that Germany must not be left behind.
After Grand Duchess Sophie of Saxony-Weimar-Eisenach agreed to
become the society's first patron, there was only one place it could
be based: right here in Weimar. Placing a Shakespeare society in the
spiritual capital of German *Kultur* might not only be convenient,
Oechelhäuser realised; it could also be a symbolic act. Bach, Cranach,
Luther, Goethe, Schiller . . . why not Shakespeare? The man was
practically a native.

The statutes decreed that the new society would meet annually,
on the 'Shakespeare-Tag' of the poet's birthday. It would encourage
philology and scholarship, publishing an academic journal,
Shakespeare Jahrbuch. It would work towards an official translation
of the complete works. Above all, it would, in the fervent jargon of
the day, *nostrify* Shakespeare: make him Germany's own. Another
founding member, Franz von Dingelstedt, a successor of Goethe
and Schiller as director of the Weimar court theatre, wrote, 'Behold,
today, as the third in the sacred trio, the Briton joins Germany's
Dioscuri. He, too, is ours!'

It is doubtful many Britons would have agreed with this, but

Germany could indeed boast something genuinely unique. When it came formally into existence at 10 a.m. on 23 April 1864, the Deutsche Shakespeare-Gesellschaft was the first academic Shakespearian society to be founded anywhere in the world.

Only one problem: I'd mislaid them. The modern-day headquarters of the DSG was nowhere near William-Shakespeare-Strasse, as I'd casually assumed. Hastening back to the centre of town after heading in entirely the wrong direction, I asked at the tourist information bureau. All I got was a flurry of furrowed brows. Eventually someone turned up Windischestrasse, a narrow lane less than a hundred metres away.

I sprinted down. There was indeed a large sign reading 'Shakespeares', but it was a bar. They hadn't heard of the society either – I'd tried tourist information? Through gritted teeth, I explained I had.

Eventually, I found it: a modest white nameplate on the wall of an office building, opposite a mobile-phone shop. In neat type, the nameplate read, DEUTSCHE SHAKESPEARE-GESELLSCHAFT, E.V., GESCHÄFTSSTELLE. It seemed to share space with a yoga centre.

The door opened, disclosing a woman in early middle age with a mass of curly brown hair: the DSG's part-time administrator, Birgit Rudolph. She smiled cautiously and welcomed me in.

'It isn't much to look at, I am sorry,' she said as we hauled our way up the steep stairs. 'It is more of an office space. We use it mainly to keep information.'

The two-room office was functional, with a forlorn touch of the GDR: a couple of desks, a few exhausted-looking pot plants and an elderly fax machine. Along one wall were neat rows of box files. Near the dusty glass of the window, a copy of the 'Flower' portrait of Shakespeare – so-called because it was once owned by the family of Edward Fordham Flower, organiser of the same tercentenary festivities Wilhelm Oechelhäuser had so despised – surveyed the scene. There was a pungent smell of old paper, mixed with wet carpet.

It certainly wasn't a patch on the offices of the Goethe-Gesellschaft, which I'd popped into briefly the previous day: an imposing suite of rooms encased within the Schloss and offering sumptuous views on to the Park an der Ilm.

Rudolph was attempting to hide her smile. 'Yes, this is true. But we are older, you know this? They are only founded in 1885. We are 1864. They are a little bit sensitive about that.'

Still, it was a wrench to see the society in such incommodious surroundings. When the DSG had convened its first meetings in the 1860s and 1870s, its ambitions – at least measured by the extravagance of its rhetoric – were almost without bound. The philosopher and scholar Hermann Ulrici wrote, 'We want to de-Anglicise the English Shakespeare. We want to Germanise him, to Germanise him in the widest and deepest sense of the word; we want to do everything in our power to make him even more and in the truest and fullest sense what he already is: a German poet.' Another scholar, Karl Fulda, was even more fulsome: 'We have an undeniable right to regard him as ours, because we have made him ours thanks to German industry, German spirit, and German scholarship.' Not for nothing had one historian of the society declared that most of these tributes to Shakespeare were 'far too embarrassing to quote'.

Birgit directed my attention to the wall, where a large bookcase was lined with a row of volumes: a full run of the bilingual *Shakespeare Jahrbuch*, still published annually and distributed to all members. She carefully pulled out a few early editions, their leather covers softened to toffee-brown but the gold lettering on the spine still bright. We peered at the faded, closely printed pages, Birgit translating as we went.

The very first issue laid out the DSG's objectives, 'show[ing] the traces of Shakespeare's great influence on all areas of intellectual endeavour', and invited scholars working in the area to help the society 'pay due attention to the performance of Shakespeare's plays and give an overview of recent literature'. Membership cost the modest sum of 3 thalers annually.

Interesting as it was that the founders had treated live theatre with the same rigour and seriousness as textual studies and critical editions – scholarly suspicion about the activities of mere thespians would last far longer in Britain and America – the arresting thing was how nakedly political the DSG's early objectives were. It was not enough to foster German appreciation of Shakespeare; the very first lines of the prospectus referred to the goal of 'naturalis[ing]' him. This was not accidental: 1864 was also the year Schleswig-Holstein in northern Germany was invaded by Austro-Prussian forces, bringing an end to Danish control of the region and a prelude to the unification of

Germany six years later in 1871. Perhaps Oechelhäuser, Ulrici and the others were attempting a similar move: by declaring Shakespeare 'Germanised' they were forging a nation of their own. Nor was he the only foreign writer to be co-opted by ardent German nationalists: the Deutsche Dante-Gesellschaft was to follow in 1865, once again the world's first.

The Shakespeare society made waves far outside Germany; much further, even, than Britain. In 1877, the great American editor Horace Howard Furness, for many years a member of the Shakspere Society of Philadelphia, published the latest volume of his gargantuan variorum edition of Shakespeare – a monument of nineteenth-century scholarship, which aimed to collate every version of every published text in eye-straining, mind-numbing detail. In a mark of academic kudos that must have sent up yells of pride in Weimar, Furness dedicated the book 'with great respect' to his cousins in the Deutsche Shakespeare-Gesellschaft. The volume, naturally, was his edition of *Hamlet*.

Birgit was clutching a gift of her own. In recognition of my visit, the Gesellschaft committee had asked her to present me with a copy of another publication produced in the early years of the society: a life-size facsimile of Shakespeare's will. The original was now in the British national archives at Kew, but in 1889 the DSG had gained permission to have it photographed using the latest technology and printed with a transcription on the facing page (necessary, if one couldn't read the lawyer's cramped Jacobean handwriting).

Das Testament William Shakespeare's was over a foot wide and nearly two feet tall, beautifully bound in red and dove-grey, printed on thick, creamy paper the texture of velvet. It was a splendid object, and a touching gift. I had not the faintest clue how I would get it home.

O HAMLET . . . Wherever one looked in the nineteenth century, it loomed. Like Old Hamlet's Ghost, the play kept materialising in the oddest places, refusing to turn up its toes and die.

It wasn't just Germany. English Romantics were infatuated with Shakespeare's Prince ('I have a smack of Hamlet myself, if I may say so,' Coleridge declared), and in both Russia and France 'Hamletism' became a fashionable malady among a certain breed of *fin-de-siècle* intellectual. From there it became an unlikely source of nationalistic pride: influenced by a series of popular lithographs of Hamlet by the Romantic artist Delacroix, both Baudelaire and Mallarmé eagerly proclaimed themselves in sympathy with the Prince's exquisitely artistic refusal to act, while the Russian Turgenev (whose fiction is littered with Shakespearian doppelgängers) asked, 'Is not the picture of Hamlet closer and more understandable to us than to the French, let us say more – than to the English?'

Yet it was in Germany that *Hamletomanie* – 'Hamlet-mania' – became a national addiction, not simply on stage but politically too. Why, though? Why not *Richard II* or *Antony and Cleopatra*, both plays that dwelt just as insistently on the semiotics of poetic inaction?

The popularity of *Werther* was one reason, behind it the northern-European urges of the *Sturm und Drang* and Lessing's admiring description of 'grand, terrible and melancholic' emotions. And it surely didn't hurt that the Prince was, after Martin Luther, Wittenberg's most famous temporary resident. But it seemed to me that things went deeper than that: there was something about Shakespeare's depiction of a hero too noble for the world that surrounded him, too fine and pure for the exigencies of existence, that resonated in nineteenth-century Germany, a chaotic jumble of princely states and former empires doing its best to find itself as a nation. In 1844, Ferdinand Freiligrath had written in the famous first lines of a poem that '*Deutschland ist Hamlet!*' ('Germany is Hamlet!') – like Shakespeare's Prince, the country simply could not pull itself together. The phrase reverberated around German culture, not just in the nineteenth century but well into the twentieth.

Never mind that this is, at best, a deeply one-sided analysis of Shakespeare's hero. What is interesting – and not often noted – is what Freiligrath goes on to say. '*Vier Akte sahn wir spielen erst!*' the poet writes, 'Four acts only have we seen played!'

Hab acht, Held, daß die Ähnlichkeit	Look out, O hero, that the similarities
nicht auch im fünften du bewährst!	Do not continue into the Fifth!
Wir hoffen früh, wir hoffen spät:	We hope early, we hope late:
Oh, raff dich auch, und komm zu Streiche,	O, brace yourself and come to blows,
und hilf entschlossen, weil es geht,	And help decide, because it goes
zu ihrem Recht der flehnden Leiche!	To the rights of the imploring
	corpse [of Old Hamlet]!

| *Mach den Moment zunutze dir!* | Make the moment of use to you! |
| *Noch ist es Zeit . . .* | Now is the time . . . |

In some ways, this assertive, devil-may-care Hamlet is closer to the action hero of the English Comedians than to the pallid victim so beloved of Coleridge or Mallarmé. At least this Prince is being called upon to *do* something.

That said, the image of a tender, more feminised Hamlet remained resonant in Germany. One of the interpretations of the play I was keen to investigate was the silent-film version by Sven Gade, produced in 1921 in Berlin. Long relegated to the sidelines of Shakespearian cinematic history, in Britain it was the stuff of specialist screenings. I'd finally turned up a DVD copy on German eBay. Huddled in bed in the chilly attic room at my guesthouse in Weimar, shadows leaping and flickering across the walls, I watched it.

The film's major attraction was also its most controversial feature: Hamlet was a woman, played by the great Danish actor Asta Nielsen. In every respect *Hamlet: Ein Rachedrama* ('Hamlet: A Revenge Drama') was one of the most marvellously strange adaptations in existence.

Nielsen had founded her own production company to make the film, basing its script on material drawn from one of the earliest sources of the play, the early-medieval chronicles of Saxo Grammaticus. This she combined with a cranky book from 1881 by the American academic Edward P. Vining – dedicated, it so happened, to Horace Howard Furness – which argued that young Hamlet had been born a woman, a fact which has been hidden from the Danish court by Gertrude because of her fears about leaving the throne without a male heir. Brought up a boy, s/he roughhouses with Laertes in Wittenberg and befriends her/his princely contemporary, Fortinbras. More teasingly, s/he develops complicated feelings for Horatio (far stronger than those s/he develops for Ophelia). Her identity is only revealed on the point of death, when Horatio clutches the hero's body and realises she is in fact a heroine. ('Death uncovers your tragic secret!')

Filmed in modishly expressionist black-and-white, the film was above all a showcase for Nielsen's acting, underlining her wistful sense of tragedy as well as her mercurial comic timing. This was one of the funniest *Hamlet*s ever committed to film. Ophelia was dispatched with one sardonically elevated, pencil-thin eyebrow ('Oh, *her*,' it seemed to

say), Polonius had his beard tugged mercilessly, and during the mad
scenes Nielsen loped around, rubber-limbed, like a cat on tranquillisers.
It was an electrifying performance, and put me in mind more than
once of *Der Bestrafte Brudermord*. One could see why she'd inspired
both Garbo and Katharine Hepburn.

There was a mischievous hint of subversion at work, too. Whereas
Vining's thesis about Hamlet's gender was a misogynistic attempt
to pathologise the Prince's fears of action ('in very deed a woman,
desperately striving to fill a place for which she was by nature unfitted'),
Nielsen placed herself in a much bolder and braver tradition, making
herself the star attraction in the mode of nineteenth-century leading
ladies such as Charlotte Cushman and Sarah Bernhardt, both of
whom played the Dane. Athletic yet gamine, both androgynous and
tantalisingly bisexual, she caught the character's flitting, gossamer
contradictions more fully than any other actor I'd seen.

There was another reason it felt appropriate to watch the film in the
city that gave its name to the Weimar Republic. During the 1920s, when
Nielsen's fame was at its zenith, Germany and its cabaret scene had
been the crucible of exactly the kind of avant-garde drama *Hamlet: Ein
Rachedrama* put on screen – gender-bending, quizzically exploratory
in its examination of sensual and sexual identities. I wondered if any
of the straighter-backed members of the Deutsche Shakespeare-
Gesellschaft had seen the movie when it first came out, and if so what
they thought. Alas, I could find no mention of it in their yearbook.

Morning was perfect: crisp and clear and still, a sky of powder-blue
with clouds as fluffy as poached egg white. As I crunched along the
footpath next to the River Ilm, early leaves were starting to show on
the linden trees, pointillist dots of pale yellowish-green. The birds were
loud, the scent of wet grass and earth strong on the breeze. I felt in a
dangerously good mood.

For once, I knew exactly where I was going. It was the morning
of 23 April, Shakespeare's birthday: a year since I'd begun plotting
my travels. A few minutes' walk from my guesthouse was the most
famous Shakespeare monument in Germany, the Shakespeare statue
in the Park an der Ilm. I'd been holding off seeing it until now.

The park was begun in the late 1770s by Duke Karl August, who, weary with Frenchified formal gardens (as everyone else was wearying of Frenchified literature), wanted something in the style becoming fashionable in England. Goethe – who else? – happily complied, busying himself with studying botany and drawing inspiration from a visit to Wörlitz near Dessau, one of the first English-style parks to be created in Germany. In Weimar, Goethe created a rugged, proto-Romantic scheme, groves of maple, ash, linden, chestnut and hornbeam draped around the river with a rough patchwork of lawns and paths leading up the hill to the other side. Goethe was careful to ensure that the Gartenhaus – the small dwelling where he had first taken up residence – was a central feature. Both writer's retreat and picturesque adornment to the landscape, it effectively made the *genius loci* Goethe himself. I could just about glimpse the Gartenhaus through the trees, a modest grey cottage with a sharply sloping roof like a witch's hat.

Into this artfully curated piece of artlessness the Shakespeare-Gesellschaft inserted their statue in 1904, a fortieth birthday present to themselves. The site was on the opposite bank of the river, giving it a generous view over the Gartenhaus and ensuring that – lindens permitting – Shakespeare would forever be facing Goethe (and vice versa). The sculptor was chosen with similar care: he was Otto Lessing, a descendant of Gotthold Ephraim Lessing, the man who had made many Germans aware of this miraculous English poet. Like the society, the monument was a first: the first statue to the poet raised in continental Europe.

I rounded the corner and there he was: bone-white, a little larger than human size, on a grey stone dais. For a man just turning 449, he wasn't looking so bad. Lessing had caught Shakespeare as a decisive-looking forty-something, perched casually, one leg lifted, on what might have been a country wall. Tucked under his loose gown, his right hand crooked against his waist, was a scroll – *Hamlet*, perhaps, freshly revised and about to be sent to the compositor. His left hand toyed with a single rose, his left foot resting on a fool's cap within which there was a skull (Yorick's?). The overriding impression was of a seasoned, somewhat blokeish member of the literati shortly to be interviewed for a late-night arts programme.

His expression was trickier to gauge. Lessing had sculpted it so that, as one circumnavigated the statue clockwise, Shakespeare's countenance brightened: an effect achieved by shaping the left side of his face into a

stern frown while the right side bore a soft smile. It was a clever device
– comedy and tragedy, I supposed – but, viewed from some angles, it
had the unfortunate result of giving him a condescending leer.

I decided not to be too hard on Lessing's work: I was journeying
in search of Shakespeare translated, reinterpreted, reconfigured; of
Shakespeares that looked different from the British version. Leer notwithstanding, this was what difference looked like.

Normally the Gesellschaft held a ceremony here on the morning of
23 April: a short speech at the statue, then the laying of roses. This year,
however, I was on my own. The annual Shakespeare-Tage festival was
being held in Munich, my next destination, and the Weimar tradition
was on ice. Apart from the fluting of the birds and an occasional jogger
scuffing along the gravel, it was deathly quiet. The only person who'd
come to bid Shakespeare happy birthday, apparently, was me.

I settled down nearby and tried to get further into *Wilhelm Meister*,
hacking my way through the thickets of its prose. It had seemed
somewhat inauspicious that the elegant cloth-bound 1894 edition I'd
brought with me from England had only half its pages cut; its previous
owner had obviously given up halfway. I'd gone at the rest with a
vegetable knife I'd borrowed from the guesthouse.

'Wilhelm had already been for some time busied with translating
Hamlet . . . What in Wieland's work had been omitted he replaced;
and he had at length procured himself a complete version, at the
very time when Serlo and he finally agreed about the way of treating
it . . .'

Serlo and Wilhelm were about to get stuck into a thorny debate
about the ethics of translation; what should be preserved and what
changed, whether there was any such thing as the original. The subject
was entirely pertinent to my travels, but, try as I might, I couldn't focus.
I kept drifting to birdsong, the scent of wet stone, the sun creeping
slowly between the trees, the sound of the breeze crackling in the
grass. Indistinctly, I wondered how Goethe had coped with the same
distractions in the Gartenhaus. Maybe that was why he left so many
unfinished projects.

I heard voices on the path nearby, and started: I'd been dozing.
Shamefacedly I stood up and made a show of fussing with my notebook
and placing a bookmark in *Wilhelm Meister*. I hadn't even brought roses.

In lieu of a birthday party, a spot of improvisation was required. Professor Tobias Döring, the president of the Deutsche Shakespeare-Gesellschaft, was based in Munich (hence the venue for this year's conference), but he put me in touch with one of his Weimar colleagues. Roland Petersohn was a DSG stalwart, the principal at a school near Jena. He could tell me more of the society's backstory, including its history in the former East Germany.

At precisely 4 p.m. Petersohn and I solemnly toasted 449 years since the birth of William Shakespeare – and 149 years since the founding of the society – in the only way that seemed appropriate, with bitter black coffee and kirschtorte at the Residenz Café near the Schloss Belevedere, where Marlene Dietrich once sang.

With his dark green jacket, tufting moustache and spade-like handshake, one could picture Petersohn leading his charges on hearty expeditions through the Thuringian forests. As well as having been vice-president of the Gesellschaft in the 1990s, he had published academic studies of Heiner Müller, the GDR's most celebrated playwright, another German heavily influenced by Shakespeare.

Through mouthfuls of torte, Petersohn told me his own history. He had first joined in the early 1980s as a student of English and German literature in Jena. Germany was then buried beneath the permafrost of the cold war; Weimar, of course, lay on the eastern side of the border. In the early 1960s, relations had broken down between members based in the East and their erstwhile colleagues in the West. The crunch came in 1963, when instead of celebrating the forthcoming 400th anniversary of Shakespeare's birth and the society's centennial, the decision was taken to divide it. The Deutsche Shakespeare-Gesellschaft (West) would be based in Bochum on the outskirts of Dortmund, while the Ossies retained their historic home in Weimar. As with almost everything else in postwar Germany, the two wings had eyed each other with disdainful suspicion.

The penny dropped: I'd been wondering why the *Jahrbuchs* on the shelves of the DSG offices had multiplied between the 1960s and 1990s, one set in Prussian blue, the other scarlet. For nearly forty years there were two different *Jahrbuchs*, West and East, commissioned by two societies with two competing ideologies.

It was the cold war in Shakespearian miniature. For thirty years, each Shakespeare-Tag there were rival celebrations, with theatre companies from the Soviet bloc making their way to Weimar and those from the west appearing in Bochum. At one stage, among a coterie of radical Anglo-American scholars, it was a badge of honour to receive an invitation to the DSG (Ost) and peep behind the Iron Curtain.

'Stephen Greenblatt came to talk to us,' Petersohn said, waving his cake fork triumphantly. 'He did not go to West Germany. They couldn't afford him.'

The two societies had formally rejoined in April 1993, three years after the reunification of Germany itself. The process had been every bit as protracted and painful as it was at federal level. Rival negotiating teams were sent to thrash out terms on neutral ground, including in Stratford-upon-Avon (which, given the events of 1864, struck me as an irony worth cherishing).

It sounded like something from a spy novel, I said.

Petersohn gave me a long look. 'It was the strangest of times.'

It was in this period that he had been vice president, attempting to heal the divisions. 'It wasn't easy. There were strong feelings on both sides – a lot of cold warriors, hardliners, *ja*? There had to be a lot of agreements not to talk about the things that happened in the 1960s.'

I was curious about his perspective on the DSG's origins. What did he think lay behind Oechelhäuser's determination to set up a society in Shakespeare's name?

'I think popularisation, most of all. He admired Shakespeare, he wanted people to watch Shakespeare in the theatre and read Shakespeare's plays. He was a man of business, and he was looking for a project. Shakespeare was the project.'

I said I found it striking how rapidly the Gesellschaft had attempted to claim Shakespeare as a German classic.

He chewed thoughtfully. 'What you have to understand is German history. In 1864 Germany was still in the process of becoming one country. In 1871 the Deutsches Reich is founded under Bismarck, the first time there is a specific German state, German national thinking. That is partly why you get the founding of the other literary societies in Germany at this point – the idea of uniting Germany through culture. You have Goethe, you have Schiller and then you have this English writer also, who is almost more ours than theirs.'

So in his view there was definitely a political impetus?

'*Ja*. I think so. A few people think of nothing else. They say, "OK, Shakespeare must be German." It is a way of owning him.'

But why Shakespeare, of all writers?

'Of course there are Goethe and Schiller; by paying tribute to him you are also paying tribute to them. Then there's an admiration for the complexity of his plays, this envy – a kind of positive envy, if that is a concept, for Englishness and what it means. Maybe if Shakespeare was French, or Serbo-Croatian, it wouldn't be quite the same.'

He leaned forward, his voice low. 'This is my private opinion, but I do think there is the German character trait of being fascinated by something that works perfectly, like in engineering. You see something that is so smooth, so fascinating, that can't be destroyed by time or ideology. This sense of perfectionism, you know.' His green-grey eyes were wide. 'Wow!'

Vorsprung durch Technik, almost?

'*Vorsprung durch Kunst!* Ha, ha.' He leaned back in his chair, patting his stomach. '*Ja*, there is something about that. I really think so!'

One major obstacle barred the path of the Gesellschaft's founders: until that point, there had not been an agreed translation of the all-important Shakespearian text. Borck's severe alexandrines, Christoph Martin Wieland's cumbrous prose versions, Goethe and Schiller's invasive rewritings: the history of adapting Shakespeare's work in Germany had been chequered, to say the least. An authorised text of the complete works in modern German was a major priority. But how was this to be achieved?

Some recommended commissioning a fresh translation, but to do so would be time-consuming and expensive – and the society was humiliatingly short of money (so much so that it failed to produce a *Jahrbuch* in its second year). Others suggested patching up an old version and issuing it under the aegis of the DSG. Even if the issue were resolved, what sort of translation should this be? Aimed at academics and students, or actors? With expansive critical apparatus, befitting a noble literary institution, or something cheap and portable enough to make Shakespeare a household name in Germany? The businesslike Oechelhäuser insisted it should be the latter. His more high-minded colleagues disagreed.

Fortunately, an answer was at hand – and like so much in German culture, its origins lay in the Romantic period. In the generation immediately following Herder and Goethe, two of the brightest stars in the critical firmament were August Wilhelm von Schlegel (1767–1845) and Ludwig Tieck (1773–1853). Schlegel, the son of a Hanoverian pastor who had become a professor at the University of Jena, shot to prominence in 1798 when he co-founded the periodical *Athenäum*, a home for Romantic criticism and philosophy. Tieck, a Berliner whose father was a ropemaker, made his name as a popular playwright and novelist at almost exactly the same time.

As might be expected given their age, Shakespeare was a preoccupation for both. Tieck, a man of the theatre whose later experiments in Elizabethan staging would lay groundwork for reconstructions of the Globe and Blackfriars, became fascinated with questions of translation, publishing in 1799 a version of *The Tempest*. Schlegel, schooled in aesthetics and philology, fostered more academic interests, finely represented in his lectures *Über dramatische Kunst und Literatur* ('On Dramatic Art and Literature', 1808–11), which had foreshadowed Coleridge. They argued forcefully – and controversially – that Shakespeare was not an untutored genius but a supreme craftsman.

In 1798, after reading *Wilhelm Meister*, Schlegel set his sights on a project that had never yet been attempted in Germany: the systematic verse translation of Shakespeare's complete plays. His intention, Schlegel wrote, was to 'reproduce [the text] faithfully and at the same time poetically, following step by step the literal meaning and yet catching at least a part of the innumerable, indescribable beauties which do not lie in the letters but hang about it like a ghostly bloom'. Tieck acted as intermittent advisor.

For the next three years Schlegel slogged away, translating sixteen plays, mainly comedies and histories, outdoing previous efforts (so much so that rival translators at first avoided working on the same texts) and helping initiate a minor Shakespeare boom. But despite the unstinting support and assistance of his wife, Caroline, he began to lose both patience and steam. After 1801, he completed only one more script, *Richard III* (1810). *Hamlet* was complete, naturally, but Schlegel left twenty plays untranslated, among them some of the heftiest works in the canon: *King Lear, Othello, Macbeth*.

Wary of being overtaken by other translations then in progress – at least three – Schlegel's publisher, Georg Reimer, attempted to persuade his disillusioned author back to the grindstone, but without success. In desperation, he turned to Tieck. The arrangement proved a nightmare. Schlegel, despite being cussedly unwilling to do anything more, was scornful of attempts to tamper with his artistry, while Tieck, an incorrigible over-promiser, focused on the project only fitfully, subcontracting much of the work to his talented daughter Dorothea and a team of other translators.

Nonetheless – largely because of Reimer's doggedness – the work was eventually completed, and in 1833 the nine-volume *Shakespeare's Dramatische Werke* was finally complete. Schlegel-Tieck was rapidly acclaimed as the greatest translation of its time, a cult in its own right. (The poet Ferdinand Freiligrath wrote that 'it has permeated the marrow and blood of the German people'; one critic described it as being 'as important as Luther's translation of the Bible'). For all that her name appeared nowhere in the printed text, Dorothea's translations were particularly praised, notably her *Macbeth*.

Aware of the valuable links with Goethe and the Romantics and eager to bolster their own Shakespeare cult, the DSG concluded that only one version should have their blessing – Schlegel-Tieck. After a degree of scholarly wrangling, they published an updated version (1867 –71), following it in 1891 with the book Oechelhäuser had wanted all along: a cheap single-volume edition. Anointed as the long-awaited urtext, it sold more copies than every other German translation combined.

I had one final appointment before I left Weimar. Given the role the Weimar court theatre had played in the revival of Shakespeare in Germany – not just in Goethe and Schiller's day but much later, with a ground-breaking cycle of the history plays in 1864 – I felt I should at least get past the statue of the two *Dioskuren* and nose around the place itself.

The diary was against me: a new *The Merchant of Venice* wasn't opening for another month, and the theatre was dark every night I was in Weimar save my last. But there was a production of Mozart's *Die Zauberflöte* on 24 April; not a new staging, but well-received. The opera had been performed here in 1794, three years after its premiere in Vienna, and was now considered a local classic. Goethe had laboured on a sequel; like so much else, it had remained incomplete. It was enough of a connection, and anyway I reasoned that I had earned a restorative evening of Mozart. I booked a ticket.

For all that the theatre had been rebuilt almost entirely since Goethe and Schiller's day, when Susann, the press officer, offered to show me the building, I said yes. As a writer on theatre with a strong aversion ever to get involved in making it, I took a tourist's naive pleasure in sneaking backstage: the clutter of discarded props; the way the stage itself, a piece of glistening doll's-house perfection when seen front of house, was in fact a sordid tangle of duct tape and trailing wires and signs screaming ACHTUNG! in exciting colours.

Leaning against the wall of the paint shop there was a huge picture of Goethe, several metres high, a blown-up reproduction of the famous portrait by Joseph Karl Stieler. Completed in 1828, it depicts the poet near the end of his life, in a sleek black silk jacket and expensively embroidered waistcoat: the very model of the artist-courtier in well-fed prosperity. But Goethe's dark eyes – sidelong, distracted, even plaintive – told a different story, more haunted and ambivalent: a man of frustrated ideas and ambitions, tortured by doubts that any of it had been worthwhile.

Goethe's distinctly Hamletish approach to Shakespeare lasted long beyond the publication of the last part of *Wilhelm Meisters Lehrjahre* in 1796. He'd stayed on at the court theatre after Schiller's death, but the fizz had gone out of it: yet another tiresome administrative appointment that kept him from his writing.

Although his own dramas drifted away from Shakespearian models – notably *Faust*, the first part of which was drafted by 1806 – Goethe did try every so often to produce the plays. In 1811, he put on a long-desired staging of *Romeo and Juliet*, which though based on Schlegel's translation had lost half of the text and acquired 488 lines of Goethe's own. Goethe regarded it as a mixed success: 'I have probably never looked more deeply into Shakespeare's talent, but he, like all ultimate things, remains after all unfathomable.' In 1817, shaken by the death of his wife Christiane the year before and sick of backstage bickering – which culminated in Karl August pressuring him to stage a French melodrama with a poodle in a leading role – he resigned.

An essay he began work on during his last years at the theatre, '*Shakespeare und Kein Ende!*' ('No End to Shakespeare!'), written over a three-year period from 1813 to 1816, rehearsed these agonised questions once again. Earlier in the day I had spent a few hours in the Goethe-Schiller Archive, a statuesque classical building high on the brow of a hill overlooking Weimar. One of the curators had shown me a scribal copy of the essay: the size of a small pamphlet, in tidy copperplate that gave little hint of its protracted gestation.

Its paradoxes were typically late-Goethean. It argued that Shakespeare was pre-eminently a man of the theatre, but also that the plays were best read aloud rather than acted; he was a modern poet but also 'naive' as per Schiller's scheme, and simultaneously – somehow – both. Niggling away was the question of whether it was even possible to stage his plays:

> Shakespeare's works are not for our physical eyes . . . Shakespeare works through the living word and this – the word – is best transmitted by reading aloud; for then the listener is not distracted as he is by a performance, be it a fitting one or not. There is no greater pleasure and none more pure than to listen with closed eyes to a reciting (not a declaiming) of a Shakespeare play that is right for it.

Was this ambivalence a hard-won lesson from the experience of staging *Macbeth* and *Romeo and Juliet*, or a demonstration that Goethe was congenitally unsuited to the job of theatre director? It was hard to say.

Wilhelm Meister refused to be banished. In 1821 Goethe published what would be his last major work, *Wilhelm Meisters Wanderjahre* ('Wilhelm Meister's Journeyman Years'), which he would continue tinkering with until a few years before his death in 1832. An experimental, proto-Joycean novel built up from many years of jottings, it sends Wilhelm – who has long since abandoned the theatre – on a cascade of adventures featuring magic boxes and hidden caves through territory that more closely resembles the world of medieval quests or magical realism than any realistic European setting.

Critics are still divided as to whether *Wanderjahre* is in a finished state, or even whether it counts as a novel at all. One bitter little line caught my eye, right at the end of the book. It comes amid a collection of aphorisms supposedly composed by Makarie, a mystic seer-like figure whom Wilhelm encounters on his wanderings:

> How much falsehood Shakespeare and particularly Calderón have subjected us to, how these two great lights of the poetic firmament

have become *ignes fatui* of us, let the writers of the future note in
retrospect.

From the great illuminator of *'Zum Shakespeares Tag'* who had given
the young writer the 'gift of sight' to an *ignis fatuus* or false fire . . . if
these were Goethe's own sentiments too, even a hint of them, it was a
bleak conclusion.

Even so, Shakespeare stayed in Goethe's thoughts to the end.
According to his first biographer Johann Peter Eckermann, among the
poet's final words was a paean to the writer who had meant so much
to him over fifty years: 'Just let someone try, with human desire and
human strength, to produce something that one could set alongside
the creations that bear the name of Mozart, Raphael or Shakespeare.'

A few days later in March 1832, as Goethe lay dying, language failing
him, it was said he had tried to write words in the air. Only one letter
was discernible: 'W'. I had a strong hunch it stood for Wilhelm.

Die Zauberflöte didn't entirely live up to the excitements of being
backstage: saying the production, over a decade old, was past its sell-by
date was putting it kindly. But for once it wasn't having Shakespeare
on the brain that made me glimpse him in the theatre that night. The
wrangles between the Queen of the Night and the magician Sarastro
in *Die Zauberflöte* had obvious echoes of Oberon and Titania, but all the
intimate resemblances were to *The Tempest*, itself a free extemporisation
on themes of magic, illusion, power, love.

Much has been made of the bizarreness of the librettist Emanuel
Schikaneder's symbolism-heavy plot, with its love quest, imprisonments,
trials of virtue and abstinence – including the well-supported theory
that it was based on his and the composer's interest in Freemasonry.
Watching it, I wondered if the story made more sense if one saw it
through a Shakespearian lens. The virtuous young lovers Tamino and
Pamina were plausible stand-ins for Ferdinand and Miranda; Sarastro
was a double for Prospero; Monostatos, the 'blackamoor' and chief of
Sarastro's team of slaves, for Caliban.

None of these similarities is surprising, if one accepts the theory that
Zauberflöte was partly inspired by *The Enchanted Island*, John Dryden
and William Davenant's 1667 adaptation of *The Tempest*. And there

are more alluring connections too. According to a single account, a dramatist called Friedrich Wilhelm Gotter had made a 'marvellous free adaptation' of Shakespeare's *The Tempest* under the title *Die Zauberinsel* ('The Enchanted Island') and sent it to Mozart soon after *Zauberflöte*'s premiere in October 1791. Desperate for money and by then gravely ill, Mozart had agreed to write the music (having, confusingly, already contributed to yet another opera by Schikaneder with a remarkably similar title). Less than three months later, however, he would be dead, the work incomplete.

Mozart's *The Tempest* was one of the great operatic might-have-beens. But then *Zauberflöte* contained enough magic of its own, I thought as I walked back through the darkened, silent streets of Weimar. For all the silliness of Schikaneder's plot, the music was transcendent, grave and mystical, filled with an exultant sense of joy but also the strange youthful gravity Mozart summoned without apparent effort. Listening, I felt the philosophical tangles of Goethe and Weimar classicism and nostrification slipping away: Mozart had the measure of me.

He certainly had a way with recognition scenes. When Pamina and Tamino were reunited in the final act, it was via a duet of heart-stopping simplicity and grace, their vocal lines winding ecstatically around each other while strings pulsed mesmerically underneath. Forget airy sprites and frolicking masquers: the transposition that introduced it, from a lambent A-flat major to a shimmering F major, was a conjuring trick that rivalled anything written by Shakespeare.

———◆———

AS I BOARDED THE TRAIN, my head was full of everything I'd seen. For all the ardent, sometimes alarming zealousness of German Shakespearians – *unser* Shakespeare, divine Wilhelm and the rest – it was possible to explain away their obsession as Roland Petersohn had done: as an exaggerated symptom of the nationalistic fervour that swept through many new European states in the revolutionary years of the mid-nineteenth century.

Shakespeare had been essential to the renaissance of German literature and drama for the German Romantics; from there, particularly once Germany had an authorised translation, it wasn't the craziest leap to declare him an honorary German. Many countries had tried to plant a flag in Shakespeare, whether it was fables about his supposed Sicilian origins or recent Canadian attempts to claim that a seventeenth-century oil painting now kept in a vault in Ontario, the so-called Sanders portrait, was the only surviving portrait done from life (and thus a more authentic relic than anything owned by Canada's two ancient rivals, America and Britain). Such nationalistic appropriations were a touch naive; but they testified, if little else, to Shakespeare's global reach and the intensity of devotion he inspired worldwide.

Another period of the Deutsche Shakespeare-Gesellschaft's past was infinitely more troubling. While at the Goethe-Schiller Archive, I'd glanced at the society's papers, ordering a couple of box files on the off chance they might throw up something. One box was from the 1930s and included a colourful copy of the magazine *Die Woche* commemorating a Weimar performance of *Was Ihr Wollt* (*Twelfth Night*, translated under its playful alternative title *What You Will*). The issue was published in 1932. I didn't have the time – or the German – to dig deeper, but it fired a question: what *had* happened to the Gesellschaft the year following, once the National Socialists had seized power?

The answer wasn't hard to find. The English-language history printed on the Gesellschaft's website restricted itself to a taut and legalistic paragraph, but was at least clear: the DSG had fallen squarely under the influence of the Nazi regime. Party officials had infiltrated the board, Jewish subscribers been forced to resign. The annual Shakespeare-Tage were remodelled to accommodate Nazi interests and ideologies.

There was barely an academic or literary institution that had not been forced into some ghastly accommodation with Hitler's regime, but it was conspicuous that the Party had shown such interest in Shakespeare. Could it be related to those nineteenth-century attempts to claim him for German culture? And what happened once the second world war had begun, when Germany and the country of Shakespeare's birth were officially at war?

The website article had been written by an academic from Hanover, Ruth von Ledebur, who had researched the Gesellschaft's history and was coming to the conference in Munich. I emailed, asking if we could meet. In the meantime, I downloaded a slew of journal articles to my laptop to read on the train.

What I read made my head throb even more. The early years aside, the DSG had done its best to keep out of the political intrigues that overtook Germany during the late nineteenth and early twentieth centuries. It prided itself on its internationalist reputation, boasting that by 1911 its members included Theodore Roosevelt and King George V of England, alongside the emperors of Austria and Germany.

Such amity did not last. One flashpoint was the first world war, when Shakespeare had – like so much else – been drawn into the conflict. As in 1864, an anniversary was responsible: 1916 was three hundred years since Shakespeare's death, the cue for events in various cities around the world, among them Prague, New York, Madrid and Copenhagen.

The story went something like this. Hearing that German Shakespearians intended to plough ahead with their celebrations despite the fact that there was a war on, an elderly British playwright called Henry Arthur Jones had written a pamphlet pouring caustic scorn on the idea that Germany could find anything at all to celebrate in Shakespeare. Jones had made a name on the late-Victorian stage with society dramas, to great commercial but little critical success. (Oscar Wilde once quipped that 'there are three rules for writing plays. The first rule is not to write like Henry Arthur Jones; the second and third rules are the same.') Now sixty-five, a semi-invalid, Jones was crabbed and cantankerous, devoted to defending his country's honour with a mania that verged on lunacy.

In *Shakespeare and Germany*, published in 1916, Jones turned his fire on German claims to own Shakespeare, which by that stage had hardened into a trope:

> It will be well for England to be prepared for the characteristic official announcement which will doubtless be made in Berlin on 23rd April for the final and complete annexation by Germany of William Shakespeare, with all his literary, poetical, philosophical, and stage appurtenances, effects, traditions, and associations, and all the demesnes that there adjacent lie. [. . .] Meantime we may ask by what insolence and egotism, what lust of plunder, or what madness of pride Germany dares add to the hideous roll of her thieveries and rapes this topping impudence and crime of vaunting to herself the allegiance of Shakespeare?

It was not incidental that Jones's title page stated that *Shakespeare and Germany* had been 'written during the Battle of Verdun'.

The pamphlet may have been deranged, but in one respect it was dead right – caught up in its own brand of nationalistic fervour, the Deutsche Shakespeare-Gesellschaft had indeed convinced itself that 1916 should be a bellicose celebration of the Germanness of Shakespeare. When president Alois Brandl addressed his colleagues in Weimar in April 1914, even before hostilities formally commenced, he insisted that 'Shakespeare belongs to our spiritual armament', and ended quoting the words of Henry V before Agincourt:

> O God of battles, steel my soldiers' hearts.
> Possess them not with fear. Take from them now
> The sense of reck'ning, ere th'opposèd numbers
> Pluck their hearts from them.

Brandl would not be the first to reach for *Henry V* during wartime – and was certainly not the last – but the effect was to entrench divisions between British and German academics. When an erstwhile colleague of Brandl's, the Anglo-Jewish scholar Israel Gollancz, was assembling a *Book of Homage* to Shakespeare for 1916, asking representatives from countries worldwide to send in tributes to the plays and poems, Germany and Austria were pointedly uninvited. Another DSG stalwart, the dramatist Ludwig Fulda, suggested that if the Kaiser's army were to win the war, a clause should be inserted into the peace treaty 'stipulating the formal surrender of William Shakespeare to Germany' (it was a 'mistake' that he had been born in England in the first place). It seems unlikely that Fulda knew of Henry Arthur Jones's pamphlet, which suggested the Germans would try to do exactly this. And it was apparently not a joke.

In March 1933, once the Nazis had seized power, the Deutsche Shakespeare-Gesellschaft was even more eager to conform. Nervous about the newly passed legislation concerning *Gleichschaltung* ('falling-into-line'), the society hurriedly recast its Shakespeare-Tag celebrations to remove any taint of opposition. Echoing Freiligrath the century before, the new keynote speaker, Max Deutschbein, enlisted none other than Hamlet to this new *Völkisch* cause, 'not only the most powerful revelation of the poet himself, but . . . at the same time the most striking embodiment of the heroic-Germanic man'.

The Party repaid the compliment handsomely. Within the year, the DSG was receiving funds from the foreign office. Fervent right-wingers soon thronged its ranks. Rainer Schlösser, a journalist and favourite of Goebbels, became a committed member, as did Joachim von Ribbentrop, later Germany's ambassador to Britain. A rubicon loomed in 1936, when the translator Hans Rothe, whose muscular, modernist versions of Shakespeare had been popular during the Weimar era, found himself under attack. Remarkably, the dispute made headlines: the SS house magazine *Der Schwarze Korps* weighed in, and in May 1936 none other than Goebbels gave a speech proclaiming that 'literary experiments' on writers such as Shakespeare were not to be tolerated. (Rothe had already fled the country.) Invited to offer scholarly judgement, the Gesellschaft dithered before eventually ruling that Rothe's translations were inferior to Schlegel-Tieck.

Things became stranger, and more sinister. Otherwise innocuous *Jahrbuch* articles began to bristle with terms such as *Kampf* ('struggle') and *Streben* ('striving'). A lowpoint came in that same year of 1936, when Professor Hans F. K. Günther, whose eugenic research had made him an object of veneration for many senior Nazis, joined the board. The author of such works as *A Racial Typology of the Jewish People*, Günther was not selected, needless to say, for his expertise in literary criticism. On Shakespeare-Tag that April, he gave a talk. Its full title was 'Shakespeare's Girls and Women from a Biological Perspective', an ominous nod to an essay on the heroines by the Jewish poet Heinrich Heine.

Even by the surreal standards of National Socialism, the talk makes for bewildering reading. Günther argued that Shakespeare was a fervent eugenicist, committed throughout his works to ideals of racial purity, whether in Sonnet 1's claim that 'from fairest creatures we desire increase' (to breed) or the way in which, at the close of *Twelfth Night*, Viola and Sebastian recognise each other because of their 'noble' ancestry.

'Some of you might be somewhat shocked at my attempt to connect Shakespeare with questions of heredity, selection, eradication and birth statistics,' Günther announced:

> and you might think that such a lecture at this celebration of Shakespeare would transgress against good taste that forbids the connecting of literature with population statistics or even medical procedures. However, I believe I can say that Shakespeare, with his spirit open to the world . . . would not have closed himself off to questions of heredity and selection.

According to the notes, his speech was received 'with applause'. The text is there, in cold print, in the 1937 issue of the *Jahrbuch*.

Later I read a translation of the resignation letter of one Dr Ludwig Goldstein from Königsberg. The letter had arrived in 1933. 'My entire life I have been a faithful and active member of the German Shakespeare Society,' Goldstein began:

> Today, however, I have to ask you to delete my name from your list of members. My entire life, I have not known any notion of *Volk* other than the German, and I have tried to serve this notion in East Prussia. However, these days, I am ostracised as a 'Jew', that is, as a 'non-German', and I am, as a consequence, restricted in matters of earning my living. Hence, I have no option but to withdraw from such valuable institutions and associations as the Shakespeare Society.

Three years later, by the time Günther stood up to deliver his speech, there would have been no Jewish members whatsoever. Ludwig Fulda, so stridently nationalistic during the first world war, was also a Jew, and had also been forced to resign. In 1939, denied entry to the United States, he committed suicide.

Waiting for my connection on the platform, I thought grimly of the train journey I had just taken. A few minutes out of Weimar, we had passed a large forest, the Ettersberg, the hunting ground for the Dukes of Weimar since at least the seventeenth century. As we had swept past, I had seen through the rich green of the trees a tall thin spire in austere grey brick. Solitary and immense, it surveyed the land for miles around. It was the monument to the Buchenwald concentration camp, less than six miles from Weimar. The trains had gone there too.

Munich was bustling and busy, with the self-righteous glow of a town experiencing good fortune it considered to be wholly deserved. While most of Europe was still clawing its way out of the credit crunch, in the well-fed heartland of Bavaria things had barely been better: unemployment levels the lowest in Germany, a flourishing economy the envy of cities worldwide. As the taxi and I jostled through the Thursday rush-hour traffic, all I could see were new-model Audis and Mercs and BMWs. Everyone on the street seemed to be on their way to or from the gym, possibly via the hair salon. In the evening sunlight, even the cars looked musclebound and tanned.

From modest beginnings, the Shakespeare-Tage had swelled into a multi-day jamboree, incorporating academic talks, seminars and workshops, theatre visits, trips to local attractions – a hybrid of academic conference and cultural minibreak. Usually events were held in Weimar, or occasionally in Bochum. But in recent years the society had begun to expand its operations. In Munich the theme, appropriately enough, was *Geld und Macht*: money and power.

As I climbed the stairs to the conference suite at the city's Literaturhaus, I was buzzing with questions: who actually came to events like these? And would anyone really talk to me about the subject that was uppermost in my mind, the society's awkward relationship with its past?

On the top floor, in a sleek, glass-walled atrium bathed in glossy spring sunshine, the members of the Gesellschaft were taking coffee and making small talk, preparing to go into the welcome address by Professor Tobias Döring. I inspected the room: perhaps 150 people; a reasonable density of comfortable footwear, tweed and corduroy but not as many grey heads as I'd imagined. A burly, bearded man of about my age was standing by the coffee point with a baby in a sling across his chest.

I was admiring the view, which swept out past the honey-coloured dome of the Theatinerkirche to the purple-fringed Bavarian mountains, when a woman appeared beside me.

'It is my first time here in Munich!' she said.

Me too, I said. We exchanged smiles.

Inge was from Dessau and had been a member of the Gesellschaft since before reunification, in 1989. She was now in her sixties, she told me in flawless English; behind her large glasses, which were framed by a smooth, carefully trimmed bob, her eyes were wide. The wife of a businessman, she had been a full-time mother; now that the kids had flown the nest, she finally had time to devote herself to her own interests. Shakespeare was one.

Whereas the Shakespeare Association of America and the International Shakespeare Association were thoroughly professionalised organisations, exclusively the habitat of academics giving position papers and peer-refereed articles, the Shakespeare-Gesellschaft had stayed true to its roots. In 1869, the Gesellschaft had 190 members; these days the membership was roughly 2,000, but only a third were scholars, with the other two thirds divided between teachers (generally of secondary-school English Literature) and members of the general public. Accountants, insurance agents, physicists, vets: the DSG roster numbered them all. The German language, precise as ever, had a noun for people who joined societies like these: *Bildungsbürgertum*, the educated, bookish middle classes.

I found the concept captivating. As a writer and critic who intermittently passed myself off as an academic I was used to attending events like this for work, but for fun? Shakespeare as a hobby, like basket-weaving or bell-ringing?

'It is so friendly, and the Shakespeare-Tage are very interesting,' Inge was saying. 'I have many friends all over Germany now, it is a good chance to have a reunion. People like me, we cannot get enough of Shakespeare!'

She'd made it a project to see every one of the plays, which meant frequent trips to London as well as theatres around Germany. Only Shakespeare's final, co-written *Two Noble Kinsmen* – so obscure that even the Royal Shakespeare Company had not bothered to include it in their 2006–07 festival of the complete works – had so far eluded her. One could not help but be impressed.

I glanced at the programme, with its seminars on Marxist investigations of *Timon of Athens* and the relationship between communism and Shakespearian cinema. Did she ever find the talks a bit . . . specialised?

She shrugged. '*Ja*, some of them are a bit boring, some are more interesting.' Her voice lowered. 'Tobias, when he was appointed, some of us older ones were a bit anxious that he would change things – make it more academic, you know? But he's been very good.'

We bid each other farewell, and I watched her being swallowed by the crowd swarming towards the lecture hall. Her notebook was already out; the expression on her face was of eager anticipation. I tried to stave off the sense, not wholly successfully, that she was more professional at this than me.

When I walked in, Ruth von Ledebur was already there: a slight figure in a corner of the restaurant. She was wearing a smart sky-blue top and matching cardigan. Her shoulders were rounded with age, a crown of snowy hair cropped short around a broad, open face. As she gestured at me to sit down, her eyes scrutinised me carefully: sapphire-sharp, with more than a hint of scepticism in them. I liked her immediately, and was simultaneously grateful not to be one of her students.

Born in 1929 into an aristocratic family, Ledebur had grown up in Hanover. After marrying and training as a schoolteacher, she returned to university in her forties, completing a PhD at Bonn on the history of German Shakespeare during the cold war. She had begun to get interested in the history of the Shakespeare-Gesellschaft, which she had recently joined: what had shaped its ideologies, the way its story had mirrored and echoed the agonies and triumphs of Germany itself. She spent weeks at a time in the Weimar archives, blowing dust off files that had remained untouched for years, burrowing backwards from the second world war through the thirties and then the twenties. She asked awkward questions. She started to piece together a narrative about the society's activities in the interwar period. Making the Gesellschaft face up to its past became her life's work.

Her voice was soft but precise. 'The dogma of the academics used to be, "We are not political, we are not political." That was the generation before my own.' Her gaze was level. 'But you understand everything is political, in a way.'

For an hour and a half, over an elegant lunch, we talked about the things her professors had not wanted to. For Ledebur the story went right back to 1864, and the way the society had become enmeshed with the mania for making Shakespeare Germany's national poet.

'It's a kind of patriotism, and it develops not just in the nineteenth century but into the twentieth century too. During the first world war there was a young scientist, and he writes – I think he is already in the trenches at this time – "Germany is where Shakespeare is born a second time."' She chuckled. 'It's a fantastic idea: that Germany would be the better place for Shakespeare to have been born. It's going up this ladder of nostrification – not saying simply, "He is ours," but, "It would be *better* if he had been ours."'

The process had continued after the first world war. The humiliation suffered by Germany at Versailles was felt keenly by the conservative middle classes, many of whom were apprehensive about the Weimar Republic. In Weimar itself – a conservative town that found itself unwillingly giving birth to a radical democratic experiment – these feelings were especially raw.

Ledebur leaned across. 'You know Weimar was one of the few towns which had a dominance of Nazi representatives before 1933?'

She wagged a finger. 'Yes, that is very important. You have come across Baldur von Schirach?'

I had heard the name: Schirach was head of the Hitler Youth, and had saved his skin by denouncing Hitler at Nuremberg after the war.

It transpired that Schirach's father Carl was sometime head of the Weimar theatre, one of the most influential cultural figures in the town. It was he who had introduced the young Baldur to Hitler after an opera in Weimar. Carl had also been on the board of the Shakespeare-Gesellschaft, and had done his utmost to push the society towards the hard right.

Everything connected, Ledebur explained. 'It was important to have full possession of German cultural superiority, and part of that cultural superiority was not only Schiller and Goethe, but also Shakespeare.'

When the National Socialists first came to power, they hadn't exhibited much interest in the Shakespeare Society or Weimar's other literary organisations. But the propaganda benefits of having such well-respected institutions on board began to dawn. A movement still regarded as the preserve of thuggish Bavarian louts could acquire valuable cultural capital by associating with a place such as Weimar.

Were other DSG members really believers, or was it just Schirach?

Her eyes narrowed. 'This is a highly ambiguous matter. At the annual meetings, there used to be one speaker only. In the Nazi period, the board came to an agreement that one year they would have an academic speaker, the following year allow one of the Nazi bosses to give the talk. So they played it both ways. Appeasement, if you wish.'

Trouble really began for the Gesellschaft when funds began to run out: it had lost most of its assets in the devaluation of the 1920s, and once Jewish members and political undesirables were ejected its membership declined still further. Ledebur's smile was colourless. 'It was the opportunity to turn the screw.'

In observing the grim proximity of Weimar and Buchenwald, I was far from alone, she explained: after the war, the relationship had become a symbol of the appalling concatenation of high art and pure barbarism. *Buchenwald liegt bei Weimar* ('Buchenwald lies near Weimar') became a rallying cry for postwar intellectuals determined that culture should never again be co-opted for political ends.

Behind this forensic quest for the truth I sensed the urge for some kind of reparation. Ledebur had been ten years old when the war broke out. What were her own memories?

She paused for a while, her thin fingers lightly stroking the fork on the table.

'I was partly conscious of what was going on, and I do remember my parents saying, "Don't talk about this outside the house." When we were about ten or eleven and were forced to join the youth movements, my mother and I did not speak about politics with my father. We knew that we would be questioned about our parents, and they knew how difficult it would have been for us. So politics was not a topic, and I am sure that among members of the society it was exactly the same – they were afraid that if they voiced criticism, they would be the next to be thrown out.' She shook her head briskly. 'But it's no excuse, it's no excuse.'

Did she feel sympathy for the position in which her predecessors in the society had been placed?

This time the pause was much longer. Outside on the street, green leaves were stirring in the sunlight.

'When I began to research this,' she said slowly, 'I felt horror: that there was absolutely no way of exculpating what they have done. And I am still strongly of the opinion that there were people who did resist, people who opposed.'

It must have been a gruelling area to research, I said.

'Awful, awful. No one had handled the archives in Weimar, they were just stored away. I started my research in the late nineties. I was the first to have these dust-covered folders in my hand. I took the folder from 1933 and in that folder, I found a postcard from a Jewish member, declaring his resignation.'

This is the one I'd read on the train, reproduced in an article; I hadn't realised that it was her discovery.

'Yes. But the really terrible thing is that the president wrote back saying, "Perhaps we will soon have happy times again and you can rejoin the society." That was the spirit in 1933. Many thought, "Oh, it will blow over." That was shocking.'

Did anyone know what had happened to Dr Goldstein?

She was arranging her napkin in front of her, fold by painstaking fold. 'Probably you can guess.'

'You know what is interesting?' she said as I helped her to her feet. 'Once the war was over, there was again an immense enthusiasm about

Shakespeare in Germany, immense! In the theatres, in the academy – a sense that we will rebuild Germany, and Shakespeare will be a figurehead of that.'

There was an odd smile on her lips as she eased herself into her jacket. 'It seems to creep up in German history whenever there is a change.'

⸻

ONE EXTRAORDINARY FACT about Shakespeare in Germany: there are now estimated to be more professional performances of his plays put on here each year than in the UK. Partly this is a result of the country's federalised structure, where even modest towns boast their own producing theatre and resident company. Partly there is the lasting German reverence for art – *die Kunst* – which results in levels of subsidy that make British theatre-makers throb with envy. (The culture budget of Berlin alone is estimated to be €1 billion annually, more than the UK spends on culture in total, and makes the American National Endowment for the Arts look like loose change.)

But I suspected there was something else going on: *unser* Shakespeare was very much alive and kicking. The strident militarism of the phrase may have made modern scholars blush (particularly in pacific, post-war Germany), but theatres operated as if it still applied. Only the plays of Schiller are more performed.

No fewer than three separate theatres were putting on Shakespeare performances during the Shakespeare-Tage. I had managed to get tickets for *A Midsummer Night's Dream* at the Residenztheater and *King Lear* at one of the most famous theatres in Germany, Munich's Kammerspiele. The new *Lear* was on everyone's lips. It was by the Dutch director Johan Simons, who even by the standards of contemporary German theatre had an insurrectionary reputation. Inge had seen it the night I arrived; when I asked her what she thought, she pursed her lips. 'You'll see,' she said enigmatically.

As I took my seat inside the Kammerspiele's jewel-box art nouveau auditorium, there was something I couldn't put my finger on; something not quite right. The set looked unexceptional: a tent-like structure in black-and-white striped cloth, with what appeared to be real grass in front. It looked like an upmarket garden fete.

After a few minutes I worked out that the thing that wasn't right was the smell: thick and ripe, with distinct farmyard overtones. It reminded me of family caravanning holidays in north Wales. Why was I smelling it in central Munich? Could there be a very un-German problem with the drains?

No. The selling point of *König Lear* was that performing alongside the human cast was a troupe of live pigs, kept in an improvised pen downstage-left. Ears flopping, the pigs trundled amiably around, the size of large wheelbarrows, occasionally menacing the scenery. Every so often, a handler in rubber boots would top up a swill tray, which provoked an orgy of snuffling and munching.

The pigs certainly had excellent dramatic timing: as Lear was howling his way through the storm, one detached itself from the herd and embarked on what I can only describe as the porcine equivalent of a soliloquy, standing in full glare of the footlights and gazing coolly down the length of the auditorium.

The gist of the production was clear enough. This was *King Lear* as satire, with Ancient Britain as a farmyard in a muddy field, and a King – flabby and rasping – at the end of his rope. Cordelia wore spangly hotpants; Goneril and Regan, both frantic for their father's attention, were swaddled in shapeless smocks. In the hovel scene the farmyard *Konzept* seemed to make sense – both human and pig flesh, I can report, have the same radiant pink hue under stage lights – but elsewhere it reduced whatever grandeur the play contains to a state of brutish disquiet. The fight between Edgar and Edmund, which lasted for a grim five minutes, resembled a scuffle between drunks in a pub car park. Compared with the humans on stage – never mind us in the audience – the pigs, it seemed to me, had a pretty good deal.

Why *were* there pigs? I wondered if it'd be any clearer if one spoke German. Once the applause was done, I asked my neighbour. She shrugged, plainly baffled; that was contemporary German theatre for you.

I had an uncomfortable night's sleep in which abattoirs and shambles sticky with blood loomed large. By 8 a.m. I was outside my hotel.

I had an appointment with Peter Longerich, a professor of German history who specialised in Holocaust studies and divided his time between Munich and Royal Holloway in London. He had recently completed a biography of Goebbels, and was also involved in Munich's long-delayed project to build a museum documenting National Socialism. I hoped he might be able to answer the question that had been bothering me: why the Nazis had been so smitten by Shakespeare in the first place. Filleting the sonnets for references to breeding was one thing, but could one really turn the author of *The Merchant of Venice* and *Othello* into the poet laureate of the 'master race'? Could *Hamlet*, the play so often co-opted as Germany's own, really coexist with the absolute will to power?

Out of nowhere, a black Alfa Romeo detached itself from the traffic and squealed to a halt next to the kerb. The door shot open.

Crouched inside was a rangy figure in a black leather jacket zipped against the morning chill, and dark, shoulder-length, thinning hair, worn in the manner of a German rock star of the late 1970s. Longerich. Over the gear-stick, a little contortedly, we shook hands.

His manner was sardonic and lightly amused; I reasoned it needed to be, if one spent much time in the company of Himmler and Goebbels.

As we swung into the line of traffic, I explained the object of my journey. He sent a spent cigarette cartwheeling out of the window.

'You came to the right place. In Munich we have more Nazis than we know what to do with.'

It was here that the Party had its origins as a fringe group founded in 1919, one of a number of *Völkisch* extremist organisations that sprang up in the chaos following the Kaiser's abdication. Hitler became the fifty-fourth person to join what was then known as the German Workers' Party. He rapidly took control, changing its name to the National Socialist German Workers' Party (NSDAP) and establishing a power base in the city. By November 1923 he had launched the so-called Beer-Hall Putsch, which culminated in a demonstration at the Feldherrnhalle ('Field Marshal's Hall') in the centre of the city. When protestors exchanged fire with police, nineteen people were killed, fifteen of them brownshirts.

The putsch failed, but although the NSDAP was banned and Hitler imprisoned in Landsberg Fortress (where he occupied himself by writing *Mein Kampf*), Munich was crucial to the movement's rehabilitation. As soon as the ban was revoked in 1925, Bavarian businessmen and society hostesses replenished its coffers, while the city's unemployed working class filled the ranks of the Stormtroopers. Membership rocketed from

25,000 in 1925 to 180,000 in 1929. By 1930, following the Wall Street
Crash, the Party was polling at 18 per cent nationally. Three years later,
Hitler was in the Reichstag.

Munich had always been central to the myth, Longerich explained.
In 1935 the city was bestowed with the title of *Hauptstadt der Bewegung*
('Capital of the Movement'), and the NSDAP – eternally suspicious
of cosmopolitan, liberal Berlin – retained its headquarters here, along
with almost every Nazi organisation. We roared along the street that
led towards the Feldherrnhalle, which the Nazis had sanctified as a
memorial in front of which Munichers were required to give the Nazi
salute (with an unlooked-for effect on pedestrian flow; the detour to
avoid it became known as the *Drückebergergasse* or 'Dodgers' Alley').

Longerich parked on the edge of Königsplatz. We walked the rest on
foot. Some of the earliest Nazi rallies and book-burnings had been held
here in 1935, the same year that the corpses of the brownshirts killed
in 1923 were reburied in so-called Temples of Honour. The square was
expanded into a vast parade ground, equipped with a state-of-the-art
lighting system for rallies and military manoeuvres.

Königsplatz was now covered in grass, and the Temples of Honour
were long gone, dynamited by the US Army in 1945, but the plinths in the
distance remained, partially shrouded beneath a dark tangle of brambles
and weeds. Sombre grey buildings, sombre grey sky; the place had a
desolate and wind-nagged air, even on a gentle spring morning like this. It
was all too easy to project the grainy black-and-white photographs in the
history books on to the scene in front of me: thousands upon thousands
of ink-black Stormtroopers standing to crisp attention, swastikas snapping
in the breeze.

The Documentation Centre was a sorry story, Longerich explained,
subject to endless postwar wranglings about the meaning of the past.
After more than a decade of impassioned in-fighting, the project had
come close to falling through, and the arguments about what should
go inside had still not finally been settled.

He gestured to a cube-like structure swathed in scaffolding and white
protective panels, on the site of what had been NSDAP headquarters:
at least the builders had begun.

'One day, you know, we might even get it finished.'

Over coffee and Danishes, Longerich and I debated how William Shakespeare had got himself mixed up in all this.

Kultur and *Kulturpolitik* had always been vital to the Nazi movement, in Munich most especially: in 1933 Hitler declared the city 'Capital of German Art', and it was here in 1937, inside an improvised space in the Hofgarten, that the notorious exhibition of 'Degenerate Art' had been held.

Moreover, the Nazis had a taste, and something of a talent, for drama. The renovations to Königsplatz transformed what had been a humdrum city square into a site for grandiose, semi-mystical ceremonies that could be replayed via newsreels across the world. Torchlit processions and military march-pasts were crafted with a director's eye, not a detail or uniform out of place. One thinks inevitably of the 1936 Olympics, which became a spectacle of fascist power on the largest stage the world could offer, all captured for cinematic posterity by Leni Riefenstahl.

Theatre was also a private obsession. Hitler's reverence for Wagner and the more bombastic bits of Beethoven was well recorded, but I hadn't known about his interest – fed by the intellectual vanity of an intelligent but poorly educated man – in drama. His own theatrics during speeches were rehearsed with actorly precision, and it was a fascination encouraged by his friendship with Joseph Goebbels, a genuinely cultured man who had a doctorate in nineteenth-century German drama and a lifelong passion for high art. Together the two made theatre trips, recorded in exhaustive detail in Goebbels's thirty-one volumes of diaries. Shakespeare was installed as a favourite author. Though I had a hard time believing that Hitler was ever much of an expert, the historian Timothy Ryback has located leather-bound translations of the plays in the Führer's private library, and Hitler was given to quoting lines from *Hamlet* and *Julius Caesar*, particularly when menacing political opponents. In a sketchbook from 1926 he had roughed out designs for a scene in act one of *Julius Caesar*, the forum where Caesar is murdered in cold blood.

Goebbels's own passion, Longerich explained, ran much deeper. At Heidelberg university he had studied with the most famous Shakespearian of the age, Friedrich Gundolf, whose *Shakespeare und der Deutsche Geist* of 1911 ('Shakespeare and the German Soul') became the canonical expression of *unser* Shakespeare (a bleak irony: Gundolf was Jewish). Goebbels had also spent the early 1920s attempting to forge a career as a writer, composing verse plays – only one of which was ever staged – and writing an expressionist novel heavily influenced by Goethe's *Werther*.

As propaganda chief, Goebbels maintained an iron grip on the news agenda and the Party's image, and he quickly set up a so-called 'Chamber of Culture' with draconian powers extending across the press, radio, film, publishing, music, visual arts and theatre. Goebbels used this not simply to regulate what was available for public consumption, but to indulge his own predilections and whims. Shakespeare was one: after seeing *Coriolanus* in 1937, Goebbels exclaimed that the playwright was 'more relevant and modern than all the moderns. What a huge genius! How he towers over Schiller!'

There was pure politics behind this, but surely something more: the excitable compulsion of the artist manqué. What Goebbels had so conspicuously failed to achieve with his own art he could accomplish as Reichsminister.

'Theatre genuinely meant a lot to him,' said Longerich. 'If you read the diaries it's clear that he's emotionally touched and driven by the experience. I don't think it's cold-blooded propaganda. He really is an enthusiast.'

'Politics had become the drama of the people,' Goebbels wrote, and it was a mantra he lived. He set up a number of 'Reich theatres' directly under his remit, involving himself in almost every aspect of their work, and appointed Rainer Schlösser, the journalist and DSG member from Weimar, to the new position of *Reichsdramaturg*. Fond of issuing unprompted director's notes (in 1936, he gave advice on a new production of Wagner's *Tristan und Isolde* at the Deutsche Oper, which the production team scrambled to put into effect), Goebbels also acted as munificent patron. Perhaps a quarter of the ministry's budget went on theatre, far in excess of its political value, and more than the amount it spent on straight propaganda. Between 1933 and 1942, audiences for German theatre roughly doubled.

The difficulty was what to put on stage. 'Degenerate' or left-wing scripts from the 1920s were obviously out; so too were works by playwrights who had any hint of Jewish ancestry – an alarming number. Goebbels's initial intention had been to mould a new *Völkisch* culture that could rival achievements in arms production or on the sporting field, but the practicalities defeated the ministry, particularly as so many artists had fled overseas. Goebbels had a brief passion for commissioning *Thingspiele*, vast outdoor theatre events – part rally, part pseudo-Nordic cult ceremony – but the logistical challenges of building 4,000 outdoor arenas proved impossible, and audiences were mystifyingly resistant. Schemes to commission symphonies and films on National Socialist themes came to little. At a talk for activists in 1935, Goebbels conceded that it was possible to 'build autobahns, revive the economy, create a new army,' but not 'manufacture new dramatists'. Goering admitted that it was 'easier to make an artist into a National Socialist than the other way around'.

As war crept up it became difficult to commission new plays anyway. It was a headache: a huge number of German theatres, and an ever-shrinking repertoire.

Longerich shrugged. 'Goebbels realises it's impossible, it just can't be done. It's a vacuum. They have to do something.'

The solution was to stage classics. But even this wasn't as easy as it sounded. Goethe proved problematic (Hitler thought him 'maudlin') and Schiller was troublesome because of his insurrectionary themes, most obviously *Wilhelm Tell*, whose hero was Swiss. (The play was taken off altogether in 1941, after a Swiss plot against Hitler.) Molière had been popular, but was banned after the invasion of France, alongside all French dramatists. Ancient Greek tragedy had the right kind of monumental purity, but was problematically southern European. Spanish Golden-Age drama was permissible, particularly after the cultural pact with Franco in 1939, but never took off. George Bernard Shaw was acceptable because he was perceived as anti-British, but was still alive, so there was the problem of royalties . . . So it went on. One of the few writers left was Shakespeare. Not only was he politically safe; everyone knew, of course, that he was German.

Proving this last fact beyond all doubt became of urgent importance. The Party issued a pamphlet called *Shakespeare: A Germanic Writer*, asserting that the nineteenth-century cult had been correct, and that Shakespeare's true home was now Germany. School curriculums emphasised the role of the 'Nordic visionary' in freeing Goethe, Herder and Lessing from the tyranny of French neoclassicism. Schirach's Hitler Youth staged Shakespeare Weeks. (Invitations were sent to London in 1937, and politely refused.) Managers produced the plays in ever-greater numbers. In 1934, a total of 235 theatres opened seasons with Shakespeare; three years later, the figure was 320. In 1936, the regime boasted that there had been more Shakespeare productions in Germany that year than anywhere else in the world.

Even when 'enemy dramatists' were banned after the outbreak of hostilities with Britain in 1939, Shakespeare stayed, now regarded – albeit after some soul-searching – as essential to the war effort. *Wille und Macht* magazine ran a special issue arguing that Shakespeare held his own in Germany 'even in the face of the enemy'. On 23 April 1940, as the Wehrmacht were preparing their final assault on France, Germany's leading intellectual lights made sure to be in Weimar to hear the Shakespeare-Gesellschaft's president declare that 'two centuries of German work on behalf of Shakespeare have given us the right to treasure the greatest dramatist of the German race'. When Munich's Kammerspiele agonised about a new *Hamlet*, they were assured by the propaganda ministry not to worry: for the purposes of paperwork, Shakespeare was officially German. It was rumoured the order came from Hitler himself.

Like every Nazi cultural policy – notably the Party's almost comically contradictory approach to jazz – this resulted in some tormented interpretational tangles. Given Nazi attempts to emulate the Roman empire, 'heroic' plays such as *Julius Caesar* and *Coriolanus* were candidates for revival (despite uncomfortable echoes between Hitler and Caius Martius). So were the 'Nordic tragedies' *Hamlet*, *King Lear* and *Macbeth*, the last of which was particularly popular, regarded as a 'ballad' about a military hero overwhelmed by fate.

Comedies such as *Twelfth Night* and *The Winter's Tale* remained successful, as much for escapism as anything else, but *A Midsummer Night's Dream* had unhelpful associations with the Jewish composer Mendelssohn. The English histories were patently unsuitable, and effectively banned. *Antony and Cleopatra* was not an option, because, as one official primly put it, 'a play in which a warlord leaves the battlefield to run after his mistress must be judged as particularly negative'.

But *Hamlet*, yet again, was in: a version starring the hugely famous actor (and favourite of Goering) Gustaf Gründgens at the Staatstheater in Berlin became riotously popular, reaching 200 performances from 1936 onwards. With no discernible irony, one critic acclaimed Gründgens as 'a Hamlet who knows precisely what he wants'. An entire Romantic tradition was overturned at a stroke.

The so-called 'racial dramas' remained an obstinate problem. The Reichsdramaturg ruled that it was possible to put *Othello* on stage, so long as the hero was presented as an Arab nobleman rather than a 'negroid' black African. But *The Merchant of Venice* caused tremors at the highest level. On paper, no other play seemed so in tune with Nazi racial policies – had Hitler not declared in July 1942 that Shylock was a 'timelessly valid characterisation of the Jew'? In theatres, though, the potentialities of Shakespeare's script proved dangerous and double-edged.

The unrepentantly anti-Semitic German actor Werner Krauss played Shylock in a notorious version in Vienna in 1943 – a few years after playing a series of identikit Jewish characters in the film *Jud Süss* – and presented what one reviewer described as 'the pathological image of the typical eastern Jew in all his outer and inner uncleanness'. But other directors fought shy of the play, wary of raising sympathy for Shylock's predicament among audiences. Could it really be possible to stage his famous appeal for tolerance in a country where millions were on their way to concentration camps, if not already dead?

> Hath not a Jew eyes? Hath not a Jew hands, organs, dimensions, senses, affections, passions; fed with the same food, hurt with the same weapons, subject to the same diseases, healed by the same means, warmed and cooled by the same winter and summer as a Christian is? If you prick us do we not bleed? If you tickle us do we not laugh? If you poison us do we not die?

Many producers balked. Nor was this the only difficulty; the elopement of Shylock's daughter Jessica with the Christian Lorenzo was impossible to stage in a country whose race laws expressly forbade miscegenation.

Remarkably, the Reichsdramaturg Rainer Schlösser agonised for at least four years over the question, attempting to sell *The Merchant of Venice* as anti-Semitic propaganda when Shakespeare's text didn't quite make that possible. Someone offered to rewrite the ending so that Jessica turned her back on marriage. In the end Schlösser suggested to Goebbels an even more convoluted solution – doctoring the script to imply that Jessica was not of Jewish blood at all, but Shylock's Christian foster child. As for Shylock himself, that bothersome speech should simply be cut.

By summer 1944, it was obvious the regime was crumbling. Allied troops were about to breach Germany's borders. Theatres were closed. Yet, despite his ever-growing list of responsibilities, the Reichsminister's mind remained on finer things. That September, one of the last major propaganda projects to pass across his desk was a lavish film of *The Merchant of Venice*, with Werner Krauss once again in the lead and directed by Veit Harlan, who had done *Jud Süss*. Goebbels greeted the idea eagerly, and pushed for production to start as soon as possible – one last chance for his cultural legacy to be assured. The scheme was patently delusional. But it said much about his sense of priorities that, even as defeat loomed, Goebbels couldn't let Shakespeare go.

I wondered about Longerich's view. Was this just frustrated ambition, or was there something deeper at work?

He sent a thoughtful stream of smoke in the direction of Königsplatz. 'If you ask me, I think it's the idea of creating a kind of alternative world, a fantasy world. The racist imagination and political utopianism are not so different. Why is Hitler so obsessed by Wagner? Because it's fantasy.'

He ground the cigarette into the ashtray and drained his coffee briskly. 'You want to go to a place and to see your fantasies becoming reality. That is theatre, yes?'

After three days spent chasing Nazi-shaped shadows, I was hopeful that Michael Thalheimer's production of *A Midsummer Night's Dream* at the Residenztheater would lighten my mood. It had never been my favourite comedy – a school production where I played a fretful and poorly enunciated Philostrate was to blame for that – but I was sorely in need of some fairy dust. Perhaps the show could provide it.

I would have been wise to have done some homework. In the most brutal traditions of *Regietheater* ('director's theatre'), Thalheimer was known for taking a scalpel to texts, the sharper the better. A version of *Faust*, staged in an empty black cube at the Deutsches Theater in Berlin, presented Goethe's hero as a self-centred egomaniac, strumming an air guitar to Deep Purple's 'Child in Time'. His production of Lessing's *Emilia Galotti* (1772) had boiled the tragedy down to an unremitting seventy-five minutes, the cast refusing to look each other in the eye throughout. 'For me theatre is the last remaining public space where a discourse is dared . . . on the misery of the world, on the true state of humanity,' Thalheimer told an interviewer afterwards.

At the Residenztheater, there was misery aplenty on offer. The lighting was harsh and monochrome, the set made of steel pipes resembling the wall of a prison. Theseus and Hippolyta appeared to be in the terminal stages of an abusive relationship, him clawing her breasts while she stared in mute horror into the wings. Hermia had almost certainly been raped by her father and was being pimped out to Demetrius; she and Lysander appeared to be in it entirely for the sex (which looked wretched). Puck, who spent most of the play half naked, had the belly of a darts player and the face of a crime boss. Even Nick Bottom, Peter Quince and co., usually a blessed piece of comic relief, were played as disgruntled union workers who looked as if they'd rather be manning a picket than mounting a piece of spineless bourgeois theatre.

Within ten minutes I had placed a series of private bets, which joylessly I watched myself win. Simulated rape? Check. Simulated anal rape? Check. Simulated blood? Check. Simulated semen? Check (a spume of beer sprayed across the stage). Full-frontal nudity, male and female? Check. Check, check, check. Not so much *Dream* as never-ending nightmare. For the first time I could recall, I yearned for there to be more fairies, perhaps even a burst of Mendelssohn.

In any case, my mind was elsewhere: still mouldering somewhere in the Third Reich. Had the Allies been so different, really? A few years after Goering's pet Gustaf Gründgens went on stage as *Hamlet* in Berlin, the British-born actor Maurice Evans – now forgotten, but a huge star at the time – had created a 'GI *Hamlet*' and performed it at military bases in Hawaii. Heavily streamlined, it made the Prince (according to *Life* magazine) into a 'rough-and-ready extrovert, delayed in avenging his father's murder more by force of circumstance than by his own pigeon liver'.

Around the same time, Fleet Air Arm lieutenant Laurence Olivier, spurred on by the Ministry of Information, remade *Henry V* as lavish, all-colour British propaganda in 1944. The movie was dedicated to the 'Commandos and Airborne Troops of Great Britain, the spirit of whose ancestors it has been humbly attempted to recapture' (a 'spirit' that required swingeing cuts to the script, including Henry's order to his troops to kill their prisoners).

Less well-known was the top-secret British wartime plan, known as 'Operation HK'. As a last-ditch measure in the event of invasion, Parliament would be evacuated to Stratford-upon-Avon and its members set up in the Shakespeare Memorial Theatre. No doubt the venue was chosen partly for practical reasons – a space of sufficient size in comparative rural safety, with plentiful hotel accommodation – but the idea of hunkering down in the home of the National Poet, deep in the heart of England, evidently provided comfort to Britain's harried wartime civil servants.

Of course one could detach Shakespeare from the uses to which he had been put. One had to. Yet the thought that the works of Shakespeare, of all people, had become involved in all this I found both exhausting and depressing. He was the most humane of writers, the most even-handed, the most keenly sceptical of received ideas: he had an uncanny knack of finding glimmers of sympathy in the most unlikely circumstances. It was impossible to see *Measure for Measure* without wondering who was right: the idealistic woman who stands by her beliefs and refuses to sacrifice her virginity to save her brother's life, or the brother who puts her in that position? The law, or natural justice? Both, neither? One couldn't watch *The Merchant of Venice* without feeling for Shylock even as he drew the knife on Antonio. That was, of course, why the Nazis had such trouble staging him: he could never be as shallow and one-sided as they needed him to be. Still, I thought wearily, when it came to using Shakespeare as propaganda: a plague on both your houses.

On Sunday morning, the DSG assembled for the final time to bid farewell to each other and, at least temporarily, to Shakespeare. We had moved to the regal setting of the Altes Rathaus on Marienplatz, a white-stone, high-gabled building that looked as though it was made out of frosted gingerbread. Beneath the broad oak spans of the grand hall – a painstaking postwar facsimile of the fourteenth-century original – we sat in polite rows, listening to a financial journalist from the *Süddeutsche Zeitung* describe how Shakespeare had predicted the credit crunch. Listening to the rough translation whispered courteously by my neighbour, I tried to forget that this was also the hall where Goebbels had given the speech in November 1938 that led to Kristallnacht.

Music helped. In lieu of laying roses at Weimar's Shakespeare statue, the most ceremonious portion of the event was the performance by a local choir of Frank Martin's *Songs of Ariel*. Despite his English-sounding name, Martin was a Swiss composer who died in 1974, little-known outside the choral and operatic worlds, and often disregarded within them. He produced an impressive body of work, among them an anguished *Mass for Double Choir* (1922–26), the *Petite Symphonie Concertante* (1946) and an intimidating number of theatre and opera scores.

Soon after the war, Martin moved to the Netherlands and began his first opera. The text he chose was the same one Mozart had never completed: *The Tempest. Der Sturm* was finally finished in 1955, and premiered at the Vienna State Opera the following year. By that time, unable to get Shakespeare's luminous verse out of his head, Martin had already completed separate settings of the five songs sung by Ariel that punctuate the play.

They were, I thought, his masterworks. To some of the uncanniest, most piercing lyrics in the English language, Martin composed music of rare absorption and wonder, suspended somewhere between the mysticism of late Ravel and the diamond clarity of Stravinsky. All five songs were remarkable in their way: Martin took childish delight in giving the basses a doggy 'bow-wow' in 'Come unto these yellow sands'. But for me the finest was the second, a setting of words sung by Ariel to Ferdinand, words of agitated and haunting beauty:

> Full fathom five thy father lies.
>   Of his bones are coral made;
> Those are pearls that were his eyes;
>   Nothing of him that doth fade
> But doth suffer a sea-change
>   Into something rich and strange.
> Sea-nymphs hourly ring his knell:
> Ding dong.
> Hark, now I hear them.
>   Ding-dong bell.

'The ditty does remember my drowned father,' responds Ferdinand in the play, flabbergasted by what he is hearing. Martin made the image absolute, draping undulating high chords in the female voices over a melodic line of phantom stillness – a shadowed corpse sunk deep beneath the rippling waves. At the close, he left the music deliberately unresolved, eerie tintinnabulations echoing around the choir before subsiding into silence.

I found it profoundly moving. As they finished, I attempted to hide my embarrassed snuffling from my neighbour.

Afterwards, with a couple of hours to spare before my train to Berlin, I drifted back through town. The afternoon was still and soft; barely anyone was on the streets. As I retraced my steps across Königsplatz, I noticed something I had failed to the day before. What had been the Führerbau – the building in which the Munich agreement was signed, granting Hitler a swath of Czechoslovakia in 1938 – hadn't been razed along with the Temples of Honour, as I'd assumed: it was right here, massive and mournful, a monumental neoclassical structure in limestone the colour of sour cheese. There was a blank gap on the facade where a bronze eagle had hung, and telltale scars from shell damage. I had seen the building, but not realised what it was.

As I walked up the steps I passed a group of ballet dancers in bubblegum-pink cardigans and legwarmers, reclining in the spring warmth. From a half-open window there came the sound of a violin sawing away. After the war, the place had been given to the University of the Performing Arts. The room where Hitler had once given dictation was now a rehearsal studio.

For all the agonising among Munich's historians about how to incorporate the past into the present, this was one monument no one had needed to update or change. Art had got its revenge. I thought it by far the finest memorial in town.

—◆—

IN BERLIN, I SHUTTLED BETWEEN APPOINTMENTS. I went to the Freie Universität to meet a graduate student who had done research into productions of The Merchant of Venice after the Holocaust. I rattled out to Spandau on the S-Bahn to visit the actor Norbert Kentrup, part of the very first troupe to perform at the not-quite-completed reconstruction of the Globe theatre in London, and heard about his return visit to play Shylock, as a German, in English. I spent a few hours in the archives at the Deutsches Theater, looking at the promptbooks of Max Reinhardt, whose experimental, high-tech productions achieved legendary status in Germany in the 1910s. (After rejecting an offer of 'honorary Aryanship', Reinhardt departed for the US in 1938.)

Still on Nazi duty, I spent a doleful morning in the Staatsbibliothek on Potsdamerstrasse, rootling among the personal papers of Gustaf Gründgens, Goebbels's favourite Hamlet, for any clue as to why that play had proved so popular. The curator and I drew a blank: the files from the 1930s until the late 1940s had mysteriously disappeared.

I went over to the Schaubühne theatre in Charlottenburg several times, to see a show and re-interview the artistic director Thomas Ostermeier, whose deconstructed, post-postmodern *Hamlet* I'd hugely admired when I'd seen it in Berlin and London a few years earlier. The production had since become a global sensation, performed nearly 200 times and travelling to locations as varied as Zagreb, Buenos Aires, Seoul, Dublin – even Helsingør, like the English Comedians centuries before. They had recently taken *Hamlet* to Ramallah in the West Bank, Ostermeier told me, and conducted workshops at the Freedom Theatre in the Jenin refugee camp. There they had found Prince Hamlets by the dozen – frustrated and angry young men battling with the question of revenge, not knowing whom, if anyone, to trust.

What did he think German Shakespeare was all about? 'I don't think the Germans are good at Shakespeare,' he deadpanned. '*Unser* Shakespeare? It's stupid, completely stupid.'

By the time I returned to the Deutsches Theater, this time to see a performance, I felt I was clutching at straws. A friend of a friend, Ramona Mosse, had kindly offered to talk about her work on postwar political theatre; we'd settled on combining this with a new production of *Coriolanus*. The show was even more self-consciously baffling than the productions in Munich: acted by five female performers wearing wigs to a soundtrack of corny eighties pop music, its logic largely eluded me.

One reason it was liberating to encounter Shakespeare in translation was that he could be the best of both worlds: both ancient and modern, both canonical and contemporary. The Romantic Schlegel-Tieck now being deeply un-hip in Germany, most theatres re-translated him each time they mounted a new production. Given everything I'd discovered about culture in the Third Reich, a suspicion of received wisdoms and the classical canon was understandable. But was this still Shakespeare? I felt we'd gone over the edge.

In all the interviews I'd done in Poland and Germany – twenty, perhaps more – one line kept boomeranging back: Ruth von Ledebur's suggestion that Shakespeare seemed to crop up at moments of political crisis or change. That was true in 1771, and true again more powerfully in 1864; it was grimly true during the second world war, when Shakespeare had been dragooned into propaganda battles on both sides, Allied and Axis. It had happened again during the cold war, with two different ideologies of German Shakespeare eyeing each other over the Berlin Wall. But why? Why Shakespeare? Why *Hamlet* most especially?

Ramona paused for a second over her beer. 'You are writing about Heiner Müller, yes? I haven't heard you mention him.'

I knew Müller's name and a little of his reputation as an East German playwright from my conversation with Roland Petersohn in Weimar, but he hadn't been high on my list. He was so little-known in Britain that I had never even seen one of his plays.

Ramona looked playful. 'Ah, then you should get to know his work. He had some interesting things to say about Shakespeare. And *Hamlet*.'

This was an understatement, it transpired. Over a fifty-year writing career, most of it based in East Berlin, Müller had adapted numerous classics, among them Sophocles' *Oedipus Rex*, Laclos' *Dangerous Liaisons* and various texts by Brecht, but had returned insistently – it appeared compulsively – to Shakespeare, a playwright to whom he was often compared (one critic called him 'a sort of socialist William Shakespeare'). Müller's 1971 *Macbeth After Shakespeare* blurred the roles of director and adaptor to an unsettling degree, jettisoning the Witches, cutting the text to a machine-gun twenty-three scenes and compressing the action into a cycle of never-ending violence. Despite its focus on the suffering of Scotland's peasants, the production landed the playwright in trouble with GDR officials for its 'historical pessimism'.

But this was as nothing, Ramona explained, to the reaction that greeted Müller's most infamous Shakespeare adaptation, 1977's *Die Hamletmaschine* ('Hamletmachine'), which was outlawed by the East German authorities for being 'decadent, anti-humanistic and pessimistic'. It was eventually premiered in Brussels in 1978. Allusive, enigmatic, savagely compressed, *Die Hamletmaschine* was a landmark text of 'post-dramatic' theatre, nine pages of cryptic fragments, shorn of any plot, which might (or might not) bear some relation to Shakespeare. It was now considered a classic.

Ramona's eyes were shining. 'It's an amazing text, a poem as much as a play. It can be broken up and performed in any way: it's like the ultimate distillation of *Hamlet*.'

The tale had a twist. Müller, far and away the most famous playwright of the GDR, had always wanted to stage *Die Hamletmaschine* in his homeland. In 1988, invited by the Deutsches Theater, the very theatre in which we'd been sitting earlier that evening, to direct *Hamlet*, Müller had decided to do so – on condition that he would also be allowed to stage *Die Hamletmaschine*, as a kind of play-within-the-play. Permission had eventually been forthcoming. The production became known as *Hamlet/Maschine*.

Nervous about how to direct the greatest play of all – a text, furthermore, that had been nagging at him for decades – Müller dithered. Initially he wanted to cast five separate Hamlets, one actor per act, until it was pointed out no theatrical agent would agree to it. Working closely with his designer, Erich Wonder, he nonetheless developed a concept every bit as epic, in which the production would open in a kind of ice age and slowly ripen into a scene of scorching apocalypse, as if at the end of history. Müller was determined that none of Shakespeare's text would be cut, being played at terrifically slow speed, so it was planned to stage the show over two evenings. Eventually that plan, too, was abandoned, but the performance still lasted a colossal seven and a half hours, beginning at 4 p.m. and ending near midnight.

As so often in German Shakespeare, history was waiting in the wings. When Müller and his cast went into rehearsals in August 1989, few realised that the GDR was beginning to topple. Yet when Hungary removed its border restrictions later that month, thousands of East Germans fled. Rallies sprang up in many cities, notably Leipzig, where police refused the GDR leader Erich Honecker's orders to clamp down on protestors chanting *'Wir sind das Volk!'* ('We are the people!'). When the fortieth anniversary of the GDR came round on 7 October, many feared that tanks would be on the streets. Miraculously, they failed to materialise.

Müller – a committed socialist who wanted to reform East Germany, not end it – did his best to plough on with rehearsals, but actors and technical staff kept disappearing to participate in protests. Gradually it became clear that, whatever they did on stage, it would be interpreted as a comment on a failing, flailing regime. On 4 November 1989, nearly a million people crowded into Alexanderplatz, a mile or so east of where Ramona and I were sitting, to demand change. Five days later, on 9 November, people began to stream across the opened Berlin Wall.

When *Hamlet/Maschine* finally had its debut the following March, a week after the GDR's first free elections, many saw the production as a requiem for a failed state. In the final days of rehearsals Müller, acknowledging that there was no way of keeping politics at bay, suggested that the invading Norwegian prince Fortinbras – who entered wearing a stiff business suit – was 'the ghost of Deutsche Bank'.

Ramona's smile was enigmatic. 'So I don't know whether this answers your question. Maybe there are no answers. I don't think this is what Müller intended, to put Hamlet on stage as the GDR ended. But it is true – Shakespeare has a habit of cropping up in Germany at strange moments in our history.'

Deutschland ist Hamlet yet again: I hadn't reckoned on the phrase being so absolute. As a ten-year-old I'd visited Germany myself on a family holiday just after reunification, and walked around saucer-eyed at the battered Trabants cluttering the streets and the new white satellite dishes mushrooming on decayed apartment blocks. Eager for a piece of history, I'd lifted a chunk of cladding from an abandoned watchtower near the border, and told myself it was as good as having my very own piece of Wall.

I sorely wanted to find out more about Müller, *Hamlet* and *Die Hamletmaschine*. But I had a flight to London the next morning.

'Then come back. How long to Berlin? An hour and a half, two hours?' Ramona rolled her eyes. 'Pffft, you British. You're so terrible at travelling.'

＊

I DID GO BACK TO BERLIN. As spring turned to summer, then autumn, then winter and spring again, I made several return trips, not quite able to let Germany go. I read and reread *Die Hamletmaschine*, teasing apart its poetic paradoxes and marvelling at the way Müller made Shakespeare's play shiver in the glare of a surveillance state:

> THE ACTOR PLAYING HAMLET I'm not Hamlet. I don't take part any more. My words have nothing to tell me any more. My thoughts suck the blood out of the images. My drama doesn't happen any more. Behind me the set is put up. By people who aren't interested in my drama, for people to whom it means nothing. I'm not interested in it any more either. I won't play along any more. [*Unnoticed by the actor playing* HAMLET, *stagehands place a refrigerator and three TV sets on the stage. Humming of the refrigerator. Three TV channels without sound.*] The set is a monument. It presents a man who made history, enlarged a hundred times. The petrification of a hope. His name is interchangeable.

I spent a strange evening in a themed beer hall – dirndl-wearing waitresses, bagpipe player – with Alexander Weigel, dramaturg on *Hamlet/Maschine*, hearing rehearsal-room tales. (Rehearsals had been torturous, mostly: Müller had been so paralysed with indecision that months had gone by without any useful work being done.) I saw Thomas Ostermeier's *Hamlet* for the third time, and was obscenely pleased to catch something that had eluded me before – a thespian in-joke about *Die Hamletmaschine*.

On a later visit I watched four hours of the murky VHS recording of the production at the Akademie der Künste on Robert Koch Platz, and spent an afternoon in an Indian restaurant with Margarita Broich, Müller's Ophelia and his sometime partner, who talked about the out-of-body experience of rehearsing Shakespeare while the GDR was collapsing.

Broich – willowy, beautiful, surprisingly shy – also talked, more sadly, of their life together. She was just twenty-one when they met, Müller in his fifties; him from the East, her from the West. She laughed ruefully as she recalled the shenanigans required: the hotel room next to the border crossing, the Stasi paperwork. She had played Ophelia just as they were separating after nine years together – the end of an era in more ways than one. As she spoke, she shook her head, as if ridding it of memories. Another country, another life.

The following day I stood, in sidelong autumn sunlight, in front of Müller's grave, a slender iron column in a quiet corner of the Dorotheenstadt cemetery. Müller died in 1996, four years after the communist country in which he so fervently believed was declared a useless experiment.

Did any of it help me answer the question of why Shakespeare, or *Hamlet*, or Heiner Müller had become so entangled in German history? Not really. More than once I thought of a line from the play, addressed by an infuriated Hamlet to Rosencrantz and Guildenstern:

> Why, look you now, how unworthy a thing you make of me! You would play upon me, you would seem to know my stops, you would pluck out the heart of my mystery . . .

Perhaps it was best to leave some mysteries unplucked. Ramona had been right: there were no more answers, but the questions seemed more interesting.

Somehow, I sensed I would end up back in Gdańsk. As I had nearly finished writing up this account, an email from Jerzy Limon dropped into my inbox. At long last the theatre was nearly finished; they were planning a grand opening, during the annual Shakespeare festival. Could I come? I booked the first flight I could.

Seventeen months after I'd last been there, three and a half years after I'd first been out, Gdańsk looked identical: same cobbled streets, same finicky mansions, same tourists drifting along Długi Targ, same high royal-blue sky. Only the Teatr Szekspirowski had changed: if before it looked like a naval frigate lying at anchor on Wojciecha Bogusławskiego, now a maximum-security prison had taken up residence, angular and forbidding, finished in menacing dark brick.

Inside, it didn't take long to locate Jerzy. He was the man of the hour, spotlit in a bank of Klieg lights brought by news crews from across Europe. Black suit shimmering, he seemed in his element, caressing the cream leather seats of the auditorium, rapping his knuckles against the wooden finishes, pointing out the building's features – fully reconfigurable stage! roof retractable in three minutes flat! – in an effervescent flow of Polish and English. The space was certainly handsome: airy and open, galleries stacked neatly on three sides, finished in honey-coloured birch and beech.

The final budget had been 93 million zloty (£16.2 million), over half of it from European Union coffers. It hadn't hurt that Poland's prime minister, Donald Tusk – about to be made president of the European Council – was a Gdańsker. Tusk would be attending the opening, was the word; goons in dark suits and shades had started to congregate.

After Jerzy finished being interrogated by a Polish lifestyle magazine, I caught his eye. I asked if he was pleased. His grin was nearly as broad as the stage.

Tusk's presence that night turned out to be a mixed blessing: eager not to be outdone by the massed presence of Poland's theatrical elite, the PM had personally prepared some brief remarks on the similarities between Shakespeare's plays and Polish politics. *Julius Caesar* held many lessons for a wise politician, he informed us, as did *Macbeth*—

The intake of breath in the room was almost audible. Tusk had invited an ancient theatrical curse, mentioning the Scottish play by name in a theatre that wasn't staging it. A well-known female director tutted loudly.

Sure enough, twenty-five minutes later, the ceremony was brought to an abrupt halt when a voice came over the tannoy. A suitcase had been discovered in an upstairs room and its owner couldn't be located. This was not a drill. Ten minutes after that, 600 VIPs were kicking their heels on the pavement outside while the bomb squad was summoned. Tusk fled. I watched the remainder on local television.

The opening production, a touring *Hamlet* from London travelling the globe, was only moderately more successful. The cast, who had been on the road for a constant six months, plainly couldn't wait to get back to their dressing rooms, if not on the first flight home. They looked as though they had come to detest every line of the play. But it wasn't just that, I realised: there was something about the concept of taking a British, English-language production around the world that seemed a relic of another age. It took no account of the things I had excitedly begun to discover, the multiplying ways in which Shakespeare had been translated and disseminated globally, how he had already infiltrated so many cultures in ways that would barely be recognisable back home. In its sense of smug cultural superiority, it struck me as typical of an attitude I had been doing my utmost to leave behind.

The following evening, I walked across to a pop-up space backstage at another of Gdańsk's theatres. The show was called *I, Malvolio*, by the maverick English theatre-maker Tim Crouch. Commissioned by the Brighton festival to create work for young people, Crouch had written a gloriously eccentric series of one-man pieces starring himself as, respectively, Peaseblossom, Caliban and Banquo. *I, Malvolio* – an alternative perspective on *Twelfth Night* from Shakespeare's drama-detesting puritan – was the latest in this rogue's gallery. Sprung from the prison into which the playwright throws him near the end of the action, Malvolio was here in Poland, two nights only.

As Crouch strutted, writhed and sneered across the stage, wearing shit-stained undergarments and a battered coxcomb, the Polish audience looked distinctly jumpy. Shakespeare – *this*? A man dressed like *that*? I could feel the panic mounting. Things got still jumpier when Crouch, attempting to ad-lib his way out of danger, tossed the surtitles to the wind and began to pick on audience members individually, even though no one appeared to comprehend English.

Gradually, the show righted itself. The audience breathed more easily, began to share in the joke. Language ceased to matter quite so much; someone began to heckle good-naturedly in Polish, which had the room in stitches. Crouch turned his ineptitude with the surtitles (no doubt planned) into a running metatheatrical gag, checking the screen for what he was supposed to say next, then attempting an outrageously poor Polish pronunciation.

'Find that funny? Find that kind of thing *funny?*' he roared, half in character, half out. By the time the applause came round, the audience was eating out of his hand.

It was a virtuosic piece of stagecraft, laughable and faintly lunatic, spiced with enough existential precariousness to make it a serious meditation on the fragility of drama. Unlike most modern touring theatre, it experimented with the barriers surrounding language and culture, bringing them into the same shared, contained space: the world and journey of the play. The reason it worked, it occurred to me, was that it was properly spontaneous; every time, every place it was performed, it was different. Created in compact with each and every audience, its flexibility made it fully alive.

Afterwards, I walked back past the Teatr Szekspirowski, fronted with fluttering pennants and brightly spotlit against a charcoal ground of sky. As I stood there in the fresh sea breeze, I realised I'd been wondering since I first came to Gdańsk what it might have been like to watch the English Comedians at work, four centuries before – those travel-stained English actors, strangers in these chilly parts of northern Europe, using Shakespeare for their own purposes in a cavalcade of languages, making things up as they went along. So little trace survived that one could only guess what it would have been like to see them in action: the tumbling clowns, the wise-cracking, smart-alec heroes . . .

One could only guess, but maybe I'd just seen some kind of answer.

Buried Richards

Staunton, Virginia · Washington DC · San Francisco ·
Nevada City, California · San Diego

I n the slate grey of too-early morning, William Shakespeare looked haggard and underslept. He gazed out from his roost in the bathroom, peering pruriently into the shower. The cotton tea towel on which he was printed shivered lightly in the breeze. Next to the bed in which I lay – oak, four-poster, with a counterpane embroidered in the manner of a Renaissance herbal – was a list detailing the 'Symbolism of Flowers in Shakespeare's Plays'. Next to that was a watercolour of Anne Hathaway's Cottage. In the dawn, its colours looked unsettlingly luminous. A motto was painted in curling script on the wall: 'If music be the food of love, play on.' Beneath it – somewhat redundant in the circumstances, I thought – was one word: SHAKESPEARE.

I groped for my phone: 4.46 a.m. I groggily surveyed my surroundings, taking fresh note of the hand-coloured engravings of *A Midsummer Night's Dream* above the headboard and the tiny casket of pot-pourri. Near the television were back issues of a magazine called *British Heritage*, with Camilla, Duchess of Cornwall on the cover. Above the magazines, attached to a board, was a pictorial guide to the architecture of 'Shakespeare's Stratford'.

Already it was starting to get warm: I could feel the humidity on my skin. Outside, through the opened mullioned window, the crickets and frogs were loud: a sharp, hot buzz, like the noise of radio static.

Puzzled and exhausted, head still thick from the sleeping tablet I had swallowed on the flight, I subsided into the pillows and tried to remember where I was. Slowly the answer came: Virginia. The United States. Jet lag certainly wasn't helping, but it was hard to avoid the

sensation that I'd flown 3,600 miles away from Britain and ended up
exactly where I'd left.

I had only myself to blame. I had been searching for a route into
American Shakespeare, a way to write about the fascinating and at times
perplexing process by which a sixteenth-century British playwright had
become absorbed into the culture and lifeblood of the United States.
Not only had a nation founded by theatre-detesting Puritans been
reconciled to Shakespeare; he had become a kind of national symbol.

Wanting to begin my trip into American Shakespeare near where
Shakespeare's work had first landed in America, I had brought my eye
to rest on a town called Staunton, Virginia. On paper, chiefly known
as the birthplace of one of the blandest presidents of the twentieth
century, Woodrow Wilson, it didn't have a tremendous amount to
recommend a visit.

But Staunton (pronounced 'Stanton', I was rapidly corrected) had
found an ingenious solution to its deficit in the presidential stakes: the
figure who had gazed down on me all night and invaded my dreams,
William Shakespeare. Here, in the late 1990s, a buccaneering local
troupe had the notion of building a reconstruction of a Shakespearian
theatre. The reconstruction wasn't, as might be expected, a version of
the Globe; it was more interesting than that, a replica of the indoor
playhouse Shakespeare and his company moved into in late 1608. The
new Blackfriars Playhouse had been running since 2001 under the
ambitious name of the American Shakespeare Center. It was the first
working Blackfriars replica to be built anywhere in the world.

Making a trip had been on my mind for years. When I first moved to
London in the early 2000s, I'd haunted the Globe, mooning over Mark
Rylance's boyish, sweet-tempered Hamlet and Kathryn Hunter's cackling
Richard III. Going there had opened my eyes – as it has since opened the eyes
of hundreds of thousands of others – to how fluid and fast Shakespeare's
scripts could be, how little paraphernalia they needed to spring into life:
oak columns, bare wooden boards, daylight. For a while I couldn't bear
to see Shakespeare anywhere else (it helped that the tickets were cheap).

But the Globe was only half the picture. It was what happened to
Shakespeare in the latter part of his career that I wanted to explore.
Able for the first time to perform all year round, the King's Men forged

for themselves a new kind of drama. All of Shakespeare's late plays, though they continued to be performed outside, were written with the Blackfriars in mind: a shadowy space, intimate, candlelit, the photographic negative of the rambunctious open-air Globe.

There were other connections, teasing ones. Virginia had been established in May 1607, when 104 English settlers had stolen land from Algonquian Native Americans and christened their settlement Jamestown after the monarch who chartered their voyage. (Virginia itself was named for James's predecessor, Elizabeth I.) As these ill-equipped gentlemen colonisers were battling disease, Indians and their own manifold incompetence, Shakespeare and his colleagues – another and rather more professional company of James's men – were mapping new worlds back in London. Stories from America and its struggling colonies would infiltrate Shakespeare's late work, most obviously *The Tempest*. Who needed *Hamlet* off the coast of Sierra Leone? Here was a more solid seafaring connection. Jamestown was only 150 miles away.

Staunton also featured the place where I was staying, Anne Hathaway's Cottage. This wasn't, as I had first assumed when I found it online, an official outpost of the American Shakespeare Center, but a guerrilla replica, set up by an enterprising B&B owner to cash in on the town's new-found appreciation for the Bard. Though it was thatched and prettily half-timbered, set in a pleasant garden, one had to squint to see the resemblance. I doubt it would have fooled Shakespeare.

Juliette, the owner, and I chatted over breakfast. Unlike the cottage, she was the real deal, an emigrée from Bath who had lived in the US for forty years. It was just possible to hear in her voice the starchy vowels of home, softened by four decades of American life. She'd had the idea for the B&B soon after the theatre opened – but I suspected it wasn't just that.

'A little home from home, that's what it is,' she said, sounding for a second terribly English.

My eye was on the corner of the room, where a thin ginger cat was skulking, eyeing the invader with a notebook.

'Oh, *his* name's King Lear,' Juliette said, all-American again. 'Don't worry. He's a real sweetie.'

That Shakespeare's work had made it out here was, on the face of it, deeply improbable. In 1607, when Jamestown was founded, the playwright was in his celebrated, prosperous mid-forties – about to get stuck into *Pericles*, and so begin his last great phase. His near-contemporaries, the earliest European settlers in America, had little time or temperament for drama. The kind of people driven to forge new lives for themselves in the unyielding environments of Virginia, Massachusetts and Maryland were, almost by definition, not minded to spend time idly watching plays.

In 1642, in the throes of a fundamentalist Christian government, England had barred the doors on its public playhouses. Across the Atlantic, an even more pursed-lip spirit prevailed. In 1687, the clergyman Increase Mather thundered, 'Persons who have been Corrupted by *Stage-Plays* are seldom, and with much difficulty, Reclaimed.' As late as the mid-eighteenth century, Massachusetts levied hefty fines on anyone who dared watch or perform them. Time and again, early American legislation associates playgoing with the most damnable kinds of iniquity. In 1682, William Penn, founder of Pennsylvania, made a point of outlawing 'stage plays, cards, dice . . . masques, revels, bull-baitings, cock-fightings, bear-baitings, and the like, which excite the people to rudeness, cruelty, looseness and irreligion'.

Accordingly, Shakespeare's work was slow to journey across the Atlantic – and did so not as theatre, but as literature. In the late 1640s, the Reverend Seaborn Cotton, son of the famous preacher John, copied out the yearning lyric 'Take, O, take those lips away' from *Measure for Measure* into a commonplace book, alongside fragments from Herrick, Spenser and Sidney. Another Harvard man, Elnathan Chauncy, fell for the charms of Shakespeare's beguiling long poem on love and lust, *Venus and Adonis*, copying a few lines into his own scrapbook in the 1660s. (*Venus and Adonis* was so popular in Shakespeare's own lifetime that only a single copy of its first edition survives: fans seem to have read it to destruction.)

The earliest date scholars can locate a copy of the collected works in the American colonies is in the library of a well-to-do Virginia planter called William Byrd II, who returned from England in 1696 with a copy of what seems to have been the 1685 Fourth Folio, a reprint of the famous First Folio assembled by Shakespeare's colleagues and published after his death. By 1723, Harvard had acquired a six-volume edition to be shelved alongside the forbidding theological and classical works that made up most of its library.

Significantly for the course of American history, the Founding Fathers were among the first to expound the delights of reading (rather than seeing) Shakespeare. Benjamin Franklin urged the Philadelphia Library Company to buy a collected works in 1746, while Thomas Jefferson – a Virginian – recommended the plays to a friend, explaining that '[a] lively and lasting sense of filial duty is more effectually impressed on the mind of a son or daughter by reading *King Lear*, than by all the dry volumes of ethics and divinity that were ever written'. Among the holdings in Jefferson's fine library at Monticello, a forty-minute drive from Staunton, are numerous Shakespearian texts and commentaries.

One of the earliest American enthusiasts for a writer he called 'the Great Master of Nature' was John Adams, who succeeded George Washington to become the second president of the United States. As a lawyer in Boston, Adams devoured the works, saturating his diaries with quotations from *King Lear*, *Romeo and Juliet*, *Troilus and Cressida*, *The Merry Wives of Windsor* and *Henry VIII*. If anything, however, the Bardolator in the Adams household was John's wife Abigail; years later, their son John Quincy Adams recorded that an edition of Shakespeare had been 'on my mother's nursery table', and that 'at ten years of age I was as familiarly acquainted with his lovers and his clowns, as with Robinson Crusoe, the *Pilgrim's Progress*, and the Bible'.

By then, perhaps inevitably, Shakespeare had been recruited on to the side of a nation fighting for independence. In October 1775, as war with Britain raged, Abigail Adams wrote to John suggesting that George III would soon be bellowing, 'My kingdom for a horse!' like the doomed Richard III at Bosworth. The following March, trapped in a besieged Boston, she urged her husband on with stirring words from *Julius Caesar*, spoken by Brutus on the eve of battle:

> There is a tide in the affairs of men
> Which, taken at the flood, leads on to fortune;
> Omitted, all the voyage of their life
> Is bound in shallows and in miseries.
> On such a full sea are we now afloat,
> And we must take the current when it serves,
> Or lose our ventures.

Although the north-eastern states persisted in their costive animosity towards theatre – New England would not relinquish its ban on public performances of plays until the late 1700s – down in the more permissive South, Shakespeare's scripts began to make their way out of libraries and on to the stage. In contrast to his more serious-minded colleagues, George Washington was a devoted playgoer in Williamsburg, Virginia, particularly partial to comedies. In July 1787, he whiled away an afternoon watching Dryden and Davenant's operatic version of *The Tempest, The Enchanted Isle*; later, as president, he hosted an amateur performance of *Julius Caesar* in his official residence at Philadelphia.

Washington's correspondence bustles with Shakespeare, particularly when it comes to the struggle against British tyranny. In October 1778, as commander-in-chief of the Continental Army, he wrote:

> They will know, that it is our Arms, not defenceless Towns, they have to Subdue. Till this end is accomplished, the Superstructure they have been endeavouring to raise 'like the baseless fabric of a vision' falls to nothing.

The words are Prospero's near the close of *The Tempest*: an image of British dominance that figures it as a wistful, poetic illusion, created for a fleeting moment before dissolving into thin air.

The British were not above using Shakespeare, too, albeit as much for the purposes of entertainment as propaganda: between 1777 and 1783 they staged a number of plays including *Richard III* in New York. Not to be outdone, the rebel army later mounted *Coriolanus* at Portsmouth, New Hampshire. An anonymous verse that circulated in the lead-up to hostilities poked fun at the British and their detested levies: 'Be taxed or not be taxed, that is the question.'

The very first performance of Shakespeare on the American continent is usually credited to an amateur: a New York doctor, Joachimus Bertrand, who advertised in March 1730 a staging of *Romeo and Juliet* 'at the Revenge Meeting House, which is fitting up for that purpose'. In a nice piece of director's casting, Dr Bertrand announced that he himself would play the Apothecary.

Two decades later, a pair of ambitious young tyros, Walter Murray and Thomas Kean, founded a theatre company in Philadelphia; forced by the mistrustful authorities to relocate to New York, they performed *Richard III* in March 1750. The show was so successful that they took it out on tour through Virginia and Maryland – making the play perhaps the first homegrown American Shakespeare hit.

But the earliest actor-manager to put down solid Shakespearian roots on this side of the Atlantic was not American, but English, Lewis Hallam. In April 1752, Hallam, his wife Sarah, their three children and a 'good and sufficient company' of ten actors embarked on a sloop called the *Charming Sally* bound for Virginia, aiming to make new lives for themselves in the New World. With them was a trunk-full of costumes, a few pieces of portable scenery and a small library of plays: light comedies by George Farquhar, William Congreve and John Gay; sober tragedies including Joseph Addison's *Cato* and Nicholas Rowe's *Fair Penitent*; and, crucially, a bundle of scripts by Shakespeare.

After docking at Yorktown, Hallam and his troupe travelled to Williamsburg and prepared a place to perform. The first advertisements went out in late August 1752, grandly announcing the arrival of 'a Company of Comedians, lately from London', and boasting that 'Ladies and Gentlemen may depend on being entertain'd in as polite a Manner as at the Theatres in London'. On the bill for their debut was *The Merchant of Venice*. As well as a patriotic dedication to King George II, the poster carried a warning: 'No Person, whatsoever, to be admitted behind the Scenes.' The London Company of Comedians would take no chances with rude-mannered colonials.

Sometimes, though, colonials had occasion to be rude. One early tale is revealing: the visit to Stratford-upon-Avon made by John Adams and Thomas Jefferson on a tour of the English countryside in April 1786. Determined to make it a pilgrimage – Jefferson kissed the ground when they arrived – the pair were nonetheless underwhelmed by the Birthplace ('as small and mean, as you can conceive', wrote Adams) and unimpressed by Shakespeare's funeral monument ('an ill sculptured head'). Adams wrote dejectedly, 'There is nothing preserved of this great Genius which is worth knowing. Nothing which might inform Us what Education, what Company, what Accident turned his Mind to Letters and the Drama.'

I wondered if this contained a clue as to why a much later group of Americans had decided to raise a seventeenth-century theatre here in twenty-first-century Virginia. Despite carving separate chips from a chair in which Shakespeare had reputedly sat (Jefferson was sceptical), the second and third presidents became two in a long line of foreign tourists to become convinced that the English had failed to honour Shakespeare – and that they, leaders of a brand-new nation, could do an infinitely better job.

The American Shakespeare Center wasn't hard to find: in a cosy town centre dominated by pillared nineteenth-century storefronts with striped awnings, it was a hulking interloper, a barn-like building in ox-blood brick.

Inside, however, the Blackfriars was a beauty, a casket in pale Virginia oak, glistening in the light. It felt tiny: the whole thing was roughly the size of a tennis court. A waist-height stage filled approximately half of the space, benches the rest, with railed galleries ranged all around. The stage itself was a scale model of the Globe's, minus the canopy and pillars: a central 'discovery space' with curtains, flanked by wooden doors, with a small curtained balcony aloft at first-floor level. With its hammer-beam roof and amber woodwork, it looked prettily like the hall of a Jacobean stately home.

The Blackfriars was the brainchild of an English professor from a nearby liberal-arts college, Ralph Cohen. He'd set up a small touring troupe in 1988 with friends, using research into Renaissance staging practices, beginning to make its way out of the seminar room: a minimum of props and scenery, Elizabethan-style doubling. When the company decided they needed a home, it seemed only logical to build a copy of one their house dramatist would have known, as exact as they could make it.

London's replica Globe was already being planned, Cohen told me cheerfully; so Staunton had gone under cover. Built on a shoestring budget of $3.7 million (£2.2 million), the Blackfriars had opened in 2001, six years after its cousin beside the Thames. He denied there was any hint of competition, but I wasn't so sure: hearing later that the Bankside Globe had plans to build its *own* indoor theatre, modelled on designs from later in the seventeenth century, the American Shakespeare Center had upped the ante. Their next project was called 'Globe II': a replica of the second, tile-roofed Globe raised in 1614 after the first Globe burnt down. Fundraising was being conducted via their phone number: (877) MUCH-ADO.

Shakespeare wouldn't entirely have recognised the American Blackfriars, Cohen admitted. Planning issues had prevented them from adding windows (which would have helped light the original, as well as providing much-needed ventilation). More controversially, the Staunton fire department had been chary about lit wicks and the smoke. The candlelight they used was electric. 'We did what we could, with the money, in the time,' Cohen said. Settling on to my wooden bench, I thought they had done an impressive job, by any measure.

I had tickets for *Cymbeline* – a late play, and so entirely suited to the space. Rude-mannered colonials were not in evidence: it was a well-groomed crowd. On the bench in front of me was a woman in her early seventies, splendidly clad in camel coat with a sweep of honeyed silver hair. Next to her was a man in an exquisite grey suit, purple silk scarf cascading from his breast pocket. Clearly when one came to the theatre in Staunton one came in one's finery.

Happenstance though it was, it was a pleasing touch. One of the main attractions of playgoing in the Jacobean period – especially in a 'private', indoor theatre – was the opportunity it offered for gawping at folk off stage as well as on. Jacobean Londoners were a fashion-conscious bunch, obsessed with luxurious fabrics, rich colours, expensive jewels and gewgaws. Ornamental hairpieces (some of which were made by Shakespeare's erstwhile landlord, the Huguenot exile Christopher Mountjoy) were pieces of art in themselves. At the London Blackfriars one could pay extra to sit on the stage and be seen – a practice the Virginia Blackfriars had joyously brought back to life, placing a row of stools either side to make seats for 'gallants'.

After a brief and energetic burst of banjo, the Blackfriars company launched into *Cymbeline*. It, too, was brief and energetic. Speeches were taken at a gallop; in no time at all, the plot was up and running. Imogen, sole remaining child of King Cymbeline, has married the commoner Posthumus Leonatus against the wishes of her father (and, even more, the wishes of her wicked stepmother). Posthumus is banished; Imogen follows him, and so begins a wild and troubling journey of self-discovery. She dons the garments of a man to recover her husband and – though she doesn't yet realise it – her brothers, Guiderius and Belarius.

The costumes were a melange of Jacobean and early-twentieth-century, but the actors' confidence in this bare, unadorned space felt entirely authentic, and Shakespeare's late, meaty dialogue sounded to my ear fully plausible with an American twang:

GUIDERIUS
  There is cold meat i'th' cave. We'll browse on that
  Whilst what we have killed be cooked.
BELARIUS   Stay, come not in.
  But that it eats our victuals I should think
  Here were a fairy.

GUIDERIUS What's the matter, sir?
BELARIUS
    By Jupiter, an angel—

Bah Jup'tuh . . . It remained an enigma, the question of how Shakespeare might have heard (or spoken) his own lines; at the London Globe I had attended performances by actors trained in so-called Original Pronunciation, which sounded to me like broad Somerset inflected with the slatey nasal twang of Lancashire. One thing everyone could agree on, however, was that East Coast American, with its neat terminal *r*s and light medial vowels (*pass* to rhyme with *ass*, *scenario* as 'scen-*ai*-rio') was much closer to the language Shakespeare and his audiences understood than the fluting tones of the Royal Shakespeare Company.

I was most intrigued by how the ASC would handle a tricky aspect of Shakespeare's late plays, their fondness for spectacular staging. Following the experiments conducted in Jacobean court masques, where no expense was spared on eye-popping scenography, the London Blackfriars was seemingly equipped with a battery of high-tech special effects: a hoist in the 'heavens' via which actors could be flown on to the stage; elaborate trapdoors through which performers were propelled at speed; a company of resident musicians to provide magical sound effects. *Cymbeline*'s stage directions call for any number of tricks to dazzle the eye – a cunning device to make it appear that the doltish Cloten has been beheaded; an 'apparition' of ghosts to musical accompaniment; the entry of Jupiter himself, who 'descends in thunder and lightning, sitting upon an eagle' before casting a thunderbolt.

There were no godly descents on offer that night: a golden-robed Jupiter simply strolled on to the upper-level balcony to the crashing of some backstage ironmongery (a device for flying in *dei ex machina* had been another casualty of the Virginia Blackfriars's tight budget). But Cloten's death had a satisfying gruesomeness, amplified by the harrowed expressions on the faces of the on-stage gallants.

I loved it. Fast, tonally all over the place, with more switchback turns than a mountain pass, the production made sense of *Cymbeline* in a way that a more austerely conceptual version wouldn't. Conducted on a stage not much larger than a tablecloth, the sword-fighting was properly perilous, and one of the most famous lyrics in the English language, spoken over the body of the disguised and apparently dead Imogen, was delivered with a touching lack of preciousness:

Fear no more the heat o'th' sun,
  Nor the furious winter's rages.
Thou thy worldly task hast done,
  Home art gone and ta'en thy wages.
Golden lads and girls all must,
As chimney-sweepers, come to dust.

It might have been the tiredness, but I was dabbing my eyes at that. Ambushed by the late plays once again.

IF YOU WANT TO GET A FIX on the importance of Shakespeare to a certain kind of American life, you have only to glance at a street plan of Washington DC.

First, trace the twin diagonals of Pennsylvania and Maryland Avenues as they rush towards the west frontage of the Capitol building. Then nudge your eye gently right. Above, to the north, sits the marble lozenge of the Supreme Court. To the immediate south is the Library of Congress's Jefferson building – a blowsy, Beaux-Arts affair, crowned with a squat pimple of a dome. Next door is the Adams building, raised in the 1930s when the library ran out of book stacks.

The building to look for is the fifth. Tucked next to the Adams, it completes the arrangement, which is as severely patterned as any Renaissance garden. It is the Folger Shakespeare Library, the world's vastest Shakespeare archive, home (at the most recent count) to 256,000 books, 250,000 playbills, 60,000 manuscripts, 200 oil paintings and any amount of other Shakespeariana. The brainchild of collector Henry Clay Folger and his wife Emily, it sits enclosed on two sides by the United States's central library, in the shadow of Congress, just across the street from the highest court in the land. In this most symbolic of cities, it is hard to see how it could be more symbolically embedded.

There is another conceit, meticulously planned by the architects. Sketch an imaginary plane back west from the library's front wall, and run it straight through the Capitol and along the National Mall. The line brushes the Washington Monument, before running headlong into the Lincoln Memorial – plumb through what the library's first director, speaking at its opening on 23 April 1932, called 'the three [men] whom Americans universally worship'.

Lincoln, Washington, Shakespeare: the Pilgrim Fathers, who had fled England precisely to avoid diabolical iniquities like Shakespearian drama, would doubtless be appalled.

Deep in my map as I came up past the Capitol, the Folger sprang out on me by surprise: a slim, art-deco cigarette case of a building, its marble shining bone-white in the sun. It looked for all the world like a minor government department, or the embassy of a small but strategically important country. Bardonia, I supposed.

I had a meeting, bang on 9 a.m., with Michael Witmore, the Folger's director. Escorted to his corner office, I tapped gently at the door, which was half ajar, and poked my head around. Glossy green carpet, helipad-sized desk, with the windows giving on to a panoramic view of the Washington skyline. There was only one word for it: presidential.

A few seconds later, Witmore appeared behind me, bearing two steaming mugs emblazoned with the Folger logo. He looked pretty presidential himself – pinstriped suit and shining shoes, sandy brown hair, a youthful mid-forties.

Quite a view, I said, looking out of the window and towards the Capitol dome, glimmering in the light.

He eased back behind the desk, mug in hand. 'In DC, our culture is politics. And Shakespeare is a writer who is very good for people who think about the world in political terms.'

A former professor at the University of Wisconsin who had done graduate work at Berkeley and UCLA, Witmore was a new arrival at the Folger. He had qualifications in scholarly fields I barely knew existed: the crossover between Renaissance rhetoric and bioinformatics; data-visualisation in Shakespeare's texts. He had only been in the post a few months.

I asked him to sum up what the job involved. He offered a well-practised smile. 'Secretary of state for Shakespeare . . . I exaggerate, of course.'

Perhaps I shouldn't have been surprised by the politico-corporate atmosphere: Henry Clay Folger had been, after all, a businessman.

Born in New York City in 1857, the son of a millinery dealer, he got a job in the nascent oil industry partly to pay himself through Amherst College. After graduating, he raced up the corporate ranks – first as a clerk at a small oil firm, then, in 1881, joining what became Standard Oil. By 1909, he was one of Rockefeller's juniors. By 1911, he had become the first president of Standard Oil New York.

All along, Folger nursed a secret passion. After paying 25 cents to hear Ralph Waldo Emerson lecture at Amherst in 1879, he had become fixated on Shakespeare. He bought a copy of a talk Emerson had given during the 1864 tercentenary, and read it cover to cover. He upgraded his one-volume complete works to a thirteen-volume edition. In a copy of Thomas Carlyle's *On Heroes*, he underlined Carlyle's statement that Shakespeare was 'the grandest thing we have yet done'.

When he met the woman who would become his wife, Emily Clara Jordan, passion became infatuation. A graduate of Vassar College, Emily wrote her master's thesis on the 'True Text of Shakespeare'. Henry's wedding gift to her in 1885 was a facsimile copy of the 1623 First Folio, so that she could 'see Shakespeare's plays as they were originally given to the world'.

'It becomes a group effort between the two of them,' Witmore said. 'They seem to have egged each other on.'

The Folgers were soon collecting: at first modestly, buying a copy of the 1685 Fourth Folio for $107.50, paid for on credit (a copy of the same edition as that probably owned by the Virginia planter William Byrd). As their wealth and influence expanded, so did their ambitions. In 1897, they acquired their first major Shakespearian haul, including rare early editions of *Romeo and Juliet* and *The Merchant of Venice* and much else besides. Among them were four copies of the First Folio, this time originals: infinitely more valuable than the Fourth.

The same rapacious deal-making that Henry practised on behalf of Standard Oil transformed the genteel world of rare book and manuscript dealing. For forty years the Folgers posted agents across Europe, operating under pseudonyms, keeping close watch on everything that looked as if it might come up for sale.

They were shameless. One precious collection was prised out of the hands of the ailing Bishop of Truro after his son-in-law was offered cash in hand. Another tranche of books was poached off a rival collector after his stocks took a nosedive. The Folgers mastered a unique kind of alchemy: transmuting black oil into Shakespearian gold. In one five-month period in 1917 they spent $780,500, nearly $15 million in today's money, all of it on books and manuscripts.

'*The Tempest* reads well anywhere but especially so at the seashore, and best of all in mid-ocean,' wrote Henry on one transatlantic shopping expedition. There were stories that when they went away they carried a card index in their chiffonier. Perhaps needless to say, they remained childless.

Witmore stood up, and gazed out at the skyline. 'I think Mr Folger genuinely loved Shakespeare and felt it spoke to him, as many Americans of his period did. But it's also a desire to possess, to get hold of a cultural legacy that was empowering on a global scale.'

Yet empowering *how*? Other Gilded Age potentates such as William Randolph Hearst and Henry Clay Frick lined the walls of their sprawling palazzi with Old Masters and Roman statuary. You couldn't do that with dusty old books. Neither of the Folgers was a professional scholar; Henry was so busy building up financial reserves and spending them that he barely had time to read. Crates piled up, unexamined, in warehouses and at their home in Brooklyn Heights (rented, so they had more money to lavish on Shakespeare). Academics desperate to steal a glance at their astonishing collection were turned away. In 1899 Folger wrote to a friend confessing that his 'modest library' was for 'the most part as yet unread'.

Witmore smiled. 'Did Mr Folger understand the full magnitude of what he was doing? I think he understood the magnitude, but not the specifics.'

A plan began to form. Quietly, in the late 1910s, he and Emily began to look at sites on Capitol Hill. They eventually settled on a row of houses on what is now East Capitol Street. Disaster threatened when the site was earmarked for an extension of the Library of Congress, but Folger, stunning lawmakers with the announcement that he had a collection of 'national significance' to offer, got his way. In 1928, the architects set to work.

'The part I find very striking,' said Witmore, 'is that he says, "Initially I thought of placing this collection in Stratford-upon-Avon next to the man's bones, and I could have built it in New York City, which is where my peers have built their libraries, but I would like to locate it in Washington as a gift to the nation, *for I am an American*."'

It was quite a thought – keeping all this Shakespeare in the United States rather than repatriating it had somehow become a patriotic act. One-nil to America.

Yet Henry Folger never saw the project through. In 1930, just two weeks after the cornerstone for the building was laid, he went into hospital for a minor operation and unexpectedly died. When the library opened in April 1932, Emily Clay Folger was left to welcome guests from across the world, led by President Hoover, on her own.

I wondered aloud if this accounted for the library's faintly morbid feel. I'd only been inside an hour, and it felt – there was no avoiding the issue – a touch deathly.

Witmore was twiddling a pen. 'You realise we're also a mausoleum?' I didn't.

'Oh *yeah*. If you go to the reading room, there's a plaque on the wall, between their portraits.' He was grinning broadly. 'Mr and Mrs Folger are right behind that. It makes us one of the few places on Capitol Hill where bodies are buried.'

Later, I looked for the plaque. It was right where Witmore had said. TO THE GLORY OF WILLIAM SHAKESPEARE AND THE GREATER GLORY OF GOD, it read. God may have been greater, but Shakespeare got top billing.

After the sober, federal-looking exterior, the Folger's interior came as a shock. The main reading room was outlandish: a brazen piece of fakery that looked as if it had been built by a Hollywood set designer striving to replicate the most maudlin aspects of an Oxford college, at a scale four times larger than reality.

Lined in baize-green carpet, it was nearly the length of a swimming pool. Suspended from the hammer-beam roof were three gargantuan iron chandeliers that could have doubled as torture implements, and, at one end, an oversized stained-glass window. Thick Renaissance tapestries lined the walls, above bookshelves in sombre oak. Huge logs lolled in a stone fireplace the size of a two-storey building. All it lacked was a hunch-backed buter playing fugues on the organ, and perhaps a spaniel or two snoozing in the armchairs. At least the scent was authentic: antique paper, drying book spines and carpet, with a top note of floor polish and air conditioning.

On the wall at the far end, I saw as I neared it, was a full-size wooden copy of Shakespeare's funerary monument in Holy Trinity church, Stratford-upon-Avon. Back in England I had always thought that this ugly Jacobean half-bust, framed by a dinky architectural surround, gave the poet the expectant air of a fairground automaton, as if his eyes might suddenly start flashing and the quill in his right hand spring into action. This morning, his American doppelgänger looked supercilious and mildly bored.

Also, it was freezing: Nordic winter to the Southern heat outside. Presumably this was for the books' sake. A handful of researchers sat bolt upright at their desks, bundled in scarves and jumpers. The pale light reflecting up from their laptops gave them the ghoulish look of medical specimens. A duteous hush prevailed, broken only by the occasional agitated flurry of laptop keys.

One woman flicked a glance at me, filed me as of limited scholarly interest, and turned back to her screen.

A Polish academic once told me – happily, I think – that you could lose yourself in the Folger's collections. Descending staircase after staircase, walking past steel bookcase after steel bookcase, I saw that it might literally be true. In the vast vaults below the reading room, the strip lights gave everything an underwater tinge. I could feel the vibration of the air conditioning in my teeth. It was like being in the refrigerated hold of a container ship. One could spend weeks down here, and no one would ever know.

I had asked to see the most treasured part of the Folger library: its holdings of early printed books and manuscripts, kept under lock and key deep beneath Capitol Hill. I was told to present myself bright and early the following morning, and meet a curator called Erin Blake.

I found Blake standing in front of a colossal steel bank door, fifteen inches thick and studded with a fearsome armature of locks and levers. An electric bell jangled as she swung open the gate inside.

She smiled mischievously. 'It goes off automatically whenever we open and close the door. If you hear one bell and not the second, watch out. We come running!'

No part of the Folger holdings is as valuable as the so-called STC collection, named after the Short-Title Catalogue, which aims to list every book published between 1475 and 1640 in Britain, Ireland, the British Empire and the United States. The Folger has some 55,000 of these precious antiques, nearly half the catalogue, including such mouth-watering examples as early printings of Chaucer's *Canterbury*

Tales, published by Caxton in 1477, and the first edition of Newton's *Principia Mathematica* (1687). Only the British Library and Oxford's Bodleian have more.

But I wanted to get my hands on something properly unique: the Folger's extraordinary collection of Shakespeare First Folios. Blake led us around the corner, into another section of the vault.

'Drum roll, please,' she said.

In front of us a wall was filled with a flock of squat books, each roughly the size of an A4 folder and a couple of inches thick, lying flat on their backs to protect their spines. The Folios were dressed in a variety of outfits. Some were bound gaudily in crimson or chocolate leather and tooled in extravagant gold filigree; others had much duller bindings, scarred and chafed with age. Blake pointed to one hulkingly unattractive copy, which looked as though it was wrapped in rhino skin that had darkened to the colour of tar.

'Seventeenth-century calf. They would have all looked like this originally. But Shakespeare was such an important figure for nineteenth-century collectors that they wanted to make sure they had bindings worthy of him, so they threw away the originals. Much to our chagrin.'

This was the world's largest collection of Folios?

'Oh, yes! By a factor of about seven. There are eighty-two, depending on how you count them – some are incomplete. About a third of the copies that exist. The world's second-largest collection is now in Japan.' She allowed herself a flicker of a smile. 'What do you guys have in the British Library? Six, now, I think.'

Trying not to feel too wounded, I asked if one could put a price on the collection.

'I don't know where you would start. A good Folio went at auction a few years ago for four and a half million dollars, and that's not even the most expensive. The one before that went for six million-plus.'

I attempted a rapid piece of arithmetic. Assuming – what, an average of $3 million per copy? More? That meant the best part of $300 million on this wall alone. But of course if you put them all on sale the market would collapse.

Why eighty-two copies of exactly the same book had ended up in a vault in the middle of Washington was one of numerous mysteries about Henry Clay Folger. By the standards of many rare editions, the Folio is dirt-common; of the 750-plus copies printed, around 230 are still in existence, in collections as far-flung as Meisei University in

Tokyo and the state library of New South Wales – a global web now so complex that one scholar, Anthony James West, has devoted a career simply to tracking them down. Individual copies vary in condition (some have hand annotations, others a particularly starry provenance) but in many respects the Folio is a reasonably straightforward mass-produced seventeenth-century book.

Blake slid out a copy from a middle shelf, and placed it carefully between us. It had a flashy gold-and-yellow binding that should by rights have enclosed copies of *Reader's Digest*. She eased it open, her fingers moving slowly across the large pages. The famous frontispiece, with Martin Droeshout's even more famously doleful engraving of Shakespeare; a fawning joint dedication to the Earls of Pembroke and Montgomery; an address 'To the great Variety of Readers'; commendatory poems; finally, in pole position on page 1, *The Tempest*.

If the Folio bore an uncanny resemblance to a tombstone, there was a reason. When a consortium led by Shakespeare's fellow actors John Heminges and Henry Condell began serious work on the book in 1621, five years after Shakespeare's death, it was intended as a volume commemorating a life's work – a compendium of thirty-six plays that had previously existed either in so-called 'quarto' format or never (in the case of eighteen texts) appeared in print at all.

Quartos were cheap pocket editions, often haphazardly produced, their name deriving from the fact that they were assembled from folding sheets of paper in quarters, meaning the print shop could squeeze four leaves or eight pages from each sheet. Folios, by contrast (from the Latin *folium* or 'leaf'), were double the size and correspondingly more prestigious – a format generally reserved for grand works of theology, history or philosophy. In Shakespeare's day, printing mere playscripts in double-columned folio was extremely unusual: Ben Jonson had been the first to attempt something so bold, publishing his own works in folio in 1616. That Heminges and Condell did the same for Shakespeare was a mark of the high esteem in which he was held. But as an object, there is little unique about the book unromantically called *Mr William Shakespeares Comedies, Histories, & Tragedies*, which went on sale in London in autumn 1623.

If you were *really* interested in Shakespeare's working methods, Blake explained, you would do better addressing yourself to the shelf nearby, on which sat perhaps a hundred slim volumes, some not much thicker than a paperback pamphlet and bound in a merry riot of black, red and gold. This was the Folger's collection of quartos. From a scholarly point of view, the quartos were often far more fascinating. The earliest printings of Shakespeare's scripts, many published during his lifetime, they revealed more about how his plays were actually acted and understood than the prim-and-proper, Sunday-best Folio.

Every quarto had a tale to tell. Several were set from the playwright's 'foul papers' or working manuscripts. Others contained telling slips, such as the cock-up in the 1599 second quarto of *Romeo and Juliet* that printed the name of Will Kempe, the star comedian who'd once visited Helsingør, instead of his character. *Hamlet* was printed in two rival quartos, in 1603 and 1604. The first was apparently unauthorised, a garbled version perhaps cut down for a touring troupe such as those played in by Kempe or cobbled together from the memory of an actor (it contains such poetical delights as 'To be or not to be, ay, there's the point'). *Hamlet*'s second quarto, loudly advertised as 'newly imprinted and enlarged to almost as much again as it was', seems to have been issued to set the record straight, perhaps by a piqued author. Other quartos are truly irreplaceable: the Folger's Q1 *Titus Andronicus*, a slender volume published in 1594, is now the only copy in existence anywhere in the world.

But the Folios have all the glamour. In the late eighteenth century the book began to acquire the patina of fabled antiquity. Stoked by reverence for the Immortal Bard, First Folios started to sell for higher and higher prices. Had you turned up at Edward Blount's bookshop near St Paul's cathedral in November 1623, you could have bought a brand-new First Folio, hot off the press and bound in plain calf, for £1, roughly equivalent to 44 loaves of bread (unbound, it was even cheaper: 15 shillings). In the 1750s it was possible to get hold of one for just over £3 (100 loaves); by the 1790s the cost had leapt to £35 (900 loaves). By the 1850s, it would cost you 5,000 loaves.

From there, prices went wild. By the early twentieth century a copy of the Folio cost roughly the equivalent of 96,000 loaves. In October 2001, when a pristine First Folio went on sale at Christie's in New York, it fetched not $2–3 million as estimated, but a stupefying $6,166,000 (£4.2 million). Near enough 6 million loaves – a lot of bread, in every sense.

American enthusiasts such as the Folgers were largely to blame for this runaway inflation. In 1902, of 158 known First Folios, 100 were in British collections and 39 in the United States. Today, the figure is almost exactly reversed – 44 in the UK, 145 in the US. Foliomania is an American fetish, one that has long since priced out less dazzlingly wealthy collectors and libraries.

In fact, despite a recent spurt of interest from Japanese collectors, many countries have never even seen an original First Folio. There is calculated to be just one copy kept in all of sub-Saharan Africa (in Cape Town, part of the former library of a colonial governor); no copies in East Asia outside Japan; and no copies at all kept in India or South America. As Folger had no doubt intended, his Folios not only beat the Brits – they bolstered American cultural hegemony.

Folger called it simply 'the most precious book in the world': a statement that reveals much about his addiction, but bears little relation to its actual bibliographical value. He collected Folios because they were there to collect, and because he wanted no one else to own as many as he did. That, apparently, was that.

His death presented the librarians with a conundrum. What on earth to do with the embarrassment of Folios cluttering the Folger vaults? It wasn't until the mid-1940s, long after the library opened, that a postdoctoral researcher at the University of Kansas, Charlton K. Hinman, came up with an answer. Analysing photographs of aerial bombardment while serving in naval intelligence during the second world war, Hinman had developed the idea of constructing a machine that could compare pages from two apparently identical copies of a book. Each book would be placed, open, on either side of a flat bed; by looking through a complex series of lenses, one could superimpose their images to see if there were any differences – a punishing process called 'collation' that until then had taken hours of toil and eye strain and was prone to error.

I had seen the Hinman Collator in a cubbyhole off the reading room upstairs: an ungainly contraption in Bakelite and sheet steel, it was the size of two hefty fridges, and looked like the mutant offspring of an electron microscope and a battlefield operating table.

Hinman dedicated his life to the task of collating Folios, sniffing out each and every variant – typos, corrections, insertions, editorial alterations – in each and every available copy of the book. He finally published his results in 1963. Five years later, he produced the *Norton Facsimile*, a so-called 'perfect' facsimile of the text – a composite copy made from no fewer than twenty-nine separate copies, error-free, the distillation of all that was wise and good in Shakespearian bibliography.

There was no doubting Hinman's brilliance, I thought as I headed back upstairs, and his work had helped scholars see the realities of early-modern printing with fresh clarity. But in one way his 'ideal' Folio was yet another index of the Folgers' baffling quest. A platonic edition, impossibly perfect, it was also illusory.

Years later, another use for the Hinman Collator was found, when the CIA is believed to have purchased one to assist in forgery cases. Courtesy of the Folgers, the Bard of Avon had done his bit for the American military-industrial complex.

On the title page of his edition of Ralph Waldo Emerson's *Essays* Henry copied out a single sentence that caught his eye: 'Build therefore your own world.' I found it fascinating that it had been Emerson who had inspired the young Folger. Of all the nineteenth-century Americans who had measured themselves in relation to the English Bard, few had done so with as much solicitude and seriousness as the Sage of Concord.

From almost his first contact with Shakespeare as a bookish, excessively religious New England teenager, Emerson was both bewitched and a touch alarmed: the works were 'sustained on the sensual', he wrote as a seventeen-year-old, and thus to be 'regret[ted]'.

It didn't take long for Emerson's pleasure in Shakespeare to become less furtively enjoyable. Within a few years Emerson was of the view that the playwright's 'taste' was 'the most exquisite that God ever informed amongst men', and by 1835, now in his thirties, he was writing, 'I actually shade my eyes as I read for the splendour of the thoughts.' 'Immeasurable', 'unapproachable', a 'fixed star', 'whole', 'a genius': there was barely a superlative he didn't use. Emerson's relationship with the man he most often called 'the Bard' was perhaps the most enduring in a long life, and certainly the most uninhibited.

Emerson had been a founding member of the East Coast transcendentalist movement of the 1830s and 1840s, a headily pantheistic religion that combined the philosophy of the European Romantics, neoplatonism, Swedenborg and American nationalism; and it was as a transcendental writer that he understood Shakespeare. Although taking issue with the Romantic view of Herder, Goethe and their ilk that the poet was a child of nature, Emerson nevertheless contrived to deify Shakespeare, elevating him to a position almost beyond humankind. His famous essay in *Representative Men* (1850) on 'Shakespeare, or the Poet' asks, 'What point of morals, of economy, of philosophy, of religion, of taste, of the conduct of life, has he not settled?' It continues in similarly vatic vein:

> He wrote the airs for all our modern music: he wrote the text of modern life; the text of manners: he drew the man of England and Europe; the father of the man in America . . . all the sweets and all the terrors of human lot lay in his mind as truly but as softly as the landscape lies on the eye.

Shakespeare was both 'representative' and utterly unique – and his blood surged through the arteries of every patriotic American.

This last was an issue Emerson returned to repeatedly in later life, attempting to square the circle whereby a poet from the Old World could be a harbinger of the New, itself searching (as Germany had earlier searched) for the 'representative poet' who could capture all that was good and fresh about the United States.

In the manuscript of his tercentenary speech given at Boston in 1864 Emerson admitted this was a paradox: 'The Pilgrims came to Plymouth in 1620. The plays of Shakespeare were not published until three years later. Had they been published earlier, our forefathers . . . might have stayed at home to read them.' Another record of the speech credited Emerson with the line that 'the climes beyond the solar road probably call this planet not Earth but Shakespeare'. It was this speech – with its teasing suggestion that the publication of the 1623 Folio might have been enough to hold back the founding of America – that Henry Folger had read as a student. Perhaps this was why he had become so fixated on the book.

The puzzle about Emerson's copious references is that so few are to actual texts: plays are mentioned, but rarely addressed in detail; quotations reprinted, but rarely developed. Despite his Bardolatry, Emerson remained somehow uncomfortable with the image of Shakespeare as a working playwright churning out scripts for a hungry audience, preferring to regard him as a 'Poet' above such trifling mortal concerns.

This opened a much more dangerous speculation – that perhaps Shakespeare wasn't Shakespeare at all. Soon after *Representative Men* was published, Emerson received a letter from a schoolteacher and failed playwright called Delia Bacon, who had become convinced that works of such noble mien could never have been written for the ignorant rabble who frequented the Elizabethan theatre ('masses . . . still unlettered'), and that furthermore Shakespeare of Stratford (a 'stupid, illiterate, third-rate play-actor') was a fraud. From supposed cryptographic investigation of the texts, Bacon had developed the theory that none other than her historical namesake (though not, in fact, her relation), Francis Bacon, was behind them.

Now in her forties, Delia Bacon was desperate to travel to England to continue her research; Emerson encouraged her. With the support of another eminent man of American letters, Nathaniel Hawthorne, her book, *The Philosophy of the Plays of Shakespeare Unfolded*, eventually made print in 1857, the grassy-knoll conspiracy of its time. After being discovered in Stratford-upon-Avon, eyeing Shakespeare's tomb purposefully and apparently intending to break in, Bacon herself was eventually confined to an asylum.

Like every subsequent attempt to dispute Shakespeare's authorship, Delia Bacon's 'philosophy' flew in the face of copious historical data, and ultimately in the face of reason. But what struck me here in the heart of Washington DC was something that had previously passed me by: the authorship controversy was largely an American invention.

Popularised in the nineteenth century by a small clique of East Coast writers, among them Bacon, Hawthorne, Walt Whitman and Emerson (who later claimed that Bacon and Whitman were 'the sole producers that America has yielded in ten years'), American anxieties about Shakespeare's true identity had planted the seeds of doubt elsewhere. In fact the authorship debate wasn't even just American, it was Ohioan – Bacon had been born in a log cabin near Tallmadge on the Lake Erie plains, the daughter of a failed pioneer; the first man to suggest that 'Shakespeare' was in fact Christopher Marlowe, one Wilbur G. Ziegler, was an attorney from Fremont, 100 miles west.

Among later sceptics were Henry James and Mark Twain, who devoted a hefty portion of his 1909 semi-autobiographical work, *Is Shakespeare Dead?*, to the certainty that the man had never even written the plays. A suspicious number of Supreme Court justices, most recently John Paul Stevens, had subsequently joined the flock, despite being headquartered a stone's throw from a library whose holdings – had they bothered to explore them – amply proved otherwise.

What drove these American doubters? Was it the yawning gulf

between what they knew (or thought they knew) about Shakespeare's life and his godlike posthumous reputation? Distrust of received nostrums? A transatlantic weakness for lords and ladies? The chance to stick it to the Brits and that dumb little tourist trap called Stratford?

Whatever the answer, it was hard to avoid the sense that while the United States hardly had a monopoly on Shakespeare conspiracy trolls, it had certainly done plenty to feed them.

The happy amateurishness of the Folgers' collecting had unlooked-for consequences. When the scholar Joseph Quincy Adams (a scion of the famous presidential family) took over as director in 1934, he quailed at the Sisyphean task before him: no plan of operation, not even an accurate list of the collections. More than 2,000 Standard Oil packing cases had to be shipped from New York and unpacked, over 90,000 items catalogued and found room for.

Some of the Folgers' bequest was well chosen: in the vaults Blake and I cradled a nineteenth-century edition of *A Midsummer Night's Dream*, adorned in diaphanous watercolours of azure and rose-pink by the symbolist artist Pinckney Marcius-Simons. But other objects had more doubtful significance. Another drawer contained a lumpen bronze of Lady Macbeth by Alice Morgan Wright, a (possibly malevolent) gift from Henry's sister that made Lady M resemble a sex toy that had lain too close to a gas fire.

So gimlet-eyed about books, when it came to other parts of their collection the Folgers allowed Bardolatry to cloud their gaze. An object listed as 'Queen Elizabeth I's corset' turned out to date from the eighteenth century. There was said to have been a box bound in red morocco containing a few auburn tresses, ostensibly 'A Hair from the Head of William Shakespeare'. I could find no trace of it in the catalogue. But the library had in the intervening period seen fit to acquire a translation of *Hamlet* into Klingon.

It took years to get everything organised, irritating academics who couldn't wait to go fossicking in the Folgers' gold mine. Someone complained that in all the fuss, this new, world-leading library hadn't thought to buy a single modern dictionary.

Gradually things settled. Following Emily's death in 1936, Adams at last got the library under control, filling it out with material that could balance and support Shakespeare. His star acquisition was the collection of the British businessman and collector Leicester Harmsworth, a spectacular array of over 8,000 English early printed books, which arrived in 1938. The second director, Louis B. Wright, ramped up the Folger's research and publication activities, transforming the library into a major force in historical and literary scholarship.

But there were risks in placing an institution like this so close to the nerve-centre of American power. Rummaging one afternoon through the typescript of a surprisingly gossipy history compiled by one of the Folger's first curators, Giles E. Dawson, I happened upon his account of what happened at the library during the second world war.

It made for eye-opening reading. After the attack on Pearl Harbor in December 1941, Adams and his trustees decided to evacuate the most valuable parts of the collection. Staff worked frantically to pack up the Folios, quartos, early books and manuscripts, having arranged to send them to Amherst College in Massachusetts for the duration. Some 200 cartons were loaded on to a freight car.

The train was dispatched and a team headed separately up to Amherst to meet it. But when they got there, the freight car had disappeared. There had been a fault with one of the axles, which had overheated and nearly caught fire. The librarians began to panic. An update arrived: the fault had been caught, but the car had been taken out of the train in Philadelphia. A gang of railroad workers, blissfully ignorant of what the boxes contained, had left them standing outside with no supervision or security.

The precious cargo eventually arrived in Massachusetts. But it was a chastening thought, to put it mildly, that the Folger had come close to losing its most precious holdings – and not once, but twice on the same day. I checked the catalogue again: it seemed Dawson's account had never been published.

Standing one morning among the federal employees and policy advisors as we queued for our daily doses of Starbucks, I found myself mulling Michael Witmore's suggestion that Shakespeare was a primarily political writer, and thus a natural fit for Washington DC. Was anyone actually staging him here? I scanned the *Washington Post* listings, but the Shakespeare Theatre Company, Washington's leading troupe, was dark – nothing doing during my visit. A young fringe group called Taffety Punk were about to present a version of the early narrative poem *The Rape of Lucrece*, and they had invited me to visit them in rehearsals, but not for a few days yet. In this most political of towns, this most political of playwrights appeared to be on furlough.

It seemed a shame. The early *Henry VI* plays, that rollicking triple-decker on the Wars of the Roses, might have made interesting viewing in light of the ongoing stand-off between Democrats and Republicans in Congress. More polarised by the minute, the two parties seemed as impossible to manage as any of Shakespeare's brawling barons, and as unlikely to come to agreement over their blood feuds. More cynically, several commentators had noted the similarities between ex-president George W. Bush and Shakespeare's Hal – another hard-drinking wastrel who undergoes a sudden epiphany, renounces his 'wild' youth, and becomes one of the most warmongering leaders in the canon.

But it was *Julius Caesar*, of course, that possessed an illustrious history in the United States, where this republican play has long been far more popular than back in Britain. Partly in deference to the surging patriotism being felt in the colonies, the Hallams' London Company of Comedians had been refounded in 1763, eleven years after arriving, as the American Company. In 1770, on the brink of war, they acted *Julius Caesar* in Philadelphia, astutely marketing it as depicting 'the noble struggles for Liberty by that renowned patriot Marcus Brutus'.

A century later, the Boston-born E. L. Davenport, one of the biggest stars of the 1860s and 1870s, excelled as a redoubtably toga-clad Brutus, setting a record for performances of the play on Broadway in 1875. In 1953, Joseph L. Mankiewicz successfully made *Julius Caesar* into big Hollywood box office with Marlon Brando as Mark Antony and Louis Calhern as Caesar (Roland Barthes poked fun at these 'gangster-sheriffs').

Julius Caesar even shaded into real-life American political tragedy. In November 1864 John Wilkes Booth, one of three actor-sons of one of the earliest American stars, the English-born Junius Brutus Booth, participated in a production in New York alongside his brothers. Junius Brutus Jr played Cassius, Edwin was Brutus, while John Wilkes took Mark Antony. In a famous photograph commemorating the event, the three brothers pose in costume – Junius reaching for his sword, Edwin making as if to restrain him. John broods, a dangerous loner, on the other edge of the frame.

The performance was a fundraiser for the Shakespeare statue later erected in Central Park. But it had ghoulish echoes when, the following April, John Wilkes crept into the presidential box at Ford's theatre in Washington and shot Abraham Lincoln in the back of the head.

The theatre-loving president happened to be watching a comedy, Tom Taylor's heavy-handed 1858 farce *Our American Cousin*. But Booth had cast himself in an altogether more serious role. A letter he wrote before heading to Ford's theatre, later published in the papers, ended with some well-known words:

> O, that we could come by Caesar's spirit,
> And not dismember Caesar! But, alas,
> Caesar must bleed for it.

'I answer with Brutus,' Booth concluded.

Lincoln, had he survived, would have caught the reference instantly. A lover of Shakespeare since childhood, he was known to lug a complete works around the White House, and had once performed from memory 'Now is the winter of our discontent', the opening soliloquy of *Richard III*, 'with a degree of force and power that made it seem like a new creation' (as described by the artist Francis Carpenter, who complimented the president on his acting). Days before his assassination, Lincoln had been rereading *Macbeth*, and, tormented by a recurring nightmare, confided to his bodyguard that 'the thing has got possession of me, and like Banquo's ghost, it will not down'.

As I walked towards the library that morning, Starbucks in hand, I thought again about the line through the centre of town connecting Lincoln, Washington and Shakespeare. More lethal than I'd reckoned.

<hr />

YEARS AGO, AT A THEATRE FESTIVAL somewhere or other, I bought a postcard. It's a map of the United States of America. At first glance it isn't much: plain black-and-white, US postal-sized, a conventional projection of the continent state by state, with locations marked in small, neat type.

You peer a little closer; peer and begin to puzzle. These places sound familiar. Tucked inside southern Texas, a short drive from the Mexican border, there's somewhere called Sebastian – a settlement of 1,864, the census tells you, not much more than a tight grid of asphalt and some industrial facilities. Far north, at the other extreme of the United States, is a town on the North Dakota prairie called Hamlet. Hamlet, perhaps appropriately, is now a ghost.

It goes on. You count no fewer than four American Orlandos, all the way from Orlando, Kentucky (an 'unincorporated community' perched on the edge of Daniel Boone country) to the famous resort city in Florida. There's a large village near Chicago, Illinois, named Romeoville. It boasts, apparently, a golf club called Bolingbrook.

The postcard, entitled *A Shakespearean Map of the USA, Featuring Towns that Actually Exist!* – by the American artist David Jouris – is, of course, a joke. It's an erudite joke, to be sure. One needs a secure apprehension of the canon (perhaps even a specialist encyclopedia) to remember that Speed in Indiana is also the name of Valentine's 'clownish servant' in the youthful *The Two Gentlemen of Verona* – a character whose chief claim to fame is one of the most tedious interchanges in Shakespearian comedy, centring on the rhetorical significance of a sheep.

Equally, you'd require a firm grasp of the history plays to recall that the various American Gloucesters pinpointed here relate to five separate characters: two Duchesses (in *Henry VI Part II* and *Richard II*), two Dukes and an Earl. One Duke is Humphrey of Gloucester, the youngest son of Henry IV in *Henry IV Part II* and *Henry V*. The other is more of a celebrity: Richard, Duke of Gloucester, later King Richard III.

Do any of these places have any Shakespearian connection at all? No, in most instances – accidents of geography, genealogy, cartography. But I'd absent-mindedly tucked the postcard into my notebook and brought it to Washington with me, and one quiet afternoon in the library, when I should have been doing a million more profitable things, I started to wonder if there was more to it than that.

A quick search online uncovered another ghost town, Shakespeare in New Mexico, rechristened in 1879 after a mining company named in honour of the playwright. North of the Canadian border, Stratford in Ontario, a former rail city, has made profitable connection with its namesake Stratford-upon-Avon: a Shakespeare festival has run there since 1953, one of the most famous in North America. (Stratford in Connecticut poached the idea, launching its own Shakespeare festival in 1955, which ran until the late eighties.) Orlando, Florida, honours its namesake in *As You Like It* with its own Shakespeare theatre, founded in the early 1970s when a professor from the university of Central Florida bought a school bus, painted it with rainbow stripes, and toured student actors around local educational institutions.

In a deeper sense, I began to realise, Jouris's map is quite accurate. Littered through the history of the United States are stories of Shakespeare cropping up in odd, out-of-the-way corners, far from East Coast libraries and theatres. As early as 1764, the English explorer Thomas Morris, mapping what would become Illinois, was astounded to be presented with a volume of Shakespeare's plays by a Native American chief in exchange for gunpowder. ('A singular gift from a savage,' wrote Morris wonderingly, apparently not pausing to consider the word 'savage' too deeply.)

I started to collect stories. I came across a vivid and nerve-jangling tale from eighty-odd years later, the early 1840s, about a touring company of actors travelling through Florida in the middle of the Seminole land wars. Journeying without military escort through an area teeming with Native American warriors determined to protect their territory from the depredations of the US government, the troupe were set upon and two actors killed. To celebrate their victory, the Indians prised open the trunk containing the company wardrobe and disported themselves as 'Othello, Hamlet and a host of other Shakespearian characters'.

For scholars, there are three famous sentences in *Democracy in America*, Alexis de Tocqueville's sprawling eyewitness account assembled from nine months spent touring the expanding United States and Canada in the early 1830s:

> The literary genius of Great Britain still casts its rays deep in the forests of the New World. There is scarcely a pioneer's cabin where one does not encounter some odd volumes of Shakespeare. I recall having read the feudal drama of *Henry V* for the first time in a log-house.

Scarcely a pioneer's cabin . . . I had long been intrigued by this reference – if only for the comical image of France's grand inspector of penitentiaries in some bug-infested lean-to, reading about his own nation being crushed at Agincourt. I'd assumed it to be exaggeration, a product of romantic infatuation with the newly United States. Now I began to wonder.

I would probably have forgotten the question altogether had I not stumbled across an article in *Shakespeare Quarterly*, the Folger's own journal. It was entitled 'Shakespeare in the Rockies', by an English professor at the university of Denver, Levette J. Davidson. The article was dated January 1953. Davidson was long dead.

He mentioned references I had already come across – a nineteenth-century fur trapper who lugged 'a copy of Shakespeare' everywhere he went; early performances of *Macbeth* in Salt Lake City to the hearty accompaniment of the Mormon Tabernacle Choir. But he went on to recount a far more unusual tale, one I'd never heard, about the explorer Jim Bridger. Bridger, the greatest frontiersman of the 1840s and 1850s, was a mountain man born and bred, perhaps most famous for mapping the Salt Lake area for the founder of the Mormon church, Brigham Young. He also established what became Fort Bridger, Wyoming, a staging post on the long trek westwards to California.

Despite being unable to read, Jim Bridger was fond of stories – one storyteller in particular. The soldier J. Lee Humfreville, who spent the winter of 1863–64 holed up with him elsewhere in Wyoming, relates how, upon hearing that 'Shakespeare's was supposed to be the greatest book', Bridger became seized by a passion:

> He made a journey to the main road, and lay in wait for a wagon train, and bought a copy from some emigrants, paying for it with a yoke of cattle, which at that time could have been sold for one hundred and twenty-five dollars. He hired a German boy, from one of the wagon trains, at forty dollars a month, to read to him. The boy was a good reader, and Bridger took great interest in the reading, listening most attentively for hours at a time. Occasionally he got the thread of the story so mixed up that he would swear a blue streak, then compel the young man to stop, turn back, and reread a page or two, until he could get the story straightened out. This continued until he became so hopelessly involved in reading *Richard III* that he declared he 'wouldn't listen any more to the talk of a man who was mean enough to kill his mother' . . .

'It was amusing to hear Bridger quote Shakespeare,' Humfreville continued. 'He could give quotation after quotation, and was always ready to do so.' (Even if he didn't always get the plot details quite right.)

I read this with surprise, then astonishment. Copies of a book circulating as part of a barter economy is one thing; Native

Americans pilfering costumes from white men invading their land another. But an illiterate trapper selling valuable cattle to acquire a text he couldn't read?

Yet there was corroboration, the testimony of Margaret Carrington, the wife of an officer in the US Army:

> [Bridger] cannot read, but he enjoys reading . . . He sent for a good copy of Shakespeare's plays, and would hear them read until midnight with unfeigned pleasure. The murder of the two princes in the Tower started him to indignation. He desired it to be read a second and a third time. Upon positive conviction that the text was properly read to him, he burned the whole set, convinced that 'Shakespeare must have had a bad heart and been as devilish mean as a Sioux, to have written such scoundrelism as that'.

Even by the colourful standards of many frontier accounts, this was startling stuff. It was an image of Shakespeare not as a remote entity from the high Renaissance, the apex of Eng Lit, but as American popular entertainment – the author of stories vivid enough to enrapture a grizzled mountain trapper, so shockingly real that the murder of the Princes in the Tower could persuade him to burn the complete works he had spent so much to acquire. I was used to the idea that Shakespeare was, in his day, a hugely successful commercial playwright, but *Richard III* as a prairie companion in Wyoming? Really? I was taking a flight to California in a few days' time; maybe here was the hook I was after. In the story of Bridger I felt I had found a clue, though to what I wasn't yet sure.

In the nineteenth-century American West, he was certainly not on his own in his passion for Shakespeare. In January 1861, an item appeared in the *Rocky Mountain News* advertising an eccentric bet by the paper's editor – that it was impossible for an amateur to play Hamlet alongside professional actors with 'only three days' study'. The prize for anyone willing to do so was $100.

The challenge seems to have fallen on deaf ears, at least until July, when the paper printed a follow-up:

> We learn that a gentleman of this city, well known in Sporting Circles, will make his first appearance as Hamlet, on Saturday evening next at the Apollo Hall. The gentleman plays the part on a heavy bet, *viz.*,

that he could not be able to study the part (one of the longest in the drama) between this day at noon until Saturday evening. Look out for an exciting time.

Sure enough, the 'gentleman' (an infamous gambler) learned the part and triumphed. This was the paper again, four days later:

The performance at the theatre on Saturday night last was a highly creditable one, the chief feature being a rendition of Hamlet by Mr C. B. Cooke of this city. The character was to our mind most faithfully represented. Mr Cooke has not a strong voice, but his reading was most capital, and his action graceful, artistic, and impressive. He is a better Hamlet than we have ever seen personified by any stock actor.

A trapper spouting Shakespeare? A gambler making the gamble of his life and winning, with *Hamlet*? I thought I had already gleaned a fair amount about the history of Shakespeare in America. I wondered if I really knew anything at all.

The longer I stayed at the Folger, the more it seemed that this monumental edifice of learning was also a kind of fortress. It was a definitive statement, writ in Georgia marble, that Shakespeare was best appreciated not on the stage, but on the page – more precisely, in the thousands upon thousands of pages kept down in the vaults, safe from prying eyes and grubby fingers.

Perhaps it was something about Washington, too. After five days here I had begun to tire of the city, its inhabitants' constant sense of being on Important Business. The chinos and trouser suits and official lanyards and trilling mobile phones I found irritating. The runners in military T-shirts trekking up and down the National Mall had begun to get on my nerves.

At night, I played truant. I couldn't stop walking. I quartered the city block by block, snapping blurry photos with my phone: the Capitol in weak moonlight; the slim point of the Washington Monument cool white against a bouillabaisse-coloured sky. The shadow-puppetry of trees and streetlights against the National Gallery of Art.

Even the FBI's 1970s Hoover building, beige and blocky and overbearing in daylight, acquired a mysterious poetry in the dark; rounding it one evening, I dislodged a flock of starlings gossiping in the shadowy recesses of its cliff-like walls. It was the loudest sound I'd heard all day.

Late one evening, in search of Shakespeares from less domisticated American locations than the District of Columbia, I spotted on the bookshelves of my B&B a novel I'd been meaning to read for years, Jane Smiley's *A Thousand Acres*, an adaptation of *King Lear*. For someone interested in the westward expansion of the United States, and of Shakespeare, it was a serendipitous discovery.

Published in 1991, the book transplanted *Lear* from the baronial castles and wind-blasted heaths of ancient Britain to the limitless plains of Iowa in the dying days of the 1970s. A thousand acres was four hundred hectares, give or take: the size of the family farm in Zebulon County, in the grip of Larry Cook, aka Lear, for as long as anyone can recall. The story was told in the flat, undeviating voice of his eldest daughter Ginny, a stand-in for Goneril. Regan was Rose. Cordelia was Caroline, who had escaped to the city and trained as a lawyer. At the story's fringes, on a collision course for its centre, was Jess Clark, a drifter recently returned from years in California; a shaggier but no less treacherous force than Edmund.

Shakespeare's main source was an old play, *The True Chronicle History of King Leir and his Three Daughters*, and the figure of Lear also crops up in Geoffrey of Monmouth's semi-mythical history of British kings, completed by 1139. But the story's roots surely lie in folk tale: a king cursed with daughters instead of sons, a kingdom divided and sent to rack and ruin. Even in Shakespeare, one has the sense that Goneril and Regan are struggling to escape the shackles of being cast as fairy-tale wicked sisters.

Smiley's was an audacious decentering. She painstakingly fleshed out these women, making them into sympathetic figures with their own tragedies – Rose, raging against breast cancer and a violent partner; the luckless, abused, browbeaten Ginny, worn almost to the bone. Caroline is an ambiguous figure: impulsive and headstrong, coddled from her father's worst excesses, she is the first to round on him when he proposes splitting up the farm, before fatefully taking his side.

For his part, Larry isn't a cuddly father figure more sinned against than sinning; this 'Daddy' is vindictive, cussed, stubbornly silent when it suits him but given to volcanic eruptions of rage. 'Perhaps there is a distance,' Smiley writes in the voice of Ginny, 'that is the optimum distance for seeing one's father':

> farther than across the supper table or across the room, somewhere in the middle distance: he is dwarfed by trees or the sweep of a hill, but his features are still visible, his body language still distinct. Well, that is a distance I never found. He was never dwarfed by the landscape – the fields, the buildings, the white pine windbreak were as much my father as if he had grown them and shed them like a husk.

Yawning Midwestern farms, the dun towers of grain elevators, fertiliser-tainted lakes – all of it emphasises the pinched interiority of these characters' lives.

For all that its most famous setting is a heath, *Lear*, too, is surprisingly domestic in scale. An early performance took place at court in front of King James I on 26 December 1606 and was perhaps restaged at the original Blackfriars. The play is obsessed by the consequences of not having enough space: too many knights, multiple imprisonments, a hovel on the heath that can't squeeze in everyone. One of its most poignant exchanges takes place between the King and his Fool:

> FOOL Canst tell how an oyster makes his shell?
> LEAR No.
> FOOL Nor I neither; but I can tell why a snail has a house.
> LEAR Why?
> FOOL Why, to put 's head in, not to give it away to his daughters and
>   leave his horns without a case.

Smiley's Midwestern landscape offered her characters something similar, I thought: more land than they knew what to do with, but not nearly enough room to breathe.

As I neared the former schoolhouse on Capitol Hill that was the Taffety Punk rehearsal space, the night air was filled with the raw clang of electric guitars and the *whump* of a drum kit. Inside, in a black-box theatre, two dancers were writhing on the floor in what looked suspiciously like carnal embrace. On a bar stool in front, a singer/performer dressed in black was speaking slowly and with flat irony into a microphone. Her words I half recognised:

> Her pity-pleading eyes are sadly fixed
> In the remorseless wrinkles of his face.
> Her modest eloquence with sighs is mixed,
> Which to her oratory adds more grace.
> She puts the period often from his place,
>   And midst the sentence so her accent breaks
>   That twice she doth begin ere once she speaks.

The poem was Shakespeare's early narrative work *The Rape of Lucrece*; this is the desperate moment just before Lucrece is attacked by her rapist Tarquin. It was the first time I'd ever seen it performed, never mind reimagined for the age of post-post-punk.

When the performers had come to a pause, I hesitantly introduced myself to the person who seemed to be in charge – a thin, wiry man in his early thirties with a scarecrow of peroxide hair and a purple T-shirt. He introduced himself as Marcus Kyd, artistic director. His eyes, cavernous with tiredness, shone with ragged enthusiasm.

Taffety Punk had got going when Kyd and a few fellow acting graduates had begun to get work professionally in the early 2000s. They'd been shuttling between acting gigs and teaching jobs when they realised that what they actually wanted to do was make a less boringly middle-aged kind of theatre than the stuff generally on offer in Washington.

Kyd had been in the world's most short-lived rock group; one time they'd performed with a few dancers, and it had seemed to work. They'd decided to form a theatre company, run on the lines of a band, playing in dirty basements and pop-up venues: live dancers, acting, guitars, tickets as cheap as they could make them. They'd named themselves after a line in *All's Well That Ends Well*, the clownish Lavatch's description of a 'taffeta punk', Jacobethan slang for a prostitute dressed in silk. Impressively – though perhaps unsurprisingly for a group based in the same city as the Folger – they had adopted the Folio spelling.

'We're all punk-rock, classically trained weirdos,' Kyd said, reaching for a tall tankard of coffee.

My contact had described them as 'cool dorks', I said.

'Yeah, *dorks*, that's way better. We're obsessed with Shakespeare, Greek material, anything older than the eighteenth century.'

The *Lucrece* project was their latest and largest so far – also their most improvisational. They'd been fiddling with it on and off for the past few years. Lucrece, Tarquin, Lucrece's husband Collatine and the poem's narrator were played by a cast of four, doubling musical instruments where possible. (Lucrece, played by Kimberly Gilbert, played bass.) Two dancers interpreted various parts of the piece, notably the rape scene. The rest was sort of made up, with the music remixed and looped live.

But the text was pure Shakespeare, Kyd grinned. 'The poem endures. We keep fucking with the rest, but we don't want to fuck with that.'

I was struck by the fact that they didn't seek to treat Shakespeare's poem, difficult and neglected as it was, as a historical curiosity.

Kyd shook his head. 'We looked at the poem, and it was just so compelling: what happens to Lucrece, the way he shows her as a rape victim. Women are still going through that all the time. We talked about that a lot as a group. Tarquin, too, the bullshit he does when he's justifying himself?' He put on a Midwestern farm-boy accent. '*Oh yuh, she wuz askin' for it, look at how she dressed . . .*'

It was nearly time to go: they only had the space for another hour, and had the whole final section to run. As Kyd was plugging in his guitar, I asked him what he thought about the Americanness of Shakespeare.

He looked thoughtful. 'You know, the whole continent, but DC especially, suffers from a certain . . . *preciousness* about Shakespeare. I think it's misleading, to tell people that plays are literature, you know, and I think that's partly the impetus of the company. Theatre is not church, Shakespeare is not church.'

He grinned and hit a power chord: *keowang!* 'It has to be contemporary, y'know? There's no other way of doing it.'

———•———

ON THE FLIGHT FOR SAN FRANCISCO, I started where I'd left off: with Alexis de Tocqueville. Tocqueville's thesis in the second volume of *Democracy in America* was that, more or less, the US had no real literature of its own:

> When one enters the shop of a bookseller in the United States, the number of works there appears very great whereas that of known authors seems, on the contrary, very small. First, one finds a multitude of elementary treatises meant to give first notions of human knowledge. Most of these works have been composed in Europe. The Americans reprint them, adapting them to their use. Afterwards comes an almost innumerable quantity of religious books, Bibles, sermons, pious anecdotes, disputations, accounts of charitable institutions. Finally the long catalogue of political pamphlets appears . . .

Shakespeare was one of these 'known' European authors. Copies of the plays had been imported from London from the 1770s onwards, and American publishers – free of copyright restrictions – eagerly reprinted them. The first self-proclaimed 'American' complete works was produced in Philadelphia in 1795 (in fact cobbled together from previous versions), and subsequent editions were printed in Boston and New York. The plays began to make their way on to the bookshelves of normal middle-class households.

Tocqueville continued, 'Although America is perhaps the civilised country of our day where people are least occupied with literature, one nevertheless meets a great quantity of individuals there who are interested in things of the mind.' It was presumably one of these 'individuals' whose *Henry V* he devoured in a log cabin at some point in 1831 or early 1832.

By that time America had been pushing west for the best part of fifty years. Late in the eighteenth century, settlers had begun to stake out territory in Kentucky, Tennessee and elsewhere, but the decisive moment arrived in 1803, when Jefferson completed the purchase of the Louisiana Territory, 828 million square miles of it, from Tocqueville's countrymen, the French. At the stroke of a pen, the size of the United States more than doubled, stretching from the Atlantic seaboard to the Rockies in the west, and from the Gulf of Mexico right up to the Canadian border.

It was into this busily expansionist United States that Tocqueville and his friend and colleague Gustave de Beaumont arrived in May 1831. They disembarked at Newport, Rhode Island, visited New York City, spent Independence Day in Albany, zigzagged north to Canada then made a grand counterclockwise loop through Cincinnati, Nashville, Memphis, New Orleans and back up through the South – a thorough frontier tour lasting some nine months. En route they quaffed Madeira wine with President Andrew Jackson at the White House ('not a man of genius'), for whom the westward expansion of the United States was, in the phrase, Manifest Destiny. A year earlier Jackson had pushed through the Indian Removal Act, which authorised the government to force out Native Americans living east of the Mississippi. By 1837, the US Army had cleared some 25 million acres (39,000 square miles). In 1845, Texas, a Mexican territory, was annexed as the 28th state of the Union. In 1846, after a strident series of US victories, the war that followed with Mexico ended in the seizure of yet another western territory: California.

It wasn't just French aristocrats exploring America's new boundaries. Actors had been touring the frontier almost since professional drama had arrived on the continent. After running into difficulties with the Quakers in Philadelphia, Lewis Hallam's London Comedians had decamped for Jamaica in 1755. After their refounding as the American Company, the actors toured the north-east, even making it into the Puritan stronghold of Rhode Island in 1761. (To ingratiate themselves they cunningly advertised *Othello* as a 'Moral Dialogue in five parts' and announced that the performance would finish by 10.30 p.m., 'in order that every spectator may go home at a sober hour, and reflect upon what he has seen'.)

Charleston in South Carolina was an important calling-point on the touring route, as were theatres in Annapolis, Baltimore, New York City, Philadelphia and Williamsburg. According to one count, plays by Shakespeare were acted professionally 180 times between 1750 and 1776, covering perhaps half the canon. Audience numbers began steadily to increase, and numbered Native Americans as well as colonialists; as early as 1752, a Cherokee chief and his wife and son were among the earliest ticket-buyers for the Hallams, watching the company perform *Othello* in Williamsburg, and in 1767 nine Cherokee dignitaries watched a command performance of *Richard III* in New York City.

America may have had its suspicions when it came to literature, but the swaggering new nation grew to adore drama. Tocqueville devoted a chapter to the subject, arguing that democracy and popular theatre went hand in glove ('love of the theatre being of all literary tastes the most natural to democratic peoples'). In the decades following independence, theatres sprang up in Pittsburgh, Mobile, Cincinnati, St Louis. By the mid-1790s, five cities – New York, Philadelphia, Charleston, Providence and Boston – boasted permanent companies. The rest were served by a dense network of touring troupes. As well as American performers, these groups were fed by a steady supply of actors from England, drawn by tales of wild profits and even more wildly enthusiastic audiences.

George Frederick Cooke, who had thrilled London audiences as a ferocious Richard III, was tempted across in 1810. In New York, an audience of 2,200 mobbed him; in Boston he was acclaimed as 'the finest actor England can produce'. Cooke went on to tour in Philadelphia, Baltimore and Providence (and, even more remarkably, managed to control his prodigious drinking).

Edmund Kean – the brooding Romantic actor whose electrifying performances had been compared by Samuel Taylor Coleridge to 'reading Shakespeare by flashes of lightning' – was another star who crossed the Atlantic. Back in Britain, Kean had been a contentious figure, rejoicing in his rake-hell reputation, which extended from his stupendous appetites for alcohol and women to his habit of keeping a pet lion. When he arrived in America in 1820, the East Coast press was hostile, though Kean silenced them with a barnstorming debut as Richard III, who had now become America's favourite antihero. (*The New York Post* gushed that he was 'the most complete actor . . . that ever appeared on our boards'.) Kean followed it with mesmeric turns as Othello, Hamlet, Shylock, Lear and Macbeth, becoming the highest paid performer the United States had yet seen.

Five years later, this time hounded out of England after being sued for adultery, Kean returned to America, hoping to make a new start. In Boston, however, he came unstuck. Still smarting from a previous encounter – underwhelmed by the size of the audience, Kean had refused to play Richard III in the city – the crowd greeted him with a 'powerful and unexpected burst of catcalls and a series of hisses'. Objects began to be hurled, at first oranges but then chunks of metal; Kean escaped to the green room, then ran for his life. The crowd turned their wrath upon the building and succeeded in almost demolishing it. Theatre riots were far from unusual in London – back in 1809, a hike in ticket prices at Covent Garden had sparked disturbances that went on for three months – but it was the first time the American theatre had seen anything on this scale.

Notoriously, it would not be the last. In this proudly independent nation, insults by Kean and his ilk rankled. The United States and the United Kingdom had technically been at peace since the last British-American war of 1812–14, but rivalries smouldered on. Frances Trollope's acidulous *Domestic Manners of the Americans* (1832) denounced everything from the quality of Americans' singing to the poisonous dullness of East Coast dinner parties. The snide observations of Charles Dickens in *American Notes* (1842) cemented the sense that Brits liked nothing more than sneering at their rude, expectorating, poorly washed, slave-owning country cousins.

The theatre, so crucial to American self-identity, became the stage on which these transatlantic rivalries were played out. In 1827, two years after Kean was hounded off in Boston, the actor James Henry Hackett (1800–71), a native of New York City who became renowned for his Falstaff, travelled across to London and stunned Covent Garden audiences by proving himself the equal of any British-born actor: the first American ever to do so. With palpable surprise, the *Athenaeum* commented, 'his is the best Falstaff that has been seen for many a day'.

But in every sense the greatest American star of the age was the strapping Edwin Forrest. Born in a working-class neighbourhood in Philadelphia in 1806, Forrest honed his acting skills on the frontier circuit (he was rumoured to have trained with the Native American warrior Push-ma-ta-ha) and made his New York debut in 1826. Billed as the 'Native Tragedian', Forrest excelled in muscular roles, usually contemporary and always full-bloodedly American. Writing in 1842, one critic compared him to Niagara Falls, suggesting that his voice, 'in its tremendous down-sweeping cadence ... was a whirlwind, a tornado, a cataract of illimitable rage!' Steamboats and racehorses were named after him.

But Forrest had a competitor: the Englishman William Charles Macready. Thirteen years older and a dignified veteran of the London stage, Macready had toured successfully to New York as early as 1826, and had returned in 1843, winning acclaim for his pensive, painterly approach to roles such as Macbeth, Othello and Hamlet.

Though the actors themselves began as friends (at least in public), their competing fans regarded them as cut-throat rivals, Macready's scrupulously intellectual acting contrasting starkly with Forrest's

gung-ho bravura. When Macready decided to make one final tour
to the US in 1848, it was seen as a showdown between the 'Eminent
Tragedian' (as Macready was nicknamed) and his 'Native' counterpart.

The best historian of the episode, Nigel Cliff, dates the rivalry to
two years earlier, when Forrest – stung by poor reviews on his own
tour to London – had hissed Macready's Hamlet. When Macready
arrived in New York in October 1848 to play Macbeth, the Englishman
unwisely thanked the audience for being on his side against his
'unknown accuser'. Hot-headedly interpreting this as an insult, Forrest
decided to chase Macready to every city he visited, playing many of
the same roles in direct competition. Hostilities escalated: one night in
Cincinnati, half a sheep was thrown at Macready's feet.

Far worse was to come in New York City the following spring.
Both actors had brought productions of *Macbeth* to town; both were
drawing capacity crowds. On 7 May 1849, at the Broadway theatre,
Forrest scored a huge laugh for his line, 'What rhubarb, senna, or
what purgative drug | Would scour these *English* hence?'

Macready, appearing at the Astor Place Opera House a few blocks
away on the very same night, was having a much tougher time. A
catcalling audience threw such a quantity of objects – including,
eventually, chairs – that the performance was halted. Macready nearly
took the next boat home, but a letter of support signed by such
luminaries as Washington Irving and Herman Melville persuaded him
to stay. He would do *Macbeth* one last time, on 10 May, with police
protection.

Even allowing for the history of this unluckiest of plays, it was not
a wise decision. Several people tried to disrupt the show and were
arrested. But this only increased the ire of the mob outside, swelled by
criminal gangs and incensed by handbills demanding, SHALL AMERICANS
OR ENGLISH RULE THIS CITY? Paving stones began to plummet through the
windows into the lobby. Macready valiantly fought through *Macbeth*'s
final act before fleeing the building in disguise. Struggling to control a
riot already out of hand, soldiers fired into a crowd 15,000 strong. At
least twenty-two people died, and many more were injured, mostly
bystanders. To this day, the Astor Place Riot is one of the bloodiest
episodes in New York's history.

Clearly there was a great deal more going on during those mad days
in May 1849 than a dispute over *Macbeth*. The feud between America
and Britain had simmered for years; class tensions in New York itself

were at boiling point. It was only a couple of years after the Birthplace affair, when the British press had been aghast at the rumour that P. T. Barnum was on the point of buying the house where Shakespeare was born. The theatre of the early and mid-nineteenth century was a rough-and-tumble environment, audiences used to showing their feelings with voices and fists. In that, of course, it was not unlike the theatre of Shakespeare's own day, regarded as so boisterous that the authorities continually attempted to do away with it altogether.

Still, I found it striking – and, despite the gruesome toll of the Astor Place Riot, somehow impressive – that Shakespeare was so revered in nineteenth-century America that the acting of him was regarded as of such titanic importance. These days, it is hard to imagine a debate over who played the better Macbeth grazing the letters page of the *New York Times*. You could bet your hat no one would have died.

⁂

IN THE HARD, CLEAR LIGHT OF MORNING, San Francisco looked chintzy and beaten-up, like a film set left to bleach in the sun. My hotel was in the Mission district, sandwiched between a liquidation store and a tattered line of nineteenth-century rowhouses. I felt vaguely pleased that I had found one area of the city that had so far resisted tech-industry gentrification. Above a tyre repair shop, there was a sign: WE LEAP INTO DEBT BUT CRAWL OUT. I liked its gimcrack optimism. Welcome to California.

By the time Edwin Forrest and William Macready were having their violent showdown regarding the Scottish Play, something else had happened to the United States, more profound than even this turbulent affair. On 24 January 1848, a carpenter named James W. Marshall employed by the settler John Sutter discovered flakes of gold in a stream bed beneath the Sierra Nevada mountains. Within weeks the news had leaked, and the Gold Rush was on. Thousands of wagons began rumbling west, through what are now Nebraska, Wyoming, Idaho and Nevada. Ships began to throng San Francisco, depositing clerks, dry-goods merchants, doctors, farmers.

All had thrown off their existing lives to recast themselves as 'argonauts', paying tribute to the accomplices of Jason, the Greek mythological character who journeyed in search of the Golden Fleece.

Perhaps 100,000 came in the first few years, and not just East Coasters. Many travelled up from Mexico, or came from Australia, Germany, Chile, Hawaii and – most especially – China, from where immigration was huge. Soon the argonauts acquired another name, the 'Forty-Niners', symbolically reborn in the Golden Year.

In 1848, San Francisco had been a slumbering, fogbound garrison town of 800 souls; twelve months later 25,000 people had surged into what was fast, too fast, becoming a metropolis. Many were on their way to the Sierra foothills to find a claim, but others decided to create a life for themselves right here, in what has nicely been called the 'instant city'. The historian H. W. Brands captures the paradox well: 'San Francisco,' he writes, '[was] unique in American history to that point: it was at once urban and a frontier.'

What brought me west was the question of how theatre had experienced its own rush in California. Actors had joined the stampede, either as miners or (more sensibly) as performers, taking advantage of the opportunities on the frontier to make a fast buck. The instant city needed instant entertainment; among many less salubrious recreations, theatre became part of the burgeoning metropolis.

My first morning in California, I arranged to visit the San Francisco Museum of Performance and Design, where Bill Eddelman, a theatre historian who taught at Stanford for many years, guided me towards a teetering stack of material. I spent the day digging into my own seam of gold.

Like everyone else, probably, I had my images of the Old West, as firmly etched as the lines in a photogravure – the wagon trains, the teeming gambling dens, the spit-and-sawdust saloons and dance halls. I dimly remembered watching *How the West Was Won* on television as a child, with Spencer Tracy intoning parables of Manifest Destiny in a voice hewn from granite, and Debbie Reynolds trilling 'A Home in the Meadow' on a Sacramento riverboat, dressed – had I got this right? – as a Venetian blind.

Gambling dens and brothels there certainly were in Gold Rush San Francisco, a dime a dozen, spread among the zinc-covered frames and dust-choked tents. But there were also other, more sophisticated ways to blow your earnings, or – far more likely – your savings. In the museum's holdings were theatrical histories of the period, compiled at the behest of the Californian Works Projects Administration during the Great Depression, when much of this material was first written up.

The twenty volumes of *San Francisco Theatre Research* were a touch feverish themselves. But they also contained hard evidence, sifted from newspaper reports, handbills and other primary sources. One statistic was captivating: between 1850 and 1859, no fewer than 1,105 theatrical productions were given in San Francisco – 66 minstrel shows; 84 'extravaganzas' (a catch-all that includes circus, ballet and pantomime); 48 operas in five different languages; 907 straight plays. A single day's entertainment listings in the early 1850s includes everything from comedy skits and *Babes in the Wood* to gala stagings of Donizetti's *Lucia di Lammermoor* and Verdi's *Rigoletto*. If an aspiring argonaut had half a day to spare, he could catch an entire Italian opera while he waited.

As it happens, California's first purpose-built theatre was in Sacramento, which – conveniently placed on the route up to the goldfields – had swelled from a forested staging post to a giddy boom town. The theatre was called the Eagle. It wasn't grand: the walls were canvas nailed on to a wooden frame, the roof was sheet iron and tin, the stage made from packing boxes. When it opened on 18 October 1849 it was acclaimed as 'this oasis in the great desert of the mind'. On 4 January 1850, the oasis lived, unluckily, up to that description: when the Sacramento river flooded, the Eagle washed away. (A replica was raised in the 1970s, but no longer functions as a theatre.)

But San Francisco itself was soon pimpled with theatres, hurriedly thrown up – perhaps seventy-five separate auditoriums between 1850 and 1861. Back east, under the lingering shadow of puritanism, it had taken decades for theatre culture to become established; here, out west, it was taken to be an immediate and essential part of life.

One thing I discovered in the archives: American soldiers in the nineteenth century were hearty fans of am-dram, willing to put on a show at the faintest provocation. In 1845, none other than Ulysses S. Grant – later nicknamed 'Unconditional Surrender' for his devastation of the South – rehearsed the role of Desdemona as a beardless, twenty-three-year-old lieutenant at Corpus Christi, Texas, awaiting action against the Mexicans. (Grant was decreed to lack 'sentiment', whereupon he was sacked for a professional actress.)

It was a volunteer company from New York, stationed at Santa Barbara during the same Mexican wars, who first brought Shakespeare to California. Bored of guard duty, they spent the summer of 1847 busily remodelling a Spanish adobe house as a theatre. The debut performance was *Richard III*, with two blankets for a curtain, wigs made from lambskin, and a grand orchestra of two guitars, a violin and a drum. Drafted to Los Angeles in the spring of 1848, they promptly erected a 300-seat theatre. Their thespian activities were only halted when news leaked about Sutter's Mill, followed quickly by the peace treaty with Mexico.

The same economic and social forces that drove westward expansion in the nineteenth century spread East Coast culture in all its forms. Shakespeare, as I had discovered on Capitol Hill, had been regarded as a central part of American identity since the Founding Fathers at least; it must have seemed only natural to many pioneers that he came along for the ride.

In the mid-nineteenth century Shakespeare was experiencing his own relentless expansion. 'Stereotype' technology, in which printers used plaster casts to take an impression from pages of pre-existing metal type (the origin of the word), enabled American publishers to produce still-cheaper editions. These made the plays available to more readers than ever before – nearly two hundred and fifty separate editions printed between 1795 and the 1860s, with fifteen published in 1850 alone.

The texts – or at least expurgated chunks of them – also loomed large in schoolrooms, where they had long been valued for their usefulness in teaching elocution. Primers such as *McGuffey's Reader*, first published in 1836, introduced generations of American schoolchildren to stirring speeches by Mark Antony in *Julius Caesar* and Prince Arthur in *King John*, and became as substantial a part of American culture as the King James Bible and John Bunyan's *Pilgrim's Progress*.

The easy familiarity with which popular writers such as James Fenimore Cooper and Louisa May Alcott cite Shakespeare in their frontier tales merely hints at the reality. In the words of the historian Ashley T. Thorndike, 'in the West the travelling elecutionist, the lecturer, the company of actors on a Mississippi showboat became his emissaries and evangels ... no other writer was so quickly assimilated into the wilderness'. The mid-nineteenth-century cult of Anglo-Saxonism, which proclaimed the idea of Manifest Destiny and the supremacy of white, English-speaking Americans over all others (especially those others who were recent immigrants), bolstered still further the importance of Shakespeare.

As Thorndike suggested, while Shakespeare may have been recited in log cabins and rehearsed by beardless lieutenants, it was because of professional travelling actors that his plays reached new and much broader audiences on the frontier than they had ever done back east. The famous seven-strong Chapman acting family bought a flatboat in Pittsburgh in 1831, and sailed it up and down the Ohio river, offering mixed bills everywhere from major cities such as Cincinnati to straggling riverside villages. Other companies played hotel ballrooms, billiard parlours, food cellars, converted barns – anywhere that would have them.

After 1849, professional performers began to descend on California in their hundreds. Although many actors stayed in San Francisco, others assembled touring companies to take on what became known as the 'gold circuit' across the Sacramento valley and up into the Sierras. Of necessity these were small groups: according to the historian Helene Wickham Koon, perhaps eight to ten people made up each, the leading man or woman usually doubling as an actor-manager – booking whatever theatre (or billiard parlour, or food cellar) they could get into.

What drew them, as it drew everyone, was lucre. For those prepared to put up with the hardships of a mountain tour, the money was dizzying: an average of $300 a night (the best part of $8,000 today). Miners were appreciative audiences. If you had a fan on the other side of the oil footlights, your share of the box office could be supplemented by a nugget or bag of gold dust tossed your way.

These actors travelled with the barest essentials: a change of costume or two, a handful of props, the whole lot thrown into an open wagon. In Britain, the movement towards historically informed design – the practice of setting *Henry VIII*, say, in elaborately researched Tudor costume or *Much Ado About Nothing* in Renaissance Italian garb – was just getting started, courtesy of pioneers such as William Macready, his contemporary Charles Kean (the rather more straight-backed son of Edmund) and the designer William Telbin. Out in California, however, these were luxuries no one could afford. According to one possibly sardonic account, 'six dresses, two wigs and an iron sword constitute an ample wardrobe for a company of six to travel in the mountains'. McKean 'Buck' Buchanan, a larger-than-life actor who cut his teeth in the US Navy, was known to play Macbeth in the gloriously inexact costume of slouch hat, cape, yellow gauntlets and riding boots.

Tight-knit troupes trekked through such sprawling, brawling tent-and-tarpaper cities as Hell's Delight, Port Wine Diggings, Skunk Gulch, Flapjack Canyon and Yankee Jim's. Koon estimates that by 1850, just a year into the Gold Rush, fifty stock companies were plying gold-mining towns.

Nearly all the immigrants to California – as many as nine out of ten – were men. But in theatre, at least, different rules applied. One of the many side effects of this topsy-turvy new world was that female actors and managers were permitted much greater autonomy than they were back east. The name of Lola Montez – a strong-featured, blue-eyed Irish immigrant whose 'Spanish dances' made her transcontinentally famous and eventually led her to the bed of King Ludwig I of Bavaria – is still spoken of with fondness. There were countless others: operatic prima donnas, leading ladies, child stars, equestrian divas . . .

I read about the life of Sarah Kirby Stark, acclaimed as California's first female tragedian, for whom the Gold Rush seems to have been the opportunity of a lifetime. Born in New Orleans, by the time she arrived in San Francisco in early 1850 at the age of thirty-seven, Sarah had already buried one husband, and her second would be dead within the year. In short order she met and married the rugged Nova Scotian James Stark. Dark-haired and slight, Sarah had a sharp intensity on stage, but also a much rarer talent – the ability to keep a theatre in business. Between 1850 and 1864, she would manage no fewer than five separate theatres in Sacramento and San Francisco.

Before they met, both Starks had travelled to London to study with Macready (somewhat ironically, in view of events in New York in 1849). Perhaps it was from Macready that they acquired an adoration for Shakespeare, but whatever the source, it would change American theatre history. Together they offered the first professional *Hamlet* to be seen on the West Coast (James as the Prince with Sarah, pre-Freudianly, playing Gertrude), and gave the Californian premieres of at least seven other plays, among them *Macbeth*, *The Merchant of Venice*, *The Taming of the Shrew*, *King John*, *The Merry Wives of Windsor*, *A Midsummer Night's Dream* and even the romance *Pericles* – one of only a handful of performances on record anywhere in the world during the nineteenth century.

Sarah seems to have seized on Shakespeare's rich female roles: according to the press her Portia was fittingly 'lawyerly', her Katherine (in *The Taming of the Shrew*) 'truthful', and her Lady Macbeth 'a woman of powerful, but ill-balanced mind, ambitious, but by no means devoid of her finer womanly qualities'. After she and James divorced, Sarah went on to marry twice more and moved to New York. In 1896, having outlasted five husbands, she retired to California, the golden state that had brought her so much.

More snapshots of the early years come courtesy of the Edinburgh-born artist and travel writer J. D. Borthwick, who had been living in New York in 1850 when – in the formula that became a catechism – he had been 'seized with the California fever'. He boarded a barque bound for the Panama isthmus (an instinctive gambler, Borthwick took his chances with malaria and the shortcut through the jungle) and arrived in summer 1851.

In San Francisco Borthwick was surprised – and impressed – to find beached ships being used as warehouses and salmon 'equal in flavour to those of the Scottish rivers'. In this hectic environment, he observed with gruff approval, 'people lived more . . . in a week than they would a year in most other places'.

It wasn't the only thing he observed. Holed up for the night in a town in the Nevada mountains called Nevada City (despite its name, neither in Nevada nor a city, but 'a mixture of staring white frame-houses, dingy old canvas booths, and log cabins'), Borthwick had just retired to his berth in a boarding house after a pleasant evening's gambling when he was abruptly awakened:

> Next door was a large thin wooden building, in which a theatrical company were performing. They were playing *Richard [III]*, and I could hear every word as distinctly as if I had been in the stage-box. I could even fancy I saw King Dick rolling his eyes about like a man in a fit, when he shouted for 'A horse! A horse!' The fight between Richard and Richmond was a very tame affair; they hit hard while they were at it, but it was soon over. It was one-two, one-two, a thrust, and down went Dick. I heard him fall, and could hear him afterwards gasping for breath and scuffling about on the stage in his dying agonies.
>
> After King Richard was disposed of, the orchestra, which seemed to consist of two fiddles, favoured us with a very miscellaneous piece of music. There was then an interlude performed by the audience, hooting, yelling, whistling and stamping their feet; and that being over,

the curtain rose, and we had [William Barnes Rhodes's farce] *Bombastes Furioso*.

Richard III yet again ... The play seemed to be everywhere. But why? Borthwick wasn't much help: '[The farce] was very creditably performed,' he concluded, 'but under the peculiar circumstances of the case, it did not sound to me nearly so absurd as the tragedy.'

In a folder at the museum collections I came across a stray photograph – a nineteenth-century theatre just over the mountains in Nevada. The photograph was in colour, dating (I guessed) from the late 1940s or early 1950s, shortly before the theatre was demolished. A low stage, pine floor, two levels of red-plush boxes either side of the proscenium arch; hard wooden chairs in the stalls. Plastered around the safety curtain, which featured a bucolic scene of what appeared to be Tuscany, were crude hand-drawn advertisements for local businesses: AMERICAN BAKERY: PIES, CAKES AND BREAD . . . RYAN & STENSON: DRY GOODS, GENTS OUTFITTERS, HATS ETC . . . SAWDUST CORNER SALOON: WINES, LIQUORS & CIGARS.

The gilt decoration was peeling, the pink-and-green paint pitted and stained with damp. On the ceiling, the plaster was coming off in sheaves. But if one squinted carefully, one could just about see a bearded figure painted above the centre of the stage: Shakespeare, presiding deity and the most popular playwright of the American frontier.

Before I lit out for the Nevada foothills in pursuit of the actors, I had a date. Following the advice of a friend, I had booked to see a show at the California Shakespeare Theatre in Berkeley. In the best Western traditions, it was a big-boned tragedy, indeed the biggest of them all: *Hamlet*. For added frontier-style authenticity, it was in the open air, at the Bruns Amphitheatre in the Orinda foothills.

'Just make sure you layer,' my friend had said. 'It gets kind of fierce up there at night.' I thought of all the times I'd attended outdoor Shakespeare in England – shivering on damp grass to the faint tang of manure – and reckoned I could survive.

The quickest route to Berkeley was east over the grey spans of the Bay Bridge, but I was determined to leave San Francisco in style: north over the Golden Gate. By the time I got there, the towers were glowing like molten steel, crimson in the late-afternoon sun. In the rear-view mirror fog was still shrouding the city, a purplish cloud from which towers and high-rises occasionally protruded. It had the pleasing appearance of a disaster scene I had narrowly escaped.

Just before Orinda I swung the car right and pulled on to a narrow asphalt track that wound up through the woods. We were only fifteen minutes past the university bookstores and gourmet coffee shops of Berkeley, but this was decisively hill country. Grasslands and knots of tawny rock reared steeply either side. The hills, beaten to gold by the heat of summer, were shading into copper. For the first time in two weeks in America, I felt as though I was outside.

The parking lot was a field; and already, with an hour and a half to go before the performance, three-quarters full. We were a genial lot, the early crowd – in our fifties and sixties, mostly, wearing hiking gear and stoutly booted. There was a worrying quantity of fleeces and gloves. One woman had two sleeping bags sausaged under her arms. I began to wish I had taken my friend's warning seriously.

The California Shakespeare Theatre was a child of the early seventies, a hippyish artistic collective that had gathered to stage *Hamlet* in a church in downtown Berkeley. Expanding into a summer-long festival majoring in Shakespeare, it had staged more than fifty productions before moving up here to a purpose-built amphitheatre in the forest.

I climbed through dense thickets of cedar and oak, the tang of pine needles strong on the breeze. Cal Shakes relished its outdoorsy reputation, even if nature had been somewhat declawed. When I reached the top of the hill, it was to benches and refreshment stalls dotting the glades. The queue for the gourmet buffet (signature dish: The Hamlich) was thriving. It reminded me faintly of the summer opera festival at Glyndebourne in Sussex, though instead of dinner jackets and evening gowns here the tailoring was by North Face. I inspected the wine menu: as heavyweight as one would expect.

Presiding over this fine example of wholesome Northern California living was Jonathan Moscone, Cal Shakes' artistic director. Stoutly built, with a silvering goatee, he was clad in a bulky cardigan and had the aspect of an ageing software developer.

If I couldn't get hold of a living and breathing nineteenth-century Californian actor-manager, I figured Moscone was a decent substitute. A San Francisco native, he had run Cal Shakes since 2000 and was by all accounts making a roaring success of it. Audience numbers were up for the third year in a row, and Moscone himself had recently received an award for his work in regional arts. The company was on a roll.

Shakespeare wasn't the only thing they produced, said Moscone, but the major reason Cal Shakes was doing well was the Bard. *Hamlet* had extended its run a week after opening, having scored the largest advance sales in the theatre's thirty-year history. I caught something I'd rarely glimpsed in the eyes of an American theatre producer: the sight of accumulating dollar bills.

'At first I thought they were mistyping the numbers. I thought we'd never make so much. *Hamlet's* a big-ass play, three and a half hours sitting outside on a bench. You've got to know it's long, right? But this time they've really gone for it.'

We talked through which other titles were safe bets. He mentioned *Romeo and Juliet*, *The Tempest*, *A Midsummer Night's Dream*, *The Taming of the Shrew* – plays that had also done well in these parts during the nineteenth century.

'They're big plays, I guess. They seem to fit here. We had the same with our version of *Nicholas Nickleby*. Big stories.' He glanced at the forest around us, beginning to twinkle with fairy lights. 'You know, the East Coast is small – the cities are big, but the states are small, the houses are small. Here, the hills are not small.'

The American festival circuit, of which Cal Shakes is a well-established part, told its own story about the success of Shakespeare in the United States. There are now at least 250 Shakespeare festivals in operation in the US, more than anywhere else in the world by a comfortable margin. Some American festivals inhabit beautifully appointed theatres in historic settings, such as the Virginia Blackfriars or the replica of the London Fortune playhouse at the Oregon Shakespeare Festival in Ashland, a few hundred miles north of where Moscone and I were sitting. Nearly all have repertoires centred on Shakespeare, but some have swelled into permanent producing houses offering everything from Marlowe to adaptations of Disney's *The Little Mermaid*. Others, in the best Western traditions, are fly-by-night travelling outfits: Montana Shakespeare tours isolated rural communities and parks with a handful of actors, covering thousands of miles annually.

According to figures compiled in the mid-1990s, over three million tickets were sold annually at Shakespeare festivals in the United States. If one factors in free events – including such institutions as New York City's Shakespeare in the Park, set up in the 1950s – nowadays the numbers would be even higher. Festivals such as these are the way most Americans still encounter live Shakespeare.

As the audience began to move towards the auditorium, I rattled on about my discoveries in the Museum of Performance and Design. Moscone knew it all, having once directed a show on the subject by the contemporary playwright Richard Nelson. I liked the play's title: *How Shakespeare Won the West*. As it happened, Nelson had also written a play about the Astor Place Riot.

I wondered if Moscone ever dreamed of the 1850s, the pit heaving with miners, the shuddering pinewood floor . . .

His eyes acquired a faraway look. 'Man. Yeah. Wouldn't it be fabulous if we could do shows like they did? People shouting the lines back with them, throwing them dollars, or they'd just stop in the middle and start playing a song?'

He pounded the table. 'That. Would. Be. Fucking. Awesome.'

The audience for *Hamlet* was on its best behaviour, and there were no songs that I could hear, if one discounted the crickets thrumming loudly all around and the occasional sorrowing howl of a coyote.

Next to me in the crowd, a man in a green cap with the logo of the Gallo winery lifted a bottle in greeting. He appeared to be on the single-estate Cab Franc.

The setting was undeniably spectacular. The broad sweep of the amphitheatre – a slender doughnut of steel girders, with a wide stage in front and stepped terraces – echoed the Globe in London, except that instead of the Thames and St Paul's cathedral we had a fine view of the Orinda hills, now mottling to dark green and grey in the gloom. Above it, the sky was the colour of sapphire.

I had come expecting this *Hamlet* to be traditional, but I was surprised. The production was set in a decaying mansion that could have been deep in the Hollywood hills or just outside Cupertino, where Apple have their headquarters. Centre stage was an empty swimming pool filled with discarded toys and smashed lawn furniture. Sharp tailoring and military uniforms were the order of the day; only the play-within-the-play was done, knowingly, in Elizabethan ruffs and doublets. Old Hamlet, blood-soaked, looked as though he'd done a stint in a zombie movie. Hamlet, played by LeRoy McClain, was a soulful tough guy who brought to mind the young Denzel Washington. He sobbed 'To be, or not to be' while clutching Ophelia in his arms. (It emerged that both actors were in fact Brits who now worked in the US: an echo of their forebears.)

Barnardo's exclamation during the night-watch opening scene, ''tis bitter cold', produced a rueful laugh among the audience. But there were consolations: it was the only *Hamlet* I'd seen where the Ghost's appearance was complemented by the rising Plough, seven pinpricks of faint light in the night sky. Just once, much later on, there was the diamond glint of a meteor.

Stumbling down to the car in the dark, I saw a poster. 'Why Go to the Movies and Be Exposed to Wanton Sex, Needless Profanity and Gratuitous Violence?' it asked. 'Experience It Live.'

I was up and out not long after dawn, sprinting for the I-80 with a motley flotilla of pickups, people carriers bulky with bikes and boats, and the rest of the demob-happy weekenders.

Passing through Berkeley the day before, I had called by the Shakespeare & Co. bookshop. The name appealed for obvious reasons, but there was more to it than that. Searching online for something appropriate to read in the mountains, I had found a copy of one eyewitness account of the touring life, Walter M. Leman's *Memories of an Old Actor* (first edition, 1886). Shakespeare & Co. had it in stock, a steal at six bucks.

The book was foxed, a little battered, but sturdy enough – epithets that also suited the author. In the frontispiece engraving, Leman's shoulder-length white hair was combed back in a shaggy bonnet, surrounding stout, squat features. Beneath bustling eyebrows, his eyes were firm and sharp. I tried to picture him on stage. Not Hamlet; more like T. S. Eliot's Prufrock, an attendant lord. An eerily plausible Polonius.

Leman certainly had Polonius's chatter. His style was breathless and gossipy, a garrulous gale of names and second-hand tales and recollections of theatrical figures I recognised dimly, if at all. Had he been standing at the crush bar, I would have shrunk from his presence. Here, between hard covers I could close at any time, I warmed to his company.

Leman was born in 1810 and had been theatre-mad from the beginning. One of his earliest theatrical memories – so he said – was watching Edmund Kean forced in ignominy off the stage in Boston. He had met the grandson (or was it the great-grandson?) of Lewis Hallam, the man who had brought professional drama to America. He claimed intimacy with Edwin Forrest, having played 'various times' with him. On this last, I believed him, particularly his doleful portrait of the later Forrest, crushed by a lengthy divorce case and reduced to doing regional tours for a pittance.

Leman had an actor's tic when it came to describing other performers – vague effusion with the occasional enlivening bout of pure bitchery. He was delightfully catty about James Henry Hackett's pretensions to tragedy ('the public never recognised his claim'), and studiedly offhand about Dickens, whom he saw in Montreal and accused of gabbling his lines.

The contents page mapped anywhere and everywhere. Leman travelled north to Portland, Maine; played Montreal and Philadelphia; then struck out for California in 1854. He had come back again and again, before chasing the Silver Rush into Nevada. There was a ton of material here. I awarded him a ceremonial scattering of Post-its, details to be investigated later.

Leman wasn't my only companion. The North American Shakespeare festival circuit had produced another boon besides ticket sales: one of the finest through-composed pieces of jazz in musical history. Before leaving Britain, I had downloaded to my iPod a copy of Duke Ellington's *Such Sweet Thunder*. Inspired by a residency at the Shakespeare festival in Stratford, Ontario, in 1956, Ellington and his long-time musical partner Billy Strayhorn had composed an entire suite on Shakespearian themes.

Thirty-five minutes and twelve movements long, longer than Copland's *Appalachian Spring* and twice the length of Gershwin's *Rhapsody in Blue*, the album had filled my hire cars on our rambles through Virginia and California. 'Lady Mac' – which began with playfully profane gospel-ish chords by the Duke before segueing into a sashaying dance number – had enlivened numerous traffic jams in Washington. 'Madness in Great Ones', Ellington's slithering, beserkly chromatic tribute to Prince Hamlet, had popped up while I was on the way back from Cal Shakes. I had a soft spot for 'Sonnet in Search of a Moor', a poignant solo for Jimmy Woode's strummed double bass, with its nobly aspiring yet fatally naive melody.

The suite's title wittily quoted Hippolyta's description of the hunting horns of Hercules and Cadmus in *A Midsummer Night's Dream*:

> Never did I hear
> Such gallant chiding; for besides the groves,
> The skies, the fountains, every region near
> Seemed all one mutual cry. I never heard
> So musical a discord, such sweet thunder.

Swapping hunting horns for the jazz variety was not only a neat spin on the Americanisation of Shakespeare; it was a mark of Ellington's aristocratic confidence in his African American art form, and what the jazz historian John Edward Hasse calls his 'repertory company', the orchestra he led for fifty years.

As the car and I loosed ourselves from the freeway on to Highway 49, we entered a different kind of America: motorhomes parked on little leanings of earth, telegraph poles dancing off in mysterious directions, cracked and pitted asphalt beneath the tyres. Sagebrush and stubby cypress trees gave way, as we climbed towards the Sierra Nevada, to solid stands of pine and cedar.

I enjoyed how the car made this backwoods transition cinematic, like a spool of film put into reverse. Cars transmogrified into battered pickups. Suburban houses shrank into dilapidated bungalows, then into battered mobile homes.

The forest was starting to grow dense now, trees clustering thickly on either side. The soil had become ferrous, raw orange in the sun. The road signs acquired a sardonic backwoods poetry: Wolf Mountain Road, Rattlesnake Road, Bonanza Way, You Bet Road.

Just as Ellington eased into 'Sonnet for Hank Cinq', a perky, trombone-heavy tribute to Tocqueville's favourite play, *Henry V*, I saw an election notice: 'Vote Richard Barb, Supervisor. More Jobs. Less Government.'

I read it at first as 'Bard'. Shakespeare on the brain.

There was another reason Shakespeare was popular in these parts. Like the Colorado gambler who learned *Hamlet* and acted it after only 'three days' study', the travelling actors ranging across the Californian mountain trails found one piece of mobile equipment most useful of all: their memories. Though they did their best to offer contemporary material, for the bulk of their work they had to rely on the scripts that everyone knew, from toughened old hands to the rawest of recruits

– those plays, like jazz standards, they could riff on and produce at a moment's notice. That meant Shakespeare. The fact that the titles were familiar and guaranteed good houses was a bonus.

Whether he was the Shakespeare we would recognise today is a substantially thornier question. As Borthwick's testimony indicated, it was usual for visiting companies to offer mixed bills, as was then standard practice on the East Coast and back in Britain. A bill might contain *Othello* or Edward Bulwer-Lytton's ponderous melodrama *The Lady of Lyons* (1838), but would also include shows like *Slasher and Crasher*, *A Rough Diamond* and *Love in All Corners*.

Some were stock farces exported from London; others were written expressly for local audiences, such as Doc Robinson's 1850 musical medley *Seeing the Elephant*. Robinson's title was the slang phrase for coming West with overhyped expectations, and his tale of gullible miners, busted claims and bloodthirsty bandits resonated with audiences who knew those realities only too well. Robinson's bleak song 'Used-up Man', with its caustic line about mosquitoes so big they'd take out your liver, became a hit. 'I's a used-up man, a perfect used-up man,' it ran. 'If ever I get home again, I'll stay there if I can.'

Shakespeare, too, was permitted – nay, encouraged – to slum it. One travelling troupe offered *Othello* featuring one Miss Celeste, 'a *danseuse*'. The San Francisco producer Joseph Andrew Rowe leavened his versions of the tragedies with equestrian circus entertainments.

Even ostensibly straight performances were anything but. The playscripts in use in the nineteenth-century United States (as back in Britain) would give most modern editors the vapours. The show advertised on playbills as *The Taming of the Shrew* was not Shakespeare's, but the 1754 adaptation by David Garrick known as *Catharine and Petruchio*, one of many spin-offs composed since the seventeenth century. This boiled down the action to a brisk three acts and made the utmost of Catharine's compliance at the end, transforming it into a heart-gladdening homily on wifely virtue. Popular for a century in the UK, it was even more so in the US, where it was preferred to Shakespeare's text until well into the 1880s. So was Nahum Tate's Restoration rewrite of *King Lear*, with its notorious happy ending.

Romeo and Juliet was usually done in another Garrick version of 1748, which increased Juliet's age from thirteen to a more decorous eighteen and reshaped the ending so the lovers were permitted one final frantic embrace. *Hamlet* was heavily cut to emphasise the hero's youthful verve, with particular attention played to the fencing scene – as well it might be, given the largely male audiences up in the mountains.

The most popular play, it seemed inevitable by now, was *Richard III*: performed once again not in either of the texts that derive from Shakespeare's script (first quarto 1598, First Folio 1623), but in the adaptation published in 1700 by the English actor-manager Colley Cibber. This slimmed the cast list to more manageable proportions – particularly welcome on the road – and spliced it with sections from its prequel *Henry VI Part III*. Shakespeare may have written only half the lines, but Cibber's version, beloved of actors and audiences on both sides of the Atlantic, was the favourite for many years to come. (Parts of Cibber even make it into Laurence Olivier's celebrated film version of 1955.)

Some American companies attempted the best of both worlds, performing farces and burlesques actually *based* on Shakespeare. The British comic playwright John Poole's *Hamlet Travestie* was an instant hit when it appeared in London in 1810, and transferred to New York the following year. It inspired a small industry in imitations, including versions of *Romeo and Juliet*, *Othello* and two separate satires of *Richard III*, plus new American titles such as *Macbeth Travestie* in 1843; *An Old Play in a New Garb (Hamlet, Prince of Denmark)* in 1853; *Capuletta, or Romeo and Juliet Restored* in 1868; and the slyly titled *Much Ado About a Merchant of Venice*, published in New York in 1858. Some made their way to California. In San Francisco in 1853 Doc Robinson performed a version of *Richard III* spliced farcically with scenes from the comedies; and bawdier, semi-scripted versions seem to have toured the mining camps.

For a sense of how these burlesques were fitted up for new audiences, there is the evidence of the 1870 Broadway revival of *Hamlet Travestie*, which was almost entirely rewritten for New Yorkers – from references to a 'skating rink' in Elsinore (probably a reference to Central Park) to satirical gags aimed at corrupt city judges. This modified version of *Hamlet Travestie* ends with a song-and-dance number for the whole cast, led by the ghost of Old Hamlet:

> Zounds. What a scene of slaughter's here!
> But I'll soon change it, never fear.
> One touch of my most mighty magic
> Shall to gay Comic change, this dismal tragic.

It was easy to imagine miners applauding that.

They might have had more complicated feelings, though, about a speech in *Much Ado About a Merchant of Venice*. The lines were spoken by Shylock, reflecting on the elopement of his daughter Jessica with the Christian Lorenzo. Following time-honoured anti-Semitic stereotype, Shylock was usually still acted in this period as an out-and-out villain. In Brougham's farce, though, the Jew is different, more sensitively presented. 'She has vamoosed far away,' he says wistfully:

> Far away from old Shylock,
> There's no one left to comfort me.
> All at my sorrows mock.

These lines would, I thought, have had plenty to say to anyone who'd gone west to seek their fortune.

What was conspicuous about these burlesques was not simply that they poked fun at the 'IMMORTAL POET' (as John Poole half-mockingly called him), but that audiences were assumed to know their Shakespeare intimately enough to get all the jokes. Back east, in the hands of Emerson and his ilk, the Bard was being propelled relentlessly up the Parnassus of high culture. Here, out west, he was still something else.

One of the books I'd read back at the Folger was a canonical survey by the historian Lawrence W. Levine, published in 1988. Its title was *Highbrow/Lowbrow: The Emergence of Cultural Hierarchy in America*. Shakespeare was Levine's prime exhibit.

He argued that in the culture wars that had dominated nineteenth-century America, one of the fiercest had been around how 'culture' itself was defined. Researching minstrel shows from the 1830s onwards, Levine had been astounded by the omnipresence of Shakespeare – astounded because this revealed an intimate knowledge of Shakespeare's works not only among those writing and performing, but even more so among working-class audiences. For shows to call themselves *Ye Comedie of Errours* or *Julius Sneezer*; or for an African American actor to segue briskly from 'To be, or not to be' into a popular song; or for Mark Twain to sneak his own *Hamlet*-and-*Macbeth* parody into *Huckleberry Finn* ('For who would fardels bear, till Birnam Wood do come to Dunsinane,' proclaims an actor Huck meets on the river); it followed that everyone had to be in on the gag, regardless of their background.

Everything I had discovered so far confirmed what Levine had suggested. Shakespeare saturated 'lowbrow' American culture, from minstrel skits to extravagantly plotted burlesques. The culture that obtained in California during the first years of the Gold Rush was undeniably that of Jacksonian America: vigorous, demotic, democratic.

As the nineteenth century wore on, Levine argued, America itself changed so that Shakespeare became 'sanctified', perceived as more remote, more highbrow: the plays were purged of textual impurities, performed in historically 'accurate' garb; in fact, less often performed. They were increasingly the purview of scholars, editors, lecturers, professionals. Mixed bills gave way to windy Emersonisms about 'fixed stars' and limitless genius (and the doubts about Shakespeare's authorship that followed). From this perspective, there is another way of viewing an event like the Astor Place Riot: not simply as a conflict between nations, but as the last gasp of a working-class culture that saw Shakespeare as something worth fighting for.

Here in California, though, I couldn't see it being that simple. For starters, while Shakespeare in the Gold Rush was undeniably lowbrow in any meaningful sense of the word, his works were also regarded as the summit of high culture and treated with the seriousness that deserved. And to call mining audiences 'lowbrow' was, I thought, hugely to underestimate their sophistication: they seemed able to take entirely in their stride everything we would call 'high', 'low', 'folk', 'popular' and almost anything in between.

Accounts of frontier theatre dwell, almost as a trope, on the boisterousness of audiences – generally taken as evidence of their shaming lack of refinement. Walter Leman records a *Richard III* in San Francisco where the Crookback had come on and declaimed, 'What does this mean?' as per his version of the script, to which the audience had offered so many salty replies that the performance had to be halted. When a struggling actor arrived in Nevada City to play Richard in December 1856, the audience arrived with 'a profusion of esculents' – vegetables – which it proceeded to hurl.

Their manners may have lacked polish, but surely this only testified to the miners' passionate engagement with what was in

front of them on stage. One of the hoariest myths about the Gold
Rush was that the men who made it out here were young, poor
and badly educated. As recent social historians have demonstrated,
however, while argonauts were certainly footloose, shiftless they
generally were not.

By its very nature, the Gold Rush was a middle-class phenomenon.
Simply to attempt the great trek west cost at least $500, roughly twice
the average American's annual wage. Many miners were married and in
their thirties; more had at least a sixth-grade education up to the age of
twelve. Among much else, the Gold Rush created a great efflorescence
of writing, with many Forty-Niners recording their experiences in
diaries, quite apart from the newspapermen and professional travel
writers who came to California in search of a story. It was easy to
see how Shakespeare would resonate with this literate, curious and
adventurous population, pining for the culture they had left behind.

And Shakespeare they knew inside-out. By today's standards, many
on the frontier were what we would regard as learned sophisticates,
able to recite speeches by Hamlet, Macbeth, Mark Antony and Brutus
from learning them at school. The accounts were full of miners
bawling out lines or jeering off performances that didn't reach their
high standards. Nor were audiences exclusively white: according to a
newspaper account from New Orleans dug up by the theatre historian
Philip C. Kolin, 'The play-going portion of our Negro population
feel more interest in, and go in greater numbers to see, the plays of
Shakespeare represented on the stage, than any other class of dramatic
performance.' The number of African-Americans in the 'free' state of
California was small compared to other parts of the United States –
perhaps 2,000 at the height of the Gold Rush – but it is a reasonable bet
that at least some did likewise.

It wasn't true, either, that popular American Shakespeare had
breathed its last in the middle of the nineteenth century. At the Folger
I'd ordered a DVD of the oldest surviving full-length American feature
film. It was blind luck that it happened to be Shakespeare (older movies
had perished), but it was nonetheless intriguing to find it was a version
of *Richard III*. Dating from 1912, the picture was 5,000 feet and 55 minutes
long, and starred the great English-born actor Frederick B. Warde. The
story of its rediscovery was remarkable: a former projectionist from
Oregon had kept it in his garage for thirty-five years, carefully looking
after the friable – and highly flammable – nitrate reels.

Richard III was in every way a prestige, 'highbrow' release: it featured hundreds of extras, elaborately medieval sets and a spectacular amount of expensive location work, including a Battle of Bosworth filmed in upstate New York that gave Olivier's version forty-three years later a run for its money.

Yet in certain ways it was gloriously populist. The most watchable thing was Warde's Richard: malevolently funny, with a limp dangerously close to an orang-utan's lope and a menacing habit of removing his leather gauntlets finger by finger. His wooing of Lady Anne was a bravura piece of acting: bursting from a hedge like a fox, he allowed himself a snigger that was practically audible, before falling to his knees. Less than a minute of screen time later, Anne was in his arms.

Made long before synchronous sound, the script was nowhere to be heard, but Warde seemed to cram in the entire text nonetheless, transforming its rhetoric into witty pieces of silent ballet (the circling of the ring around Lady Anne's finger, a light kiss of the fingers bidding adieu to his unlucky brother Clarence). This *Richard III* was streets ahead of any filmed Shakespeare that had yet been produced back in Britain – a two-reel, twenty-minute version of the play from 1911 starring the renowned Stratford actor Frank Benson was infinitely less sophisticated, largely static scenes shot in front of painted flats.

The film was also, it occurred to me, something much more precious: a living link with the Richards of the nineteenth century. Until its rediscovery, Warde was the great lost hero of American theatre, omitted from most histories despite a career that stretched over half a century, from the 1860s to the 1920s. Born in Oxfordshire in 1851, he had trained as a 'utility' or general-purpose actor before coming to America in 1874. Unlike many actors, who preferred to remain in the comforts of New York, he arranged a touring schedule that took him to every whistle-stop and one-horse town he could reach by rail, from Nashville to Little Rock to San Francisco to Bloomington, Illinois. For twenty-four years, Warde played up to two hundred and twenty shows a season, specialising in Shakespeare productions cut to the quick.

New York audiences, by then accustomed to their Bard being presented with more finesse, disdained him; it was out on the circuit that Warde found his audience. In LaCrosse, Wisconsin, Warde's Lear was acclaimed as 'powerful in every scene'; in Baton Rouge, Louisiana, his Mark Antony in *Julius Caesar* was 'beyond all praise'. One journalist wrote: 'These old legits, according to our quiet ideas, rant and rave

. . . in a way that would doubtless prove highly amusing to our white-gloved, low-voiced beperfumed New York audience, but it is too bad for the sake of youthful theatregoers we cannot have a short season with these old players once a year, just to show us from what we are advancing – or deteriorating.'

And the tradition of Shakespeare-inspired burlesque, too, continued just as contentedly. Shortly before I left England a friend had sent me a little piece of video, a YouTube clip of something called *Shakespearian Spinach*. It was a black-and-white Popeye cartoon made in 1940 by Fleischer Studios. Popeye the sailor was cast as a Shakespearian actor playing Romeo; the villainous Bluto his top-hatted, cape-wearing antagonist. Olive Oyl, being Popeye's rightful sweetheart, was of course Juliet (complete with ear trumpet).

The plot runs something like this. Hearing that he has been replaced on the bill, Bluto is bent on revenge and deploys every dirty backstage trick available, from attempting to bump off Popeye with the front cloth to locking him in a costume trunk. Popeye retaliates in inimitable fashion: after Olive throws him a wreath made from his favourite iron-rich brassica, he windmill-punches Bluto into the flies of the theatre, and gets the girl in time for curtain-down. 'Parting is such sweet sorrow,' he growls joyously over his recumbent enemy. All in six and a half minutes.

There was even a knowing spin on Shakespearian cross-dressing, with the pipe-smoking hero slipping into Juliet's costume in order to biff Bluto in the kisser. And was it possible to see in this grudge match between an Eminent Tragedian and a plucky Native a hint of Macready and Forrest and the Astor Place Riot? I wouldn't put it past the Fleischers, canny New Yorkers both.

The roads up into the Sierras were twisting rat's tails, winding and jackknifing every which way. Within moments of leaving the highway I was into dense forest, stacks of pines either side of the road and sharp cliffs of rusty rock stippled with dry scrub. Though there was the occasional small settlement, most houses were solitary, buried in their own little fastnesses, offering little more to the nosy passer-by than a postbox and perhaps a trash can or two. The only buildings with any prominence were the fire stations, of which there seemed to be considerably more than there were houses.

The roads told a story about the past, but what it was, I could only guess. Lady Bug Lane, Stagecoach Way, Nugget Lane and Black Bear Lane slid past. Slave Girl Lane was straightforward enough – a depressing reminder of California's Native American population, thousands of whom were sold into servitude by settlers. But Mystery Lane? It was a mystery.

My first destination was a place that went under the picturesque moniker of Rough and Ready (named for 'Old Rough and Ready' Zachary Taylor, a hero of the Mexican wars who became president just as the Gold Rush hit). At its zenith Rough and Ready was one of the largest towns in California, home to nearly 4,000 souls and, moreover, so confident of its own importance that in 1850 its citizens voted to secede from the Union entirely and form the Great Republic of Rough and Ready – the only recorded instance of such a thing in American history. The breakaway nation lasted just three months; all over, like so many things in America, by 4 July.

But where was it? Barrelling along the Rough and Ready Highway – an impressive name for an anorexic strip of blacktop – I shot straight through Rough and Ready itself without noticing. I was ten minutes past before I skidded to a halt and rechecked the map. Was that really the town?

Coming the other way, I successfully registered the red-brick fire department and a worn clapboard structure marked 'General Blacksmith'. But I couldn't work out for the life of me where Rough and Ready actually was.

It was only when I swung the car around for the third time that I saw it, or saw something: a fire bell and a toy-sized saloon, in front of a tawny stretch of flattened grass. A covered wagon was planted against a fence, opposite a dainty collection of freight cars. Above a miniature post office, Old Glory fluttered lazily. Stencilled on the side of the too-small water tower, in counterfeit nineteenth-century type, was a sign: THE LITTLE TOWN OF ROUGH AND READY.

Rough and Ready had not only dematerialised; it had suffered the insult of being scaled down to one-third life size. This was, apparently, Ye Olde Wilde West erected by some backwoods entrepreneur, a photo stop that compressed the Gold Rush into a single convenient frame.

The reason I had wanted to come to Rough and Ready was that there was also a theatre, or had been, on the second floor of what was once Downie's hotel. Stanley Kimmel's *The Mad Booths of Maryland*, which tells the history of the Booth acting dynasty in spirited detail, records that Rough and Ready's inhabitants refused point-blank to attend the theatre in Grass Valley, four and a half miles away, believing their own auditorium to be the finest in the area. This, unfortunately, didn't correlate with its durability: one company were applauded with such frenzy that the floor collapsed.

Where was the hotel now? No sign, unless it was buried underneath the miniature water tower. I paid my respects at the cemetery and drove on.

I had been prepared for little from the Gold Rush to have survived, but it was nonetheless a shock to find how much had gone. Back in London, archaeologists had recently discovered the foundations of the very first theatres Shakespeare had worked at, the Theatre and the Curtain, built in 1576 and 1577 respectively in Shoreditch, just north-east of the City of London. In each case the remains weren't much more than a handful of Tudor bricks, but the sites had still yielded precious evidence – broken drinking vessels, shards of the earthenware cash boxes that gave the box office its historic name. (The great innovation of Tudor theatre was to make audiences pay before they saw the show rather than handing round the hat afterwards – in London, at any rate: one touring company demanded the same in Norwich in 1583, and provoked a riot from locals unused to such metropolitan affectations.)

Here in California, though, J. D. Borthwick was dead right: life moved at blinding speed. A hundred and sixty years, a series of fires and the particular desuetude that comes from a live-fast-while-you-can culture had worked the destruction of centuries.

A town called Auburn, which I drove down to next, had a handful of surviving Gold Rush buildings, but no sign of a theatre. Same story in Placerville, *née* Hangtown. So much had gone. By the time Walter Leman had arrived in California in 1854, 'almost every mining town possessed a building devoted to theatrical uses'. This didn't mean an actual theatre, he was quick to point out: one was a 'schoolroom, crowded to suffocation'; Placerville's was an old hall where a huge pillar blocked the middle of the room (which 'Buck' Buchanan managed to turn to his advantage as Shylock, seizing it on the lines, 'You take my house, when you do take the *prop* | That doth sustain my house').

Another had a stage knocked together from two billiard tables. In Calaveras County, a hundred miles south, the Chapmans were said to have played on the stump of a giant redwood tree. In several others, Leman wrote, it was impossible to perform *Richard III* without 'Bosworth Field [being] knocked all to pieces . . . for want of room to get on and off the stage'.

My final destination that day was both beautiful and melancholy: the immense Malakoff Diggins State Historic Park, high in the Sierra Nevadas, forty-odd miles north of Auburn. As the road corkscrewed around and up, I concentrated on glueing the car to the yellow centre line. Every so often an expanse of mountains, blue and hazy in the heat, flashed past before the trees closed in. The FM signal was getting dickery, and the Christian rock station, the only one I could find, kept disappearing. Eventually it sank beneath a sea of profane hiss.

Malakoff Diggins had its origins in 1852, when a group of miners set out from lower ground to find virgin territory. That territory, like so much of the United States, was of course already occupied, here by the Hill Nisenan. Those Indians that had not been killed by marauding parties of soldiers or miners, or died of diseases that had been introduced by the Spanish, now saw the habitat they relied on wiped out. Much good Manifest Destiny and the spread of white culture did them.

I'd been looking for marks of the past: well, they were all around me. Foul-looking lakes in the hollows of canyons, with water the colour of industrial disinfectant, laced with mercury left over from the gold-ore refining process. Entire hillsides rinsed clear of topsoil, a few stubby long-needled pines clinging desperately on. Apart from the water, the colours were all grey and bruise-red. Bad things had happened here.

I parked next to a sign heralding North Bloomfield, the town founded by the miners, since abandoned. By the 1850s North Bloomfield had a population in the hundreds, then, rapidly, the thousands; now, it was 'pop. 8–12'. The road was a wide tree-lined avenue that would not have looked out of place in a Parisian suburb; either side ran white picket fences and a small street of houses. Many were freshly painted. The park rangers must have been responsible (you could book to stay here in the summer), but it gave North Bloomfield the wary, suspenseful air of *Picnic at Hanging Rock*, as if everyone had popped out and simply melted away. The only sound was the rustling of the forest and the crackle of pine needles beneath my feet.

I scuffed along the deserted Main Street, peering into the restored buildings. At the druggist, lined with bottles on freshly painted shelves, it looked as if someone had simply gone out back to make up a prescription. The post office was piled high with still-to-be-sorted mail. Inside the clapboard chapel, its paint gleaming, was a life-size statue of St Francis welcoming his flock, so lifelike he might have been about to saunter across and seize my hand. I realised I was shivering, despite the heat.

Trying to ignore my heebie-jeebies – amplified by the warning notices about bears and the fact that I had no mobile phone signal – I stood in front of the saloon. It had rough timber walls, a scattering of battered tables and chairs, a piano pushed to one side, a long wooden bar. Lager and whiskey bottles glinted on the shelves. It wasn't at all hard to imagine visiting actors putting on a show here. But the sense that their ghosts were hovering was rather too strong for my liking. I snapped a few pictures and hastened back to the car.

'It's a darn pity, that's what it is. You've come just as we've closed *Antony*.'

I had arranged to meet John McDade at 10 a.m. Squinting in the sun, I had seen only shadows. Abruptly, one shadow detached itself and resolved into the thin, stooping figure of a man. He wore glasses, a faded Hawaiian shirt, black trousers worn to a lizard sheen, and had a lugubrious, seen-it-all-before air. He shook my hand distractedly. I wondered whether Leman and his colleagues had in their repertoire a stock character called Theatre Manager.

From the street, the Nevada theatre didn't look much: two windows, two doors, a modest two-storey facade in russet brick. But the interesting thing about the Nevada was its history. If the accounts I'd read were accurate, this was California's oldest working theatre. Located in Nevada City – where J. D. Borthwick had his surprise nocturnal encounter with *Richard III* – it was the seventh theatre to be raised in the town, which at its height was the third-largest settlement in the state. The Nevada was the only one to have made it to the present, a lone survivor from the earliest days of Californian drama.

Were my sources correct? I asked McDade as we headed in. *Was* this actually California's oldest theatre?

He sorted his words with care. 'The correct definition is it's the oldest *original-use* theatre building. If push came to shove, I would have to say the Eagle in Sacramento is older, but that's a reconstruction. The oldest *theatre* is in Monterey, but it's currently closed.' He pursed his lips in melancholy satisfaction. 'I don't reckon it meets earthquake standards any longer.'

The Nevada's story was eloquent about the hardships of life in Gold Rush California, but also the buoyant optimism of those who participated. It was built on the ruins of a hotel that had burnt to the ground in 1851, then again in 1856, then once again in 1858. Reopened in 1860, the hotel lasted just three years before again going up in one of the fires that ravaged every jerry-built, overpopulated Gold Rush town.

Perhaps reasoning that the gods had made their views clear when it came to hotels, Nevada City residents formed a theatre association, with the aim of erecting a more splendidly appointed auditorium than the town had yet seen. Despite yet more bad luck when the scheduled opening was delayed by the nationwide mourning for President Lincoln, it finally opened in September 1865.

The Nevada's original facilities were impressive – gas lighting, with an elaborately painted scenic drop curtain, a stage 45 feet wide and 28 feet deep and a 10-foot basement. There was no lobby, meaning that it could cram in 750 seats, with more audience standing.

We were now in the auditorium, modestly sized, painted vermilion and scarlet, with a blocky proscenium arch and shallow stage behind. None of the original ornamentation had survived; it had a functional appearance, deliberately unfancy. The wavering bumps and lumps in the brickwork made it look as though someone had tried to iron the walls flat and failed. Like all theatres seen during the daytime, the place had a raffish and disreputable air. I knew and liked it well: the heavy scent of seat cloth and antique gloss paint. In the shaft of sunlight streaming through an open fire escape, the dust lifted and tumbled in lazy clouds.

Its spells as a movie house in the early twentieth century had taken their toll, McDade explained, pointing out the 1930s seating and a balcony added in the 1940s. A shallow rake had gone in, and the flies above the stage had been removed. But in all other respects, the Nevada was essentially the same as when companies played here in the 1860s.

It seemed impressive, I said, that the building had been entertaining people almost non-stop for 140 years.

McDade allowed himself a smile. 'Hundred-fifty, coming up.'

Rather too aware of my experiences in North Bloomfield, I wondered if he ever thought of the spirits of performers past.

He prodded his glasses thoughtfully up his nose. 'I ain't never seen the ghost. But we've had paranormal investigators here a couple times.'

There was an *actual* ghost?

'That's the story. Hell if I know. But historical ghosts? I don't worry about those too much. We've gone from Mark Twain to Mötley Crüe.'

He left me standing in the middle of the stage. I wasn't entirely sorry to have missed *Antony and Cleopatra*: its absence meant that the space was bare, largely as it would have been originally. Twelve or so rows of maroon leatherette seats were ranged below me, the back wall almost close enough to touch. It looked a comfortable size for Shakespeare.

Standing there in the empty theatre, I found myself thinking of what I'd learned in Poland and Germany about travelling actors in the sixteenth and seventeenth centuries, the English Comedians who had taken Elizabethan drama with them on the highways and byways of northern Europe. One reason, surely, that Shakespeare's scripts proved so portable was the way they combined supreme dramatic sophistication with crystalline dramaturgical simplicity.

To stage *Hamlet* or *Macbeth* you didn't need elaborate sets, or a huge store of props. Doubling of roles was assumed, indeed built into all of Shakespeare's texts. (*Romeo and Juliet* has something like forty parts written for a cast of perhaps sixteen; the sophistication of its construction beggars belief.) And if those texts were further adapted and pared down . . . While ever-larger armies of supernumeraries were cluttering ever-larger stages on the East Coast and back in Britain, here the old rules prevailed.

The late comedies were more extravagant in their requirements – perhaps the reason they were less popular in the Old West (difficult to stage *The Tempest*'s masque in a saloon in Rough and Ready, still less on the sawn-off trunk of a giant sequoia). But in most of Shakespeare's plays, stage directions were famously minimal. It was a professional requirement to make it up as you went along. That must have appealed to many a barnstorming nineteenth-century ham.

Thinking about the rambunctious audiences, the improvised venues and scenery, the bear-baiting and gambling, the fine costumes dragged around on horseback, I found it impossible not to think that Gold Rush miners had experienced something even Henry Folger, with all his filthy riches, could never have bought: a theatre Shakespeare himself would have understood.

The question still remained of why the pioneers responded so keenly to Shakespeare. Sure, they'd learned him in school and by rote, but wasn't the Gold Rush a once-in-a-lifetime chance to escape all that? Most Forty-Niners made very little money – if anything, they lost it. Part of the attraction of going west must have been the opportunity to get out of the rat race, to find a new life for yourself. The myth that lay behind it, Manifest Destiny and the rest, was that this was a chance to forge an entirely new civilisation, an American one. What could an Elizabethan playwright possibly have to say to you out here?

An answer came to me at the North Star mining museum in Grass Valley, just down the road from Nevada City. I was peering at a photograph of a hydraulic mine in operation some point in the late 1850s. Hydraulic mining was not a sophisticated art: you took a high-pressure hose (initially powered by mountain streams, later by water wheels), pointed it at a hill, and washed the hillside away, running the gravel through sluices to separate the gold. The photograph depicted a hose in operation, pummelling a hillside stripped bare of every living thing. The water described an elegant white arc that belied its horrendous force. All around towered hundred-foot pines, clustering gloomily at the edges of the frame. Near the hose – I nearly missed him at first – was the tiny shape of a man, knee-deep in sludge.

The scene was dismal and awesome all at once: the trifling figure dwarfed by the immensity of nature, and conquering it nonetheless. It was a kind of unvarnished real-life equivalent to the huge Western landscape paintings by Albert Bierstadt and Frederic Edwin Church I had seen in the De Young Museum in San Francisco, done in the 1850s and 1860s: thunderous waterfalls, epic chasms, mighty crags, towering clouds, beetling peaks. The Triumph of the Sublime. Man versus Nature.

Was it too rhapsodic to think that Shakespeare had a similar totalising force? The repository of immense, larger-than-life stories? The chronicler of passionate and fatally troubled men? If Coleridge had described watching Edmund Kean as like reading Shakespeare by flashes of lightning, a galaxy of Romantic critics had been equally overwhelmed, especially in Germany: Shakespeare the demigod sitting on a mountain, roaring sea at his feet (Herder); an Alpine avalanche crushing everything in its path (Schlegel). Was a similar movement abroad in the nineteenth-century United States? Edwin Forrest had been compared to Niagara; indeed, so had Shakespeare, in a speech given by the writer William Cullen Bryant on the inauguration of the Shakespeare statue in Central

Park ('among the poets he is what the cataract of Niagara is among waterfalls'). Emerson had gone even further, comparing Shakespeare to a planet.

It seemed to make sense. What statistics there are show that while comedies were certainly popular on early Californian stages, they weren't Shakespeare's. It was the tragedies, with their weighty central roles, that were performed most often: *Hamlet, Macbeth, Othello*. No one seemed sure why.

I tried to approach the plays as a Forty-Niner might. *Macbeth* is the story of an isolated, underrewarded and ambitious man making the best of the hand he's been dealt; out of nowhere he's offered a path to riches. *Hamlet*, for its part, has bleak humour by the bucketful, a hero far too intelligent for the situation he finds himself in, and an obsession with death that must have struck a chord with miners forever burying comrades dead of cholera, scurvy or just plain exhaustion. The play even has a thrilling brawl at the end.

Othello really interested me. Nowadays we tend to think of it as an investigation of racial politics, but before the twentieth century it was most often played – by, of course, a white actor blacking up as the Moor – as a tragedy of tormented passion far away from home. It mapped on to the Gold Rush almost too well. Most of it takes place far away from the fleshpots of Venice (San Francisco), in the remote location of Cyprus (the mountains), in the musky male stink of a military barracks (mining camp), and features a character, Cassio's lover Bianca, who is probably a prostitute (no translation necessary). One didn't have to be a doctoral student to see how the theme of sexual jealousy might resonate with lonely, frustrated men who had left families behind, or how they might identify with the hero's tortured words to Iago:

> By the world,
> I think my wife be honest, and think she is not.
> I think that thou art just, and think thou art not.
> I'll have some proof. My name, that was as fresh
> As Dian's visage, is now begrimed and black
> As mine own face.

Similar agonies coursed through letters by miners I had read, despondent about the lives and loves they had left back east. There was a good reason the play was popular in the military (it had to be, if you cast Ulysses S. Grant as Desdemona). And that 'begrimed' must have got a rueful laugh, at the very least, in Rough and Ready.

I had a suspicion I was indulging in the fatal flaw of literary critics and solitary travellers: inappropriate over-reading. Probably these scripts were popular here simply because they were popular, as they were popular elsewhere in the United States. But there was one play above all that struck a chord here, and which had stalked me on my travels through America. It was far and away the most performed drama in the Old West, as it seems to have been in the emerging United States: *Richard III*.

On the face of it, for *Richard III* to be a big hitter in California seemed strange: hard to imagine that pioneer audiences had much time for the tangled skeins of the Wars of the Roses, still less for the Tudor Myth. One could see why it would be popular with companies – that jewel of a star part – and, in Colley Cibber's version, eminently tourable through the mountains. But why with miners, so particularly? I remembered watching Al Pacino's 1996 documentary, *Looking for Richard*, in which Pacino spends most of his time explaining to befuddled contemporary American actors and audiences who King Richard actually was, let alone why they should perform in or watch his play.

Critics have ventured a number of explanations for *Richard III*'s runaway popularity in eighteenth- and nineteenth-century America. Theatre historian Kim C. Sturgess calls Richard a 'tyrant fit for a rebellious population', suggesting that the play offered a kind of 'oral essay' about the excesses of the English monarchy that made it appealing in the heady independence days of the 1760s and 1770s. The critic Mark Thornton Burnett, investigating film spin-offs from two centuries later, suggests something else – that Richard was a prototype Horatio Alger figure, an embodiment (albeit malign) of the pull-yourself-up-by-your-bootstraps American Dream.

Looking around the museum for something that snagged my interest, I saw a Perspex case containing a rusty Colt revolver, a whiskey flask and a little travelling box of the card game Faro. Like the photograph, it touched an idea. Gambling was a religion in the Old West. Miners would bet on just about anything – horse races, cock fights, bear fights, dog fights, bull fights, fights between themselves. The historian Susan Roberts argues suggestively that gambling – far and away the most popular activity in the diggings, usually Faro or a

Mexican three-card game called Monte – took on 'a special significance in a setting like California, where it shared with the primary economic activity, placer mining, elements of unpredictability and irrationality'. That was surely true: what was the Gold Rush, if it wasn't the biggest gamble of everyone's lives?

And who is Shakespeare's biggest gambler, if it isn't Richard Gloucester? The Crookback, 'cheated of feature by dissembling nature', who nonetheless wins the crown and almost everything, before losing it all again in battle? The greatest puzzle about Shakespeare's Richard is what really drives him: relentless ambition? crazed bloodlust? buried childhood trauma? Surely a more straightforward explanation is that he can't resist throwing the dice. As he chortles after successfully wooing Lady Anne over the coffin of her uncle:

> Was ever woman in this humour wooed?
> Was ever woman in this humour won?

One could say something similar about other antiheroes popular with Gold Rush audiences, notably Macbeth and Iago in *Othello*. But in Richard, surely, it is crystallised, this restless need to improvise, the relentless determination to risk it. He is an inveterate chancer who begins with nothing and gambles, and gambles again; who woos and wins, and charges through the play with a snarl and a wisecrack on his lips.

Like Richard, Californian miners had put everything in jeopardy in the hope of a passage to riches. Like him, many of them ended up dying in the attempt. I thought of Bosworth – in California often a room above a saloon, being bashed to pieces by the boots of touring actors – and what are very nearly Richard's last lines in the play:

> I have set my life upon a cast,
> And I will stand the hazard of the die.

'Cast' and 'die'; Richard even had the lingo. It wasn't hard to see how these words would reverberate with gambling men stranded in their own 'field'. Even his desperate final wager, 'A horse! A horse! My kingdom for a horse!', must have had an eerily authentic ring.

And nineteenth-century American actors knew how to hold an audience, no matter who or where they were. The poet Walt Whitman

remembered seeing Edwin Booth's father, the famously volatile Junius
Brutus, as Richard III, and never forgot the experience. This is his
account of Booth's tent scene near the end of the play, where Richard
is visited on the eve of battle by the ghosts of everyone he has killed:

> From the couch where he had been writhing in the agony of his dreams,
> from the terror which the palpable images of those whom he had
> murdered inspired, he rushed forward to the footlights, his face of the
> ashy hue of death, his limbs trembling, his eyes rolling and gleaming
> with an unearthly glare, and his whole face and form convulsed with
> an intense excitement. It was the very acme of acting . . .

There was another tale about Junius Brutus Booth: that one of his
favourite stunts on tour, half-wild on booze, was refusing to die at
Bosworth – he would simply pursue his opponent off the stage and on
to the street. Audiences must have adored that impromptu rescripted
end.

The Canadian critic Russell M. Brown once suggested that the
grounding model for much American fiction was Oedipus, the hot-
headed, club-footed runaway who murdered his father, as America had
fought its way to independence from Britain. (The model for Canada, by
contrast, was the timidly father-worshipping Telemachus.) I wondered
if another fine archetype mightn't be Shakespeare's Crookback: the
villainous victor, the ultimate go-getting, self-reliant, self-made man.

———•—•———

THE FIRST CALIFORNIAN GOLD RUSH was over in the blink of an eye: done
and dusted by 1856, when the amateurs packed up and either moved on
to other rushes elsewhere (British Columbia, Nevada, eventually the
Klondike) or retreated back home with their tails between their legs.
After the 1850s, gold mining was the specialism of large conglomerates.
The great levelling dream that had brought so many to California –
that anyone with a pan and a golden glint in their eye could strike it
lucky – rang increasingly hollow. In 1854, San Francisco was thrown
into panic by a drop-off in gold production. Banks went bust and a
third of the city's businesses closed their doors.

Shakespeare went bust, too, in a more roundabout fashion. The frail combination of circumstances that had seen thousands of miners hooting at *Richard III* and *Hamlet* in tiny tarpaper settlements passed. Communities either evolved into small, tough mining villages dominated by the companies, or else vanished off the face of the earth. Theatres closed, and the work for travelling actors shrank; fewer and fewer came to do tours in California, instead heading for more profitable gigs elsewhere. Some performers decided to make a new life out west. Others simply returned from whence they'd come.

That isn't to say the curtain came down on Californian drama: it was the reverse. Many theatres survived the bitter recession of the mid-1850s, but by drastically trimming their sails. The taste for cast-heavy Shakespeare was expensive. Cheaper entertainment – melodeons and music halls, vaudeville, variety acts – became the norm. Theatres that had hosted great dramas of race such as *Othello* and *The Merchant of Venice* now preferred minstrel shows: inexpensive, popular, reliably profitable. More hearteningly, San Francisco's jumble of cultures played its part. Chinese-language theatre, serving one of the city's largest immigrant communities, planted a foothold in 1855 when the Shanghai Theatre Company set up permanent shop on Dupont Street, the first Asian troupe to do so.

Perhaps there was a touch of Levine's highbrow/lowbrow, too: as the nineteenth century wore on, it began to be accepted in America, as in Britain, that Shakespeare deserved special treatment. Texts were sanitised, performance practices changed. The Bard was increasingly regarded as a subject for reverential study, to be examined in the cloistered hush of libraries and gentlemen's clubs, or in lumbering picturesque productions. Henry Irving's *Hamlet*, which toured the East Coast and Canada from London in 1883, lasted a punishing five-plus hours and required a cast of sixty and several tonnes of scenery. No chance of getting that up to the mountains, even if there had been an audience.

But Shakespeare did not change everywhere. Down in San Diego, my final destination, I thought I'd found a holdout of a rougher, ruder kind of theatre, one that had lasted long into the twentieth century and beyond. From all that I'd read, it was still going strong.

In the late summer of 1934, the San Diego Chamber of Commerce put on a show. Deep in the Great Depression, the town needed to liven up its moribund economy. The Chicago World's Fair, then coming to an end, gave the city fathers an idea – their own world's fair, right here in Southern California.

It required eight months of round-the-clock building and a hefty chunk of federal money. But when it opened in Balboa Park the following May, the California Pacific International Exposition was a wonder to behold. You could watch astonished as a life-sized robot called Alpha ambled across the grounds and fired a pistol on command. You could marvel at the Ford Building, a futuristic concrete cylinder designed to resemble a V8 engine. You could visit the House of Pacific Relations, a collection of cottages in different national styles, or explore the 'Indian village', complete with rattlesnake pit. The Gold Rush, naturally enough, made an appearance: there was a twenty-one-acre funfair called the Gold Gulch Mining Camp, complemented by (as *Time* put it) 'an old-time saloon, ogling dance-hall gals and some bearded characters in hickory shirts splashing in a muddy wallow with pans'.

Much the greatest attraction at the exposition, at least in some quarters, was the Zoro Garden nudist colony, at which women and some men – hired performers rather than actual nudists – gambolled around in G-strings and played volleyball in the mild Pacific air. Visitors could pay for admission, or simply hoick up their Panama hats and gawp through holes in the fence. By the time the exposition closed in September 1935, nearly 4.8 million visitors had come through. Flushed with unexpected success, the Chamber of Commerce did it all again the following year.

Here, among the rattlesnakes, next to the nudist colony, was William Shakespeare. Taking their cue, again, from Chicago, where one of the most popular exhibits – much to the organisers' surprise – had been a 'Merrie England' replica of the Globe, the San Diego organisers decided to raise a replica of that replica in Balboa Park. Theirs would be more authentic: the weather being balmier, they could get away without a roof.

The Old Globe, as the new one was known, was staffed by a team of bright-eyed acting graduates paid a pittance to perform streamlined versions of nineteen plays. Each afternoon, commencing at 1 p. m., the players would come on to the open-air thrust stage and race through cut-down 'tabloid' versions of five or six texts, each a maximum of an hour long, with ten-minute intervals in between. There was no scenery; each actor played as many as six different roles a day. Elizabethan costumes were compulsory, and for one photocall the

Globe Players acted out an historical banquet with an actress got up as Gloriana herself. Audiences dined more modestly, at 85 cents a plate, at the Falstaff Tavern next door.

No one expected Shakespeare to survive in San Diego. The theatre was little more than a circular wooden frame boarded over and painted in mock-Elizabethan style; it had been jerry-built with so little regard to the weather that an awning had to be rigged up to prevent audiences collapsing from heat exhaustion. When the exposition finally came to an end in 1936, the authorities prepared to tear it down.

But fans had other ideas. A committee to preserve the Old Globe, and rebuild it along less disposable lines, was formed. Their target was $15,000, with half the funding coming from the city and labour provided free by Roosevelt's Works Progress Administration. An appeal went out for San Diegans to find the remaining $7,500. Donations, many just one or two dollars, flooded in. A few months later, in winter 1937, the Old Globe was pronounced saved.

My motel was opposite the white cliff-face of a military facility belonging to Lockheed Martin, on a roaring six-lane highway: hardly territory for a quiet stroll. But I was feeling antsy after a week in a car, so I got the taxi to drop me downtown and decided to walk the last couple of miles.

Even mid-morning, the heat was punishing. Beige-coloured asphalt wavered in the sun. I quickly realised that the neat grid of my tourist map had been hiding something: San Diego was built across a series of canyons, which wound and dipped beneath the city like crazy paving. Laurel Street, which had started so reasonably on the straight and level, had developed a bad case of the inclines.

At long last, I dragged myself across the roadway bridge into Balboa Park. Beneath me, cars thundered through the canyon. Every few minutes, a jet bound for the airport, its undercarriage and flaps trailing untidily, shrieked overhead.

Hemmed in by a screen of palm trees and miraculously insensible to the noise, the San Diego Lawn Bowling Club were just polishing off a game: nut-brown seniors in baseball caps and high socks, neat little tummies protruding over their shorts. They looked rapt in concentration, like figures in an eighteenth-century landscape.

Seasick in the heat, I began to see things. Above the trees, shimmering woozily in the haze, was a campanile. As I trudged through a Renaissance-style gatehouse, there sprang up a fantasy of baroque tracery, pilasters and ornamental columns in Spanish colonial style. This surreal mirage wasn't early symptoms of heat exhaustion, after all: it was the California Building, constructed for an earlier exposition.

The Old Globe was tucked around the corner, behind a walled garden. Given that I'd only seen pictures of the thimble-sized 1930s original, its scale took me aback. It was perhaps 40 metres wide, seated 600 people, with a broad courtyard out front and a gable-ended pavilion next door. With a jaunty tiled roof where thatch should have been and an air-conditioned indoor stage, it put the 'mock' firmly into 'Tudor'. (Indeed, the Old Globe isn't even a globe: only half the theatre is round.) But it looked cheery enough, with its mullioned windows and its half-timbering. After the California Building, it seemed positively restrained.

In a meeting room inside, the Old Globe's official historian, Darlene Gould Davies, told me its story; she had witnessed much of it herself, having arrived in San Diego in 1951, a theatre-crazy eleven-year-old. As an actor, her first main-stage show had been at the age of thirteen, she said. 'Opposite Dennis Hopper!'

Like the Nevada theatre, the Old Globe had a fiery past. Reborn as a permanent theatre in December 1937, it had been destroyed by an arsonist in 1978. It rose once more and reopened in 1982, whereupon calamity struck a second time when the temporary stage that had been used in the meantime was also burnt down. The Old Globe in which we were sitting was in fact rather new, having been remodelled in 1995.

There were now three theatres: the main house, a studio space and the outdoor festival theatre, which is where I would be seeing a show tonight. From its humble origins, the Old Globe now ran a summer Shakespeare festival, in addition to a year-round programme that made it one of the linchpins of West Coast theatre. Each year some 200,000 people came to the Old Globe, 50,000 of them to see a play by Shakespeare.

I was interested in the movement the Old Globe and its Chicago predecessor had started. Courtesy of the eccentric but visionary British theatre-maker William Poel (1852–1934), attempts to recreate Elizabethan staging techniques had been going on since at least 1881. I'd run into Poel's shade in Gdańsk, because of his staging of *Der Bestrafte Brudermord*, that wildly modified early German version of

Hamlet. Decades before that experiment, Poel attempted something almost as extraordinary – an original-practices production of the 'bad' first quarto of Shakespeare's play itself (the text that features lines such as 'To be or not to be, ay, there's the point'), in Elizabethan costume and with Elizabethan music. Poel spent the rest of his career trying to convert numerous theatres into temporary Globes after London County Council, regarding him as a dangerous obsessive, refused his request for a site on which to build a permanent one. Experiments continued in mainland Europe in 1889, when a Hungarian director named Jocza Savits built a platform out from the proscenium arch and over the orchestra pit in a theatre in Munich.

In America, however, the interest in replicas, like the interest in First Folios, properly took flight. Shakespearian Globes became must-have accessories at no fewer than four world's fairs of the 1930s: Chicago, Dallas, San Diego and Cleveland in Ohio. There are now at least nine dotted across the US, of varying degrees of authenticity.

These early American Globes were freewheeling affairs, based on the scantiest research. But they left a substantial historical imprint. At Cleveland's Globe a quick-witted seventeen-year-old Jewish American actor called Sam Wanamaker spent the summer of 1936 performing with an outfit called the New Globe Players. Thirty years later, now a respected actor and political activist who had fled to Britain because of McCarthyism, Wanamaker turned his mind to raising yet another replica – this time as accurate as scholarship could make it – as close to the original site on London's Bankside as possible.

In the event, the London Globe took nearly a quarter of a century to build, in the face of aggrieved opposition that numbered everyone from Southwark Council to left-leaning academics who derided what they saw as Wanamaker's attempts to erect a Disneyfied piece of Merrie England on their doorstep. Wanamaker had to fight a court case and raise the money himself, a significant portion of it American, which led to frequent roastings in the press. He died in 1993, before the Globe project was complete. It would be years before the monumental scale of his achievement – and the insights yielded by a working model of Shakespeare's outdoor theatre – could be realised.

There was a powerful irony here, one that brought me back to the Blackfriars replica in Staunton. Not only had one of London's major heritage attractions been created by a Yank, it had its origins in the glorious inauthenticity of the world's-fair Globes, and in 'tabloid'

Shakespeare performed to holidaying audiences for a handful of dollars. The very idea of 'authentic' Shakespeare, not as sober scholarly experiment but as popular, money-making exercise, was inherently American. Only under considerable duress had the British allowed it to be exported back to the UK.

I sensed another irony, too, in the ghostly presence of Gold Gulch, now lost somewhere beneath Balboa Park. When the Old Globe first opened, audiences for Shakespeare probably hadn't been so huge in California since the Gold Rush. Calling this theme-park entertainment didn't have to be an insult. It was in the finest American traditions.

Early evening in San Diego was as sweet as the day had been fierce: a clear and vacant sky, suffused with diluted violet, palm trees streaked with the last red-gold of the sun. Flocks of visitors were roaming the park. Everywhere there seemed to be roving professional photographers, manhandling well-dressed couples into glades or draping them artfully against Spanish colonial walls. Above them, on picturesque cue, was a rising moon, chalky yellow. Over the contented ripple of conversation and the quiet *tsk-tsk-tsk-tsk* of the evening joggers, I could hear the soft buzz of cicadas. Every so often, somewhere in the distance, there was the lowing of the railroad.

After several weeks' travelling, I had finally found myself back at the beginnings of Shakespeare in America: a performance of *Richard III*, the play that had become a home-grown hit in New York in 1750 and gone on to be so hugely popular in the nineteenth century. It would be mildly fraudulent to claim this was pure happenstance: of the dozens of festival listings I had browsed, this had been the only staging I could find. Whatever power Richard Gloucester once had over the American theatregoing imagination, it had waned. But, having come this far, I wasn't going to miss a chance to meet him in person.

The Old Globe festival theatre wasn't dissimilar from Cal Shakes: a broad stage surrounded by a horseshoe of tiered seats, with a latticework of telegraph poles holding up the lighting rig. I'd seen folk festivals with more sophisticated set-ups. With the trees crowding behind and the scatter of moths in the lights, it had a pleasingly bucolic air.

The audience was of a different order from the one I'd seen in Orinda. Maybe it was the weather, but everything felt several notches more relaxed. Blonde girlfriends in stilettos and tiny cocktail dresses were taking their seats; middle-aged dudes with goatees and sunglasses moseying around in wide cargo pants and baggy T-shirts. There was plenty of white hair sprinkled through the audience, but it was a younger crowd than I'd seen at a performance of Shakespeare for as long as I could remember.

There was only one word for *Richard III* itself: muscular. Richard Gloucester, played by the Seattle-born Steppenwolf graduate Jay Whittaker, sported a leather biker jacket and trousers that were worryingly tight. With lip curled in permanent disdain and a scream that resembled an F-16 taking off, he even managed to make the limp into a kind of macho strut. While researching the production I had come across an interview with Whittaker about his prowess on the surfboard. In San Diego, even Richard Crookback caught waves.

Subtle it wasn't. With its camouflage netting and helicopter sound effects, it was rather too obviously indebted to post-Gulf War productions of the history plays that had become over-familiar in Britain (the director was a visiting Brit, Lindsay Posner). But its vivacity and energy reminded me why *Richard III* was one of Shakespeare's earliest hits, and why it was never out of print in his lifetime.

It is, of course, the ultimate actor's play. Even when Richard is ostensibly doing nothing, he's doing everything: fidgeting, skittering across the stage, pushing and prodding, directing events ('Bustle, bustle,' he urges his followers before Bosworth), relentlessly bending circumstances to his will. Shakespeare channelled much of that energy from his main source, an anonymous play called *The True Tragedie of Richard the Third*, which, though printed in 1594, soon after Shakespeare's version went on stage, likely dates from much earlier. This Richard, too, is forever the hustler:

> KING Carry George Standley to prison.
> GEORGE Alasse my Lord, shall I go to prison?
> KING Shall you go to prison, what a questions that?

In both plays, Richard is director in all but name.

The Old Globe's staging also possessed something I'd been craving since Washington: politics. The Earl of Richmond, blonde and blue-eyed, could have stepped out of a campaign poster; I half-expected to see his victory over Richard at Bosworth attended by cheerleaders. Yet so bleak was the production's view of power that even this moment – the founding of the Tudor dynasty, for generations held up by critics as Shakespeare's obedient celebration of the Tudor Myth – had a metallic tang of irony. During his stump speech on the eve of battle Richmond announced:

> God and our good cause fight upon our side.
> The prayers of holy saints and wrongèd souls,
> Like high-reared bulwarks, stand before our forces.

One could imagine the lines on a Tea Party T-shirt.

Something else struck me as I watched: even given the nationality of the director, how all-American the play seemed. Many people I'd talked to on my journey had brought up the vexed relationship between the United States and Britain when it came to Shakespeare – if not quite, these days, a full-blown Forrest–Macready rivalry, something a little more anxious and subcutaneous. Broadway was awash with British productions; British theatre names had become huge stars on American TV and film. Whenever a UK company brought Shakespeare across to America, it was regarded as somehow the real deal – Shakespeare as it should be done. The cut-glass British accents, inauthentic though of course they were, only helped maintain the illusion.

Here, in a festival theatre on the Pacific seaboard, something different seemed to be going on: a connection to an older, properly American kind of Shakespeare, with some similarities to its British cousin but also invigoratingly distinct. This Shakespeare was rougher and less cautious, more energetic – more alive, I thought. It was hugely heartening to see an American actor making great strides as Richard III, as his predecessors had done a century and a half before.

I thought back to the American Richards I'd encountered in the last weeks – Abigail Adams's ardent hope that George III might be left bawling 'a horse, a horse', Frederick B. Warde's scuttling silent-movie villain, Abraham Lincoln doing 'Now is the winter . . .' from memory, Walter Leman performing Bosworth on a billiard table, Junius Brutus Booth refusing to go down at the end and playfully, doggedly fighting on. It was common to regard Richard as a villain, perhaps one of Shakespeare's most malevolent. He was also one of the most appealing characters – the smartest, the funniest – in the canon.

On the way out through the lobby, I passed a bust of Shakespeare: a bronze by the French artist Albert Carrier-Belleuse. It caught the poet in a moment of supernal inspiration, head nobly tilted down, garments billowing around his neck like Lear in the storm.

There was one cosmetic modification: half his cranium was missing. The bronze had been in the Old Globe the night it went up in flames in March 1978 and was hit by a piece of falling masonry. Borne aloft from the burning building, it had been placed here as a sign of the Old Globe's Blitz spirit. Shakespeare looked long-suffering, but also as though he'd survive.

Nor was Richard dead and buried in America, not just yet. Months after I got back, well into plotting the next phase of my journey – and just as worldwide excitement was building about the discovery of the remains of the real King Richard III beneath a car park in Leicester – I saw an article in the *New Yorker*. It was about a new drama soon to air on Netflix; a gamble for the website, a thirteen-part series only available online. It was a political saga, the story of a savagely ambitious congressman, Frank Underwood, who hacks and slashes his way to the vice-presidency. David Fincher and Beau Willimon produced, Kevin Spacey starred. Their title was *House of Cards*.

As an over-earnest, over-politicised twelve-year-old I'd watched the original BBC *House of Cards*, scripted by Michael Dobbs and Andrew Davies, and thrilled to its skulduggerous portrayal of Westminster life. There were back-stabbings galore, all manner of plot and counterplot, but in every sense the dark heart of the drama was Ian Richardson's icily ironic Francis Urquhart, Tory chief whip. A self-proclaimed 'back-room boy', he coolly manoeuvred his way right to the front.

What I missed then, I realised now: Urquhart, too, had a doppelgänger. Richardson had been an eminent actor at the RSC; Urquhart's rise and eventual fall were closely patterned on *Richard III*. The echoes were everywhere one cared to look – Richardson's drawling soliloquies to camera (one memorably conducted at a urinal), the blithe and systematic silencing of his enemies, the eerily sexless seduction of a younger woman; most of all, perhaps, the depiction of power-lust as a raw, unhaltable force.

The Crookback was back. Spacey's most recent stage role had been a touring production of *Richard III* done in the best barnstorming, nineteenth-century style, which had started at London's Old Vic before heading to San Francisco, New York and other cities worldwide. He and Fincher had dropped numerous hints about the new script's indebtedness to Shakespeare – not just *Richard III* but *Othello* and *Macbeth*. There was an amplified part for Underwood's scheming wife and a likeably gullible president who, though white, bore more than a passing resemblance to the Moor of Venice. Like its nineteenth-century forebears, the script was heavily doctored, but the film-makers had found a Shakespearian poetry of their own: shots of scurrying spiders, a Civil War subplot, Spacey relentlessly breaking the fourth wall . . .

The only thing missing from the *New Yorker* article was the sense that this had happened before, 160 years earlier, when *Richard III* was acclaimed as the greatest American play of them all.

But perhaps that didn't matter. It was good to see Shakespeare back in prime time, and with a shot at vice-president to boot. Something told me he would make it to the White House.

Gurudeva

Mumbai · Pune · Kolkata · New Delhi

In the mid-1960s, a young Indian-American production house called Merchant Ivory was in trouble. Their first movie, 1963's *The Householder* – an ambling comedy about the marital difficulties of a schoolteacher and his wife – had not been a success. 'The best to be said for their effort is that it represents an earnest try at reflecting middle-class life in modern India,' sniffed the *New York Times*, labelling the pace sluggish and the acting 'ponderous'. The critic Bosley Crowther was especially irked by one of the cast, Harindranath Chattopadhyay, 'a name so long I can hardly spell it' – which he proved, by misspelling it.

Merchant Ivory's next project, a short documentary called *The Delhi Way* (1964), made even less of a splash. Fifty minutes long, mostly shot years before, it was the pet project of director James Ivory, who had run out of money halfway through production. When the film finally came out, most of the critics failed to notice. It sank almost without trace.

In 1965, though, Merchant Ivory struck lucky. While making *The Householder*, its male star, Shashi Kapoor, had introduced Ivory to a family called the Kendals: an eccentric Anglo-Indian clan who doubled as an acting troupe called Shakespeareana. For twenty years, the Kendals had pounded the highways and byways of India, taking versions of Shakespeare to schools, convents, village squares, maharajas' palaces; anywhere that would cover their costs, from the North-West Frontier Province in what became Pakistan down to Travancore in the south. Geoffrey Kendal was paterfamilias and star actor – Hamlet, Lear, Othello, Antony. His wife Laura Liddell took the female leads, joined by their daughters Jennifer and Felicity, both practically brought up on stage. The family was complemented by a flexible cast of extras – some

English expats, others who became major names in Indian theatre and cinema: Kapoor himself, Utpal Dutt, Anwar Mirza, Marcus Murch.

At one time Shakespeareana boasted Countess Mountbatten as a patron, but by the time Ivory met the Kendals things were considerably less exalted. Interest in their brand of touring, English-language Shakespeare was dimming. Felicity had already left to make her name in England; Geoffrey and Laura would follow in the 1970s. If not quite on their uppers, they were perilously close.

Ivory sensed that there was a film here, one that touched large themes: the turmoil of India as it fought to find a post-independence identity; the changing face of Indian entertainment; colonial and postcolonial loss. Above all, the film could describe the paradoxical position of the Anglo-Indians, a class who had once ruled India but were now stranded between a country that no longer wanted them and a British 'home' many had never even visited. Perhaps this could be the movie that explained – as *The Householder* had singularly failed to – the contradictions of India to the west.

Ivory himself, a Californian, would direct, with the renowned Bengali director-composer Satyajit Ray writing the music. Ismail Merchant, born into a Muslim family in Mumbai, produced. A German-born Jewish emigrant who had spent many years in India, Ruth Prawer Jhabvala, would write the script. The Kendals and Kapoor could play themselves, thinly disguised as a troupe called the Buckinghams.

The film this wobbly-legged multinational conglomerate made – the earliest success of their remarkable forty-year partnership – was called *Shakespeare Wallah*. It was a hit.

By the time I came to watch Merchant Ivory films as a teenager in the 1990s, they were well on their way to being despised. They were written off in the cleverer newspapers (the ones I tried to read) as heritage porn: *Reader's Digest* on 35 millimetre, classic novels seen through the soft-focus lens of Laura Ashley or Ralph Lauren. Film buffs scorned them; even fans grew weary of their morbid period detail and blue-blood casting. The perspective on England and Englishness offered by *A Room With a View* (1985) or *Howards End* (1992) was more National Trust than National Front. But still: not serious cinema, even though I quietly had a soft spot for them.

Thus it was with some trepidation that, years later, I sat down to watch *Shakespeare Wallah*. Conditioned by late-period Merchant Ivory to expect something in the mould of the plushly upholstered *The Jewel in the Crown* television adaptations or David Lean's *A Passage to India*, I was disconcerted to find myself watching what appeared to be experimental postmodern cinema.

The film's opening is startling, a surreal silent tableau in which the Kendal/Buckingham family, strangely clad in periwigs and breeches, perform in front of what seems to be a French chateau beside a lake. The period locations are present and correct, but (with the exception of that chateau, a folly near Lucknow) they are dingy expat digs, not stately homes. Instead of over-saturated period colour, the film is in austere black-and-white, the hot glare of the subtropical sun fraying the corners of the frame. There is Ray's music, deft and sprightly, performed on flute and tabla with the occasional vivacious flurry of strings. And of course India, not England, is the movie's subject as well as its location – a society both complex and tantalisingly elusive, a place where the film-makers' interest in postcolonial tensions can bubble and simmer.

One thing is consistent with the Merchant Ivory brand, though: *Shakespeare Wallah*'s unrepentant nostalgia. Ivory and Jhabvala shift the timeframe from the late 1940s (the period Shakespeareana had been in their pomp) to the early 1960s, fifteen years after independence, making the Kendals seem more hopelessly out of date than they had ever been in reality. *Shakespeare Wallah* translates as 'Shakespeare seller', Geoffrey Kendal's real-life nickname, but it becomes mournfully clear that India is no longer in the market for what the Buckinghams have to offer. Their vehicles repeatedly break down, a heavy hint that their travelling days are done. An elderly cast member abruptly dies. A performance of *Romeo and Juliet* collapses into a fist fight. Tony Buckingham's response to this sea of troubles chimes with everything being felt in painfully post-imperial, about-to-become-postcolonial Britain: 'It's a rejection of everything I am.'

Shakespeare's name is inscribed deep into this narrative of loss – lost ground, lost culture, lost empire. Just as India has shaken off the British yoke, so it is attempting to shrug off Britain's National Poet. 'I've been to see *Hamlet*,' Shashi Kapoor's playboy Sanju announces to his girlfriend Manjula, played with delicious archness by Madhur Jaffrey. 'Who?' she asks.

In the wings of *Shakespeare Wallah* looms a bogeyman, the Indian film industry – a creature that also seems to be out for Shakespeare's blood. As well as being involved with the *filmi* star Manjula, Sanju has also become disastrously entangled with the strolling player Lizzie, and this becomes a metaphor for the movement of the movie. As well as a love rivalry, it is also a contest between theatre (educated, highbrow, old, English) and cinema (jejune, populist, new, Indian). Sanju talks Manjula into attending the Buckinghams' version of *Othello*, but when she arrives in the auditorium it causes such a stir among the movie-mad audience that the show is held up.

The conclusion drawn by *Shakespeare Wallah* is stark: Shakespeare is all but finished in India, and Bollywood is almost entirely to blame. One might even adopt the title of another Merchant Ivory film (one I also secretly liked): these are the remains of the day.

I spent months trying to work out where truth ended in *Shakespeare Wallah* and fiction began. I dug out Geoffrey Kendal's diaries, published in 1986, and read them cover to cover. They were enjoyably garrulous, retelling Kendal's first glimpse of Mumbai with the Entertainments National Service Association, sent out to perform for British troops during the second world war, and his return with the troupe that became Shakespeareana in 1947. Though full of colourful tales and hair's-breadth escapes – the earthquake that hits halfway through a show; the actor who drives across the Himalayas in a 1935 Wolseley ambulance – the diaries nonetheless seemed remarkably incurious about India or Indians, other than as (generally) polite witnesses to the Kendals' English-language performances. Despite the film's many fictions, its downbeat mood seemed accurate enough: it was with tangible bitterness that Kendal recorded a Shakespeareana performance in 1962, where the locally produced poster advertised the presence of Shashi Kapoor – then beginning to make a name for himself in films – but omitted the name of Shakespeare.

Yet this wasn't the whole story. On a rushed three-day trip to India in 2012, researching a newspaper piece on two acting companies preparing to come to the Globe in London, I'd managed to glean enough about contemporary Indian theatre to realise that Kendal's gloom (like much else in an extravagantly contoured life) had been excessive.

Shakespeare hadn't evaporated when the British slipped away on liners bound for foggy Tilbury: on the contrary, there were plentiful modern adaptations of the plays. Indeed, an entire festival near Chennai was dedicated to Shakespeare translated into Indian languages – proof of the vibrant life of Shakespeare on the subcontinent.

What I was struggling with were linkages. I was missing a sense of how this contemporary theatre connected with the kind of Shakespeare that Kendal and his colleagues were acting – if it connected at all. Were the traditions entirely separate? Was there any traffic between the blood-and-thunder, English-language Shakespeare being done by Shakespeareana and the Indian traditions of translation and adaptation? And what of Indian movies, where Shakespeare has a continued and vivacious presence?

It wasn't until I stumbled across a slim pamphlet that the pieces began to slot into place. It was entitled *Shakespeare in India* and it was by the British academic Charles Jasper Sisson. I dimly remembered Sisson's name from the dusty corners of an MPhil reading list – a don at University College London, he'd written a book on Shakespeare's lost plays and another on an Elizabethan inn-yard in east London. I wasn't expecting to see him here, rubbing shoulders with theory-heavy monographs on Indian Shakespeare, their titles stiff with words like 'postcolonial' and 'diasporic'.

The pamphlet's subtitle was 'Popular Adaptations on the Bombay Stage'. It was the date that really caught my eye: 1926. This was far earlier than anything else I'd been reading – the height of the Raj, or very nearly. Why had a British specialist in Jacobethan stage practice written a book on Shakespeare in Mumbai? And what on earth did he mean by 'popular'?

Based on his experiences teaching at Elphinstone College, part of the university of Mumbai, Sisson's account had all the exuberant, pent-up enthusiasm of a man who has stepped outside himself, perhaps for the first time. It began by declaring its lack of interest in 'the influence of Shakespeare upon the cultured classes in India'. What Sisson wanted to address was a Shakespeare who had become increasingly remote in Britain (as by now in America), a Shakespeare who was still down-and-dirty popular entertainment. He wrote:

There is but one country in the world, to the best of my knowledge, except possibly Germany, where the plays have of recent times formed the safest and surest attraction to the indiscriminate masses who attend popular theatres, where the proprietor of a theatre could count on a profit on a Shakespeare production. That country is India, and the theatres in question are a group of theatres in the city of Bombay, clustered together in the heart of a poor Indian population.

These theatres were spread around Grant Road in Mumbai; the plays weren't performed in English, but in Marathi, Gujarati, Hindi, Urdu. Tickets cost a handful of rupees. Aside from himself, the only Europeans who had been inside these places, Sisson thought, were policemen on the prowl for pickpockets.

Warming to his theme, he went on:

> The orthodox Shakespearian would experience many a shock if he ventured into this strange temple of his idol. He might accustom himself to the Oriental costume and *mise-en-scène*, to the disturbing medley of the audience, even, with some study, to the foreign language. But he would be amazed to find that he was being provided with an opera and a ballet as well as a play . . . and horrified when he realised the extreme liberties that were being taken with the text and plot.

The liberty-taking shows Sisson discovered, working with M. R. Shah, an assistant professor at the university of Mumbai, stretched back to the 1890s, perhaps earlier. They were a vigorous and remarkable series of Shakespeare adaptations in the Parsi theatre of Mumbai, named for its inventors in the Parsi community.

Sisson and I were alike in one respect at least: these adaptations were unlike anything either of us had encountered before. They included *Vasundhara*, an adaptation of *Macbeth* from 1910 that retold Shakespeare's story not from the hero's perspective, but from Lady M's, for whom it was renamed. There was also *Bazm-e-Fani* ('Mortal Gathering'), an Urdu version of *Romeo and Juliet* in which the balcony scene was, Sisson gleefully remarked, 'pretty completely rewritten' (he included a translation). He was particularly entranced by the Mumbai taste for shoehorning comic subplots into even the soberest of tragedies, particularly plots poking fun at Indians excessively devoted to British manners.

Lest anyone think he had gone dotty in the subtropical sun, Sisson included photographs: fey-looking male students from the New High

School in Mumbai in doublets and hose; a mysterious shot of an extravagantly moustachioed man apparently about to behead another with a scimitar (captioned 'typical costumes', but providing no clue as to which play they were typical of).

As Sisson described with wonderment the 'frequent songs and dances', the socially varied audiences, the pell-mell competition for tickets, the elaborate staging techniques and lust for theatrical novelty in Parsi theatre, one sensed him eyeing sceptics at the back of the lecture hall. What about authenticity and scholarship, old chap? What does any of it have to do with *our* Shakespeare, the British Bard we know and love?

To that, Sisson had a triumphant answer:

> The Bombay popular stage offers in many respects a parallel to the Tudor stage in England. Its adaptations of Shakespeare, disconcerting at first sight, show his plays to be things that are still alive and in process of becoming new things, being ever born again, even as they were on the Elizabethan stage.

Things that are still alive and in process of becoming new things . . . Here was another, more enlightening perspective on how Shakespeare's work might operate in India, ways that were largely alien to the English-speaking Geoffrey Kendal and his ilk; ways many British people would still struggle to recognise as 'Shakespeare' at all.

More, in the twenty-first century, the tradition is very much alive. No one seems sure of current numbers, but there are now estimated to be several hundred adaptations of Shakespeare plays into nearly all of India's twenty-plus official languages, and more versions of Shakespeare in Indian cinema than anywhere else on the globe.

Film I found an especially enticing subject, and not only because of *Shakespeare Wallah*: the world's oldest synchronised-sound version of *Hamlet* turned out to be Indian, from 1935, and Shakespeare has been cited as the most-adapted writer in Bollywood history. There were echoes of the plays – so I read – in even the most unlikely Indian films, if one knew where to look: action thrillers, rom-coms, gangster movies, farces.

There was surely something here. Even by the time Kendal arrived in India in 1944, three years before independence, Shakespeareana was already past its sell-by date, but not because Shakespeare had lost India or India had discarded Shakespeare. If Sisson was correct, Indian urban culture had absorbed Shakespeare – translated him, adapted him, localised him, remade him, and by the time Merchant-Ivory-Jhabvala were shooting their film, had been doing so for the best part of seven decades. What *Shakespeare Wallah* figured as something made waste was, viewed another way, the creation of something else new. It's just that Kendal and co. didn't realise it. Perhaps they didn't want to.

———

INNOVATION IS GREAT . . . BRITAIN

HERITAGE IS GREAT . . . BRITAIN

CULTURE IS GREAT . . . BRITAIN

SHOPPING IS GREAT . . . BRITAIN

At the airport, the British tourist board was out in force. Five or six metres long and almost as tall, the posters marched down the concourse, a blur of fantastical scenes: the tail fin of a formula one racing car, Bodiam Castle in East Sussex, Norman Foster's swooping roof for the British Museum, someone's designer stiletto.

What these posters were doing in the arrivals terminal at Mumbai was anyone's guess. I tried to work out what kind of Britain they were intended to evoke: a proud nation of stiletto-wearing, castle-haunting racing drivers, perhaps. *O brave new world that has such racing drivers in't* . . . Whatever it was, I was delighted to be fleeing it.

To orientate myself in India's movie capital, I had arranged to meet a film critic called Nandini Ramnath. She wrote for *Mint*, a slick, business-orientated newspaper with links to the *Wall Street Journal*. Her reviews were sharp and cosmopolitan, her tone just this side of libellously sardonic. If anyone could guide me safely through the hyperbole of the Indian film industry, I hoped it would be her.

On the evening of my arrival, we arranged a rendezvous by the Flora Fountain in the old Fort district of South Mumbai. This was the heart of Raj territory: down the road from the Byzantine-Gothic pile of Chhatrapati Shivaji Terminus, formerly Victoria Terminus; on the same street as Elphinstone College, where C. J. Sisson had taught. An appropriate place to debate the colonial reach of Shakespeare, I thought as I walked down from my hotel. In the rust-red dust of the Oval Maidan, bathed in honey-coloured evening light, whippet-thin boys in trousers and shirtsleeves were playing cricket beneath the shadow of the university clock tower. Had it not been for the heat, we could have been in Hyde Park.

In contrast to her surroundings, Nandini resembled a character in a 1930s American newsroom comedy: fast-walking, furrow-browed, an unruly tangle of dark hair bunched over her fashionably thick-rimmed glasses. She barely broke stride as she collected me, disposing of one cigarette and lighting another in the same fluid, virtuosic movement.

'You need to learn the Bombay shuffle,' she yelled over her shoulder as she crossed the road, executing a neat lower-body swerve through the maelstrom of lurching, blaring steel. The closest I could get was two paces behind.

Nandini talked as fast as she walked. In the first ten minutes, drinking warm lager at the roof bar of the Sea Palace hotel, we had raced through my plans for South Africa, the influence of Jacques Derrida on Indian university education, the state of the British newspaper market and her views on my publisher.

She moved on to *Shakespeare Wallah*, which I had watched again on the flight.

'Oh, I *love* that film,' she said, brow momentarily unfurrowing.

I had my doubts, I said; the politics, the colonial-era nostalgia . . .

She expelled an impatient rivulet of smoke in the general direction of the sunset. 'Oh, *that*. That's not the important thing. The important thing is how important Satyajit Ray is to the film. As well as writing the music, you can see his influence in how beautifully it's shot. He chose some of the locations, loaned them his cinematographer, sat in the editing studio telling Ivory to *cut, cut*. All the later Merchant Ivories are just so corseted, so *cosseted*, you know? That one's kind of free.'

What I really wanted was a primer on Bollywood. I'd read books and seen a small handful of Hindi movies, but was lacking an overall sense of how the industry worked. What made it tick?

'You have to remember where it came from. Indian cinema has always relied on things borrowed from all over the place. There's the *nautanki* tradition – a kind of variety act or vaudeville – a bit of acting, a bit of singing, as well as bits from the Sanskrit epics, the *Ramayana* and the *Mahabharata*. Until about ten years ago – maybe less so now – the typical Hindi film was exactly like that. A real composite.'

She smiled wickedly. 'There's even an industry term: the "unofficial remake". You get the official remake, then you get the unofficial remakes, sometimes several of them. That happens to western films, to Indian films also. Many different versions of the same story.'

Even the term 'Bollywood' was a composite, and often misapplied. Originally a term of affectionate abuse created by the Indian English-language press in the 1970s, outside India it has come to stand for any Indian-made film. In fact the subcontinent is home to a number of different local movie industries, operating in many of its official languages and in an awe-inspiring variety of forms, from art-house indie films to lumbering commercial franchises.

Nandini marked them out with the glowing end of her cigarette. 'Three main industries: Tamil film from the south, Telugu film from Andhra Pradesh, which is huge now, Hindi here in Bombay. But the list goes on, many different languages. And of course Bengali cinema.' She sniffed. 'That's a cut above.'

'Bollywood' – the mass-market, Hindi-language, Mumbai-based movie industry – produces perhaps 200 movies annually. All told, though, there are something like 1,000 films produced in India each year, double the output of Hollywood.

What these industries shared was a hunger for making money. According to a report by the consultants KPMG and crawled over by a slavering Hollywood Reporter, revenues in Indian cinema were around 94 billion rupees in 2013 (£0.9 billion), with growth pegged at 10 per cent-plus annually. This was half what Hollywood brought in because of the difference in ticket prices, but far higher in terms of sales. Over 3 billion seats were flogged in India each year, and the subcontinent was still what the analysts called heavily 'under-screened' – lacking in cinemas per head of population. No wonder mass appeal was the name of the game.

'Of course there are a lot of modernist trends in Indian cinema, some art-house, but that's broadly where the popular stuff comes from. That's the overarching idiom: a big audience, getting bigger, who must be entertained at all costs.'

I was curious as to where the notion of artistic originality came into things. Even at the major Hollywood studios there was an emphasis on making product distinctive. Did the same obtain here?

'I don't think it's so important. What is more important is, do you make people laugh, do you make them cry? Can you appeal to a family audience? Can you sell tickets? I'm speaking very broadly. But I think that's true.'

So if one saw echoes of, say, Shakespeare in Indian cinema, they wouldn't necessarily be there for factors of high culture or prestige? There'd be more functional factors at work?

Nandini ducked her head. 'Got it. You pick and choose as a film-maker. You may not have read *As You Like It*, but you think – wow, great idea, girl dressed as boy. You want to get to a particular place in a film, but you haven't found a way, and it turns out Shakespeare has solved it for you. You just borrow it, and disguise the source – if you can be bothered.'

Surreptitiously, I glanced at my watch: 9 p.m. We'd been talking for an hour and a half. Nandini's evening was far from over; there were still two events to go to, a book launch and a drinks party hosted by a film-director friend. My head was throbbing, though whether from the working practices of Bollywood, jet lag or the cigarette smoke, I wasn't sure.

'Good luck with your project,' she called as she strode purposefully into the night, past the recumbent shadows of people sleeping rough on the pavement. 'You might even have fun!'

Holed up in my hotel room, waiting on a series of appointments, I tried to get to grips with what C. J. Sisson had been watching all those years before.

Parsi theatre combined two of the most important things in Mumbai: pleasure and profit. Parsi Zoroastrians began arriving in India perhaps as early as the 700s, driven by persecution in what is now Iran. By the early nineteenth century, they were one of the city's most important communities, with powerful interests in shipbuilding and trading, and an eagerness to do business with anyone and everyone. Cricket was one early obsession: the Parsis were among the first Indians to become obsessed by the game, and in 1848 formed the Parsi Oriental Cricket Club in Mumbai, perhaps the oldest on the subcontinent. Horses and polo were other obsessions, particularly among well-to-do Parsis – of which there were many.

British-style theatrical entertainment was yet another fascination. In 1840, a consortium of leading Mumbai citizens led by the successful merchant Jagannath Sunkersett lamented to the British governor about the lack of a 'place of public amusement in the Island' and appealed to be allowed to build one, claiming that 'such a measure would promote good humour and tend to induce a desirable tone of feeling in Society at large'. The result was the erection in 1846 of the Grant Road theatre on what were then the northern fringes of the rapidly expanding city. A fifth of the size of its approximate model, the Theatre Royal, Drury Lane in London, with a tight capacity of 337, it became the crucible for Indian drama in Mumbai.

Back in the eighteenth century, drama had been performed for and by British employees of the East India Company as an alternative to other principal ways of passing the off-hours in Mumbai – playing cards at home or shooting rabbits on Malabar Hill. At the Bombay theatre on Bombay Green, built in 1776 at the heart of the British settlement, amateur troupes assuaged their homesickness by staging versions of fashionable London comedies and farces. But interest gradually shrank and the Bombay theatre fell into disrepair, until it was acquired in 1835 by another eminent Parsi businessman, Jamsetjee Jeejeebhoy (whose statue still lords it over the Oval Maidan, and who once sent four Arab horses to Queen Victoria as a gift).

Once they had control of the playhouses, Parsi producers began to change the scene. Shows in English were gradually replaced by plays in Gujarati, Urdu and Hindustani (a mixture of Hindi and Urdu), serious works drawn from the Persian epics as well as lighter pieces. By the 1850s, theatregoing had become a fashionable pastime among the upwardly mobile Mumbai middle classes.

At first, Parsi theatre was amateur only: small drama clubs performing among their own community. Yet within a decade Parsi theatre had become a fully fledged professional, commercial operation. By the 1890s, as many as twenty companies were vying for audiences, each with teams of actors and playwrights, their own playhouses in the Grant Road area and rival publishing businesses to print scripts. According to one historian, this new drama 'created perhaps the largest ticket-buying audience in Indian stage history'.

Despite the name, Parsi theatre, like the city that gave birth to it, was by no means monocultural. Parsi money fed the operation, but actors and spectators were drawn from many different communities and religions. Nor was it just Mumbai: rival Parsi troupes eventually operated in every corner of the subcontinent. Using the fast-growing infrastructure of the railways, companies went on tour, sometimes taking over entire trains with sets, costumes, equipment and armies of stagehands and actors. Several troupes took steamships far south across the Bay of Bengal to what is now Sri Lanka; others travelled to Burma and Singapore. One even made it to London for the Indian and Colonial Exhibition of 1885, led by Khurshed Mehrvan Balivala, one of numerous actors acclaimed as the 'Irving of India' after the renowned British star Henry Irving.

The drama they offered was a swaggering, eclectic amalgam of anything that would dazzle the eyes and stir the hearts of audiences. Early Parsi scripts had been based on the Persian *Shahnama* and the Sanskrit *Mahabharata*, but before long the Arabic *Arabian Nights* were being raided for stories, as were Victorian melodramas and the *nautanki* private theatre seen in north Indian royal courts.

Also here at the birth of popular Indian drama, as Sisson realised, was Shakespeare. Estimates vary, but between seventy-five and a hundred Shakespearian translations were created during this golden era of Parsi theatre. The first recognisable adaptation was of *Cymbeline* in 1871; others followed thick and fast. As Sisson also recognised, these adaptations were not remotely purist, even by the indulgent standards of the versions I had encountered in the western United States. Texts were gutted for their moving parts and reassembled into appealing commercial formulas: sensation was amped up, plots and characters more strongly delineated. An improving moral gloss was invariably applied.

Music was central in every sense. Space was made for 'orchestras', usually assembled from the classical core of harmonium plus tabla and nakkara drums, also amplified by western instruments such as the clarinet. The critic Ania Loomba describes an Urdu version of *Othello* performed in 1918 that opens with Brabantio entertaining the hero with dance and music, followed by a duet between Roderigo and Iago. Sisson noted a version of *Titus Andronicus* that squeezed in an English music-hall number.

Parsi actors worked a great deal harder than most of their British brethren: they were required to sing, dance and do acrobatics, as well as have voices strong enough to carry across auditoriums packed to the rafters. Women were initially forbidden from performing, so there was competition to find sweet-voiced, girlish young men who could play female parts. Even once professional actresses began to appear from the 1870s onwards – to howls of outrage from traditionalists – men predominated, often named for their most famous roles. One, the honey-voiced Pestanji Framji Madan, became known as 'Pesu

Avan' after the character he played in a Gujarati adaptation of *Pericles*.

Competition was cut-throat. There are tales, as in Elizabethan England, that companies paid spies to attend rival performances and copy down what they heard and saw. Other companies hired claques to hiss their opponents. Audiences expected a great deal: one critic took a production of *Ali Baba and the Forty Thieves* to task for having fewer than forty thieves on stage (though conceded that the company had imported a live tree from England). The latest theatrical technology offered spectators ever-more awe-inspiring effects: trapdoors, flying beds, dazzling lighting changes, real running water.

For a flavour of what it might have been like to sit among the audience, there is the testimony of a nineteenth-century actor whose company brought a Marathi version of *Macbeth* to Mumbai:

> On the night of its first production the tumultuous enthusiasm of the audience reached such a high pitch that they continued shouting 'once more!' (meaning repeat the sleepwalking scene), declaring that they would not allow the play to continue until they were satisfied. Then the great Ganapatrao, who played Macbeth with distinction, came forward and lectured the audience: 'This is not a music-hall, where you can encore a song as many times as you like. If you still persist in your demand, realise that such a consummate piece of acting cannot be repeated devoid of its context. Yes, I shall start the whole play again, and will need three more hours to reach this point. It is already one in the morning; but I have no objection if you get the necessary police sanction.' The effect was instantaneous; the play proceeded.

There are reports of such dire warnings not succeeding, and the action shuddering to a halt in order to allow songs to be sung three, four, five extra times. Some shows dragged on until dawn.

Above all, this was Indianised Shakespeare: as well as being translated into Indian languages, the plays were freely relocated to the subcontinent and adjusted for local conditions. In the New Alfred Dramatic Company's Urdu *Twelfth Night* from 1905, Dilera, Princess of Baghdad (Viola), and Jafar (Sebastian) are travelling on a train rather than a ship when they are caught in bad weather. A bridge collapses, the twins are flung into the water far below – Shakespeare's storm reimagined for the largest railway nation in the world.

Worlds often collide in Parsi scripts, mirroring the cosmopolitan

make-up of Mumbai. A Parsi *Hamlet* renamed *Khoon-e-Nahaq*
('Unjustified Killing/Blood') from 1898 featured stage designs closely
based on reports of Henry Irving's hugely popular British production,
but was set in a medieval Indian court filled with Kathak dancers, and
out of respect to its Muslim context Gertrude was poisoned with a
glass of milk rather than wine. An Urdu *Comedy of Errors* from 1912
by the well-known playwright Narayan Prasad Betab, nicely renamed
Gorakh Dhandha ('A Puzzle'), opens with, of all things, a spectacular
scene in a coal mine. 'It has not,' writes the scholar R. K. Yajnik,
whose 1933 study of Indian theatre is still invaluable, 'reverence for
the original.'

Yajnik was perhaps missing the point. Parsi theatre managers and
playwrights had little interest in reverence; their driving need was to
cram in audiences and beat their competitors. The Lucknow-born
playwright Syed Mehdi Hasan Ahsan, who began working in the
Parsi theatre in the late 1890s and was one of the earliest to translate
Shakespeare into Urdu – *Khoon-e-Nahaq* is his – put it like this in the
preface to *Bazm-e-Fani* (1898), the adaptation of *Romeo and Juliet* Sisson
had mentioned:

> I have not taken the help of Shakespeare's poetic imagination, but built
> a little mosque of my own design because, in my opinion, Shakespeare's
> way of thinking does not harmonise with the Indian way of thinking.
> That is why the plays have been greatly altered.

'A mosque of my own design': the metaphor chosen by Ahsan, a
Muslim, is revealing. Shakespeare may have provided the foundations,
but Parsi playwrights felt little compunction about demolishing his
dramatic fabric and rebuilding plays from the ground up.

To me, one of the most appealing facets of these adaptations is
the way they sometimes cock a snook at the very people who had
exported Shakespeare to India as part of the noble colonial project,
the British. An early version of *The Taming of the Shrew* performed at
Surat in 1852 has the literal title 'A Bad European Woman Brought to
her Senses'.

Even more deliciously, the scholar Poonam Trivedi records a Hindi
version of *The Comedy of Errors* from 1882 by Munshi Ratan Chand that
bears some fascinating changes. In Shakespeare's version of the story,
just as the plot builds to its climax, there is a scene in which the horrified

servant Dromio – continually being mistaken for his twin brother – tells his master how he is being pursued by a 'kitchen wench . . . all grease' who has convinced herself he is her lover. 'She is spherical, like a globe,' Dromio says, then launches into a laboured series of similes identifying precisely which bits of the 'globe' she reminds him of:

ANTIPHOLUS In what part of her body stands Ireland?

DROMIO Marry, sir, in her buttocks. I found it out by the bogs.

ANTIPHOLUS Where Scotland?

DROMIO I found it by the barrenness, hard in the palm of her hand.

ANTIPHOLUS Where France?

DROMIO In her forehead, armed and reverted, making war against her heir.

ANTIPHOLUS Where England?

DROMIO I looked for the chalky cliffs, but I could find no whiteness in them. But I guess it stood in her chin, by the salt rheum that ran between France and it.

ANTIPHOLUS Where Spain?

DROMIO Faith, I saw it not, but I felt it hot in her breath.

ANTIPHOLUS Where America, the Indies?

DROMIO O, sir, upon her nose, all o'er embellished with rubies, carbuncles, sapphires, declining their rich aspect to the hot breath of Spain, who sent whole armadas of carracks to be ballast at her nose.

ANTIPHOLUS Where stood Belgia, the Netherlands?

DROMIO O, sir, I did not look so low.

It is rough stuff: that line about the 'heir' must have got a boozy groan at the law college of Gray's Inn, where *Errors* was performed in December 1594. But this comic Grand Tour must also have resonated with Shakespeare's well-to-do audience, who would have heard of the places Dromio mentions, even if they had never visited.

Working on his adaptation – wittily entitled *Bhramjalak Natak* ('A Web of Confusion') – Ratan Chand realised that although his own audience in late-nineteenth-century Mumbai was more cosmopolitan, the scene needed an overhaul. Several of his alterations are worth observing. First, the 'Indies' (here referring to America) are gone; and instead of a nod to England's 'chalky cliffs' at Dover, it is India that stands, patriotically, 'in [the woman's] face, for just as Hindustan is the best of all countries, so was her face the best part of her person'.

Second, England doesn't disappear entirely – it is relegated to the location occupied by the Netherlands in Shakespeare's text, the bottom. 'This was such a tiny country,' Chand's Dromio character scornfully remarks, 'that exceedingly hard as I looked, I could find it nowhere. It must be hidden among those parts of the body I didn't look at.'

I found this gratifying: Shakespeare's text not only translated, but used to reorder the world according to an Indian perspective. The tiny, frigid British Isles were exactly where they should be – at the arse-end of nowhere.

DOUBLE CHIN REMOVAL, read the sign. JAW LINE ENHANCEMENT.

I was outside the address, or thought I was, but all I could see were dilapidated apartment blocks, paint coming off the concrete, and a scattering of small businesses. I wasn't expecting armies of men carrying clapperboards, but I'd been hoping for more from my first visit to a Bollywood studio than this. Was the studio doubling as a Botox clinic? Could it be hidden inside the estate agent's next door?

Just after 9.30 a.m., I was already dead on my feet. Jostling north through Mumbai at rush hour had been like swimming through an onrush of warm tar. It had taken the taxi the best part of two hours to get here from my hotel in the southern district of Marine Lines, a journey of roughly sixteen miles. The driver had pleaded to take the Worli suspension bridge, which elegantly solves the problem of Mumbai's geography – the fact that much of it is concentrated in a narrow spit of sand less than a mile wide – by ignoring it altogether, swooping out from Worli beach in a lordly sweep before reconnecting with dry land a few miles further north. Miscalculating the exchange rate of the toll, I'd insisted we go through the city instead. Every so often, as we got wedged in a hooting mob of motor rickshaws or overflowing buses, young men clinging casually to the doors, I caught his weary glance in the rear-view mirror. I had a lot to learn about Mumbai.

Fretful about the time, I tried to extract the phone number of my producer contact from the tangle of notes and figures on my pad. I'd got lucky, getting this interview (which is to say it had taken a phalanx of phone calls and the intercession of a friend of a friend). I was in danger of losing my slot.

Vishal Bhardwaj was high on my Bollywood hit list. A composer-director from the rural northern state of Uttar Pradesh, he had burst on to the international scene in 2003 with his film *Maqbool*, a startling remake of *Macbeth* that translated the play into a sleazy underworld version of modern-day Mumbai. Renowned Bollywood tough guy Irrfan Khan played a hit man bent on taking over a Muslim crime gang; the Witches were recast as corrupt cops obsessed with *kundli* astrology. Bhardwaj had followed this surprise hit with the lavish *Omkara* (2006), in which a muscle-bound enforcer called Omkara/Othello – the illegitimate son of a low-caste mother – romances the high-born, 'fair-skinned' Dolly, played by the screen siren Kareena Kapoor.

Smartly contemporary, made with an eye on the box office as well as anxieties about crime rates and caste tensions, Bhardwaj's were a new breed of Indian Shakespeare adaptation. They had made the outside world at long last pay attention to the fact that Shakespeare was a major presence in the subcontinent.

After several phone calls and twenty minutes' searching, I located VB Productions on the fifth floor of an accommodation block marginally more run-down than the rest. Released from the tiny cage elevator, I was rushed through a dark apartment, crammed with young faces crouched over laptops. It looked more like a student flat share than a movie office.

Near the back was a space roughly the size of the front room in my one-bed London flat. It had been converted into a recording studio. In a glass booth on one side, not much larger than a phone box, a teenage male singer with bee-stung lips was pouting into a microphone. On the other, sitting in front of a small red harmonium and surrounded by a bevy of technicians, was Bhardwaj himself: a small figure with plump, genial features and a pudding-bowl haircut frizzed with grey. I was issued a cup of sweet tea and directed to a corner stool to observe.

They were halfway through recording one of the songs for the new VB movie, a ghost thriller called *Ek Thi Daayan* ('Once There Was a Witch'). Seeing them record was a drama in itself. Bhardwaj would issue a stream of instructions in rat-a-tat Hindi, his right hand cresting the air in little curlicues and waves. The singer watched him apprehensively, as if trying to remember a complex series of road directions. Then a pre-recorded guitar track, a sultry love ballad, would blast out at full volume. The singer would croon a couple of notes, whereupon

Bhardwaj would interrupt to correct some indiscernible accent of phrasing or gesture – a shade more vibrato here, less of a swoop there. They would go again, Bhardwaj occasionally demonstrating on the harmonium. There was one English word I understood amid the Hindi. 'Heartfelt,' he kept saying. 'Heartfelt.'

They spent fifteen minutes on the first section of the first phrase alone. Many popular Indian films relied on a hit song – and the free air time and advertising – to turn a profit, but it wasn't just this: the songs Bhardwaj wrote were miniature masterpieces, crafted with the kind of care that was going out of fashion in mainstream Hindi film. Watching him at work was like seeing a poet in the frenzy of creation.

After half an hour, the wrung-out-looking singer was dispatched to take a break, and Bhardwaj guided me through yet another door to a corner office. It contained little more than a desk and two chairs, with a scruffy divan folded in the corner.

He was an accidental Shakespearian, he admitted. He'd been forced to learn Shakespeare in English Literature lessons at school, but hadn't thought much of him – deadly boring, painful to read. He mimicked throttling someone. 'If you see him alive, you want to kill him.'

All that changed in the early 2000s when Bhardwaj went to collect his godson for the holidays. They'd been travelling on a train to Mussoorie in the far north, a five-hour journey. Casting around for something to read, Bhardwaj had borrowed his godson's *Tales from Shakespeare*.

At the time he'd been trying to develop a gangster film, a tribute to *The Godfather* with shadings of Japanese *noir*. He'd been stuck: no plot. But when he found himself reading, then rereading, Charles and Mary Lamb's 1807 prose adaptation of *Macbeth*, he realised there could be a script that combined this story with hints of Coppola and Kurosawa, all set in Mumbai. Back in the city, he got hold of a copy of the play itself. He had his script.

I'd watched *Maqbool* again on DVD a few days before coming out; what I hadn't realised before arriving was how it caught the mood of the city: its stifling atmosphere, its swampy mist and murk, the sea always lapping at its ankles.

Bhardwaj laughed shyly. 'Yes, the city became the character, the hero of the film, almost. But I was ignorant. I didn't know the weight and burden of Shakespeare.'

Did he really find it a burden?

'Obviously, who doesn't respect Shakespeare, but I try not to keep him on that pedestal, do you know? When I see British or American films, they are so over-burdened. I treat him more like my co-writer.' He waved distractedly at his office: the divan, the pile of papers in the corner. 'I ask him to come down and sit with me and have a drink, let's talk it out.'

Had Shakespeare's name been good for box office?

He looked incredulous: clearly I didn't understand the first thing about Indian movies. 'With *Maqbool*, one of the financers told me, "Script is good. But one thing – please – I will give you money – take out Shakespeare's name. If people see that it is being based on Shakespeare, they won't come to watch the film."' He laughed. 'Money-minds think all alike. Lucky he was wrong.'

Shakespeare's presence had been a blessing in disguise; not only had Indian audiences watched and enjoyed the film, it had got Bhardwaj noticed on the international festival circuit. *Maqbool* had been invited to Toronto, *Omkara* shown at Cannes: rare honours for a non-art-house Indian film-maker.

He was currently on the hunt for another play to adapt. He was wavering between *Hamlet* and *King Lear*.

His eyes glittered. 'You tell me, you are the scholar. Which one should I do?'

Both could be interesting prospects, I said. What was he looking for?

'For me, character is important. Like in *Macbeth*, I find Lady Macbeth the reason to make the film; in *Othello*, Iago was the reason. If I make *Lear*, Edmund will be the reason. Sleeping with both the sisters, the sisters kill each other . . .' He laughed. 'This father–daughter thing is fine, but for me Edmund is the person. Oh God, he's so full of *masala* – spice, you know.' He wriggled his head. 'Such a good character.'

Given that he was a Kurosawa fan, I wondered if he had seen *The Bad Sleep Well*, a skulking 1960 adaptation of *Hamlet* that recast the Prince as a quiet salaryman adrift in a world of grief. Its downbeat mood, set in the shadows of postwar Japanese society, might appeal.

'A contemporary work?' He scribbled something on a pad. 'It will be very interesting to see.'

Months later, I read that Bhardwaj had announced his next film. *Hamlet* it was to be.

On 7 July 1896 the event occurred that would, eventually, change Parsi theatre for good. A French chemist and entrepreneur named Marius Sestier, en route to Australia via Mumbai, staged an exhibition showing off the brand-new gizmo he had brought with him. *The Times of India* carried adverts for 'the marvel of the century, the wonder of the world'. The venue was Watson's, one of the city's grandest hotels. Only Europeans were allowed entry.

The device Sestier brought was ingenious. A wooden box the size of a small briefcase, it had a lens at the front and a hand crank behind. Pointed one way, it was a motion-picture camera; opened up, with a magic lantern shining through, it became a projector. Sestier's employers, Auguste and Louis Lumière, called it the *'Cinématographe'*. The new art form it made possible – moving images captured wherever the camera could be taken, and replayed for a watching audience – they christened *cinématographie*.

The machine had only previously been seen in Paris, Brussels, New York and London. On the bill in Mumbai were the short films that had astounded French audiences: the thirty-eight-second *La Mer*, with its haunting depiction of waves piling on to the beach and bathers leaping into the flood. The fifty-second *L'Arrivée d'un train en gare de La Ciotat*, whose depiction of a moving train had caused, according to one witness, 'fear, terror, even panic' when it was shown in France. (In Mumbai, *L'Arrivée* seems to have been watched with equanimity, its inhabitants perhaps more accustomed to the goings-on of railways.) The *Bombay Gazette* was particularly taken with *Workers Leaving the Lumière Factory*, which brought 'a whole crowd of moving humanity onto the canvas'. Within weeks, shows were a near-nightly occurrence. India's movie craze had begun.

Among the audiences for an early screening – one that admitted Indians – was a photographer from Maharashtra called Harishchandra Sakharam Bhatvadekar, better known as Save Dada. Entranced by what he saw, Dada ordered a motion-picture camera from London and used it to film what was around him – Indian scenes of 'moving humanity', ones that would appeal to local audiences. Dada's first 'Topical' was a wrestling bout at Mumbai's Hanging Gardens, and in December 1901 he shot the return from Britain of the Indian mathematics student Raghunath Paranjpe, who had scored triumphant success at Cambridge.

But Indian audiences were also hungry for fiction. A thousand miles east in Kolkata, another photographer, Hiralal Sen, and his brother, Motilal, had the idea of doing something novel with the new technology: filming plays. The Sens' first moving picture seems to have been a dancing scene from the popular drama *The Flower of Persia* filmed in 1901. Intrepid entrepreneurs, they were responsible for another first, making perhaps the earliest Indian cinema adverts, for Edward's Tonic and Jabakusum hair oil.

One of the biggest names in early Indian cinema, the legendary J. F. Madan, professionalised the movies and made them into an Indian industry. Brother of the famous 'Pesu Avan' who had starred in that Parsi *Pericles*, J. F. had begun his career as an actor in Mumbai, playing Shakespearian adaptations. Later, he became a ferociously successful businessman, and in the 1890s, acquired the Elphinstone and Khatau-Alfred Parsi theatre companies. By 1902, as well as motley interests in insurance, pharmaceuticals and food-and-drink imports, he had relocated to Kolkata to set up what became Madan Theatres, an early theatre monopoly. When the company decided to retain the services of two enormously successful Parsi playwrights – Narayan Prasad Betab and Agha Hashr Kashmiri – the Shakespearian circle was complete.

Betab's name I recalled from that perplexing-sounding version of *The Comedy of Errors* set partly in a coal mine; Hashr, meanwhile, would be the one who most clearly bridged the gap between Shakespeare and cinema, and whose life story reveals much about changing tastes in Indian entertainment.

Born in Varanasi in 1879 to a Kashmiri family of shawl-makers, Hashr became fluent in both Urdu and Hindi, later learning Persian and Arabic. He published his first play at the precocious age of eighteen, whereupon he decamped to Mumbai and began writing for Parsi troupes. A photograph of Hashr taken in his late thirties or forties depicts a studious, otherworldly-looking man at his desk, a book open on his knees. But the plays that made his name were anything but academic. *Bilwa Mangal* is named for a poet who falls in frenzied love with a prostitute; *Aankh ka Nasha* ('Intoxication of the Eyes') is set in a brothel. Hashr's Urdu adaptations of pre-existing texts went further, pushing the boundaries of what it was acceptable to show on the Indian stage.

Scholars have dismissed him as a hack, but I found Hashr's reinterpretations of Shakespeare engrossing. He raided the plays with encyclopaedic efficiency, ransacking them for hair-raising moments and effects but paying almost no attention to context. Lady Macbeth's sleepwalking scene crops up almost verbatim in his *Khwab-e-Hasti* ('Dreams of Grandeur') from 1909, fitted into a plot that bears little relation to the original; while *Said-e-Havas* ('Captive of Desire', 1907) filches a melodramatic scene from *King John*, in which the virtuous young Prince Arthur is threatened with murder by an assassin, and squeezes it into a storyline drawn from *Richard III*. Even ostensibly original plays by Hashr are so suffused with Shakespeare that scholars can't agree whether they are adaptations or not.

Hashr's *Shaheed-e-Naz* ('Martyr to Charm', 1902) is an eloquent example. It borrows many of the elements of *Measure for Measure* – disguised ruler, lecherous deputy, sinful brother, virtuous woman – but rearranges them as if on a chessboard. Instead of Duke Vincentio adopting disguise to spy on his morally dubious deputy Angelo (who falls for the virtuous Isabella when she comes to plead for her brother's life), Hashr's play opens with a bodyguard attempting to murder a ruler who has been too merciful to the man who propositioned *his* sister. Only then does the ruler adopt disguise.

Despite the contortions of this new plot, it is hard not to feel that some things are an improvement – notably the bed trick in which the Angelo character is gulled into sleeping with the wrong woman. In *Measure for Measure*, as in *All's Well That Ends Well*, the device strains credibility (would a man not realise?) but Hashr accomplished it easily: his Isabella character simply gets the Muslim, non-drinking Angelo drunk.

After working for various organisations in both Mumbai and Kolkata, Hashr decided to form his own troupe around 1910. In tribute to the writer who had gifted him so much, he called it the Indian Shakespeare Theatrical Company. In time Hashr became known as *Shakespeare-e-Hind*, the 'Shakespeare of India'. In 1916, he joined Madan Theatres, then busily remaking itself into a film company.

Initially, Parsi troupes coexisted peacefully with the movie industry, particularly during the silent period: little competition from grainy black-and-white shorts. But when a director called Dadasaheb Phalke released the first full-length Indian feature film, the forty-minute *Raja Harishchandra* (1913), based on the same mythological sources that furnished many Parsi playwrights with material, theatre-makers began to panic. Actors and writers decamped; dramatic companies rushed to rebrand themselves as film studios.

In March 1931, when synchronous sound finally arrived in India with the spectacular historical drama *Alam Ara*, billed as 'all-talking, singing, & dancing', it was the death knell. Not only did the movie boast seven songs, beating the theatre companies at their own game, it was based on a popular Parsi play. A film made the following year, *Indrasabha* ('Indra's Court'), had an awesome seventy songs. The Parsi troupes that were left either folded or were unceremoniously thrown out of their theatres so that they could be converted into cinemas. By the mid-1930s the movie business was second only to textiles as the main industry in Mumbai.

Hashr, though, was fortunate: film, which he'd been wise enough to join early on, conferred on him a kind of immortality. When the playwright passed away at the age of fifty-six on 28 April 1935, cinemas and studios across India closed their doors in mourning. Shakespeare-e-Hind had become the most famous playwright, poet and screenwriter the country had ever known.

If modern Hindi films had a Hashr, I was told, it was a man known as Gulzar. As writer, screenwriter, lyricist and director, Gulzar *saab* had bestridden Bollywood for decades: the nearest thing Mumbai movies had to a living patron saint. He was about to be given the Dadasaheb Phalke prize, the highest award in Indian cinema, not to mention an Oscar and a Grammy for lyrics he composed for a song in Danny Boyle's *Slumdog Millionaire*. Nearly eighty, he had been in the business for fifty years – old-school Bollywood royalty.

After weeks of correspondence that made my attempts to track down Vishal Bhardwaj seem effortless, I was finally granted an audience. Nasreen, a British Indian documentary-making friend who had helped with the fraught late-stage diplomacy, offered to help translate. I suspect she doubted it would actually happen.

The house was in the exclusive suburb of Pali Hill, a winding incline draped prettily with gulmohar and almond trees that made the mania in the rest of Mumbai seem like a bad dream. As the electric front gate hushed closed behind us, a female assistant welcomed us into a cool, shaded entrance hall and whisked away our shoes. We were ushered through yet another antechamber into the main office-cum-lounge, lined with books and expensive-looking *objets*. From a wall full of DVDs, the sculpted bust of what looked like Nefertiti gazed implacably out.

Next to Nefertiti, and nearly as forbidding, was a ramrod-straight figure in a white kurta. He sat behind an enormous black desk crowded with books and papers. His white hair was swept into a high fringe; a luxuriant moustache, also white, gave him an austere, schoolmasterly air. He placed down his iPad, and inclined his head modestly to greet us.

The reason I'd been eager to interview Gulzar is that he had kept alive a tradition begun by writers like Betab and Hashr, one that seems near-impossible in the cinematic world of the west: making Shakespearian comedy into big, broad box office.

One of his most famous films was *Angoor* from 1982, a classic starring the late-lamented star Sanjeev Kumar. The remarkable thing about *Angoor* (remarkable at least to me) was that it is a faithful update of *The Comedy of Errors* – two pairs of identical but separated twins, mistaken identities, shipwreck, the lot. Barring the Rodgers-Hart musical *The Boys from Syracuse* and the BBC's earnest television version of 1983 (a contractual obligation of their complete-works series), *The Comedy of Errors* has never been filmed in anything like its original form in the west. To have made *The Comedy of Errors* into a movie at all, still less made it a commercial success, seemed an unlikely achievement.

In India, however, Gulzar explained, the story has always been a hit. Fittingly for a script about multiple sets of twins, something like six separate cinematic versions had been made in the past fifty years. *Angoor* itself was based on two earlier movies: a literary Bengali version called *Bhranti Bilas* (1963); and a Hindi one wittily called *Do Dooni Char* ('Two Times Two Equals Four', 1968).

He emitted an avuncular chuckle. 'You know the Bollywood interpretation of copyright? We call it the right to copy.'

Sanjeev Kumar, by then one of the most recognisable faces in Bollywood, had been persuaded to make *Angoor* on the basis that he would get quite literally double the screen time, playing both Antipholus characters, here called Ashok. One Ashok is living a contented if not wholly blameless life in a quiet modern-day Indian town with his wife, sister-in-law and a mistress around the corner; the other Ashok just happens to be in the area. The character actor Deven Verma played the Bahadurs, servants to the

Ashoks. Screen trickery did the rest. *Angoor* means 'grapes' in Hindi. Gulzar permitted himself a smile: it was as wilfully nonsensical as anything else.

'There are plenty of stories of twins, but two sets of twins – that was only Shakespeare. There is no other example in literature anywhere that I have come across. So I wanted to adapt it.'

There was even a cunning Shakespearian joke for those watching out for it, right at the film's conclusion, when the series of confusions came to an end and the two sets of twins were finally reunited.

ASHOK I OK, tell me. Do you have a mole on your right shoulder?
ASHOK II No.
ASHOK I Neither do I. We must be brothers, then! [*laughs*]

The reference is to the climax of *Twelfth Night*, when Viola and her long-lost twin Sebastian confirm each other's identities by describing the 'mole' on their father's brow. I thought it a nicely nonchalant touch.

Gulzar shrugged. 'We talk about adaptation, but of course this is the same process for Shakespeare: he himself is adapting, from Plautus, from other comedies. That's how it is.'

I wondered if there was another reason *The Comedy of Errors* proved attractive to Indian film-makers. As its critics were forever lamenting, Bollywood had long been dominated by the requirements of genre, expectations about character types or plot development as rigid as medieval chivalric codes or the operation of the Japanese tea ceremony. Despite its Shakespearian ancestry, *Angoor* also fitted neatly into the category of so-called 'lost-and-found' movies.

Films such as *Kismet*, *Awara*, *Waqt* and the most renowned classic of all, *Mother India* (1957), portray nuclear families broken up by circumstances beyond the characters' control – an errant or absent husband, natural disaster, the intercession of violence or evil. *Waqt* ('Time', 1965) begins with an earthquake that sunders a husband, wife and their three sons. The action-comedy *Amar Akbar Anthony* (1977) features a plot line that would have given even Shakespeare migraines: three brothers are separated as children and raised in three separate households in three different religions. After a preposterous series of coincidences, all are reunited to take revenge on their mutual foe.

The lost-and-found genre didn't merely allow for a blizzard of joyous confusion. It was also, like many things in Bollywood, a way to reflect Indian audiences' concerns and anxieties back at them. Millions of families had been wrenched apart during the partition of India and Pakistan in 1947; increasing urbanisation had separated millions more. Religion, class, caste, wealth: India remained, as the newspaper headlines kept insisting, a country fractiously divided. In a land of 1.25 billion people and growing, it would not be hard, like the Ashoks, to lose yourself.

There was one moment I was especially keen to know about in *Angoor*: the final few frames, which depicted a portrait of Shakespeare played by an elderly Indian actor sporting beard and ruff – a frank acknowledgement of Gulzar's source, but also (it seemed to me) a kind of repossession, a literal demonstration that Shakespeare was now Indian.

Gulzar smiled thinly: top marks. 'I didn't want to make Shakespeare English. I didn't want him to be a stranger to the audience. You know, one reason Shakespeare is so good is that he is a mix. You have heard of *nautanki*?'

Nandini had mentioned it, the folk theatre popular in northern India; it had influenced Parsi theatre too.

'*Nautanki* is a mixed form, prose, poetry, songs, music. A comedian also, for a relief for the audience. Those shows went on all night. Indian screenplays, they're long – three hours, four hours. We used to have regular comedians, too, as part of the subplot, to engage the audience. Shakespeare does that, like the gravedigger in *Hamlet*. He knows how to keep the audience engaged.'

Rising to show us out, he paused. 'I was talking to Vishal Bhardwaj just now on the phone,' he said. 'You know he is thinking about a new movie? I encouraged him. I said, "The ground belongs to Shakespeare, you have built your house on it."'

A learned reference to Syed Mehdi Hasan Ahsan's 'mosque', or happy coincidence? Bollywood was full of copies, after all.

He bowed formally and, Hollywood-style, also offered me his hand. 'This is the right way of putting it: the land belongs to Shakespeare, the house belongs to us.'

Everything in Mumbai had a touch of melodrama. The sober broadsheet pushed under the door of my hotel room was a hair-raising read, full of cartoonish journalese that wouldn't have disgraced William Randolph Hearst's hacks at their yellowest. 'Gay Man Faces Cops' Chin Music,' read one headline about a man who'd been violently attacked by police. 'Dalit Honour Killing: Kin Against Tardy CID Probe,' read another. Even dull-as-ditchwater stories about rail fares were given the gee-whizz subediting treatment. Indian CNBC's coverage of the forthcoming budget was being advertised on billboards forty feet high.

These were as nothing, though, compared to the real news: Bollywood and its comings and goings. Every paper had a lavish colour section containing the latest *filmi* gossip, and on the web things were more breathless still. I tried to get my head around the cast of characters: a parade of interchangeable nymphets, typically papped on the arms of rugged older men on their way into tedious-looking PR events. The stories were tissue thin: a male actor was proclaimed to 'have feelings' for a female colleague because a dance sequence had been mildly rearranged; a minor disagreement on Twitter had spiralled (opined a source, anonymous of course) into a venomous 'cat fight'.

Even so, Bollywood seemed innocent, certainly compared with the hard-bitten celebrity coverage of the US or Britain. There was talk of 'crushes' and 'dating'; a screen kiss in this still-conservative society was a major event. And it was a world on first-name terms: Sallu, SRK, Big B, Bebo, Chi Chi ('little finger' in Punjabi, but which had somewhat ruder connotations when applied to the actor Govinda). Bollywood seemed simultaneously to share the characteristics of a shimmering royal court and the dysfunctional family just down the street.

I delighted in the lingo. 'B-Town' was, grandiosely, a Bollywood metonym for Mumbai. A 'grey role' was one in which an actor who specialised in villainous characters attempted to transition to more sympathetic ones. 'Item number' I'd heard before: the dubious tradition of shoehorning in an arousing dance sequence regardless of the plot ('item' being a derogatory term for the women who danced). To my disappointment, a 'starer' wasn't a film one *stared* at in horror or surprise, but a film *starring* someone big (*videt*, 'multi-starer'). I liked the concept of 'acting pricey' – getting above yourself, especially on set.

No wonder lexicographers agree that Indian English – melded by the newest technologies, hungrily absorbing parcels of languages such as Hindi and Punjabi – is not just a dialect but a language in its own right. In the west, it's often treated as the butt of a joke: there is a bestselling book called *Entry from Backside Only* devoted to what are perceived as the Mistress Quickly-level malapropisms of 'Indlish' or 'Hinglish' – turning the concept of 'passing time' into a noun, 'timepass'; or 'preponing' (instead of postponing) appointments by moving them forward, etc.

Such things are still often dismissed with a snigger, particularly as many of these linguistic innovations come from the ground up, from the millions of Indians working their way out of poverty by taking English lessons and getting a middle-class job in the IT or service sectors. But I relished the language. It made the English that came out of my own mouth sound ponderous and auntly. I couldn't help feeling that Shakespeare – a worshipper of the crowdedly over-extended metaphor and the crafty half-buried meaning – would have warmed to it, too.

There is certainly one way he would have found the Indian film world congenial. Gulzar was dead right: Shakespeare's plays, like a significant percentage of commercial Indian cinema, are magnificent in their unoriginality.

For all that people instinctively regard him as a supreme creator, it is more accurate to describe the playwright as a uniquely gifted magpie who plundered everything around him for clues, hints, suggestions, anything that could fire an idea. The written sources he read and digested were in the hundreds, and are still being chased down; less durable influences (phrases borrowed, people met or observed) will surely never be recovered. The more time one spends with Shakespeare, the more one realises his world is a glittering collage of others' worlds; that his brilliance lies in his ability to make something fresh from the most trite and cliché-ridden of materials.

The post-Romantic obsession with solitary, remote genius would have been near-unrecognisable to Shakespeare and his contemporaries. During the Renaissance, the concept known as *copia*, the ability to present humdrum matter with abundance and grace – and thus exhibit one's learning – was a cornerstone of the education system. Grammar-school boys like Shakespeare were expected to be copious, and drilled relentlessly so they might become so: inscribing set phrases from writers ancient and modern into their commonplace books, memorising and regurgitating biblical quotations, learning to scan and fillet texts for anything recyclable. Desiderius Erasmus's textbook *De duplici copia verborum ac rerum* ('On the Twofold Abundance of Expressions and Ideas', 1512), famously includes several hundred different ways to say 'thank you for your letter'.

For moderns, the word 'imitation' carries the taint of something plagiarised, knocked-off; for Elizabethan writers, schooled in the Erasmian arts of *imitatio*, it was high praise. The critic Robert Miola puts it nicely: 'The genius lay not in the invention but in the translation.'

Translation was what Shakespeare spent much of his life engaged in: literally from sources in languages such as Latin, ancient Greek, French and Italian; but also from English texts in many forms – histories, books of philosophy, avant-garde poetry, sermons, official documents, broadsides, other plays. The most thoroughgoing attempt to trace and reprint these texts, Geoffrey Bullough's monumental *Narrative and Dramatic Sources of Shakespeare*, fills eight stout volumes, occupied its author from 1957 to 1975, and even then is judged incomplete. Shakespeare apparently found it impossible to write without first examining from every conceivable angle what others had done with similar material, only then working out how to overmaster them.

Take *Othello*, the play Vishal Bhardwaj had so smartly remade as *Omkara*. Shakespeare's primary source was a tale from 1565 by the Ferrarese scholar Giambattista Giraldi, nicknamed Cinthio, which gave him the outline of a scheming ensign who convinces his Moorish captain that the captain's wife has been unfaithful. (No English version seems to have been available in the early 1600s when Shakespeare was writing the play, so he must have read Cinthio in Italian or French.) To this Shakespeare added picturesque real-life details drawn from a translation of Gasparo Contarini's account of Venetian government, Richard Knolles's *The Generall Historie of the Turks* (1603), Pliny the Elder's *Natural History* and a travelogue from 1550 by the Tunisian diplomat and writer Leo Africanus, translated into English as *A Geographical Historie of Africa* (1600).

Leo, born a Muslim and enslaved by Christian pirates, was freed by Pope Leo X (hence his adopted name) and converted to Christianity; his unusual life story might have supplied a model for the character of Othello, as might the 1600 visit to London of the Moroccan ambassador Abd el-Ouahed ben Messaoud ben Mohammed Anoun. Even the hero's name – one thing none of these sources supplied – is not entirely original. The first version of Ben Jonson's play *Every Man in his Humour* (1598) has a jealous husband called Thorello; Shakespeare borrowed the idea, changing the syllables just enough to get away with it.

Another example of Shakespeare's shameless willingness to borrow from others comes in *Antony and Cleopatra*. Enobarbus's lustrous set-piece speech about the Egyptian queen is deservedly famous:

The barge she sat in, like a burnished throne
Burned on the water. The poop was beaten gold;
Purple the sails, and so perfumèd that
The winds were love-sick with them. The oars were silver,
Which to the tune of flutes kept stroke [. . .]

Yet the play is so intimate with its source, Plutarch's *Lives of the Noble Grecians and Romans* in the 1579 translation by Thomas North, that the similarities are uncanny:

To take [Cleopatra's] barge in the river of Cydnus, the poop whereof was of gold, the sails of purple, and the oars of silver, which kept stroke in rowing after the sound of the music of flutes, howboys, citherns, viols, and such other instruments as they played upon in the barge. And now for the person of herself: she was laid under a pavilion of cloth of gold of tissue, apparelled and attired like the goddess Venus commonly drawn in picture; and hard by her, on either hand of her, pretty fair boys apparelled as painters do set forth god Cupid, with little fans in their hands, with the which they fanned wind upon her . . .

Here *copia* comes perilously close to outright copying. Despite being renowned as an example of Shakespeare's surging late style, Enobarbus's speech is largely in the voice of Plutarch filtered through Thomas North. Only a few deft poetical touches lift it from workmanlike historianese into scintillating brilliance: 'beaten gold' for the poop; 'tune of flutes kept stroke' rather than 'kept stroke in rowing after the sound of music of flutes'.

Shakespeare may have sometimes borrowed too much, even by broad Jacobethan standards. In 1592, when the Warwickshireman was emerging as a dramatist in London, the playwright Robert Greene accused Shakespeare of plagiarism, calling him 'an upstart Crow, beautified with our feathers' – a young pretender who stole from his older, better-educated betters. Shakespeare perhaps remembered the slight, and got his own back. Nearly two decades later, his rival long since dead, he filched a story from Greene's novella *Pandosto* of a king who becomes convinced that his wife has slept with his best friend. The play became *The Winter's Tale*.

'Translation, not invention': I thought of Bollywood, and what the film critic Tejaswini Ganti has theorised as the process of 'Indianising' pre-existing cinematic material, either films from the west or older Indian classics – not quite remakes, exactly, more a subtle process of ingestion and digestion that went back to Indian cinema's origins in Parsi theatre and its own extravagant amalgam of sources. Gulzar's description of Indian copyright as the 'right to copy' was glib (and, for that matter, second-hand – I heard the line in India at least twice), but it wasn't a million miles from the truth. The Indian Copyright Act, amended in 1999, has an unusually wide conception of what exists in the public domain, and vests originality in how an idea is *expressed* rather than the idea itself. In the UK and US, the law focuses on the idea's intrinsic originality, which results in something much more restrictive.

Shakespeare, who worked in a world where intellectual property was at best an uncertain and emerging concept, would surely have fitted into this environment with ease. It was sometimes said that if he were alive now, he would be working as a Hollywood screenwriter. I wondered whether he mightn't have been happier right here in Mumbai.

Needless to say, the British had intended none of this. Determined to impose their own brand of education upon their subject populations, they had brought Shakespeare to the newly founded schools of India and other colonies partly as an instrument of political control. It was in the classroom that the colonial master could be obediently copied, a new class of Indians forged.

Though English had been taught in missionary schools from the early eighteenth century, it wasn't until the beginning of the nineteenth that the project became systematised. After the signing of the Charter Act of 1813, which brought the Indian territories controlled by the almighty East India Company under the direct control of the British crown, western-style academic institutions began to flourish. The first, the Hindu College in Kolkata, was founded in 1817; similar colleges followed in Mumbai, Pune, Chennai and elsewhere. But a thorny issue arose: what should these new colleges teach? A curriculum that reflected local conditions, languages and customs, or one imported from England? The question raged between so-called 'Anglicists' and 'Orientalists'. In the end, the Anglicists won: if India was to be dragged out of backwardness and barbarity, then it needed the guiding light of European education.

One man who certainly believed so was Thomas Babington Macaulay, who in 1834, still many years away from completing his epic *History of England*, travelled to India and returned to Britain flushed with reforming pedagogical zeal. Macaulay's 'Minute' on the subject, based on a speech he gave to parliament in February 1835 during the debates about Indian education, has become justly notorious. 'I have no knowledge of either Sanskrit or Arabic,' the Honourable Member for Leeds announced:

> but I have done what I could to form a correct estimate of their value. I have read translations of the most celebrated Arabic and Sanskrit works. I have conversed, both here and at home, with men distinguished by their proficiency in the Eastern tongues. I am quite ready to take the oriental learning at the valuation of the Orientalists themselves. I have never found one among them who could deny that a single shelf of a good European library was worth the whole native literature of India and Arabia.

That single damning sentence – a solitary shelf of a 'good' European library worth more than the output of several different languages stretching back thousands of years – proved momentous. When the English Education Act was passed later in 1835, it allocated funds to western-style educational projects only. Sanskrit and Arabic, so nonchalantly dismissed by Macaulay, were out; Shakespeare and his language – the language of government, administration, literature, empire – were in.

To get the tenor of this debate, the way it recast shabby commercial and political self-interest as an act of selfless intellectual endeavour, one need only look up the January 1850 edition of the *Edinburgh Review*, which published an account of a select committee report on the subject of 'Colonisation' given to the House of Lords in 1847. It contains the following passage:

> It is a noble work to plant the foot of England and extend her sceptre by the banks of streams unnamed, and over regions yet unknown and to conquer, not by the tyrannous subjugation of inferior races, but by the victories of mind over brute matter and blind mechanic obstacles.

A yet nobler work is it to diffuse over a few created worlds the laws
of Alfred, the language of Shakespeare, and the Christian religion, the
last great heritage of man.

'Yet nobler . . .' In this account, the imposition of Shakespeare is quite
literally God's work.

Macaulay's Minute explicitly stated that his reforms were aimed at
creating 'a class of persons Indian in blood and colour, but English in
taste, in opinion, in morals and in intellect'. This, too, became reality.
In 1844, the governor general, Henry Hardinge, passed a resolution
'assuring preference in selection for public office to Indians who had
distinguished themselves in European literature'. In doing so, he ensured
that generations of aspiring Indian civil servants would experience the
night terror recorded in this anonymous mandarin's ditty, of not having
revised the doyen of late-Victorian Shakespeare critics, A. C. Bradley:

> I dreamt last night that Shakespeare's Ghost
> Sat for a civil service post.
> The English paper for that year
> Had several questions on *King Lear*
> Which Shakespeare answered very badly
> Because he hadn't read his Bradley.

Mountstuart Elphinstone, the man whose name bespatters so much
of Mumbai, was firmly on the other side of this debate. He had been
a passionate Orientalist, a knowledgeable admirer of traditional
government in the Maratha states and a respectful proponent of
Maratha culture, and as governor of Mumbai had resisted the
introduction of English. It was one of many gloomy ironies that the
college founded in his name in the city in 1856 – and at which, sixty
years later, C. J. Sisson would get a job teaching Shakespeare – became
a bastion of the new learning.

I FOUND MUMBAI A MAZE, quite apart from the traffic and the people (20
million of them, someone said, though there were so many informal
settlements no one was really sure). The city's drive to decolonise had

rendered the street plan a tangle of double meanings that would have taxed the most ingenious of semioticians. Most people still used the old names. There seemed to be a cheerful acceptance that none of us could say with certainty where we were.

What did one even call the city? The change from 'Bombay' to 'Mumbai' had happened in 1995 at the behest of a hard-line right-wing state government. The government argued that 'Bombay' was a corruption of the name for the Hindu goddess Mumbadevi, and that the city should be renamed accordingly. Others utterly rejected this theory on combined etymological and political grounds, arguing that in fact 'Bombay' derived from the Portuguese *bom bahia* ('good bay') after the old European settlement, and that to deny the city's colonial inheritance was both ignorant and ideologically dangerous. Which side one was on revealed much about one's attitude to life and politics. Wary about causing offence, I took to mumbling the name of the city until the person I was speaking to had declared their hand.

I was also trying to navigate past a number of investigative dead ends. None of the researchers I'd spoken to had been able to help me get access to Parsi theatre scripts – difficult to find, almost never translated back into English. ('I would love to get a PhD student to work on the archive,' a professor told me, 'but no one wants to do it. It's so unfashionable now, and there isn't the funding.')

A morning trip to Elphinstone College itself – a teetering nineteenth-century pile that had the morbid whimsy of a Victorian sanatorium – also turned up little. In a dank classroom deep inside the building, staff and students had listened politely as I prattled on about the nocturnal activities of C. J. Sisson. But there were no marks of his presence, or of the university dramatic societies that had given birth to the first Parsi companies in the 1850s. Shakespeare *was* still taught, one academic sighed as we patrolled the Gormenghastian corridors, but kids these days wanted 'business English': more useful on the job market. It was hard to dispute the logic.

One afternoon I walked through the crowds down Grant Road (now Maulana Shaukat Ali Road) in search of the theatres that had once clustered there. Nearly all had gone, and the early cinemas that had replaced them in the 1920s and 1930s were shuttered and forlorn, victims of multiplexes and cheap DVDs. The area known as Pila House – a corruption of 'playhouse' – had reverted to a previous incarnation: it was now the name of a famous brothel, part of the red-light district of Falkland Road/Patthe Bapurao Marg. Some forms of entertainment never went out of fashion.

At the junction of Grant and Falkland Roads, amid a jostling flow of pedestrians, yellow-and-black taxis, motorbikes and peanut-wallahs, I stood in front of the famous Alfred Talkies. It was one of the few remaining survivors, having begun life as the Ripon theatre in the 1880s, home to many Parsi plays, before converting to a picture house in 1932.

The Alfred was still an impressive sight: recently painted a daring shade of peach, it had a resplendent three-storey facade boasting a trio of Corinthian pilasters and an irregular arrangement of windows that gave it a raffish, gap-toothed appearance. A hand-painted marquee stretched the length of the first floor, advertising a battalion of macho, gun-toting Bollywood heroes. Just behind, partially obscured, I could see the older sign in blocky black letters: RIPON THEATRE. It was said that behind the screen there was still a functioning stage.

Dashing through a gap in the traffic, trying to shut out the roaring din all around me, I scrutinised the bill. The Alfred appeared to specialise in so-called 'morning shows', softcore porn spliced into old action movies or romances. An academic paper had declared these yet another example of hybridising *masala* culture, multiple ingredients stirred together to create a uniquely Indian fusion. Did I have the courage to find out? I felt my nerve failing me. I wasn't sure I could stomach a morning show, especially one seen at 4 p.m. on a Sunday.

Movies, movies, movies. Every spare millimetre of wall was covered with posters, twenty or thirty at a time. Explosions, helicopters, the smouldering eyes of lovers, pendulous bosoms, striding men in sunglasses packing heat: the requirements seemed as severe and unyielding as the Petrarchan sonnet. SUPERHIT, MEGAHIT, BLOCKBUSTER, TOP GROSSER, they yelled.

The hornet-striped rickshaws buzzing around town were emblazoned with home-made tributes: Salman Khan in the new *Ek Tha Tiger*, a stencil of Big B in the old movie *The Great Gambler*. Songs from the movies warbled from every roadside barber's stall, keening, seductive women's voices enveloped by swooning strings. One day I passed a Christian church. The sign read, 'The Oscar for Best Supporting Actor Goes to . . . God Almighty.'

Surrounded by such imprecations, it seemed churlish to resist. But I'd read so many conflicting accounts of early Indian cinematic adaptations of Shakespeare that I hardly knew where to begin. There was cautious consent that a version of *The Merchant of Venice* called *Dil Farosh* (a punning title that means 'The Seller of Hearts'/'One who Has Sold His Heart'), produced in 1927 and based on Syed Mehdi Hasan Ahsan's wildly popular adaptation from 1900, was the first full version of Shakespeare to be seen on the Indian screen. Thereafter, though, the historians splintered into vehement disagreement.

Khoon-e-Nahaq ('Unjustified Killing/Blood'), a rendering of *Hamlet* from 1928 again based on Ahsan's earlier Parsi script, might have come next; unless it was a silent version of *Cymbeline* drawn from Betab, *Meetha Zehar* ('Sweet Poison'). Some rejected this sequence entirely, insisting that *Savkari Pash* ('Moneylender's Clutches', also known as 'The Indian Shylock') from 1925 by the Marathi-Hindi director Baburao Painter was in fact the earliest *Merchant of Venice* because of its central theme.

I didn't much care who was first across the line, but how could one not adore the titles? *Zan Mureed* ('Henpecked Love'), an *Antony and Cleopatra* released in 1936; *Hathili Dulhan* ('The Stubborn Bride'), a Parsi-influenced *Taming of the Shrew* from 1932. None of these pictures had appeared in any of the British- or American-published filmographies of Shakespearian cinema I'd consulted; in fact most of them contained barely a single non-white director. Shakespeare film studies, so modish in the western academy, had done its utmost to ignore Indian cinema's rich seam of adaptations.

Were any of these movies still extant? Could one watch them? I ransacked every shop and street stall I passed. DVD boxes accumulated in my hotel room, a colourful jumble of remastered classics with eye-searing period covers, cheap pirated copies, and sleek modern releases. *Chori Chori* (roughly translatable as 'With Utmost Stealth'), a warmly admired comedy from 1956, starred Nargis – the immortal star of *Mother India*, whose portrayal of a saintly village woman battling for the sake of her sons helped the movie become one of the most famous in Indian cinematic history. Her love interest in *Chori Chori* was the suave lothario Raj Kapoor; technically the film was an unofficial remake of Frank Capra's *It Happened One Night*, but it was also reputed to borrow from *The Taming of the Shrew*. It went on the pile.

Raj was the elder brother of Shashi Kapoor, who'd begun in

Shakespeareana with the Kendals; though he'd never performed with the troupe himself, Raj had obviously been bitten by the Shakespearian bug: a later film he directed, *Bobby* (1973), was supposedly a version of *Romeo and Juliet*. Teasing out the Kendal connection, I also managed to find *36 Chowringhee Lane*, a film from 1981 starring Jennifer Kendal (sister of Felicity), about an Anglo-Indian teacher living in Kolkata and teaching Shakespeare. These went on the pile too.

Anything earlier than *Chori Chori* was a definite no-go, I was told: best to ask at the National Film Archive in Pune a hundred miles southwest. I was still trying to get someone there to answer my calls, but I booked a train ticket anyway.

I was luckier with modern films, ones that bore little relation to classic Bollywood. The Malayali *auteur* Jayaraj Rajasekharan Nair had produced two well-regarded adaptations, *Kaliyattam* (1997), which places a version of *Othello* around a performance of the incantatory Keralan dance form theyyam; and *Kannaki* (2002), which has heavy echoes of *Antony and Cleopatra*.

I chased down ever-more tangential titles. *The Last Lear* (2007), a creaky vehicle for the actor Amitabh Bachchan about a retired thespian who knows all the plays by heart. Sangeeta Datta's *Life Goes On* (2009), another *King Lear*, this time set in the British Bengali community. As I watched shop assistants scurrying from store cupboards to stock computers and back again, I asked myself if there existed Indian films that weren't based in some way on Shakespeare.

Wondering whether it would be possible to find traces of anything earlier, I took myself off to the Chor Bazaar flea market. I'd heard of a stall called Bollywood Bazaar, a famous centre for the secondary market in movie-related items. I might not be able to buy the films, but perhaps there'd be a Shakespearian gleam or two in the dust. A poster for *Sweet Poison*? A publicity still for *Henpecked Love*?

When I arrived, the place looked promising. It was a joyous clutter, a cross between a junk shop and a shrine, barely roomier than the taxi in which I'd got there. So many items dangled above the door – three Indonesian masks, a sombrero, an electric guitar, a bronze fire bucket – that it was perilous to duck in.

The owner started on the patter even as I was adjusting to the gloom. I was interested in posters, artefacts, props, all original, all super-good quality? Right place, no question.

There was the sweet scent of mothballs and damp paper. In the back of the shop was what appeared to be a full set of Roman armour.

The owner rapped it smartly with a knuckle: *ding!* 'Bollywood, 1960s! Excellent price!'

I stressed that I was researching the history of Shakespeare in Indian cinema, a big book, very serious project. He didn't skip a beat. Nodding gravely, he scanned my list with cool professionalism.

He clicked his tongue. 'Some, some. But these very rare films.'

After about ten minutes, working in tandem, we had turned up a few posters, but they were titles I'd already come across: interesting to see, but hardly the cinematic rarities I was after.

I spotted a pile of photographs in a corner. He walked me over sadly. 'Very minor movies, sir . . .'

I flipped through: head shots. The faces were seductive, coy, noble, stern, gazing full of long-lost meaning into a permanent middle distance. I was no expert, but I didn't recognise a single one.

Then I came across a face I *did* recognise: that of Raj Kapoor. Here he was, looking terribly young, being cradled by an actress I didn't know. The gesture was of – what? Exhaustion? Forgiveness? Consolation? It was maternal, somehow, and I thought immediately of Gertrude and Hamlet. There were many versions of *Hamlet* in Indian film, but none starring Kapoor that I knew of (a pity: he had a damaged grace that might have suited the role).

The actress was unbearably beautiful: a swan-like neck, dark almond eyes, with the hint of something remote in her looks – Tibet? Nepal? She wore an expression of sadness and forbearance.

The owner ran a fingernail along the text at the bottom: *Main Nashe Mein Hoon*.

'Late fifties, I am thinking. Title means, "I am drunk".' He tipped his thumb towards his teeth. 'Raj Kapoor often drunk!'

Who was the woman?

'Ah, Mala Sinha! Very beautiful. Many movies, big, big star.'

The name stirred something – had *she* been in a Shakespeare? Which one?

But the shopkeeper had already moved on. With a conjuror's flourish he pulled out an A5-sized copy of a poster. In the centre was the title, huge and bold, white-on-black on a curlicued frame: *Romeo and Juliet*.

This was more like it. I remembered reading about the movie: another Nargis film, it was meant to be based on the Hollywood version of 1936 with Norma Shearer and Leslie Howard. It was filmed during 1947, the year of independence and partition – an interesting time, to say the least, to make a film about love across the barricades.

At the top of the poster Nargis looked adoringly up at D. K. Sapru's Romeo, who wore a European-style jerkin with a gold chain. The text proclaimed, 'NARGIS ART CONCERN presents the world's greatest love story . . . Romance supreme against a background of clashing swords, brought to thrilling reality.' Below was an inset panel: 'THE FAMED BALCONY SCENE: Moments of rapturous bliss stolen while danger awaits . . .' The address of the studio was in tiny type: 335 Grant Road. I must have walked past it the other day.

I was determined to watch Nargis's *Romeo and Juliet* at the National Film Archive, and finding a poster – particularly a poster I had never seen reproduced – was a step closer. This was definitely coming with me back to England, along with the photo and a couple of other posters.

'All together . . . four thousand rupees.'

At Indian prices, it was a shockingly high amount: £40. The photo looked authentic, but the posters were only copies, for all that they had been aged with what looked suspiciously like tea. I'd fondly imagined I might have been able to get originals for that.

The owner looked at me in genuine pity. 'Originals much, much more expensive.' He steepled his fingers together. 'Sir – sorry – I would not sell original if you give me . . . one thousand dollars!'

We settled on R2,000. 'I am not making business with you, sir,' he said as we concluded. 'This is *pleasure* for me.'

I was surprised that he had such intimate knowledge of the history of Shakespeare in Indian cinema. He looked gratified, and lowered his voice.

'BBC call me,' he said. 'Man from BBC. They make TV programme about Shakespeare. They come here to Bollywood Bazaar. They film right here!'

I remembered. There had been a documentary, presented by Felicity Kendal, telling part of the story of Shakespeareana and her early years in India. Bhardwaj had briefly been interviewed; was there also a scene in a shop? Possibly.

I felt suddenly deflated: bruising to have been beaten to the scene by a British television crew. Indian cinema's lack of originality was catching.

As I made a fuss of gathering up my photocopies, I noticed a small bust, a couple of inches high, leaning against a snuff box decorated with a Mughal miniature. Shakespeare.

'From Goa,' the owner said. 'Very, very old.'

It seemed unlikely; I suspected a canny piece of TV set dressing. This was Bollywood, after all.

In spare hours between interviews, in the cool of the morning or the thick, treacly heat of evening, I hunkered in my hotel room, feeding my laptop with DVD after DVD and searching for corner-of-the-eye glimpses of Shakespeare in Hindi cinema.

The first film I watched was *Bobby*, Raj Kapoor's 1973 classic. Regarded as taboo-breaking for having introduced illicit teenage romance to mainstream Bollywood, it did so with extensive debts to other, older stories. Depicting the tortured romance between the plutocratic son of a Mumbai businessman (played by Raj's son Rishi) and Bobby, the daughter of an impoverished Goan fisherman, its basic plot device owed plenty to *Romeo and Juliet* – most obviously in its portrayal of a love affair against the odds, but more interestingly (I thought) in the way it addressed some of the polarities that divided Indian society: rich versus poor, young versus old, Hindu versus Christian, modernising/westernised versus conservative/traditional.

When Kapoor senior shot the film in the early seventies – licking his wounds after a failed affair with Nargis – India was going through one of numerous bouts of abrupt change. A headstrong young generation demanded much greater freedoms than their parents felt able to offer; there were deep worries about the pernicious influence of the west. It struck me as not unlike Elizabethan England, likewise riven by tensions between social classes and debates about the ethics of arranged marriage – even if *Bobby*'s denouement, in which the renegade lovers are kidnapped by hoodlums, was an undeniable swerve from Shakespeare's play.

Farhan Akhtar's *Dil Chahta Hai* ('The Heart Deceives', 2001) was the product of a different kind of Indian film industry – globalised, street-smart – but just as revealing of its era, as laden with BMWs and Sony laptops as *Bobby* had been with migrainously patterned miniskirts and over-coiffed hair. The film was lavish in length (three-plus hours, divided by the traditional interval), scale (shot in Mumbai, Goa and Sydney) and ambition, narrating the coming-of-age tale of three male schoolfriends as they journey bumpily towards love and self-knowledge.

Akhtar paid numerous tributes to Bollywood's own history, but the obvious reference was *Much Ado About Nothing*, which furnished the movie's central section with a Beatrice-and-Benedick-style romance between Shalini and Akash, the warring, wisecracking leads, who find romance after disastrous beginnings.

There were deeper Shakespearian themes, too. Shalini and Akash discover their feelings for each other while watching an opera called *Troilus and Cressida* (not William Walton's, but a Bollywood knock-off). And the framework story of Akash and his two pals had affinities with *Love's Labour's Lost*, itself the story of a group of young men and their faulty attempts to balance their own friendship with the demands of real romantic love. Was I being over-ingenious? Apparently not: Akhtar included a cheeky shot in which Shalini stands on Sydney Harbour in front of a yacht named *Much Ado*.

On and on the Shakespearian trail went – through *Chori Chori* (whose debts to *The Taming of the Shrew* were fairly incidental, I thought) to a contemporarised, indie version of *A Midsummer Night's Dream* called *10ml Love* released in 2010, whose director, a young film-maker called Sharat Katariya, was kind enough to invite me to his apartment for a screening. (His title, he explained, referred to Puck's magic juice, placed on the eyes of the competing lovers.)

By far the most unexpected encounter came in *Bodyguard* (2011), a lumbering comedy-action blockbuster by the journeyman director Siddique. Tipped off that the film contained a nod to Shakespeare, I had added the DVD to my collection.

In time-honoured fashion, *Bodyguard* was not so much a remake as a re-re-re-remake, the third version of a Malayalam movie about a rich daughter who falls for her minder, with obvious debts to the saccharine Hollywood picture from 1992 starring Whitney Houston and Kevin Costner. Chiefly a vehicle for bovine hard man Salman Khan and Kareena Kapoor (who'd also been in *Omkara*: yet another Kapoor scion, a granddaughter of Raj), it seemed an unlikely site for a Shakespearian tribute, and I had nearly given up when, an hour and a bit in, the plot began to take a distinctly familiar turn.

Piqued by the overbearing presence of her bodyguard (Khan),

rich-girl Divya (Kapoor) concocts a scheme whereby she will text and call him, pretending to be a secret admirer, Chhaya, and hoping he will get so distracted that he leaves her alone. Gradually the inevitable happens: the bodyguard (ironically named Lovely) falls head over heels for this imaginary woman, while Divya realises her own feelings for him are genuine. Everything comes to a head in a park, when Divya takes Lovely by the hand and asks him to pretend that she is his mysterious beloved, the fictional Chhaya, so he can rehearse his lines:

> DIVYA Look into my eyes and it will automatically convey your feelings.
> LOVELY That's even more difficult, madam.
> DIVYA Nothing is impossible in love, Lovely.
> LOVELY Coming, madam, coming . . . [*gathering himself*] Chhaya, you do love me, don't you? I hope you are not joking. When you said that you love me I couldn't say anything. But it felt nice. I love you too.
> DIVYA [*unsettled by her own emotions*] Say the same thing to her honestly. She will be yours for ever.

Even discounting the prosaic Hindi-into-English subtitles, this was hardly Elizabeth Barrett Browning; but was it imagining things to think the entire scenario was cribbed from act three, scene two of *As You Like It*, where Rosalind (disguised as a man) persuades Orlando to do exactly the same thing, rehearse his love for a woman who is none other than herself? Swap doublet and hose for mobile phones, the forest of Arden for a park in Pune, and the exchange was near-identical.

And were there hints, too, of *Twelfth Night* in the story of a glum killjoy gulled into falling in love with his mistress? There was a lingering shot of the Bodyguard standing in front of a mirror, trying to crack an unaccustomed smile while wearing a yellow T-shirt, the same colour favoured by Malvolio . . .

Perhaps, perhaps. What really captivated me is how lightly the references were worn. Of course there are western rom-coms based on literary sources – *Clueless* (1995) recasts Jane Austen's *Emma* as a Beverly Hills teen comedy, while 1999's *Ten Things I Hate About You* does something similar with *The Taming of the Shrew*, set in an American high school knowingly named Padua. But the literary overtones are heavily played up, part of the ironic in-joke – a postmodern gag on 'highbrow' culture slumming it for the purposes of mass entertainment. Irony was hardly absent in Indian cinema, but it seemed to me that something more straightforward was going on, at least in *Bodyguard*: a borrowing from Shakespeare that treated him with a refreshing lack of reverence.

There had been several western versions of *As You Like It*, notably Paul Czinner's 1936 movie with the young Laurence Olivier and Kenneth Branagh's 2006 movie. The Czinner was a piece of ersatz Elstree pastoral, shot on a leaf-strewn sound stage that resembled *The Adventures of Robin Hood*; the Branagh a campy exercise in hey-nonny-nonny, set weirdly in Japan with a British-American cast. In both, the fact that the scriptwriter was William Shakespeare was entirely the point. I tried to imagine a British or American director stealing a scene from *As You Like It* and stitching it quietly into, say, a Sylvester Stallone movie, and gave up. I couldn't.

Nonetheless, after three days of cramming movies into strange corners of the day, I felt my interpretative skills coming dangerously unstuck. Indian movies seemed to bleed endlessly into each other; they were halls of mirrors, each reflecting yet more sources and influences, on and on into infinity. Were any of these films really Shakespeare? Was that even the point? C. J. Sisson's line kept returning: 'Things that are still alive and in process of becoming new things . . .' It was all but impossible, however, to say where the new things began and the old things ended.

If one were searching for an efficient way to go mad, I decided, one could do worse than go source-hunting through the output of Bollywood.

———•———

I RESTED THE BACK OF MY HAND against the heat of the train window, watching the last ragged pieces of suburb float past like clumps of froth on the tide. The sun, high now, made the marks in the pane scatter and glare, a spider's web frozen in hot glass.

We had been travelling for an hour and a half, forty-five minutes late and getting later. It had taken that long simply to crawl up the Mumbai peninsula, wriggle out across the top corner of Navi Mumbai on the east side of the bay and swing slowly south-east for the run down to

Karjat, Lonavala and Pune, home of the National Film Archive. The
plain was monotonously clear and flat, the colour and texture of
coarse sandpaper. It was stubbled with khaki bushes, the low outlines
of purplish hills behind. Soon we'd be up in the cool of the mountains.
It seemed unimaginable.

Reluctantly, I dragged myself back to my books. How about
pinpointing the earliest translation of Shakespeare on the Indian stage?
This wasn't necessarily an easier task than it was with the movies.
R. K. Yajnik, so delightfully scandalised by the depredations of Urdu
and Gujarati playwrights, had helpfully tabulated the translations
he'd found up to the 1930s. I worked down his table with a pencil:
the earliest was from 1853, a Bengali version of *The Merchant of Venice*
called *Bhanumati Cittavilasa* by Hara Chandra Ghosh, reportedly the
first Indian version of any foreign play at all.

The date snagged my eye before I remembered why. California. The
Gold Rush. James and Sarah Stark. Just as Ghosh was settling down to
translate *The Merchant of Venice* in Kolkata, the Starks were preparing
the very same play in San Francisco, 8,000 miles away – the first time
it had been staged on the West Coast. Sarah and Ghosh could almost
have exchanged rehearsal notes, if the mail had let them. But then
Ghosh became a prominent lawyer; it was an amusing thought that he
might have been too grand to correspond with a mere travelling player,
let alone a woman.

The play snagged me for other reasons, too. *The Merchant of Venice*
was far and away the most popular title to be adapted in India: Yajnik
listed no fewer than twenty-one other versions, the majority nineteenth-
century – not forgetting, of course, Hashr's *Dil Farosh* (1900), so
successful that it had made it into the movies. It was surprising, to
put it mildly, that a play so locked into a Judaeo-Christian framework
– to the point where it was sometimes considered too controversial
to stage, particularly in the US and Israel – resonated so loudly in a
culture with quite different religious and ethnic tensions. But perhaps
those tensions weren't so different after all: vengeful majorities
and embattled minorities (and vengeful minorities and embattled
majorities) are everywhere. And one could argue that the play was as
much about money and trade as it was about religion, both subjects
that must have recommended it to residents of Kolkata, a trading post
every bit as powerful as Renaissance Venice. I remembered reading
somewhere that *The Merchant of Venice* was also hugely popular in

China, for reasons no one could fathom. I filed away the thought away for future use.

In India, the comedies and tragicomedies seemed to provide the most fodder for early translators. This, at least, was straightforwardly explained. Tragedy in the Greek or Shakespearian sense was alien to Hindu dramatic traditions; in classical Sanskrit texts it is almost unknown for major characters to experience the vicious reversals of fate described by Aristotle. According to the *Natyashastra* ('Science of Drama'), compiled two millennia ago by the priest Bharata and thought to be the oldest study of stagecraft anywhere in the world, Indian plays were divided into distinct and rigidly defined genres. The closest to tragedies were *natakas*, featuring epic characters such as gods and kings and matters of serious or historical import – but with the major difference that, instead of suffering and expiring at the end, they triumphed.

Maybe this was also why *The Comedy of Errors* had been so successful in India (twelve theatrical versions by the 1930s, according to Yajnik). It bore uncanny similarities to another major genre outlined by Bharata, *prakarana* – stories of invented human characters and their foibles, focusing on the comedy of money, love, justice, mistaken identity and the like.

Even more striking was the popularity of the late tragicomedies, especially given their neglect elsewhere: four translations of *Pericles*, a play that vanished from the stage almost entirely for two centuries in London; and seven separate *Winter's Tales*.

In the west, the delicate balance between laughter and heart-wrenching sorrow in *The Winter's Tale* has often been regarded with bewilderment: Dryden dismissed the play as 'so grounded on impossibilities . . . that the comedy neither caused your mirth, nor the serious part your concernment'. Between 1634 and 1802 it was staged, heavily adapted, a mere handful of times. Yet the play seems to have found a home here in India, perhaps more attuned to dramas more heterogeneous in form, less straightjacketed by genre.

Cymbeline, too, seized my attention. This troubling, sprawling late play had been saved from neglect in the Victorian period by the virtuous character of Imogen, who offered British actresses such as Helen Faucit and Ellen Terry the chance to display both their formidable talents and their irreproachable piety. For all that I'd managed to catch it in Virginia, it remained an eccentric rarity for most producers in the west. Yet in India it was a favourite: by Yajnik's count, there had been twelve separate translations between 1868 and 1910, and he ranked it '[one] of the most successful comedies' he had come across. A particularly popular Marathi version called *Tara* by the scholar and schoolmaster V. M. Mahajani was staged frequently and went through several editions in print.

As it happened, *Tara* – first performed in my destination, Pune – was also the subject of one of the earliest accounts by a foreign writer to have witnessed an adaptation of Shakespeare in India in, as it were, the wild. It was printed in *Macmillan's Magazine* and was by an Anglo-Irish academic who was teaching out in India, Harold Littledale. It came from 1880, a year after the play was written; I had brought it with me on the train.

Littledale had been fortunate enough to attend the double marriage festivities of the ruler of Vadodara and his sister – festivities that had been carried out, he wrote, 'on a scale of magnificence unusual even in ceremonious India'. Many performers came to Gujarat specially; others ('jugglers, snake-charmers, dancers, acrobats') simply rolled up. Among them was a company of touring actors.

The play didn't start until 10 p.m., an hour later than advertised, but the fact that there was a delay meant Littledale had a chance to poke around the theatre. A temporary structure constructed from canvas and bamboo poles, it surrounded an oval whitewashed sandbank stage twenty feet wide and forty feet deep, fronted by a drop curtain, 'on which an elephant- and tiger-fight was depicted, and by a proscenium of canvas, adorned with full-length portraits of three-headed gods and mythic heroes in strange attire'. An audience of around five hundred, mainly men and children, squatted in an improvised amphitheatre dug from the sand. Light came from kerosene lamps affixed to the trees.

If the decor struck Littledale as 'strange', this was as nothing to the show. It was preceded by a musical offertory to the god Narayana on voice, sitar and tabla, which (opined Littledale) 'sound[ed] most like an unavailing attempt to smother the squeals of two babies with the din of a bagpipe'. But once the play finally commenced Littledale fell under its spell: won over partly by the splendid costumes, but most of all by the emotional intensity of the acting, at a pitch far exceeding anything he had witnessed back home.

The cast, like the audience, was all-male; central in every sense was the teenage boy he saw playing Imogen:

In the cave scene, where Imogen was seemingly dead, and was bewailed by the two boys, many of the spectators brushed aside their tears,

while one old rajah fairly blubbered outright. Much of this was no
doubt a tribute to the original pathos of the character, but some share
of credit for so powerfully exciting the emotion of pity must be given
to the young actor himself.

I'd blubbered myself at exactly that moment, back in Virginia.

The action was shifted to two fantastical locations (Suvarnapuri, or
'golden city', for Britain; Vijaipura, 'land of victory', for Rome), and a
Brahmin astrologer was introduced to help administer the fairy-tale
happy ending. Littledale admitted, somewhat grudgingly, that these
were improvements. After staggering out six hours later, at 2.55 a.m.,
he was surprised to find he had enjoyed himself.

As I read his account, particularly in the light of my discoveries in
California, it was possible to feel something Littledale himself grasped
only dimly. The performance he witnessed in Pune achieved something
that British Victorian theatre producers, increasingly obsessed by
grandiose sets and finicking historical 'accuracy', were doing their
damnedest to eradicate: a sense of spontaneity.

Here, as in the Sierra Nevada, props were minimal to non-existent,
the acting style non-gestural and lacking in 'ranting and raving'. The
swordplay, Littledale wrote, 'would have astonished Mr Irving' in its
deftness. The all-male casting he thought revelatory, particularly when
it came to the boy playing Tara/Imogen's adoption of male clothing:
'His disguise as a boy looked exquisitely girlish, and his manner, timid
yet collected, exactly conveyed the impression of Imogen, trembling
with womanly fear.' Ellen Terry evidently had competition in Vadodara.

There was perhaps another reason Cymbeline resonated with Indian
audiences – its echoes of the Hindu scriptures. The image of a virtuous,
morally unimpeachable wife who travels to the ends of the earth has
parallels in the Panchakanya (iconic heroines) of Hindu mythology. One
such paragon is Sita, heroine of the Ramayana, who, like Imogen, is
schemed against by a stepmother, exiled to the wilderness, and suffers
numerous trials for the love of Rama, her husband. Another heroine
in the Ramayana is Tara: though her story is somewhat different from
that of her namesake in Mahajani's play (she is abducted by her evil
brother-in-law after her husband, Vali, is presumed killed in battle),
she still embodies the virtues of chastity and constancy in the face of
near-insurmountable odds. Shakespeare's talent for creating strong,
self-sacrificing female characters, from Portia in The Merchant of Venice

to Hermione in *The Winter's Tale*, obviously had much to recommend it to a Hindu culture that still prizes such things as pre-eminent female virtues. Perhaps Victorian England and contemporaneous India weren't so different after all.

Also, I couldn't help noticing a change Littledale barely registered: a tweak to the character of Cloten, the clottish stepbrother who, in Shakespeare's play, tries to woo Imogen despite the fact that she is already married. In order to display the character's peculiar combination of obstreperous idiocy and teetering self-regard, the Marathi actor not only equipped him with a stutter; he was also given a fondness for western classical music. In other words, it seemed the 'despicably idiotic' Cloten was presented as a Brit. The joke seems to have passed Littledale by.

The National Film Archive of India didn't much resemble a place where fairy-tale transformations were likely to occur. A low-slung complex in grubby grey concrete, it dated from the 1990s but looked several decades older. Scowling from behind the trees, it reminded me of a police headquarters, a functional building in which bland but unspeakable horrors were routinely performed. It was studded with warning notices: NO PARKING, NO SMOKING PLEASE, CHILDREN NOT ALLOWED.

In the legal sense, I was not allowed either: I didn't have an appointment. I had eventually managed to get the NFAI's director on the phone – a furtive conversation in which it was clear that only some appalling secretarial oversight had enabled me to be connected at all. I had been asked to supply information on the purpose of my project and the films I wished to research, and had received a curt note reminding me of charges liable, which I acknowledged. Silence had then ensued. 'Just turn up anyway,' Nandini had advised. 'They'll have to let you in.'

They had, but it was unclear to what effect. The other researchers I'd seen at the entrance had melted away. The building had a melancholy out-of-term feel. I wandered the dirty and desolate corridors, trying in vain to find out where I should go.

Eventually I was directed to the film-preservation office. I knocked on the door, then swung it cautiously open. No one home. The room reminded me unpleasantly of a prison cell, windowless, the walls scuffed, a desk crowded high with cardboard files and unruly stacks of A4 paper. A dusty computer sat in a corner, surrounded by piles of VHS tapes.

I took a seat in front of the desk. Twenty-five minutes went by, then another fifteen. No one came in. I went for a walk.

By the time I got back, the office was at least populated; in front of the computer sat a small-framed man with a thin moustache. He looked up impatiently as I knocked. His browser window was open on TripAdvisor.

I explained my project; would it be possible to talk to someone about the history of Indian cinema? A curator, perhaps? I had tried to make an appointment, but had been experiencing some difficulties—

'There is no one available with expertise in that matter,' he said tightly.

Was the director available?

'The director is elsewhere on business.'

Would it at least be possible to view one or two of the early Shakespeare films in the collection? I had travelled a long way, and would be most grateful for any assistance.

'Which titles does this request concern?'

I showed him my list. He glanced at it for a few seconds and handed it back.

'We have only the *Hamlet*, 1954. You may watch that at 2.30 p.m.'

It was now 11.15 a.m. It wasn't possible to see anything before that? Or another film? I was only in Pune a few days.

He waved his hand irritably.

'Watch that first film, then you may come back. We talk then about the others. You may use the library in the meantime.'

He swung his chair back towards TripAdvisor. Our interview was over.

Fighting the sense that my expedition down here had been wasted, I tried to see if the library contained anything I hadn't already discovered back in Mumbai.

It was tough going. The reference books were outdated, and barely listed any Indian Shakespeare movies at all. The only relevant work was western: Kenneth S. Rothwell and Annabelle Henkin Melzer's

Shakespeare on Screen: An International Filmography and Videography from 1990. Inclusive on Europe, Japan and the United States, and impressively open-minded about what it considered 'Shakespearian' – including spin-offs such as *Hamlet and Eggs*, an American short from 1937 – it had a yawning black hole where world cinema should be. *Khoon-ka-Khoon*, the groundbreaking 1935 Hindi-Urdu version of *Hamlet* by the great Parsi actor Sohrab Modi – the world's first sound film of the play – was briefly mentioned, but the only other Indian Shakespeare film was *Shakespeare Wallah*; not really Indian, not fully about Shakespeare.

The online catalogue wasn't much better: it contained some of the films on my list, but by no means all. The silent movies I'd read about so eagerly – *Khoon-e-Nahak*, *Dil Farosh* – were nowhere to be seen. Neither was *Khoon-ka-Khoon*. There was *Hamlet* by the prolific actor-director Kishore Sahu, the one I'd been permitted to watch, but it came from much later (Hindi, 1954, 35 mm, 15 reels, B&W). Nargis's *Romeo and Juliet*, the film I'd been hoping more than anything to locate, had also gone awol. I tried again, working methodically through my list. DOCUMENTATION NOT FOUND GO BACK, DOCUMENTATION NOT FOUND GO BACK. Even the computer sounded stressed.

Trying another tack, I trawled through back issues of *Filmindia*, India's first movie magazine, founded by the journalist and impresario Baburao Patel in 1935, not long after the talkies arrived. This was more worthwhile: in the March 1948 issue, a few pages away from a colour photograph mourning the recent death of Gandhi, were shots taken on the set of *Romeo and Juliet*. (The costumes made it look like Disney's *Snow White*, Nargis adorned with flowers and sporting a tulle cloak.)

The review of *Romeo and Juliet* a few issues later was positive, if rather too cap-doffing to the Hollywood film of twelve years earlier. 'Nargis Proves Equal Of Norma Shearer', the headline read. 'Indian Film Version Of Shakespeare's "Romeo And Juliet" Copies MGM Pattern'. Apparently it had taken a total of two years to film, which had caused some troubling continuity issues. 'Judged from the standards of modern realistic, psychological plays,' the reviewer sniffed, 'it is an old-fashioned melodramatic tear-jerker.' Of the film itself, other than denunciations of its technique and lighting, there was frustratingly little description.

Filmindia was more helpful when it came to Kishore Sahu's *Hamlet*: the cover of the September 1954 issue was a painted portrait of Sahu himself brooding against a vivid blood-red background, skull in hand.

Sahu had begun in the golden studio era of the early forties with Bombay Talkies before setting up on his own; this was his biggest picture yet. The publicity agents had obviously been working overtime, judging by the number of tenuous preview stories they had managed to sneak into the magazine. Patel's regular 'Bombay Calling' column was surmounted by an enormous still of the young girl playing Ophelia. 'Coy and innocent and yet so engagingly sexy,' it purred.

The girl's face looked familiar, but it took me a few moments to work out why. It was the same face I'd seen in that pile of photos in Bollywood Bazaar: the actress clutching Raj Kapoor, an expression of infinite forbearance etched on to her features. I'd tucked the photo into the cover of my notebook as a kind of mascot. Her name was Mala Sinha. So *this* was the Shakespeare she'd been in.

I tapped away on my phone: yes, the same Mala Sinha. She'd become a huge star, acting with everyone from Raj Kapoor to Raaj Kumar, Dev Anand to Biswajit Chatterjee, and for directors including Guru Dutt, Bimal Roy, Yash Chopra – anyone who was anyone in Indian cinema. Playing Ophelia for Kishore Sahu in 1954 had been her breakthrough role.

I opened up a fan site to check when she was born – 1936 – then realised with a start that she was still alive. In the unforgiving language of Mumbai film journalism she was a 'yesteryear actress', retired and somewhat reclusive. There wasn't much background on her. But she was shortly to be honoured with a Phalke award for lifetime achievement. I wondered if there was any way I could locate her. I texted Nasreen, who had helped me get hold of Gulzar. It was worth a punt.

I read on in *Filmindia* with renewed appetite. The few academic articles that had mentioned Sahu's *Hamlet* had written it off as a poor imitation (naturally) of the British version of 1948, produced and directed by Laurence Olivier. Baburao Patel wasn't much kinder – in fact considerably less. He might have found Mala Sinha 'engagingly sexy', but for the film itself he had only scorn. Under the headline 'Sahu's "Hamlet" Flops at the Met', he accused it of 'slander[ing]' Shakespeare's memory, with its 'stinking selfishness'. Claudius was portrayed as a 'stupid drunken clown'; Laertes came in for especial criticism, with his 'callow and silly face'.

Hamlet sounded rather good; I began to look forward to seeing it.

Somewhat to my surprise, when I came back at 2.15 p.m. Kishore Sahu and *Hamlet* were waiting. I was shown to a screening room, through corridors piled hazardously with canisters of aluminium and bright green plastic.

The room made the film-preservation office look like an operating theatre. It was window-high with more canisters and a tide wrack of DVD boxes. Pushed back against the wall was a huge Steenbeck reel-to-reel editing machine in hospital-blue steel, balanced on which were stacks of old accountancy ledgers. On the table opposite, next to a battered filing cabinet piled with a scree of papers, was a venerable-looking VHS machine. A flat-screen TV was attached to the wall. (This at least appeared to date from the twenty-first century.) On top of everything was a rime of thick, gluey dust. It gave the strong impression of having been burgled, maladroitly, a couple of decades ago.

In the centre of the chaos a chair had been laid on. Trying not to cause an avalanche, I gingerly put down my bag and pulled out the copy of the complete works I'd brought with me (no subtitles, I'd been warned).

After reading so much about how Sahu's movie was an inferior imitation of Olivier's, I was thrilled to discover in fact how different it was. Visually, for sure, there were debts: the same *noir*-ish, tenebrous black-and-white, the same brooding low-angle shots, in fact many of the same sequences – Hamlet sitting alone, clouded in thought, after the wedding banquet at the play's opening; or forcing his mother on to her bed in Freudian lust. Sahu's art director, V. Jadhav, had done a fine job replicating Olivier's crepuscular castle sets and faux-medieval costumes.

But in deeper ways, *Hamlet: A Free Adaptation*, seemed to me exactly that – free. From the jaunty title music onwards (Sahu had wisely drawn the line at mimicking Walton's tremulous score), it kept offering sly surprises. One was Sahu himself, who, in contrast to Olivier's carefully calibrated interiority, made the Prince into a swashbuckling Parsi hero, forever swooping his cloak and flaring his nostrils like a wildcat on the prowl. Whereas Olivier played 'to be or not to be' with portentous symbolism, balancing on a rocky promontory overlooking the crashing waves, Sahu's approach was commendably lacking in fuss: he fingered a dagger to the tolling of the castle bell.

Yet the revelation was Mala Sinha, who in this famously lopsided play was granted almost equal status. Whereas in most versions of

Shakespeare's text, Ophelia warrants something less than 5 per cent of the script, in Sahu's version she was an unignorable presence, barely off-screen for scenes at a time. We first glimpsed her stepping daintily down a staircase like a wind-up doll, but she soon proved herself more than a match for Sahu's Prince, turning on him with the incendiary ferocity of Nora in *A Doll's House*. She even gained a whole extra scene, a flashback sequence in which she cavorted around a fountain, singing sweetly of love.

The songs were the great innovation. An Indian audience took their presence for granted, but in the hands of composer Ramesh Naidu and lyricist Hasrat Jaipuri, not to mention Sinha's own sad-sweet voice (unusually, she sang her own songs instead of relying on a playback singer), they attained a poetry that matched the script. I loved the gravediggers' duet: a perky number heavy on twanging sitar, done to a demented dance sequence worthy of the Marx Brothers. With Sinha's final song, offered as she gazes into the brook in which she is shortly to end her life, I sensed *Hamlet*'s narrative arc being subtly recoded. In contrast to Jean Simmons's simpering girlchild in Olivier's movie, Sahu and Sinha dared to make Ophelia a strong-willed Bollywood – perhaps even a Hindu – heroine.

The dialogue was peppered with quotations from Urdu classical poets; the translation not drawn directly from Shakespeare, but based on Syed Mehdi Hasan Ahsan's *Khoon-e-Nahak*, with nods to Sohrab Modi's *Khoon-ka-Khoon*. While these earlier versions – and the Parsi plays they were based on – might have not survived, in a ghostly sense both lived on.

As we headed towards a breakneck version of the fencing match, Sahu bounding up the castle stairs like Errol Flynn, it seemed to me that this was not, as the critics had claimed, a slavish remake of a British classic at all. It was a version in knowing dialogue with its predecessors, both in India and the western tradition. Every *Hamlet*, it can be argued, is a kind of seance: an encounter with the spectres of everyone who has staged this most famous and haunting of tragedies. Olivier wrestled with the shades of John Gielgud, John Barrymore, Edwin Booth – a whole parade of Princes stretching back to Thomas Betterton in the seventeenth century and even Shakespeare's own, Richard Burbage. Sahu, though, was one of the few who directly incorporated, not fought, the past. Doing so, he managed to exorcise a few of the old ghosts.

'You managed to see it? They showed it to you?'

It was hard to tell whether P. K. Nair was joking. Propped up on a daybed in the gloom of his apartment, within grabbing reach of a steel crutch, his expressions were unreadable. He seemed fragile, sallow-looking, with fleshy features and a corona of white hair that straggled negligently over his ears and down his neck. When I arrived, he'd pointed to the cotton wool in one ear: a little deaf. But his eyes were alert, and his mind was busy and bright.

Born in 1933, Nair was Indian film history in fleshly form: a one-man memory bank who had made it his life's mission to rescue the cinematic past from dust and oblivion. As a movie-struck kid in Kerala in the 1940s, he'd sneaked out to attend late-night screenings while his parents were asleep, paying for 'floor tickets' on the sand. He'd talked his way into being an assistant on *Mother India*, and sat at the knee of the great neorealist Bimal Roy. The National Film Archive was his doing: as a researcher and historian, he had begun it almost single-handedly in 1964.

Nair *saab* was a man around whom legends accrued. It was said that he had watched some films hundreds of times, sitting in the dark with flashlight and notebook; that he had hosted jamboree student screenings of the sections of movies snipped out by the censors for being too rude. He'd spent years rummaging through basements at long-shuttered studios and sweet-talking relatives of their founding fathers to part with precious reels of nitrate. The NFAI had preserved a total of 12,000 titles, 8,000 of them Indian. It was only a slight exaggeration to say that without Nair there would be no Indian film history at all.

'Today, did they show you the print or the DVD?'

We were talking about Kishore Sahu's *Hamlet*.

VHS, I replied.

He nodded slowly. 'Yes, I am worried about that. The print was not good when we got it. It was a used print, you know, from some distributor, not brand-new. It was the only one we could get. But I don't know what the condition is like now. I worry these prints are not being looked after.'

I had come to Nair to resolve my questions about the relationship between Shakespeare and early Indian cinema. Despite his dazzling panoply of knowledge, it was dismal going. The earliest Shakespearian film of all, *Dil Farosh*? Long-lost. *Meetha Zehar*? Destroyed, perhaps by the studio. Sohrab Modi's *Khoon-ka-Khoon*? Now on the most-wanted list. The beguiling photos I had seen of the world's oldest synchronous-sound *Hamlet* – Modi agonising in his chair, head in hands; a bearded Ghost wearing enormous white wings, like something out of an avant-garde film by Jean Cocteau – were all that was left. None of these early movies survived.

He registered my look of dejection. 'You have to understand,' he said gently, 'that almost nothing exists from the early time. In the silent period India made nearly fifteen hundred feature films. Of fifteen hundred we have only about nine or ten left, and most of them are incomplete. We have posters, pictures, but the reels . . .' He left the sentence hanging. 'It is a dark period.'

So Sahu's *Hamlet* was indeed the earliest Indian Shakespeare in existence? Not even Nargis's *Romeo and Juliet* had survived?

Settling himself on the daybed, he tried to explain. 'When we started in the sixties, maybe only thirty per cent of movies made before 1950 were available. We saved twenty per cent. My priority when I was starting the archive was to find as many early films as I could. I thought, "Oh, the fifties films can wait." I didn't give them priority. And by the time I came to the seventies or eighties . . .'

India was hardly the only country to have experienced the problem: the great Hollywood founder Sam Goldwyn's silents had been destroyed because the insurance costs were too high, while Universal Pictures washed and recycled old stock to reclaim the expensive silver-nitrate emulsion. It was miraculous that the rediscovered *Richard III* from 1912, which I'd watched in America, not only survived but had been in a playable condition; to preserve a film that antique requires extraordinary sensitivity and care. In India, Nair aside, such care had been lacking. And the sheer quantity of films made, corner-cutting distribution, poor preservation techniques, the climate: all of it meant that the scale of loss here was immense.

Nair told me of his heartbreaking attempts to secure a copy of *Alam Ara*, India's first talkie. He had visited the elderly Ardeshir Irani, its director, and his son Shapoorji in the late sixties. Ardeshir was adamant that there were still three reels in existence, but as Nair was leaving Shapoorji confessed he'd recently got rid of them, stripped of their silver for a few rupees.

'What is it possible to do?' he said. 'Even in the film industry people are not much concerned with the future of the archive.'

Nor was the archive itself especially concerned, it seemed. Since Nair's retirement in 1991, it had been run by a succession of bureaucrats with little or no background in film. It wasn't surprising that the current director was away; he was rumoured to have two jobs. The archive's facilities were poorly maintained, many of its treasures in danger of being lost. Nair had himself moved back from retirement in Kerala to try and limit the damage.

'I used to take personal care of each and every place in the archive,' he said, his voice rising. 'But the people they were getting in just didn't have the training. All these things I tried to do just vanished.'

The nadir had come in January 2003, when a fire ripped through the NFAI vaults. As many as 4,000 priceless reels had gone up in acrid smoke, 450 of them from before the 1950s. The Indian losses were irreplaceable: early talkies in Marathi and Hindi, the first Indian film to win an award at Venice . . . It was said the fire had started because flammable reels had been stored in unsafe conditions.

'So many times I brought these things to notice, but they keep on arguing, "Oh, he is now not in the organisation. He is keeping on criticising," you know. So I thought of stopping that.'

I suddenly realised why it had been so hard to get inside the place. Everyone I had spoken to back in Mumbai agreed the archive was in danger. But what to do about it, that was the issue. India had so many pressing problems . . .

'So when you ask am I worried, yes, I am worried,' Nair said. 'I have real worries.' He seized his crutch and clenched it as if it would break. 'Every day, as far as I know, some film is getting damaged beyond repair.'

It was after 9 p.m. by the time I got back to the hotel: early by Indian standards, but I couldn't face finding a restaurant outside. There was a café of sorts in the lobby. I dumped my bag on the closest table and, not bothering to glance at the menu, ordered the largest beer they had and a portion of daal and rice. Aside from a fleet of waiters checking their phones, there was just one other diner, a porcine businessman in a striped shirt pecking at his laptop.

It is a hazard of travelling alone that one's emotions become Himalayan extremes: the highs exultant, the lows desperate. But I reasoned that I had some cause to feel despair. Granted, I had managed to see *Hamlet*, the oldest surviving Shakespeare film in India – but that a movie from the mid-1950s was considered uniquely antique had come as a shock.

By the evanescent standards of my usual trade, theatre, film had always seemed to me almost alarmingly permanent: all you needed to do was hang on to the stuff. But it appeared almost no one, bar P. K. Nair and a few others, wanted to bother. There he was, in his gloomy little room, while films rotted into nothing a few hundred yards away. The thought was incalculably depressing.

No doubt films were being preserved, and the chances of a few lost reels popping up in someone's attic were really rather high. Digitisation made it harder to delete things. India was at the forefront of technology: the wi-fi on the train to Pune had been faster than it was in my London flat. But in its scrambled hurry to modernise, the country seemed sometimes to regard its own past as an impediment. I remembered a line I'd read somewhere. 'India has a rich past, but a poor history.' It was a cliché, but hard to deny.

I thought back to C. J. Sisson's essay, the point at which I had begun my journey. One of the things he most admired about Parsi theatre was how it resembled Elizabethan drama: its exuberant commercialism, its restless creativity, its bumptious optimism. In Mumbai, he had written, '[Shakespeare's] plays . . . are still alive and in the process of becoming new things, being ever born again.' That was surely true, and true about Bollywood too – but what was also true was that this hunger for invention turned the industry into an inattentive custodian of the old. If you could simply remake a film, why bother to save the original? It was just last year's movie, just cluttering up someone's floor.

But then, as I'd discovered at the Folger library, the Jacobethans hadn't been much good at preservation, either. If the First Folio hadn't been published in 1623, eighteen of Shakespeare's plays would probably never have survived. The overwhelming majority of Renaissance playscripts are in exactly the same condition as India's silent cinema: long since lost in action.

Not quite everything was lost. Back in Mumbai a few days later, on my way to interview another film-maker, I felt my phone buzz.

Nasreen. The text was mysterious: a postal address in Mumbai and a phone number. I was wondering what on earth this signified when the phone buzzed again. 'MALA SINHA,' the message read. 'NO IDEA IF STILL CURRENT. GOOD LUCK!!!!'

Mala Sinha: the beauty on the film poster clutching Raj Kapoor, the unexpected heroine of Sahu's *Hamlet* – the great screen actress herself. I tried calling from the rickshaw and couldn't get through. Once the phone seemed to be answered, but the line was so poor it was difficult to tell. The voice on the other end – if it was a voice – was a faint susurration in a language I couldn't understand. The whine of the engine, reverberating through my teeth, made me wonder if I was imagining it.

I had a flight to Kolkata booked in a day and a half's time and a diary full of appointments. But the address was only a few miles away, in the upscale district of Bandra. On a whim, I decided to cancel my film-maker and direct the rickshaw to Bandra instead.

Forty minutes later, damp with sweat, I was there. The area had a grand past, judging from the rambling deco-style villas either side of the road. One or two were in fine condition, their cream and sorbet-yellow paintwork spotless, like steamers with matronly lines. Others had been converted into boutiques or business centres. One was in the process of being torn down, presumably to make space for the twin of the brusque new tower to its right.

I went past the address several times before I registered it behind a dark screen of rain trees. Even by the standards of genteel shabbiness unique to Mumbai, the house – a villa that might once have been even grander than its neighbours – looked like a ruin. Mould blackened the exposed plasterwork around the front door and porch. Lines of damp stretched along the frontage in great grey waves. Dark windows gazed blankly out. I'd arrived half a century too late. If this had once been a film star's house, it was now in *Sunset Boulevard* territory. Actually, it wouldn't have made a bad set for *Sunset Boulevard* . . . I took a few photographs to commemorate my near-brush with stardom.

A stray impulse made me try the gate. It wasn't actually sealed as I'd thought, but wedged with a screw. I prodded the screw, which clattered to the ground on the other side. The gate yawned open with a slow, horror-movie creak. Perhaps someone *did* still live here.

Heart thudding, I ducked through. All I could hear was the traffic and the rustling of the trees. No one came past.

Reasoning that I might as well, I tiptoed across the drive and tried the bell: nothing. I wasn't even sure it had rung. I pressed my ear to the door. Still nothing. I pulled out my notebook and started scribbling a note. How did one address a 'yesteryear star'? Miss? Mrs? Mala? Did she come from the era before cutesy Bollywood nicknames?

Suddenly, there was a ferocious roar in my left ear and I felt the security screen in front of the door buckle and thrash. A dog was corkscrewing wildly behind it, barking as if desperate to be let loose. Instinctively I flinched away. When I looked back up there was a pair of narrow eyes, human, glaring at me from around the door.

'What' – *bark* – 'think' – *bark* – 'doing here?' – *bark* – 'who do you' – *bark, bark* – 'trespass' – *bark, bark, bark* – 'bitten'.

Attempting to recover my composure, I squawked a reply: I was a British writer, deeply sorry, had been hoping to leave a message . . .

Steadily the barking subsided, then ceased with a gruff sound as the dog's owner grabbed its collar.

I put on my most haplessly English voice. I was actually trying to get in contact with Mala Sinha, the actress, I explained. Did she still live here?

A curt silence.

'She might,' said the voice, which was female.

'Is there any way I could talk to her?'

Another curt silence.

'She's sick. She can't talk to you today.'

'Another day? Any day at all?' In desperation I reached for my trump card. 'I'm an enormous fan. I've come out all the way from London to meet her.'

This time the silence seemed warmer. The door yielded another few inches. Behind it was a woman in her indeterminate forties, wearing jogging bottoms, hair scraped back. One hand held the collar of a large, shadowy dog.

'I'm sorry about him. He's very excitable, aren't you, darling?'

She crouched down and started to kiss its nose. It growled, unpersuaded.

I kept talking, going heavy on the fandom. Information trickled back. Mala Sinha did live here, but she was elderly now. She didn't accept many callers. She never talked to journalists. But perhaps a young man who had come all the way from London just to meet her . . .

I did my best to look like a young man who had come all the way from London just to meet her.

'I can't promise anything, I will be honest. But I will ask her. You may call me tomorrow.'

As she scribbled down the number in my notebook, I studied her face: something familiar about the eyes.

'I'm Pratibha,' she said, keeping her gaze on me as she handed back the pad. 'The daughter,' she added.

When I called the number, I was astonished that the phone was answered immediately. I could make tea? 4 p.m. that afternoon would do?

But what to wear for tea with a Bollywood film star? Anxious to present myself as an ordinary, personable human being who didn't make a habit of breaking into gardens, I had dug out my least crumpled shirt and left it hanging in the hotel bathroom; but my jacket was so hopelessly crushed that it hardly mattered. In the heavy heat on the doorstep, the sweat was trickling down my back. In a gesture of what I hoped might be interpreted as sophistication, I had bought macaroons at a cake shop nearby. I strongly suspected they were already melted.

After a few minutes, the door swung open, this time mercifully canine-free. Behind it was a tiny figure, wearing a cream-coloured silken sari, black hair neatly tied back, eyes dark behind thin gold glasses. It was really her: Mala Sinha. She was almost indistinguishable from the teenage girl I'd been watching in faded black-and-white in Pune a few days before. With a quiet smile, she ushered me through. She moved lightly, thin silver bangles tinkling on her bare arms.

Given that it looked from the street like a wreck, the house's interior took me unawares: a rococo fantasy of pink-veined marble, glossy walnut and rosewood panelling. Against one wall of the huge reception room, next to a curved art-deco bay window, was a bar that would have looked fully at home in a Los Angeles country club. Next to that was a cabinet filled with statues in shimmering silver and gold. A spiral staircase wound down from a mezzanine floor above. Bollywood goddesses really did live in palaces.

'You are very welcome here,' Sinha said formally, gesturing me towards a sofa the size of an aircraft carrier. Pratibha, clad in a dark-blue summer dress, materialised from a side door followed by an elderly labrador, which waddled over to join us. This must have been the fearsome creature that had menaced me the day before. It began to sniff the underside of the sofa. Sinha's husband, Chidambar, came in with a tea tray.

Ten minutes later, I was showing Sinha clips from *Hamlet* I'd surreptitiously recorded on my phone. She had only ever seen the film once, she said, at the glitzy Mumbai premiere in 1954. That was nearly sixty years ago.

'I am singing, the mad girl?' she said, watching the screen greedily. 'This is my own voice, you know. My own singing voice.'

She pointed a slender finger at the phone. 'Why am I becoming mad?'

I explained it was because Hamlet had left her, then murdered her father.

'Oh,' she said, then looked quickly back. 'I was very beautiful then.'

Having grown up in Kolkata in a Nepalese Christian family, Sinha had been spotted by the great Bengali director Ardhendu Bose, who had persuaded her father to let her act. Sahu – then one of the most renowned names in Indian cinema – saw her, and decided he had found his Ophelia. When she came to Mumbai, she was unknown. She was just sixteen.

She laughed; a girlish laugh, unrestrained. 'I was very scared of him. He was a perfectionist, very strict – always down-faced, you know. We said that he was happy when he looked unhappy!'

We settled into a rhythm: my questions, Mala's answers, Pratibha's interjections-cum-translations, polite entreaties from Chidambar to take more tea, the barking of the dog. Little by little, memories released themselves, like bubbles wobbling to the top of a glass of water.

Though *Hamlet* had been savaged by the critics, it had made Sinha's name. Offers flooded in from Bollywood and abroad.

'They wanted her to go to Hollywood,' said Pratibha. 'She had international looks, but her father wouldn't let her go.'

So Sinha had become a star right here in Mumbai. She appeared in another four movies in 1954 alone. Her work rate was formidable; by the end of the fifties she had made over thirty more. Comedies, social movies, spy thrillers, the majority Hindi, some Bengali – often filmed simultaneously, dashing between sets for different takes. She was one of the first female stars to have roles bigger than her male counterparts, and get top billing. She had known everyone, acted with everyone, for everyone.

She had even worked with Sohrab Modi of *Khoon-ka-Khoon* fame, and remembered him as a brute. 'Very hard taskmaster. When he used to pass through my make-up room, he would tell us to stop smiling. He said, "This is working place, not joking place." Just like headmaster. But he was a very stylish actor.'

Gently I guided her back to her own *Hamlet*. She remembered that a man had come specially from London with the costumes. Her dress was almost too heavy to walk in, the wig itchy and hot under the lights.

Her hands flew suddenly to her lips. 'I remember my drowning.'

The scene had been filmed in, of all places, Mumbai Zoo. 'I jumped into the pond. It was very dirty water, above my head, with all the ducks.' She nodded decisively. 'Whatever my director told me to do, you know, I did.'

I wondered if she missed it – the attention, the energy of it all? She insisted not, but I sensed a tinge of regret.

'You must keep moving,' she said firmly. 'That is the secret to a long life.'

Still, a touch of the diva remained. Curious to see what had become of her at the Phalke awards, I checked online when I got back to Britain. With regal magnificence, she had spurned her lifetime award at the last minute. The organisers had insulted her by forgetting to put her name on the invitation card. 'I am an artiste,' she told the press. 'An artiste never dies.'

Shakespeare Wallah was never intended to be the last word. After the movie's unexpected success in 1965, James Ivory and Ismail Merchant toyed with the idea of a sequel, and commissioned a follow-up script from Ruth Prawer Jhabvala. It was called *A Lovely World* and it followed Felicity Kendal's character Lizzie Buckingham back to England, to her new life in newly swinging London. Struggling to make it as an actor, she eventually renounces the stage, settling instead for a conventional marriage with a ditchwater-dull older man – pining all the time for the India she has lost.

In the end, *A Lovely World* never got made; the only records of it now are eight thin folders in Ivory's archives at the University of Oregon. But although the Kendals, too, were long-departed – Laura died in 1992, Geoffrey in 1998 – they hadn't entirely disappeared from India.

In fact I'd heard there were sightings of them near Juhu beach, very much alive.

The place was called Prithvi Theatre. A stone's throw from the beach in the well-appointed middle-class north of the city, Prithvi has a reputation as one of India's most important centres for new drama, running a manically busy series of performances, workshops, seminars and festivals, nearly 600 shows a year. In a city whose heart is at the movies, it is a busy outpost of live theatre.

A travelling company called Prithvi had been set up in 1944 by the pioneering film and theatre actor Prithviraj Kapoor. Bankrolled by Kapoor's film work, the troupe – sometimes eighty strong – took consciousness-raising drama in both Hindi and Urdu on the road, aiming to unite the fledgling nation. Before it finally shuddered to a halt in 1960, the company had performed an estimated 2,662 shows in over 100 towns across the subcontinent. Prithviraj was also the father of the great Kapoor acting clan: Raj was his eldest son, Shashi his youngest. Even now, the Kapoors were regarded as the first family of the Indian film industry. As so often in India, everything connected.

If this story of travelling actors sounds familiar, there is a reason. While in Kolkata in 1956, Shashi had met Jennifer Kendal, Geoffrey and Laura's eldest daughter, then acting with Shakespeareana. They fell in love and – in defiance of their families – married two years later. Twenty years on, Jennifer's parents having returned to England, they united the companies too, and built a permanent theatre on land that Prithviraj had earmarked for the purpose. If *Shakespeare Wallah* had a legacy in India, it was in front of me: a 200-seat auditorium in a grey building the size of a small barn, overlooked by apartment blocks and shaded by palm trees. It, too, had become Indianised.

At Prithvi I met Kunal Kapoor, Shashi's son, who had run the place with his sister Sanjana after their mother Jennifer's early death. Now in his fifties, built like a bison, with a jet-black moustache that wouldn't have disgraced a Texan ranch owner, he was invigorating company. For an hour on my last evening in Mumbai we talked about his father Shashi, his uncle Raj Kapoor, his grandparents the Kendals; and, of course, about Shakespeare. 'What you have to understand is that Shakespeare is in our DNA,' he said.

As we climbed the teetering stairs to his attic office – more ship's gangplank than staircase – he pointed out water-stained costume drawings from the Shakespeareana days: an earringed Petruccio with his arms around Katherine in *The Taming of the Shrew*, Tony Lumpkin in *She Stoops to Conquer* sporting hunting pinks and a skew-whiff horse-riding helmet.

Why did Kunal feel that India had such a connection to Shakespeare?

'So many reasons. Education from the nineteenth century onwards, the mission schools, people being forced to learn it by rote. But it's more than that. Perhaps it sounds bizarre, but these are *Indian* stories, you know? The love, the jealousy, the loyalty, the melodrama, the sense of family – they're such identifiable Indian values. In some ways the plays make more sense here. Tybalt and Juliet are cousins – the intensity of that relationship, I'm not sure it makes sense instinctively in Britain or America. Put them into an eastern setting, India or wherever, and it all starts to be much more real.'

So he didn't buy the theory that India had abandoned Shakespeare after independence, as *Shakespeare Wallah* implied?

He snorted. 'Not at all. For a start my grandparents stayed here a lot longer, which isn't in the film. They were still acting scenes from Shakespeare until they left. And of course Shakespeare went everywhere else.'

He clapped my shoulder and pointed behind me. I'd missed it: a gilt frame above the door, four feet by three, containing a crimson flag. Across the flag, in gold gothic lettering, hand-painted, was one word: SHAKESPEAREANA. After thirty years of peripatetic existence, the company colours, hoisted wherever they played, had found a resting place here in north Mumbai.

Downstairs, it was night-time, fairy lights glimmering in the trees and the open-air café buzzing with suave young Mumbaikers in silk shirts and salwar kameez. Next to them, on a tiny improvised stage in the courtyard, the show had already begun – a young troupe performing a tribute to *commedia dell'arte*. I had little difficulty catching up with its story of bumbling constables and conniving tricksters and wizened misers in the finest Venetian traditions. Not so different from *The Comedy of Errors*, come to think of it.

It was peculiar, watching this medieval European art form to a soundtrack provided by the Indian night. The gossiping of crickets was loud above the distant rumble of traffic and – just discernible – the shushing of the Arabian Sea. But the four actors were whip-smart and the crowd was gulping it up. Some things really did need no translation.

I'D ALWAYS ASSUMED THAT what the history books said was correct: the British had left India in 1947. Not in Kolkata, they hadn't. They seemed to be everywhere I turned. I saw them in the cathedral spire of St Paul's floating above the trees, a dead ringer for Canterbury. They were here in the lions that guarded the gates of Fort William, flanked by a massive – and massively dyspeptic – monument to Queen Victoria. The mustard-yellow taxis, Hindustan Ambassadors, had an accountantly British manner: modelled on 1950s Morris Oxfords, their small round headlights gave them a peering aspect, as if they were perennially displeased by what they saw. The British were even here, somehow, in the grass and leaves: after nine days in the dust and smog and haze of Mumbai, Kolkata seemed almost indecently green.

They were certainly out in force in South Park Street Cemetery at the heart of the old city. I trekked across several fields of Brits. When the cemetery opened in the mid-eighteenth century, it was the largest Christian burial site outside Britain and America. Calcutta had become Kolkata, Park Street Mother Teresa Sarani, but its erstwhile residents clung grimly on, occupying numberless sarcophagi that looked – as doubtless they were intended to – as if Doomsday itself couldn't make them budge. The Indians they had been sent out to rule had no chance. In the honeyed afternoon light I wandered among cenotaphs and urns and obelisks and columns, overgrown with lichen and mould but still standing proud after two hundred years.

Kolkata was where the story of the British in India properly began. The East India Company had been on the subcontinent for the best part of a century by the time its agent Job Charnock, sent east to establish a new trading post, selected a village called Kalikata on the river Hugli in 1690. By the end of the eighteenth century, the village had expanded into a defensive encampment known as Fort William. In time it became the seat of the so-called Bengal Presidency, a trading post that allowed the Company to consolidate its influence into an unbreakable military-politico-industrial complex. After the military strongman Robert Clive reclaimed the city for the British at Plassey in 1757, Warren Hastings, India's first governor general, began moving the colonial administration to Kolkata in 1772. When crown rule was established in 1858, bringing an end to the era of Company government, the city – with its regal palaces and its stately esplanades, its mansions and its gardens – was the natural choice for capital of the Raj.

Even before this, drama had formed an important fulcrum for colonial life in Kolkata, earlier and more thoroughly than it had elsewhere in India. The first English theatre here dated from 1753, twenty-odd years before its equivalent in Mumbai. A new space, the Calcutta theatre, followed in 1775; none other than David Garrick back in England lent his support by sending out one of his assistants, copies of playbooks and rolls of scenery. (The grateful gentlemen of Kolkata shipped him chintz fabric and Madeira wine for his trouble.)

Other playhouses followed, with casts and audiences drawn from the cream of Kolkata society. One of the most renowned was a private theatre built by the society hostess Emma Bristow inside her house in 1789, described as a 'perfect theatre differing only from a public one in its dimensions'. That same year, scenes from *Julius Caesar* were staged, with Mrs Bristow herself playing Brutus's servant Lucius.

While Kolkata's British-born, high-tea brigade seem otherwise to have contented themselves with light skits and farces, Shakespeare was a major presence on the bills at the Calcutta theatre, alongside heavyweights such as Philip Massinger, a later playwright for the King's Men; famous Restoration dramatists Thomas Otway and William Congreve; and the eighteenth-century comedian of manners Richard Brinsley Sheridan. In 1784, *The Merchant of Venice* was staged; according to one report, 'Shylock never appeared to greater advantage.' *Hamlet*, *Romeo and Juliet* and *Richard III* were all acted in the closing years of the eighteenth century and into the early nineteenth.

Such was the zeal for theatre in Kolkata that when the Calcutta theatre closed its doors in 1808, a new playhouse sprang up almost immediately afterwards: the Chowringhee, set up in a fashionable area of the city by a consortium of backers including the pioneering Shakespearian critic D. L. Richardson and Dwarkanath Tagore, grandfather of the great poet Rabindranath Tagore.

The Chowringhee played host to a remarkable string of Shakespeare performances from 1814 onwards. Despite the apprehensions of the *Calcutta Gazette* that a *Macbeth* that April would be 'murdered by a body of amateurs', the production was widely acclaimed, and other plays including *Coriolanus*, *Richard III* and Garrick's adaptation of *The Taming of the Shrew* were successfully done. Ties to the motherland remained strong: a performance of *Henry V* was staged in 1816 to benefit families of soldiers 'killed or maimed' at Waterloo. Armies of English actors trooped out to Kolkata, bringing with them the latest European tastes and trends.

Perhaps the greatest of these visitors was Mrs Esther Leach: acclaimed as the 'Mrs Siddons of Bengal' after Sarah Siddons, the tragic muse of the London stage, she died in the service of her art in 1843 after oil lamps set fire to her gown during *The Merchant of Venice*. (Terribly burned, she expired two weeks later.) The Chowringhee itself had already gone up in smoke a few years before, but the theatre that replaced it, a splendid edifice in the Grecian style known as the Sans Souci, attracted stars by the boatload from London and Australia.

The early cantonment theatres were strictly whites only: no 'natives' allowed. But Shakespeare began to percolate more widely. As in Mumbai, educators were largely responsible. In 1831, a group of Bengali school students founded what is thought to be the first indigenous-owned professional playhouse anywhere in India, the Hindu theatre, specifically intended for the performance of Shakespeare. Their opening show included scenes from *Julius Caesar*, staged alongside an English translation of the seven-act play *Uttararamacharita* ('The Later Deeds of Rama') by the classical Sanskrit playwright Bhavabhuti. According to the faintly dismissive account in the *Calcutta Courier*, 'Some young Hindoo gentlemen admirably schooled in the Histrionic art exercise their talents for the amusement of their native and European friends.'

A few years earlier, in 1822, a thirteen-year-old Anglo-Indian boy called Henry Louis Vivian Derozio acted Shylock in a school production of *The Merchant of Venice* – perhaps the first Indian in history to do so. Derozio would go on to found the free-thinking Young Bengal movement, which, inspired by ideas gleaned from the French Revolution, rebelled against the strictures of conservative Hindu society. With Derozio's death in 1831 at the age of just twenty-two, Young Bengal foundered, but it helped inspire what became known as the Bengali Renaissance, the great flowering of Bengali literature and thought that swept through Kolkata in the nineteenth century, many of whose leading lights received a thorough grounding in Shakespeare as part of a western-style education.

More explosive cultural minglings were to occur. In August 1848, a performance of *Othello* opened at the Sans Souci. White actors had blacked up to play non-white characters for years in Kolkata, but in order to drum up business, the theatre manager decided to try something novel: a young Indian actor called Baishnava Charan Adhya in the lead. The *Calcutta Star* ran an advert promoting 'a novel evening's entertainment . . . Shakespeare's Tragedy of *Othello* . . . By a Native Gentleman'. More sensationally still, Esther Leach's daughter, acting under her stage name Mrs Anderson, would play Desdemona, joined by a similarly white cast.

Kolkata was agog: an Indian appearing on stage with white people! Seducing an Englishwoman! Crowds built up outside the theatre and the police were summoned. Fearing the worst, the garrison commander intervened and ordered the soldiers in the cast not to perform, meaning that opening night had to be moved back by a week.

Once the show had finally opened, the press damned Adhya with thin, sneering praise. The *Englishman* proclaimed that 'scarcely a line was intelligible', before adding that 'the performance was wonderful for a Native'. A month later, it sent a correspondent back to have another go: 'tame, languid, affected, tedious and imperfect, and a cruel infliction, undeservedly imposed upon a kind-hearted and indulgent public'.

Another paper, *Bengal Harkaru*, strove to be more generous but still declared Adhya's delivery 'cramped'. The general tone seems to have been that of Samuel Johnson on the similarity between female preachers and dogs walking on their hind legs: not done well, but surprising to find it done at all. An English correspondent wrote to the *Calcutta Star* chortling over his attempts to witness what he referred to as 'the real unpainted nigger Othello'.

The inference was clear: Indian people could take exams, study poetry, become obedient colonial administrators, even read Shakespeare if they wished. But for them to think of performing him in English – least of all in a white theatre for white audiences – was quite different. It was a joke.

While I had managed to spend ten days in Mumbai and see barely half an hour of live drama, in Kolkata it was all I could do to avoid the stuff. The afternoon after I arrived I interviewed Professor Ananda Lal, an expert on the history of Shakespeare in Bengal, who promptly invited me to join him at a contemporary retelling of the ancient Sanskrit play

Shakuntala, a roaring hit for Prithviraj Kapoor in the 1940s. The British Council were petitioning me to come to several events. Someone else was keen to show me Bengali folk theatre, if I could spare a few hours . . .

There was one performance I was kicking myself for not having seen. It had opened six months earlier, and – while not quite on a par with Adhya's *Othello* – had caused a major stir in the tight-knit, fervently politicised world of Kolkatan theatre. It was a version of *Macbeth* by a young theatre company named Swapnasandhani, and it had, unlikely as it sounded, run into trouble with the state government.

The trouble was this: the translation they had used, by the playwright Ujjwal Chattopadhyay, had made unflattering references to Mamata Banerjee's populist Trinamool Congress party (TMC), which had recently swept to power in West Bengal after thirty-four years of Left Front rule. Banerjee had been a trusted lieutenant in the Indian National Congress before launching her own party on a wave of anti-Left Front feeling. Into a speech of Malcolm's near the end of the play, Chattopadhyay had slyly inserted a quote from one of Banerjee's speeches. In TMC circles there was outrage; the playwright, a state employee, came under pressure to recant. The next time *Macbeth* went on stage, the quote had mysteriously vanished.

Censorship? Political pressure? Publicity stunt? Theories were legion, and *The Times of India* had picked up the story. Even by the fissiparous standards of Bengali politics – 'No matter how long you live here,' someone told me, 'you never really understand them' – this was a diverting turn of events.

When I called him, the director, Koushik Sen, was happy to talk. Could I come to a venue near the cathedral? He would corral some colleagues and we could discuss all things Shakespeare and Bengal, perhaps show me a little of their work.

When I stepped inside the Academy of Fine Arts, the atmosphere was febrile. Technicians were hurrying around backstage. A man strode past towards the dressing rooms, three bright blonde wigs slung over his arm. An assistant guided me through to the auditorium – Sen was busy right now, she said, but he could talk afterwards.

After what, though? I'd arrived expecting an interview-cum-group-discussion. Apparently I'd walked into a full-scale *Macbeth*.

Full-scale was the phrase: the setting was urgently contemporary, with the shock troops of Macbeth (who was played by Sen himself) in camouflage fatigues and glistening knee-high boots that put me in mind of *Star Wars*. A voluptuous Lady Macbeth shimmered malevolently in ballgown and tiara; the Witches, spitting and seething like caged snakes, were extravagantly cross-dressed (this was where the blonde wigs had ended up). When the Macbeths finally ascended to power, it was to a throne of human bones.

The Bengali translation was beyond me, and I'd left my complete works behind at the guesthouse. But I comprehended the metaphors clearly enough: power was corrupt and corrupting. Direful ambition lay at every turn. Even the good were not immune: Macduff was a shrewd politician, and it looked only too likely that Duncan's son, Malcolm, would likely be a chip off the old tyrant. (There was a small cheer from the audience as he finished one speech; the Banerjee quote had evidently been reinserted.)

I glanced at the programme. 'We fear that the disease that plagued Scotland during Macbeth's tyrannical rule has also infected our land and times,' read the director's notes.

After the performance was over, I was directed through to the gallery next door. Fifteen or so people were waiting, most in their twenties or early thirties – directors, actors, designers, a translator or two. A portrait of Mother Teresa gazed gravely down on us from the wall.

They were talkative and passionate. I'd arrived in the middle of a Bardic boom, they said. Following a Bengali translation called *Raja Lear* in 2010 starring the veteran actor Soumitra Chatterjee, revered for his collaborations with Satyajit Ray, there had been no fewer than eight separate Shakespeare productions in Kolkata, a staggering number given the home-grown Bengali drama that usually fills the city's stages. *Raja Lear* itself had been staged nearly forty times, and was still in the repertoire; Bangla productions of *As You Like It*, *Julius Caesar* and *A Midsummer Night's Dream* had followed. *Macbeth* had been seen more than thirty times already.

A few minutes later Koushik Sen came in, shining with sweat, still in costume. His army fatigues gave him the disquieting appearance of a junior officer about to send the whole bunch of us to military prison.

He had chosen *Macbeth* for unashamedly political reasons, he said: though it was ostensibly about medieval Scotland or Jacobean England, the Banerjee situation had made parallels right here in West Bengal.

'Shakespeare is a way for us to keep thinking. Macbeth is thinking when no one else is thinking: this is why he wins.'

Another director shouted from the back: 'We want to say what we want, through a Shakespearian text.'

Had they really come under pressure to censor the performance?

'There were various pressures,' Sen said, his expression difficult to read. 'But we talked among ourselves, and we decided that we would put the references back in.'

Macbeth had a deep history in these parts. The play had been translated by the revered father of Bengali drama, Girish Chandra Ghosh (1844–1912), who staged it at the Minerva theatre in 1893 in the midst of the Bengali Renaissance. The performance was acclaimed as an artistic and political landmark: the *Hindu Patriot* considered it a 'new departure in the dramatic history of Bengal', and even the *Englishman* admitted that although 'a Bengali Thane of Cawdor is a living suggestion of incongruity . . . the reality is an astonishing reproduction of the standard convention of the English stage'.

As I talked with Sen and his colleagues, one name came up more than any other: that of Utpal Dutt. One of the most important theatre-makers of the post-independence generation, Dutt had also become a huge star in Bollywood. I tried to recall when I had first heard of him, then remembered: he'd made a cameo in *Shakespeare Wallah*. He had been a good friend and former collaborator of the Kendal family.

Born in 1929, twenty years after Geoffrey, Dutt had joined the Kendals while still studying at St Xavier's College in Kolkata before striking out with his own company, the Little Theatre Group, which produced cut-down versions of Ibsen, Tagore and Shaw and toured them across India. Of the many remarkable figures I had come across during my travels, Dutt was among the most captivating: one of the most prolific film actors of his generation, responsible for making over 200 Hindi and Urdu movies, most of them entirely forgettable, he had another, more disconcerting, life – as a Marxist political activist in West Bengal.

As Indian politics had intensified in the 1950s and 1960s, Dutt started to write his own plays and joined the underground Maoist Naxalbari movement. In 1965, after the ruling Congress party took umbrage at his drama *Kallol* ('Waves') about government complicity in the 1946 Mumbai naval mutiny, he was imprisoned for several months without trial. Dutt spent the rest of his days living a fantastical life, somehow supremely Indian: famous actor in Bollywood potboilers by day, leftist guerrilla by night. Shakespeare was the glue that held together these two very separate identities.

Shakespeare haunted Dutt, or perhaps the other way around – most obviously during his career in mainstream theatre, where his Othello was acclaimed as the greatest in Indian history, so famous that in a 1961 Bengali melodrama called *Saptapadi*, which featured a scene from the play, it was the rasping-voiced Dutt who had redubbed the Moor's speeches because it was said no one else was qualified to do them. (Revenge for Baishnava Charan Adhya, perhaps.)

But Shakespeare also nourished Dutt's politics. In the 1960s, declaring that he was finished with staging English-language performances for uncomprehending audiences ('they sat there with clenched fists – pretending to enjoy it'), he resolved to adapt and act the plays in Bengali. He began with a modern-dress *Julius Caesar* (described as 'through contemporary eyes') in 1964, with Dutt himself as Caesar. The idea developed of taking the plays out of western-style theatres in the city and touring them to an altogether more challenging constituency – impoverished rural audiences in far-flung corners of the state.

Bengal had a boisterously popular folk-theatre tradition known as *jatra* (from the Sanskrit 'setting out on a journey'), and Dutt realised that Shakespeare could make excellent sense in the form. Traditional *jatras*, rumbustious melodramas bursting with noise and music, went on all night long, but Dutt's adaptations, created with a team of veteran actors, were abbreviated to make them available to farmers, labourers, housewives and tea-plant workers doing shifts. They were staged most often in the open air, preceded by a free musical performance designed to pull in audiences. Dutt estimated that sometimes they played to 30,000 people at a time, under fierce carbide lights, tannoys sending the dialogue booming out across the fields.

Their Shakespeare was condensed: *Romeo and Juliet* became a folk play called *Bhuli Nai Priya* ('I Have Not Forgotten, My Love'); *A Midsummer Night's Dream* was relocated from the forests outside Athens to the Bengal mangrove forests. Dutt had done *Macbeth*, too – in fact several times, first in 1954 in a 'fast-moving, noisy' version that toured Bengal villages; then again in September 1975, in response to the state of emergency declared by Indira Gandhi, during which Dutt's own scripts were banned.

Dissatisfied with pre-existing Bengali translations, Dutt wrote his own version of the Scottish play, sharpening its left-wing politics by inserting extra scenes for a cast of Bangla-speaking peasants and filling it with music by Shostakovich and Khachaturian as well as Stravinsky.

When the show came to Kolkata, Dutt printed embittered words spoken by Ross on the front of the theatre programme:

> Alas, poor country,
> Almost afraid to know itself. It cannot
> Be called our mother, but our grave, where nothing
> But who knows nothing is once seen to smile . . .

'We knew that we couldn't find a better play against autocracy,' Dutt said. Koushik Sen smiled quietly: his sentiments exactly.

A passionate Shakespearian who was also a passionate polemicist; a Sanskrit-speaking intellectual who could recite Virgil from memory and mingled with factory workers and farm labourers; a radical Marxist who was also a good pal of the Kendals and made movies for Merchant Ivory – whatever paradoxes I was trying to resolve about the many identities of Shakespeare in India, Dutt seemed to contain plenty, not to mention some I hadn't even thought to consider.

While in Mumbai it had been a struggle to find any traces of Shakespeare at all, in Kolkata he seemed – like the British – to be everywhere. There was a whole street named after him, Shakespeare Sarani (formerly Theatre Road, rechristened in 1964 for the 400th anniversary of the poet's birth). There was a dauntingly active organisation called the Shakespeare Society of Eastern India, run by an affable, Falstaffian academic called Amitava Roy, who welcomed me into one of their Sunday-evening meetings and plied me with sweet tea and disconcertingly knowledgeable questions.

'Shakespeare is in everyone's hearts here,' Roy beamed, to fervent nods from his congregation. 'No one else is like him, no one across the world. You know the Indian word *Gurudeva*? It is what Mahatma Gandhi called Rabindranath Tagore. *Guru*, you know, "one who leads". *Deva* is "maker". Shakespeare, Rabindranath, Homer – they are *Gurudevas*. They show you the way, and they show you the truth.'

I had seen the statue to Shakespeare on Shakespeare Sarani? I must find it at once and pay tribute, Roy's group said. Feeling a little shaken by the fervour of their belief, I promised to try.

History, as ever, had a great deal to do with this. The shadow of English literature fell across countless Kolkatan writers of the nineteenth century – not only Young Bengal playwrights such as Michael Madhusudan Dutta and Dinabandhu Mitra, who pioneered drama at the new playhouses during the 1860s and 1870s, but poets, novelists, philosophers, musicians. The lyricist Dwijendralal Ray penned epic dramas much influenced by the English history plays, while the father of the Bengali novel, Bankim Chandra Chattopadhyay, borrowed as liberally from Shakespeare as he did from Thomas Hardy and Walter Scott. Bankim based the heroine of his early novel *Kapalkundala* (1866) partly on Miranda in *The Tempest*, and in an essay pointed out how slow the British had been to 'grasp the import of [Shakespeare's] wonderful plays'. A modern critic put it well, and in terms that the evangelical Shakespeare Society of Eastern India might have supported: among the English-educated intelligentsia of nineteenth-century Bengal, Shakespeare became a source of 'non-denominational spirituality'.

One writer engaged with Shakespeare assiduously, the most famous Kolkatan of all: Rabindranath Tagore, India's first Nobel laureate. As a child growing up in a phenomenally wealthy Brahmin family, Tagore was given a thorough western education alongside schooling in classical Indian languages, religion and literature, and read widely in Sanskrit, Bengali and English, including poets such as Byron and Coleridge, as well as Dante in English translation. According to his first English biographer, Tagore was forced by his tutor to produce line-by-line translations of Kalidasa's *Kumarasambhava* ('Birth of Kumara') and *Macbeth* as punishment for poor behaviour.

Tagore read more when he travelled to Brighton and London in 1879 as a gauche eighteen-year-old, taking classes at University College on *Coriolanus* and *Antony and Cleopatra* (which he 'liked very much'), but admitted that he was disillusioned by his experiences in the seat of Empire. Before he arrived, he wrote later, he had supposed Britain 'so devoted to higher culture that from one end to the other it would resound with the strains of Tennyson's lyre'. Real life bore little resemblance to literary fantasy. In a letter home he complained bitterly how some English seemed astonished that Indians knew anything about culture at all. It was a tension that would trouble Tagore for the rest of his life, particularly when he began to call for independence from Britain. Having been knighted by George V, he renounced the award in disgust at the Jallianwala Bagh massacre of 1919, in which protestors in Amritsar had been fired on without warning by British troops, leaving at least 400 dead and 1,200 wounded.

Some of the same ambiguity touched Tagore's relationship with Shakespeare. It was clear that he was influenced by the older writer a great deal, not least in the playscripts he wrote. In the preface to *Malini* (1896), whose tough-minded heroine owes something to Shakespeare's own female leads, he admitted, '[his] plays are always our dramatic model. Their manifold varieties and extensiveness and conflicts had captured our mind from the beginning.'

In 1916, invited by the Anglo-Jewish scholar Israel Gollancz to contribute to a commemorative volume for the 300th anniversary of Shakespeare's death, Tagore composed a brief Bengali verse comparing Shakespeare (in the translation Gollancz printed) to a sun whose 'fiery disc' had appeared near 'England's horizon', but whose rays now stretched across the world:

> Therefore at this moment, after the end of centuries, the palm groves by the Indian sea raise their tremulous branches to the sky murmuring your praise.

Despite this extravagant tribute, Tagore – unlike many of his Bengali contemporaries – was not an uncritical admirer. Where Bankim had adopted Miranda as one of his own heroines, Tagore took issue with the very substance of *The Tempest*, devoting a critical essay published in 1902 to it and *Shakuntala*, revered as one of the greatest works by the Sanskrit writer Kalidasa. Tagore observed numerous echoes, for instance in the romance between Shakespeare's Miranda and Prince Ferdinand, which resembles that of the innocent young nymph Shakuntala and the wayward King Dushyanta, and in the way both texts use an idyllic remote setting in order to intensify the drama (in Kalidasa's case a secluded forest, in Shakespeare's the near-deserted island).

But Tagore's comparison is not to Shakespeare's favour. While Kalidasa uses the seduction of an all-too-innocent girl as potent dramatic irony – Dushyanta, as the audience well knows from the story's origins in the *Mahabharata*, will abandon Shakuntala – Tagore argues that Shakespeare's Miranda is a more sentimental figure, 'girt round by ignorance', seen almost entirely through her relationship with her father and Ferdinand, her lover. In contrast, Shakuntala is truly a child of nature, 'linked in spirit to her surroundings', whose connection to the forest is implicit and essential. Where Shakespeare, Tagore argues, simply drops his characters like chess pieces into their environment, Kalidasa genuinely understands both his cast and where they end up – and thus the older play has a much more subtle understanding of the relationship between mankind and nature.

It would be easy to argue that Tagore misunderstood, that the object of *The Tempest* is not the 'isle' it is set on but the power-plays of the humans stranded there. Still, I felt that his argument was persuasive, particularly when it came to the troubled relationship between master and servants in the play. Contrary to the best efforts of British Victorian critics, who fell over themselves to argue that Prospero was a benign foreign ruler bringing enlightened civilisation to the island and its natives, Tagore identified a bleaker truth about the relationship between coloniser and colonised: '[Ariel] wishes to be free, but, bound and oppressed by human force, he is made to work like a slave. He has no love in his heart, no tears in his eyes.'

In *Shakuntala*, he wrote, there was 'love, peace and fellowship'. *The Tempest*, meanwhile, offered 'oppression, rule, rigour'. It would take western scholars decades to reach similar conclusions.

My final day in Kolkata flew past in a blur – dinner at the house of a theatre critic, followed by a surreal evening in the company of Amitava Roy, who gamely offered to take me to the last night of a *jatra* festival. Together he and I crammed into a dusty auditorium in a run-down district of Kolkata, overflowing with stout middle-aged couples, and watched an hour of wild and indecipherable melodrama: a cross (as far as I could construe) between *Dallas*, the Hindu epics and the more tumultuous sections of a revivalist prayer meeting, all to the raucous accompaniment of electric guitar, keyboard and drums. The show's title was *Anurager Chhoya* ('The Touch of Love').

Over ten million tickets are said to be sold for *jatra* performances each year in West Bengal, and perhaps a hundred companies are active, touring far-flung villages in the poor rural parts of the state. This is one of the few corners of the world where theatre remains more popular than cinema. Despite their mythological origins, *jatra* shows now draw on everything from news events to Bollywood movies and American television shows; there is even reputed to have been a *jatra* based on James Cameron's film *Titanic*.

It wasn't just the dry ice, strobe lights and chest-thumping acting that made me wonder if this was what Parsi theatre would have been like to watch: *jatra*, yet another Indian melting pot of cultural influences, was surely one of its offspring. And it suddenly occurred to me that this, too, was what it might have been like to watch theatre in the California Gold Rush – except here in India the tradition was vigorously, full-bloodedly alive. Utpal Dutt had described this kind of folk theatre as 'tempestuous incantation'. Having seen it live, I felt I understood exactly what he was trying to summon.

I had one place remaining on my itinerary: Delhi, where I was due at a conference being held by the Shakespeare Society of India (no relation to the Shakespeare Society of Eastern India, it appeared: yet another Indian doubling). I'd wangled an invitation by offering to speak about the World Shakespeare Festival. I also hoped that, after two and a half weeks of hectic travel, the conference might offer a pause for reflection – a way of putting into focus the many colliding Shakespearian images I had accumulated in India, America and Germany. Many of India's leading Shakespeare scholars were due to be in attendance. At least some of them might be able to tell me what was really going on in global Shakespeare.

A little after 4.30 p.m., I boarded the Rajdhani Express, pushing through the hooting crowds of red-turbaned porters on the platform. Only one other passenger was in my compartment: a small, neat man in his late fifties, with bulldog jowls and a tidy grey moustache. He was buried in the *Times of India* crossword; we gave each other absent nods, like seasoned commuters.

Twenty-five minutes later, right on time, we slid out of Howrah station. The sun, fierce orange, was sinking into the west, burnishing the marshy streams and lakes as we slipped out of the city. Every so often there was a glimpse of the darkening River Hugli. As we gained speed, the shuddering and creaking of the train settling into a ponderous, bottom-heavy sway, I experienced a sensation that had evaded me since arriving in India: something approaching peace.

FOR MY LAST THREE DAYS IN INDIA, I played at knowing what I was doing. I rose early in my spartan student quarters at the University of Delhi guesthouse, attempting not to electrocute myself on the power socket placed inexplicably beneath the shower. I walked for twenty-five minutes through the morning haze to Indraprastha College, bought a glass of freshly pressed orange juice from the juice-wallah by the gates. I attended lectures and seminars, asked questions, filled most of another notebook with neat lines of ink. On manicured lawns, I sipped sweet chai and made small talk with students and professors. I gave my paper. It was mediocre.

Whatever clear ideas I possessed about Shakespeare in India, I sensed them slipping away. It wasn't the organisers' fault: the sessions were insightful on everything from differing translations of *Macbeth* to the relationship between Shakespeare and Kalidasa (yet another Shakespeare of India: the subcontinent was groaning with them).

No – it was me who was to blame. Whatever story I was trying to tell, I was losing track of it. Tamil Shakespeare, Kannada Shakespeare, Shakespeare and Hindu philosophy, Shakespeare and Tagore, Shakespeare and Gandhi, postcolonial Shakespeare, post-postcolonial Shakespeare, remakes of Shakespeare, re-remakes, re-re-remakes, re-re-re-remakes: too many Shakespeares, for my cluttered brain at least. Too many Indias.

One elderly academic, white-haired, shrunken inside his overlarge suit, kept trying to show me his magnum opus, a titanic compendium of Indian writings in praise of Shakespeare. The book was nearly a thousand pages long. Had I known about its existence when I arrived, it might have been a useful companion, if somewhat bulky. Now, though, it was the last thing I wanted to read. It seemed an all-too-pointed reminder of how little I knew about India – and, for that matter, about Shakespeare.

Back in Mumbai I'd spent a morning with a playwright, Ramu Ramanathan. He told me about a project he'd done with students in which he'd asked them to go out on the streets and imagine Shakespeare's plays happening right there in the city: Shylock spotted on the concourse at Masjid Bunder station, Cleopatra sunning herself on Versova beach. I'd loved the idea of a cast of Shakespearian characters on the loose – a glimpse of Ophelia here, a half-caught Coriolanus there. But one could spend a lifetime searching for their faces, and never quite succeed. It struck me as not so different from the journey I was on.

It wasn't just India; I felt all the different Shakespeares I'd encountered juddering and blurring into each other. Grey concrete and green ice and biting Baltic air; King Lear amidst the grain elevators of the Midwest; Richard III in a saloon bar in Malakoff Diggins; a smirking Romantic statue in Weimar; a punk singer yelling out Shakespearian couplets in a basement in Washington DC. And this was before one even got to Shakespeare's myriad Indian faces: Gulzar's elderly actor in beard and ruff, winking knowingly over the credits to *Angoor*; that *Star Wars*-style *Macbeth* in West Bengal in the shadow of the government; the girlish figure of Mala Sinha, sinking beneath the water's surface . . .

Perhaps it had been unwise to commence a journey with *The Comedy of Errors*: the metaphor seemed rather too obvious. What was it that Antipholus said – 'in quest of them, unhappy, lose myself . . .'? I had long since lost myself. At the end of the summer I was due in South Africa, to chase down a whole new set of Shakespeares. The thought made me dizzy.

During a break late one morning, I sat on a chair on the grass, putting off returning to the overheated lecture hall. In a few days, the forecast said, the *loo* winds would start to blow, and Delhi would surrender to high summer. By then, I would be above them, in a plane bound for London. High over the Himalayas, angled towards Turkmenistan and the Caspian Sea.

Everyone had gone back in. Or nearly everyone: a few chairs away was a professor I had met the previous day. His research on Hindi cinema I had found hugely useful when planning my journey; I had been glad to make his acquaintance.

'Bunking class?' he said, fanning himself with his programme. 'Me also. After a few days at these things I begin to switch off.' He tapped his temple. 'The old brain, you know.'

A white-jacketed waiter was carrying tiffin boxes across the lawn. We watched the shadows shifting and shimmering in the hot breeze.

'How's your trip? Getting what you need?'

I admitted I was finding it difficult to join the dots. So many theories about Shakespeare, about India, about Germany and the US, so many cultures, interpretations, languages – I was having trouble working out if any of them combined. Mumbai, Pune and Kolkata had left my head in even more of a scramble than usual. All these different adaptations . . . It felt as though one could go on for ever, and never reach the end.

I sensed he was stifling a smile.

'Old chap,' he said softly, 'isn't that rather the point?'

On my penultimate evening in Delhi, I took the metro south. It was a long journey, over an hour, but the carriage was quiet and I was glad of the air conditioning and the chance to be alone with my thoughts. The train rocked softly as we ticked through the stations: Green Park, Malviya Nagar, Saket, Qutub Minar. As we came above ground, I watched the city flickering past, bulky silhouettes of office buildings and a clutter of low-rise apartment blocks shrinking into the haze. When the carriage doors hissed open at each stop, I caught the scent of the city: dust and drying earth, grass, burning rubbish, diesel fumes, woodsmoke from the fires of nightwatchmen huddled over braziers. The sun was slowly making its way down through the sky, tinting everything the colour of weak tea.

Down the steps at Ghitorni station, a party was readying itself for the off. Bulbous light fittings in crimson and gold were being lugged off a truck, and a small band of musicians was crouching by the side of the road next to their instruments. In their scarlet jackets and pressed white trousers, they looked as if they were about to be planted on top of a cake. Behind them were the gates of a large hotel. A wedding, I guessed. As I went past, a young man in the band grinned and raised his cap in mock-salute. Its pom-pom bobbed crazily on his head.

I had come out here for an old Indian favourite: *The Winter's Tale*. The play was being staged by the young Delhi company Tadpole. The setting was outdoors, and the performance would be promenade-style. I had heard good things at the conference; anyway, it was an excuse to sneak away.

They had done well with the location, at least, I thought. The venue was a yoga-retreat-cum-arts-centre near the city limits, down a winding lane just off a main road. As I came through the gate I saw a low, pretty collection of buildings draped across the grass around a small and shadowy lake. Lanterns had been lit, white orbs floating in the tree branches.

I was directed up through thickets of bamboo towards the playing space: a sand-covered drum on top of a small mound, perhaps the radius of a baseball infield, with a large tent-like canopy in bamboo and wicker, open on all sides, draped with pieces of white fabric that stirred slightly in the cool evening breeze. I grinned as I came close: it wasn't dissimilar from the outdoor auditorium Harold Littledale had seen while watching *Cymbeline* in Vadodara in 1880. Would there be anti-British jokes? I hoped there would.

The audience were sitting in cane chairs and benches and on rugs spread around. There was a scattering of Europeans and Delhiites, neat young men in chinos and Nehru waistcoats, women wearing bright scarves in lemon and sea-green. Beyond the buzz of pre-show conversation the evening was noisy with the clucking of crickets and frogs and the keening of peacocks. I inserted myself on the ground next to a man in a Puma T-shirt and Birkenstocks and waited for the performance to begin.

It did so with a tableau: a woman, heavily pregnant, stepping into the light. She looked around at us sadly, as if in foreknowledge: a young wife, Hermione, about to have her world wrenched apart. Gradually a cast assembled itself, twelve actors in all, one of them playing Hermione's young son, Mamillius. With two servants gossiping about the state of affairs between Sicily and Bohemia, we were pitched into the world of the play.

I had seen more highly polished versions of *The Winter's Tale*, but rarely performed with such grace and deftness. It was alive with Indian and African drums, singing and dance. The actors were barefoot, clad in long, elegantly tailored tunics. A parlour game became deadly serious when Leontes invited Polixenes, whom he suspects of being unfaithful with Hermione, to play for his life. The stage was bare – by turns a dance floor, Mamillius's sandpit, and, when jealousy took hold of Leontes, the arena for a predator on the loose. When Hermione was eventually summoned to answer for herself, she was dragged across the sand with such violence that the woman opposite me flinched.

The directors, Anirudh Nair and Neel Chaudhuri, had defined the play linguistically. Shakespeare's English was used in the Sicilian court scenes, with the servant characters speaking in accents a shade heavier. When the action moved to the countryside of Bohemia – the on-stage narrator Time hurrying us forward sixteen years, the cast exchanging their fine tunics for patchwork shirts and jackets – the language shifted to Hindustani. We moved, too, to another space on the opposite side of the garden. As the shepherds prepared for their sheep-shearing celebrations with wild dances, the audience began to yell and cheer.

I wasn't able to judge the translation, but it seemed to me an expressive solution to the shifting geographies of the play – and, perhaps, only possible in a multilingual, multivocal country like India. Hindustani itself is an Indian sort of compromise: chunks of Hindi alongside gobbets of Urdu, mixed with Persian Farsi, Sanskrit and Arabic. The language has a colonial history – promoted by Orientalist educators in the nineteenth century as a way of keeping the Raj intact – but the theatre-makers told me later they hadn't intended to invoke it. For them Shakespeare was a fully Indian writer, not British property. They wanted to make a production that moved beyond the colonial past; which, as far as possible, broke free from it. As *The Winter's Tale* demonstrated, there were issues at stake larger even than postcolonial politics – love, jealousy, birth, death.

It has usually been assumed that *The Tempest* was the last drama Shakespeare wrote on his own, with three co-written scripts, probably done with his younger colleague John Fletcher, coming later: *Henry VIII* or *All is True*, the lost play *Cardenio*, the bittersweet and troubling romance *The Two Noble Kinsmen*. In truth, as with so many things about Shakespeare, there is no way of knowing in which order the late plays came. It is autobiographical over-reading that makes us yearn to associate the magician Prospero who breaks his staff and drowns his book with Shakespeare bidding farewell to his art.

Myself, I had always preferred the theory that *The Winter's Tale* was Shakespeare's goodbye note, if such a thing existed. There was something about its gleeful hop-skipping across improbabilities: the shepherds who stumble across a baby in its basket on a hillside ('Thou metst with things dying, I with things new-born'); the budding Bohemian romance between the girl Perdita, brought up in innocence of her royal birth, and a disguised prince, the son of her father's mortal enemy. Then there was the crowning impossibility, the most theatrical of all: that a statue of a long-dead wife might yet turn out to be really her, and alive.

By now we had moved yet again, to English and the side of the lake. On the opposite bank, a female figure clad in white stood motionless, silhouetted against the dark trees – Hermione. A drum began steadily to beat. Leontes stepped towards her, and faltered; then reached out a hand to touch. 'O, she's warm!' he exclaimed. It was left to Paulina, Hermione's fiercest and most faithful friend, to deliver Shakespeare's riddling explanation, and with it all the paradoxes of theatre:

That she is living,
Were it but told you, should be hooted at
Like an old tale. But it appears she lives . . .

The American critic Anne Barton, who lived for many years in Britain, put it well. 'The last plays,' she wrote, 'appeal so poignantly to our sense of how we should like the world to be, and know that it is not.' It took supreme art to contrive happiness from such wreckage; a kind of artlessness, too.

Walking slowly back to the metro afterwards, I realised there had been one other noise, alongside the frogs and grasshoppers and peacocks – the noise of frantic drumming. It was the wedding I had passed earlier. As I climbed the stairs to the platform, I looked down and across: the party was in full swing. The hotel grounds were ablaze with crimson and pink spotlights, tables dotting the grounds. On the grass, people were whirling in dance, arms high above their heads. I looked for a long time, but couldn't see the couple.

William Shake-the-Sword

Johannesburg · Kimberley · Durban · Cape Town

I
t was July 2012. I had come to the private view of a new Shakespeare exhibition at the British Museum in London. Gallerists, art-world types, theatre folk, hacks, hangers-on: we were gathering in the Great Court, balancing canapés and glasses of warm white wine. Serving staff slid neatly through the crowd. Refracted and diffused by the swelling glass roof, the hubbub was building into a soft, contented roar.

Drifting with some warm white wine of my own, I eavesdropped. A group of actors was midway through a satisfying disquisition on the awfulness of a colleague's show. Someone was talking clamorously about securing Olympics tickets against the odds. A frisson went around when a team of security men materialised near the entrance. The frisson flattened, then evaporated: it was merely the retinue of the culture minister, widely despised.

Unable to spy anyone I knew, I wandered off and did what one is never meant to do at private views: view the exhibition. For a Shakespeare obsessive, there was much to savour. On one wall was the portrait of the Moroccan ambassador to the court of Elizabeth I, Abd el-Ouahed ben Messaoud ben Mohammed Anoun. Depicting the ambassador scowling splendidly, scimitar at his side, white turban neatly knotted, this was thought to be the first portrait by an English artist of a Muslim. From what I had learned in India about Shakespeare's eagerness to pluck inspiration from anywhere and everywhere, Messaoud played a more intriguing role here, too: he was (just possibly) the original for Shakespeare's Othello.

I was unexpectedly entranced by the skull of a brown bear, perhaps female: a sad, broken wedge of bone, the colour of old toffee. Excavated

from the site of the original London Globe, it had been donated to
Dulwich College, the boys' school in south London founded by a great
rival of Shakespeare's, the actor-manager Edward Alleyn. The bear had
been baited, her teeth filed down to make her less lethal to the mastiffs
who tormented her, so prolonging her death. I wondered if playwright
or actor had heard her bellow in pain. Alleyn, who owned bear pits and
brothels as well as theatres, might well have supervised her demise.

A few cabinets away was a 'hornbook', a wooden pallet about the
size of a small restaurant menu, enclosing a slip of paper on which
were printed the letters of the alphabet and the Lord's Prayer, with
a translucent piece of horn in place of a glass panel. *A e i o u, ba be bi
bo bu, ca ce ci co cu* . . . The young Shakespeare would have used one
exactly like this. There was something uncommonly affecting about
the thought of the boy's lips shaping the sounds.

In a corner was a fragment of 'Herne's Oak', the tree in Windsor
Great Park that witnesses Falstaff's humiliation at the hands of
Mistresses Ford and Page in *The Merry Wives of Windsor*. The scene is
a fiction, of course, but the oak was real enough: it had blown down
in 1863, a sad but accurate augur of the tercentenary fiasco. Here it
was, neatly catalogued and archived, testifying to little more than
the Victorian fetish for making relics – any relic at all, no matter how
circumstantial – from the National Poet.

Lost in thought, I took a little while to notice the buzz of activity
near the gallery exit. In the middle of the shadowed space, illuminated
by a shallow pool of warm light, a crowd had collected around a display
cabinet. Faces pressed close against the glass, they stood there in mute
contemplation. Behind them, others were politely waiting in line. I
looked around: the rest of the gallery was almost empty. Whatever
was in that cabinet, it was the star of the show.

I sidled closer. It was a book. Compared to the treasures I'd been
looking at a few moments before, it wasn't much: modern, small,
dumpy, its scuffed pages propped open on an acrylic stand. On the
spine were printed the words 'The Complete Works of Shakespeare'
in faded blue type. The dustjacket was lined with what seemed to be
Hindu prayer cards: images of gods and goddesses in pink and garish
yellow.

As I was watching, two women solemnly bowed their heads. They
looked as though they were venerating a holy object.

In a way, they were. Hindu camouflage notwithstanding, the book was the so-called Robben Island Bible: a copy of the complete works owned by Sonny Venkatrathnam, a former South African political activist who spent six years on the island penal colony during the late 1970s. The book was a cheap, mass-market, single-volume edition of the plays and poems first published in the 1950s, named the 'Alexander' text after its editor, Peter Alexander. There are thousands, perhaps tens of thousands, of identical copies in existence; indeed, the one that accompanied me on my travels through Germany, America and India was a reprint of exactly the same edition.

For once, the fuss attending the book wasn't about whether Shakespeare had written the words it contained: it was about what happened to the copy in Venkatrathnam's care. A member of the African People's Democratic Union of South Africa (Apdusa), he had been imprisoned in Robben Island's 'leadership section', and, approaching his release in 1978, had passed the copy around his cellmates and asked them to sign their names. Many had become major figures in the ANC-led government after 1994. Former secretary general Walter Sisulu had signed, as had ANC guiding lights Ahmed Kathrada and Govan Mbeki, father of Thabo – all heroes of the struggle. In total, thirty-three prisoners had inscribed their signatures, with one anonymous mark in addition.

But the book's real claim to fame was that it contained the biggest name in South African history: Nelson Mandela. Mandela, imprisoned a few cells away from Venkatrathnam, had highlighted six lines of *Julius Caesar*, and inscribed his signature and the date in crisp blue ink: 16 December 1977. The words he chose are spoken by Caesar in act two of the play, just before the Roman leader takes the cataclysmic decision to go to the Senate, ignoring warnings that his life is in danger:

> Cowards die many times before their deaths;
> The valiant never taste of death but once.
> Of all the wonders that I yet have heard,
> It seems to me most strange that men should fear,
> Seeing that death, a necessary end,
> Will come when it will come.

Primed to observe the Mandela connection, the global media had thrilled to the book's arrival. The *Guardian* led its story with the news that it had lent 'solace and inspiration' to the political leaders on

Robben Island. The *Telegraph* described it being 'passed around from cell to cell and read secretively'. *The Times of India* helpfully explained that the cards on the cover were Diwali greeting cards and had been placed there by Venkatrathnam as a way of hiding the book's identity. It was this that had given the book its soubriquet: Venkatrathnam told a guard it was his 'bible' as a way of keeping it illegally in his cell.

Dora Thornton, the British Museum curator, took the biblical analogy further: 'The book was used in the same way as the Bible has been used down the ages: as a constant reference for debating the moral issues of the day.' Other reports said the copy had been 'smuggled' on to Robben Island and read in secret. In what might generously be described as a flourish of sub-editorial creativity, the BBC had promoted the book to 'Nelson Mandela's Shakespeare edition'.

As I stood in line, waiting to see this precious tome, my curiosity was piqued and a little puzzled. In an exhibition devoted to antiquities from the worlds inhabited and imagined by Shakespeare (Elizabethan tapestries, Jacobean flag designs, early-modern playscripts, seventeenth-century copies of Roman busts), the Robben Island Bible struck – I thought – a discordant note. It was neither from a world that Shakespeare knew, nor part of any world he had put on stage.

Perhaps unsurprisingly, given that his European contemporaries made only fitful attempts to penetrate further than the coast of southern Africa, Shakespeare exhibited little curiosity about life at these latitudes, for all his imaginative globetrotting elsewhere. The word 'Africa' or 'Afric' appears just a smattering of times in the plays, always used with what appears to be calculated vagueness. When Africa does take more substantial form – such as in the Tunisian wedding that the shipboard party in *The Tempest* have attended, or that possible Moroccan inspiration for *Othello* – it seems that North Africa is what the playwright has in mind. Assuming that the story about the performance of *Hamlet* in Sierra Leone was wishful thinking, Shakespeare's work itself wouldn't arrive on the African continent until the turn of the nineteenth century. There was no denying that the story behind the Robben Island Bible was compelling, but for a sliver of South African history to be here at the British Museum struck me as decidedly odd.

It wasn't just this exhibition: in the years since it had first gone on display in Stratford-upon-Avon in 2006, the Bible had acquired the sanctified glow of a genuine relic. It had inspired numerous articles and at least two books. Radio and television documentaries had featured it. A play by the American writer Matthew Hahn was based on interviews with some of its signatories. The South African-born actor Antony Sher had rhapsodised about its significance to the history of his country, as had Sher's partner, Gregory Doran, artistic director of the Royal Shakespeare Company. After it had finished its stint in London the book was booked to visit the Folger in Washington DC, next to all those First Folios.

As I came out of the gallery, I saw a stooped figure pinned in the glare of a television light. Small in his dark suit, he looked older than the photograph in the display case, but still recognisable – Sonny Venkatrathnam. He was now in his late seventies and had travelled from South Africa for the opening of the exhibition. He was leaning heavily on the arm of his granddaughter and looked a little uncertain on his feet.

Once the television light had been extinguished, I introduced myself and explained my project. Venkatrathnam was warm and courteous and listened to my questions with quiet concentration. Sitting on a bench near the gift shop, we talked briefly about his experiences on Robben Island and his battles with the prison authorities to acquire reading materials and education. But he was plainly exhausted: it had been a long flight, he had been doing interviews back to back. The museum staff were hovering. He apologised profusely; he wasn't as young as he was.

'You're coming to South Africa?' he asked. That was the plan, I replied.

'Sorry we didn't get much time. I'm in Durban. Come and see me. We can talk some more. I'll show you the book.'

In truth, another book was on my mind that summer. I'd come across it before departing for India. It was a compendium of tributes to Shakespeare, compiled by the former chairman of the Shakespeare Association in Britain, Israel Gollancz. Its title was *A Book of Homage to Shakespeare*. Other than the fact that the great Bengali writer Rabindranath Tagore had contributed, all I really knew about it was that it had been published in 1916 in honour of the 300th anniversary of Shakespeare's death, and that – 1916 being the depths of the first world war – German and Austrian writers had not been invited to join the party. On a slow afternoon I snuck off work and cycled down to Gollancz's alma mater, King's College London, to take a look.

Nearly 600 pages long and three inches thick, dauntingly hefty in the hand, the *Book of Homage* was less a book than a monument. It was expensively bound in cream and gold, and gorgeously printed on thick, luxurious paper. Physically at least, it was considerably more impressive than the Robben Island Bible. On the contents page I counted 165 tributes in over twenty languages, from nations including the United States, France, Greece, Belgium, Denmark, China, Russia, Persia, Japan and Armenia. Apparently I was far from the first to wonder about how Shakespeare's work had been received and understood in other countries and cultures. In fact I was nearly a century late.

Team GB was well represented – Thomas Hardy, John Galsworthy and Rudyard Kipling had contributed, backed by a veritable squad of dons: A. C. Bradley, E. K. Chambers, W. W. Greg, A. W. Pollard, their initials giving them the pleasing appearance of a batting order in an Edwardian cricket team. A platoon of diplomats were also present (the Spanish ambassador writing 'To Shakespeare, from a Spaniard'; His Majesty's man in Rome offering an Italian 'Thought'), alongside various lords spiritual and temporal, and several leading thesps.

But the *Book of Homage* was not, as I had expected, a tub-thumping piece of patriotism in honour of the British Bard. Colonies and former colonies such as India and Canada were present, but so too were countries far beyond the scope of the Empire. Scholarly lectures mingled promiscuously with rococo panegyrics, in a babel of different languages. The Egyptian neoclassicist Muhammad Hafiz Ibrahim volunteered an Arabic poem pointedly reminding everyone of the cultural politics behind celebrating a white, western writer ('if justice were done to the Oriental authors, there would be feasts in their honour in both East and West', as the English summary put it). Gollancz's decision to present non-English contributions in their original form had the effect of making this supposedly universal, transcendent being called 'Shakespeare' (or Шекспир, or שייקספיר) seem stranger and more thrillingly unusual than his readers can ever have expected.

One name on the contents page snagged my eye – or, rather, one absence of a name. The essay was entitled 'William Tsikinya-Chaka'; its author was simply described as 'A South African'. It was the only piece from the African continent. It was also the only piece in the book to be anonymous.

I read it, and was immediately taken. In contrast to the elephantine braggartism on display elsewhere, this South African essay was crisp and concise, a masterpiece of cool wit. Just four pages long – a main text in the southern African language Setswana with an English translation alongside – it related the story of how its author had first encountered Shakespeare, and been remade by him.

The writer told of growing up in the remote mining town of Kimberley in the Northern Cape, and of seeing a performance of *Hamlet* in the mid-1890s, when he was eighteen. Impressed, he acquired a copy of the complete works, and read *The Merchant of Venice* from beginning to end, marvelling at its realism and dramatic force, and the vigour of Shakespeare's language.

But it was while reading *Cymbeline*, with its complex and fraught journeys of discovery and near-loss, that something more momentous happened: the author met 'the girl who afterwards became my wife'. Shakespeare was not merely present at this burgeoning romance – the poet's language made it possible:

> I was not then as well acquainted with her language – the Xosa – as I am now; and although she had a better grip of mine . . . I was doubtful I could make her understand my innermost feelings in it, so in coming to an understanding we both used the language of educated people – the language which Shakespeare wrote – which happened to be the only official language of our country at the time.

'It may be depended upon,' he added slyly, 'that we both read *Romeo and Juliet*.'

It was the essay's homespun clarity, its lack of idolatry, that I found appealing. Whereas so many of Gollancz's contributors offered prolix generalisations about the Bard's ineffable appeal, this nameless, Setswana-speaking South African was attempting to work out what Shakespeare might mean in the here and now. Here and *then*, in the South Africa of 1916.

His homage seemed all the more meaningful because it suggested equivalence. More than equivalence: equality. Shakespeare was a fine storyteller, the writer suggested; but then so too were his own people, the Tswana. It was possible that Shakespeare's plays and Setswana stories shared similar folkloric origins. The essay's title, 'William Tsikinya-Chaka', was a playful free translation of the poet's name, meaning 'William Shake-the-Sword'.

That is not to say the essay avoided politics. In fact the closer one looked, the more loaded those politics seemed. It was far from accidental that the 'language of educated people' in South Africa at the time was English: it had been imposed by the British administration in what was then the Cape Colony. As in India, educationalists who had brought English to Africa also brought Shakespeare; courtesy of mission schools, his plays had been part of the colonial education system almost from the beginning.

But the way the writer described Shakespeare wasn't, as I had encountered in so many Indian accounts, as a tool of colonial oppression. He was a bridge of translation, of connection. Shakespeare was the writer who enabled two young people – one Tswana, the other Xhosa – to romance each other in the words of immortal lovers, just as his works enabled communication between European cultures and those of Africa.

One issue haunted the essay: that of race. Marrying a woman from a different language and culture, the author wrote, had been challenging enough to their respective families; but it was as nothing to the way white people had become accustomed to regard blacks. He described going to see a screening of a film that depicted the crucifixion of Jesus:

> According to the pictures, the only black man in the mob was Judas Iscariot. I have since become suspicious of the veracity of the cinema and acquired a scepticism which is not diminished by a gorgeous one now exhibited in London which shows, side by side with the nobility of the white race, a highly coloured exaggeration of the depravity of the blacks. Shakespeare's dramas, on the other hand, show that nobility and valour, like depravity and cowardice, are not the monopoly of any colour.

I checked up: the second film referred to was almost certainly D. W. Griffith's silent epic, *The Birth of a Nation*, which even in its day, 1915, caused uproar for casting white actors in blackface and lionising the Ku Klux Klan. It was against this 'gorgeous' entertainment that Shakespeare's plays stood as potent rebuke: 'nobility and valour, like depravity and cowardice, are not the monopoly of any colour'. This was one of the earliest accounts I'd discovered to argue that Shakespeare was colour-blind; all the more striking if – as seemed likely – the writer himself was black.

That evening I cycled back from the library, my brain busy with questions. Who on earth was this anonymous 'South African'? And why was he the only African writer invited to contribute to Gollancz's book? One of his final lines on Shakespeare kept ringing around my head: 'We of the present age have not yet equalled his acumen.' Given what would happen to South Africa in the decades after 1916, they struck a bleak and baleful note.

———◆———

LYING AWAKE ON MY SECOND NIGHT IN JOHANNESBURG, I reflected that there was one stubborn problem with my scheme to research Shakespeare in this part of the world: Johannesburg itself.

I'd visited South Africa once before as a student, a few years after the optimism of the 1994 elections, the first in which black people could vote, and been shocked by what appeared to be a society still in a state of war. Arriving in the otherwise picturesque town of Plettenberg Bay in the Western Cape, all I'd seen was razor wire and electric fences, erected (I was told) by security-obsessed Jo'burgers who'd retired there. The Afrikaner landlady I'd been billeted with spent most of breakfast complaining – in full hearing of the live-in black maid – about the price of domestic help. This democracy business was all very well, she said, her voice rising querulously, but *what* did I think about *that*?

Fourteen years later, if the razor wire and electric fences were any indication, things seemed to have got worse. Melville, the area where I was staying, was an upmarket, slightly boho neighbourhood only a couple of miles from the centre of Johannesburg. But even Melville appeared to lead a double life as an open prison: fences with spikes, electric gates, guard huts, prowling utility vehicles emblazoned with fearsome names (24/7 Security, Stallion Security, SOS Protec, Night Guard). The 86 per cent of Johannesburg's population who were black or mixed-race seemed to spend most of their time guarding the 14 per cent who were white.

I CAN MAKE IT TO THE FENCE IN 2.8 SECONDS, read a sign down the street, next to a silhouette of a German Shepherd. CAN YOU?

When I'd arrived, I'd asked where would be safe to walk – I was keen to stretch my legs from the flight and see the *koppies*, the stone outcrops for which Johannesburg was celebrated.

I was met with blank looks. Walk? Up there? On my own?

'Maybe during the day, with a guide,' said the owner of the guesthouse. 'Maybe. *Buuut* early evening . . .' He whistled through his teeth.

How about the city centre? Was it safe to walk there?

No, even during the day. OK, maybe some streets, but as a tourist – safer just to take cash with me, no cards, and leave my mobile phone.

But I needed my phone for work, I bleated.

'Get a local one. A cheap one.'

It went on. Public transport a no-no. Trains especially. Best to hire a driver. Not expensive – get one for the day if need be.

What if I didn't want to be ferried around like a white lording? What if I wanted to be spontaneous? Surely it was safe to walk around Melville itself?

His expression was flat. 'You look like a tourist a mile off. Stick to being *spontaneous* somewhere else.'

Piece by piece, I put flesh on my mysterious South African. It wasn't just me who was foxed by his identity: several accounts named him as William Tsikinya-Chaka, mistaking the subject of the essay for its author.

Eventually an article gave me what I wanted, and a small trail of breadcrumbs besides. He was a man called Solomon Tshekisho Plaatje, a journalist, linguist and political activist. For all that I'd never heard of him until a few months before, Plaatje was one of the most important figures in twentieth-century South African history. He was the founding secretary general of the South African Native National Congress (SANNC), the organisation that became the African National Congress, a leading light in the early struggle for equal rights in South Africa.

I combed through reference books, databases and secondhand bookshops in search of him, each morsel of information more enticing than the last. Plaatje had a name that was Dutch in origin, given by an Afrikaans settler to his grandfather (it was pronounced *Ply-kee*, I was told), but he was indeed a black South African, part of the Tswana tribe.

Born in 1876 on a mission station outside Kimberley, the Northern Cape town where the colonialist and diamond magnate Cecil Rhodes had made his fortune, Plaatje lived through the early mining booms that transformed South Africa from a loose cluster of African kingdoms to a profitable piece of the British Empire. As a young man he had experienced at first hand the Siege of Mafeking – now Mafikeng/Mahikeng – during the second Boer War of 1899–1902, later composing a memoir of the experience, the only one by a black eyewitness. He became a crusading journalist, founding one of the few South African newspapers in the control of a black editorial team, and, scandalised by what he perceived as Britain's betrayal after the foundation of the Union of South Africa in 1910, joined the campaign for native rights.

It was here that Plaatje came to wider attention. *Native Life in South Africa*, his caustic account of the cruelties of the 1913 Natives Land Act, the first grim step towards apartheid, alerted the world to the injustices being perpetrated in his homeland. In the 1910s and 1920s he toured Europe and the United States, rabble-rousing for the SANNC and meeting civil-rights pioneers, among them one of America's greatest campaigners for racial equality, W. E. B. Du Bois. By the time of his death in 1932, back in Kimberley, Plaatje was perhaps the most widely read black writer on the African continent.

The tales related by his more enthusiastic biographers strained credulity: could he really memorise entire books at a glance? Recite whole plays after only one hearing? But other stories, which sounded equally far-fetched, were well documented. Despite only having received an elementary education, Plaatje was proficient in eight languages. Prime minister David Lloyd George, who met him, confessed himself 'greatly impressed'. He had written a bestselling book in praise of sexual relations between the races, as well as a novel in English, the first by a black South African. There appeared to be nothing the man couldn't do.

And then, of course, there was Shakespeare. The playwright was entangled in Plaatje's life in ways that were especially enticing. After he had seen *Hamlet* as a teenager, the plays seemed to shadow his every move. His journalism repeatedly quotes Shakespeare; *Mhudi*, the novel, is saturated by references. And then there were the translations, six of them: *The Comedy of Errors, Julius Caesar, Othello, The Merchant of Venice, Much Ado About Nothing* and *Romeo and Juliet*. If my sources were accurate, these were not only the first full translations of Shakespeare plays into Setswana; they were the earliest translations into any African language at all. Plaatje deserved a place in the pantheon simply for this.

And yet information was maddeningly hard to come by. None of the standard Shakespeare reference works mentioned him. *Mhudi* excepted, his books were on the hazy fringes of out-of-print. His biography and a selection of his journalism – both fine scholarly works by a British researcher called Brian Willan – were almost impossible to find. Back in Britain I'd asked Shakespeare experts for leads on Plaatje; none were even aware of his existence.

It was a conundrum. As I scanned the haphazard pile of volumes by or about Solomon Plaatje that had filled my suitcase, I thought: when it came to the global history of Shakespeare, who had written him out?

A graceful classical portico menaced on every side by brutalist concrete faculties and labs, the William Cullen library at the University of the Witwatersrand, known locally as 'Wits', looked painfully out of place, as if someone had lifted an orangerie from Versailles and placed it in the middle of a high-security penitentiary. The university's most precious collections are housed at the Cullen, including the papers of Solomon Plaatje. I had booked an appointment for the day after I arrived in Johannesburg, hoping it might answer at least some of my questions.

As I came near, the place looked closed. The lights were off. Strange – it was 3 p.m., definitely opening time. Then I noticed a small sign pinned to the wall, in a looping and haphazard hand: 'Library Closed No Power'. There had been electricity outages on and off all winter, a combination of South Africa's creaking network and rumbling union disputes. The previous week gold miners had walked out. The atmosphere was sour, full of mutterings that the ANC government under president Jacob Zuma was crumbling.

But there was really only one story in South Africa that September: the ailing Nelson Mandela. A few weeks earlier, the former president had been rushed into hospital in Pretoria. Crowds had massed in the street, expecting the worst, but Mandela had rallied and, to widespread rejoicing, had made it to his ninety-fifth birthday. Three days before I landed, he'd been brought back home to the exclusive suburb of Houghton, a few miles away. The Mandela compound had been one of those hit by the power cut the previous night; an emergency generator had to be used to keep his intensive-care equipment online. The papers were full of outraged headlines: MADIBA POWER SCARE. For once, it wasn't a metaphor.

An hour and a half later, once the lights had finally gone back on, I got inside the Cullen. The Africana reading room was a genial clutter of books, pot plants, posters and murals. Over the banisters leading up to the mezzanine there was a huge banner, reading THE PEOPLE SHALL GOVERN! – a relic of the university's history as a bulwark of the anti-apartheid movement. Across every inch of wall were black-and-white photos of protests and rallies on campus. It seemed fitting that this was where Plaatje – some parts of him, at least – had ended up.

Plaatje was born on a mission station some 30 miles away from Kimberley, about 280 miles south-west of Johannesburg: a quick hop on the plane I was scheduled to take early the following week, but many hours by dirt and dust track.

The mission was run by a German, the Reverend Gotthilf Ernst Westphal, and at school Plaatje seems to have been a remarkably talented and responsive pupil. As well as speaking his own Setswana and learning other local tongues, he would have been taught German and 'Cape Dutch', the language that became Afrikaans. He received extra tuition from Reverend Westphal's wife, Elizabeth, who introduced him to literature and music. There was talk of him going to secondary school – a rare privilege for a black child in South Africa at that time.

It was not to be. In 1894, at the age of seventeen, Plaatje abandoned education for a job as a messenger at the Kimberley post office. He lived in the Malay Camp, a mixed area of town, and became involved with the newly formed South Africans' Improvement Society, which hosted regular talks, concerts and events. In 1898, he married the sister of a friend, Elizabeth Lilith M'belle – the woman he had courted with *Romeo and Juliet*. The following year, he left to take up a job in Mafikeng as an interpreter in the legal courts. By now, he could speak and write in Setswana, Sesotho, English and Dutch, and speak isiXhosa and German.

The second Anglo-Boer War had followed soon afterwards, and in the Cullen was the manuscript of the diary he'd kept during the Mafikeng siege: a thin wodge of yellowing foolscap, one of the few surviving texts in Plaatje's hand. Written in rapid but legible script – mainly English, with a few Afrikaans and Setswana words thrown in

– it was a surprisingly larky read, telling of daring escapes from Boer bullets and giving valuable eyewitness detail on what life was really like in a British encampment under fire.

What there wasn't anywhere at the Cullen, at least anywhere I could see, was evidence of Plaatje's passion for Shakespeare: no manuscripts, no notes on his translations. Aside from the diary, the only hint that Plaatje had any interest at all in that direction was a letter dated 17 January 1931, seven months before his death, appealing for funds to help publish 'native literature'.

The photographs, however, were eloquent. One showed a young man, perhaps in his mid-twenties, wearing a dark jacket and white bow-tie, his watch-chain shining, holding what appeared to be a piece of sheet music. Though he was a little plump, his features were finely formed: square jaw, broad forehead. His posture was alert; his eyes, directed at the camera, were bold and cool.

The other picture was later, and sadder: a small print of an old man, exhausted-looking, sitting at a typewriter. A homburg sat jauntily on his head and a tie was neatly knotted at his throat, but his pale linen jacket was too big. His shoulders were slumped, his gaze unfocused. He looked substantially older than his fifties. I wondered what forces had transformed one Solomon Plaatje into the other.

There was something else in the library. Passing through London on a speaking tour, Plaatje had visited the Zonophone record company at Hayes in Middlesex, where he had recorded three discs of African music, presumably to aid his consciousness-raising efforts. They were in Setswana and isiXhosa, a combination of hymns and folk songs, sung by Plaatje himself with Sylvia Colenso (daughter of the Bishop of Natal) accompanying. The shellac originals were now too fragile to play, but the Wits librarians had digitised them.

Sitting on my own in the library, the red late-afternoon sunlight burning into the wall behind, I strained my ear to the tiny speakers of an antique PC. Through a thick soup of hiss I could just about pick out hymn-like piano chords and a man's thin voice. 'Singa Mawela', a gently lilting song, was suited to their talents: Miss Colenso's rippling arrangement gave it a pleasant touch of the Edwardian salon, with the unexpected addition of the pops and clicks of the isiXhosa language, produced by Plaatje with obvious enjoyment. At last, a voice to match the face.

I selected another track. There was a whoosh of static and Plaatje's

voice soared high above, sounding easy and smooth. It only took me a
few moments to recognise the words and tune, whose jaunty optimism
I had always found deeply moving:

> *Nkosi sikelel' iAfrika*
> *Maluphakanyis' uphondo Iwayo . . .*

Lord, bless Africa, may her spirit rise up . . . It was the South African national
anthem, the first time in history it had been recorded. At the chorus, a
female voice joined in – Miss Colenso, I guessed. She and Plaatje sang in
harmony before the music faded into crackle and silence.

Soon after composing his account of the Mafikeng siege, Plaatje's
interest in politics had hardened into direct campaigning. In 1901, he
took over the editorship of a new Setswana-language newspaper,
Koranta ea Becoana ('The Tswana Gazette'). His tone intensified; in one
fire-brand editorial published in September 1902, he launched a spirited
attack on the British, under the headline 'Equal Rights'. 'We do not
hanker after social equality with the white man,' it read. 'We do not
care for your parlour, nor is it our wish to lounge on couches in your
drawing rooms . . . All we claim is our just dues; we ask for our political
recognition as loyal British subjects.'

But British influence over this part of the world was waning.
Following an uneasy victory in the Anglo-Boer War, the British
government came to a compromise with Afrikaner nationalists. In
1910, the former British colonies in the Cape and Natal joined with
the Boer republics of Transvaal and the Orange Free State to form the
Union of South Africa. The interests of the overwhelming majority of
South Africans – those South Africans who were black – were excluded
from the deal.

Plaatje sensed his own people being sold down the river. In 1909,
a group of four black delegates had come together in Waaihoek,
Bloemfontein, and agreed to create a permanent organisation to fight
for black legal and political rights. Three years later, in January 1912,
when the South African Native National Congress was finally formed,
the Zulu John Dube was elected president. Plaatje became secretary
general.

In 1913, the nascent SANNC faced its rubicon: the passing of the Natives Land Act, which at a stroke outlawed black South Africans from either owning or renting eight tenths of the land in the Union – anywhere outside 'reserves' set aside for their use. Black landowners were evicted and tenants forced off land they had farmed for generations. Millions became refugees in their own country. Denied representation in the South African parliament, the SANNC made frantic plans to send a delegation to London. When they made the trip the following year, Plaatje would be among them.

In the meantime, though, he responded more characteristically, as a reporter, picking up a bicycle and heading out on the road to see the effects of the Land Act for himself. What Plaatje witnessed in these journeys of July 1913, in the middle of the cold South African winter, became the essence of *Native Life in South Africa*, the book that would make his name.

That evening, back in my room in Melville, I read *Native Life* from cover to cover. It begins with a sentence that has since been etched deep into the history of apartheid: 'Awaking on Friday morning, June 20, 1913, the South African native found himself, not actually a slave, but a pariah in the land of his birth.' The book goes on to cover in meticulous and unsparing detail how four and a half million black South Africans found themselves made 'pariahs' by the Land Act.

Native Life in South Africa also makes harrowing use of eyewitness material, retelling journeys Plaatje took through the length and breadth of South Africa, from his homeland in the north to far south in the Cape. One of its most distressing passages describes the moment Plaatje encountered twenty-four women who had taken part in protests against a law requiring them to carry passes proving they were on the payroll of a white employer – a foreshadowing of the Pass Laws imposed by the government from the 1910s onwards. 'Tears rolled down our cheeks,' Plaatje wrote, 'as we saw the cracks on their bare feet, the swellings and chronic chilblains, which made them look like sheep suffering from foot-and-mouth disease.'

Critics have drawn attention to the echoes in Plaatje's text of Daniel Defoe's *A Journal of the Plague Year* (1722) and William Cobbett's *Rural Rides* (1830) – likewise a journey around a people in the process of being dispossessed. But another writer seemed to me to underpin the movement and energy of *Native Life in South Africa*, at some points directly, at other times just beneath the surface: Shakespeare.

About halfway through the book, stepping back from the catastrophe convulsing his country, Plaatje permits a few shafts of autobiography to penetrate. His and Elizabeth's young son, named Johann Gutenberg after the inventor of moveable type, had been born in September 1912; he died in January 1914, at the age of just sixteen months. With spareness and gravity, Plaatje describes Johann's funeral procession winding around the streets of Kimberley, and is suddenly taken back to the image of a young family he had seen on the road. 'What have our people done to these colonists,' he asks, 'that is so utterly unforgivable, that this law should be passed?'

These thoughts on land and ownership, on need, on loss, on family, on fatherhood, take him to one play in particular:

> Are not many of us toiling in the grain fields and fruit farms, with their wives and their children, for the white man's benefit? Did not our people take care of the white women . . . whose husbands, brothers and fathers were away at the front [during the first world war] – in many cases actively engaged in shattering our own liberty? But see their appreciation and gratitude! Oh, for something to
> > Strike flat the thick rotundity o' the world!
> > Crack Nature's moulds, all germens spill at once!
> > That makes ingrateful man!

The play is, of course, *King Lear*. Though most often interpreted as a harrowing psychological study, there is another side to Shakespeare's tragedy, less often explored by contemporary directors: its politics. For its earliest audiences the play contained cruel echoes of the Enclosure movement, which – like the Natives Land Act – saw entire populations dispersed or dispossessed. As the landowning Shakespeare well knew, Jacobean England was full of Lears and Poor Toms, masterless men forced to wander the countryside after being ejected from fields that were rightfully theirs.

Plaatje, so it seemed to me, drew on this older, deeper aspect of the play – figuring himself as a monarch who has been ejected from his own country, left to call for retribution against a bitterly unfair world. To demand justice increasingly seemed like a form of madness.

One afternoon I sat on a sofa in the middle of a private garden in the middle of Johannesburg, trying to keep out of the fierce sun high overhead. Rugs were spread across the lawn; all around me the trees cut blocks of dark shadow into the dusty grass. It had rained the night before: early spring rain, much-needed. The scent in the air was of dry concrete and damp earth. By the wall, a jacaranda tree was blossoming in a fizz of purple petals. Birds shrieked somewhere in the distance.

Around the garden men and women stood in pockets of two and three, chicly dressed, picking at finger food and frowning at their iPhones. A man nearby was having a vehement conversation with his neighbour about the prospects for the African art market. His mirrored shades sent scatters of light across the cushions.

'We're next after India, heh? India is totally over. People are fucking *hungry* for this stuff.'

The neighbour was nodding intently.

'India is *over*, man, I tell you. Over.'

I had wangled an invitation to a lunchtime reception at a Johannesburg arts festival on the basis that I was a journalist visiting town. These grounds were spurious: my attention was actually focused on the other end of the garden, where a group of men – nine or ten, all of them black, a mixture of ages from their early twenties through to fifties – huddled.

In a moment, they had turned to face us. One man stepped out, and began to speak in a low voice, his hands bunched by his sides like a boxer willing himself into the fight. His accent was strong, and it took me several seconds to place what he was saying:

> If there were reason for these miseries,
> Then into limits could I bind my woes.
> When heaven doth weep, doth not the earth o'erflow?
> If the winds rage, doth not the sea wax mad,
> Threat'ning the welkin with his big-swoll'n face?
> And wilt thou have a reason for this coil?
> I am the sea. Hark how her sighs doth blow.
> She is the weeping welkin, I the earth.

It was perhaps Shakespeare's first truly great tragic speech, spoken by the Roman soldier Titus Andronicus in the third act of the early play named after him. The words are of desperation and incipient insanity, at a moment in the action when – Titus's daughter having been raped and mutilated, his sons arrested, Titus's own hand cut off – it seems as if things cannot get worse. The play being *Titus Andronicus*, they do. This tragedy is sometimes interpreted as a rehearsal for *King Lear*.

I glanced around. The crowd looked suitably dumbfounded. Even the man in mirrored shades had shut up.

After the performance, I made my way over. A small, bullet-shaped woman with long, reddish-dark hair was fussing the group back into the corner. Her name was Dorothy Ann Gould. An actor, she was something of a legend in South Africa. As well as maintaining a busy career in teaching, on television and stage, she ran a weekly workshop in the deprived inner-city neighbourhood of Hillbrow. Her weapon in this campaign was Shakespeare.

'You liked it, heh? The *Titus*?' she said, shielding her eyes against the sun.

I said I had never seen anything like it.

She sniffed at the surroundings. 'Not really our usual setting, but it's good experience. Plus it's a useful audience, all these arts folk. Good for the project, getting it known.'

The scheme had been running just over a year; it had begun as a drop-in centre for men and women (mostly men) who were homeless or struggling with addiction, or both. She'd suggested the idea of drama training, and the participants had eagerly agreed. Rehearsals were held weekly by Dorothy and her assistant Marcus Mabusela. The participants had chosen their own name: Johannesburg Awakening Minds, JAM for short. It sounded good; and it was time, they figured, that they had a little sweetness in their lives.

Gould was determined not to patronise them. 'Right from the beginning, we started on Shakespeare. The first thing was "No longer mourn for me when I am dead", Sonnet 71, you know. I took them through what Patsy Rodenburg, the voice coach at the Royal Shakespeare Company, did with me in Stratford.' She thrust a bundle of scripts decisively into a bag. 'They loved it.'

Just nine people had come to their debut performance. But then some of the group had got gigs as film extras, and small fees; they started to build a reputation. They were trying to work up to something fully staged. She had her eye on *Hamlet*: they'd been rehearsing a group rendition of the Prince's 'What a piece of work is a man!' speech.

I thought of its troubling, ragged early line ('I have of late – but wherefore I know not – lost all my mirth') and was struck that she'd focused on tragedies. *Titus* especially: it seemed an obscure choice.

She shook an accusatory finger at the city beyond. 'Well, *they're* not shocked by Lavinia having her tongue cut up and her hands cut off, and being raped, if that's what you mean. In Johannesburg that's what happens every day. Every single phrase in that *Titus* speech means something to them. Yes, it develops their voice, it develops their breath production, it forces them to be still and powerful and discipline their bodies. But it's also because in real life they can't shout, "Why am I unemployed, why is there such poverty in South Africa?" Through *Titus*, they can. They can be in tears. It makes it OK to cry.'

She looked as if she was daring me to disbelieve her. 'It's powerful stuff. They don't want *woozy* stuff. It wouldn't . . . make any sense.'

After we'd finished the interview, I helped carry her bag and some equipment back to the car. As I turned to go in, I heard the sound of an electric window winding down. Gould was leaning out, silhouetted against the glare of the city beyond.

'Come see for yourself,' she bellowed as the wheels churned in the dirt. Behind her there was only red dust.

Before leaving Britain I'd arranged to visit Pretoria, forty miles north, to keep an appointment with an academic, Daniel Matjila, who taught in the African Languages department at the University of South Africa (Unisa). Matjila had a special interest in Solomon Plaatje and had recently co-edited a biography. He was also of Tswana heritage and fluent in the language. I hoped he would be able to give me some insight into how Plaatje had translated Shakespeare's words. I also hoped he could help me answer a deeper question, harder to fathom: why Plaatje had decided to translate Shakespeare at all.

The story seemed to begin in June 1914, when Plaatje was sent to London as part of that SANNC delegation. In between meetings with British civil-rights activists (who did their best to exploit the delegates for their own ends) and British civil servants (who worked tirelessly to ensure they would never meet anyone of influence) Plaatje mingled with the liberal intelligentsia of London. When the rest of the delegation hurried back to South Africa after Britain declared war on Germany that August – all but burying their campaign – Plaatje decided to remain. In the three years he ended up staying in Britain, he would address over three hundred public meetings up and down the country, educating Britons about the injustices of the Land Act, and trying to finish and find a publisher for *Native Life in South Africa*.

It was around this time that he had come into contact with Daniel Jones, a young phonetics expert at University College London who was (among much else) George Bernard Shaw's inspiration for the character of Professor Higgins in *Pygmalion*. Jones was fascinated by African languages, and the two developed the idea of compiling a book of Setswana proverbs, capturing the spoken language in all its vividness, and also some kind of reader-cum-teaching-manual. Their collaborations soon bore fruit. A slim volume, *Sechuana Proverbs with Literal Translations and their European Equivalents*, was published, rapidly followed by *A Sechuana Reader in International Phonetic Orthography*. It was also around this time that Plaatje met Israel Gollancz and made his short Setswana-language contribution to the *Book of Homage to Shakespeare*. All three books would come out in 1916 – plus, once a publisher had finally been persuaded to take it, the first edition of *Native Life in South Africa*.

Although the British celebrations marking the tercentenary of Shakespeare's death in April and May that year were muted, they were far from non-existent. Schools up and down the country put on events, and at the Drury Lane theatre in London there was a gala performance of *Julius Caesar* attended by King George V. It ended with a pageant featuring tableaux from the plays performed by a cast some 200 strong, including the veteran Ellen Terry as Portia. The evening was capped in splendidly patriotic – not to say metatheatrical – fashion when Frank Benson (another of Gollancz's contributors) was knighted by His Majesty with a prop sword, still in bloodied toga as Caesar.

Plaatje was swept up in the Shakespeare fever. He was there at *Julius Caesar*, which he reported as being performed with 'great skill', and also visited Stratford-upon-Avon. Ever alert to the political ramifications, he addressed a meeting of Stratford's Brotherhood movement, where he was billed as a 'well-known Shakespeare scholar'.

Concluding his essay in the *Book of Homage*, Plaatje had expressed his fervent hope that 'with the maturity of African literature, now still in its infancy, writers and translators will consider the matter of giving to Africans the benefit of some at least of Shakespeare's works'. 1916 seems to have reminded him that there were few people so qualified as himself, and no time like the present. He began work the following year, as soon as he was on the ship back to South Africa, putting the play he had so recently seen, *Julius Caesar*, into Setswana.

According to an interview given much later to the Johannesburg *Star*, Plaatje followed this up with *Othello* ('translated partly in 1923 on a voyage from Quebec to Cherbourg and completed on a journey from Southampton to the Cape a year later'), *The Merchant of Venice*, *The Comedy of Errors*, *Much Ado About Nothing* and *Romeo and Juliet*. All but the last three, I suspected, he had seen on stage.

There was one maudlin note. The article in the *Star* would not be published until July 1930, two years before Plaatje's death. The project would take over thirteen years, and in the end outlive him.

I was early, but beneath the concrete cliff-face of the Unisa building Daniel Matjila was already waiting. Heftily built, with a ready grin, he folded my hand into one large paw and pumped it enthusiastically. I surmised that it had been a while since anyone had come to interview him about Solomon Plaatje.

In his office high up in the superstructure, with a commanding view over the hills back to Johannesburg, he gave me a brief language lesson. Setswana is a Sotho tongue, its speakers living primarily in what are now the north-eastern areas of South Africa and Botswana ('Place of the Tswana'). Although it was one of the earliest African languages to acquire a written form, it had little tradition of written literature. In Plaatje's day, other African languages, notably isiXhosa and Sesotho, had begun to develop a contemporary literature of their own – Thomas Mofolo's Sesotho novel *Chaka* (1925) had been a strong success – but Setswana limped behind. It was this that Plaatje had been determined to address.

Matjila's theory was that Plaatje's interest in Shakespeare had earlier roots than the performance of *Hamlet* he'd seen as a teenager. He might well have encountered stories from the plays as part of the Tswana storytelling culture, and other black South Africans of his generation had been taught Shakespeare in mission schools. (There is a story that part of *Twelfth Night* had been translated by a Setswana-speaking Christian priest in Bloemfontein as early as the 1880s.) But there was politics, too, in choosing to put Shakespeare into Setswana and publish the results.

'He wants to demonstrate that we have a language that can handle the very same ideas as English. Just as Shakespeare writes about Greek monarchs or Italian monarchs, we have a culture which is just as sophisticated. *Macbeth* has royalty; we also have chiefs.' Matjila tapped his chest. 'There is an *equivalence* there. This is what Plaatje realises.'

Although *Julius Caesar* was the first play Plaatje translated, the first translation actually printed, in 1930, was *Diphosho-phosho*, which translates literally as 'Mistakes upon Mistakes' – *The Comedy of Errors*, a play I'd encountered back in London courtesy of the Afghan group Rah-e-Sabz, and which had cropped up with surprising frequency on my journeys. Plaatje had completed the work by stealing time from political activism and paid journalism, but publishers, once again, weren't interested. He was forced to fundraise privately. The stark reason why his translation of *The Comedy of Errors* made it into print was that this – the shortest play in the canon – was the cheapest to produce.

From a shelf behind his desk Matjila fished out a modern reprint of *Diphosho-phosho* and flipped it open. The dimensions of a paperback, it was more pamphlet than book, just fifty-two pages long. The title page read 'The Sayings of William Shakespeare', in blocky and rough type. It looked an underwhelming way for Shakespeare to embark on a new life at the other end of the world.

But *Diphosho-phosho* was a quietly radical act of translation, Matjila explained – one that recast the relationship between the greatest poet in the English-speaking universe and an African language. In his essay for the *Book of Homage*, Plaatje had emphasised the vigorous oral traditions within Tswana culture. Translating *The Comedy of Errors*, he went one step further; he made the writer he playfully called 'William Tsikinya-Chaka', William Shake-the-Sword, an oral storyteller too, in the most honoured Tswana style.

Although Shakespeare's comedy contains its share of fruity jokes, Elizabethans seem to have been particularly attracted by its elegance and gloss – its mellifluous wordplay, its clever-clever reworking of the conventions of Roman comedy. Plaatje detected something different. The Latin names and locations were approximately transliterated (Antifoluse oa Efesuse/Antipholus of Ephesus and Antifoluse oa Sirakuse/Antipholus of Syracuse were the two leads; Agione/Egeon their father), but to the playtext itself Plaatje made sweeping changes. Stoutly set in Africa, it became a rambunctious family farce.

In place of Shakespeare's stylised and highly patterned poetry, Plaatje offered idiomatic and salty Setswana prose, seeded with day-to-day aphorisms. The text made local reference to the farms and fields, livestock and wild animals and Northern Cape landscape he and fellow Tswana knew intimately. Adriana and Luciana addressed each other as *nnaka* ('younger sister') and *nkgone* ('elder sister'). The two Dromios called their respective masters simply *mungwaka* ('boss') and their wives *Mmisis*, a borrowing from the English 'Mrs'.

Whenever Plaatje encountered a figure of speech that struck him as over-ingenious, he didn't hesitate to replace it, usually with something more geographically appropriate:

> When the sun shines, let foolish gnats make sport,
> But creep in crannies when he hides his beams.
>> *Gnats only fly when the air is humid; but as soon as the fiery sun bakes everything, they lie in hiding.*

> Thou art an elm, my husband; I a vine.
>> *You are a cave, my husband; I am the rock reptile.*

Where Shakespeare made reference to the legendarily icy 'Poland winter', Plaatje neatly substituted an example that would make more sense to his southern-hemisphere readers: 'the cold month of June'.

Plaatje's relish in the work is palpable, but this wasn't simply for fun; at the back of his mind was the brute fact that Setswana was fast losing out to colonial languages such as English and Afrikaans, especially in schools. 'It has not been an easy task to write such a book as this in Setswana,' he wrote in the introduction:

> it has been both difficult and intricate. But we are driven forward by the demands of the Batswana – the incessant and shrill cries of people exclaiming, 'Tau's Setswana will be of no use to us! It is becoming extinct because children are not taught Setswana! They are taught the missionary language!'

Perhaps that also accounted for Plaatje's decision to translate *The Comedy of Errors* rather than a more familiar set text; its homespun, knockabout qualities would make it ideal for schoolrooms. I wondered how many Setswana-speaking children had been given the opportunity to roll their eyes at the preposterous goings-on of Antifoluse oa Efesuse and Antifoluse oa Sirakuse. Given how few copies remained in existence, not nearly enough.

One critic described Plaatje's translations as 'linguistic activism'; it struck me as a neat and accurate phrase. Perhaps, in fact, I'd been approaching all this from the wrong angle. Plaatje's Shakespeare translations weren't really about Shakespeare at all. Shakespeare was being hitched to a much braver ideal: saving an entire culture.

On my mind was something I'd been mulling since seeing so many foreign-language productions at the World Shakespeare Festival. The commonest British complaint about Shakespeare from overseas was that there was barely any point in seeing the plays in translation. Deny the language, and you denied the essence of what makes Shakespeare Shakespeare.

Yet of course every performance, in whatever language, is a form of translation; and most contemporary British audiences or students have only a hazy sense of the depth and fullness of Shakespeare's English. There is a reason why most scholarly editions contain far more explanatory notes than they do text, and why there is a brisk market for translations of Shakespeare into modern English, for use in the English-speaking world. As time passes, the early-modern language Shakespeare used inevitably becomes more and more remote from the English most contemporary English-speaking people speak. Translation is one way among many of keeping the texts alive.

Plaatje, I felt – like similarly creative translators in India and Germany – understood these issues deeply, and realised how much could be achieved by separating Shakespeare from his language: for his own people, for Setswana, for South Africa. It had been bold to claim in 1916 that an African language was capable of containing the greatest writer in the British Empire. Plaatje made it do so nonetheless.

Translation was generally figured as a loss. At a profound level, I began to realise, it could also be a gain.

When I asked how I might get down to Hillbrow to visit Johannesburg Awakening Minds, I went through the health-and-safety charade all over again. I'd be lucky to find a driver who'd drop me anywhere near. Even in the middle of the day it wouldn't be wise to walk the streets.

In *Hillbrow*? As so often in Johannesburg, it was impossible to gauge where sensible advice ended and white middle-class paranoia began.

I called Dorothy. She sounded amused. No big deal. If I could make it to her place, she'd be happy to take me.

As we jounced down through Johannesburg in her ancient white Mercedes, she told me more about the project. Despite a grant from the Shakespeare Society of Southern Africa, JAM were in a constant battle for funding, and (I sensed) struggling to find a focus. Some members wanted to write and perform their own material, focusing on HIV and gender awareness; others preferred classic texts. Some of the group had failed to show for a recent performance – they'd either managed to find paid work elsewhere or were struggling with the commitment.

'It's hard enough for professional actors in South Africa, theatre is so marginal and badly paid here. And when you've been sleeping on the streets and there's all this other stuff going on . . .'

We were coming into Hillbrow. On all sides angular grey housing blocks loomed, floors packed as tight as eggboxes, roofs studded with white satellite dishes. There weren't many cars, but the streets were bustling with gangs of teenagers and pedestrians lugging shopping bags. Bar the odd shuttered or broken window, the shops looked busy. It was hardly downtown Zurich, but it wasn't the Armageddon I'd been promised either.

In the apartheid era, Hillbrow had been designated whites-only. Later it had become one of the few places in the inner city in which different races could mix and mingle. But an influx of population from rural areas and the townships during the 1980s, compounded by middle-class flight to the suburbs, had made it one of Johannesburg's most notorious slums. The area was still battling high crime rates and unemployment, mere blocks away from the offices and hotels of the city centre. The Hillbrow Tower, a slender spear of late-sixties concrete that had once been one of the nation's proudest symbols, soared above the high-rises. Into a square kilometre, Hillbrow packed many of the problems and paradoxes of modern-day South Africa.

Inside the church hall it was cold, with walls of unfinished plaster and chill light streaming on to the white-tiled floor. In the centre of the room were twelve or thirteen brown plastic garden chairs. Five men were seated, several of whom I recognised from the performance a few days before. They were hunched in jackets and hats, sipping steaming cups of instant coffee. More men wandered in. I took a seat at the back.

Dorothy wasn't joking about treating them like professionals: I had seen rehearsals at the National Theatre less taxing than this. They began with a fifteen-minute warm-up, then moved on to vocal exercises: singing, shouting, reciting short pieces from memory – chunks from Marlowe's *Tamburlaine*, Shakespeare's Sonnet 12 ('When I do count the clock that tells the time'). The shuffling, uncertain men who had walked in began to carry themselves differently; more boldly, I thought. They looked as if they actually expected to be there.

A large part of me was sceptical about the idea of Shakespeare as self-improvement: it smacked of the Victorian schoolroom, with its finger-wagging insistence that culture paved the road to clean living. And I was unsure, too, about associating the horrors of *Titus Andronicus* – rape, mutilation and the rest – with the mean streets of Johannesburg: too many echoes of the scare stories told by white folk about the animalistic depravity of the inner city. (A British-originated production starring Antony Sher and a South African cast had been roasted when it came here in 1995, regarded as violent cultural tourism.)

But watching these men work, I began to wonder. It seemed unlikely that anyone before now had bothered to worry about their breathing, or asked them to fill a space with their voices, or made a group of well-dressed, rich folk stand obediently by and listen to them. No doubt one could do this with many kinds of outreach project. But I thought of Plaatje's Lear, raging against the Natives Land Act and 'ungrateful man'. Why not Shakespeare?

At the tea break I got talking to one of the participants. His name was Thando Matodlana. He was twenty-seven. He'd grown up in Port Elizabeth in the Eastern Cape, and had come up to Johannesburg and struggled to find work. He ended up sleeping in a shelter, sometimes on the streets. He was now in a secure flat; no running water, but it was at least his own. He had ambitions to train as a sound engineer.

He'd been one of the first to sign up for Dorothy's classes. 'We used to go and play cards and read stories. But we didn't really have anything to do, nothing concrete. I wanted to learn acting, so I got involved.'

How had he found the sessions?

'It feels great, reading the pieces of Shakespeare. Dorothy is introducing us into Shakespeare. I learned a little Shakespeare in high school, but I didn't understand a lot. Here it is different.'

Was it hard, adjusting to the language? He scratched a scar above his nose. 'I can say it's all in the mind. Even though the words are difficult, bombastic words, you have to work on them with a dictionary.' He smiled. 'It's good, man! It's inspiring. If you are angry and you perform the piece, it helps you get it out of the way.'

He clapped me on the back. 'Anything is possible, man, you know? You have to believe and trust!'

Afterwards, we sat in rows as another actor stood, performing Titus's soliloquy once again. As he reached the final lines his body shook, breath shuddering in and out of his chest like a swimmer fighting for air:

> Then must my sea be movèd with her sighs,
> Then must my earth with her continual tears
> Become a deluge overflowed and drowned,
> Forwhy my bowels cannot hide her woes,
> But like a drunkard must I vomit them.
> Then give me leave, for losers will have leave
> To ease their stomachs with their bitter tongues.

As he finished, even the roar of the city seemed to fall quiet.

———◆———

TWO DAYS LATER, I WAS IN KIMBERLEY. An hour's flight south-west of Johannesburg over the barren, khaki-coloured stretches of the Highveld, it had seen better days. The epicentre of the nineteenth-century diamond industry and the first city in the southern hemisphere to install electric light, Kimberley now looked gaunt and dusty, as if the twenty-first century had given it the cold shoulder. The centre was filled with low cinderblock buildings from the 1960s and 1970s, a few grand Victorian facades the only hint of its illustrious past. Even the palm trees looked exhausted. KIMBERLEY: THE CITY THAT SPARKLES! read a sign. Not today it didn't.

I scuffed up and down the main road, dodging the huge mining trucks that lumbered and groaned through. My guidebook had devoted only a couple of pages to Kimberley, focusing on the former De Beers mine, now unpoetically known as the Big Hole: a yawning, seventeen-hectare gash in the townscape that, from the plane, made it look as though Kimberley had been hit by a meteor. The Big Hole seemed all too symbolic of what would happen when the diamonds finally ran out.

Almost nothing from Plaatje's time here had survived, I'd been warned: the mixed area of town where he'd lived had been razed during the apartheid era, and the cityscape was almost unrecognisable. But there was a museum at 32 Angel Street, the house where he'd lived for the last decade of his life. Since 1992 it had been a national monument.

By 11 a.m., the sky looked like toughened glass, the sun an angry white glare. Attempting to keep to the shadows, I walked in the dust of the road past battered, tin-roofed houses fringed by high fences and straggling shrubs.

Number 32 was between a playground and a pawnshop. It wasn't much more than a shack: two barred windows facing the road, brick facade, a verandah and a corrugated-iron roof. The bell was broken, so I banged on the gate. SOL PLAATJE MUSEUM AND LIBRARY read the sign, above a terse note that viewing was by appointment only.

Inside, 32 Angel Street was, if possible, even more dispiriting. A largeish central room had been lined with bookshelves and turned into a small library, with a melamine table in the centre and a scattering of chairs. A sizeable crack ran down one wall. Despite two strip lights buzzing noisily above, it was dark and smelt strongly of damp. Above the desk was a painting of Plaatje, in dark suit and wing collar, clutching a sheaf of books. Gingerly, I lifted open the visitors' book. I was the only visitor so far that month.

Perhaps I shouldn't have been surprised by the state of the house. It was simply the last pausing place in a remorselessly peripatetic life. Though Plaatje made his way back from England in 1917, once *Native Life in South Africa* was safely in print, he only stayed another two years before he was off again – at first back to England, on a second SANNC deputation and another round of speaking tours, then to Canada and the United States.

It dawned on me that perhaps another reason he had translated Shakespeare, often at sea, was as a way of evading loneliness. Shakespeare was someone knowable, a companion on all those ocean voyages, when his wife and children were thousands of miles away and the cause of black South Africans looked as impossibly remote as ever. Maybe it wasn't pure happenstance that he'd been drawn to *The Comedy of Errors*. Themes that seemed so strong when I'd seen the play in London – madness, separation anxiety – must have had tangible force for a man who was on the move for the best part of fifteen years.

It didn't help that he was permanently broke. In August 1923, stranded in London and lacking the money to pay his passage home, Plaatje had been forced to appear in a stage production about Africa called *The Cradle of the World*. There were two photographs in the front room at 32 Angel Street: one a group shot of seven performers clad in leopardskins standing stiffly behind pot plants; the other of Plaatje himself, sporting a necklace and a feather hat that looked as though it had been dug out of a jumble sale. Though Plaatje was characteristically chipper, writing to a friend that 'I learnt a lot during the month', it must have been a humiliation.

By the time he made it back to South Africa in November 1923, having completed his version of *Othello* on the voyage, the political situation in South Africa had changed beyond all recognition. Despite the SANNC's attempts to appeal directly to Britain, the Union government made it abundantly clear that it had no intention of letting its erstwhile colonial masters meddle in South Africa's affairs. Earlier that year, the Native Urban Areas Act had come into force, clamping down on black immigration into cities and laying the groundwork for racial segregation. The SANNC had been reborn as the African National Congress, but in all other respects it was in disarray, hobbled by lack of funds, outflanked by new, more militant organisations. The older and more moderate generation of activists began to lose their influence. Plaatje in particular felt he was being sidelined.

Private tragedies echoed public ones. Plaatje had been in the US in July 1921 when he received news about his beloved daughter Olive; she had been taken ill during a train journey back from Natal with the after-effects of rheumatic fever. Prevented from entering a whites-only waiting room, or resting on the whites-only seats, she had died on the platform.

Plaatje himself had been ill for many years with a chronic heart problem. In June 1932, during yet another frantic journey from Kimberley to Johannesburg to push for the publication of yet another book, this time of Bantu folk tales, he caught influenza. On 17 June, determined to keep an appointment with the printers, he collapsed on the way back. Two days later, at the age of fifty-five, he, too, was dead.

The Shakespeare translation project all but died with him. According to his biographer Brian Willan, only a few scraps of *Romeo and Juliet* survived in manuscript – a couple of pages at most, dug out decades later from boxes of his papers. Of *Much Ado About Nothing* and *Othello* there was now no sign whatsoever. Whatever Plaatje's true thoughts on Shakespeare's study of a black man striving to find his place in white society, it was likely that no one would ever know them.

Julius Caesar was eventually published, though in conditions that made a mockery of Plaatje's struggles for his culture. In 1937, five years after his death, a white professor at the university of Cape Town, Gérard Lestrade, was handed the manuscript of *Dintshontsho tsa bo-Juliuse Kesara* ('The Death of Julius Caesar'). He edited with zeal, abandoning Plaatje's carefully constructed phonetic system and taking it upon himself to 'correct' the text. Lestrade's introduction argued that Plaatje

> diminished what Shakespeare had written by omitting words, lines, dialogues or verses. More often than not the omissions had altered the meaning of Shakespeare's words. In some cases, Plaatje added his own words; most often these additions had nothing to do with the original. At times Plaatje committed outright errors of translation, possibly because he did not understand English very well, or else he was not paying close attention to what he was doing. Again, most often than not, these mistakes had altered the meaning and diminished the beauty of Shakespeare's words.

Even disregarding the supercilious dismissal of Plaatje's expertise and intentions – adding his 'own words' was surely the point – one didn't have to look far to see another motive behind Lestrade's attack. A black man was surely incapable of translating the greatest white writer there was.

Plaatje's translation of *The Merchant of Venice* had likewise disappeared, but on a shelf at the museum I found an earlier and fuller edition of *Native Life* than the one I'd been using. At the top of the same chapter in which he'd quoted *King Lear*, Plaatje had originally placed lines from *Merchant*, in English and lightly adapted:

> He hath disgraced me and laughed at my losses, mocked at my gain, scorned my nation, thwarted my bargains, cooled my friends, heated mine enemies; and what is his reason? I am a Kaffir. Hath not a Kaffir eyes? Hath not a Kaffir hands, organs, dimensions, senses,

affections, passions? Is he not fed with the same food, hurt by the
same weapons, subject to the same diseases, healed by the same
means, warmed and cooled by the same summer and winter as a
white Afrikander? If you prick us, do we not bleed? If you tickle us,
do we not laugh? If you poison us, do we not die? And if you wrong
us shall we not revenge? If we are like you in the rest, we will
resemble you in that.

The speech is Shylock's, an anguished appeal for tolerance to the
Christians of Venice. For 'Jew' Plaatje had written 'Kaffir', a deeply
offensive term for a black South African; for 'Christian', 'Afrikander' (a
variant spelling of 'Afrikaner'). In the play, as in the South Africa of his
day, the words fell on deaf ears.

At Plaatje's death in June 1932, Kimberley turned out to mourn him.
Zaccheus Richard Mahabane, the president general of the ANC,
conducted the service. Newspapers across South Africa lamented the
passing of a great scholar and statesman. The London *Times* carried a
brief but respectful obituary, declaring him 'a prominent figure in the
South African Native Congress'. Later, I searched the *Times* archive:
despite Plaatje's extensive connections with Britain, this was the only
time Britain's newspaper of record had thought to acknowledge his
existence. Clearly it was safer to praise a black South African activist
while burying him.

But then British journalists weren't the only ones unsure of
Plaatje's place in history. Hearing of his Shakespeare translation
project, Clement Doke, a pioneering South African linguist, wondered
whether 'other types of literature are not at present much more
urgently needed in Setswana than this'. The critic and playwright
Stephen Black told a friend that he had written to Plaatje warning him
off entirely: 'Instead of wasting his time on translating Shakespeare, he
should translate something which contains humanity, the one quality
of which Shakespeare is entirely devoid . . . What in God's name the
Tswana want to read Shakespeare for I don't know, unless it is that they
want to feel more like worms than ever.'

In literature as in politics, by attempting to bridge two cultures,
Plaatje had trapped himself in no man's land. His novel *Mhudi* had

suffered a similar fate when it was eventually published in 1930. A courageous attempt to tell the story of his own people in a form that owes much to the historical epics of Walter Scott and with language that borrows from the King James Bible and Bunyan's *The Pilgrim's Progress*, it, too, was an attempt to bridge cultures. It, too, was judged a failure. According to an anonymous review in the *Times Literary Supplement* in 1933, Plaatje should have abandoned his pretensions to 'Europeanism':

> One wonders what secret fountain of African art might not have been unsealed if, in interpreting his people, a writer of Plaatje's insight had thought and written 'like a Native'. That might well have been the first authentic utterance out of the aeons of African silence.

No matter that this was the first novel published in English by a black South African: Plaatje's problem was that he was not 'authentic' enough, not enough 'like a Native'. In presuming to write a novel – or wear a suit, or meet with Lloyd George, or translate Shakespeare into Setswana – he had exceeded the position allotted him by the hue of his skin.

Plaatje's wider ambitions lay unrealised. His hopes for South African education were bulldozed by the Bantu Education Act of 1953, which enforced a discriminatory curriculum in schools across South Africa: Hendrik Verwoerd, its architect, said the Act's intention was to warn the 'Native' off 'the greener pastures of European Society where he is not allowed to graze'. Every major political battle Plaatje fought, from the 1913 Land Act to his attempts to reason with Union president Jan Smuts, ended in failure. In 1936, four years after his death, the non-racial Cape franchise he had fought so fervently to keep was abolished. Within fifteen years a hard-line nationalist government would take charge and formalise the policy Plaatje and his colleagues feared more than anything else: apartheid.

Perhaps most devastating of all, as the situation in South Africa became ever more intractable, the ANC grew distinctly uncomfortable with its founding fathers. In the radical heat of the 1960s and 1970s, to be a 'native intellectual' – a phrase popularised by the anti-colonial philosopher and activist Frantz Fanon – was tantamount to being complicit with the racist colonial power. In the face of outrages like the Sharpeville Massacre of 1960, when police fired on township protestors without warning and killed at least sixty-nine people, who wanted to celebrate a Shakespeare-loving egghead? Plaatje was buried all over again.

While I was in California, I met the expatriate South African scholar Natasha Distiller. Distiller had written perceptively about Plaatje as a 'coconut' – a derogatory word for someone who was 'black' on the outside and 'white' on the inside. Far from being a term of casual abuse, Distiller argued, in Plaatje's case it touched something precise: his attempts to forge a hybrid persona that borrowed aspects from European culture while promoting his own heritage and language. In a multicultural, twenty-first-century world of hyphenated identities (African-American, British-Indian), it didn't seem such a difficult balance to strike. But the world in which Plaatje lived regarded the concept of hybridity as a dangerous affront to the principles on which it was organised.

And what if the universality of Shakespeare was an illusion? What if it really was a Eurocentric fantasy to think that Shakespeare naturally had relevance everywhere? In my hotel that night, I looked up a famous encounter between Shakespeare's works and African storytelling traditions that posed exactly these questions. It had occurred in West Africa sixty-odd years ago, and been reported by an American anthropologist named Laura Bohannan. The article appeared in *Natural History* magazine in 1966.

The story began in the early 1950s, when Bohannan left her adopted home in Britain to travel to West Africa. Her aim was to study the Tiv people, who still live flanking the great Benue river, the longest tributary of the Niger, in what was in the process of becoming the Federation of Nigeria after nearly seventy years of British colonial rule.

Although this was serious research, Bohannan was also fulfilling a bet. Back in Oxford, an Englishman had taunted her with an old libel – that Yanks don't get the Bard:

'You Americans,' said a friend, 'often have difficulty with Shakespeare. He was, after all, a very English poet, and one can easily misinterpret the universal by misunderstanding the particular.'

I protested that human nature is pretty much the same the whole world over; at least the general plot and motivation of the greater tragedies would always be clear – everywhere – although some details of custom might have to be explained and difficulties of translation might produce other slight changes.

The two of them agreed to a wager. Bohannan would take *Hamlet* to Africa, and see if her theories held water.

The play indeed became an object of fascination, though not in the way she intended. As the swamps rose after the harvest, the Tiv ceremonies she'd come to observe ceased – to her immense frustration – and the boozing commenced:

> People began to drink at dawn. By mid-morning the whole homestead was singing, dancing, and drumming. When it rained, people had to sit inside their huts: there they drank and sang or they drank and told stories. In any case, by noon or before, I either had to join the party or retire to my own hut and my books. 'One does not discuss serious matters when there is beer. Come, drink with us.' Since I lacked their capacity for the thick native beer, I spent more and more time with *Hamlet*.

After a while, her hosts admitted they were confused – wondering what this weird American woman was doing, sitting alone staring at 'paper' rather than joining in the fun and games. Bohannan tried to explain.

The account of her storytelling occupies the rest of the article. The Tiv, as it turns out, have no time for *Hamlet*: are bewildered by its premises, perplexed by its plot, alienated by its bizarre belief systems, at odds with its moral compass. The ghost of Hamlet's father cannot be a ghost, they say; he must be an omen sent by a witch. Gertrude's marriage to Claudius is not 'o'er-hasty'; it is a prudent move that guarantees the security of the family. They don't share Hamlet's queasiness about his aunt-mother, but, operating in a polygamous culture, are scornful that Old Hamlet was so neglectful as to have had only one wife. They are horrified by the death of Polonius, but – experienced hunters with hair-trigger reactions – largely because he allowed himself to be taken by surprise behind the arras. They are openly stricken that Hamlet should avenge himself on an uncle who has so generously taken him in.

Rereading Bohannan's essay that night, I realised this wasn't simply a narrative of mutual incomprehension. It challenged the idea that Shakespeare had central significance in global culture, was relevant wherever you travelled. If, as Solomon Plaatje had suggested, Shakespeare was just one storyteller among many, perhaps he didn't even matter all that much. There were plenty of storytellers out there. And it reflected back on us: why did *we* think the story of *Hamlet* said so much? Did we really have any clue what it was about, this 400-year-old version of a millennium-old text?

Once Bohannan finally reaches the end of her storytelling session, beaten down by her sceptical audience, the old men who have been listening seem satisfied with the outcome of their transcultural dialogue. 'Some time,' one of them remarks, 'you must tell us some more stories of your country':

> We, who are elders, will instruct you in their true meaning, so that when you return to your own land your elders will see that you have not been sitting in the bush, but among those who know things and who have taught you wisdom.

I admired the style of literary criticism practised by the Tiv. I copied the lines into my notebook and reminded myself to look at them more often.

On my last afternoon in Kimberley, I met up with Sabata-mpho Mokae. As well as co-founding a literary festival in Plaatje's name, Mokae was a journalist, biographer, novelist and writer of short stories. He was also a historian, a translator, a curator and an aspiring film-maker. He seemed busier than the rest of Kimberley combined.

On the stroke of midday a small silver car creaked up. At the wheel was a young man in his mid-thirties, dressed in a crisp orange T-shirt and jeans, with shoulder-length braids and thick, square glasses that were a little askew. He had a serious, bookish air and a habit of frowning when he talked.

He wanted to show me something. After driving past a monument to Cecil Rhodes, Kimberley's great robber baron, he edged us into a nondescript car park in front of the city police headquarters. It took me a moment to realise where he was pointing: at a squat block of stone, a few metres high, with two holes incised into the top. I had passed it the day before and assumed it was a particularly cryptic piece of public art.

It was actually a plinth: a few years back the ANC-dominated provincial government had commissioned a statue of Plaatje, but the family and many others objected.

Mokae lifted his fist out of the car window in the black-power salute. 'He was standing, with his arm raised like this, you know? Totally inauthentic. That symbol didn't even exist when Plaatje was alive. It was typical; they wanted to make him something he was not.'

The government had the statue installed in 2009, only to be forced to remove it again a few weeks later. An older statue was hurriedly taken out of storage and placed at another site in the centre of town. It was a more fitting representation, depicting Plaatje seated in front of his books, but the ANC still made sure to dominate proceedings, dispatching President Zuma to administer the unveiling.

Mokae smiled wryly, and straightened his glasses. 'The first statue is now in a storeroom in the town museum. They're too embarrassed to melt him down.'

As he swung the car round and drove us towards the cemetery where Plaatje was buried, I wondered where he stood on the question of identity politics. Was Plaatje really a 'coconut', a traitor to the cause for having believed so fervently in Shakespeare?

Mokae looked to be concentrating hard on the traffic. 'I think he wants to see beyond colour, he genuinely believes that,' he said eventually. 'He had black and white friends, he exchanged letters with people in Europe and America, he wrote to the prime minister in South Africa. People could say that he aspired to whiteness, but I think that's not right. Plaatje was ahead of his time.'

By now we were on the outskirts of town, a road fringed with gum trees, their ragged outlines wavering in the heat. The light was blinding. Silhouettes tramped past, women mainly, carrying heavy bags or balancing bundles on their heads. A little group of boys in shorts lingered in front of a corner supermarket, sheltering under the shade of an umbrella. The outlines of everything were razor-sharp; the land looked dry enough to combust.

We came through the cemetery gates, raising a rough cloud of grey dust. Mokae parked the car and we stepped out: a flat expanse of scrub-grass and gravel, pockmarked with stubby cypresses and cacti.

Here the graves were fitfully spaced, some little more than piles of broken stone, cluttered with rubbish. The wind sent an empty Coke bottle and a torn ice-cream wrapper skittering along the path. Other than the crunch of our shoes on the gravel, the only noise was the faint sighing of traffic on the highway.

Mokae pointed to a thin obelisk, a little distance from the others. I recognised it from a photograph of a visit by Mandela, years before: the monument at Plaatje's grave, raised in 1935, three years after his death. It looked painfully small.

I read out the inscription: 'To the Sacred Memory of Solomon Tshekisho Plaatje, Journalist, Author, Temperance Organiser, Social Worker and founder of the Brotherhood Movement of SA.' Below was a small note in Setswana, *I Khutse Morolong: Modiredi Wa Afrika*. Mokae translated: 'Rest in peace, Morolong, Servant of Africa.'

I bent down and lifted a wreath lying upside-down a few feet away. The fine dust stuck to my hands.

Mokae leaned down beside me. He was running his fingers along the script.

'See? They got the date wrong.'

I looked more closely: it was true. Plaatje had died on 19 June 1932; this said 18 July. Whoever carved the memorial got mixed up, and no one had bothered to correct it.

Perhaps things weren't as grim as they looked. In recent years the powers that be had woken up to the power of Solomon Plaatje. There was now a Sol Plaatje institute at Rhodes University in Grahamstown, and several literary awards in his name. Most momentously, Kimberley was about to get a university, its first – also the first South African university of the post-apartheid era. The aim was to attract students from poor, non-urban backgrounds who might not otherwise be able to attend. Zuma had announced that it, too, would be named after Sol Plaatje.

Plaatje's Shakespeare had not entirely evaporated either. *Diphosho-phosho* was still awaiting a debut performance, as far as I could find out, but in 2001 a Johannesburg-born theatre director, Yaël Farber, had placed sections of his *Julius Caesar* into a reimagining of the play called *SeZaR*. Staged during a time when some were debating whether Shakespeare should be removed from the South African curriculum altogether – that same year, the advisory board for the Gauteng education department had decreed *Julius Caesar* 'sexist' and *Lear* 'full of violence and despair', as well as recommending that Plaatje's own *Mhudi* should be dropped – *SeZaR* was a bold assertion that Shakespeare was an unnegotiable part of South African history.

Nor was this was the only production of *Julius Caesar* to re-engage in the linguistic battles fought so fervently by Plaatje. Back in Johannesburg, talking to an academic at Wits University, I discovered that a student company had recently been working on their own version of the text along remarkably similar lines. It had begun as a kind of research workshop, but had mutated into a semi-professional performance touring schools and townships. They were playing a fringe space. Apart from that, all I really knew was the show's name, which gave little enough away: *The Julius Caesar Project*.

As I sat there in the auditorium on a Sunday afternoon, there didn't seem anything especially unusual about the performance, at least at first. Eight cast members came silently on, four women and four men, a mix of ethnicities, dressed in identikit white vests and khaki combat fatigues. The set was sparse to the point of non-existence: three wood-framed panels suspended in the air, likewise khaki, mottled with what looked dubiously like blood.

The students were good, and conjured the scene almost instantly. A Roman street; wise-cracking carpenters and cobblers; two tribunes, nervily trying to keep a lid on things. Everyone on stage was multitasking: crossing genders, playing senators, commoners, conspirators.

The scene changed. Cassius – a thin, urgent boy, black, with sharp, precise movements – began to put pressure on Brutus, a female student with dark blonde hair and a faint Afrikaans accent. Brutus confessed his/her doubts to Portia, another woman. The crowd muttered, in a combination of Shakespeare's English and what sounded like isiXhosa. Death was in the air.

But during the meeting of the conspirators to plot the assassination, things began to go awry. Someone else seemed now to be playing Cassius, and Brutus had transmogrified into Casca; or was it the other way around? Muddled after ten days on the move, I tried to remember the order of the plot: surely Antony should have come on by now?

By now we were back with the crowd of plebeians, this time turning on the poet Cinna – hounded to death for unluckily having the same name as one of the conspirators. Wasn't that meant to happen after Caesar was killed? Come to think of it, what had happened to the assassination scene? Caesar appeared to have gone awol.

This was less a performance of *Julius Caesar*, more a live remix of the text. The action had been juggled so that different plot strands

were isolated: first the scenes with the commoners, then scenes with
Caesar, then with Brutus. The actors were swapping fluidly between
roles, making it hard to tell who was playing whom. It said a great
deal about the flexibility of Shakespeare's scripts, their openness to
recontextualisation and reconfiguration, that one could tear apart the
play like this and it still just about make sense. And it achieved one thing
I'd never expected from *Julius Caesar*: the most famous assassination in
history came as a surprise.

Afterwards, the students and I sat around on the stage, dissecting
their dissection. All eight were studying English and drama. *Július
Caesar* was a set text. They had known they wanted to do something
performance-based, but couldn't agree on a director; also, the group
wasn't large enough to do the play in its entirety – it has forty-plus
roles, many of them speaking.

An associate professor at Wits called Sarah Roberts had initiated
the project and acted as director. She suggested reassembling the text
to clarify its themes. One inspiration was a British television series
from the early 1980s called *Playing Shakespeare*, presented by the Royal
Shakespeare Company's co-founder John Barton, which explored
the meaning of the plays through democratic, actor-led workshops.
Another was a book on improvisation. Could they somehow combine
the two? How would that even work?

The result was a kind of game, with elegant if brain-bending rules:
every actor would learn the script in its entirety, and only decide who
was playing which part in the seconds before they went on stage. The
cast could also exchange roles at a moment's notice: if someone started
speaking, say, Caesar's lines in a particular scene, everyone else would
have to scramble to catch up.

It sounded like a recipe for insanity, I said. They grinned: it made
things fun.

Emma Delius, who had played Brutus before migrating to Casca,
explained that everyone in the group, from different schools across
South Africa, had had different levels of exposure to Shakespeare, so this
was a way of making the playing field even. But the project had taken on
its own momentum. It was Shakespeare – but improvised Shakespeare.

Another student, Sinako Zokufa, nodded vigorously. 'The way we
do *Julius Caesar*, it's literally never the same show – that's what people
always say about theatre, I know, but here we deliberately make it a
surprise. The audience shares the surprise.'

I liked the concept, not simply because it offered a fresh way into an overfamiliar text, but because it released many of the questions buried within *Julius Caesar*. Who is really in charge? Where does power reside – in the dictator about to be crowned king, or the citizens lining the streets? Tribunes or senators? Conspirators or cobblers? It seemed a pertinent approach in post-apartheid South Africa, a country still grappling with the workings of democracy.

Political process was very much on their minds, agreed Karl Thurtell, a tall, blonde boy who had briefly taken on Caesar. 'By highlighting particular stories in the play – say the story of the citizens – we've highlighted something that might otherwise go missing. It shows what it means to be an active citizen. Most of our theatre history in this country is embedded in protest theatre. This was our way of making *Caesar* in that tradition.'

One thing was undeniably South African, and fully in the mould of Solomon Plaatje. In a country where most of the population spoke at least two languages, it had been felt necessary to incorporate at least some of those languages into the production. I'd been right to identify isiXhosa, but scraps of isiZulu, Sesotho, Afrikaans and siSwati also jostled alongside Shakespeare's English – all of them, like the acting, left up to chance. If someone wanted to speak a particular language at a particular moment, they could.

Setswana too?

Yamikani Mahaka-Phiri, who'd briefly played Cassius, nodded. 'A few more, sometimes.'

The next question was obvious: how about race? The students came from a variety of ethnic groups; was this also part of the point? A way of putting the rainbow nation on stage?

There was some awkward shuffling. 'Look, it's difficult,' said Thurtell eventually. 'I'm white, a second-language Afrikaans speaker, and I know the political weight that brings. If I start the first scene in Afrikaans, playing a tribune trying to control the masses, then I know a large portion of the audience will interpret that as something from the apartheid state. In some places it will work, but not elsewhere.'

Zokufa was frowning. 'In this country, theatre is political. It gets politicised, everything gets politicised. This ensemble is mixed-race, and we have to be aware of messages we're sending, even if they're unintentional. But we don't want it to be *about* race.'

What did they think about the argument, still raised every so often in South Africa, that they shouldn't be doing Shakespeare at all – that to do so was simply to reinscribe a colonial heritage?

For the first time, they looked entirely nonplussed: Shakespeare was simply part of South African life, along with so many things, good and bad.

Delius spoke up. 'Just because the text happens to be by Shakespeare doesn't mean we can't use it!'

Mahaka-Phiri was visibly incensed. 'It should not sit on a shelf somewhere in England.' He threw out his arm expansively. 'It should be *here*, on a South African stage.'

In the taxi back home, I remembered what one scholar had called Plaatje's translations: 'linguistic activism'. It seemed a pretty fine description of what I'd just seen.

THE FOLLOWING MORNING, sitting in the Johannesburg sunshine, I sat down and took stock. I had become so enveloped in the story of Plaatje and his legacy I was in danger of forgetting the reason I had come to South Africa in the first place: the Robben Island Bible.

My brief conversation with Sonny Venkatrathnam in London had left me with a teeming series of questions. How had Shakespeare been read on Robben Island? *Had* he been read? What was Shakespeare's significance in a later period of apartheid from that experienced by Solomon Plaatje? Had Shakespeare been – as the media were so keen to make out – a familiar part of prison life, or did his works have a different significance in South Africa's most notorious political penitentiary? In London 100,000 visitors had queued to see the exhibition. What had we all been looking at?

I'd been exchanging emails with Venkatrathnam's granddaughter, Teneille. Durban was only an hour-long hop away by plane; would they mind if I paid a visit? The answer came back straight away: of course. Sonny was a man of his word.

I found him watching cricket in the glare of a Durban afternoon. As I came inside the house, a large flat-screen TV was showing England playing Australia in Cardiff – a wide shot of turf, as green and smooth as a billiard table, beneath an eiderdown of soggy Welsh cloud. The scene looked as freakishly alien as if it were being beamed back from the Moon.

'You like cricket?' *Crrrickutt.* 'I like cricket. It's slow. Good pace for me these days.'

He was frailer than I remembered, even from fourteen months before: as thin as a marionette inside a worn green checked shirt and loose flannel trousers. Though his handshake was strong, his face was pinched and sharp, eyes dark and pebble-bright. As he sat down in a leather recliner, exposing a bony pair of ankles, he gestured towards a framed photograph propped on a small table. A single candle was placed in front. His wife Theresa. She had been ill, I recalled him saying. She had died later that summer.

I mumbled my condolences.

He smiled distantly, as if it were I who had lost somebody. 'She was my rock, my support, all the way through my detention.'

Sonny's wife had played an important part in the story of his copy of Shakespeare. But before we talked about that he wanted to discuss his old life. Brought up in the Sea View district of Durban, he had majored in English Literature at the university of Natal in the late 1950s. A set text was *Clarissa*; Sonny had become one of countless undergraduates worldwide to be defeated by Samuel Richardson's 970,000-word leviathan.

He brushed away a hand in distaste. 'Pffft, so boring, it didn't inspire me at all. Useless, pain in the butt.'

But he also discovered something more suited to him: Shakespeare. Several plays were set texts at school – *Julius Caesar* stuck in his mind – but he'd not paid a huge amount of attention. Then, during his final year, he'd written a short dissertation on the role played by fools, those riddling philosophers – from Touchstone in *As You Like It* and Feste in *Twelfth Night* to *King Lear*'s Fool – who stand at an oblique and ironic angle to the action, alone licensed to tell the truth about what they see.

The interest reflected Sonny's own fragile position in South African society. As one of the country's million-strong Indian-heritage population, he was granted greater liberties than black South Africans, but apartheid had its own fanatically detailed rules when it came to Indians, too, and the white elite never came close to regarding them as equals. Sonny – born Surinarayan – made common cause with activists of all ethnicities, joining the Unity movement.

In June 1971 he was arrested in Pietermaritzburg and charged with inciting a military uprising. The sentence was stinging: twelve years. He was bundled away to Leeuwkop prison in Johannesburg, then on to Robben Island, five miles off Cape Town in the chill seas of Table Bay. Because he was one of the 'terries' – convicts under the Terrorist Act – he faced heavy suspicion. Conditions were brutal. Hard labour, breaking stones and chopping wood from morning until night.

Initially political prisoners were prevented from having any reading material at all save the Bible – of limited interest to Sonny, brought up in the Hindu faith – but they petitioned for access to books. Grudgingly they were permitted to use the prison library. One deliriously happy day, it was announced they would each be allowed a book of their own, to be sent by their families.

In the absence of anything more controversial (hardly likely they'd allow texts on African politics), Sonny decided his must be a copy of Shakespeare. It would be something he could read and reread, and which would help keep his mind active through the indignities and inanities of life on the island. Theresa, at home in Durban and supporting their three children, bought a copy. In May 1972, it arrived.

This is where the story got a little confusing. I had read, I said, that the book was smuggled on to the island and kept there in secrecy. Was that the case?

He produced a shallow laugh: no way anything could be smuggled across the bay, past all those guards. 'It *was* confiscated, two months after it arrived – they were having a clampdown or something. They put it away in the storeroom, in our section. Then one day, a Sunday, I was standing at the gate and a warder comes up and says, "Tell the fellows that the church is here." "Church" meant priest, you know. I said, "OK, but let me get my Bible, it's in the storeroom." So he opened it, I took out my Shakespeare and showed it to him. I told him, "It's the Bible of William Shakespeare." So he let me have it.'

So it was this that had given the book its nickname: not because it was a quasi-devotional text, but because of an off-the-cuff remark. Something similar accounted for the Hindu greetings cards that lined the cover. They had been sent by Sonny's family for Diwali: touching gifts, when one considered they portrayed Lakshmi and Vishnu, Rama and Sita – gods and goddesses who have been united after numerous travails – but not otherwise of significance. Sonny himself was agnostic, and had cut them up and used them to cover the book – not because Shakespeare was banned, but to discourage the poorly educated, God-fearing Afrikaner warders from touching it. It wasn't in any case a camouflage that would have withstood much scrutiny: Shakespeare's name was plainly visible. The book had never been confiscated again and had remained there undisturbed for the rest of Sonny's time on the island.

I wondered how often he and the others read Shakespeare. Was the book passed between them?

Again, yes and no. When his copy of Shakespeare first arrived, he had been kept in a communal cell. One of his Apdusa confederates, Joseph B. Vusani, had read from the book to other prisoners, many of whom struggled to read for themselves, adapting stories and retelling them at night in isiXhosa – not dissimilar from Plaatje's oral tradition, perhaps. But once conditions had improved and Venkatrathnam and others had been relocated to single cells, then permitted to study by correspondence course, Shakespeare had fallen by the wayside: simply no time. Caught in the baffling, maze-like intricacies of a bachelor's degree in accountancy (chosen because it fitted the remaining duration of his sentence), Sonny reckoned he had not read it for the last four years of his incarceration on the island.

The book might have been used as a promptbook at end-of-year performances, when prisoners were permitted to put on small dramatic readings, but he couldn't swear to it. It was all a long time ago.

So the Bible hadn't been a bible, not really, nor had it been smuggled or widely read. After the colourful accounts I had read of its significance – and of the wider significance of Shakespeare on the island – it was dismaying to hear that Sonny's actual engagement with the book had been so slight.

It was a relief that the signatures in it were indisputably authentic. In late 1977, as he was approaching the end of his sentence and preparing to be transferred back to the mainland, Venkatrathnam had passed it around fellow occupants of the leadership section, asking them each to choose a passage and sign their name – Mandela, most famously, being one.

But even here the book was not quite what it seemed. Though some prisoners had gone through the text with great precision, carefully identifying a passage or poem that seemed appropriate to their situation, others had been far more cursory, scribbling a signature in the approximate location of a relevant passage or simply choosing a well-known line. It had taken Sonny months to get the book to all thirty-four men. Some inmates had held on to the book for days or weeks; others had barely flipped through. It wasn't clear how many of them had laboured over or discussed their choices, or simply scribbled their names as a favour to a friend. Whatever else it testified to, the Bible didn't reflect what the British Museum curator described as 'a constant reference for debating the moral issues of the day'.

Perhaps some of this ambiguity accounted for a curious news story, ignored by the British press, that had appeared a few days after the British Museum put the Robben Island Bible on display. It appeared on the website of the Toronto *Star* and was headlined 'ANC Disputes "Iconic" Status of Robben Island Bible'. The paper quoted the ANC national spokesman saying that the book was 'iconic to those who want to make it iconic. To us, it is not.' He went on: 'We know so many other documents that are iconic in the ANC's eyes. We didn't know anything called the Robben Island Bible.'

What did Sonny think lay behind this story?

He hit the heel of his hand on the glass tabletop, making the ashtray jump. 'Well, I think they are ashamed. If you go through the passages that the leadership has chosen, many of them, you'd be ashamed what they chose and what they did.'

Taken aback by the ferocity of his reply, I wasn't sure I understood – he was saying that the corruption and political scandals that had mired the ANC were somehow a denigration of Shakespeare? That this was why they were keen to distance themselves from the book?

He nodded curtly. 'Sometimes I tell my children that I am ashamed that I call them comrades.'

I suspected the reason was simpler, and sadder: that the book had a smaller significance in the story of the struggle than had been made out. While the Bible had experienced growing fame all over the world – Britain, the United States, elsewhere – here in South Africa it was neglected. The book had never been displayed publicly; the Robben Island Museum had made approaches, but Sonny wasn't convinced they would take care of it. He was in two minds about whether to sell it – not for the money, more to make sure that it could be kept on display. He was considering donating it to the Shakespeare Birthplace Trust in Stratford-upon-Avon.

Wouldn't that be a tragedy, I said, for it to leave South Africa?

He brushed away his hand once again. 'I don't see that much interest in South Africa.'

I asked if I could take a quick peek for myself; I'd seen the book, but only behind glass, in front of the blank gaze of a security guard. I'd heard he normally kept it beneath his bed.

Sonny looked stricken. 'Andrew, I'm so sorry. It's gone to Washington in America. Library called the Folger? They're putting it on display, a big new exhibition. You just missed it by days.'

Perplexed by what my conversation with Venkatrathnam had thrown up, I arranged to speak to another man who'd been imprisoned alongside him, and who had also signed the book. I was hopeful he might help me get nearer the truth about the Robben Island Bible – or at least some version of the truth. His name was Ahmed Kathrada.

A member of the Indian Congress party and one of the activists sentenced at the notorious Rivonia trial of 1963–64, when an entire swath of the ANC leadership were imprisoned, Kathrada had been a friend and colleague of Mandela, Sisulu and others from the 1940s. He had served a gruelling twenty-six years and three months in prison, eighteen of them on Robben Island, afterwards becoming Mandela's parliamentary counsellor. One of the handful of senior figures from the early days who were still alive, he had kept a dignified distance from the scandals that had tainted many in the post-1994 leadership.

But it wasn't just his CV that made me keen to speak to Kathrada; it was his relationship with Shakespeare. He studied for four degrees during his incarceration, in politics, history, criminology and library science, and for a time had been Robben Island's librarian. His letters to family made reference to the plays, and he filled notebooks with quotations from Shakespeare and others. If anyone could help me understand more about how Shakespeare was read and understood on the island, it was surely Kathrada.

Over email he gave me an address back in Johannesburg, an apartment in the well-to-do neighbourhood of Killarney. It was elegant and homely, crammed with books and mementoes of the struggle. Kathrada was in his mid-eighties but as active as ever, trim in a green Robben Island-branded polo shirt. He was polite and deliberate, but it was clear why he commanded such respect. His dark eyes were on me throughout as we talked.

I'd had a hard time persuading him to talk: he was faintly sick of the whole thing, it transpired. In fact, seeing as I was here, he had a few things to get off his chest. First, it was a myth that Shakespeare had been banned on the island – and he should know, because when he had arrived in June 1964, among one of the earliest batches of 'politicals', there were two books among his belongings, Arthur Quiller-Couch's much-reprinted *The Oxford Book of English Verse* (a book Mandela also owned) and his own copy of Shakespeare's complete works. The books had come with him from Pretoria jail, and remained in his possession until he was discharged.

They were on his shelf right now, in fact; did I want to see?

He padded into the next room and returned with two stout tomes, patched and worn – one bound in Oxford blue, the other in faded bottle-green. On the flyleaf of the Shakespeare (the same Alexander edition as Venkatrathnam's) was the sales label of a Johannesburg bookshop and a flourishing signature in blue biro. 'Pretoria Jail – 1964' and 'Robben Island – Aug 1964' were inscribed beneath.

'Now I don't want to contradict anybody,' Kathrada announced carefully, placing the books on the coffee table between us. 'This is my own experience, but Robben Island had absolutely no problem with books, even though I was not yet registered to study. We only registered in 1965. But they allowed me to keep both these books.'

The other myth was that Shakespeare loomed large in prison life. Again he could only speak to his experience, but he could not remember a single detailed discussion about Shakespeare on the island. Some prisoners had studied the plays as set texts for school certificates or degrees, sure, but the idea that Shakespeare had been a major subject of debate – still less formed a constant point of reference – was, in his view, far-fetched. He had studied *Macbeth*, but only because it was a set text.

How about his degree in library science?

A ruse, he replied: a double major with African Politics, it had allowed him to get around the regulations concerning books that *were* banned, those that contained controversial historical or political material.

He smiled thinly. 'I had no interest in library science, none whatsoever. Everything I did in my studies was with an ulterior motive. What subject can I register for, which books can I get?'

So why had he brought Shakespeare with him in the first place?

He shrugged: something to read. 'I can never claim to be well informed about Shakespeare. I don't read Shakespeare as an academic book. I enjoy it while I am reading it, and if you have a discussion a week after, I won't be able to . . .' He paused. 'Well, it's that type of book. But it was interesting. I had to while away the time. And as for the Oxford poetry book, there were particular poems that I was very fond of, from school days.'

This wasn't to say that Shakespeare had been irrelevant; it was clear, talking to him, that he had read among the plays widely. But this had been a solitary experience, something private and personal – a retreat, like note-taking, a way of communing with himself.

With his permission, I picked up his complete works. The pages fell open at *Othello*, with neat, precise pencil marginalia on the page. I noticed he'd drawn a line next to Brabantio's flagrantly racist words to Othello, expressing his disbelief that Desdemona would ever have 'run . . . to the sooty bosom | Of such a thing as thou'.

Why had he marked those lines – did he remember?

'That was 1965, I think. I had quickly read through and come to the foolish conclusion that Shakespeare was a racist. Othello, Shylock . . . It was a very quick reading. Neville Alexander and Dennis Brutus, who were inmates too, they were academics, and I made the foolish mistake of confronting them, saying that Shakespeare was a racist.' There was a flicker of a smile. 'They shot me down.'

So they did discuss Shakespeare occasionally?

'Maybe once or twice.'

What was more surprising was that he had no clear memory of signing Sonny Venkatrathnam's copy. I'd seen a photograph of the page, with Kathrada's signature crammed next to the famous speech from *Henry V*, 'Once more unto the breach, dear friends, once more', and the date December 1977, the same month that Mandela had signed. Kathrada's choice of speech had exercised the interpretative powers of several critics: was he saluting his experience in the military wing of the ANC? Rallying the troops? Quietly hinting at the costs of war?

Honestly, he couldn't say why he had chosen those words. 'It's possible Sonny was a bit nervous to get this thing signed before he finished his sentence, so that he didn't miss people. In my case, I did not necessarily choose my favourite passage. What I chose, I chose on the spur of the moment, so much so that I can't even remember now what I chose. It must have been done in a great hurry.'

Why did he think the book had been autographed by so many prisoners? Because of their abiding respect for William Shakespeare?

He shrugged. 'I think it was of great sentimental value – like if you go to a book launch, people want to have the book signed. That's just a natural thing. But from there it just took a momentum of its own, various people got involved, professors started writing about it. I remember shortly before Neville Alexander died, I happened to raise this with him, and he just laughed.'

His fellow prisoner laughed because the story of Shakespeare on Robben Island had become overblown?

He slipped off his bifocals and held them up against the light. 'Yes, there were too many claims made.'

It was one of the many costs of being a survivor, he explained: you became a symbol, but you had little control over what you symbolised. Particularly anything that touched Mandela.

He shook his head in irritation. 'One chap went on television to say that he spent eighteen or twenty years next to Mandela. He lies; he was never even *in* that section. Now that Mandela is not well, people have come out with all sorts of things – "I know Mandela the longest, he's been a friend." People take advantage of that.' He sighed wearily. 'I am used to people making claims, all sorts of claims. It's one of those things.'

So he didn't feel that Shakespeare had something unique to offer in South Africa?

His smile was steady and patient. 'If you take the whole of Shakespeare,' he said slowly, 'you will find relevance to every country.'

As I left the flat, slowly walking down the stairs and out on to the bright street, I tried to measure my feelings. After all I'd heard and read about the Robben Island Bible and its totemic significance, it was impossible not to feel despondent about what seemed to be the realities: the fact that the book hadn't really been read, even by its owner or those who had signed it; the fact that Shakespeare had barely been discussed, even among those prisoners who had an interest.

But then again, was any of this surprising? Was it really plausible that prisoners in one of the most inhumane penitentiaries in the world had devoted enormous amounts of time to the hermeneutics of Shakespeare? If you were given the opportunity to improve your education – and wanted to put it to use in the struggle – would you choose Elizabethan drama over law or politics? After nearly two weeks here, I was slowly realising the truth behind something I'd been told on the first day I arrived: when it came to making sense of the recent

South African past, everything was less straightforward than it seemed.

None of this was Sonny's fault. He could have made a great deal of money out of his experiences – like many of his former colleagues, now high on the hog – and I very much doubted he had. Nor had he claimed anything about the Bible that wasn't true. The exaggerations and embroiderings were all other people's.

But then of course, I thought gloomily, he hadn't needed to: desperate to believe that Shakespeare played a pivotal role in the defining human-rights struggle of the twentieth century, the rest of us had done it for him.

———◆———

YET MAYBE THERE WAS A DIFFERENT STORY to be told about the connection between Shakespeare and apartheid: not in prison cells on Robben Island, necessarily, but in university seminar rooms and theatres across South Africa.

Browsing one lunchtime in a second-hand bookshop, I came across a slim lilac paperback. Its title was *Shakespeare Against Apartheid*, and it was by Martin Orkin, an academic who'd taught at Wits. It had been published in 1987, a period when revolts against the hard-line P. W. Botha administration were at their height and yet another nationwide state of emergency had been declared. Many feared South Africa might tumble into outright civil war.

Various people had told me about *Shakespeare Against Apartheid*. Over lunch, I read it. The book was absorbing, hectoring, optimistic, doom-mongering and persuasive by turns. It was aimed at (predominantly white) South African undergraduates who had passed through an apartheid education system still dominated by the teachings of liberal humanists such as A. C. Bradley and the New Critics of the 1940s and 1950s. Its aim was insurrection by stealth.

Orkin argued that it wasn't true (as those critics had claimed) that the Almighty Bard was above the rough-and-tumble of contemporary politics; to believe so was to close one's eyes to the injustices and violence raging all around. Instead, Shakespeare could – should – be employed in the here and now. American new historicists and Marxist-influenced British cultural materialists had become increasingly fascinated by the political contradictions and pressures that shaped Shakespeare's working life: intrigues at court, of censorship, the devastating divisions of the Reformation. Orkin argued that it was high time South African teachers did the same.

Leading by example, Orkin attempted to introduce Shakespeare to the pressure cooker of 1980s South Africa: a pariah state of suspicious deaths and torture in custody, a racist judiciary, an army flagrantly out of control. An essay on *Hamlet* linked King Claudius's attempts to dispose of the hero – sending him to England in the company of assassins, then arranging a suicidal duel with Laertes – with the death in September 1977 of the black activist Steve Biko, who had been stripped and beaten in a police cell. Instead of dwelling on hoary debates such as why Hamlet delays his revenge (Bradley diagnosed a case of 'profound melancholy'), Orkin suggested the Prince was already manning the township barricades:

> The young men and women in Soweto and elsewhere in South Africa, who know they are living in a system which is less than just, despite its official claims, will recognise many aspects of the situation depicted in *Hamlet* . . . Not all such men and women may be interested in Shakespeare, but the experience of *Hamlet* is in their blood.

Later in the book, I was caught by the presence of a play that Ahmed Kathrada had mentioned, and which I felt had been eluding me until now: *Othello*. Taking his cue from Solomon Plaatje's suggestion that 'Shakespeare's dramas . . . show that nobility and valour, like depravity and cowardice, are not the monopoly of any one colour', Orkin outlined the hypocrisy of denying that the play's essential subject was race. In contemporary South Africa, it could not be about anything else. Furthermore, he bore down on a long and dishonourable line of white critics who had sought to resolve the 'problem' of how a black African Othello married a white woman in the first place. Samuel Taylor Coleridge had notoriously asserted that 'it would be something monstrous to conceive this beautiful Venetian girl with a veritable negro', but this was merely the start. Squadrons of commentators had been drawn to the issue, attempting to reconcile their own deep-held prejudices about people of colour with the issues thrown up by the play.

When it came out, *Shakespeare Against Apartheid* was pungently controversial, decried as well as worshipped, but it did something crucial – insist that Shakespeare might indeed have something to say about how things really were in South Africa.

I thought back to Solomon Plaatje's renaming of Shakespeare as 'William Shake-the-Sword'. At the time, it had struck me as an erudite, slightly ironic joke. Maybe it was also a call to arms.

Othello had played its own highly particular role in the politics of race in South Africa. The tragedy had a long history in these parts – perhaps, I was surprised to learn, the longest of any Shakespeare play on the African continent. The first recorded performance dated back to the early nineteenth century, less than two decades after any of Shakespeare's work had first been acted in Africa and only twenty-four years after British forces seized the Cape from the Dutch. A hardy band of 'a gentleman and three ladies from the Theatre Royal Liverpool' arrived in the garrison of Cape Town in the spring of 1818 and quickly joined forces with a local amateur stock company.

On 24 October, a newspaper announced that 'under the sanction of His Excellency, The Governor . . . This Evening the amateur company will perform the *Tragedy of Othello* with the musical farce *The Poor Soldier.*' The combination of main-course tragedy with a farce or comic opera for dessert (this one by the Irish playwright John O'Keeffe) was entirely standard in the period, and, as I had discovered in California, would last happily for decades yet. Try as I might, though, I could find out no more of this Liverpudlian attempt on Shakespeare's play, or whether the 'gentleman' played Othello or Iago (my guess was the latter, it usually being regarded the better role).

In 1829, another visiting Englishman, H. Booth, gave what the *Cape Commercial Advertiser* regarded as a 'judicious and effective performance' in the lead, offering extracts alongside *Romeo and Juliet* and *Richard III*. Other *Othellos* followed in 1831 and 1833. In 1834 an amateur company attempted it once again, their lead actor praised for his 'dignity and feeling' in 'several of the most trying scenes'.

As I read about these early performances, one thing struck me: that no one seems to have an inkling that the racial politics of Shakespeare's play had anything to do with those of the emerging South Africa. From scant paragraphs in a few newspapers, it wasn't clear whether this was wilful blindness or a fact so obvious it barely needed repeating. Whatever the truth, *Othello* became one of the most popular Shakespeare plays in the colony.

In 1836, yet another new version appeared, translated into Cape Dutch. This time there is no mistaking its intentions: the title was *Othello, of de Jaloersche Zwart* ('Othello, or the Jealous Black') and was perhaps based on a popular – and shamelessly racist – parody that had circulated in the Netherlands. Judging from a letter sent to the *Commercial Advertiser*, the show provoked strong feelings among audiences. The correspondent fulminated:

> In frequenting the theatre, do not professing Christians pointedly violate their baptismal vows? . . . In listening to . . . *Othello*, do they not unnecessarily contract a horrible familiarity with passions and deeds of the most fiendish character . . . and give up their minds to be polluted by language so gross? Is not the guilt of such persons great, and their danger imminent?

The language was straight out of the English sixteenth century, or the American seventeenth: zealots like Philip Stubbes and Stephen Gosson were forever railing against the pestiferous iniquities of stage-players. (Stubbes's own formulation was that plays were incitements to 'idleness, unthriftiness, whoredom, wantonness, drunkenness, and what not', which sounded pretty good to me.)

But in this talk of 'passions' and 'grossness' the issue took on a nasty new topicality whose origins were not hard to intuit. Slavery had been abolished on the Cape two years before, in 1834, a fact that left many bitter that their 'property' was being taken away by a remote and lordly British government. That black characters should appear on stage was not merely damnably un-Christian – it was a damned insult.

Productions of *Othello* kept coming – 'the defining dramatic expression of South African society in the Shakespearian canon', in the words of Rohan Quince, an authority on South African theatre history. Another version was staged courtesy of a Dutch society in 1837, this time with Iago played by 'a Gentleman lately arrived from India' (European, it is fair to assume); then again in 1842, remade as an 'operatic burlesque' with men playing both Othello and Desdemona (again, both white). Here the play's racial context was acknowledged, albeit for laughs – Mr Macdonald's Desdemona won applause for his 'little endearments towards his black "hobby" [husband]'. Iago was reportedly played as a buffoonish Irishman, another kind of racial slur. The show was riotously popular.

What lies behind the rib-nudging tone of these accounts becomes clearer when the celebrated Victorian actor Gustavus V. Brooke visited Cape Town in 1854. A scheduled performance of Bulwer-Lytton's *The Lady of Lyons* was quickly replaced with *Othello*, because, the advertisement read:

> [*Othello* is] better understood here than any of Shakespeare's plays. Its hero (a *coloured* man) who has moved and won a *white* lady, ships, bays, soldiers, a castle, and a governor, being all familiar to the Colonists' ear, 'as household words'.

The tone was larksome – a *coloured* man who marries a *white* woman! – but it nonetheless signalled a hardening of attitudes.

In the twentieth century, real life would make a nonsense of anything that Shakespeare depicted on stage. The beginning of the apartheid era is conventionally dated to 1948 and the victory of the National Party, but the word *apartheid* ('separateness') was first used by Afrikaner racial theorists as early as the late 1920s.

One landmark piece of legislation was the first incarnation of the Immorality Act (1927), outlawing 'extramarital carnal intercourse . . . between whites and [black] Africans'. This was later enlarged to cover all sexual relations, married or otherwise, between whites and any other race. *Othello's* subject matter – with its depiction of a marriage between a black man and a white woman – became, in effect, illegal. The play was never officially banned, but was increasingly regarded as too controversial to stage or even teach. In Port Elizabeth in 1962, it was removed from high-school courses.

The Population Registration Act of 1950 divided South Africans into three racial groups, in steeply descending order: white, coloured and black ('Bantu'), with a fourth category, Indian, added later. 'Coloured' designated someone who was mixed-race, usually descended from Europeans who had had relationships with black Africans or slaves, but in practice the term was notoriously imprecise, applied to anyone who didn't look 'white' enough. Under the Separate Amenities Act of 1953, theatres were segregated. This legislation was further toughened by the various Group Areas Acts and regulations imposed in 1965, which stipulated that 'no racially disqualified person may attend any place of public entertainment' – outlawing both mixed audiences and mixed casts, not to mention mixed sport, music or any other cultural activity.

Although during apartheid the majority of Shakespeare performances were played by white actors in front of white audiences (even, on rare occasions, *Othello*), courtesy of politically conscious performers Shakespeare began to become involved with the struggle. As was the case in communist Eastern Europe, one attraction was that subversive political messages could be smuggled into ostensibly uncontroversial texts – almost impossible for the authorities to object if the script was by the deadest of dead white males. It is an irony worth enjoying that some of the strongest Shakespearian responses to apartheid were staged by Afrikaans-speaking directors and actors in state-funded, whites-only venues.

One of the most mischievous was the German-born director Dieter Reible, who in 1970 broke the newly initiated cultural boycott to work in South Africa. Reible's Afrikaans production of *Titus Andronicus* was set in a fascist Roman state with clear contemporary echoes, and lingered – to the obvious discomfort of some critics – on the passionate love affair between Queen Tamora of the Goths and the black character Aaron. The following year, Reible used *King Lear* to go even further. Although the rules required the actors to be ethnically white, Reible made liberal use of make-up and set the play in something resembling a Zulu or Xhosa village, knowing full well that President Fouché would attend the premiere. Incensed, one paper suggested that Reible should apologise for this grave affront to the president's dignity (and that of his wife).

Another Afrikaans-speaker, the playwright André Brink, made grim comedy out of apartheid with a 1971 version of *The Comedy of Errors* called *Kinkels innie Kabel* ('Twists in the Cable'), set in a fishing village on the Cape. Cleverly using Shakespeare's twins to poke fun at the ludicrous divisions of the system, it featured a skit on the fact that in real life South Africa had recently dispatched not one but two candidates to the Miss World competition ('Miss South Africa' and 'Miss Africa South'). After a performance by all-white performers, the play was staged in the comparative freedom of Cape Town's Little Theatre, with a racially mixed cast in front of integrated audiences.

But it was *Othello* that provoked one of the most thoughtful critiques of apartheid. In the same year, 1971, the British playwright Donald Howarth moved to South Africa, setting himself up in a tiny flat in Hillbrow. Horrified by the death of the activist Ahmed Timol, murdered in police custody that October (officers claimed Timol had voluntarily thrown himself out of a tenth-floor window), Howarth wrote a play called *Othello Slegs Blankes* ('Othello Whites Only'), its title referencing the signs plastered on everything from drinking fountains to beaches. Although the script was never intended to be staged, the playwright was persuaded to put it on at the newly opened Cape Town Space in June 1972.

Though the Space evaded the regulations forbidding mixed casts by setting itself up as a 'private club', Howarth's version operated as if the laws had the same force in the auditorium as they did outside on the street. Othello, deleted from the cast list, never once appears; his lines are parcelled out among the rest of the cast, one of whom is a police informer who conspires to kill Desdemona. On going into the theatre, audiences were handed an official-looking form by a man dressed as an immigration officer. 'Are all the persons concerned in the presentation of the play of pure white descent?' it asked.

Shakespeare's *Othello*, though a tragedy, scatters behind it a few seeds of hope: Iago is eventually unmasked and arrested; Othello realises his tragic mistake and dies kissing the dead Desdemona on the lips. Howarth allowed his South African audiences no such consolation. Here Lodovico, the Venetian official who arrives to take charge at the end, doesn't simply refuse to punish Iago – he promotes him, in words of stinging irony:

> From now on his power and his command
> Shall be vouchsafed in honest Iago, deserving
> Champion of our discriminating laws,
> Watchdog and defender of our principles.

Othello Slegs Blankes, wrote one critic, helped 'lay bare the absurdities that so many of us accept as commonplace'.

Inspired by the example of Cape Town's Space, in 1974 an actor and director of Jewish-Lithuanian extraction, Barney Simon, and Mannie Manim, a white producer and lighting designer, decided they wanted to create a similar theatre up in Johannesburg. Free of government involvement, it could give a home to black writers and actors who couldn't find outlets for their work. Perhaps most importantly, audiences would be desegregated and tickets priced at a level even the poorest could afford.

When Simon and Manim came across the dilapidated shell of what had been the Indian fruit market in the inner-city area of Newtown, they decided this would be their new home. The Market theatre, as it was named, opened with a production of Chekhov's *The Seagull* in June 1976 – the same month as the student-led Soweto Uprising, which led to nationwide protests that left nearly 600 dead. Soon it was being called 'the theatre of the struggle'; soon after that, South Africa's unofficial national theatre.

In its early years the Market established a reputation for contemporary, politicised work – *Woza Albert!* (1981), which satirically reimagined the second coming of Christ in apartheid South Africa; scripts by Athol Fugard, whose *Sizwe Banzi is Dead* and *The Island*, created in collaboration with young black actors, presented lacerating depictions of the passbook system and long-term incarceration.

But in 1987 – the same year *Shakespeare Against Apartheid* came out – the Market staged a performance that would become famous internationally, and suggest, as Orkin had done, that classic writers could also comment powerfully on the cruelties and injustices of the South African system. The show, again, was *Othello*.

The production had come about when Janet Suzman, a Johannesburg native of Jewish heritage (and niece of the famous anti-apartheid campaigner Helen Suzman), who had made her name as an actor with the Royal Shakespeare Company, decided she wanted to use the experience she'd gained in Britain to assist in the struggle. She planned to work with John Kani, one of the actors who had collaborated with Fugard on the protest scene. She wanted to do something bold: cast a black African as Shakespeare's Moor.

It wasn't quite the first time that a black actor had played Othello on a South African stage: four years earlier, in 1983, Joko Scott took the role in a cut-down production directed by Phyllis Klotz in Cape Town, with a cast of just six. But the Market version became a watershed, partly because of Suzman's contacts overseas but also the symbolic resonance of the venue.

And *Othello* had, Suzman argued, only become more apposite. By 1987 the Immorality Laws had been repealed, but were still fresh in everyone's minds; Shakespeare's portrayal of a lawful mixed-race marriage that cracks under the pressure of circumstance seemed, if anything, more clairvoyant. It would be impossible for the censors to object, given that the script was penned by the greatest playwright in the English language.

The major worry, Suzman later told me, was whether *Othello* would sell tickets. Shakespeare had barely been done at the Market before. Would an audience reared on hard-hitting protest drama cope with a 380-year-old play in Jacobean English done in doublets and hose? Would the cast? Would anyone even turn up?

In the event, when *Othello* opened in September 1987, it provoked a firestorm. Almost literally – after threats from right-wing organisations, the auditorium had to be swept for bombs. There were audience walkouts. Hate mail was sent by the sackful, much of it to the blonde, white actor playing Desdemona, Joanna Weinberg. There was a scandal when a photograph of Suzman with her arm around Kani was printed on the cover of the South African Airways in-flight magazine. A member of parliament fulminated that 'allowing a photograph of a black man and a white woman in close proximity' was 'integrationist policy' by stealth.

South African critics – white, mostly – were equally wary. One declared that Suzman had committed a momentous error in 'allowing Othello and Desdemona to exhibit their sexual bond in public'. Kani, who had won a Tony award on Broadway for his work with Fugard, was accused of 'making mincemeat' of the Bard's immortal verse. One critic dismissed the production for its 'patronising liberalism'. Another wrote, 'One is almost tempted to side with [Iago].'

But the international press, starved of good news about South Africa, was overjoyed. The *New York Times* proclaimed that 'it has broken new ground here both on and off the stage'. Reviewing a recording of the production later broadcast on British television, a critic proclaimed Kani 'the most moving Othello I have ever seen'. The *Guardian*'s review was headlined simply, 'The Moor Who Speaks for a People'.

Far more importantly, South Africans came in their droves – around 40 per cent of them black, a higher percentage than had ever been seen for a European classic at the Market. There were stories of people travelling up from Cape Town, nearly 900 miles, to see it. The theatre management were stunned. 'Had we known how successful it was going to be,' said a spokesperson, 'we would have let it run for three months or more.'

Two years earlier, it would had been illegal for a real-life Othello and Desdemona to kiss in South Africa, never mind marry or have sex. Now Kani was kissing Joanna Weinberg every night, in full view of 500 people, in a script written by Shakespeare. Suzman and Kani got what they wanted. *Othello* hit a nerve.

Unlike a hundred other productions I had come across in my travels, this one I was actually able to watch. Suzman had persuaded a TV company to film *Othello* in the theatre and it had subsequently been transferred on to DVD. I had thrown the copy in my suitcase just before I left, with the dimmest recollection of having seen it as a student.

Returning from an evening at the Market where the only sign of the production had been a photograph of Kani and Weinberg in the bar, I watched it again. It was a revelation. Curled up in the room of my guesthouse, squinting at the tiny screen of my laptop through the soft fuzz of 1980s television haze, I felt as if I had rarely seen *Othello* so clearly.

It wasn't perfect. The setting was stolidly conventional, Renaissance archways and flickering lanterns, and looked at grave risk of toppling over. Some members of the cast were more secure than others. The jerkins could have done with a dry-clean.

But so much else seemed fresh-minted. Rarely had the opening scene, in which Richard Haines's bullying Iago and Frantz Dobrowsky's limp-as-lettuce Roderigo exchange insults about heathens, lascivious Moors, Barbary horses and the rest, felt so plainly shocking:

> 'Swounds, sir, you're robbed . . .
> Your heart is burst, you have lost half your soul.
> Even now, now, very now, an old black ram
> Is tupping your white ewe.

Iago's speech, rousing Desdemona's father from his bed with the news that his daughter has eloped and married a man of another race, could have been transplanted with barely any updating to the dank bar-rooms populated by members of the South African National Front.

One person I recognised with a jolt: Emilia, Iago's wife. It was Dorothy Ann Gould, whose work with homeless men I'd witnessed in Hillbrow; this must have been one of the first productions she did after returning from the UK. She was one of the finest Emilias I'd seen, full of sorrow and sharp outrage, especially at the end of the play, where she is the first good character to realise that Othello has been duped and that Desdemona is innocent ('O gull, O dolt, | As ignorant as dirt!'). Having heard her talk about the problems of contemporary South Africa, I wondered if this was acting.

But Kani and Weinberg, as the hero and heroine, were at the centre of everything. Safely reunited in Cyprus after a wild sea voyage from Venice, they kissed each other with lingering passion – no doubts here that this was their wedding night, nor possible to forget that until recently they would not have been permitted to share it. Even the little things caught me: I had never before noticed how rarely Othello is addressed by his name, how often he is called just 'the Moor'. The word made him sound like an alien species.

In some ways the critics were right: Kani's delivery was not immaculate in the cut-glass style of the RSC. There was a rawness to him, a timorousness. But to me that made sense. He looked like a man unsure of his footing, standing on ground that could slip away from under him at any moment. In the face of Iago's insinuations about Desdemona's unfaithfulness, the decorated general seemed to revert to a previous version of the world – one in which white men, not he, did the ordering around.

As often with *Othello*, it was Iago's show, but this Iago drew his power from the fact that he was a belligerent, bulging-eyed racist. Haines stuck his fingers in his nose in piggish imitation, rolled his eyes and grabbed his crotch, hee-hawing like an ass. There barely seemed a moment in which he wasn't in control: taller and broader than Othello, he butted against him, spoiling for a fight. Once he touched the hero's forehead, and with great deliberation wiped his hand afterwards to clean it. In company Haines affected something approaching an upper-class English accent. In soliloquy his voice was rougher, with the whip-crack vowels of Afrikaans lying just beneath, like a threat. 'Cassio's a *proper* man,' he said in the mincing accent of an upper-class officer, before abruptly switching gear: 'Let me see now | To *git heez plaice.*'

I had arrived in South Africa with doubts about whether *Othello* could work as agitprop: its perspective on race was surely too complicated for that, its constructions of ethnicity and identity too finely balanced. Earlier that summer, I had watched a production at the National

Theatre in London – smart and smartly contemporary, set in what was perhaps the modern-day British Army – where it had seemed almost irrelevant that Othello was black. In a world of colour-blind casting, performed in the heart of liberal, multicultural Britain, it was a study of jealousy gone disastrously wrong.

Here, unavoidably, the play was something sharper, more splintered and raw. Colour-blind casting was something no one could imagine in the South Africa of 1987.

What did it actually mean to play Othello? I was anxious to ask John Kani, but I wasn't having much luck. The Market, who were shortly to rename their main auditorium after Kani, couldn't locate him. His agent had been trying since before I arrived. He was rumoured to have five mobile phones; I had been ringing and texting one of them for three days straight, and hadn't yet been granted a reply.

As insurance, I thought it might be prudent to spend an afternoon finding out what other people had made of the Moor. For black performers, *Othello* has a tormented history, and not just in South Africa. I'd long been drawn to the life of the pioneering black American actor Ira Aldridge, by the time of his death in 1867 one of the most famous performers anywhere in the world. Denied the possibility of making a career in his homeland, the 'African Roscius' (Roscius was a great Roman actor; Aldridge liked to encourage the rumour that he'd been born in Senegal rather than New York City) made a career in Britain and mainland Europe. Shakespeare was his passport. He excelled in many plays, notably as Shylock and Lear, but his signature role was Othello – described when Aldridge toured Russia as 'voic[ing] the far-off groans of his own people, oppressed by unbelievable slavery'. Showered with honours by European heads of state, Aldridge proved that actors of colour could make Shakespeare their own.

The role was something similar for Paul Robeson, who identified closely with Aldridge and played the Moor several times, notably opposite Peggy Ashcroft at London's Savoy theatre in 1930. (The previous year, doing *Show Boat*, Robeson had been unable to get a table at the Savoy hotel next door.) In an era when it was still customary for white performers to smother their faces with black make-up – as they would continue to do in Britain and America until the early 1990s

– taking a plum part such as Othello was nothing less than an act of emancipation.

But in the years since, the play has once again become controversial. With the notable exception of Verdi's *Otello*, directors and audiences in most western countries now feel deeply queasy about the idea of casting a white performer in the lead. Given the grim legacy of minstrel shows and the like, 'blacking up' is seen as unacceptable, and the fact that there are so few major classical roles for actors of colour makes it even harder to defend.

But then some black performers have problems with Othello, too. James Earl Jones has expressed his unease, despite doing the play on Broadway in 1982 to huge success. The British-Ghanaian actor Hugh Quarshie has declared that 'Othello is the one [role] which should most definitely not be played by a black actor'. (Long after I was in South Africa it was announced Quarshie would play the part at the RSC, opposite Lucian Msamati, who is of Tanzanian heritage, as Iago.)

Many of these debates hinge upon Shakespeare's conception of the role. It is generally agreed that he created three characters who can be described as 'black': the villainous Aaron the Moor in *Titus Andronicus*, the blundering Prince of Morocco in *The Merchant of Venice* and, of course, the Moor of Venice himself. Others make their way on stage, or drift tantalisingly close: Aaron's child with Queen Tamora in *Titus Andronicus*, described as a 'tawny slave', so presumably mixed-race; the nameless 'Negro' girl made pregnant by Lancelot Gobbo in *The Merchant of Venice*; the 'King of Tunis' who marries the daughter of the King of Naples just before the action of *The Tempest*. But other figures are more elusive. How should the ethnicity of the Egyptian Cleopatra, who describes her skin as 'with Phoebus' amorous pinches black', be played? Or Caliban? And what the playwright intended by making characters 'African' – if the intention is consistent – is an even larger question. In the era of postcolonial criticism, few questions have used up so many gallons of scholarly ink.

There is much to disagree on. For a start, 'blackness' – the scare quotes seem necessary – was a complex and unstable notion for Shakespeare and his contemporaries. For much of the sixteenth and early seventeenth centuries the number of people in England who were non-white was minuscule, even in the multicultural metropolis of London. Although Elizabethan privateers were only too pleased to ship African slaves to America and the Caribbean, England itself had no regulated slave trade, unlike other European countries such as Portugal or Spain.

A small number of black Africans – mainly West Africans, along with Berbers from northern Africa – had been brought to England, where they were overwhelmingly employed in domestic work. Queen Elizabeth I had a black maidservant, as did high-profile members of her court. Some seem to have found employment as entertainers: one 'John Blanke, the blacke trumpeter', played regularly for Henry VII and Henry VIII, while James I employed black entertainers.

Even so, the line of tolerance was thin. Despite there being so very few black people – perhaps a thousand in total, half of one per cent of London's population – official anxiety increased sharply in the late sixteenth century, particularly in the recession-struck 1590s. Queen Elizabeth may have been content to be served by people of colour, but she issued numerous edicts ordering the expulsion of a group of black men captured from a Spanish colony in the West Indies, proclaiming in 1596 that 'there are of late divers blackmoores brought into this realm, of which kind of people there are allready here to manie' and that it was her 'good pleasure to have those kinde of people sent out of the lande'. The queen repeated the call in 1601, complaining about the 'great numbers of Negars and Blackamoors'. Declaring them 'infidels, having no understanding of Christ or his gospel', she again called for them to be thrown out. (It seems unlikely any actually were.)

It was a contradiction. On the one hand, as England came increasingly into contact with the non-white world, people of African heritage gained work as servants and performers, and on occasion were treated with exaggerated respect, as when the Moroccan ambassador, whose portrait I had seen at the British Museum, visited Elizabeth's court in 1600 to negotiate trade and diplomatic relations. On the other, they were regarded as brutish heathen, relegated by the colour of their skin – and suspicions about their faith, even if they had converted to Christianity – to the condition of exotic and alien other.

On to this complex and contradictory jumble of ideas about ethnicity, class and religion all manner of stereotypes and suspicions were projected. 'Blackamoors' had been commonplace in European literature since the medieval period, and one theory holds that English Morris dancing has its origins in the impersonation of *moriscos* or Moors. White performers blacked up to play devils and damned souls in miracle and mystery plays. At the court of James I, it was briefly fashionable to slum it in blackface: in Ben Jonson's *Masque of Blackness* (1605), a troupe of high-born ladies donned dark make-up in order to play 'Africans'. (Jonson may have borrowed the idea from *Othello*, written a year or two earlier.)

On the infrequent occasions black characters appear in Elizabethan drama, they are cast in the role of calculating villain, as in George Peele's *The Battle of Alcazar* (c.1588–89), a history play dominated by the machiavellian schemings of the Moorish Muly Mahamet, and Thomas Dekker's co-written *Lust's Dominion* (1598–99), in which a Barbary prince, Eleazar, manoeuvres to the summit of the Spanish aristocracy. Black performers were unknown on the public stage, so both characters were almost certainly played by white actors wearing make-up.

Aaron in *Titus Andronicus* is squarely in this tradition. A snarling villain who plots Titus's downfall while simultaneously conducting an affair with Queen Tamora, he represents the forces of devilish ambition, gleefully comparing himself to a 'black dog'. But even Aaron contains complexities – not only do his intelligence and wit make him the most compelling character on stage, but his apparently loving relationship with Tamora is a rebuke to Jacobethan stereotypes about black men's unrestrained sexuality. His desperation to save their child from death is one of the most humane aspects of a notoriously inhumane play.

Yet it was in *Othello* that Shakespeare forced his audiences to re-examine their deepest prejudices. At one level, as Quarshie argued, the play enacts a crude racist fantasy: a black man marries a nice white girl and murders her in a fit of sexual jealousy. But up close *Othello* makes those interpretations impossible to sustain. The Moor is highly valued by the white Venetian senate, and his relationship with Desdemona is a consensual love match. He is also, of course, the hero for whom the play is named, the unwitting victim of events rather than their scheming author.

Though the text is saturated with imagery of white and black, light and dark, good and evil, Shakespeare renders those categories all but meaningless. Iago and Roderigo might slander Othello as a 'thick-lips' and an 'old black ram', but the hero is described by the Duke of Venice as 'far more fair than black'. Othello himself later frets that Desdemona is a 'fair paper' who has been blackened by adultery, and it is Iago, a white man, who exults that he will 'turn her virtue into pitch' and compares himself to a devil who indulges in 'the blackest sins'.

It is all but certain that Shakespeare created the role for his long-term collaborator, the actor Richard Burbage. What did the audience who watched the play at James I's court in November 1604 see? How did they interpret Burbage blacking up to play a 'Moor' who has at some point been 'sold to slavery', then converted to Christianity, and is now a general in the Venetian army on assignment in Cyprus, fighting the Muslim Turks? It was surely impossible to say, other than that all their expectations were confounded.

The critic Jonathan Dollimore puts the paradox: 'Does the fate of Othello confirm, qualify, or discount the charge that this play is racist? Certainly the play enacts a series of displacements of the aberrant and the abhorrent on to the alien. But is it endorsing that process, or representing it for our attention?' That, surely, is the question.

On my penultimate evening in Johannesburg, my phone buzzed. John Kani. The text offered the curtest of apologies. I still wanted to meet? Tomorrow? Could I get to the new shopping mall at Rosebank?

Rolling into the restaurant an hour late, wearing a blue blazer, matching trousers and a baseball cap, the great man briefly acknowledged my presence, then turned away to sign autographs. I wondered if the cap was intended to hide his identity, or advertise it. As a leggy, gym-toned woman went into a pantomime of cardiac arrest, I suspected it was the latter.

He looked very little like the uncertain figure I'd seen on screen. Now seventy, equipped with half-moon glasses, a neat salt-and-pepper goatee and an indulgent, slow-burning smile, Kani had grown into the role of elder statesman with ease. He was a dead ringer for former president Thabo Mbeki: indeed, the pair were old friends from the resistance days. Mbeki would have been easier to get hold of, I thought.

'Sorry,' he said eventually, flashing a pearlescent film-star grin and offering the lightest of shrugs. This is just how it was when you were John Kani.

We began at the beginning. Born in 1942 into an isiXhosa-speaking family in New Brighton just outside Port Elizabeth, along the coast from Cape Town, he was one of eleven children. At school he'd worked hard and was lucky – the Bantu Education Act hadn't fully come into force, and his class were exposed to the Eng Lit-heavy curriculum of the former Cape Colony: Chaucer, Milton, Wordsworth, T. S. Eliot, Shakespeare.

Kani had little regard for the works of Shakespeare ('we didn't know who he was') until one day when he was fifteen, when his isiXhosa teacher brought into class a translation of *Julius Caesar*. Kani was asked to stand up and read Mark Antony's speech addressed to the dead Caesar, 'O pardon me, thou bleeding piece of earth'. Declaiming the words in his own language, he sensed how powerful it felt to be an actor. He joined the drama society and began to dream of a life on stage.

Though his eldest brother's arrest for involvement in the ANC meant that he was forced to take a job at Port Elizabeth's Ford car plant, Kani became involved with an amateur group called the Serpent Players, run by Athol Fugard, then just beginning to make a name for himself as a playwright.

Their early work together, much of it created with Kani's former schoolmate Winston Ntshona, was almost exclusively political – Brechtian, minimalist, often improvised, usually performed to township audiences. Their biggest success together was *Sizwe Banzi is Dead* in 1972, set in Port Elizabeth. Kani played a photographer who encounters a businessman who's stolen a dead man's identity in order to beat the passbook system. Premiered in Cape Town, it transferred to London's Royal Court, then to the West End, then on to Broadway. Soon afterwards Kani moved to Soweto and became involved in the Market.

There was little practical difference between making consciousness-raising drama and taking part in the struggle, he explained. The security services took an obsessive interest in their activities; once, during a curtain call, Kani was seized by police and spent twenty-three days in jail. An uncle did time on Robben Island. His younger brother Xolile was later shot dead while participating in a protest.

But Kani didn't want to be stereotyped as an actor-activist. With Ntshona, he did *Waiting for Godot*, set in a thinly veiled version of their homeland. They were directed by the same man who had written *Othello Slegs Blankes*, Donald Howarth. In 1985, with the Immorality Act still on the statute books, Kani agreed to take the role of the valet Jean in August Strindberg's *Miss Julie*, who has a destructive affair with the mistress of the house, played by the white actor Sandra Prinsloo. One night half the audience walked out in orchestrated protest. Later in the run, Kani was set upon by a gang, and left with eleven stab wounds.

Suzman had contacted him about *Othello* not long afterwards. 'I said, "Janet, I've just come through a terrible time. I did *Miss Julie*, it got me eleven stab wounds. I don't think white people will like this." And she said, "Then why are you doing theatre? We do theatre to empower people, we do theatre to present our case." I thought – OK, on condition that the entire cast is white, only Othello is black, and that we stick to the text.' He sipped on his green tea. 'So we started the process.'

Was it a role he'd ever considered? Did he know its history?

'I remember when I was a kid seeing *Othello* in Port Elizabeth. There was this white actor, wearing black make-up, who had on this old black hat and he was called a "Moor". Our teacher explained to us, we mustn't confuse the Moor with a black African. It is a shade within dark, perhaps lesser white, but still white – nothing to do with race.' He looked ironic. 'That is what my teacher said.'

Not having studied Shakespeare since school, he ended up putting much of the text into isiXhosa in order to learn it. 'I was translating mentally as I spoke. Janet looked at me and said, "God, they are going to kill you in England; they are going to kill you." I said, "That's a chance we're going to have to take."'

The critics were the least of their problems. After he was arrested yet again on the way in from Soweto, what followed was one of the most fantastical experiences of his life: a seminar in Shakespearian close reading from the Special Branch of the South African police force.

Kani reenacted the scene before my eyes, voices and all. 'They pull out a script! They go to page seven, where it says, "Othello takes Desdemona into his arms."' He shifted into a brute Afrikaans accent. '"*You kissed her on her lips for seven-and-a-half seconds! It's not in the script!*" Page twenty-four, when they arrive in Cyprus, "*You embraced her and you kissed her all over her face and you touched her breast!*"' He was laughing hard, chest rocking. 'Like this, for hours.'

Suddenly he looked serious. 'But compared to Joanna Weinberg, the hate mail to her, being called a Jewish slut . . .'

For him, was the play about combatting racism?

'If this play *avoids* racism, I'm not in it. It has to deal with racism, but also go beyond racism, go to human attitudes, human deficiencies, moral degradation, lies, expediency, betrayal. Everything. It's not the only play to deal with race. *Merchant of Venice*, "If you prick us, do we not bleed?" *Titus Andronicus*, where Aaron is with his child, who is black? That's the most powerful black-is-beautiful speech there is.'

He had reunited with Suzman to do Claudius in *Hamlet* in 2005, and played a Mandela-ish Caliban opposite Antony Sher in 2009. He was optimistic that he and Suzman would work together again, this time on the big one: *King Lear*, with Kani in the lead. He'd also done *Othello* again in 2010, this time directing, with his son Atandwa – oh, to be a young man again . . .

I sneaked a look at my watch. We had been talking for nearly two hours. Maybe this was why Kani was permanently late: it was impossible to shut him up.

He looked sheepish. 'I told my wife I would only be short.'

As he grabbed his car keys, I said I had one final question: whether performing *Othello* was a political act.

He patted me genially on the shoulder. 'Andrew,' he said, 'I was going to ask what at that time was *not* a political act.'

Over dinner in Melville later that night, tussling in the pages of my notebook, I attempted to put everything I had seen in the last few weeks into some kind of order. Plaatje's project to translate Shakespeare had come to almost nothing, dangerously ahead of its time. Yet finally (and with no small irony) his achievement was starting to be recognised – a model of what the multilingual, multi-ethnic, cosmopolitan new South Africa might achieve. For its part the Robben Island Bible was not what it had seemed to be, as far as I could make out, but equally Shakespeare *had* been dragooned into the struggle against apartheid – though the very play used for those purposes had often been accused of racism.

Perhaps it was myself I was struggling with. In contemporary Britain or America it often seemed anathema to talk about Shakespeare and politics in the same breath. Theatre directors might make a production 'political' – like that American *Richard III* – by setting the play, say, in fascist Europe or post-Saddam Iraq, but this was often a ruse designed to inject novelty into an otherwise off-the-peg interpretation. Politics was a design decision, like lighting or costume. When I was an English Literature student at Cambridge in the smooth and Blairite late 1990s, politics had been a tainted word, tinged with connotations of obsessiveness, careerism or (worse) both. In lecture halls we were trained to examine ideology with a scepticism verging on border-guard hostility. In the seminar rooms I haunted as a postgraduate, an approach to Shakespeare like that suggested by John Kani would have been heard with pained politeness, then placed on the slab where it could be butchered and deboned.

Johannesburg made such cool academic distance seem preposterous. Two decades after the end of apartheid, I had yet to see a single white person doing a job that could be described as menial. Cleaners were black, street-sweepers black, servers in fast-food restaurants black. Security guards were black: there were five of them right here outside the restaurant, 'car guards' who, for a few rand, watched your wheels while you sank your teeth into your wasabi-seared sirloin or nipped into the organic supermarket. Scrawny-looking men in fluorescent tabards, they loitered in packs, looking twitchy. I wondered where they slept at night.

News about Mandela seemed more depressing by the hour. The previous day a story had broken about a police investigation into fraud at several of his charities. South Africa's Serious Economic Offences unit had attempted to investigate, but been called off because of the embarrassment it would cause the ANC. Mandela himself was still being kept alive by machines. Driving past his house in Houghton, I'd got the driver to stop near the caravanserai of satellite trucks and news vans parked outside the compound. I asked the CNN and SABC correspondents what waiting felt like. 'Like *Waiting for Godot*,' CNN deadpanned.

One thing I had worked out. In the same bookshop where I'd found *Shakespeare Against Apartheid*, I'd come across a book by the Johannesburg-based photographer David Goldblatt, who has been shooting scenes from South Africa since the 1960s. He'd begun by capturing apartheid – three National Party men on horseback, pig-snouted beneath their trekker's hats; a touching photograph of a young white farmboy with his black nursemaid. More recently, he'd photographed the changing faces of democratic South Africa (mayors, councillors, municipal managers) in a wonderful 2005 series called *Intersections*.

But the photograph that resonated with me was an early one, taken at the Randfontein Estates Gold Mine in the Transvaal in 1966. The image, in stark monochrome, is of a man, black, in his twenties or perhaps older. It is impossible to be sure: Goldblatt crops out everything apart from his torso. A mine technician, his chest bristles with authority and the tools of his trade: steel rulers, notebooks in his pocket; jack knife and stopwatch at his belt. His fingers look powerful and assured. On his arm is a shining steel identity tag: BOSS BOY, it reads.

Boss boys were managers, responsible for running a team of black workers in the mine. Their authority was curtailed by having to answer to a white superior – something assured by the fact that they (like many other black servants) were always called 'boy', irrespective of their age. Garden boys, house boys, boss boys: one could be in one's eighties and be a boy. Take on one of the most hazardous jobs in South Africa, be as qualified and as competent as any white man, and you were still a child.

I couldn't see Boss Boy's face, but I thought I recognised him nonetheless. He looked like Othello.

—•—

IN THE SHARP MORNING LIGHT Cape Town looked even more like a frontier settlement than usual. As I walked down the incline of Buitenkant Street towards the centre, the clapboard frames of colonial-style dwellings and red-brick warehouses glinted prettily in the sun. The day I arrived it had been raining hard, the city and its surrounds all but invisible beneath a porridgey blanket of mist and cloud. Now the air felt cool and apple-crisp; a week of late-winter storms had scrubbed Cape Town up and made it as fresh as paint.

I glanced behind me and saw the flat chiselled surface of Table Mountain, stark and dark and huge against a sky of pure, high blue. It was the first time I'd seen it since arriving. In the Khoikhoi language it had a much nobler name, *Hoerikwaggo*, 'Mountain in the Sea'. If I lived here, I thought, I would never look at anything else.

I was bound for Robben Island. It seemed a strange destination on a day as beautiful and cheery as this, but at the quayside the crowds were out in force, in straggling lines that stretched from the ferry terminal to the Ethiopian gourmet coffee stand, past the joint selling organic banana muffins.

I had been forewarned about the Madiba effect. Up in Johannesburg, Mandela was still very much alive – on the internet and rolling news there were hourly bulletins on his health – but the nationwide obsession with his condition, and the realisation that these were surely his final days, had reminded South Africa about what it generally preferred to forget: the past. The Mandela museum in Soweto was thronged with visitors, and the same was true here in Cape Town. Places on the ferry out to the island had been booked up for weeks.

I joined the line, planting myself in the middle of a Christian spring camp from KwaZulu-Natal, boisterous teenagers in coordinated hoodies, and a group of elderly African American ladies from Alabama in fleeces and fawn pedal-pushers. Slowly we funnelled down a ramp towards a large white double-decker boat, past a glossy display on the island's history.

'Welcome to jail!' shouted the crew. On the gangplank we grinned for the official photographer: merry temporary inmates.

Within a year of it finally being closed to prisoners, Robben Island's journey into the realm of the symbolic had begun. In 1996 it was nominated a National Monument, then in 1999 a Unesco World Heritage Site. The decision was made to keep the prison exactly as it had been; former inmates, many of whom had struggled with life outside, were recruited as 'EPP' (ex-political prisoner) tour guides. A few months earlier, President Obama had come, one of 200,000 visitors a year, and been shown around by Ahmed Kathrada.

Sped across the sparkling blue bay, we were there in less than half an hour. Herded on to buses marked 'Driven By Freedom', we crept past the lime quarry, obediently taking photos of the 'reunion cairn' created by a thousand ex-prisoners. We took photos of the dog kennels, larger than the solitary-confinement cells. We took more photos at a viewing point at the edge of the island, facing on to the broad water of Table Bay, with the dark thunderhead of Table Mountain behind. After a while I stopped taking photos.

As we walked under the famous gate ('We Serve With Pride, *Ons Dien Met Trots*' still stencilled above), we were introduced to our EPP, Mncedisi Siswana. He was one of the angry young student radicals dispatched to the island in the late seventies – roughly the time Sonny Venkatrathnam was leaving. He served five years in Section E, reserved for the newest arrivals. Bull-necked, deliberate, he spent several days a week reliving one of the most painful pieces of his past.

'Robben', a derivation of the Dutch *rob*, 'seal', refers to the animals that still throng the bay. Identified by the Portuguese explorer Bartolomeu Dias in 1488, initially the island was a refuelling stop for ships on their way around the Cape, an easy calling point for fresh water and supplies. William Keeling's East India Company expedition cast anchor here in December 1607 after stopping in Sierra Leone – a pleasing coincidence, but which still didn't make the Shakespearian connection of Keeling's voyage any more plausible.

When the Dutch East India Company representative Jan van Riebeeck founded the first permanent European settlement on the Cape in 1652, on land that had been variously settled by Xhosa, Zulu, San and Khoikhoi peoples, the island became a place of punishment. Legendarily, the first prisoner was a Khoihkoi man called Autshumato, who had the temerity to protest when the Dutch stole his cattle. Banished to the island in 1659, Autshumato and two followers managed to flee the following year by purloining a rowing boat. They are thought to be the only people ever to have mounted a successful escape.

Under the British, the island became a leper colony in the nineteenth century, then a military base. In 1960, following the violent protests that exploded after the Sharpeville Massacre, arrests soared. Faced with hundreds of black 'terrorist' convicts, the government decided it needed an ultra-high-security facility. The following year *Robbeneiland* became a prison once again, this time a political one.

Conditions for the first batch – among them Mandela, Ahmed Kathrada, Walter Sisulu and Govan Mbeki – were even tougher than those experienced by Sonny Venkatrathnam a few years later. Gang leaders on criminal sentences were encouraged to intimidate 'politicals'. Hard labour – in the limestone or bluestone quarries, collecting seaweed – led to eye and respiratory problems because of the blinding light and omnipresent dust. Cell raids by guards – white, of course – were common, as were beatings, strip-searches and solitary confinement. Prisoners of different ethnicities were issued different diets (seven ounces of meat or fish a day for whites; six ounces for coloured inmates, four times a week; and five ounces for blacks), but the food was frequently inedible. The island's topography, surrounded by icy Atlantic currents and buffeted by violent gales, offered cruelties all its own.

Yet, as always in South Africa, multiple ironies were in play on Robben Island. One was the fact that many inmates were better educated than their captors: a source of aggrieved resentment at first, but which helped build bridges. Another was that the government's determination to keep these prisoners in a wind-blasted Atlantic hellhole had the effect of unifying them as never before. Rivalries between different groups – ANC versus PAC, elder statesmen versus youngsters who arrived in the seventies, Namibians versus the rest – softened in the face of a common enemy.

One fateful development stemmed from the apartheid state's mania for classification, which led them to isolate the 'Big Team' of Mandela, Mbeki, Kathrada, Venkatrathnam and others in the leadership wing. Not only did this make it abundantly clear whom the authorities most feared and respected; it enabled communication along the line of solitary cells. Coordinated hunger strikes gradually produced a more acceptable regime. Even the hated lime quarry became a site for education.

Reading prison memoirs, I was struck above all by the passion for learning. It was reportedly Mandela who first appealed for 'the atmosphere of a university [to] prevail here on the island', and the trope was repeated in almost every account. From 1966 some prisoners were permitted to study via correspondence course for school certificates and degrees; others received informal tuition, or gave it. Govan Mbeki took part in a late-sixties literacy drive, teaching other prisoners to read in their own tongues or English. Some who arrived on the island with little more than basic primary education left it with degrees. In the words of Dikgang Moseneke, who took bachelor's qualifications in English and Law, 'many people have emerged to survive Robben Island largely because of their studying'.

It wasn't just textbooks. As in any prison, sport became of obsessive interest. Mandela and others were permitted to run, and in the mid-1970s, clubs were set up for football, tennis and rugby. In the archives of the prison are hand-printed certificates issued by the 'Robben Island Academy of Fine Arts'.

Mandela recalled concerts, chess and draughts tournaments, and cultivated a small patch of dusty ground as a vegetable garden. Nearly everyone piled into the makeshift cinema built during the 1970s to watch *The Mask of Zorro*, *The King and I*, Joseph L. Mankiewicz's *Cleopatra* and, later, South African movies. Kathrada's letters record that he became an unlikely devotee of *The Cosby Show* (despite earnest doubts about its representation of African American politics). According to the historian Fran Lisa Buntman, there were keenly fought ballroom-dancing competitions.

Many read as widely as possible. Neville Alexander, who had taken a PhD in the late nineteenth-century dramatist Gerhart Hauptmann before being sent to the island in 1964, relished the chance to broaden his already considerable horizons:

> I read books in prison which I would never have had the time or the opportunity to read when I was outside: classics of European litera-ture, Gibbon, Shakespeare, the authorised version of the Bible a few times, Dickens; also African history, international law, economics, languages . . .

Alexander's reading list may have been unusually sophisticated, but he was by no means alone in his eagerness to use the prison library.

Before taking the ferry I'd managed to get hold of another former Robben Island prisoner on the phone: Eddie Daniels, a Cape Town native. Arrested in 1964 for sabotage, he was sentenced to fifteen years. Daniels was a contemporary of Kathrada and, despite being from a different political party, a friend of Mandela; he, too, had signed Sonny Venkatrathnam's copy of Shakespeare.

His perspective was different again from theirs: as a kid from a working-class, mixed-race family (he detested the term 'coloured'), he had left school after grade eight and been sent to get a job. He went to sea and worked for a time as a diamond miner, but his formal education had halted at the age of fourteen.

The island enabled Daniels to study, at first for high-school exams, then BA and BComm degrees. 'To me prison was a blessing in disguise,' he told me. 'I met wonderful people – Mandela, Sisulu. And I got my education.'

His Unisa degree had indeed featured Shakespeare: he'd studied *Romeo and Juliet* and *Macbeth*. In Sonny's book he'd signed his name next to a famous speech from the latter, 'Tomorrow, and tomorrow, and tomorrow, | Creeps in this petty pace from day to day . . .'

It seemed a powerful speech to choose, with its emphasis on entrapment and futility, I said. Did he feel it echoed his situation in prison?

He seemed surprised by the question: not especially. He had come across it as a set text, and simply thought the words were beautiful. 'Reading Shakespeare, I loved it. To me it opened up a whole world. I just drank it in.'

So, like Kathrada, he didn't feel there had been a special resonance between Shakespeare's text and the struggle?

'Not for me, no, I don't think so. It was more that I had just never read anything like this before.'

One thing he did remember: the Section B prisoners had staged *Julius Caesar*, or part of it, in the yard. He was hazy on the details and couldn't place the date or how long they'd rehearsed, but Neville Alexander had organised the performance. Daniels himself had played Mark Antony. He had strong memories of reciting 'Friends, Romans, countrymen, lend me your ears . . .'

'I was so emotional that at the end there were tears coming out of my eyes and they were saying, "Look, look, he's crying."' He chuckled softly. 'But this is all a long time ago.'

He thought there might have been another production, of *Waiting for Godot*, but again the details were blurred. Drama performances had stopped soon afterwards. He'd love to help, but if Shakespeare had played other roles on Robben Island, he couldn't recall.

When the group went into the Namibian wing, I lingered in the wind and sun with my notebook, thinking again about Sonny's copy of Shakespeare and the scraps of text beside which thirty-three prisoners had inscribed their names.

Working from the transcription supplied by the Robben Island Museum, I had marked them up in my own complete works. In spare moments of my journey across South Africa I'd often returned to them, pondering the choices the prisoners had made.

It was conspicuous how many had gravitated towards the same plays – three signatures each beside passages from *As You Like It*, *Julius Caesar*, *Hamlet* and *King Lear*; two each for *A Midsummer Night's Dream*, *Twelfth Night*, *Richard II*, *Henry V* and *Macbeth*. Five prisoner had selected sonnets (Neville Alexander had chosen two). Three signatories had selected quotations from, respectively, *The Tempest*, *The Merchant of Venice* and *Antony and Cleopatra*. Sonny Venkatrathnam had simply signed the book on its title page. One, Kadir Hassim, did the same on the first page of the introduction, with no apparent reference to Shakespeare's words at all.

I thumbed through. Some selections were surprisingly light, given the context – both Kwede Mkalipi and Elias Motsoaledi had marked their names on the last page of *A Midsummer Night's Dream*, near the famous epilogue spoken by Puck:

If we shadows have offended,
Think but this, and all is mended:
That you have but slumbered here,
While these visions did appear;
And this weak and idle theme,
No more yielding but a dream . . .

Might there be a hint of dreamy wish-fulfilment, of waking up to find the living nightmare of apartheid over? Perhaps they were simply attracted to Puck's tripping, fleet-footed rhymes. Or maybe they were just filling an inviting blank space in a book full of dense print. (Mkalipi, given the opportunity to choose again, went for a different passage entirely.)

Other passages seem to have been singled out largely because they were famous. Govan Mbeki had selected the first page of *Twelfth Night*, most likely for Orsino's 'If music be the food of love', while Joseph Vusani had marked his name and the date (2 January 1978) in neat copperplate, placing an asterisk next to Jaques's 'All the world's a stage, | And all the men and women merely players'. A day later, the Botswanan activist and ANC member Michael Dingake had planted his own signature under the 'precepts' offered to Laertes by Polonius in *Hamlet*:

Give thy thoughts no tongue,
Nor any unproportioned thought his act.
Be thou familiar but by no means vulgar.
Those friends thou hast, and their adoption tried,
Grapple them to thy soul with hoops of steel . . .

'To thine own self be true,' Polonius concludes, a piece of advice that was corny even when Shakespeare wrote it. Had it attracted Dingake because it seemed comfortingly familiar, or because being imprisoned for the colour of your skin made the idea of being 'true' seem passionately important? I thought of what Eddie Daniels had said: he just liked the sound of the words. Maybe this was the case here too.

Not all the inscriptions seemed circumstantial. I was interested by the prisoners who had chosen sonnets, perhaps because they were more rigidly self-contained (the word *stanza* literally means 'room'), maybe also because the narrative 'I' of each poem – though slippery and unreliable over the course of 154 sonnets – seems more directly applicable to a solitary reader in a solitary cell:

> Since brass, nor stone, nor earth, nor boundless sea,
> But sad mortality o'ersways their power,
> How with this rage shall beauty hold a plea,
> Whose action is no stronger than a flower?
> O how shall summer's honey breath hold out
> Against the wrackful siege of battering days
> When rocks impregnable are not so stout,
> Nor gates of steel so strong, but time decays?
> O fearful meditation! Where, alack,
> Shall time's best jewel from time's chest lie hid?
> Or what strong hand can hold his swift foot back,
> Or who his spoil of beauty can forbid?
> 　O none, unless this miracle have might:
> 　That in black ink my love may still shine bright.

Sonnet 65 had been one of Neville Alexander's choices. It struck me as a potent choice, summoning both the island prison ('sea', 'battering days', 'rocks impregnable', 'gates of steel') and reiterating the sonnets' great obsession, the erosive workings of 'time'. Time was also the subject of Alexander's first selection, Sonnet 60 ('Like as the waves make to the pebbled shore, | So do our minutes hasten towards their end'), one of the few poems that plays knowingly with its position in the sequence that make up the quarto of 1609.

The theme seemed to make sense. Sentenced to ten years during the island's most brutal first period, Alexander and other prisoners had plentiful opportunity to ponder the unremitting power of time, particularly as wristwatches and other timepieces were banned. Mandela himself had written in *Long Walk to Freedom*, his autobiography, how 'time slows down in prison; the days seem endless . . .' It also reminded me of Solomon Plaatje's translations; perhaps Shakespeare was a way of keeping loneliness at bay.

But there was an irony here, too, of which Alexander must have been aware: that what Feste in *Twelfth Night* nicely calls the 'whirligig of time' also brought in its revenges. Nothing would outlast time – not apartheid, not the prison in which he marked up these words, not himself. After years of ill-health Alexander died in 2012, just after Sonny Venkatrathnam's book went on display in London. Kathrada may have been right that his colleague had been dubious about the hype surrounding the Robben Island Bible; but Alexander had clearly thought long and wisely about Shakespeare. I dearly wished I could have asked him.

By now our group was in the leadership section, a long corridor with a white ceiling and surgical-green walls. There were strip lights above, identical wooden outer doors with scuffed barred gates behind, bars on windows inner and outer. A single metal light switch and alarm bell were next to each. A crush had formed outside cell 5, Mandela's for eighteen years; silently we jockeyed to see Mandela's blankets, bedroll, stool, slops bucket, meal tin. Was I being too suspicious, wondering if they *were* Mandela's? When I got to the front, the cell looked bare and monkish, unrecognisable from the photographs I had seen, when it had been crowded with books and prints.

Similar complexities surrounded the question of Mandela's own engagement with Shakespeare, on which the real fame of the Robben Island Bible hung. Aside from scattered references in his correspondence and later speeches – written, of course, by professionals – the only hint of Shakespeare to make it into *Long Walk to Freedom* was Mandela's account of the night before sentencing at Rivonia. Expecting to hear he would be executed, he claimed to have recalled 'Be absolute for death', Duke Vincentio's stoical words to the imprisoned Claudio in *Measure for Measure*, a speech that advises the condemned man to regard life as 'a thing | That none but fools would keep'.

It was a neat reference – if anything, I thought, too neat. Claudio is also facing legal but wrongful execution; he, too, will eventually be saved. Though *Long Walk to Freedom* was begun on the island, it was heavily edited and tidied up for publication many years later. Like much else about Mandela, it is not always what it appears to be.

There were also ambiguities about his selection from *Julius Caesar* in Venkatrathnam's book, the lines beginning 'Cowards die many times before their deaths'. On the face of it this was a straightforward assertion of bravery ('death ... will come when it will come'), but it was also something more shadowy, given that the words are spoken by a leader about to be assassinated. Was Mandela making subtle reference to the real dangers he faced, or was this a meditation on the fragile nature of leadership? Both? It was a fine conundrum.

But perhaps this was the lesson to draw from Sonny's book and its inscriptions. The South African critic David Schalkwyk has called the book a 'palimpsest' because of its openness to interpretation, its accreted layers of meanings (and the meanings others have placed on it). This is surely right: there is no single code. There is no right or wrong way to interpret it, much as there is no right or wrong way of interpreting Shakespeare's text itself, or for that matter the history of Robben Island.

Some of the prisoners' signatures were undeniably casual, done on the spur of the moment as a favour to a departing cellmate. A stray line or thought appealed, or illuminated a distant memory. A favourite passage already bagged, a hurried riffling through for other options, a quick signature scribbled. Others reflected a deeper and more involved engagement with Shakespeare, whether encountered in school or here on the island. Some choices were escapist, fantastical; others seemed to catch the dreary realities of prison life. Two prisoners, Justice Mpanza and Mohamed Essop, both chose the mournful final words of Edgar in *King Lear*, 'The weight of this sad time we must obey, | Speak what we feel, not what we ought to say'.

In some cases, the fact that these words were written by Shakespeare must have been largely irrelevant – the book was simply a storehouse of commonplace wisdoms, as it has been for generations of readers. On other occasions, as perhaps for Venkatrathnam himself, the fact that they were composed by the greatest poet and playwright in history was the only thing about them that mattered. Every prisoner had his reasons, whether in the moment or deeply felt; perhaps, even, the two were inextricable.

As we were hustled towards the exit, our tour complete ('Same gift shop back on the mainland, madam,' a staff member announced), I thought about two other passages from the book. Walter Sisulu had selected a speech from *The Merchant of Venice*, the only prisoner to choose anything from that play. The words were Shylock's, and here at least the sentiments were not hard to map on to the experience of apartheid South Africa:

> Signor Antonio, many a time and oft
> In the Rialto you have rated me
> About my money and my usances.
> Still have I borne it with a patient shrug,
> For suff'rance is the badge of all our tribe.
> You call me misbeliever, cut-throat, dog,
> And spit upon my Jewish gaberdine,
> And all for use of that which is mine own.

I wondered whether Sisulu had known that Solomon Plaatje, his great predecessor in the ANC, had translated the play, and scribbled a version of a different but equally famous speech ('Hath not a Jew eyes . . .?') in his notebook. Perhaps it didn't matter. The resonances were plain to see.

The thought brought me back to one of the very first signatures in the book, left by the Indian Congress member Billy Nair on 14 December 1977. It marked a short speech in act one, scene two of *The Tempest*, spoken by Caliban. Had Nair, who died in 2008, known the words already, or read them for the first time on the island that Christmas?

> This island's mine, by Sycorax my mother,
> Which thou tak'st from me. When thou cam'st first,
> Thou strok'st me and made much of me, wouldst give me
> Water with berries in't, and teach me how
> To name the bigger light, and how the less,
> That burn by day and night; and then I loved thee,
> And showed thee all the qualities o'th' isle,
> The fresh springs, brine-pits, barren place and fertile—
> Cursed be I that did so!

This island's mine . . . Cursed be that I did so . . . The words leapt off the page, not simply for their incantation of this particular 'isle', but for the near-inexpressible anguish that lay beneath them. A little rocky piece of land, stolen from its rightful owners and then turned into a prison; a place of inexpressible beauty and also of inexpressible torments. Deeper still, the bewilderment and stunned humiliation of betrayal.

As I took my seat on the boat, a sentence spoken by Caliban later in the scene came to mind: 'You taught me language, and my profit on't | Is I know how to curse.'

Back on the mainland, I checked for news of Mandela: still no news. I wondered if he'd slip away while I was in South Africa, and offer my story a gravid, *Lear*-like conclusion: old ruler dies, kingdom stands (or falls). Sad stories of the death of kings, et cetera.

Thankfully, though, he was still hanging on, and rumours were that he'd improved. That section in *Julius Caesar* he'd highlighted should have been issued by the ANC press office, attention all media: 'death, a necessary end, | Will come when it will come.' Or will come, I thought cynically, when the ANC decides it will come.

Speaking of the ANC, I had failed to get clarification on whether the party really did have a view about the significance or otherwise of the Robben Island Bible. Repeated petitions to their national spokesman came to nothing. I supposed that was my answer. There was a rumour that the book, after returning from Washington, would soon be off again – this time to Glasgow, for an exhibition celebrating the 2014 Commonwealth Games.

I was waiting for a final appointment. Back in England, an academic contact who was doing research into South African education emailed me details of something called the Shakespeare Schools Festival South Africa. It had been founded by an energetic and enthusiastic high-school teacher from Cape Town called Kseniya Filinova-Bruton. Set up in 2011, the SSF SA had expanded rapidly into a nationwide festival with outposts in four of the country's nine provinces. The first year, 20 students had participated; 850 were scheduled for this year. While most of the South African theatre I'd encountered was struggling to find its way – no funding, declining audiences, a loss of purpose following the end of the struggle – here was something that seemed to be genuinely alive and kicking.

Filinova-Bruton and I had met briefly at an SSF SA event back in Johannesburg; she was ardent and talkative, with the no-nonsense manner of a big-firm lawyer and dark blonde hair cut in a smartly tailored bob. She suggested we meet up again here in her home town. She'd be happy to take me out to the township of Khayelitsha, where one of the keenest participants in the SSF SA programme, Chris Hani Secondary School, was based.

As we drove east out of the city, ducking behind Table Mountain and on to the broad expanse of the Cape Flats, Filinova-Bruton explained how the project had started. She was Russian, born in St Petersburg to parents who were actors; she emigrated to South Africa in her twenties and began teaching. She set up a drama society before hearing about the British Shakespeare Schools Festival, which had been running since 2000. Surprised to discover that South Africa had no equivalent, she resolved to set one up. Even she seemed astonished by how fast it had grown.

'I had no idea it would take off,' she said in rapid-fire English, her newly acquired South African accent not entirely obscuring the occasional hint of Slavic. 'It was just one school, one class of my boys, me on my kitchen table with all these spreadsheets and scripts.' She pointed at the programme in my lap, which listed their numerous activities. 'Now look where we are!'

It remained a cottage industry; this year's festival had been done on R100,000, approximately £6,000. Filinova-Bruton was still teaching full-time. Schools paid a registration fee of R550 (£30), which gave teachers tuition in directing and a half-day workshop for the class, plus cut-down scripts and resources. Each team was invited to perform in a professional venue. She was proud that many less well-off schools had signed up; even if money had to be begged or borrowed, no one should be turned away. It was the first time many had collaborated, or even met: private schools next to government schools, kids from prosperous suburbs performing alongside kids from the townships.

'It's a great leveller. You see them when they arrive in the morning, they're nervous, they don't know each other, but by the end of the day, it's like one big happy family, it really is.'

After three weeks in South Africa I had grown doubtful about such claims on the rainbow nation. But Filinova-Bruton's optimism was hard to resist. I kept my doubts to myself.

Why had she chosen Shakespeare? Why not Athol Fugard – or, for that matter, Chekhov?

We swerved past a small fleet of minibus taxis trailing diesel fumes and spray.

'He wrote about everything, and for everyone. Everyone can approach him. I really believe that. I think that's a good thing to have in South Africa right now.'

We passed through the garden suburbs of Pinelands and Rondebosch towards the run-down outpost of Athlone, which under the Group Areas Act became a dumping ground – along with most of the Cape Flats – for communities the apartheid state wanted to forget. Tidy villas and gated, tree-lined estates gave way to industrial estates and business parks, then sandy scrub and trees crouching beneath the wind. In the wing mirrors, impossible to escape, was the squat shadow of Table Mountain, its top bruising a heavy, lead-grey sky.

Gradually the houses reappeared, progressively more dilapidated: at first boxy bungalows and apartment blocks that looked like prison accommodation, then, past the airport, the townships – hectic collages of tin and corrugated steel, tumbledown wooden shacks painted yellow and salmon and sea-green against the sandy grey of the earth. Some were little larger than garden sheds with bright-blue portable toilets outside.

People reappeared: women, mainly, wearing thick fleeces and hats and carrying shopping bags, or sitting in plastic garden chairs in front of stalls selling live chickens. A few streets on, across the lane that divided two shacks, someone had hung their washing out to dry: six identical blue shirts and two Babygros, hanging within inches of a tangle of power cables.

If one were in search of an essay on how much still needed to be done in South Africa, I thought, one could do worse than drive for twenty minutes out of Cape Town.

Located on Govan Mbeki Road and named for another ANC martyr, Chris Hani Secondary School, recently rebuilt, was in a better state than I'd feared – three cheerful storeys of orange brick lording it over the shipping containers converted into shops and dwellings that surrounded it. Its 1,370 pupils were some of the most active at music and drama in the Western Cape. In the impoverished and almost entirely black township of Khayelitsha, where over half the population was living in what was eupehmistically called 'informal' accommodation, it was an unlikely and cheering beacon of success.

I was bustled inside the principal's office and shown the school's precious trophy haul: a plaque from the Safe School Project, citations from the Western Cape education department. In a cabinet was a yellow certificate from the inaugural SSF SA festival. Next to an image of Shakespeare's head were words from *Twelfth Night*: 'be not afraid of greatness.' In the play they were a warning not to get above one's station – in a snobbish practical joke the steward Malvolio discovers them in a forged letter he thinks is from Olivia, his mistress. Here they had a braver ring. Anything is possible, they said. Wilton Mkwayi had marked exactly the same lines in Sonny Venkatrathnam's copy of Shakespeare.

Outside, in the chill wind gusting across the flats, boys in grey uniforms were scooting a football through the puddles. The sun flashed through a scrap of torn cloud, turning the water the colour of polished nickel and making the grass a vivid, sharp green.

I was escorted across into a drama studio. It was hardly luxurious –

lime-coloured walls with steel desks pushed up against them, mirrors and a dance barre down one side – but it looked well maintained. Waiting inside were two drama teachers, Lize-Marie Smalberger and Darlington Sibanda, and seven tenth-grade students aged fifteen and sixteen, bundled in coats and hats against the cold.

Chris Hani had been one of the first schools to sign up for the fledgling SSF SA. They'd taken their productions to Artscape, a professional venue in central Cape Town – the first time that many students had been into the city, just twenty miles away. The first year they had done *Macbeth*, following it up with *Julius Caesar* and *Romeo and Juliet*. They proudly showed me pictures: *Macbeth*'s shock troops dressed like the ANC Youth League in black berets and yellow singlets, with the Witches robed like ancestral spirits.

Most had not even heard of Shakespeare before taking part; he wasn't on the curriculum. But they'd fallen greedily on the stories: a ruler wanting to seize power, a young couple falling in love against the wishes of their parents.

The words were hard, they admitted. Nearly all the students at Chris Hani were isiXhosa-speaking, which meant that English was a second language – Shakespeare a third.

'The language, it was a big challenge to us,' said a girl, Zintle. 'But it makes it easier to read it in the drama lesson.'

'*Ja*, that is a big help,' cut in Sesethu, another female student. 'Our teacher explains the words to us – sometimes.' She dissolved into giggles.

Doing the texts as drama rather than literature was a help, Ms Smalberger explained: it meant the students had no preconceptions, and forced them to tease out what was really going on. 'The language really helps them with their analytical skills. You have to work twice as hard. There was a huge transformation of understanding: you could see it happening.'

'We were so nervous before we went on,' said a boy, Nzaba. 'But when you're with an audience, you're talking to them. You are connected.'

On my mind was a grimmer fact, what one of the teachers had told me in the principal's office about the high rates of domestic and sexual violence in townships like Khayelitsha. One of last year's cast, a thirteen-year-old, was HIV-positive, having been raped by her stepfather; many parents were not involved in their children's lives, or were forced to live far away for work.

Did they feel the plays connected with their own experience?

Othello did, a boy said solemnly: 'We respect our ancestors. So if you marry a white girl there is going to be trouble.'

A girl, Azola, brought up *Romeo and Juliet.* 'It makes a problem about love,' she said. 'Our parents choose for us, but sometimes we don't feel that. So we hope our parents give us a chance to choose.'

Someone mentioned *ukuthwala*, the practice of forced marriage prevalent among families in the Eastern Cape, many of whom were from poor rural backgrounds.

'Your parents choose for you a husband,' she said. 'Sometimes it can be an old man and you are fourteen – you have to marry, like, a fifty-year-old man, a sick man.'

So the theme of the play wasn't simply theoretical?

She sounded sad. 'They will discuss these things without you. Those men just take you. We have to accept this.'

For all the obvious hardnesses of their lives, I thought them lucky in at least one regard: they encountered Shakespeare's words not in a textbook or on an exam paper, but as his first actors had encountered them – as speeches to be performed, pulses and sounds crackling with energy.

Sesethu was smiling broadly, snapping her fingers. 'I really like the rhythm of Shakespeare. He has an excellent beat.'

Throughout my journey I had often heard about the so-called 'Born Frees', young people born after the 1994 elections. In the minds of everyone over the age of approximately twenty the Born Frees were held to be heedless, cosseted, ruinously ignorant of South Africa's politics and recent past.

Anyone with that view should come to Khayelitsha and spend twenty minutes talking to the serious-minded grade tens at Chris Hani school, I thought. They knew more about South Africa than people three times their age.

Eager not to be left out of the discussion, one of the boys leapt to his feet and recited lines I hadn't heard for years:

> Death, be not proud, though some have called thee
> Mighty and dreadful, for thou art not so;
> For those whom thou think'st thou dost overthrow
> Die not, poor Death, nor yet canst thou kill me.
> From rest and sleep, which but thy pictures be,

Much pleasure; then from thee, much more must flow
And soonest our best men with thee do go,
Rest of their bones, and soul's delivery.
Thou art slave to Fate, chance, kings, and desperate men,
And dost with poison, war, and sickness dwell,
And poppy or charms can make us sleep as well
And better than thy stroke; why swell'st thou then?
  One short sleep past, we wake eternally
  And death shall be no more; Death, thou shalt die.

I'd last heard Donne's holy sonnet being tweezered apart in a university seminar room. It occurred to me that I'd never properly attended to: the battering, belligerent strength of Donne's belief, the urgency of his terms. There was no missing them here. The boy's voice was quiet and steady. When he finished, there was a moment of silence.

Chris Hani had big plans: they were excitedly organising a trip to the British Shakespeare Schools Festival, if they could raise the funds, and were keen to stage *Macbeth* again, make it tighter and better.

I wanted to ask more, but they were keen to get going. Today was the last day of term. Shakespeare was all very well, their body language said, but I should get some things in perspective. School holidays were school holidays.

As they were zipping up their jackets and pulling on their mittens, I asked the question I had wanted to ask all along: what they thought about the idea that Shakespeare wasn't someone kids like them should spend time with – that, as some people still argued in South Africa, he was just some dead white guy, no concern of theirs.

A girl was in the group. She had been sitting quietly by, huddled in her green-and-brown-striped hoodie, listening intently but not speaking. She was standing near the door, her brow knotted.

'From my own opinion,' she said carefully, 'Shakespeare is for everyone. I can learn from Shakespeare when I am from South Africa. I don't need to be European. I think they are wrong if they are saying that.'

Shyly, she ducked her head and headed out into the afternoon.

Strange Tales

Beijing · Shanghai · Taipei · Hong Kong

I n June 2011, Wen Jiabao, then premier of China, arrived in Britain on a three-day state visit. A pressing list of issues awaited his attention. One was the relationship between China's latest five-year economic plan and the Eurozone crisis. Sino-British defence goals were in urgent need of harmonisation. More delicately, there was what the official press release called 'enhancing mutual understanding' – diplomatic-speak for fence-mending after wrangles over China's record on human rights. In London, it was announced, Wen would be officially welcomed at 10 Downing Street by prime minister David Cameron, and would make a speech among 'Friendly Personages' at the Royal Society.

Instead of his plane putting down at Heathrow or somewhere close to the capital, however, Wen's officials directed it further north, to the small airport outside Birmingham. Partly this was convenient for a visit to the MG car plant at Longbridge, now under the control of the mighty Chinese state-owned SAIC conglomerate. But there was another reason, too. Before embarking on official business, premier Wen wanted to indulge in a spot of pleasure. He wanted to visit Stratford-upon-Avon.

On a bright, blustery summer morning, Wen spent an hour and a half in Stratford, twenty-five minutes longer than his minders had scheduled. He was escorted around Shakespeare's Birthplace and shown a copy of the First Folio, then invited to admire the only surviving letter to the poet, from fellow Warwickshireman Richard Quiney. (It is unclear whether it was pointed out to Wen, vis-à-vis the UK's ballooning trade deficit with China, that Quiney was asking Shakespeare for a loan.)

Afterwards the Chinese premier sat on a bench in the sunshine, accompanied by the British culture secretary, to watch a scene from

Hamlet. Beneath a fluttering Chinese flag, Ophelia presented him with a sprig of rosemary for remembrance.

Wen had his own remembrances: he'd been a fan of Shakespeare since he was a lad. 'His works are not to be read only once or even ten times,' he observed sagely to the assembled media. 'They must be read up to a hundred times to be fully understood.' The official Xinhua news agency let it be known that the premier had even been boning up on criticism during the flight. He was particularly taken by Goethe's reverence for the poet, and had cited a line from '*Zum Shakespeares Tag*' as proof.

Before leaving the Birthplace, Wen donated a copy of *Love's Labour's Lost*, translated into Mandarin by the scholar Liang Shiqiu. In the visitors' book, he composed his own homage, in elegantly drawn Chinese characters:

> He brings sunshine to your life,
> Gives your dreams wings to fly.

The premier was also reported to have made a wisecrack about *Hamlet*, though no one I spoke to afterwards could recall what it was.

I consulted journalistic colleagues about what was really going on here. During a trip burdened with major geopolitical issues and trade negotiations worth billions of pounds, for a Chinese leader to take time out for a jolly seemed unusual. In Hungary, his previous port of call, Wen had disappeared rapidly into meetings with prime minister Viktor Orbán; in Berlin, where he headed next, a bilateral summit about the euro with Angela Merkel had been top priority. The British PM, meanwhile, had been left kicking his heels in London while his counterpart cooed over a First Folio and two pretty young actresses.

Politics were not, of course, absent from Wen's visit to Stratford: culture, my colleagues reminded me, was an instrument of soft power, in twenty-first-century China as much as sixteenth-century England. Sitting on his bench at the Birthplace, the premier made a point of stating – lest anyone forget – that China had its own Shakespeares: 'The literary figures of China have produced a myriad of literary works, and reading these works will help one better understand the course of the development of our great nation.'

But, from what anyone could divine, that was it. The real explanation for Wen starting his visit with Shakespeare was probably the simplest: he was a fan. 'At least it wasn't Harry Potter,' said a friend.

Wen was certainly not alone: Chinese visitors were thronging the UK. According to the Office for National Statistics, there are now something like 196,000 a year, more than ever before. When I should have been rationalising my notes from South Africa, I spent a morning frowning over ONS spreadsheets. The numbers were modest compared with France (3.9 million visitors annually) and Germany (3.1 million), but when one considered the expense of getting to Britain, let alone the expense of staying, they were astounding. An economy flight from Beijing to London cost something like 6,000 RMB (£600). Say fourteen nights, factoring in accommodation, food and the rest . . . One wouldn't get much change from 30,000 RMB (£3,000) per person, even if one came as part of a tour group. Some operators demanded a deposit of many thousands of yuan before they'd even accept your booking, not to mention the difficulty and expense of securing a visa.

And why put Stratford on your once-in-a-lifetime itinerary? London is obvious: shopping, must-see sights. The historic cities of Edinburgh or York are clear attractions, likewise hops to Oxford and Cambridge or a stately home such as Blenheim Palace. But a detour to a small town in the Midlands whose chief export is theatre? I'd been sixteen years old before I'd bothered to go to Stratford, and it was only two and a bit hours down the motorway.

I called a Chinese travel agency with offices in Nottingham and Heilongjiang province. Was it really the case that Chinese tourists were eager to go to Stratford-upon-Avon? Absolutely, they said: increasingly so. Of the 40,000 visitors they handled each year, roughly a quarter insisted on a visit. Others organised tours locally, perhaps as a summer holiday after doing a postgraduate degree. In excess of 80,000 Chinese students were in UK higher education at the time, and on master's programmes nearly as many Chinese postgraduates as there were British.

Wen's visit had only increased this surging Bardolatry, not least because the Shakespeare Birthplace Trust had cannily installed a photograph of the premier in the 'World Pilgrims' section of its museum. The Heilongjiang agency told me that one of their most popular tours combined two great British brands: Stratford and the Cadbury's chocolate factory at Bournville. And did I know that Birmingham airport was about to start accepting direct flights from Beijing, the first British city outside London to do so? Staff were being taught Mandarin in readiness for a tidal wave of yuan-clutching Chinese.

Why Stratford? I asked, just to check I wasn't missing something.

The manager sounded bemused by my question. 'For the famous British author, of course.'

As the months went by and the countries on my itinerary crossed and recrossed, China and I kept blundering into each other. I was fascinated to discover that Shakespeare was banned from theatres and schoolrooms during the Cultural Revolution, and that within hours of the ban ending, people had queued around the block to buy copies of the plays. (Wen's youthful passion must have been illicit: the Cultural Revolution only ended when he was thirty-four.) I read that 21 million Chinese fourteen-year-olds studied the trial scene from *The Merchant of Venice* each year – why that play, though, no one seemed sure. Shakespeare-fever had claimed some unlikely victims: according to a report in the *Shanghai Daily*, the bestselling author Zhang Yiyi was undergoing reconstructive surgery to make him look more like the Bard, at a cost of 1.4 million RMB (£150,000). Zhang told the press that 'life is a process of striving to become a better person'.

I wasn't alone in my burgeoning obsession with all things Chinese: the British government was only too eager to return Wen's overtures. In December 2013, the prime minister, David Cameron, his chancellor and a jumbo-jet-load of business leaders embarked on a three-day trade mission to China. Deals worth £5.6 billion were brokered in everything from satellite technology to health care. Diplomats seemed particularly enthused by a £45-million contract to export British pig semen to Chinese farmers. 'We're doing all we can to ensure that businesses up and down the country reap the rewards of our relationship with China,' a government spokesperson said.

This time, culture was unnegotiably part of the deal. Britain's and China's culture ministers signed a memorandum of understanding. And I got a tip-off that a major new announcement was on its way. Organised in conjunction with the Royal Shakespeare Company, it was of a project to translate the complete works of Shakespeare into Mandarin, along with a number of Chinese plays into English. Its cost, expected to be £1.5 million and a shock addition to the culture ministry budget – which was otherwise enthusiastically cutting subsidies for British arts organisations – would be borne by the taxpayer.

Pig semen and Shakespeare, I thought on my way to Heathrow. It was good to know the British still had something to sell.

———

'RATHER A BUILDING, IS IT NOT?'

The voice belonged to a young and faintly harassed-looking man. He wore a dark cotton jacket and was clutching a white iPhone and leatherette briefcase. He gestured at a soaring curtain of glass and silvered metal, curving upwards towards apparent infinity. Outside, in the late-morning sun, a lake glinted, its surface so still and smooth it might have been a tray of mercury.

The man bowed modestly and pressed a business card into my hand. On one side it read, 'Zhang Sihan, Overseas Media Representative, National Centre for the Performing Arts, Beijing'. On the other side was what I presumed to be the same in Mandarin.

He offered a creased smile. 'But – please to – call me Harry.'

I'd arranged to meet Harry (he was politely insistent) because, looking for a place to begin exploring the journey of Shakespeare through China and its culture, I'd decided I could do worse than begin at the centre of Chinese culture.

At least geographically, it looked like a solid decision. Located off Tiananmen Square and just across from the Forbidden City, the NCPA, known locally as the 'Egg', rose like a pale mirage behind the Great Hall of the People, the home of the Communist Party of China. Surrounded by water, its entrances and exits buried underground, it had a mystical and impregnable aura, and appeared from the outside – disconcertingly, I felt – to be floating in mid-air. Inside, it was no less awesome: 150,000 square metres of curved glass and titanium, a taut ellipsoid skin covering half a city block. Entering was like boarding a spacecraft from another and considerably more sophisticated planet. Harry was right: it was rather a building.

As we patrolled the curved front wall, he rattled through the statistics. Designed by the French starchitect Paul Andreu, the Egg had taken twelve years to build, and cost roughly 3.2 billion yuan (north of £300 million). It cost a third of that each year simply to run, heavily subsidised by the Chinese government. When it was pointed out that the upfront expenditure came to half a million yuan (£50,000) per seat, roughly what it would cost to have each one studded with jade and covered in silk, the powers that be had magnificently replied that the arts were 'not for profit'. Opened in the run-up to the 2008 Beijing Olympics, the NCPA showed the world that the Chinese were serious about culture. Very serious indeed.

This much I'd been expecting. Along with billions of others, I had watched the grandiose Olympics opening ceremony and goggled at pictures of the megalomaniacal structures by Koolhaas and Foster and Arup that now stippled Beijing's skyline. What I had not appreciated was that, in China's National Centre for the Performing Arts, the Chinese arts were a rarified commodity. Barring a few half-hearted displays in the lobby, in fact, I couldn't see any of the stuff at all. The complex contained three state-of-the-art auditoriums. The main house, which seated 2,416, was designed specifically for European opera, the music hall for symphony orchestras. Though the smallest space – which, at 1,040 seats, was only a whisker smaller than the British National Theatre's largest auditorium – could accommodate *jingju*, traditional Beijing opera, its *raison d'être* was western drama and dance.

Zhang proudly escorted me through a CD shop stuffed with western classical music and an exhibition heavy with Puccini, Verdi, Donizetti, Bizet. In the six years of its existence the NCPA had staged nearly 70 new opera productions to an average of 80 per cent capacity. Many tickets cost under 80 yuan, less than the price of a decent meal.

A lift whisked us soundlessly to the top floor, which led to an open gantry from which we could gaze over the full sweep of the building. The ellipsoid curved giddily away beneath, blending into the polished marble floor so that it appeared never to end. In the foyer far below, a soprano was mounting a full-frontal assault on the 'Queen of the Night' aria from *Die Zauberflöte*. Top Fs pinged shrilly off the glass.

As Harry rushed off to locate a disorientated Spanish television crew, I drifted into yet another exhibition, this one devoted to the building itself: flowcharts and graphs, showing dizzying rises in audience numbers, online membership, VIP card holders, web visitors. Even if the whole lot were blithe fiction, it was impressive. 'Since its opening,' one panel read, 'NCPA has been adhering to the guiding principle to be "an important engine for the development and prosperity of socialist culture" and to be "World-class with Chinese characteristics".'

There was no mistaking the nod to Deng Xiaoping's famous formulation, first uttered in 1982 and since adopted into the Communist Party manifesto. Wily moderniser that he was, I felt that Deng might have balked at the phrase being used to advertise a French-designed shrine to Wagner and Verdi.

As I turned around, a poster announcing a festival caught my eye. SALUTE! SHAKESPEARE it read, in bilious yellow text on a hot-pink background. Next to it was a face I hadn't seen for a while – though for novelty's sake the artist had superimposed a migrainous pattern of swoops and swirls in magenta, vermilion and tangerine. It looked as if Shakespeare had been assaulted by Andy Warhol while recovering from an LSD trip.

In Britain, the 450th anniversary of his birth in April 2014 had caused a modest flurry of interest, most of it centred around a jokey feature in the *Sun* newspaper – 'FOREST FAIRIES FIASCO' for a spoof news report on *A Midsummer Night's Dream*; 'HUBBLE BUBBLE THIS SPELLS TROUBLE (GHOST OF BANQUO: AMAZING PICTURES)' on *Macbeth*. The excitement had soon fizzled. I assumed it would barely have made an impression 6,000 miles away.

Not for the first time, I'd assumed wrong. Checking the news on the way in from the airport, I discovered that *Life Week*, China's bestselling current-affairs magazine, had just placed Shakespeare on the cover of a commemorative issue. In addition to the Salute Shakespeare festival there was at least one other festival, in Shanghai, not to mention the brand-new Asian Shakespeare Association, whose inaugural conference in Taipei I was due at in just over two weeks' time. A British Council survey had pronounced Shakespeare one of the five British 'icons' most adored by the Chinese, beating even Benedict Cumberbatch and the Queen. If China was hot for western culture, it was positively randy for Shakespeare.

I bent down and attempted to decode the listings. Touring productions of *A Midsummer Night's Dream*, a Chinese-Japanese *Macbeth*, a Chinese *Romeo and Juliet*, Verdi's *Otello* . . . The thing was going on for seven months.

Harry had rematerialised. He pointed to the poster, beaming. 'China Central Television filming last week, big press conference!'

In China, apparently, the party was just getting started.

By the standards of every country I had so far visited, China was a blushing newcomer on the Shakespearian stage. Two millennia of 'closed-door' economic and cultural policies meant that no hint of Shakespeare's existence – in common with knowledge about a great deal of western culture – reached mainland China until nearly halfway through the nineteenth century.

Irked by the Middle Kingdom's isolationist policies, the British made periodic attempts to prod the sleeping giant. They were given an excuse in 1839 after the Qing emperor Daoguang banned the sale of opium, one of Britain's most valuable imports to China from India, inside his territories. Promptly declaring war, the British navy overwhelmed the Chinese fleet at Hong Kong and an expeditionary force mounted aggressive assaults against several Chinese cities culminating in the Treaty of Nanjing in 1842, the first of what are still bitterly called 'unequal treaties'. It demanded the cession of Hong Kong and the opening of five treaty ports to British trade.

Yet again, where the East India Company trod, Shakespeare followed – but in China the story had a twist. The very man given the task of confiscating the Company's opium, the diplomat Lin Zexu, took it upon himself to become better acquainted with the enemy by supervising the part-translation of an *Encyclopedia of Geography* by the Scottish writer Hugh Murray. Lin's aim was to introduce his countrymen to the ways of the clever-clever English (pleasingly described as 'greedy, tough, alcoholic, yet skilful in handicrafts'). The translation was published in 1839, the year hostilities broke out. Shakespeare's name featured in a list of famous British authors – the first time it had appeared in any Chinese publication. Despite Murray's florid assertion that 'Shakespeare stands unrivalled among ancient and modern poets, by his profound and extensive knowledge of mankind, his boundless range of observation throughout all nature', nothing made it through to the Chinese version other than the terse statement that he was 'prolific'.

More details trickled through. In 1856, an English missionary translated a Chinese textbook in which there was mention of a mysterious writer called 'Shekesibi'. In 1877, the first ever Chinese ambassador to London observed in his diary that the most renowned writer of his adopted country was 'a talented playwright living in England about two hundred years ago. His stature is comparable to the Greek poet Homer.' In 1895, the scholar Yan Fu translated yet another reference work, this time dilating on *Julius Caesar*:

Shakespeare wrote a play recounting the murder of Caesar. When Antony delivers a speech to the citizens while showing the body of Caesar to the public, he uses logic to stir up the citizens cleverly because Brutus warned him that he would not be allowed to redress a grievance for Caesar and blame the murderers. The citizens are greatly agitated by the speech and their resentment against Brutus and his comrades is running high. We should attribute Antony's success to the function of logic!

This view of Shakespeare as a supreme embodiment of western rationalism was influential. Determined to end their country's ancient resistance to outside influences, in the early twentieth century a group of intellectuals began to argue that if China had any hope of modernising, it was high time to engage with western culture. In 1907 the young writer Lu Xun, studying in Japan – itself forced to open up at the barrel of a western gunboat – wrote an astringent article arguing that Dante, Goethe, Byron, Milton, Pushkin and Shakespeare were 'warriors of the spirit', and that China must recruit and train its own spiritual warriors. The call would often be repeated.

Despite this, when Shakespeare was finally translated into Chinese, it was not as drama, but bedtime stories. Back in the nineteenth century, the British brother-and-sister team Charles and Mary Lamb collaborated on a book entitled *Tales from Shakespeare, Designed for the Use of Young Persons,* first published in 1807. Containing twenty stories drawn from the most popular plays, *The Tempest* to *Othello, Tales from Shakespeare* cleverly stitched pieces of the original text on to a narrative webbing supplied by the Lambs themselves, embroidering the plays into attractive moral samplers. Originally intended, in the words of the Preface, to 'be submitted to the young reader as an introduction to the study of Shakespeare', they were aimed at young female readers most especially, less likely to be given education. *Lamb's Tales*, as the book became known – in early editions only Charles was credited – has never been out of print in the English-speaking world since.

Much as the abbreviated scripts toured around Europe by the English Comedians in the 1600s helped propagate Shakespeare's stories in cultures where his work was unfamiliar, so too did the Lambs' *Tales* two centuries later. Short, cheap to publish and a great deal more straightforward to translate than Renaissance playtexts, they became enormously popular worldwide, especially in Asia (the film-maker Vishal Bhardwaj, who I'd spoken to in Mumbai, was one of many satisfied Indian readers). Though bowdlerised and heavily edited, they helped Shakespeare become a globally recognised name, reaching audiences far beyond the British children they were originally intended to serve.

First translated into Japanese in the 1870s, the *Tales* were printed in nearly a hundred separate editions in Japan in the next sixty years. Chinese readers had to wait until 1903, when an enterprising translator – unfortunately anonymous – published a selection of ten stories in classical Chinese. Each was given a sensationalistic heading, designed to snag the eye of male book-buyers: 'Proteus Sells Out his Close Friend for Lust' for *The Two Gentlemen of Verona*; 'Playing Tricks, the Devoted Wife Steals the Ring' for *All's Well That Ends Well*. The book's introduction emphasised the theme of Shakespeare as a global icon:

> His plays and stories became fashionable in England for a time and have been rendered into French, German, Russian, Italian and read by people all over the world. Nowadays Shakespeare is recognised and praised by the Chinese academic circle.

The subtext was clear: Shakespeare, already the world's poet, was long overdue in China. In recognition of this novelty, the publishers proudly called the book *Xiewai qitan* – 'Strange Tales from Overseas'.

It took another version of the Lambs' *Tales*, this time the complete set of twenty, to plant Shakespeare's stories firmly in the imaginations of Chinese readers. Lin Shu (1852–1924), perhaps the most prolific Chinese editor-translator of his period, forged a highly profitable career making foreign texts available to eager consumers, translating writers including Dickens, Hugo and Balzac, and *The Arabian Nights* – with the help of a team of assistants, as Lin himself knew no foreign languages. In 1904, they brought out a new book entitled *Yingguo shiren yinbian yanyu* ('An English Poet Reciting from Afar on Joyous Occasions'), which rendered all the Lambs' stories into semi-classical Chinese for the first time.

Lin's introduction went to some trouble to explain that, despite his title, these Shakespearian tales were an excellent match for Chinese sensibilities, where *shenguai xiaoshuo*, fantastical stories of gods and spirits, were established genre fiction. 'Shakespeare looked to fairies and monsters for his inspiration, themes and language,' Lin argued, continuing, 'the intellectual elite of the west is so fond of Shakespeare's poetry that every household in the country seems to be reading and reciting his lines all day long.'

The Merchant of Venice, the first volume in the collection, became *Rou quan* ('A Bond of Flesh'). *Hamlet* was given the evocative title *Gui Zhao* ('A Ghost's Summons'). *A Midsummer Night's Dream* evolved into *Xian Kuai* ('Cunning Fairies') while *Romeo and Juliet* became the enticing *Zhu Qing* ('Committing the Crime of Passion'). Lin's translators also recalibrated the texts for Chinese consumers: *Hamlet* became a Confucian parable on the importance of filial duty and respect; others were adjusted to make them resemble popular Qing-era love stories.

An English Poet sold so well that it was reprinted eleven times in the next three decades. In 1916, the 300th anniversary of Shakespeare's death and the same year that Israel Gollancz was assembling his goliath *Book of Homage* (which included just one tribute from a Chinese writer, Liu Po Tuan), Lin followed it up with another batch of tales, this time ones the Lambs had ignored, the Roman and history plays. China may have been slow to fall for Shakespeare's charms, but, courtesy of Lin's business acumen, a mass readership was soon devouring the stories of 'Sha Weng' or 'Old Man Sha'.

Throughout, one question dogged publishers – what should Shakespeare's formal Chinese name be? *Shekesibi, Suoshibier, Yesibi, Xiakesibier* (pronounced 'Sh-iack-ess-ee-bee-yer'): every translator tried a different option, attempting to squeeze these unwieldy consonants and diphthongs into a shape that Chinese mouths could form. Eventually an academic, Liang Qichao, came up with a sleeker alternative, *Shashibiya*. Not only pronounceable, it sounded plausibly Chinese. It stuck.

I wasn't entirely innocent of Shakespeare with Chinese characteristics. Sent out to Beijing the previous year to interview one of contemporary China's leading theatre-makers, Lin Zhaohua, I had seen his epic staging of *Coriolanus*. It was a colourful if somewhat outlandish experience. Translated into contemporary Mandarin and featuring a cast of nearly a hundred extras dressed in druidic robes like something out of *The Lord of the Rings*, the show was accompanied by two on-stage heavy-metal bands, going under the fearsome names of Suffocated and Miserable Faith. As the breastplate-wearing soldier-hero – a statuesque actor called Pu Cunxin, hugely famous in China – roared his way through speeches pouring scorn on cowards and commoners alike, the twin bands supplied a soundtrack of caterwauling guitars and pounding bass. It made the productions I'd seen in Germany look bashful.

When I interviewed Lin, I asked him why he had decided to amplify Shakespeare with hard rock. The maestro had smiled cryptically. He liked the noise, he said.

Coriolanus was being revived as part of the Salute Shakespeare festival, but not until later in the month. In the meantime, there was another home-grown production on stage at the Egg, *The Taming of the Shrew*, performed by a young troupe from Shanghai. Harry asked whether I wanted to come. Courtesy of that anonymous Shanghainese translator, *Shrew* had been among the first of the Lambs' *Tales* to be done in Mandarin, and one of the earliest Shakespearian productions on the Chinese stage. I most certainly did.

This new version was advertised as a smartly contemporary rom-com, something of an experiment in China, where Shakespeare was still often regarded as the purview of western companies or experimental directors such as Lin. I was interested to see what they made of it – even more interested as to whether the Beijing audience would reveal the same encouraging taste for William Shakespeare as they displayed for grand opera.

The first surprise was that the show was booked out. There was not a seat to be had, so much so that urgent calls were made to Shanghai to secure me a ticket. The second surprise was that I was nearly the oldest person there. I'd been told that live theatre in China was popular among the millennial generation born since the mid-1990s, and hadn't entirely believed it. Looking around the auditorium, it seemed to be true. I hadn't seen a crowd this eager and fresh-faced since attending a Harry Potter superfan event some years before (for work, I feel it important to point out).

Forewarned that there were no surtitles, I had downloaded a Shakespeare app on to my phone, figuring that I could bury it in my programme and consult the text by stealth. This precaution proved unnecessary: the arrival of the actors seemed to be a subliminal signal for everyone in the audience to slide out their smartphones, only occasionally pausing to consult the stage. A man two rows in front of me spent most of the performance checking stock-market prices on his Samsung. The fingers of a girl to my side flew busily over WeChat, the Chinese equivalent of WhatsApp. The auditorium was dotted with glimmering tiny blue screens.

In any case, the show needed little translation. Set in a 1930s-ish Shanghai, it was done in minimal fashion with a cast of eight. Some scenes had been rearranged, but the play had been boiled down to its essence: a cautionary tale about the dangers of women not obeying men. Katherine, the headstrong 'shrew' of the title, refuses to be married off, to the lasting irritation of her dutiful sister Bianca, who is besieged by suitors but banned from marrying until Katherine does so first. The gold-digging Petruccio is persuaded to make a bid for Katherine and does so with gusto, 'taming' her into obedience by a combination of badinage and bullying tactics. Somehow all ends happily.

It was both captivating and chastening to watch. In Britain and America, *The Taming of the Shrew* is generally regarded as a problem comedy because of its streak of violent misogyny: how else to portray a world where women are bartered and sold like sacks of grain? Or in which a wife is starved and subjected to sleep deprivation by her husband so she might become more pliant to his will? Earnest debate centres on the final scene, in which Petruccio sets up yet another blokeish bet, as to who has the most obedient wife. Not only does the newly tamed Katherine appear promptly when called, she delivers a forty-four-line speech on spousal duty. 'A woman moved is like a fountain troubled,' she declares, later continuing:

> I am ashamed that women are so simple
> To offer war where they should kneel for peace,
> Or seek for rule, supremacy, and sway
> When they are bound to serve, love, and obey.

In the western tradition, particularly since the pioneering work of feminist critics such as Juliet Dusinberre and Lisa Jardine in the 1970s and 1980s, the speech is a famous crux. Is Katherine being wilfully ironic? Is this a private joke between her and Petruccio? Should she mumble the lines, spirit crushed, like a victim of torture? I'd seen any number of variations on stage, but never a hint that Katherine might be serious, and seriously suggesting that – as she goes on to say – a woman's rightful place is beneath her husband's 'foot'.

Here in China, however, the play seemed to be something else entirely. Petruccio was played as a professional wide boy and gambler,

Katherine as a sharp-as-knives vixen whose six-inch heels added genuine danger to her athletic kung fu. I tried hard, but could sense little apparent anxiety about the gender politics: as Petruccio grabbed Katherine and flung her on top of the on-stage piano, pausing only to bash out Mendelssohn's 'Wedding March' from *A Midsummer Night's Dream*, everyone in the audience guffawed loudly. When it came to her concluding speech – delivered without a flicker of irony – even Samsung Man lowered his screen and cheered. A group of teenagers nearby were roaring with laughter, their faces flushed with pleasure.

As I headed out, I pondered my reaction. There'd been numerous stories in China about what were grimly called *sheng nu* ('leftover women'), women in their late twenties who had focused on getting an education and developing a career instead of playing the dating game. Despite a cursory amount of debate over the obvious sexism of the term, it seemed to be assumed that if women were 'leftover' it was entirely their fault, especially in a China where, as a result of the one-child policy, there were around 20 million more men than women under the age of thirty. If the response I'd seen in the theatre was any guide, the only way of looking at independent-minded single women in China was that they were 'shrews' in serious need of taming.

But then of course one could argue that this was authentic. However ironic or otherwise Shakespeare's retelling of the story (or his response to earlier folk traditions), it would have been an irony lost on large sections of an Elizabethan audience, most of whom would no doubt have responded exactly as this Chinese one had done – with whoops and cheers of delight at the sight of a woman finally doing as she's told. The unreconstructed humour might not have suited my taste, but one thing seemed clear, at least tonight: Shakespeare had found his audience.

Still, in a country where Mao had once famously claimed that 'women hold up half the sky', I found it disheartening. When Lin Shu and his team rendered the story in 1904, they gave it a simpler name: *Xun han* ('Taming a Shrew'). It sounded disturbingly like an instruction manual.

'What we must understand about Shakespeare,' said Shen Lin, 'is that it is *ideological*.'

He gestured benevolently outside his window – trees in leaf, chattering birds, a children's play area, a woman shuffling into the building opposite with a basket of washing – and swung back, his eyes mischievous.

'But then, naturally, *everything* in China is ideological.'

This homily was only slightly undercut by the fact that Professor Shen, head of theatre studies at the Central Academy of Drama, was addressing me from the end of his double bed. I had been heading out to his office when a text message arrived, asking if I could come to his apartment instead. Forewarned about the self-importance of certain Chinese academics, I had put this down to haughty behaviour. The reality was more humdrum: Shen had broken his ankle and was housebound.

Adjusting his position on the bed with a grimace, he launched into a detailed definition of ideology in a Marxist-Leninist context. Somewhere in the narrow apartment a kettle rumbled; a young student was busying herself with spring tea and rice cakes.

I had arranged to meet Shen because I was hoping for guidance on something that seemed near-impossible: squaring the works of William Shakespeare with Chinese communist ideology. Shen had kindly offered to give me a brief tutorial. He spoke energetically, in lightly accented English, but the tutorial did not look like being especially brief.

Lesson one: everything was ideological. Lesson two was equally important – that it had been so from Shakespeare's earliest arrival in China. Lin Zexu, the diplomat whose 1839 translation of a British encyclopedia had introduced the 'prolific' Shakespeare to the Chinese, had been working for a government fighting the British. Later, the earliest enthusiasts for Shakespeare's works were modernisers, seeking to wrest China out of (as they saw it) the intellectual dark ages. Lin Shu, the energetic translator-adapter who turned the plays into *shenguai xiaoshuo*, tales of gods and monsters, had his own ideology, making ancient Chinese culture commensurate with the best from the west.

When communism arrived, it was no different, Shen explained; but then one could not explain this without introducing the relationship between Marx and William Shakespeare . . .

The student arrived with the tea. I abandoned my notebook.

What I had not fully grasped was that Karl Marx, fiercely iconoclastic in so many ways, was a model Bardolatrous German. Introduced to the works as a young man in Trier, he memorised passages from the plays in both English and Schlegel's German translation. (His daughter Eleanor later recalled that 'Shakespeare was the Bible of our house'.) Marx's reverence for Shakespeare was such that while living in London he joined a Shakespeare society, and thus had a walk-on part in the ill-starred tercentenary celebrations in 1864.

Marx peppered his articles and correspondence with Shakespearian allusions, was disconcertingly well-schooled in textual studies, and showed himself an alert critic. As a journalist and agitator, he deployed Shakespeare to score satirical points or to ram home a thesis. He drew frequently on *The Merchant of Venice* for its themes of justice and mercy, and returned more than once to Shylock as the image of the money-grubbing capitalist who uses high finance to turn human flesh into mere exchange value.

But it was in one of the most neglected texts in the canon, *Timon of Athens*, that Marx found an exemplum so perfect that it could almost have been designed to illustrate the radical social philosophy he had begun to develop in the early 1840s. The fable-like tale of an Athenian plutocrat who uses, abuses and loses his wealth, then is driven into the wilderness, *Timon of Athens* has been seen as a trial run for themes explored in agonising depth in *King Lear*. Both plays were most likely written around 1604–06, in the nervy, uncertain early years of James I's reign.

Like *King Lear*, *Timon of Athens* is tormented by questions of value and worth, specifically monetary value. Marx seized on them. In a series of manuscript notes for *Das Kapital* made in 1844 he quoted Timon's scathing denunciation of gold, that 'yellow slave':

> Gold? Yellow, glittering, precious gold?
> No, gods, I am no idle votarist:
> Roots, you clear heavens. Thus much of this will make
> Black white, foul fair, wrong right,
> Base noble, old young, coward valiant.

'Shakespeare excellently depicts the real nature of *money*,' Marx scribbled in his notes, seizing on Timon's suggestion that capital is a violation of the natural order, divorcing objects and people from their true worth. By permitting the raw demands of the market to determine value, money allowed everything to become its opposite.

Shen smiled triumphantly. 'These lines made Shakespeare *famous* among Chinese intellectuals!'

It was also important to note the role of the USSR. After the founding of the People's Republic in 1949, Soviet technicians were sent out in their hundreds to help Chinese industries and universities modernise; alongside chemists and structural engineers were theatre directors and literature professors. Marxist books and essays on Shakespeare were translated and placed on curriculums. In Russia, Shakespeare had been revered since the eighteenth century; in this as in much else, China copied its 'Elder Brother'.

Chinese scholars obediently analysed the plays in dialectical terms, ransacking them for examples of class conflict. One critic described *King Lear* as 'the portrayal of the shaken economic foundations of the feudal society'. *Hamlet* became not a study in savage introspection, but a 'social tragedy' whose hero's solemn duty is to free the *Lumpenproletariat*. The description of the Renaissance offered in *Dialectics of Nature* by Marx's co-author Friedrich Engels (yet another passionate Shakespearian) as 'the greatest progressive revolution that mankind has so far experienced, a time which called for giants and produced giants', was often quoted. That Shakespeare had been a shareholder in a profitable entertainment business was conveniently glossed over.

So it went on, Shen explained: China became one of the only countries in the world where *Timon of Athens* – neglected academically, barely staged – was not only read but keenly debated. Even Shakespeare's star-crossed lovers became subject to remorseless dialectical-materialist forces: I had heard *Romeo and Juliet* described in many ways, but never before as a reflection of 'the desire of the bourgeois class to shake off the yoke of the feudal ethical code'.

I sensed I was being a dull student. Shen briskly shook his head. 'Yes, this Marxist interpretation of Shakespeare is not very original, much of it is just imported from Russia. But Marxist analysis did make a dramatic impact on Chinese interpretation of art and history.'

Did he have a favourite play?

He barely paused. '*Coriolanus*. *Coriolanus* is my favourite play.'

Could he give me a Marxist reading?

He grinned narrowly. 'Class war. Nothing new to China. Shakespeare is a very keen observer of this class war.'

Where did he place himself, politically?

'I would be put on the left side. But it depends.' He grinned again. 'Another truth about China: change is all!'

Outside on the street, the atmosphere was of a sedate, slightly beery carnival. I had forgotten: it was May Day, the socialist holiday and in China the start of a three-day public festival. As I walked down Wangfujing towards the central shopping district, the crowds were out in force, enjoying as much of the spring sunshine as could be detected through a bilious filter of smog. Young fathers with chubby toddlers on their shoulders, wives in hot pants sporting serious-looking handbags, sharply dressed teenagers by the score: I threaded my way through them all as they mounted a combined offensive on the citadels of Starbucks and Zara and Gap.

On a corner I saw a camera store. One window proudly displayed portraits of Mao and Deng Xiaoping; the other glittered with hundreds of imported Canons and Nikons. It seemed as clear a metaphor as one could want for the present state of China.

Strange Tales from Overseas . . . When Shakespeare had first been translated into Chinese, via the Lambs, it had been as stories from the remote and exotic Occident. It took significantly longer for the plays to appear as they'd originally been written: dramas to be performed on stage.

Partly this was because – not dissimilar from India – China had its own vigorous and highly characteristic theatrical traditions. By western standards, the drama of the Middle Kingdom is almost unimaginably ancient. Its deepest origins, possibly religious or shamanic, are obscure, but by the Shang dynasty (which began around 1600 BCE, a millennium before Thespis, the first recorded Greek actor, stepped on stage) hunting rituals had become codified into dances and performances. By the time of the Zhou dynasty (c.1046–256 BCE), these had become chorus dances. Grand spectacles known as *baixi* ('hundred entertainments') became popular at the imperial court, a smorgasbord of music, miming, magic, martial arts and dancing.

Back in my apartment, I studied photographs online: Tang-dynasty tomb figurines from c.700 CE were especially vivid; graceful renderings of dancers with sexily sashaying hips and long, flowing sleeves. Had it not been for their chipped paint, they could have been sculpted yesterday.

The Tang emperors were especially passionate about drama, staging lavish spectacles – the most remarkable of which, laid on for a Turkish embassy during the seventh century, required a kilometre-square stage and several thousand acrobats, dancers and magicians. Many early playtexts date from this period. Surviving scripts include one entitled *Tayao niang* ('The Dancing, Singing Wife'), in which a husband who beats his partner receives his just deserts (a nice riposte to *Shrew* the other evening, I thought), and a vaguely *Hamlet*-ish story called *Buotou buotou* ('Head for Head') telling of a youth whose father has been killed by a tiger and is bent upon revenge.

Many of these forms are preserved in Chinese opera – which, though codified much later, is a pottage of ancient ingredients. Beijing opera, the form best known in the west, is just one branch of traditional opera (known overall as *jingju*, *jing* meaning 'capital city'). There are local variants throughout China, encompassing a dazzling variety of techniques – martial arts, mime, dance and acrobatics alongside singing, acting and costume / make-up.

In Britain a few years before, I'd watched a company from Shanghai perform a version of *Hamlet* called *The Revenge of Prince Zi Dan*. It was my first exposure to live *jingju*, an art form as remote from my previous experience as Aboriginal Dreamtime dance or Tanzanian hip-hop. Visually, the piece was spectacular, the stage crammed with actors in flowing robes and elaborate headdresses, with Hamlet as an athletic and dauntingly active warrior prince balancing on platform heels five inches high. The music was even more memorable: to an artillery of clanging percussion and squealing fiddles, the performers affected a nasal, fearsomely virtuosic singing style that sounded as though it could penetrate a brick wall at a thousand paces. I left the performance both deafened and impressed.

A morning's research and a visit to the Zhengyici theatre, one of the very few traditional 'tea-house' opera houses left in Beijing – built in 1688 and beautifully restored, a lustrous jewel box in crimson, emerald and gold – helped me understand a little more. That the acting is heavily stylised was already obvious, but what I hadn't appreciated is that similar imperatives govern plot and character.

Jingju is an actors' art. Just four basic roles exist – *sheng* (male), *dan* (female), *jing* (painted-face male) and *chou* (male clown). These divide into subtypes of age or disposition (*laodan*, old woman; *daomadan*, young female warrior; *huadan*, 'flower girl', a coquette). Traditionally performers are taught in specialised schools from a young age, and spend many years in gruelling physical training, acquiring the strict requirements of their character type – the trembling falsetto of an adolescent boy, or the flashing sword skills of a virile young warrior (this must have been Hamlet, I realised). They might sometimes graduate within that type – ageing gracefully from *xiaosheng* (young scholar) to *laosheng* (elderly scholar) – but they would almost never leave it. Of the thousand-plus operas considered part of the repertoire, nearly all are centred on these types. Players spend entire careers performing just one character, honing it to flawless perfection.

Shakespeare would have recognised one aspect of *jingju* at least: female performers were initially banned from participating and only began to do so in the late nineteenth century. A few companies keep the old ways alive. At the Zhengyici I watched a male actor who specialised in the *qingyi* ('green robes') role of a mature or married woman wafting dolefully across the stage, resplendent in robes rippling with chrysanthemums and plum blossoms. Beneath a teetering headdress encrusted with pearls and flowers, his face was painted chalk-white. His voice was high and thin, but affecting in its fragility. For the first time, I understood why the sound was so piercing – it needed to project unamplified above the crashing and caterwauling of the orchestra. Sad and sweetly funny, he would have made a splendid Nurse in *Romeo and Juliet*.

But the rigorous refinements of *jingju* made it a prison. Inspired by the scholars calling for Chinese literature to open itself to outside influences, reformers argued that traditional opera was incapable of communicating genuine dramatic truth. They began to agitate for different kinds of theatre on Chinese stages. Following the collapse of the Qing dynasty in 1912 and the founding of the Republic, interest grew in *wenming xi*, 'civilised drama', based on western models.

One model was provided by the schools and universities founded by missionaries in treaty ports such as Nanjing and Shanghai, which had exposed Chinese students to western-style education – including Shakespeare – and the rudiments of translation. Students had been taking part in English-language performances of the plays since at least the 1890s, including stagings of the trial scene from *The Merchant of Venice*.

Enter *Shashibiya* and, again, Lin Shu. In July 1913, an adaptation called *Rou quan* ('Bond of Flesh'), based on Lin's version of the

Lambs' retelling of *The Merchant of Venice*, was acted by the National Renewal Society of Shanghai. A box-office hit, it sparked a fashion for Shakespearian dramas, both comedies and tragedies – notably *Othello*, *Romeo and Juliet*, *Hamlet*, *Much Ado About Nothing* and *The Taming of the Shrew*.

Whether these count as 'Shakespeare' is moot, because, even more so than equivalent versions in India, these were adaptations of adaptations of adaptations, and furthermore not conventionally scripted but given to the actors as set scenarios (*mubiao*) to be improvised around.

A 1916 advert in the *Republican Daily* for yet another version of *The Merchant of Venice* entitled *Nu lushi* ('The Female Lawyer') is a case in point. The synopsis sounds enticing, though perhaps implies that something has been lost in translation: 'It involves cutting off a piece of one's own flesh to borrow money, while the heroine, though a woman, nevertheless becomes a lawyer.'

The publicity materials for a 1914 version of *Much Ado About Nothing* called *Yuan hu* ('Bitterness') boast an even bigger sell, Shakespeare's global celebrity, rendered in the tremulous language of Hollywood copywriters:

> In Britain there are theatres that specialise in putting on Shakespeare's plays. You can imagine how expensive the tickets are! *Bond of Flesh* has won high acclaim. Today we present *Bitterness* to you, in which men and women deceive each other from the beginning to the end. The bickering couple become happy foes, and this makes you laugh to death. Later, the bridegroom stirs up trouble in the wedding hall, and the bride screams for justice. This makes you cry your eyes out . . .

Although to modern eyes *wenming xi* would look impossibly stiff, it helped shape a fledgling form known as *huaju* ('word drama'). This flourished not in the imperial city of Beijing, where *jingju* reigned supreme, but in cosmopolitan Shanghai, more exposed to imported cinema and drama.

Early *huaju* scripts were adapted from nineteenth- and twentieth-century classics, notably those of the Norwegian pioneer of naturalistic theatre Henrik Ibsen and the crusading social realist George Bernard Shaw, both seen as more in touch with the modernising spirit of the times. Then, in the early 1920s, the dramatist Tian Han tried something simultaneously new and old: translating into Mandarin one of Shakespeare's plays from the original. Deeply affected by the assassination of his uncle, who worked for Sun Yat-sen, founder of the Republic of China, Tian decided to adapt the most grief-stricken play in the canon, *Hamlet*. Published in book form in 1922 as *Hamengleite*, it was followed three years later by a version of *Romeo and Juliet*. These were new kinds of translations for China, drawn line by line from a reliable text, cross-checked with a Japanese translation.

But it was nearly another decade before a professional staging of a full Shakespeare play was first mounted in China, wildly late by global standards. In spring 1930, the Shanghai Drama Assembly staged – yet again – *The Merchant of Venice*. Performed in the Central Assembly Hall, the show ran for two seasons and was acclaimed for the lavish 'accuracy' of its staging, featuring a fountain, a Venetian garden and Italian-style costumes. It set a lasting trend in China – for Shakespeare in what the theatre historian Li Ruru wittily calls the 'original sauce': as a foreign writer who shows tantalising glimpses of exotic distant lands.

This necessitated some invasive cosmetic adjustments. Chinese actors were routinely equipped with false noses, wigs and blue eye make-up (later, blue contact lenses) to match their European costumes. When the *New York Times* drama critic Brooks Atkinson was dispatched to Asia to cover the second world war, he cabled back a review of a *Hamlet* he caught in Chongqing in December 1942. He couldn't get over the noses:

> The Kuo-Tsi actors have built up a series of proboscises fearful to behold. The king has a monstrous, pendulous nose that would serve valiantly in a burlesque show; Polonius has a pointed nose and sharply flaring moustache of the Hohenzollern type; Hamlet cuts his way through with a nose fashioned like a plowshare . . .

Such appendages remained routine in performances of western drama until the 1980s.

Given my transcultural discoveries in India, I was fascinated to read about a production of *Romeo and Juliet* mounted in Shanghai in 1938, which blended Tian Han's translation with dialogue taken from the Hollywood film version of 1936 with Norma Shearer and Leslie Howard. I was even more entranced by a film called *Yi jian mei* ('A Spray of Plum Blossom'), an ambitious 110-minute silent version of

The Two Gentlemen of Verona from 1931. Partly available on YouTube, the film is imaginatively relocated to contemporaneous Shanghai and Guangzhou and depicts two strong-willed modern women as they journey in search of their wayward men. In one daring scene Shi Luhua / Silvia, played by the huge movie star Lin Chuchu, even dons uniform, having supplanted Hu Lunting / Valentine as the chief of the military police.

From the late 1930s onwards, however, theatre was heavily curtailed, first by the war with the Japanese and then by the conflict between the nationalists and the communists. Theatres were closed, actors and directors called up to fight. In the museum at the Beijing People's Art Theatre I saw their photographs, beaming young recruits joyfully preparing to do battle against the hated Japanese.

One picture made me pause. It came from 1942 and a cultural symposium held in the city of Yan'an – a black-and-white group shot, taken at the start of talks to develop the guiding principles of Chinese communist art. In the centre, despite the graininess of the image, was a figure immediately recognisable. He wore a donkey jacket, thick black hair sprouting either side of his bald pate. Mao Zedong.

It wasn't just the NCPA trying to find a new audience for Shakespeare in anniversary year. A few months before I arrived, the National Theatre of China's new *Romeo and Juliet* had opened. The production was big news, starring Li Guangjie and Yin Tao, both screen idols – Li known for boyish roles in Hong Kong movie rom-coms and action flicks, Yin for an eyelash-fluttering series of empresses and concubines in television historical epics, China's hugely popular period drama.

The director was Tian Qinxin, one of the few female theatre-makers to have developed a career in China. Trained in Beijing before living for a time in New York, she represented a different brand of theatre to that made by 1980s-trained directors such as Lin Zhaohua: aware of Chinese traditions but export-friendly and savvily commercial. With a sharp eye for a headline, Tian had called *Romeo and Juliet* a 'Chinese love story' and pointed up its relevance to contemporary debates about marriage. She also made it known that the idea of doing the play had occurred to her while visiting Stratford-upon-Avon – yet another Chinese tourist to stand where Wen Jiabao stood, outside the Birthplace.

Three days after I arrived in Beijing I was sitting in a light-filled modern studio across from Temple of Heaven Park. While acolytes fussed and Tian prepared tea – an elaborate ritual that revealed there to be a hot-water tap somehow plumbed into the desk – I sized up the room. Glossy design books, downlights, expensive-looking porcelain glistening on the blonde-wood shelves . . . Only a discreet row of neat gold statuettes on the other side of the room hinted that Tian's real business was theatre.

With neatly cropped short hair, and clad in an elegantly tailored linen trouser suit, she was open and affable. By the time she was born in 1969 in Beijing, her family had resided in the imperial capital for nearly three centuries. As a child she had wanted to be a painter, but the Cultural Revolution, which had begun three years earlier, made this impossible. Under permanent suspicion because of their aristocratic connections, her family had dispatched her to a traditional opera school.

She first became excited by foreign drama as a teenager, when she attended China's first-ever Shakespeare festival in 1986 – a pivotal moment in Chinese appreciation of the playwright, during which the newly founded Shakespeare Society of China oversaw a remarkable twenty-eight productions in Beijing and Shanghai over a two-week period. Tian had seen as many of the shows as she could, and recalled with particular fondness an *Othello* by the China Railway Drama Company. Although her homeland was hardly free of tensions between the Han majority and other ethnic groups, it was a measure of how different Chinese understandings of the play were, she explained, that it was staged not as a tragedy of race but of class.

Her interest had swelled in 1993, when Tian was among an early generation of Chinese people allowed to indulge in the ultimate cultural luxury: the package tour to the UK. In Stratford, she bought a statue of the playwright (£7, she remembered: a lot of money for a Chinese tourist at the time) and, upon returning to Beijing, placed it carefully alongside the statue of the Buddha in her apartment. She laughed: she had 'invited' Shakespeare into her life, as one might a deity.

Her early theatre work had been contemporary, but in 2008 Tian was invited to direct a version of *King Lear*. Taking a cue from television, she adapted it as lavish historical epic. Lear became a fourteenth-century emperor; instead of daughters he had sons. It was called simply *Ming Dynasty*. She had been struck by similarities between the life of Zhu Yuanzhang, who under his official name Hongwu became the first

Ming emperor, and that of Lear. A peasant who rose to power because of his military genius, Hongwu became increasingly unpredictable and despotic in old age.

'In *King Lear*, there was this question of who would inherit the throne. There are many similarities. One man's confusion led to the catastrophe of a whole country.'

Catastrophe, however, was not on the cards in *Ming Dynasty*. Tian, like the Restoration playwright and adapter Nahum Tate, had given *King Lear* a happy ending. The tragedy became a play-within-the-play, performed for the edification of the real emperor and his court; an augury of what could happen if China was not ruled correctly. 'This was a learning experience for him, an experience of growth and reflection.'

So in her version Lear survived?

She nodded. 'All the fights among his sons were only tests, to see who would be ready. In the play-within-the-play, everyone dies, but in the *real* play the emperor gave his throne to the youngest son. The Chinese believe the emperor is the son of heaven, so it's heaven that makes all the decisions, not the emperor. The emperor was clear-minded, he knew what he wanted. It was not a man going mad.'

It was an arresting thought, *King Lear* without the madness, but already we were on to her new *Romeo and Juliet*. I was surprised to hear that it was not in fact new, but an adapted version of a staging Tian had first created in 2012 with the National Theatre of Korea. That had been quite different, she said. The setting there was the Cultural Revolution: Romeo was a Red Guard, Juliet a young dancer. Although Mao was never depicted on stage, Romeo quoted his speeches liberally.

Why had she chosen that setting?

'I was still in elementary school when the Cultural Revolution ended in 1976, so my memories aren't distinct. But I do remember that although for adults it was a time of pain and suffering, for children it was a time of anarchy. That was how I imagined *Romeo and Juliet* to be.'

But this was also where problems had begun. Working with the Koreans, Tian was given free rein to depict historical events as she wished, but difficulties arose with the possibility of a transfer to China with Chinese actors. Tian was vague on the details, but it seemed that she had come under pressure to alter the scenario to something less problematic. Most of the script stayed, translated from Korean back into Chinese, but the action now took place in a fictional mainland town during something resembling the present day, with what China Central Television (who devoted a glowing report to the show) described as 'bicycles, sunglasses and hip-hop dancing'. With its lingering shots of gyrating youngsters, the CCTV report gave no clue that the earlier production – or its vexatious setting – had ever existed. All the newspaper articles I read did likewise.

What had happened? I couldn't get Tian to say. If she found the requirement to compromise problematic, she gave no hint of it. 'Personally I'm not very interested in politics,' she said. 'Setting a play in that period isn't a matter of politics.'

Setting *Romeo and Juliet* in the Cultural Revolution wasn't political?

I sensed the translator stiffening. Tian smiled, and started again. 'The government of today is still reflecting on the Cultural Revolution. They don't like their old wounds to be shown again to the rest of the world.' The smile was polite but steely; I could push if I wanted, but the door was closed.

The routine was wearily familiar. Speaking again to Lin Zhaohua at the Beijing People's Art Theatre a few days earlier, I'd found it impossible to get him to admit there was any political dimension to his work. His collaborations with the dissident writer Gao Xingjian, who had later fled China? No comment. A production of *Hamlet* staged a few months after the Tiananmen Square massacre in 1989, where the student hero morphed into a faceless bureaucrat? No relevance to contemporary events. A version of *Richard III* where the hero bore remarkable visual similarities to former premier Jiang Zemin? Purely accidental. Even *Coriolanus*, a story about a military commander who cannot adjust to the sordid compromises of *realpolitik*, was nothing to do with politics, Lin insisted. It felt like a dance, or a boxing match, ducking and weaving around what could and could not be said.

Talking with Tian, I felt I understood a little more. Making theatre in China – especially in a large state-funded arts complex – was a sophisticated game, involving a delicate series of negotiations. One might imply any number of things in a production (especially if the parallels were subtle), but if anyone asked, it was best to smile and plead innocence. Politics was for other people. Keep the controversy on stage.

Tian and I edged into talking about a recent play, *Chimerica*, by the British playwright Lucy Kirkwood, which had become a West End hit. Tian had seen it during a visit to London. Semi-fictionalised, the script focused on the so-called 'Tank Man', the nameless Chinese citizen who had famously been photographed standing in front of a row of tanks during the Tiananmen Square protests. The image – along with any mention of the protests – had been erased from the record in mainland China, and was still blocked on search engines by the 'great firewall'. At first, Tian said, she assumed the whole story was made up.

Would it be possible, I asked, to stage *Chimerica* here?

She laughed lightly. 'Those questions should be left to the government.'

I couldn't resist one final shove. She claimed that setting *Romeo and Juliet* during the Cultural Revolution wasn't a political decision; would it have been if she had followed *Chimerica*'s lead, and set the play during the 1989 protests instead? A youthful cast, warring generations, love across the barricades . . .

Tian placed her teacup carefully on the desk. Her answer did not come immediately. 'I cannot imagine this yet,' she said.

Keen to find out how Shakespeare operated in print as well as on stage, I arranged a meeting with Jo Lusby, managing director of Penguin China. The Penguin offices were in a gleaming silver tower near Beijing's unromantically named Third Ring Road.

While I waited at reception, seven floors up, I looked down at the city below: a vast and relentless expanse of towers, turrets, parks and flyovers, all slowly being dipped in the molten sun. At street level, I'd found Beijing overwhelming, almost steroidally huge. The six-lane highway, ostensibly a normal road, that roared past the door of my apartment. The towering cliffs of hotels and office blocks, emblazoned with neon signs so weirdly intense that at night they painted everything – walls, trees, windscreens, litter bins, grass verges – with strange colouring.

It hadn't helped that for my first four days here, the air was so polluted it had been almost unbreathable: skies the colour of dirty bathwater, dusky and deadened light that made it look as though the city was permanently in the grip of a solar eclipse. The night before, though, there had been a ferocious storm; today the atmosphere was clear. I'd been astonished to find it was possible to walk around outside for longer than ten minutes without my throat burning and my eyes beginning to stream.

Lusby appeared beside me: smartly dressed, with wispy blonde hair and a bluff Mancunian accent. She indicated the sky outside the windows. 'Normally we call it Beijing blue.'

Beijing blue?

'You know, not *actual* blue. Blue that isn't really blue. Beijing blue.' She sighed contentedly. 'But today, I think it's blue.'

Wry and engagingly direct, Lusby had an experienced outsider's perspective on the joys and frustrations of working in China. She'd been here for seventeen years, first coming out after teaching English in Japan, then wangling a job with a Chinese magazine publisher. In 2005, she heard that Penguin were looking to set up an office in China, and had run it ever since.

In a sleek white meeting room jammed full of Peter Rabbit merchandise and a rainbow of Jamie Olivers, she guided me towards the bottom line. In Europe and America, publishing had been in a dark place: declining sales and increased digital competition, stuck in the jaws of the credit crunch. In China, however, the outlook could barely be brighter. Book sales were growing at over 10 per cent annually. The 2013 figures suggested they stood at 50 billion yuan (about £5 billion) each year, numbering in excess of 400,000 titles. Bestsellers regularly sold more than 3 million copies, well into *Fifty Shades of Grey* and *Da Vinci Code* territory. Little wonder that foreign publishers wanted a slice of the action.

Like all alchemy, however, it wasn't as easy as it looked. Strict governmental rules meant that official publishers, over 400 of them, were state-owned. Foreign houses were not allowed to publish in their own right, necessitating complicated deals with a Chinese publisher for each and every title.

That was before you started on censorship. Despite profligate piracy, armies of Chinese bureaucrats policed the internet, broadcasting, press and publishing. It was a byzantine system, Lusby explained: publishers employed their own censors, following guidelines provided by the General Administration of Press and Publication, which furthermore had the power to demand cuts or halt publication entirely. The Chinese edition of Khaled Hosseini's *The Kite Runner* had been doctored to remove criticism of the Soviet occupation of Afghanistan. Chinese authors who wrote on sensitive topics faced pressure to edit, with the threat of losing the right to publish ever again.

Looking for an opening, Penguin had hit upon something its rivals couldn't match: Eng Lit British writers were highly valued in China, 'classic' works above all. The company had made its English backlist, over 1,000 titles, available for import, and would soon have 50 Penguin Classics in translation. The fact that the books were essentially uncensorable was a major plus.

'You know our highest-selling import? *Nineteen Eighty-Four.'*

Really? The censors didn't have a problem with Orwellian dystopia?

Lusby arched an eyebrow. 'It's a classic, and it's not seen as about China, it's about Russia, so it's OK. If it's not written as critique, then it's not interpreted as critique. They're pretty literal.'

Western classics also offered a priceless and seductive USP: foreignness. As recently as the 1970s it was forbidden for anyone outside the Party elite to read literature from abroad, but since the rules had been relaxed, Chinese readers – as in Lin Shu's day – had proved themselves voracious consumers of anything and everything in translation: established favourites such as Arthur Conan Doyle and Dickens, but also J. K. Rowling, Gabriel García Márquez, Haruki Murakami, Dan Brown. And not only in translation: the autobiography of Alex Ferguson, the former manager of Manchester United, had become a shock bestseller the previous autumn, even before it was translated into Chinese.

Where did all this leave Shakespeare? Lusby handed me over to two young Chinese colleagues, publisher Wang Jianqi and marketing associate Liu Yunqian. Somewhere between Dickens and Man United, seemed to be the answer.

Wang ran through the current situation. Penguin had a valuable Shakespeare backlist centred on the popular paperback New Penguin Shakespeare playtexts, first published in the UK in the late 1960s and extensively reprinted. Imported into China, these sold decently, along with a few works of criticism. Although Penguin didn't themselves publish a translation of the Lambs' *Tales from Shakespeare* in this territory, the book was still very much in print: new editions had been published as recently as 2004 and 2008.

Translation, Wang explained, was the golden egg. The number of Chinese people who could read English well was still small, perhaps 1 per cent of the population, and fewer still could cope with Shakespeare in the original, even if they had learned the odd passage at school. To be in with a chance of decent sales, you had to put Shakespeare into Mandarin.

Penguin were exploring the possibility of publishing fresh versions of not one but two separate translations of the complete works in 2016. The first was by a translator called Zhu Shenghao, who had rendered a large number of the plays in the 1930s and 1940s in versions that were now China's most popular. The second – if they could negotiate the rights – would use the newer and more precise translations by the renowned scholar Liang Shiqiu. 'They have different feelings,' Wang explained. 'Readers can choose the original translation, or the imaginative one.'

In the meantime, Wang and Liu were doing their best to marketise the Bard. A display of historic Penguin editions was touring trade conventions and publishing fairs in different Chinese cities, advertising the publisher's rich Shakespearian heritage. Here in Beijing they were working hard on a strategy to support the 2016 project.

'Everyone is the player of your own life,' Liu said. 'This is the idea we are working on.'

They walked me through the plan – multimedia happenings both on- and offline, reader discussions, public events. The challenge was that Shakespeare was perceived as both old and difficult to read, so they'd come up with an ingenious solution: making Shakespeare into a luxury product, like imported Scotch or Range Rovers.

'I think in China the best way to talk about Shakespeare is as a lifestyle,' Wang said.

A *lifestyle*?

She blinked rapidly. 'As Chinese people want to be more international, they want to have something to talk about with westerners. This is our message: for this reason you'd better read Shakespeare. It will benefit your social networking, and your lifestyle.'

They were brainstorming a media campaign. Chinese celebrities would be invited to choose a favourite play. A big-name lawyer could talk about *King Lear* and why it illustrated the need to set up a legally watertight will (a major issue in China, where the rise in the number of people owning property had put huge pressure on the country's vague inheritance laws). A famous property developer might talk about *Romeo and Juliet* . . .

'We want to say that for the money you spend on a cup of coffee you could buy the greatest love story,' Wang said.

How about a TV chef talking about *Titus Andronicus*? A drinks magnate on Falstaff? A female lawyer on *Merchant of Venice*?

Wang and Liu looked at me doubtfully, uncertain whether I was being facetious. I wasn't entirely sure myself.

'It will depend on the resources,' Wang said slowly. 'If there is a big production of a play, this can help us very much.' A wistful look came into her eyes. 'If there is something like *Downton Abbey* for Shakespeare . . .'

This was yet another prestige UK import. Seen by an estimated 160 million Chinese viewers (with many more watching pirated DVDs or downloads), Julian Fellowes's lumbering period saga appeared to have displaced Sherlock Holmesian fog – or even the royal family – as the vital symbol of Britain in Asia.

'Yes,' said Wang. 'Something like this television series would be very good.'

In the corridor on the way out I saw evidence of a previous marketing wheeze – a bicycle painted a jolly shade of red and covered with Penguin branding. It was a Flying Pigeon, Beijing's traditional bicycle, thought by some to be the bestselling vehicle of all time. Its design was ripped off from a 1930s British model: a cautionary mascot for a foreign company trying to get ahead in Asia.

As I passed, I patted the saddle. The bike looked as though it would go far.

———•———

257 . . . 272 . . . 284 . . . 293

The red numbers on the screen at the end of the carriage flickered and wavered, finally settling at 300 km/h. Outside the window, the scenery had dissolved from a series of identifiable scenes to a soothing and meaningless blur. The noise was barely louder than a hum, like the air conditioning in an expensive hotel.

Eyes pricking with tiredness, I watched Beijing being dragged soundlessly away. Above were tendrils of cloud, pale mauve, slipping across a bleached sky. It looked like a smoggy day ahead. Not real blue; Beijing blue.

I was on the 0700 G101, the first train of the day to Shanghai. The line had only been open a few years, part of China's headlong sprint into the twenty-first century. At the behest of the go-getting minister of railways, Liu Zhijun (known as 'Lunatic Liu'), some 9,000 miles of high-speed track had been laid in the last decade, more than the rest of the world combined. Even when two high-speed trains crashed in Zhejiang province in July 2011, killing forty and resulting in Liu's high-speed ejection from office, the pace barely slowed.

The line I was travelling had opened that same year. The government boasted that the project had used twice as much concrete as the Three Gorges Dam. In 2004, travelling between the two cities took fourteen hours-plus; this morning, I was due in to Hongqiao station at 12.37. The swiftest trains did the journey in four hours forty-eight minutes.

Unable to look out of the window without feeling seriously dizzy, I returned to my notes. I had been interested to hear that Penguin's plans included two separate editions of Shakespeare's complete works in Chinese: Liang Shiqiu's, published in the late 1960s, and the 'original', by Zhu Shenghao, who came from the city I was heading for, Shanghai. I wanted to find out more about Zhu. Both his life and his life's work seemed to say much not just about Shakespeare, but about China's turbulent history in the twentieth century.

Zhu had been born in Jiaxing, a town just outside Shanghai, in 1912, the same year the Republic of China was founded. Raised in a middle-class family, he went to the prestigious Zhejiang University, studying Chinese literature and, like many of his peers, developing a keen concern for China's cultural reformation. After graduating in 1933, he moved into Shanghai and got a job with a publishing company.

After the success of Tian Han's *Hamlet* in 1922, something of a translation boom had followed, with versions of the plays already familiar to Chinese readers, such as *The Merchant of Venice*, *The Taming of the Shrew*, *As You Like It* and *The Merry Wives of Windsor*, all being redone in the late 1920s, this time with reference to Shakespeare's texts. In literary circles, the next step began to seem urgent: translating the complete works into Mandarin. In 1930, a committee of scholars was set up to address the issue, paid for by American aid money, but struggled to get itself organised. Egged on by his family and his university tutor, Zhu decided to beat the greybeards at their own game. He would do the whole lot himself.

In its way, the project was not dissimilar from the high-speed-rail boom of the 2000s: a way for China to prove that it was the equal of the world. In spring 1935, at the age of twenty-three, Zhu began preparatory work on *The Tempest*, setting himself the Lunatic Liu-style deadline of translating all thirty-six plays in the First Folio in two years. It was an impossible task, but he nonetheless made impressive progress, translating eight texts in the first year.

His timing, however, was desperately unlucky. In July 1937, China was plunged into war with Japan. Just a month after the declaration of hostilities, Shanghai, a plump and attractive target only 500 miles across the East China Sea, came under attack. Fleeing the Japanese advance, Zhu was forced to abandon the substantial library of texts and critical studies he had acquired. Far worse, the translations he'd completed were destroyed when the publisher went up in flames. Undeterred, Zhu seized his one-volume edition of the complete works and a dictionary and found new accommodation, determined to continue his task.

In 1938, he took a job with a newspaper agency, writing anti-Japanese articles during the day and continuing his translations by night. Leading what he later called a 'vagabond's life', he laboriously managed to retranslate the plays he had already done, but in December 1941 Japanese forces swept into the International Settlement. This time, his manuscripts were in the newspaper building. Again, his work was lost.

In 1942, by now married to his university sweetheart, Song Qingru, Zhu devoted himself wholeheartedly to Shakespeare. He and his new wife moved back to Jiaxing and into her family home. Salvaging what manuscripts he could, Zhu redid the comedies for a third time and started work on the remaining texts. Despite poverty and mounting ill-health, he managed to finish a remarkable thirty-one plays in the following twenty months before succumbing to tuberculosis in December 1944, two acts through *Henry V*.

According to his widow, Zhu said, 'Had I known I would not rise again after this illness, I would have exerted all my efforts to complete this translation.' Seven decades on, his versions are still regarded as favourites, endlessly praised for their 'poetic' and 'timelessly Chinese' qualities.

Zhu's story was reported in every book I had read about Shakespeare in China and had often been recirculated by the domestic media. Obviously, irresistibly, it was a David and Goliath tale – a heroic solo effort completed (or very nearly completed) in the face of near-insurmountable odds. It had, too, a strong strain of nationalism; it seemed entirely to the point that Zhu had been a passionate patriot who nobly continued his work despite the depredations of the Japanese.

But was it really true? From the fragments I had gathered, it seemed there was now some kind of museum to Zhu in Jiaxing. The city was only an hour or two outside Shanghai, and I was hopeful that a contact at a university would be able to help. I'd promised to call him as soon as I arrived.

In the meantime, I returned to a subject I'd encountered many times during my travels: the question of translation. How did one actually translate a writer such as Shakespeare? *Could* one really do it?

The English way of looking at it was roughly: no way. The language in which Shakespeare wrote was highly characteristic and particular, a bubbling stew of Anglo-Saxon, legal French, half-remembered schoolboy Latin and Greek, Warwickshire dialect, as well as vocabulary borrowed from the many corners of the world London was beginning to do commerce with.

Then there was what Shakespeare did with the tools at his disposal: his eye and ear for multiple meanings, half-buried senses, assonance and rhythm, beguiling imagery and metaphor. Scholars have long been obsessed by the question of how many words Shakespeare had invented (*excitement, frugal, lacklustre, savagery*: there are more, many of which haven't stuck), but – as with his deft skill at working with pre-existing sources – it was his facility with the language he heard around him that I found more remarkable. He had a sly skill at reanimating ossified meanings, an eagerness to push the most humdrum nouns and verbs in novel directions. His use of the language was so intricate and specialised that it had spawned what was in effect a customised dictionary, C. T. Onions's *A Shakespeare Glossary* (1911), 259 densely packed, double-columned pages.

And that was just vocabulary: things got still more complex when one considered sentence structure, or investigated Shakespeare's remarkable skill at conjuring voices and accents, each as distinct as an inked fingerprint on the page. Then there was his handling of verse, the surge and snap of the iambic line, the complex fugues of rhythms, and more. Although many lines were perfectly comprehensible on the surface, the more one teased apart their warp and weft the richer and more soaked with meaning they seemed. Not for nothing did his Elizabethan contemporary Francis Meres call Shakespeare 'mellifluous and honey-tongued'.

I pulled my copy of the complete works out of my bag and plucked a line almost at random:

To crown my thoughts with acts, be it thought and done [. . .]

Macbeth, act four, scene one. Eleven curt monosyllables, spoken by Macbeth as he decides to storm Macduff's castle and murder his family. I copied the line into my notebook. What mysteries did it contain?

For forty-five minutes, I attempted my own timid piece of translation, from English into English. The closer one analysed the line, the stranger and more slippery it got. Although its gist seemed clear ('To follow up my thoughts with actions, I'll attack Macduff's castle'), its deeper meaning kept slipping out of focus, like the illusory dagger that leads Macbeth to Duncan's bedchamber.

'Be it thought and done' was a pat phrase, the equivalent of 'no sooner said than done', but, doubleness being a major theme in *Macbeth*, the line also seems to toy with the double meanings of the words *crown* (the verb 'to add the finishing touch to' and the noun 'royal crown') and *act* ('actions' but also, metatheatrically, 'performance'). But it was the sentence structure that caught the ear, a weaselling piece of subjunctive grammar ('be it thought') that announced Macbeth's *intention* to make his intentions actions without ever fully admitting ownership – arguably the play's dominant theme. Spoken in a handful of seconds, the line was nonchalant in its brilliance. I couldn't begin to imagine how one might do it justice in another form.

And how did one do so in Chinese? Mandarin wasn't even the most complex of Sinitic languages, and, from the little I understood of its make-up, already seemed forbiddingly remote; not only because of the 20,000 characters regularly in use (with another 60,000 in reserve), but its strict tonal system, its huge variety of syllables, its thickets of compound nouns ('wash-hair essence' for shampoo, 'separate/combine device' for a car's clutch, 'protect risk' for insurance).

The great literary critic William Empson – also, as it happened, a devoted sinologist who spent years in China – produced a witty catalogue of Shakespearian language in *The Structure of Complex Words* (1951), attempting to unpick every meaning of the word 'sense' in *Measure for Measure*. Ingenious as he was, Empson cheerfully admitted one could never quite get to the end of *sense*'s senses, which ranged from 'sound good sense' to carnal sensuality, with every shade of meaning in between. 'Almost all of them,' he wrote, 'carry forward a puzzle which is essential to [the play's] thought.' Surely that puzzle would be utterly insoluble in Chinese?

Zhu Shenghao, writing in the months before he died, had been clear about what he had tried to accomplish, and even clearer on what he could not:

> I did my best to conserve the flavour and features of the style of the original. In case I failed to reach this goal, I would try to communicate the ideas . . . clearly and faithfully in an elegant and comprehensible Chinese. I considered it indecent to translate word for word without expressing the ingenuity and vigour of the original.
>
> Whenever I felt unable to render an English sentence into Chinese adequately, I would work a long time on it, and strive to reveal the English poet's ideas clearly, risking a completely different arrangement of the words of the original sentence. Every time I finished translating a paragraph, I used to read it carefully as [if I were] the first reader . . . [to see] if there were any ambiguities, and at the same time I would consider myself an actor for examining if the tone of the version was harmonious and the rhythm agreeable.

This is a thoughtful and flexible philosophy, unusually alive to the fact that Shakespeare's texts are scripts designed to be performed. But Zhu was working at a fearsome pace – twenty-five-odd plays in under two years, if the stories were to be believed – and whatever agonising he did must have been cursory at best. Also, he was vague on the details: what did 'features of the style' mean when one was transforming Early Modern English into Modern Standard Chinese? How was it possible to paraphrase 'clearly and faithfully' if the English version, as I'd discovered, was often anything but clear? The 'ingenuity and vigour' of Shakespeare's language one could certainly agree on, but it demanded as much ingenuity again from the translator, if not many times more.

I looked up from my tray-table. By now we were well south of Nanjing. The Yangtze river, the colour of mulligatawny soup and crowded with barges, flashed by faster than I could reach for my camera. The journey had been so smoothly rapid that whenever we paused at a station I had the vertiginous sensation that the landscape was continuing to move. Buried in my books, I had failed even to make it to the dining car.

When the doors hissed open, the humidity was like being smothered by a warm, wet sponge. It had been late winter when I'd got on the train. In Shanghai, the best part of a thousand miles south, we'd skipped to early summer. As I pulled my case through Hongqiao station, appallingly vast, I found myself shedding clothes. By the time I had got up to ground level, my jacket was gone; a half-kilometre further, so were my jumper and overshirt. By the time I settled myself into the ripped mustard upholstery of an elderly Volkswagen taxi, I had an armful of redundant clothes. The driver eyed me dubiously. It looked as though I had attempted a striptease on the concourse.

At the hotel I made enquiries about a trip to visit the museum at Jiaxing, but in the meantime I had an appointment with a modern Zhu Shenghao: Professor Zhang Chong of Fudan University, one of China's most august academic institutions. Zhang was part of the team behind yet another complete works. First published under the general editorship of the respected Chinese scholar Fang Ping in 2000, it had recently been updated.

I found Zhang in a spartan, modern office on the main Fudan campus. Like the office, Zhang was neat and unshowy, a slim figure in a dark checked shirt with sleeves folded tidily above the elbows. High eyebrows and a bald crown gave him an expression of polite, mole-like surprise. Every so often, the eyebrows would jump far above his glasses and he would look sorely troubled; more often, his enthusiasm was difficult to contain. He was that rarest of creatures, a scholar who was also a born teacher.

His translation career had begun, unusually, with *The Two Noble Kinsmen*, the neglected and troubling tragicomedy, co-written with John Fletcher, that was almost certainly Shakespeare's final contribution to the stage. On a visiting fellowship to Harvard in the early 1990s, Zhang had come across the play in an American edition. Not having read it before, he excitedly assumed this was some kind of rediscovered text; then realised it was simply that it had never been translated into Chinese. He'd done it himself for fun. He had gone on to tackle *The Winter's Tale*, *Cymbeline* and *Pericles*. Obsessed with the late plays, he was a man after my own heart.

Before we got down to the nitty-gritty of how this all worked, he wanted to show me a thin paperback. It was a facsimile of Tian Han's *Hamlet* of 1922, the first complete Shakespearian playtext published in China, the original now enormously rare. The cover was a riot of Chinese characters, but I had no trouble decoding the frontispiece – an engraving of Shakespeare derived from the so-called 'Chandos' portrait in the National Portrait Gallery in London. Even though most contemporary experts now thought it was a portrait of someone other than Shakespeare, its rugged, dashing features had attracted generations of admirers. It was an unexpected pleasure to see it here.

Zhu Shenghao was far from alone, Zhang explained: a number of heroic translation projects had been initiated in the 1930s, with varying degrees of success. A translator called Cao Wei Feng had had a similar idea in 1930, and hit similar obstacles to Zhu; he had only finished eleven plays, which were eventually published in 1943. Liang Shiqiu had also gone his own way, and taken even longer to finish – after being forced to relocate to Taiwan with Chiang Kai-shek, leader of the Republic, and the Nationalists after the 1949 Revolution, he didn't finish his translations until 1967. There were now at least five separate versions of the complete works available in Mandarin, and many more plays had been translated individually. A few translations were in verse; most – following Zhu – were in prose. With such bounteous options already in circulation, one had to wonder why on earth the British government was spending £1.5 million doing it all again. But then of course that was all about politics, and very little to do with plays.

The challenges to effective translation were almost innumerable, sighed Zhang: it was hard to know where to begin. First one had to choose a source text, a ticklish question in itself. He himself followed the popular American Riverside complete works, but cross-checked it with the new Oxford edition. There were countless differences.

Once you had decided what to translate, the next difficulty was the words themselves. Translators distinguished between 'dynamic equivalence' and 'formal equivalence' – sense-for-sense rather than word-for-word – but in practice the distinction was hazy, especially for a writer such as Shakespeare, who used words with such profound awareness of their teemingly multiple senses.

As straightforward a line as Lear's 'Nothing will come of nothing' was surprisingly laborious, owing to the fact that Mandarin has no single nounal form for 'nothing'. The closest one could get was 'not having anything', which has rather a weaker ring. The most famous phrase in the canon, 'To be or not to be', despite its apparent simplicity, posed exquisite nightmares for Chinese translators. English is unusual in having a verb form that encompasses the concept of being alive, and the much broader ontological sense, to do with the state of *being* – so is Hamlet here riddling about the nature of existence, or deciding whether to stab himself in the chest? In Chinese you couldn't have both. A tantalising interpretational knot had to be sliced through.

Metaphors were another stumbling block, either requiring laborious spelling-out or modification into something else entirely. Isabella's description of the 'glassy essence' of man's nature in *Measure for Measure* ('His glassy essence, like an angry ape | Plays such fantastic tricks before high heaven | As makes the angels weep') posed such a dilemma. The image of shattering fragility was lost when one used the most straightforward Chinese equivalent, which implied 'soft/yielding nature'. Zhu Shenghao had translated this as *liu-li-yi-sui-de-ben-xing* ('the nature [of human beings] that is easily broken like ancient glass tiles'), which had a nicely Chinese ring, but hardly tripped off the tongue.

Zhang smiled. 'And of course we are talking here only about Mandarin. China has over fifty ethnic groups, hundreds of dialects. In Hong Kong they speak Cantonese, which is even more complicated, more tones . . .'

Because of the pronunciation differences between English and Mandarin (notably Mandarin's lack of an *r* sound resembling the one in English) characters' names had to be rendered phonetically, with a great deal of approximation: 'Luomiou' for Romeo and 'Luoselin' for Rosaline, 'Hamuleite' or 'Hanmolaide' for Hamlet. And what to do with Bottom in *A Midsummer Night's Dream*? Some translators took the coward's way out and simply called him *Zhigong*, 'Weaver'. Zhang's colleague Fang Ping had come up with *Xiantuan-er*, meaning 'reel of thread', with its connotations of going on and on (as Bottom does). This was clever, but lacked the earthy scatological pun of the original. Bawdiness – one of Shakespeare's abiding talents – was a major problem for early Chinese translators such as Zhu, who drew a discreet veil over many of the dirtiest words.

Zhang smiled again, this time a little grimly. 'You see, it is very interesting. These are the dilemmas of translation.'

Painful decisions about metre followed. Zhu had simply aimed for readable Chinese prose, but Fang Ping and his team decided to attempt something more sophisticated – a verse form that echoed the original. For all the richness of classical Chinese poetry, there is nothing that resembles the muscular and flexible ten-syllabic structure of Shakespearian blank verse, a 'mighty line' forged by Christopher Marlowe and purpose-designed to echo around Elizabethan theatres. An entirely new scheme had to be concocted.

After long months of trial and error, Fang developed a strict ten-syllable system, using caesuras or breaks to replicate the *di-dum, di-dum, di-dum, di-dum, di-dum* pulse of iambic pentameter. It was devilishly complicated to work in. Zhang showed me an example from *Romeo and Juliet*, Friar Lawrence's response to Romeo's admission that he has abandoned his early love for Rosaline and fallen for the beauteous Juliet. The original sits alongside a literal back-translation:

> The sun | not yet | thy sighs | from hea- | ven clears.
> Thy old groans | yet ring | in | mine an- | cient ears.
> Lo, here | upon | thy cheek | the stain | doth sit
> Of an | old tear | that is | not washed | off yet.

> tai-yang-hai | wei-ba-ni | tan-xi-de | yun-wu | sao-jin
> *the sun has not made your sighs' cloud clear*
> wo-er-bian | hai-xiang-she | ni-na | shen-yin-de | hui-yin
> *in my ear still ring your groaning echoes*
> qiao, | jiu-zai-ni | lian-shang | wo-yi-ran | neng-bian-ren
> *look, just on your face I still can see*
> ni-na | shang-mei-you | tui-jin-de | xi-ri-de | lei-hen
> *your still-haven't-disappeared old time's tears*

In order to keep within the verse structure, even more compromises had to be made: colourful images abandoned, precise equivalences painfully rejected. It was like re-tailoring a suit jacket to someone else's body; you painstakingly let out a hem or made a tiny adjustment to a sleeve, only to find the back had ripped in two without you noticing.

Zhang looked rueful. 'Because of the differences of the language, you can only translate as much as possible. So that leaves much work for teachers and students. That is why I always advise my students, if possible, do not read the Chinese translation.'

He was a translator who advised his students not to read translations?

He shrugged. 'Translation is always inadequate. At *best*, it's inadequate. At worst, it's misleading, quite misleading. So keep to the original.'

Nonetheless, he was optimistic about the state of Shakespeare in China, something new translations could only help. Just the other week he had taken part in a flash mob to mark the 450th anniversary of Shakespeare's birth and World Book Day. Academics and actors had crowded into central Shanghai to read from the works in both Chinese and English.

He proudly pulled out his commemorative copy of *Life Week*. I hadn't been able to find one in Beijing; this was the first time I'd seen it. There Shakespeare was, cover boy – a cartoonish rendering, done in lurid green, depicting the playwright sitting pensively in a fireside chair, the characters he'd created writhing through the smoke. The issue featured long articles on his life, Chinese interpretations of the plays, competing translations and much more.

'Just a couple of days ago, a student wrote to me. She never believed that she would be interested in Shakespeare because he was such a classic, and because he wrote in ancient English. She came to a couple of sessions in my class, we studied the language and talked about translations.' His eyes gleamed. 'She found great fun in Shakespeare!'

He was keen to show me the grounds. In the spring sunshine we strolled across tidy walkways and green lawns. At the centre of the university complex was a huge statue of Mao, one of the few still standing in Shanghai. The chairman stood to attention, greatcoat austerely buttoned, an inscrutable smile playing across his lips. He seemed to be enjoying some private joke.

I thought suddenly of Solomon Plaatje in South Africa. It must be risky, I said, being a translator: bridging two cultures, one was always at risk of being stranded.

Zhang chuckled. 'You know the story? The central translation bureau were asked by the government to retranslate the complete works of Marx and Engels into Chinese. The translations needed updating, they had not been looked at for years. When the new translators looked into the text, they found the original translators had made so many errors – Marx didn't mean that, Engels didn't mean that! A catastrophe, the whole thing would have to be redone. But when they produced the report saying this, the Party decided to forget the whole project and bury it.'

His smile was broader than ever. 'It would have called into question the entire Chinese Revolution!'

As the photograph of Yan'an I'd seen back in Beijing testified, the Great Helmsman had shown a sizeable degree of interest in literature and art, even before the Revolution. A speech he had given at the conference in 1942 outlined what he described as 'the proper relationship between our work in the artistic and literary fields and our revolutionary work in general'. The principles will be familiar to anyone acquainted with Soviet socialist realism. 'Elitist art' that served the 'exploiters and oppressors' should be overturned, in favour of an ideological art aimed at the toiling masses. (In 1949, perhaps as many as 80 per cent of China's population was illiterate.) As well as promulgating revolutionary art, Mao placed artists and intellectuals alike on stern notice:

> Experts should be respected; they are very valuable to our cause. But we should also remind them that no revolutionary artist or writer can produce any work of significance unless he has contact with the masses, gives expression to their thoughts and feelings, and becomes their loyal spokesman.

At first it seemed likely that Shakespeare could be recruited to this brave socialist mission. Rubber-stamped by Marx and Engels, swooned over by Russian academics, he experienced an astonishing boom in popularity in the years after the 1949 Revolution. Having finally been published in twelve volumes in 1954, a decade after his death, Zhu Shenghao's translations were rapidly reprinted, with as many as 300,000 copies sold by the early 1960s. Perhaps another 200,000 copies of individual plays entered circulation.

The works also benefited from an upswing of interest in theatre, created when Mao, eager to revive Chinese culture, diverted state resources to set up drama schools and troupes. Perhaps 160 companies came into being in the first decades of the People's Republic, with Shakespeare and other western dramatists providing the core of the repertoire. Courtesy of the cosy relationship with Russia, Shakespeare also began to appear on Chinese movie screens, with nationwide screenings of Sergei Yutkevich's *Othello* (1955) and Laurence Olivier's

Hamlet (1948) and *Richard III* (1955). (Many people I met, especially those over the age of fifty, still spoke of Olivier – '*Aolifo*' – in honoured terms.)

May 1956 was when things began to get more complicated. Uttering the words, 'Let a hundred flowers blossom and a hundred schools of thought contend,' Mao announced a welcome switch in policy. Narrow ideological observance was out, to be replaced by a spirit of openness and tolerance. The Party could be criticised, new thoughts aired, particularly by intellectuals – many of whom did exactly that, mounting increasingly vocal attacks on the way China was being run. As his critics flooded into the open, Mao abruptly ordered a U-turn. (It is an open debate whether this had, in fact, been the intention all along.) In the crackdown that followed, opposition leaders were dispatched to labour camps or executed. The revised version of Mao's speech noted balefully there were both 'fragrant flowers and poisonous weeds'. The year it was delivered, 1957, the chairman published his own collection of artful poetry in classical Chinese forms. No irony was apparent.

The Hundred Flowers campaign paled beside what came next. Mao's Great Proletarian Cultural Revolution, launched in Shanghai in August 1966, engulfed the People's Republic. Schools were closed, fanatical young Red Guards dispatched to attack the 'four olds' (old ideas, old customs, old habits, old culture). Schoolchildren were urged to denounce parents, married couples to turn on each other. Revolution became anarchy. Millions were sent to work in the fields or factories, or imprisoned. Over a million more died. The catastrophic economic reforms of the Great Leap Forward (1958–61) may have killed more people – as many as 45 million dead in four years – but the Cultural Revolution tore China apart from top to bottom.

Teachers and academics ('the same old corpses', in the chairman's chilling phrase) were rounded up and forced to do penance, or simply shot. Shakespeare was suddenly regarded as an anti-revolutionary influence. As early as January 1964, an article in the government-controlled newspaper *Liberation* argued that 'to suppose that Shakespeare is some sort of god who cannot be surpassed is to lose direction and proceed contrary to the spirit of this epoch'.

Among millions of books, the Shanghai Theatre Academy's historic copy of *Rou quan*, that early version of *The Merchant of Venice*, was consumed by the flames. Tian Han, the revered playwright who had translated *Hamlet* as an honour to his country, was denounced as a 'bourgeois revisionist' and tortured.

Although nearly all foreign authors were banned, it seems that special venom was reserved for Shakespeare. I had difficulty working out why, until I came across the story of Jiang Qing, better known as Madame Mao. Jiang was instrumental in the Cultural Revolution: it was at her behest that 'anti-revolutionary art' was banned, a category that initially covered plays and books criticising the Party, but which grew to encompass anything she deemed unacceptable. Mao's doctor, Zhisui Li, claimed that Jiang had once spent a long conversation with him listing Shakespeare's shortcomings, and arguing that the works of a long-dead Englishman had no place in a progressive, forward-looking country like China. 'Just because Shakespeare's plays have ghosts doesn't mean we have to have ghosts too,' she said, warning him to 'pay attention' to her words. 'The chairman has discovered many problems in literature and art.'

In 1964, cancelling plans for the celebration of the 400th anniversary of Shakespeare's birth, Jiang announced a national festival of '*Jingju* on Contemporary Themes'. It launched the movement for so-called Revolutionary Operas, which junked the 'emperors, kings, generals, chancellors, maidens and beauties' of traditional *jingju*. Replacing them were storylines that venerated the People's Liberation Army, the stout courage of the masses and – naturally – Mao himself.

Titles like *Taking Tiger Mountain by Strategy*, *The Red Detachment of Women* and *Raid on the White Tiger Regiment* displaced everything else from Chinese stages for the entirety of the Cultural Revolution, as well as appearing on posters, cigarette cases, stamps, school curriculums and being blasted from loudspeakers in every public place. Although more operas were eventually written, the well-worn joke was that for ten years 800 million people watched eight shows.

It shouldn't have been surprising to learn that Jiang had been an actor in a previous life. Having come to Shanghai in 1933 to perform professionally, one of her most successful stage roles had been Nora in *A Doll's House*, after which she had become well-known in movies. Long before meeting Mao, she had tried to catch the attention of Tian Han, then one of the biggest names in Shanghai drama, but felt slighted by him; some have speculated that his downfall thirty years later had been Jiang's way of getting revenge. Perhaps this was also why she had taken such an exception to Shakespeare. As far as I could make out, Jiang had never appeared in one of his plays. It seems a pity. She would surely have made a fine Lady Macbeth.

One afternoon, having coffee with a theatre producer at the Shanghai Dramatic Arts Centre, I played a game. I had heard many dire stories about censorship in contemporary China, and wanted to know where the boundaries really lay.

Could one criticise the government on stage? He shrugged. 'Happens all the time.' Senior officials? 'Generally OK. Lot of people hate them.' Make fun of Mao? 'Not a problem, ancient history.' Sex, violence, swearing? His grin was broad. 'Nudity a problem, but we do our best.' How about a play on Tibet or the Hundred Flowers Campaign? The grin disappeared. 'That might cause you issues.'

It is easy to be scandalised by a world in which some things are regarded as too sensitive to put in a theatre. In Britain, since the 1968 Theatre Act, it has been more or less impossible to get anything taken off stage for reasons other than obscenity or libel. Following the chaotic, embarrassing court case over Edward Bond's 1965 play *Saved*, which had caused controversy for – among much else – a scene in which a baby is stoned to death, the ancient right of a royal flunky to censor plays prior to performance was revoked. The day after the Act was passed and the Lord Chamberlain's powers annulled, the musical *Hair*, with its copious scenes of hippyish nudity, opened in the West End. English drama was henceforth allowed to let it all hang out. Barring intermittent assaults on freedom of speech such as the witch-hunts mounted by the House Un-American Activities Committee during the 1940s and 1950s, in contemporary American drama things are, if anything, freer still.

Shakespeare would have found such freedoms astonishing. Operating in conditions infinitely more tense and circumscribed than those of the modern west, playwrights of the Elizabethan and Jacobean eras worked in continual fear of losing their livelihoods, or much more. When a scabrous comedy called *The Isle of Dogs* ('a lewd plaie . . . contayninge very seditious and sclanderous matter') went on stage in summer 1597, not only was every London theatre temporarily closed, but some of the cast were also flung in jail. Ben Jonson, who had co-written the script, only narrowly escaped having his nostrils slashed and his ears cut off.

Back in 1581, Elizabeth I had appointed Edmund Tilney as the Master of the Revels (the Lord Chamberlain's antecedent) and issued a patent requiring 'all and every plaier or plaiers . . . to presente and recite before our said Servant' every new script before performance would be allowed. Tilney ran the Revels office until his death in 1610, nearly all the years in which Shakespeare was writing for the stage.

The rules over what might give offence were vaguer and consequently more terrifying than anything dreamed up by the most capricious and power-hungry Communist Party apparatchik, and required sophisticated antennae. Foul or overtly sexual language was discouraged (one reason among many Shakespeare became so adept at puns). So was material that might incite sedition or which criticised the Church of England and/or the monarch. The scurrilous anti-Scottish jokes of the city comedy *Eastward Ho* (1605) caused George Chapman and Ben Jonson (again) to be clapped in jail for offending James I, which so petrified Jonson's mother that she prepared poison for him in case he received a death sentence. Offending powerful courtiers was likewise a bad idea, if one wanted to hang on to one's ears.

Shakespeare suffered nothing so extreme, but he certainly had tangles with authority. Around the early 1590s, still making his name as a dramatist, he contributed to a co-written play, *Sir Thomas More*, on the life of the Catholic martyr, which never got past the censor. As well as providing what appears to be the only source of Shakespeare's handwriting on a playtext, the manuscript, now in the British Library, is notable for Tilney's exasperated annotations.

Another incident occurred a few years later when Shakespeare adopted the name Sir John Oldcastle for the corpulent knight in an early version of *Henry IV Part I* – the same name as a fourteenth-century martyr. Oldcastle's descendants hotly objected, whereupon Shakespeare scrambled to change Oldcastle to Falstaff. There also appears to have been controversy concerning the abdication scene in *Richard II*, which disappears altogether from early printed quartos, presumably too sensitive to perform while Elizabeth I – sometimes compared to the profligate, corrupt, childless Richard – was on the throne.

Bad language, then as now, was a constant source of vexation. In 1606, a new Act 'to Restrain Abuses of Players' was passed, levying a fine of £10 for every time an actor 'jestingly or profanely' took the name of the Lord in vain. Shakespeare's scripts, in common with everyone else's, were scrubbed clean of references to God or Jesus Christ, and many of the mealy-mouthed euphemisms that resulted are enshrined in the 1623 First Folio ('O heaven!' for 'O God', 'O why!' for 'zounds'/'God's wounds' and so on). Generally, however, Shakespeare's antennae (and ears) were in excellent working order, judging by how rarely he appears to have troubled Tilney or his successor George Buck.

One reason I'd first thought of following Shakespeare around the world was that he rarely set plays in his own country or during his own times, something I'd interpreted as evidence of his eager curiosity about the world beyond English shores. It was that, certainly, but of course there was another reason too. Setting plays in far-flung destinations – Vienna, Verona, Venice – and writing about Italian or French nobles rather than their English equivalents was a matter of professional caution. It offered something extremely useful for a playwright who wanted to keep his nose un-slit: the cloak of deniability.

I liked Shanghai: I liked its way of doing business, its style, its brazenness, its bling. From everything I'd read about China's most thrusting modern city, I'd expected a landscape entirely composed of jutting skyscrapers and futuristic steel spires. Skyscrapers and spires there were, more every week, but the city also looked delightfully jumbled, as if someone had negligently dropped a few arrondissements of Paris into the bustling heart of Asia.

After the inhuman grid of Beijing there was something comforting about the clutter of the French Concession, the way knock-off clothing shops sat hugger-mugger with chic boutiques, bicycle-repair stalls next to tiny French bakeries. Cranes and building sites were cheek by jowl with streets of wooden-framed houses, the skies between the buildings congested by power lines and brash overhead signs. Going for drinks at the rooftop bar at the Peninsula hotel on the Bund, Shanghai's waterfront, was pleasant – a triumphal avenue of water sparkling with a futuristic light show – but it was in the crammed and clamorous avenues of Xuhui, the heart of the old French district, that I felt most at home. I wandered late into the warm night among the barbecue stands and the hole-in-the-walls, where wizened men sat sharpening knives or repairing clothes with foot-pedal Singers.

Most of all I liked watching the fashion-obsessed millennial kids of Shanghai, in tribes as anthropologically distinct as anything analysed by Claude Lévi-Strauss: scowling 1950s-style Teddy boys with gelled quiffs; art-studenty girls in ra-ra skirts and cowboy boots; preppy, fey-looking kids in blazers, moon-sized spectacles, bow-ties and loafers. Gourmandising on sticky pork dumplings, I sat for hours at open-windowed bars, watching the Shanghai *passeggiata* in its pomp.

Despite extensive attempts, I'd failed to get hold of Zhang Yiyi, the young Shanghainese author supposedly spending RMB 1.5 million on plastic surgery to make himself look like Shakespeare, the ultimate act of Bardic tribute. It turned out Zhang had a reputation for crazed publicity stunts designed to do well on social media. Even when he did appear in front of the public many months after I left, showing off his remodelled eyes, nose and lips, it was hard to spot the difference.

But I wondered if the city made sense of something else that had been bugging me: why *was* it that *The Merchant of Venice* was so popular in China? Although I had come to doubt the statistic that 21 million Chinese fourteen-year-olds studied the trial scene from the play (the figure turned out to have been cooked up by the Beijing office of the British Council and took little account of teaching in different provinces), many people I asked had been set excerpts from the text at school.

History was obviously part of it. *The Merchant of Venice* was one of the earliest Shakespearian scripts to be rehearsed by Chinese students in the nineteenth century, which perhaps encouraged Lin Shu to make *Rou quan* ('Bond of Flesh') the very first story in *An English Poet Reciting from Afar*. An adaptation of *Rou quan* was also the earliest professional Shakespeare production ever to be staged in Shanghai in 1913. In 1930, when it came to staging the first faithful translation of a Shakespeare text, the Shanghai Drama Assembly chose, once again, *The Merchant of Venice*.

On the face of it, it seemed strange that a script now seen as being primarily about anti-Semitism had found a home in an entirely different cultural context, China, a place moreover where the Jewish population was tiny. As I'd found, it was a similar issue in India, where *The Merchant of Venice* had likewise been hugely (to my mind surprisingly) popular.

As in Kolkata, I wondered whether Shanghai's history might have something to do with it. One of the few ports to be opened to western influence in the nineteenth century, the city became a pivot for international trade, and Jewish businesses were among the first to set up in the foreign concessions. The Sassoon family – known as the 'Rothschilds of the East' and based in Mumbai – traded in tea, cotton and opium, and set up profitable outposts in Shanghai, Canton (now Guangzhou) and Hong Kong. Other Jews followed, swelled by Ashkenazi emigration from Russia in the late nineteenth century. After the Russian Revolution, the Jewish population of Shanghai was small but influential, with several synagogues and yeshivas. The Jewish population of the city numbered perhaps 25,000 before the founding of the People's Republic forced nearly all non-Chinese to flee.

Was it any surprise the Shanghainese developed such a passion for this play, set in a seething entrepôt that so closely resembled their own? No doubt the concept of a woman donning the garments of a lawyer was an exotic attraction (Zheng Yuxiu, often described as China's 'first female lawyer', had an office in Shanghai in the 1920s and 1930s), and perhaps the Jewish element also struck some chord of familiarity.

But it wasn't just that. Venice was a byword for global trade in the Renaissance, as was Shanghai in the early twentieth century. The merchant of the title, Antonio, has fingers in as many pies and 'argosies' (merchant ships) in as many ports as any Chinese import-export business. There is languid talk of Tripolis, Mexico, the Indies. Shylock has bought jewels in Frankfurt. Even the wealthy heiress Portia, waiting in Belmont for a deal to be done over her marital future, receives suitors from as far afield as North Africa, France, Germany, Spain, Scotland and England.

As Marxist critics delight in pointing out, the language of value is hard-wired into the play; indeed, one of its central tensions is whether the word 'worth' applies to a moral-cum-spiritual condition, or is a matter of cold cash. 'Nor is the wide world ignorant of her worth,' says the young blade Bassanio of Portia: a Shakespearian double meaning if ever there were one. Everyone is indebted to someone else – Bassanio to Antonio, Antonio to Shylock, Antonio and Bassanio to the disguised Portia, who rescues Antonio from the terrible consequences of the loan he has taken out. The network of financial and emotional obligation winds around and across the story until it enmeshes everyone.

Scanning headlines about the newly established Shanghai free-trade zone, the surging property market, unrestricted foreign exchange, the global companies rushing to invest, I wondered whether a piece of the Rialto wasn't being created right here on the river Huangpu.

Perhaps there was also a clue here about the object of my journey – understanding Shakespeare's place in the world and how it came about. Cultural thinkers have borrowed the (strikingly ugly) postmodern philosophical term 'rhizomatic' as one explanation for Shakespeare's global omnipresence. The word comes from *rhizome*, a botanical word for a variety of plant that, instead of shooting its roots down and growing up, sends them out in many different directions at once. These roots then send out leaves, in effect becoming new plants of their own, adjusting to local conditions and after time growing into something quite different. Consequently they are nearly impossible to eradicate: chop off one section and another will simply sprout again somewhere else. For globalisation theorists, a rhizomatic way of looking at the world is to see it as an interconnected network with no beginning, end or obvious centre, and where the connected points are all of equal importance.

Despite the implication that Shakespeare had become the Japanese knotweed or al-Qaeda of global culture, I found it a powerful idea – an image of his influence as a series of interconnected stems rather than deriving from a single 'authentic' source, rooted in one place and time. Not a doughty British oak whose leaf canopy stretches across the world, but an ever-flourishing, ever-changing plant that belongs to many places simultaneously. *The Merchant of Venice*, a complex lattice of money and emotional relations, is surely a rhizomatic text, particularly in China, filtered through the Lambs' nineteenth-century *Tales*, themselves imported via the Japanese. One could say the same of many other plays, too, themselves based on a collage of pre-existing sources. I thought of C. J. Sisson's line, written about Indian drama but surely applicable to almost everything I'd come across since beginning my journeys in Germany: 'things that are still alive and in process of becoming new things, being ever born again . . .'

Back in the UK, a director had recently set a production of *The Merchant of Venice* in a version of Las Vegas, converting ducats to dollars and casting Shylock as a casino moneylender. Many British critics had been aghast, rejecting this as a global transposition too far. I wondered how they would react if someone set the play right here in Shanghai.

At the station gates a stooped, crumpled-looking figure was waiting. He was dressed in a frayed grey jacket and rubber boots cut off at the ankle. His hair was thinning; above an open, somewhat boyish face his eyebrows were dark and thick, giving him an expression of mild alarm. Between his fingers he was twisting a furled umbrella.

Ya Zhou, my translator, rushed towards him: Zhu Shenghao's only son, now in his seventies. My contact had managed to get in touch with the family, who were only too delighted for me to visit the house museum in Jiaxing. A tour of the city library, where his manuscripts were now preserved, had also been arranged. Zhu Shanggang, the son, would meet us from the train.

Lifting the umbrella to ward off the spattering drizzle, he bowed repeatedly as he directed us towards the car, smiling anxiously in my direction. I had the uncomfortable sensation that I had been promoted to VIP status without my knowledge.

Fifteen minutes later we were at the museum: an ample farmhouse surrounding an open courtyard, now on a busy and featureless main road. As we went inside, we were descended on by a photographer, a woman from the local government culture department and a small flock of assistants. Attempting to get into the role of visiting dignitary, I seized the hand of a man who turned out to be the gardener. Everyone laughed gaily. At least it broke the ice.

As the museum and its entourage indicated, Zhu had attained a special position in the pantheon of Chinese literature, far above what might be expected of an amateur translator who had died in obscure rural poverty at the age of thirty-two. His versions of Shakespeare had now sold millions of copies – which meant, if my maths was correct, he was probably the world's most read Shakespearian translator in any language. The first translations to reach a mass Chinese audience, Zhu's were so popular that even seasoned scholars favoured them over later, more faithful versions – or, in some cases, the English texts.

While Zhu would no doubt have been gratified by this success, it was clear as Zhu Shanggang talked that it had been in some sense his mission. The lack of a serviceable translation of Shakespeare into Chinese was especially keenly felt because Japan, yet again, had got there first: Tsubouchi Shōyō had translated the complete plays and sonnets in 1928.

'He wrote a letter to my uncle to tell him of this matter,' said Zhu Shanggang. 'My uncle told him that some Japanese people said that China is a country without culture because they have no Shakespeare translations – so if you can translate Shakespeare into Chinese you will be a national hero.'

Where rival translators had expressed despair at the difficulties (one wrote that 'the pain caused by translation is no less than that

of delivering a child'), Zhu found the task ennobling. He wrote to
Qingru, Zhu Shanggang's mother, that working on *The Tempest* was
so absorbing that he failed to notice being bitten by bedbugs. Even the
loss of his manuscripts twice over failed to dent his optimism: 'I am
very poor, but I have everything!' Qingru later reported he had said.

Why had Zhu chosen Shakespeare? I asked Zhu Shanggang.

He smiled gently, showing a cemetery of yellowing teeth. 'Of course
he liked many English authors, like Shelley, Wordsworth, and Keats.
But he loved Shakespeare: he read the plays more than ten times from
beginning to end. Once this task got started, it was a huge project. You
cannot stop in the middle and give up.'

I studied the large photograph of Qingru and Zhu that dominated
the museum. He looked suave and faintly cocky, almost implausibly
youthful, with slicked-back hair; but it was she who held the eye – alert
and engaged, with a bright, avid gaze.

It turned out that Zhu Shanggang's mother had a far greater role than
advertised. A talented linguist and a published poet, she not only nursed
her husband in his frantic final months but edited his manuscripts,
negotiating with publishers to ensure that their great life's work would
not turn to dust. I didn't possess the linguistic skills to confirm it, but I
had a hunch that anyone doing detailed research into the translations
credited to Zhu would find Qingru's fingerprints all over them.

In 1947, three years after Zhu's death and once Shanghai was back
under Chinese rule following the end of the war, twenty-seven of his
translations were published in three volumes. The rest followed in 1954,
bringing the total to thirty-one plays out of the thirty-six in the First
Folio. The plan was for the remaining texts to be completed as China's
contribution to the 400th anniversary in 1964. One of Zhu's colleagues,
Yu Erchang, set about the task.

But Mao's officials – or, as I thought, Mao's wife – intervened. By the
time Yu Erchang finished his work, it was 1966, the beginning of the
Cultural Revolution. It became impossible to circulate the translations
in China proper. It was not until 1978 that Zhu Shenghao's completed
texts were finally published in Beijing, two years after Mao's death and
forty-three years after they were started.

In the house, the air was thick with the smell of fresh paint. The
museum had recently been restored, but it only served to emphasise
how little of Zhu Shenghao remained. In one glass case were his grey
cloth boots, worn with age. In another was the battered wicker case

in which he'd hauled his books during the flight from Shanghai. Up a wooden flight of stairs, precipitously narrow, was the desk where he'd done most of the work. Fifteen minutes and we'd seen the lot.

Zhu's precious one-volume copy of Shakespeare was now under lock and key, but the view from his study was intact, over a quiet courtyard of trees, their leaves a vibrant green. Pretending to investigate his torn copies of *The Merry Wives of Windsor*, an American import, and Thomas Hardy, I listened to the sighing of the leaves and the spatter of the rain. The title of the Hardy was *Life's Little Ironies*.

After a ceremonious and drawn-out lunch in a local restaurant, we were driven to Jiaxing's central library, where a group of white-gloved female archivists were hovering in an upstairs room. Warily they pulled out a number of small parcels, wrapped in white paper and tied with ribbons like gifts. Inside were exercise books bound with brown parcel paper. Zhu Shanggang carefully teased one open: *The Tempest*, the first play his father had translated. The yellowing pages were as thin as tracing paper.

Ben Jonson famously claimed of Shakespeare that 'the players have often mentioned it as an honour ... that in his writing (whatsoever he penned), he never blotted out a line'. Zhu really did seem to have barely blotted a line, particularly as his translations progressed – page after page filled with neat rivulets of text in a quick, precise hand.

The Mandarin I had no grasp of, but it was impossible not to admire the density of the work. Dark black characters were scribbled right into the spines of the books, crowding the sides and spilling on to the scrap paper that had been used to bind them. The homemade cover of *Romeo and Juliet* was a page cut from an English-language Shanghai newspaper, including a gory story about a sixteen-year-old apprentice murdering his master with a 'large butcher's knife' in the German Concession.

I had arrived in Jiaxing sceptical about the claim that Zhu had really translated thirty-one plays in less than two years, but this part of the story seemed to be absolutely true: there was barely time, or paper, for anything else. Thirty-one plays in twenty months – a play every two and a half weeks. Liang Shiqiu's translation, the one Penguin China had their eye on, had taken its author thirty-eight years. By any standards, not only those of a man succumbing to TB, Zhu's was an awesome achievement.

This wasn't to say it was perfect. It was a delicate fact that, while not quite blotted with errors, Zhu's translations – done with a tiny handful of reference books – were creative, and sometimes plain wrong. A few days earlier yet another translator, Yiqun Wang, had taken me line by line through different versions of *Julius Caesar* and *Coriolanus*, sorrowfully pointing out places where Zhu had either ignored the primary sense of Shakespeare's lines or apparently misconstrued them, mistaking words and sometimes entire concepts.

I raised the issue as gently as I could. Zhu Shanggang looked unruffled. 'His only resources were an Oxford English dictionary, a Chinese–English dictionary and Shakespeare's original works. In a letter to my mother, he said he thought about looking at Liang Shiqiu's translations as a point of reference, but found it difficult for him to move on with his own; so from that point on, he was determined not to refer to others' translations.'

How had his father's work survived the Cultural Revolution, when so much else relating to western literature and culture had perished?

His mother had been working as a teacher, he explained; teachers had been especially vulnerable, and despite the fact that she was then in her fifties, she had been sent to do manual labour. In one of the myriad petty cruelties of the system, she had been reassigned as a cleaner in the very school where she had taught.

Zhu smiled, but his eyes were elsewhere. 'They said the school toilets had never been so clean. But she kept the manuscripts safe in Jiaxing, even though they confiscated the revisions she had made.'

If the government had known she had all these originals, they would have destroyed them too?

'Of course.'

Since then, there had been yet another switchback turn in ideological direction. Shakespeare was now deemed a symbol of openness and internationalism; it was declared that China should revere both him and Zhu Shenghao. A lavish multiple-volume facsimile edition of the manuscripts had recently been published. And the previous VIP to have come to Jiaxing to look at these pages was none other than Wen Jiabao. He had made the trip soon after returning from his jaunt to Stratford-upon-Avon, presumably eager to see how China had served a writer who 'must be read up to a hundred times to be fully understood'.

How did it make Zhu Shanggang feel, that the same Communist

Party that had once tried to annihilate everything his father achieved now honoured him as a hero?

Zhu Shanggang smiled wanly. 'People are different now from back then.'

Before I came to China, I asked a Chinese academic who now teaches in Britain whether I would get anywhere by asking people about the Cultural Revolution. The phone line had gone quiet.

'Honestly, I am not sure,' she said at last. 'The subject is still so personal, often painful. You will need to be cautious.'

The opposite had happened. Almost without my trying, stories about the awfulness of those years had tumbled out – the Beijing theatre director in his fifties who remembered watching his *jingju* actor father being paraded in humiliation through their town in full make-up and costume; the *Guardian* colleague who told me about interviewing a man who, as a zealous teenager, had testified against his own mother, testimony that meant she'd been shot.

The day after getting back from Jiaxing I had lunch with yet another theatre director, who, in the middle of a conversation about an *Othello* she had done in the 1990s, said she'd chosen the play because the hero's alienation from society echoed her own feelings about her wild-eyed contemporaries clutching their little red books.

Nearly forty years had passed since the end of the Cultural Revolution, and as China had cautiously opened up, a more confessional culture had crept in, albeit firmly one-sided in its revelations (while it was hard to talk about your family being persecuted, it was infinitely harder to admit that you or your relations had been complicit). On the mainland, books, films, TV shows and articles on the subject were still carefully censored, but outside its borders, from Jung Chang's *Wild Swans* on, memoirs and fiction itemising the horrors of China's lost decade had become a publishing sensation. Even in China there were reports that increasing numbers of people were seeking psychotherapy (itself banned under Mao), trying to lay the ghosts of the recent past.

The Party remained uneasy about open debate, but a cynic could see the political advantage of allowing certain carefully edited snapshots to make their way into the public domain. It struck me as not dissimilar from the impulse behind the propagandistic Elizabethan chroniclers Halle and Holinshed, filleted by Shakespeare for his histories, as they reflected on the carnage that tore Britain apart in the Middle Ages: *See how we are different, how our country is better. Do not endanger this.* Perhaps the Cultural Revolution was China's equivalent of the Tudor Myth, by which Elizabethans attempted to convince themselves that they would never again return to a country so fractiously divided as during the Wars of the Roses.

Digging in the archives at the Shanghai Dramatic Arts Centre one morning, I came across a photograph. It was in black-and-white, of a man leaning against a woman next to an arched doorway, vaguely Italianate. His left arm rested casually above her head, his knee grazing hers; a flirtatious gesture, perhaps a touch protective. Her smile seemed genuinely warm. Both wore Elizabethan garb. One had to peer closely to see they were Chinese: he was wearing an elaborately shaggy wig and what appeared to be a false nose; her make-up had been so thickly applied that her face looked as flour-white as the organza shawl around her shoulders.

I checked with the archivist: it was a production of *Much Ado About Nothing* from 1979 staged here in Shanghai. The couple were Beatrice and Benedick, played by actors called Zhu Xijuan and Jiao Huang. So this was what Shakespeare in the 'original sauce' looked like, with Chinese actors trying to erase every trace of their ethnic identity.

But what really caught me was that the actors, and for that matter their costumes, looked suspiciously familiar. I was sure I'd seen them earlier.

I dug back through the albums and slid out one I'd flicked through a few minutes before. These photographs were much smaller and more roughly shot, but it was clear they depicted the same production of *Much Ado About Nothing*. One by one I scrutinised the images. The masked ball; the ill-fated lovers Hero and Claudio at the altar; the denunciation scene, in which Hero is accused of sleeping with another man: all were the same. Even the sets – a bucolic panorama studded with Tuscan pines, an Italianate palazzo swathed with ornate wall hangings – looked identical.

But these photos were from 1961, not 1979. I laid both albums carefully on the table, side by side, and found the rival photos of Beatrice and Benedick; him in front of her, the doorway, her smiling. The couple were Zhu and Jiao, no question. Their poses were almost identical, as were their clothes. They were twins, the only real difference being the age of the photographs. Eighteen years apart.

In London or New York, shows were always transferring between different theatres, or being revived a year or two later. But such pauses were generally brief; and even Agatha Christie's *The Mousetrap*, which has theoretically been running uninterruptedly since 1952, had changed its cast and creative team so often that it was like the proverbial shovel that stays the same despite five new handles and twenty-eight new blades.

Why stage the same *Much Ado About Nothing* with what seemed to be an identical cast, eighteen years later? I reached for my books. The answer haunted all those conversations I'd had: the Cultural Revolution.

In the Dramatic Arts Centre café, I pieced together the story, which had been written about by the theatre historians Li Ruru and Alexa Huang. The *Much Ado About Nothing* I'd been looking at was indeed the same show, though in its original form it was even older: it dated from 1957, and had been created during the period when China and the USSR were intimate siblings. A well-regarded Soviet director, Yevgeniya Konstantinova Lipkovskaya, was part of a cultural delegation sent out from Leningrad to help set up the Shanghai Theatre Academy. She had stayed two years and directed two productions; *Much Ado About Nothing* was the second. Her cast were students. The translation was Zhu Shenghao's.

When it first went on stage in autumn 1957, Lipkovskaya's version of Shakespeare's summery comedy was acclaimed as a 'magnificent' demonstration of what Chinese *huaju* could learn from the west. Designed to look as if the actors had stepped out of a *quattrocento* fresco, it presented an enticingly distant world, one safely removed from the uneasy realities of the Hundred Flowers campaign. As the curtain rose on the shimmering Sicilian city of Messina, recreated in painstaking detail down to the roast goose on a silver salver, even the title – translated as *Wushi shengfei* ('Looking for Trouble in Trivial Matters') – seemed to illustrate the point. This was Shakespeare as sunny, escapist fantasy.

But *Much Ado About Nothing*, like everything else, found itself sucked into China's tumultuous cultural politics. Originally intended to be revived in 1958, the production had to be halted in the chaos of the Great Leap Forward, and it wasn't until 1961 – Lipkovskaya long gone and the USSR and China no longer on speaking terms – that it made its way back on stage. Hu Dao, Lipkovskaya's assistant, directed. Again it was a hit. Alongside the production photos I found a shot of a long line of people queuing outside the theatre, clutching parasols against the fierce Shanghai sun.

No one knew it, but when the curtain came down on *Much Ado About Nothing* two months later it would be one of the last times that Shakespeare would be seen on the professional Chinese stage in nearly twenty years. The following year there was a production at the Shanghai Film School of *Twelfth Night* – another comedy, again a revival – but that same summer, 1962, there was a scandal around a satirical play referencing Mao, and Madame Mao had her excuse. Its author was arrested. Four years later the Cultural Revolution would be in full, murderous sway and Shakespeare forbidden entirely.

So what of the 1979 *Much Ado About Nothing*, apparently identical in every respect to its 1961 incarnation? Incredible as it seemed, as well as being nearly the last professional production of Shakespeare to be seen before the Cultural Revolution, it was the very first to go on stage afterwards. Three years after Mao's death – the same strange, suspenseful year that the Chinese premier Deng Xioaping met US president Jimmy Carter to negotiate a policy of detente – as many of the original performers as could be found assembled in a rehearsal room and prepared to do *Much Ado About Nothing* one final time. The scripts were retrieved from the archive, along with the director's notes. The set was carefully reconstructed. Zhu Xijuan and Jiao Huang and other members of the 1961 cast relearned their lines. Costumes, design, choreography: everything the same. It would be as if nothing had happened.

Li Ruru, sent to work in the fields as a teenager, had seen the production as part of the first cohort of students to study at the Shanghai Drama Academy after the Cultural Revolution. I found her account of it almost unbearably poignant. '"Much ado about nothing" in Chinese seemed such a beautiful expression,' she wrote. 'We hoped it could excise our bitter experience with the easy and confident wisdom that the title implies.'

I found Benedick. Now seventy-nine, Jiao Huang had become one of China's biggest theatre stars and was a reliable presence in television historical dramas. He agreed to an interview. Shakespeare was one of his favourite writers; he would be overjoyed to discuss the great English poet.

When I arrived at his apartment, Jiao was in expansive mood: resplendent in American jeans and snakeskin cowboy boots, with wide, pronounced features and hair slicked back in a flamboyant quiff. On the way up the stairs, he thumped a metal breastplate attached to the wall – his costume in a recent production of *Antony and Cleopatra*. Above it was a terracotta plate, a gift from the Shakespeare Society of China.

Yes, he chuckled through a nimbus of cigarette smoke, he had indeed been in that *Much Ado About Nothing*. Not twice, though: all three times. In 1957 he had been too young to take a main role; he and his student colleagues had been cast in bit parts – knights, servants, guards, spear-carriers, all adding to the grand Italianate effect.

In 1961 it had finally been his turn; in Hu Dao's revival, he was chosen to play Benedick. From the shelf next to him, crammed with gold statuettes, he prised an album and found the relevant page – Jiao stripped to his doublet in the duel scene; looking rogueish in his officer's uniform. It was definitely the same production. In the background was the splendid stained glass of a church, meticulously imitated by Lipkovskaya's technicians. It made a tiny stage in Shanghai look like the cathedral of Notre Dame.

'It all wove together seamlessly,' he said. 'The music and dance was beautiful; the dances were choreographed by another Soviet expert, I think. At the academy, we had dance classes for two years – two classes on western dancing, two on Chinese dancing. Eight classes in total including review sessions, every week.'

He looked rapturous at the memory. 'The body movements, the pace and the speed – Shakespeare's plays in particular, you cannot do them without this knowledge.'

How had audiences reacted?

'Every show was a full house, every night for two months. It was so lively, no one had ever seen anything like it. Everyone walked out of the theatre with a big smile on their faces.' He turned to me with a wink. 'A few years ago, I saw a British film version of *Much Ado About Nothing*. I think our performance was just as good as theirs.'

Did he ever feel uncomfortable wearing western costumes – the hairpieces, false noses and the rest?

He emitted an explosive bark of laughter, and fired up another cigarette. 'To perform a foreign play, you cannot be Chinese. Lin Zhaohua in Beijing, he transforms Shakespeare's plays into something completely Chinese. Myself, I don't like this. What is the point of creating something if there is no difficulty at all? For each play I perform, I must change completely, from inside out, like a rebirth.'

Beneath the swaggering bravado I detected something else. As we talked more, its source became clear. Once the Cultural Revolution began in 1966, Jiao and his fellow actors were given a stark choice: appear in revolutionary operas, or abandon any hope of performing at all. Jiao chose the latter, and was dispatched to do farm work in the countryside outside Shanghai.

'I didn't perform for nine years. Foreign plays were all criticised. If you were passionate about western plays, you would be so severely criticised that you couldn't lift your head . . .'

He stopped. The translator, embarrassed, was staring at her feet. Jiao had begun to cry.

When he restarted, his voice was hoarse. 'I lived in a cowshed. I experienced everything. My house was destroyed.'

Many people in the west would find it bizarre, I said, staging exactly the same production in exactly the same way after the Cultural Revolution, as if those ten terrible years had never happened.

His gaze was level. 'I was even more passionate about performing Shakespeare's play. I poured all my energies into it. It is part of civilisation, is it not? How can anyone abandon it?'

Had it been hard, revisiting something from much happier times?

'Every single performance was different from before. The way we looked was not different, but the feelings and emotions were never the same.'

In 2012 he'd directed *Antony and Cleopatra*, a lifetime's ambition. It was an unashamedly old-fashioned production, he said, showing me photos that proved the point. He read out a passage from the essay he'd written for the programme. It was hardly poetry, particularly in translation, but I was caught by his suggestion that 'history is like a mirror of the sky, reflecting the changes of society and human beings'. Perhaps Shakespeare's plays could provide a kind of consolation for the bitter sorrows and humiliations of human experience. Mirroring history, they also helped make sense of it.

At the back of my mind was a book by the American critic C. L. Barber called *Shakespeare's Festive Comedy*. Published in the late 1950s, when Jiao and his colleagues had been preparing the first version of their escapist *Much Ado About Nothing*, it argued that the concept of festive renewal lay at the heart of the comedies, connecting them with ancient folk rites and myths, medieval mumming plays and May games – images of good conquering evil at the most basic, primal level. Barber's insistence on the healing power of happy endings had been dismissed as sentimental hogwash by younger critics, brought up in a more cynical era, but I thought the idea had real resonance here. Comedy equals tragedy plus time; by acting happily-ever-after, perhaps you could make it real.

Jiao lit yet another cigarette, his tenth in forty-five minutes. Through the smoke he looked impregnable, mysterious.

'Life has a lot of hardships, difficulties, but this is actually very important for an actor. These experiences should accumulate in your heart. Intellectuals in Britain are more innocent. They may not have accumulated such suffering and hardship as their Chinese counterparts have.'

It was hard to disagree, I said.

TWO DAYS AND A SHORT PLANE TRIP LATER, I was sneaking into the back of a room at National Taiwan Normal University. All I could see was a scrum of photographers and hands with cameraphones attached to them waving high in the air. The room was hot and bright. In the background was pre-recorded Elizabethan lute music, though it was hard to tell over the yelling and the clattering of camera shutters.

On a dais at the front, a group of dignitaries was blinking in the TV lights. Behind them was a poster depicting a cartoonish skyline – a child's compendium of global cities, the Eiffel Tower next to Tower Bridge next to a chunk of the Forbidden City. Romping across this interconnected global megalopolis, like a balding Godzilla, was a figure just about identifiable as William Shakespeare. The ruff was there, as was the goatee, but he looked distinctly Asian. Also, there were three of him. One was doing the V-for-victory sign like a Chinese teenager posing for a snapshot. Various people had told me during my odyssey that Shakespeare was taking over the world, but I had never yet seen the image rendered literally.

As the Q&A session got going, I crammed myself next to the

Taipei Times and pulled out my notebook, wondering vaguely if an academic Shakespeare conference had ever before attracted a roomful of hacks. Almost certainly not. But it appeared the Asian Shakespeare Association had realised it was a story.

I'd first heard of the ASA in Delhi the previous year. Fed up with attending international conferences in Europe or America, a group of academics had banded together and decided to set up a pan-Asian society of their own. The ASA would be run by Asians, for Asians. Among the membership were scholars from India, Japan, the Philippines, Korea, Malaysia and Singapore, not to mention a sizeable team from Taiwan, Hong Kong, Macau and the mainland. This was the ASA's debut gathering.

While the Chinese journalists shouted questions, I scanned the programme – three full days of plenary papers, seminars, round tables, acting and events, featuring many big names from the global academic scene. There were sessions on Shakespearian acting and contemporary Asian politics, cross-cultural performativity, translation and adaptation, early-modern travel.

Arguably, though, the ASA mattered less for what it included than what it signified. Global Shakespeare was becoming a hot academic field, but – like most of academia – its power bases were overwhelmingly in the west. The best jobs, the resources, the funding, the journals: all were still in Europe and North America. Even within Asia, 30 per cent of the world's land mass, scholars didn't engage with each other. Locked in their specialist geographical areas, the Indians didn't talk to the Japanese, or the Filipinos to the Koreans. The ASA would change all that, was the idea. The conference theme, somewhat pointedly, was 'Shakespearian journeys'. In Shakespeare, as in global politics and economics, Asia was in the ascendant.

The microphone was handed to the flustered-looking Australian chair of the International Shakespeare Association, who promptly claimed that Shakespeare was born in London and worked in Stratford, which caused a minor diplomatic incident when it was relayed in Chinese.

He tried again, sweat visibly beading on his forehead. 'The founding of the Asian Shakespeare Association proves enormous interest in and engagement of the people of Asia with Shakespeare.' This time there was enthusiastic nodding.

I listened hard as the chair of the ASA, Bi-qi Lei, stepped forward to give her closing remarks in Mandarin. The only word I recognised was the name '*Shashibiya*'. Slim, with a cascade of black hair, she had the look of a petite praying mantis dressed by Armani. Unlike the Europeans, she looked in full control of the situation.

Taipei was a useful place to distil some of the thoughts I had collected in two years of intermittent travel. I spent a few hours in a session on Chinese Shakespeare, in which it transpired that my struggles to engage theatre directors in conversation about the Communist Party were far from unusual – not so much because anyone was frightened about retribution (though funding was certainly an issue), but more because politics was seen as a huge turn-off in the brave new China.

The Australian academic, Peter Holbrook, looking relieved to have escaped the Taiwanese press, talked engagingly about the idea of motion in Shakespeare's texts – something that suffuses them at every level, from the deft bird imagery that gives the early narrative poem *Venus and Adonis* such energy and life (noted back in the 1930s by the British critic Caroline Spurgeon) to the expansive worlds of the late plays. Holbrook offered a gorgeous example from *A Midsummer Night's Dream*, where Oberon rhapsodises to Puck of a fantastical vision he has seen, 'a mermaid on a dolphin's back'

> Uttering such dulcet and harmonious breath
> That the rude sea grew civil at her song
> And certain stars shot madly from their spheres [. . .]
> That very time I saw, but thou couldst not,
> Flying between the cold moon and the earth
> Cupid, all armed. A certain aim he took
> At a fair vestal thronèd by the west,
> And loosed his love-shaft smartly from his bow
> As it should pierce a hundred thousand hearts.
> But I might see young Cupid's fiery shaft
> Quenched in the chaste beams of the wat'ry moon,
> And the imperial vot'ress passèd on,
> In maiden meditation, fancy-free.

Oberon's speech has attracted the interest of scholars because it draws on what may have been childhood memories of an entertainment Shakespeare had seen staged by the Earl of Leicester at Kenilworth near Stratford for Queen Elizabeth I, perhaps the 'imperial vot'ress' in question. But chiefly it is remarkable for the joyous speed of the writing, the liquid movement of its metaphors, its world-encompassing energy. Oberon's speech is scarcely required by the plot, merely a preamble to his describing the location of the 'herb' that Puck will use to dose the lovers' eyes. One feels almost that Shakespeare is letting his quill run away with him in sheer delight at what it could do. Hearing the words, Puck – no slowcoach – declares that he'll 'put a girdle round about the earth | In forty minutes'.

I wished I had Puck's pace, not to mention his immunity to jet lag. But as I listened to the talk, I wondered if there was something here that touched on ideas I'd been carrying with me since I started my own journeys. Many of his contemporaries singled out Shakespeare's quick-wittedness, the agile speed of his thought – the fact that he barely blotted a line, or as his colleagues Heminges and Condell put it in their preface to the First Folio, that 'his mind and hand went together'. At the deepest of levels Shakespeare's writing is bewitched by ideas of changefulness, mutation, shifting value, time's whirligig, the flexibilities embodied in metaphor (the word itself comes from a Greek root meaning 'carrying from one thing to another'). And if one were looking for an answer as to how one man wrote forty-plus plays, two long narrative poems and a hundred and fifty-four sonnets in something like twenty-five years, quick-wittedness wasn't a bad place to start.

Did this explain why his work had proved so agile and flexible, when it encountered other cultures? Not in itself. But the idea seemed compelling, if one could see the agility and flexibility encoded in their very substance.

I filed it for the moment alongside numerous other theories as to why Shakespeare had gone global, and made haste for the next seminar.

As so often, it was the conversations not on the official programme that were the ones to have. I picked up Hong Kong tips – mainly bar-related – from a young Northern Irish lecturer of Chinese heritage, useful for when I arrived there later in the week. I learned about the perils of teaching Shakespeare in Qatar, where salaries were dizzying (by academic standards) and the confluence of Renaissance studies and Islam suggestive, but one could be deported at any minute if it was declared one was in fact promulgating Christianity.

I had an informative chat with a senior academic from Nottingham, who had recently joined the university's overseas campus at Ningbo near Shanghai. 'Asia is where things are at!' she declared, waving her Starbucks coffee. No doubt the Chinese travel agent I had spoken to in Nottingham would agree.

One lunchtime I sat down with an academic from Beijing, Li Jun (David, he preferred), who had given an absorbing paper on performances of Shakespeare on the mainland in marginal or politically charged contexts. One of his exhibits was a *Romeo and Juliet* staged in 2006 in Beijing for migrant labourers – the forgotten tribe of the economic miracle, sometimes referred to as China's 'untouchables'. It was from David that I learned a fact that stayed with me long after I left China: that in *Super Girl* and *Super Boy*, the Chinese equivalent of *Pop Idol*, 800 million SMS votes had been cast, the largest and freest popular vote in Chinese history.

These weren't the only politics on campus. The previous evening there had been a screening of a film going under the name of *Shakespeare tong tai* ('Shakespeare Must Die'). Despite its blood-and-thunder title, this wasn't – mercifully – a historical thriller about Christopher Marlowe and the authorship controversy, but an adaptation of *Macbeth*, completed in 2012 by the Thai film-maker Ing Kanjanavanit.

Set in a sleek contemporary version of Bangkok, with Macbeth as a careerist military officer who becomes a populist political leader, the film was smoothly executed, but hadn't seemed especially startling when I'd seen it, particularly compared to much more radical East Asian rewrites such as Kurosawa's *The Bad Sleep Well*, his salaryman *Hamlet*, or his 1957 *Kumonosu-jō* (*Throne of Blood* in English), which transformed the play into a brooding warrior epic. Almost the most unusual thing about *Shakespeare Must Die* was its prodigious length: unusually faithful to the First Folio text, 172 minutes long despite the relative brevity of the script, it gave Kenneth Branagh's baggy 242-minute *Hamlet* – almost certainly the longest Shakespeare film ever made – a run for its money.

It wasn't so much the movie that was interesting as what had happened after it had left the editing suite. *Shakespeare Must Die* had been banned. After a protracted saga lasting most of 2012, the Thai censors declared the film unfit for public consumption, on the grounds that it was 'in conflict with peaceful social order'.

Ing K (her professional name) and Manit Sriwanichpoom, her

producer and off-screen partner, cried foul, but to no avail. Adding to the farcical irony – not least of which was that a 407-year-old text had been deemed immoral – was the fact that *Shakespeare Must Die* had received 3 million baht (around £54,000) in funding from the Thai government. The same department that had helped pay for the film was now banning it.

It was a perplexing situation, one that touched on many of the issues I'd been asking about, largely fruitlessly, back on the mainland. The ASA had negotiated rights to screen *Shakespeare Must Die*, one of the few times it had ever been seen in public, and also its sequel, a documentary that Kanjanavanit had made about her exhausting experiences with the film-classification board. Kanjanavanit had been persuaded to get an eight-hour flight here to Taipei, and would be answering questions after the screening.

As I took my seat in the darkened lecture theatre, it occurred to me ruefully that I'd at last found something I'd been searching for my entire trip – someone using Shakespeare to comment on censorship and the role of state power. It hadn't happened in China, but 2,000 miles away from Beijing at the other end of Asia.

The documentary was called *Censor Must Die*. It was gripping – not so much a making-of as a genre new to me, and presumably everyone else in the audience: a banning-of. Shot using a handheld camera, it trailed the producer Sriwanchipoom around a sequence of frowsty government offices as he attempted to understand why an adaptation of *Macbeth* – one funded by the government, no less – was causing such high anxiety. We sat with him in waiting rooms and car parks as he attempted to do battle with the pettifogging bureaucracy by which authoritarian regimes do their dirty work. Although not without doleful humour (the censors announce that they must delay one meeting to attend an urgent screening of the family movie *Dear Doggies 2*), it was cast as a Kafkaesque tragedy, with Sriwanchipoom as a wretched Joseph K failing to find out what, if anything, he has done wrong.

Some had accused the film-makers of sensationalising their plight for publicity, but it was clear the moment Kanjanavanit stood up afterwards that the whole saga had been horrendously unpleasant. Blinking behind large round spectacles, she spoke in a halting voice that had constantly to be redirected towards the microphone. She had the appearance less of a rabble-rouser than a librarian pining to return to the stacks. She looked hollow with tiredness.

As she slipped out of the door I pounced: did she have time for a few more questions? I was a *Guardian* journalist, writing a book—

She was smiling. 'I read the *Guardian* when I was a teenager.'

There'd been copies in Thailand?

She giggled. 'Boarding school in Godalming. You know – Surrey.'

A cigarette was already in her hand, so we forsook the cool of the lecture theatre for the heat and humidity outside. Though much younger-seeming than her fifty-five years, she spoke in courteous, faintly old-fashioned English that made her sound as though she'd just stepped off the King's Road in Chelsea.

She began from the day that she and her partner were told that their version of *Macbeth* wouldn't wash.

'Normally they decide immediately – first screening, it's done. When Manit went two times and still no, he had to go to a third round. I said, "OK, I'm coming with you."'

Kanjanavanit – who had begun her career as an investigative reporter – brought along her camera. At first the idea was simply to film a legal record; but as the case dragged on, it became obvious that her next film was making itself before her eyes.

I confessed it was still unclear to me exactly what had caused the problems: *Shakespeare Must Die* had seemed like an elegant but uncontroversial rendering of *Macbeth*. What was I missing?

Pushing her hair out of the way of her glasses, she explained. You had to understand Thailand, and in particular the role of Thaksin Shinawatra, the populist telecoms tycoon who had become prime minister in 2001 and then been ejected in a coup five years later. The film had originally been funded when Thaksin's rivals were in power and Thaksin himself in exile. It was when Thaksin's sister became prime minister – Thai politics, as well as being unusually prone to coups, is deeply incestuous – that their difficulties began. The parallels between Thaksin and Kanjanavanit's Macbeth/Dear Leader were the issue. A man who had made fortunes by working back-room contacts, Thaksin was accused of bullying tactics against rivals. In its depiction of a similar figure, the film was regarded as sailing far too close to the wind.

In a burst of surreal interpretative genius, one of the modifications the censors had suggested was that Kanjanavanit should film an entirely new scene to appear at the end of the movie, featuring an elderly, sweet-looking couple solemnly discussing its meaning. Audiences must be made to understand that *Macbeth* was fiction – nothing more.

Shakespeare's script was itself most likely an allegory, though a shadowy one. Written for James I soon after he inherited the English throne in 1603, flattering both the monarch's lineage (James was a distant descendant of the real-life Banquo) and his interest in witchcraft, it was also, surely, a coded warning about the dangers of ambition – a newly promoted King's Man addressing his king about the limits of regal power. Theatre directors had set it in everything from Stalinist Russia to contemporary Libya. In India just fourteen months earlier, I said, I had seen it being used to criticise the West Bengal government.

'I used Thaksin to illustrate Shakespeare, not the other way around,' she replied. 'If I wanted to criticise him I could just shout rude words on the street; plenty of people do. It'd be much less trouble.'

For now they were stuck in limbo. *Shakespeare Must Die* was still banned, although to compound the confusion *Censor Must Die* had been allowed to pass, on the basis that it depicted 'events that really happened'.

The case wasn't uppermost in her mind, Kanjanavanit confessed: she was itching to get back to Thailand, where anti-government protestors had been camped out for months. She had been out filming them and was waiting to see how it would end. A military coup was on its way, some said.

What was her working title?

She wore the faintest of smiles. '*Bangkok Joyride*.'

The light was becoming sallow. Above the warm, close smell of the forest surrounding Taipei, there was a sour metallic tang, like copper. A storm was on its way. For almost the first time, I felt a pang of homesickness. Perhaps it was simply talking to someone who sounded British. The previous day, able for the first time to access international news websites, blocked on the mainland, I'd greedily stocked up on world events. Back home it was mid-May: photos of delicate pink cherry blossom and white hawthorn frothing into bud had been doing the rounds on Twitter. Twitter was banned on the mainland too; this was my first glimpse of the British spring. I found it weirdly affecting.

As we walked towards the university gates, through lines of students streaming out of lectures, Kanjanavanit hesitated. 'You will write about this? In the paper? You never know, it might help.' She smiled apologetically. 'International coverage.'

Months later, long after the article had come out, I emailed her from London. The coup had indeed happened, just five days after we met. Military rule had been imposed and a sinisterly named National Peace and Order Committee had taken control of the government. Everyone in Bangkok was waiting to see how it would play out.

Shakespeare Must Die was on hold, but there was happier news about *Censor Must Die*: it had just won a documentary award in Beirut. She was still working on *Bangkok Joyride*. She wouldn't be submitting that one to the censors, she said.

The conference was nearly done. Final speeches were given, votes of thanks proffered and received. An elderly professor from Taipei was presented with a lifetime-achievement award (of shower gel, for reasons I never fathomed). In the humid fug outside the lecture hall we nipped at warm, sweet wine and made small talk. The inaugural meeting of the Asian Shakespeare Association was proclaimed a triumph. We raised our glasses. 'For Asia, for Shakespeare, together we're writing a new page in history,' someone declared. We swapped business cards and, flushed and a little unsteady on our feet, promised to be in touch.

For me, it was not quite the end: I was booked on a flight to Hong Kong first thing the following day. But the farewell party, I was solemnly informed, was compulsory. All serious Shakespearians must attend. Anxious to be considered a serious Shakespearian, I agreed.

Boarding a fleet of minibuses, we were deposited at the doors of a large nightclub in the centre of Taipei, a vast black hall lined with strobes and spotlights and with what appeared to be a pole-dancing platform at one end.

It was empty; the ASA had booked the place out. The lights flashed woozily pink and purple. The music thudded heavily. There was spirited talk of karaoke. The Filipino contingent, first at the bar, commandeered the dance floor. A senior Taiwanese academic, who had surreptitiously changed into a miniskirt, was in earnest conference with the DJ. The British and American scholars hung back, looking ill at ease. I gathered that karaoke was not a regular feature of the Shakespeare Association of America.

It took me three luminous vodka-tonics and two shouted conversations to realise that I had to make an exit. I couldn't see straight, my head felt as though it was being assaulted by a piledriver and I had to be up in five hours to make check-in.

As I was leaving, I heard a 1980s power ballad kick in. I had the haziest of senses that the song was by Def Leppard. The Taiwanese academic in the miniskirt was standing on the platform, in worrying proximity to the pole. Team Filipino were cheering her on. Anxious about what worlds Asian Shakespeare might explore next, I made myself scarce.

———

IN A TINY, SHORT-LET STUDIO APARTMENT, twelve floors above the clamorous, fish-smelling streets of Sheung Wan, I squinted at a map of Hong Kong, trying to get my head around how so much could be crammed into so little. Over 3 million people lived on Hong Kong Island and Kowloon; this was one of the most densely populated territories on earth. On the island side, where I was, the city was squeezed into a narrow smear of flat-ish land that ran around the coast, less than a kilometre wide. Most of it was plainly not flat at all – there were so many levels that the lanes leading up to Victoria Peak resembled the squiggled and looping curves on the surface of a human brain.

On all sides, through the greasy windows of the apartment, protruded tower blocks, yellow and dirty white, so slim and tall and close that I felt I could lean across and topple them. Through the narrowest of gaps I could see the roaring elevated road that circumnavigated the island and a few silvery millimetres of Victoria Harbour.

In the apartment directly opposite – equally tiny, it looked – a middle-aged woman was unconcernedly laying the table for lunch. She was twenty-five feet away at most. I could almost have jumped across, levered myself in and joined her.

So this was Hong Kong: the gateway to Asia as well as the British Empire's last stand; still, despite stiff competition from Shanghai, the city of the Chinese future. A 'Special Administrative Region', the goose that laid the golden eggs, and politically and economically the freest place in China, Hong Kong was a cautious experiment for Beijing – an attempt to see if 'one country, two systems' could hold together. Despite tectonic rumbles, recently activated by the pro-democracy

Occupy Central movement, so far it had. It seemed an appropriately paradoxical place to complete a journey through the teeming paradoxes of the present-day People's Republic.

I had six days here, and a notepad scrawled with leads. I was keen to find out more about Shakespeare in Chinese education, a subject I'd left under-explored until now. David in Taipei had primed me on the annual Shakespeare festival hosted by the Chinese University of Hong Kong, happening the week of my arrival and packed with student groups from across China. I'd also arranged an appointment at the Hong Kong Academy of the Performing Arts, the most important conservatoire in this corner of Asia. A translator had agreed to talk about the very different challenges of putting Shakespeare into Cantonese.

But I was uncomfortably aware that there was only so much time to do more research, soak up yet more material. After two years of intermittent journeying, my travelling days were almost done. Despite the odd glimmer of insight, my head felt soggy with jumble and mess: tangled threads, dots that should have joined but didn't. Questions had a dismaying habit of drowning out answers. Theories I'd jerry-built en route were worryingly prone to collapse. At some point I was going to have to sit down in a room roughly the size of this one and do the journey all over again, this time turning it into the pages of a book. That journey, unlike the one I was currently embarked on, would need to make some kind of sense. In my current travel-shocked state, making sense of anything more sophisticated than the route to the nearest coffee shop seemed unlikely.

I thought of the world map with which I'd started, with its neat little marks and lines. It had seemed a charming conceit, the idea of following Shakespeare out into the world, chasing him down to locations even he could never have imagined. I'd been astonished at some of the places he'd shown up; just as often, he'd winked slyly and given me the slip. The wiliest and most seasoned of travellers, he was smoothly expert at camouflaging himself like a local and slipping back into the crowd.

But then maybe Hong Kong was a good spot to dwell on such thoughts, and turn them into something useful. If the sights and noises of the city were any indication, it contained more than enough jumble and mess of its own. I wondered if I'd be able to find a way through the confusion.

In mainland China, the connection between Shakespeare and the colonial reach of the British is slight: it is true that Lin Zexu, the Qing-dynasty diplomat who introduced a certain 'prolific' British dramatist to Chinese readers, had done so in the context of the opium wars, but that was as far as it went. Shakespeare was taught in missionary schools in treaty ports like Shanghai, Guangzhou and Nanjing, but, unlike in India and parts of South Africa – Britain not having made deep enough inroads into the Middle Kingdom – the Bard was never officially a servant of Empire.

In Hong Kong things were different, as ten minutes strolling around its streets reminded me. If Kolkata had seemed haunted by the ghostly presence of the British, in Hong Kong they were hiding in plain sight. It might have been the best part of two decades after the handover, and Hong Kong more globalised than ever, but Britain was everywhere I looked: in the dumpy, right-hand-drive double-decker buses; the little green men at pedestrian crossings; the fact that people instinctively wove left on the pavements. I charged my laptop via a solid British three-pin. People talked to me of 'ground floors' in a way they hadn't done for weeks. When I dialled a number I was rewarded with a doleful British *bleup-bleup*, not the chirpy single tone of China. Taipei had made me feel indistinctly homesick; Hong Kong reminded me all too pungently of why I'd wanted to get away. I began to regret that I had a flight back to London at the end of the week.

The same opium war that had encouraged Lin to commission a translation of the *Cyclopedia of Geography* in 1839 resulted in the loss of Hong Kong to the British in 1842. The island became a military stronghold, and when the Second Convention of Beijing was signed in 1898 – and with it the famous ninety-nine-year lease over the island and the territories that surrounded it – Hong Kong became a British linchpin in the region.

One of the more unexpected discoveries I had made in India and South Africa was that wherever British colonialists hung up their pith helmets and mosquito nets, sooner or later they found themselves disporting themselves on stage. Hong Kong was no different. In December 1844, just two years after the island was ceded, officers from the garrison founded what became known as the Hong Kong Amateur Dramatic Club. (No women were permitted to join, and members were pseudonymous for fear of bringing the army into disrepute.) The club's repertoire – perhaps the first spoken drama in Cantonese-speaking China – consisted almost exclusively of light theatrical farces imported from London. In 1867 they staged the London barrister-cum-playwright Francis Talfourd's burlesque *Shylock; or, the Merchant of Venice Preserved* (1852), which makes ponderous fun out of Shakespeare's play and Thomas Otway's sensationalistic Restoration tragedy *Venice Preserv'd*. Talfourd's title page proclaims, tongue lumpenly in cheek, that this was 'an entirely new reading of Shakespeare . . . printed from an edition hitherto undiscovered by modern authorities'.

Inauthentic though this version was, I found it instructive that the Hong Kong amateurs had chosen *The Merchant of Venice* as their first foray into Shakespeare; yet more proof that the play had a special resonance in trading cities like these. It was revived in 1871, but Shakespeare (even in diluted form) did not appear again on the playbills of the HKADC until 1913, when the players staged *Twelfth Night*, following it in 1922 with *The Tempest* (one wonders how sensitive they were to the colonial context).

Shakespeare took far longer to penetrate the world of Hong Kong's Chinese population, strictly segregated from their masters. The first Cantonese translations of the play did not arrive until the 1950s, a full half-century after the earliest Mandarin stagings in Shanghai. In April 1954, the Sino-British Club arranged a festival to mark the 390th anniversary of Shakespeare's birth, including what seems to have been the earliest version of Shakespeare in Cantonese, a scene from *Romeo and Juliet*. It was another ten years, 1964, before an attempt was made to stage a full play in colloquial Cantonese. Students at the Chinese University of Hong Kong took part, wearing ancient Chinese costume in a nod to the traditions of Cantonese opera. The play, again, was *The Merchant of Venice*.

There is a reason students were so heavily involved in the dissemination of Shakespeare. As in India and South Africa, the playwright became a fixture on colonial curriculums, particularly once the British had their feet under the table in Hong Kong. The select committee report on Colonisation given to the House of Lords in 1847, suggesting that it was 'a nobler work to diffuse over a few created worlds the laws of Alfred, the language of Shakespeare, and the Christian religion', didn't just pertain to the subcontinent; those principles were applied zealously in East Asia too. They were certainly shared by Frederick Stewart (1836–89), founding headmaster at Hong Kong's first government school, who saw fit to declare that 'the Chinese have no *education* in the real sense of the word'.

Shakespeare was used to remedy this supposed deficiency. In 1882, the plays began to be taught in schools; six years later, they were instituted as part of the entrance examination for the Imperial Maritime Customs Service. In 1902, one of Stewart's successors wrote, 'Shakespeare requires the employment of all the commonest phrases in connection with matters of everyday life, as well as in expression of emotion and humour.' If one wanted to get on in Edwardian Hong Kong, one had better learn English, which necessitated brushing up on one's Shakespeare. As late as the 1960s, anyone sitting the Hong Kong Certificate was required to study one of the plays.

I spent an afternoon wandering through the Museum of History, with its walk-through displays of colonial Hong Kong – tailors' shops, a green tram, a full-size general store stocking Woodbine cigarettes, wares to make even the most flinty-hearted expat pine for home. The route culminated in a cinema playing footage from the 1997 handover. I sat in the dark, watching strange rituals I hadn't seen since they appeared on television the summer I did my A-levels: the Union flag being lowered over Government House to the quavering of the Last Post; the soon-to-be-ex-governor, Chris Patten, standing stoically in the pouring rain while the Royal Navy streamed aboard the royal yacht *Britannia*. These, too, felt like relics from a bygone age.

In accordance with the terms of the Sino-British Joint Declaration, British rule had ended on the stroke of midnight on 1 July 1997, when Hong Kong had exchanged one set of imperial masters for another. Shakespeare, as so often, had stayed.

Housed in splendidly brutalist headquarters on the island's north shorefront, with a billion-Hong-Kong-dollar view across to Kowloon, the location of the Hong Kong Academy of Performing Arts bespeaks its significance. Founded in 1984, the APA runs courses in drama, dance, music and Cantonese opera from undergraduate up to master's level, and supplies a stream of graduates to the huge Hong Kong film and television industry.

I was interested in the APA because, celebrating its 30th anniversary and Shakespeare's 450th, the academy had elected to put on a show that, to my surprise, had popped up several times in my peregrinations across China: *The Taming of the Shrew*. This production couldn't have been more different from the slimmed-down version I'd seen back in Beijing; in the best traditions of intercultural dialogue it was being staged as a melange of Cantonese opera, traditional dance and postmodern western-style drama. There were 150 people in the cast. From the reports, it sounded both brilliant and bizarre.

I'd emailed Ceri Sherlock, its director and the dean of drama. I was in luck; though the run was over, workshops were continuing, with a view to giving the show a future life. I'd be welcome to come along, if I didn't mind singing for my supper – the students could do with some feedback, and they'd love it from a British critic.

Wasn't the show in Cantonese? 'Come along anyway,' he said.

Waiting in the APA's huge, concrete foyer, expecting 'Ceri' to be a Cantonese name, I was disconcerted to find myself shaking hands with a smiling, apple-cheeked Welshman. Sherlock was one of Hong Kong's many thousands of expats. After a career in Welsh theatre, opera and television, he had first visited as part of a judging committee. A job had come up. He'd stayed for a year, which had become two, then three, then four . . .

As we walked towards the rehearsal room, Sherlock explained that this was a boom time for Chinese drama. After the handover, there had been an explosion of interest in Cantonese culture. New plays had revisited ancient Chinese texts, or drawn on stories from Hong Kong's own history. After decades in the shadow of Britain, the island was belatedly discovering its Chinese side – both similar to, and crucially distinct from, the over-mighty mainland.

So why do Shakespeare? Why not something Chinese?

A smile flickered across his lips. 'Ah, but this is *Chinese* Shakespeare. Much more exciting.'

As we took our seats in a pocket-sized studio, he explained how the production had come about. The APA had been searching for a graduation piece that could showcase students from all of its schools, and *The Taming of the Shrew* had come up – not so much for its gender politics, the obvious talking point in the west, but for the fact that it was technically a play-within-a-play.

Though the framework is usually abandoned by modern directors, the text of *The Taming of the Shrew* begins with an 'Induction' in which a drunken tinker, Christopher Sly, falls asleep and is discovered by an aristocrat, who persuades Sly when he awakes that he is in fact a wealthy 'lord' for whom an entertainment is to be performed (the episode closely resembles a tale in *The Arabian Nights*). The storyline usually regarded as the play proper, the lopsided affair between Katherine and Petruccio, is in fact a self-enclosed drama played out by a cast of actors for the benefit of Sly and a watching onstage audience. It is one of Shakespeare's earliest experiments in metadrama – a lingering fascination that also produced Bottom and co.'s horny-handed attempt at 'Pyramus and Thisbe' in *A Midsummer Night's Dream* and the play-within-the-play in *Hamlet*.

Sherlock had seen it as something more practical, a way of uniting the talents of his various students with their different but complementary disciplines. The Induction could be a Chinese opera, with drama students trained in modern-dress naturalism acting out the play-within-the-play, the war between Katherine and Petruccio. Shakespeare might have approved: like all the best dramatic decisions, it was both hard-headed and conceptually smart.

'The gender politics come as a bonus,' Sherlock whispered as the actors took their places.

After too many days on planes and in seminar rooms, it was a treat to be in the middle of some live drama. The students acted as if their lives depended on it. Though not in full costume, the boys wore angular suit jackets and trilbies that gave them the look of 1950s Triads in training. The girls were in vampish high heels; Katherine wore leggings, with her goodie-two-shoes sister Bianca in a frilly A-line skirt. The pace was fast and dangerous, and the relationship between the sexes utterly believable – the men growling and hissing like tomcats, the women skittish and playful, fragile yet assertive. The Cantonese was beyond me, but it seemed a fine fit, earthy and demotic. Listening to a blistering rant from Katherine, I asked Sherlock's student assistant if the translation was much different from the English script I had in front of me. He flushed pink. 'Cantonese can be very rude.'

The day before, I'd met the Cantonese translator, Rupert Chan. The point he'd emphasised was that – far more than Mandarin – Hong Kong Cantonese was a living, evolving language, continually in flux. It borrowed shamelessly from all across Asia, and was stuffed with loan words from English and elsewhere. In its assimilative urges and hunger for novelty, it reflected Hong Kong itself.

Perhaps it was a few days' wandering amid grandiose corporate headquarters and skyscrapers, but it hit me how much *The Taming of the Shrew* is about money as well as sex: Petruccio bragging about how he can make his fortune by bedding a woman with a rich father; the imbalanced marriage market that sees the pliant and saleable Bianca fending off suitors while the strong-willed Katherine is left with none.

After they'd run through the first act, the students took a break. For twenty minutes, in a mixture of Cantonese and English, we talked about patriarchy and relationships in contemporary China, particularly the pressure for women to conform. The subject had been on my mind since Beijing; I was pleased that at last I had someone to ask.

'This is a big problem in China, particularly on the mainland,' a boy said solemnly.

'Hong Kong too,' a girl on the other side of the room flashed back. It was the girl playing Katherine. 'It happens in our world. We want to say, we can change this. We can use Shakespeare to change this.'

Another girl brought up the Occupy movement; they had friends who'd been in the protests that lasted from September to December in 2014, demanding greater electoral freedom from mainland China. The atmosphere on the island was jittery; no one was sure how things would go. 'There is much to change in Hong Kong, many issues,' she said.

Politics aside, I wondered how they felt about Shakespeare: did he feel British, here in this former colonial outpost? They looked at me blankly. Most were native Cantonese; in 1997 they'd only just been born. The British era? Prehistory.

'I think Shakespeare is a writer from everywhere,' someone said in careful English. 'In Cantonese, he is a Cantonese writer.'

The girl who'd played Katherine spoke up again. 'His words are very poetic in English, so for me it is quite hard to put myself into these words. For the British, I think it is hard to understand all the poetry. Maybe we here don't get all that poetry. But in Cantonese we can find something that relates to us now, in Hong Kong, in this society.'

I wanted to ask more, but they were eager for feedback. My turn – supper-singing time. Fourteen faces leaned anxiously towards me. I filled for a few minutes, blathering about Elizabethan marriage codes and property laws. What I really wanted to say was this: I thought they had entirely nailed the play.

Later that afternoon I sat in the sleek bar of a hotel above Government House, sipping green tea and soaking in the Hong Kong skyline. The view across the cloudy green water to Kowloon was spectacular, framed by the gaunt grey exoskeleton of Norman Foster's HSBC headquarters and the angular glass fortress of I. M. Pei's Bank of China. At the feet of the skyscrapers and mansion blocks was dark, lush forest, carpeting the hills leading up to the Peak. No wonder the British felt such lordly self-confidence in Hong Kong, a confidence inherited by the multinational financiers who now controlled the island. Up here, it was easy to convince yourself you ruled Asia, if not the world.

I thought back to the image of Shakespeare I'd seen in that press conference in Taipei, with the Bard clambering over the globe like a plumper, goateed Godzilla. Did Shakespeare, too, rule the world? Is that what I'd really discovered on my travels?

Hunting through my notebooks, I searched for connections and linkages. I followed the thread back to the place where I'd started, twenty-three months earlier: at Shakespeare's Globe in London, watching a scratch company from Afghanistan perform a play little-regarded in the west, *The Comedy of Errors*. Powerfully moved by the experience, I'd spent that summer searching for Shakespeares that looked different from Britain's National Poet, digging among competing theses as to why he was now the world's writer.

Some of those theories had certainly borne fruit. No ignoring – particularly here in Hong Kong – the heavy tread of the British Empire, nor the way Brits carried Shakespeare across whichever waves they ruled, from Kolkata on the Bay of Bengal to the Cape on the south-west tip of Africa; to Canada and the American colonies right round through East Asia to Australia and New Zealand. In almost every territory that blushed imperial pink, Shakespeare put in an appearance, a reliable piece of colonial equipment, either performed on stage or part of the education system (and often both).

It was also true that the US-driven global spread of the English language had helped cement his reputation in those territories the British had never reached. Even if I had become increasingly dubious about the claim made by the Royal Shakespeare Company and the British Council that half the world's schoolchildren now study Shakespeare – despite the researchers' best efforts, the evidence was shaky – it was surely true that enormous quantities of people now encounter Shakespeare in some form or another, if not in formal education then via internationally successful television shows and movies such as Baz Luhrmann's *Romeo+Juliet* (1996), or in story form – novels, Japanese manga Shakespeare (hugely popular across Asia), the Lambs' *Tales*. Even if only, say, a quarter of the world's population brushed past Shakespeare at some point, that was still nearly 2 billion people.

Perhaps most excitingly, a large proportion of these people must have little idea that what they are watching or reading *is* Shakespeare. With the recent explosion in Indian and Chinese cinema, particularly among the expanding Asian diaspora, the Shakespeares streaming across the globe are now more multifarious than ever.

This was something I genuinely hadn't computed before I left: what a minority sport English-language Shakespeare now is. In all but one of the countries on my route, English-language texts had far less effect on the dissemination of Shakespeare than translations into myriad local tongues, from Bengali to isiZulu. If an academic paper I'd heard in Delhi was correct, far more people now encounter Shakespeare in modern translation than in Early Modern English, rendering it an absorbing question as to who really 'owns' Shakespeare's texts. Whoever it is, it certainly isn't the British.

I hadn't become any more reconciled to the word, but the concept of Shakespeare as a 'rhizomatic' cultural figure – decentred, present in many places at once, his roots entwined with many different kinds of local histories – seemed more and more appealing. More, if one pushed the metaphor further, one could think of Shakespeare as a kind of living organism, continually evolving: much of the same genetic code was present, but mutated, so that the organism itself took ever more diverse and wondrous forms. The Cantonese students I'd been talking to earlier, equally influenced by traditional opera, old Hong Kong movies seen on YouTube and third-wave American gender theory, would surely recognise a Shakespeare who emerged from everywhere rather than a bald man with a ruff and MADE IN BRITAIN stamped upon his base.

How about another theory with which I'd set off – that Shakespeare's global significance was down to his benign universality, the fact that he was the same everywhere you went, an emblem of our common humanity? Though I'd lost count of the number of times people had told me there was something 'universal' about Shakespeare, this hadn't been my experience at all. There were reflections and echoes, yes, but it was more accurate to describe him as a Rorschach blot that never looked the same twice. It didn't seem to me that interpretational fixedness or solidity was anything like the defining characteristic of the texts I'd seen performed or read: it was the contrasts and competing inflections that were telling. In search of Shakespeare, I'd found him different at every turn.

Even where people had apparently tried to use Shakespeare as a bridge of shared humanity – Solomon Plaatje and his Setswana translations were a telling example – the reality turned out to be more ambiguous and complex. There was something about Shakespeare that made people want to *own* him, to claim him as one of them, to give cultural status and legitimacy to their ambitions or concerns, whether it was '*unser* Shakespeare' and the cause of German nationalism in the nineteenth century or the agitated political situation in present-day Thailand. It seemed to me that no one could reasonably claim that any of these images of Shakespeare were alike. They were defiantly plural; *Shakespeares*, not Shakespeare.

So perhaps the globalisation theorists had it right, that Shakespeare was a multinational brand, a free-floating symbol that transcended national borders and could attach itself to many different kinds of cultural artefacts. If so, the process had begun even within his lifetime – if not off the coast of Sierra Leone on board an East India Company ship, then at city fairs and princely courts in German-speaking northern Europe. The translated and abbreviated Shakespeare performed by the English Comedians early in the seventeenth century was barely recognisable, just as the heavily adapted Shakespeare so crazily popular in nineteenth-century Britain and America would now be regarded with horror in both those places. The inescapable fact was that, for most of the last four centuries, 'Shakespeare' was a concept at best hazily related to the playscripts the man himself had written. But this, in a sense, was the point. Ben Jonson's famous obsequy in the 1623 First Folio, that his dead colleague was 'not of an age, but for all time', contained the grains of a potent idea – that one secret of Shakespeare's global success is that he is endlessly variable, reinterpretable, translatable, can never be pinned down to exactly one thing.

Yet there was another crucial fact, one I'd discovered reading up on Sierra Leone and had been reminded of in South Africa: that, searching for Shakespeare in many different cultures, one saw his silhouette everywhere, even places he'd never been. Many societies, particularly in the economically poor global south, rubbed along perfectly fine without the works of William Shakespeare, and would continue to do so long into the future. The anthropologist Laura Bohannan's parable about *Hamlet* and the Tiv, in which the most famous play by the world's most famous author failed to impress a group of Nigerian tribal elders, was an essential caution. Not only did it relegate Shakespeare to the status of just one storyteller among many, but it reminded us (reminded *me*) that some things were stubbornly and unavoidably local. This, too, was something I had only dimly grasped before I began to travel. It was a valuable lesson.

Back in Hong Kong, it was becoming dusk. The apartment blocks and skyscrapers had become speckled with warm points of light and the sky, murky and sullen, had deepened to purplish-grey. The Bank of China tower was illuminated with sharp bars of electric white, broken into crooked reflections by the mirrored glass. Next to it reared the crest of the International Finance Centre, its summit swallowed by the gathering murk. A storm looked to be on the way. For a few minutes, as it stole soundlessly in, I watched the illuminated city meet its twin on the blackening water.

Looking back through my notes, I snorted at where they'd led me: to the image of Shakespeare as an untethered symbol of trans-national, free-flowing capital. Where else would one find a Shakespeare who looked like that, but right here in Hong Kong?

That was another strange thing about Shakespeare: he had a disconcerting habit of reflecting your own self back at you.

At the Chinese University of Hong Kong, the foyer was a medley of Shakespearian characters. Using the programme I'd been issued, I attempted to identify them: the girl with the belly padding and the appliqué moustache had to be Sir Toby Belch. The boy wearing streaky dark face-paint must be Othello, but was he the Othello from the University of Macau, Renmin University or Ludong University? How about the three students in Chinese-opera costume and full make-up? Anyone's guess. The characters wafted around, freezing robotically into pose as selfies were captured and filed, and forming ever more unlikely Shakespearian couplings: Juliet with her arm around Imogen; Prospero cosying up to Macbeth. The Nurse had clearly taken a shine to Othello.

It seemed a good way to spend the penultimate day of my trip, and only partly because this free-associating parade of Shakespearian characters resembled the mangled state of my brain. The Chinese

Universities Shakespeare Festival was the largest and longest-running event of its kind in China. Over the ten years of its existence, hundreds of students had taken part, from 92 universities in 27 provinces. Theoretically it was all about cooperation, but no one was fooled. In the best Chinese traditions it was ferociously competitive: 44 universities had applied this year, only 12 making it to the finals. Students had been rehearsing for months, had taken days off class and all-night coach journeys to get here.

Despite the smiles and the selfies, the atmosphere was jittery. Professors were huddled in corners, with the hunched air of professional sports coaches. There was much trading of tips: would it be CUHK's year, or was being the home team a handicap? Might Nanjing regain the glory days of its past?

After a few minutes' speechifying and applause, we were introduced to the judging panel: the former head of the Australian National University drama department, the artistic director of Shakespeare Western Australia and the dramaturg at the California Shakespeare theatre. A strange coincidence, re-encountering Cal Shakes: it was where I'd watched *Hamlet* many months before. It seemed peculiar after everything I'd learned about colonial history that the students were Chinese and the judges white, but I kept the thought to myself.

The head of the CUHK English department said something about art being a bridge to our shared world. There was warm applause. Global Shakespeare in action. More warm applause. The sponsor, an oleaginous businessman who had taken a gallant interest in the female students, tapped the microphone. 'There is a saying in Chinese, it takes ten years to plant a tree . . .' I doubted it, but it was a noble thought.

As the teams streamed backstage to take their places, the head of department gave me a lowdown on the rules. Each team would perform a handful of scenes from the play of their choice, not exceeding twenty minutes. Only three actors were allowed per team. The scripts had been edited, but all were in Shakespearian English. This was as much a test of comprehension and diction as it was of acting.

I said I found it an odd idea, Shakespeare being used competitively, like college football.

The head's eyes were on his phone, searching for the festival's Twitter hashtag. 'That's China for you. Survival of the fittest. Work here for long enough and you don't notice it.'

First out of the blocks were CUHK, with an all-female cast tackling early scenes from *Romeo and Juliet*: the tussle between Juliet and her mother over plans for Juliet's arranged marriage, followed by a silent tableau of the ball scene. It was a well-mannered performance that put me in mind of Disney's *Cinderella*. Juliet wore a ball dress and pouted like Alicia Silverstone in *Clueless*; Lady Capulet was nicely haughty, with an excellent line in eye-rolling at her teenage daughter's capricious recalcitrance. Romeo was nowhere to be seen, invoked only by name: a nicely feminist take on a play somewhat over-stuffed with brawling young men.

Trying to get into the judging spirit, I looked for demerits – their pronunciation was pitch-perfect, to be sure, but was there more than a hint of finishing school? All were Hongkongers, but one would have had a hard time telling it; with their American high-school vowels and their prom-queen sheen, there seemed nothing remotely Chinese in what they were doing. But maybe that was a western way of looking at it. Maybe it was authentically Hong Kong to pretend you weren't from Hong Kong.

The letter scene from *Twelfth Night*, performed by Tsinghua University, was more enjoyable. Setting the play in the early-twentieth-century Republic of China, the student director and creative team had gone in for vaguely P. G. Wodehouse-ish outfits, with the striking exception of Malvolio, clad in gown and tights of a vibrant yellow hue (traditionally indicating high office as well as the colour of lust, it was explained afterwards). The tights were deployed repeatedly and with great vigour, which generated much audience excitement – at least more than Shakespeare's wordplay, which (unwisely, I thought) had mostly been retained. It was the first time I'd ever heard Malvolio's normally reliable line, 'these be her very c's, her u's, and her t's' – exclaiming at what he believes to be Olivia's handwriting – fall flat. I glanced at the ninth-grader next to me: not a titter. Cunt jokes presumably worked better in Cantonese.

Macau University's *Othello* came and went. My mind wasn't entirely on the task in hand. The storm had eventually blown in the night before, and I had been woken at 3.30 a.m. by a window-rattling crash so violent I thought at first it was a car bomb in the street. Disorientated, heart thudding, I had lain there for what felt like minutes, looking at the pale sheen of the streetlights on the ceiling and trying to remember which country I was in. China? India? I had eventually concluded it was Taiwan. As I fell asleep, an image had swum into my head of London painfully clear and sharp: drizzle, cloud, the soft smell of charcoal smoke over Victorian back-to-backs, the green shimmer of trees in the park . . .

I sat up in my seat and tried to keep hold of the present. Xiamen University of Technology had taken the stage. They were regarded as a long shot, coming from a new-ish university in Fujian province whose strengths lay in engineering and science rather than the liberal arts. They were underdogs. I decided to root for them.

I needn't have bothered; their version of *Cymbeline* was by far the best performance, thoughtful and emotional, portraying two pivotal scenes – Posthumus's banishment and separation from Imogen, followed by the grimly insinuating dialogue in which the dastardly Giacomo implies that Posthumus has been unfaithful to his wife while away. Their English was precise and believable, expertly navigating the whirlpools and eddies of late-Shakespearian verse, but the action had been directed in the style of Chinese opera. The cast were garbed in white facepaint and silken gowns the colour of icing; there was much coy fluttering of fans. I had no idea how authentic this *jingju* was, but for once that didn't seem the point. The production captured the play's fragile beauty and poise, how so much of its language was about the way things were seen, or not seen:

> I would have broke mine eye-strings, cracked them, but
> To look upon him till the diminution
> Of space had pointed him sharp as my needle;
> Nay, followed him till he had melted from
> The smallness of a gnat to air, and then
> Have turned mine eye and wept.

Imogen was here describing a leave-taking she had not, in reality, been permitted to observe: Posthumus was long gone, the lovers already separated, and would not be reunited for nearly the duration of the play.

Cymbeline is one of the last scripts Shakespeare wrote on his own: the astrologer Simon Forman saw it in 1611, which places it alongside *The Winter's Tale* and *The Tempest*. Deeply influenced by the Stuart masques its author must have witnessed at court, the play suited translation into another courtly form, Chinese opera. Imogen's speech had a haunting, evanescent beauty that matched the elegance and composure of *jingju*, its balance between constrained poetic formality and something much more pregnant with meaning.

Though the word is now unfashionable, *Cymbeline* is sometimes still called a 'romance', and of all the late plays it most deserves the term. It is a narrative of quest, or quests: Cymbeline's journey towards becoming a better father, Posthumus's limping progress towards self-knowledge, Imogen's odyssey to find her brothers, through what looks very much like death – she drinks a sleeping draught and falls into a deathlike slumber – and then into mythic rebirth. Xiamen's director, a tutor going under the equally romantic name of Ballet Liu, had wisely made this abbreviated version more or less Imogen's drama, dominated by an intense central performance from a student called Zhang Peipei.

As Zhang took her bow, I realised with a start that behind her trembling fan real tears were in her eyes. They weren't far from mine.

In the raucous rush of a wood-panelled French wine bar, surrounded by braying Brits and Aussies, I spent a final evening in Hong Kong. It was a Tuesday evening, but felt later in the week. The suits and shirtsleeves were spilling outside; through the open windows the sound of the city was loud. Competing with the yowling sirens and the squealing of brakes were the low roar of air-conditioning units and the strident, angular intonations of Cantonese businessmen gossiping on the street. In the humid, dog's-breath air, the city itself felt like a living creature, one possessed of its own jittery, jumped-up energy.

I realised there was another reason I'd found *Cymbeline* so unexpectedly poignant that afternoon. I had seen the play at the Blackfriars in Staunton, Virginia, eighteen months before, near the beginning of my journeys. *Cymbeline* had also been the play read by Solomon Plaatje while he was romancing his wife, and it was a *Cymbeline* in Vadodara in 1880 that had convinced a previous traveller, Harold Littledale, of the strange beauties of Indian theatre. He, too, had been bowled over by Imogen (played, as she would have been in Shakespeare's day, by a male actor). Head deep in Chinese Shakespeares, I'd wiped these rival *Cymbelines* from my brain.

Were they rivals? The two productions I'd seen in the theatre couldn't have been more different. The Staunton *Cymbeline* was melodramatic, a rollicking tale with a loud twang of the American frontier, acted in a theatre Shakespeare would have recognised the moment he stepped inside. Here in Hong Kong the play seemed much more delicate, performed in a cultural context that would have left its author bemused, but which contained an aristocratic grace he might perhaps have understood. The famous thing about *Cymbeline*, of course, was that it was an incomprehensible mishmash: Dr Johnson called its plot 'unresisting imbecility'. An amalgam of sources from a typically eclectic variety of places – Holinshed's *Chronicles*, Boccaccio's *Decameron* in a version translated via Dutch, Elizabethan prose romances and a number of others – it was a melting pot. It was also a compendium of motifs from two and a half decades of writing and the final play to be printed in the First Folio. That the *Cymbelines* I'd seen were both the same play and utterly different, a world away from each other and not, seemed entirely appropriate.

Globalisation theory was all very well, but was there something in the works themselves that explained how they had come to be reinterpreted so many times, all across the world? It was a tantalising – and tantalisingly hard – question. Shakespeare's own porousness and receptiveness to the world that surrounded him was certainly part of the answer, his nimble curiosity about what Prospero in *The Tempest* calls 'the great globe itself' (and his interest in putting that globe on stage at the Globe). I also liked the theory, acquired in Taipei, that his very language was alive with quickness and mutability, movement and change. If the plays and poems provoke us to do anything, it is surely to think more rapidly, to be light on our feet, to see things three-dimensionally and from many different angles – not one thing, many things. One thinks of the Prologue to *Henry V*, with its stirring call to make 'imaginary puissance', to combine in a shared effort of will to transform the invented scenes in front of us on stage into embodied reality. One thinks, too, that for Shakespeare and his company theatre was a lively, collaborative art – the creation of wigmakers as well as writers, stagehands alongside dancing masters, audience as well as actors.

Equally pragmatic, and no less important, is the fact that Shakespeare's scripts are unusually flexible, open to adaptation and possible to stage in any number of different forms. How many *Hamlets* had I encountered en route? Seven or eight, on stage and on screen? More, when one factored in scripts or narrative versions I'd read. For the same play – and a notoriously complex play at that – to work equally well as a Goethean *Bildungsroman* as a Parsi-influenced Hindi movie, a Wild West swashbuckler as well as a deconstructed, postmodern piece of *Regietheater* was an achievement so rare I felt it must be unique. For the multilingual, semi-improvised *Julius Caesar* I'd seen in Johannesburg still to be Shakespeare's *Julius Caesar* – just about – said much about how far his texts could be stretched and twisted before they began to buckle.

Was there something more, too? I'd been searching for an answer almost from the moment I'd watched that Afghan *Comedy of Errors*. There the play struck me as an exploration of travel, not just because of the arduous journeys, physical and emotional, taken by its cast; but in the way joyous confusions and jumbled identities went to the very core of what the drama was about. In two years of travel, I'd experienced a fair degree of comedy myself, and embarked on errors and wild goose chases too numerous to mention. Sometimes I, too, had run into myself coming the other way.

But then one could argue that travel and migration were ideas that occupied Shakespeare through the length of his writing career – more consistently perhaps than any other. Before I began travelling, I'd never fully appreciated how the motif infiltrates so much of his writing. From *The Two Gentlemen of Verona* (c.1590) to *The Two Noble Kinsmen* (c.1614), there is barely a work in which journeying doesn't underpin the wider movement of the action.

One could say this is unsurprising, given that the quest narrative is one of the most ancient in all literature. But it did seem inescapable how obsessively Shakespeare encircled and returned to the theme. The storms and shipwrecks are alarmingly, and famously, frequent (*The Comedy of Errors, Twelfth Night, Pericles, The Tempest*). So too are the exilic journeys on which he repeatedly sends his characters – the disguised Rosalind and Celia in *As You Like It* and the lovers in *A Midsummer Night's Dream*, alike banished to forests; Viola in *Twelfth Night*, saved from drowning and washed ashore in Illyria ('What country, friends, is this?'); Hamlet and his escapades with pirates in the frigid seas between Denmark and England. To these can be added Othello and Desdemona, dispatched from Venice to Cyprus on a voyage from which they will never return; Lear and his journey into the wilderness; and Imogen, with her own solitary quest through the wilds of Wales.

The sonnets resound to the theme:

> O never say that I was false of heart,
> Though absence seemed my flame to qualify—

As easy might I from myself depart
As from my soul, which in thy breast doth lie.
That is my home of love. If I have ranged,
Like him that travels I return again,
Just to the time, not with the time exchanged,
· So that myself bring water for my stain.
Never believe, though in my nature reigned
All frailties that besiege all kinds of blood,
That it could so preposterously be stained
To leave for nothing all thy sum of good;
   For nothing this wide universe I call
   Save thou my rose; in it thou art my all.

Sonnet 109 is characteristic of this portion of the sequence, in which the poet describes what seems to be an extended absence from his beloved (perhaps the 'lovely boy' of Sonnet 126), with the barbed hint that he has been unfaithful somewhere on his 'travels'. Dangerous though it is to associate that poetic 'I' with Shakespeare himself, it occurred to me that a man who spent nearly all his working life away from his family and his home town must have had plentiful opportunity to ponder what it feels like to be separated. He might never have left England; but did he need to?

Not always is the theme tragic. *Pericles*, which went on stage in 1608, the year before the sonnets were published, is especially fraught with journeys. The hero for whom it is named is sent, Odysseus-like, from 'bourn to bourn, region to region' across the ancient eastern Mediterranean – Antioch, Pentapolis, Tyre, Mytilene, Tarsus – suffering misadventure after misadventure, shipwreck after shipwreck, losing his wife in childbirth on board, then becoming separated from his daughter, named Marina for the sea on which she is born.

Against every apparent likelihood – and against everything Shakespeare's audience must have expected after the great run of tragedies that occupied him in the early 1600s – husband, wife and daughter are eventually, mystically, united. The scene is one of the most heart-stopping in all Shakespeare. 'Give me a gash,' Pericles pleads with his friend Helicanus:

              put me to present pain,
Lest this great sea of joys rushing upon me
O'erbear the shores of my mortality
And drown me with their sweetness! [*To Marina*] O, come hither,

Thou that begett'st him that did thee beget,
Thou that was born at sea, buried at Tarsus,
And found at sea again!

The first of the romances and the beginning of Shakespeare's great last phase, *Pericles* returns to themes – migration, separation – he had touched on in *The Comedy of Errors*, over a decade and a world earlier. A late voyage, even before *The Tempest*, in a lifetime of imaginative voyaging.

I looked down at my notes. My handwriting curled away on the page, black and cumbrous, looking like the product of someone else's brain. Two fat notebooks for China alone. The thought of reading them back made me want to cry.

Suddenly exhausted, I flicked a wad of Hong Kong dollars on to the counter and slid, somewhat unsteadily, off my stool. Time to think about going home.

In the departure terminal at Hong Kong airport, in the snug darkness of an evening that would go on for sixteen hours yet, I sat drinking vinegary Malbec and watching a British Airways 747 slide in to land. A band was playing, two teenage boys on piano and guitar. Their Adam's apples bobbed in time to the music.

For once, I didn't mind the wine, or the band. I was basking in the unrighteous glow of a misspent final day. There were still phone numbers to call, at least one interview I could have chased. I should really have gone back to the second session of the Chinese Universities Shakespeare Festival, and found out whether Xiamen were in with a chance. I hadn't. At 7 a.m., I'd opened the blind to find the harbour winking in the sunlight and a sky as clear and iridescent as polished crystal. I'd abandoned the city altogether and gone to the beach. It was early, a Wednesday morning, and for ten minutes I had the run of the place. The warm sand was the colour of fresh breadcrumbs, the water a delirious green-blue. I'd left my notebooks at home.

In the afternoon, I'd retreated further into type by going bargain-hunting in the antique shops on Hollywood Road. In my mind's eye was the celadon glaze of ceramics I'd glimpsed in museums in Beijing and Taipei: that unearthly, luminous milky green one sees on dishes, basins, lotus bowls. That was Ru ware and impossibly rare, but celadon was a mass export from China in the fourteenth and fifteenth centuries. There are plenty of surviving examples.

I found one promisingly dusty shop, lacking air conditioning and with an owner who resembled a bullfrog in slacks, and installed myself for a sweaty two hours, disdaining the Revolutionary Opera figurines he fished out of the back and lifting pieces of porcelain to the light with what I hoped was connoisseurship.

Eventually I chose one bowl, inscribed inside with gentle swirls, like the marks left in water by the tails of fish. There were no identifying symbols. Fourteenth-century, he insisted: late Yuan, early Ming. Without the faint flaw on the rim – the tiniest of nicks – it would be ten times the price. We settled on 1,200 Hong Kong dollars, about £100. I thought it was as likely to hail from the porcelain section of the Shenzhen Export Processing Zone, but I didn't care. Being fleeced in an antique shop was surely as traditional in Hong Kong as a detailed knowledge of feng shui and a conviction or two for insider trading.

It wasn't the only thing I bought. Heading back into town via Tsim Sha Tsui, I had passed a Japanese bookshop on Chatham Road. On a whim, I went in: I was curious to see if they had any Shakespeare manga, which I'd tried and failed to get hold of on the mainland. The students at CUHK had said they read it as a way of preparing their performances; other people I'd met had talked about its astonishing popularity across Asia. A British publisher had produced an English-language manga series, but I was after the hard stuff: Japanese originals. I half-suspected my sources of exaggerating: Shakespeare had permeated many aspects of pop culture, but Asian comic magazines?

At the counter, planting myself next to a waist-high pile of Hello Kittys, I did my best to sign-language what I wanted, mouthing every Asiatic variant of 'Shakespeare' I could think of: *Shashibiya, Sheshibiru, Shaykuspiru?*

At last the assistant decoded my tongue-tied pronunciation. *'Sheykusupia!'* he exclaimed. I nodded gratefully.

He darted across to the other side of the store, and came back proffering a tiny green-and-yellow book, ten or so centimetres tall, printed in what I recognised as katakana characters. On the cover, in yellow and pale green, was a series of stylised manga images, faces in close-up: faces yelling, screaming, weeping. I didn't recognise the play. But inside the dustjacket was a reproduction of the Chandos portrait, and dates in western format, 1564–1616. I bought it on the spot.

At the airport, as the jazz band eased into a soft-focus version of 'Bewitched', I pulled the book from my satchel and opened the covers, remembering to start back to front, right to left. The cells, four or five to each page, looked stark – black, white and grey, with small, precise speech bubbles in Japanese. The drawing was wonderfully sharp and sculptural. After an illustrated list of characters, the story commenced. There were scenes of devastation, halting beggars in the shadows. Raptors circled lazily beneath a woozy, feverous sun. In the distance, a medieval castle. One of the history plays? *Richard III? Hamlet?*

It was page five before I knew where I was – a severe stone chamber, a king enthroned high on a dais, tiny beneath the weight of his crown. Before him, flanked by rows of robed, stiff-backed knights, knelt three sons. I looked closer: long hair. Daughters.

Outside the curved glass windows of the airport, lights pulsed and shimmered, scattering colours into the black night: crimson, amber, emerald, pearl. Every so often there was the roar of a take-off, almost imperceptible. It sounded like the distant rumble of a storm. The wine in my glass barely trembled. Someone else's storm.

I looked back down at the book. *Japanese* Shakespeare, now this seemed interesting . . .

I turned the page and started to read.

Select bibliography

The books, articles and films I have been inspired by, dipped into or borrowed from while researching and writing this book are too numerous and varied to list, and that list would certainly be too vast to read. Instead I have compiled a compendium of suggested reading that acknowledges my debts to key sources, but which also – I hope – points the way for anyone making their own journeys into the rich and ever-expanding field of global Shakespeare.

Where possible titles are listed geographically, in the chapter order in which I employed them; I have prioritised works that have been translated into English. The opening section includes books and articles that range across more than one geographical area (as many do), and the final section lists works of general reference. Books and essays I found particularly helpful are marked with an asterisk. Many of the films listed are available on DVD or YouTube.

Anyone looking to orientate themselves country by country would do well to start with the excellent (and free) 'Shakespeare in . . .' online essays published by the University of Victoria in Canada, at: *internetshakespeare.uvic. ca/Library/Criticism/shakespearein*

Citations from Shakespeare in the main text are keyed to Stanley Wells and Gary Taylor (eds), *The Complete Works*, 2nd edition (Oxford, 2005).

Prologue and global Shakespeares

PRIMARY SOURCES

Purchas, Samuel, *Hakluytus Posthumus, or Purchas his Pilgrimes*, 5 vols (London, 1625).
Rundall, Thomas, *Narratives of Voyages towards the North-West, in Search of a Passage to Cathay and India, 1496–1631* (London, 1849).

SECONDARY SOURCES

Barbour, Richmond, *The Third Voyage Journals: Writing and Performance in the London East India Company, 1607–10* (New York, 2009).

Bate, Jonathan, *The Genius of Shakespeare* (London, 1997).

*Bishop, Tom and Alexander C. Y. Huang (eds), *The Shakespeare International Yearbook 11: Special Issue, Placing Michael Neill – Issues of Place in Shakespeare and Early Modern Culture* (Burlington, VT, 2011).

Brusberg-Kiermeier, Stefani and Jörg Helbig (eds), *Shakespeare in the Media: From the Globe Theatre to the World Wide Web* (Frankfurt-am-Main, 2004).

Chaudhuri, Sukanta and Chee Seng Lim (eds), *Shakespeare Without English: The Reception of Shakespeare in Non-Anglophone Countries* (New Delhi, 2006).

Cunningham, Vanessa, *Shakespeare and Garrick* (Cambridge, 2008).

*Desmet, Christy and Robert Sawyer (eds), *Shakespeare and Appropriation* (London, 1999).

Dionne, Craig and Parmita Kapadia, *Native Shakespeares: Indigenous Appropriations on a Global Stage* (Aldershot, 2008).

Dobson, Michael, *The Making of the National Poet: Shakespeare, Adaptation and Authorship, 1660–1769* (Oxford, 1992).

——, *Shakespeare and Amateur Performance: A Cultural History* (Cambridge, 2011).

Donaldson, Peter, '"All Which it Inherit": Shakespeare, Globes and Global Media', *Shakespeare Survey* 52 (1999), 183–200.

Edmondson, Paul, Paul Prescott and Erin Sullivan (eds), *A Year of Shakespeare: Reliving the World Shakespeare Festival* (London, 2013).

Gillies, John, *Shakespeare and the Geography of Difference* (Cambridge, 1994).

*Hadfield, Andrew and Paul Hammond (eds), *Shakespeare and Renaissance Europe* (London, 2005).

Hair, P. E. H., '*Hamlet* in an Afro-Portuguese Setting: New Perspectives on Sierra Leone in 1607', *History in Africa* 5 (1978), 21–42.

Hoenselaars, Ton (ed.), *Shakespeare and the Language of Translation* (London, 2004).

Holderness, Graham and Bryan Loughrey, 'Arabesque: Shakespeare and Globalisation', in S. Smith (ed.), *Globalization and its Discontents: Writing the Global Culture* (Cambridge, 2006), 24–46.

*Huang, Alexander C. Y., 'Global Shakespeares as Methodology', *Shakespeare* 9 (2013), 273–90.

*Hulme, Peter and William H. Sherman (eds), '*The Tempest*' and its Travels* (Philadelphia, 2000).

Joughin, John J. (ed), *Shakespeare and National Culture* (Manchester, 1997).

Kennedy, Dennis, *Foreign Shakespeare: Contemporary Performance* (Cambridge, 1993).

Kerr, Heather, Robin Eaden and Madge Mitton (eds), *Shakespeare: World Views* (Newark, DE, 1996).

Kliman, Bernice W., 'At Sea about *Hamlet* at Sea: A Detective Story', *Shakespeare Quarterly* 62 (2011), 180–204.

*Loomba, Ania, *Shakespeare, Race and Colonialism* (Oxford, 2002).

Loomba, Ania and Martin Orkin (eds), *Post-Colonial Shakespeares* (London, 1998).

Maquerlot, Jean-Pierre and Michèle Willems (eds), *Travel and Drama in Shakespeare's Time* (Cambridge, 1996).

Marshall, Gail, *Shakespeare in the Nineteenth Century* (Cambridge, 2012).

*Massai, Sonia (ed.), *World-Wide Shakespeares: Local Appropriations in Film and Performance* (London, 2005).

Prescott, Paul and Erin Sullivan (eds), *Shakespeare on the Global Stage: Performance and Festivity in the Olympic Year* (London, 2015).

Rebellato, Dan, *Theatre and Globalization* (Basingstoke, 2009).

Robins, Nick, *The Corporation that Changed the World: How the East India Company Shaped the Modern Multinational* (London, 2006).

Shapiro, James, *Shakespeare and the Jews* (New York, 1996).

Taylor, Gary, '*Hamlet* in Africa 1607', in Ivo Kamps and Jyotsna Singh (eds), *Travel Knowledge: European 'Discoveries' in the Early Modern Period* (London, 2001).

——, *Reinventing Shakespeare: A Cultural History from the Restoration to the Present* (New York, 1989).

Trivedi, Poonam and Minami Ryuta (eds), *Re-playing Shakespeare in Asia* (London, 2010).

Poland and Germany

PRIMARY SOURCES

Bate, Jonathan (ed.), *The Romantics on Shakespeare* (Harmondsworth, 1992).

Freiligrath, Ferdinand, *Freiligraths Werke in Einem Band,* ed. Werner Ilberg (Berlin, 1980).

Goethe, Johann Wolfgang von, *Early Verse Drama and Prose Plays,* ed. Cyrus Hamlin and Frank Ryder (Princeton, NJ, 1995).

——, *Faust I and II,* trans. Stuart Atkins (Princeton, NJ, 1994).

——, *Goethe on Shakespeare,* trans. Michael Hofmann and David Constantine (London, 2010).

——, *The Sorrows of Young Werther,* trans. David Constantine (Oxford, 2012).

——, *Verse Plays and Epic,* ed. Cyrus Hamlin and Frank Ryder (Princeton, NJ, 1994).

——, *Wilhelm Meister,* trans. Thomas Carlyle, 2 vols (London, 1894).

Halliday, Andrew, 'Shakespeare-Mad', *All the Year Round,* 11 (21 May 1864), 345–51.

Jones, Henry Arthur, *Shakespeare and Germany: Written During the Battle of Verdun* (London, 1916).

Le Winter, Oswald (ed.), *Shakespeare in Europe: Selections from Lessing, Voltaire, Goethe, etc.* (Harmondsworth, 1970).

Moryson, Fynes, *Shakespeare's Europe: Unpublished Chapters of Fynes Moryson's Itinerary*, ed. Charles Hughes (London, 1903).

Müller, Heiner, 'Die Hamletmaschine', in *Adaptations of Shakespeare: A Critical Anthology of Plays*, ed. Daniel Fischlin and Mark Fortier (London, 2000), 208–15.

——, *Heiner Müller After Shakespeare: Macbeth and Anatomy of Titus – Fall of Rome*, ed. Carl Weber (New York, 2012).

Schiller, Friedrich, *Five Plays*, trans. Robert David MacDonald (London, 1998).

SECONDARY SOURCES

Barnett, David, 'Resisting the Revolution: Heiner Müller's *Hamlet/Machine* at the Deutsches Theater, Berlin, March 1990', *Theatre Research International* 31 (2006), 188–200.

Bate, Jonathan, 'The Politics of Romantic Shakespearean Criticism: Germany, England, France', *European Romantic Review* 1 (1990), 1–26.

Bonnell, Andrew G., *Shylock in Germany: Antisemitism and the German Theatre from the Enlightenment to the Nazis* (London, 2008).

Boyle, Nicholas and John Guthrie (eds), *Goethe and the English-Speaking World: A Cambridge Symposium for his 250th Anniversary* (Columbia, SC, 2001).

Cohn, Alfred, *Shakespeare in Germany in the Sixteenth and Seventeenth Centuries* (London and Berlin, 1865).

*Foulkes, Richard, *The Shakespeare Tercentenary of 1864* (London, 1984).

Gadberry, Glen W. (ed.), *Theatre in the Third Reich, the Prewar Years: Essays on Theatre in Nazi Germany* (Westport, CT, 1995).

Habicht, Werner, 'Shakespeare Celebrations in Time of War', *Shakespeare Quarterly* 52 (2001), 441–55.

*——, 'Shakespeare in Nineteenth-Century Germany: The Making of a Myth', in *Nineteenth-Century Germany: A Symposium*, ed. Modris Eksteins and Hildegard Hammerschmidt (Tübingen, 1983), 141–57.

——, 'Topoi of the Shakespeare Cult in Germany', in *Literature and its Cults: An Anthropological Approach*, ed. Péter Dávidházi and Judit Karafiath (Budapest, 1994), 47–65.

*Hortmann, Wilhelm, *Shakespeare on the German Stage: The Twentieth Century* (Cambridge, 1998).

Howard, Tony, *Women as Hamlet: Performance and Interpretation in Theatre, Film and Fiction* (Cambridge, 2007).

*Jansohn, Christa (ed.), *German Shakespeare Studies at the Turn of the Twenty-First Century* (Newark, DE, 2006).

Korte, Barbara and Christina Spittel, 'Shakespeare under Different Flags: The Bard in German Classrooms from Hitler to Honecker', *Journal of Contemporary History* 44 (2009), 267–86.

Larson, Kenneth E., 'The Origins of the Schlegel-Tieck Shakespeare in the 1820s', *The German Quarterly* 60 (1987), 19–37.

*Limon, Jerzy, *Gentlemen of a Company: English Players in Central and Eastern Europe, 1590–1660* (Cambridge, 1985).

London, John, *Theatre Under the Nazis* (Manchester, 2000).

Longerich, Peter, *Goebbels: A Biography* (London, 2015).

Makaryk, Irena R. and Marissa McHugh (eds), *Shakespeare and the Second World War: Memory, Culture, Identity* (Toronto, 2012).

Murphy, Andrew, *Shakespeare for the People: Working-Class Readers, 1800–1900* (Cambridge, 2008).

Pascal, Roy, *Shakespeare in Germany, 1740–1815* (Cambridge, 1937).

*Paulin, Roger (ed.), *The Critical Reception of Shakespeare in Germany, 1682–1914: Native Literature and Foreign Genius* (Hildesheim, 2003).

——, *Great Shakespeareans: Voltaire, Goethe, Schlegel, Coleridge* (London, 2010).

Pfister, Manfred, 'Germany is Hamlet: The History of a Political Interpretation', *New Comparison* 2 (1986), 106–26.

——, 'Hamlets Made in Germany, East and West', in *Shakespeare in the New Europe*, ed. Michael Hattaway et al. (Sheffield, 1994) 76–91.

Sillars, Stuart, *Shakespeare and the Victorians* (Oxford, 2013).

Stříbrný, Zdeněk, *Shakespeare and Eastern Europe* (Oxford, 2000).

Strobl, Gerwin, *The Swastika and the Stage: German Theatre and Society, 1933–45* (Cambridge, 2007).

Stroedel, Wolfgang, '90th Anniversary Celebration of the Deutsche Shakespeare-Gesellschaft', *Shakespeare Quarterly* 5 (1954), 317–22.

Symington, Rodney, *The Nazi Appropriation of Shakespeare: Cultural Politics in the Third Reich* (Lewiston, NY, 2005).

*Williams, Simon, *Shakespeare on the German Stage: 1586–1914* (Cambridge, 1990).

FILMS

Hamlet: Ein Rachedrama, dir. Sven Gade (Germany, 1921).

United States

PRIMARY SOURCES

Borthwick, J. D., *Three Years in California* (Edinburgh, 1857).

Emerson, Ralph Waldo, *Essays and Poems*, ed. Joel Porte, Harold Bloom and Paul Kane (New York, 1996).

Leman, Walter, *Memories of an Old Actor* (San Francisco, 1886).

Ludlow, Noah, *Dramatic Life as I Found It* (St Louis, MO, 1880).

Nelson, Richard, *How Shakespeare Won the West* (New York, 2010).

Shapiro, James (ed.), *Shakespeare in America: An Anthology from the Revolution to Now* (New York, 2014).

Smiley, Jane, *A Thousand Acres* (New York, 1991).

Smith, Solomon Franklin, *Theatrical Management in the West and South for Thirty Years* (New York, 1868).

Tocqueville, Alexis de, *Democracy in America*, trans. Harvey Claflin Mansfield and Delba Winthrop (Chicago, 2000).

The True Tragedie of Richard the Third (London, 1594).

SECONDARY SOURCES

Ashley, Mabel Celeste, 'Gold Rush Theatre in Nevada City, California', unpublished MA thesis, Stanford University (1967).

Berson, Misha, *The San Francisco Stage: From Gold Rush to Golden Spike, 1849–69* (San Francisco, 1989).

——, *The San Francisco Stage: From Golden Spike to Great Earthquake, 1869–1906* (San Francisco, 1992).

Bristol, Michael D., *Shakespeare's America, America's Shakespeare* (London, 1990).

Burnett, Mark Thornton, 'Parodying with Richard', in Sarah Hatchuel and Nathalie Vienne-Guerrin (eds), *Shakespeare on Screen: Richard III* (Rouen, 2005), 91–112.

Carrell, Jennifer Lee, 'How the Bard Won the West', *Smithsonian* 29/5 (August, 1998), 99–107.

Cliff, Nigel, *The Shakespeare Riots: Revenge, Drama and Death in Nineteenth-Century America* (New York, 2007).

Curry, Jane Kathleen, *Nineteenth-Century American Women Theatre Managers* (Westport, CN, 1994).

Davidson, Levette J., 'Shakespeare in the Rockies', *Shakespeare Quarterly* 4 (1953), 39–49.

Dawson, Giles E., *History of the Folger Shakespeare Library, 1932–68*, unpublished typescript (1994).

Dunn, Esther Cloudman, *Shakespeare in America* (New York, 1939).

Engler, Balz, 'Shakespeare, Washington, Lincoln: The Folger Library and the American Appropriation of the Bard' [http://shine.unibas.ch/shine-folgerwf.htm].

Ferington, Esther (ed.), *Infinite Variety: Exploring the Folger Shakespeare Library* (Washington DC, 2002).

Grant, Stephen H., *Collecting Shakespeare: The Story of Henry and Emily Folger* (Baltimore, 2014).

Johnson, Susan Lee, *Roaring Camp: The Social World of the California Gold Rush* (New York, 2000).

Kimmel, Stanley, *The Mad Booths of Maryland* (New York, 1940).

Koon, Helene Wickham, *Gold Rush Performers: A Biographical Dictionary of Actors, Singers, Dancers . . .* (Jefferson, NC, 1994).

*——, *How Shakespeare Won the West: Players and Performances in America's Gold Rush, 1849–65* (Jefferson, NC, 1989).

Lanier, Douglas, *Shakespeare and Modern Popular Culture* (Oxford, 2002).

*Levine, Lawrence W., *Highbrow/Lowbrow: The Emergence of Cultural Hierarchy in America* (Cambridge, MA, 1988).

Mazer, Carey M. (ed.), *Great Shakespeareans: Poel, Granville Barker, Guthrie, Wanamaker* (London, 2013).

Rawlings, Peter (ed.), *Great Shakespeareans: Emerson, Melville, James, Berryman* (London, 2011).

San Francisco Theatre Research (18 vols), various authors and editors (San Francisco, 1938–42).

Scully, Christopher, 'Constructed Places: Shakespeare's American Playhouses', unpublished PhD thesis, Tufts University (2008).

Shapiro, James, *Contested Will: Who Wrote Shakespeare?* (New York, 2010).

*Shattuck, Charles H., *Shakespeare on the American Stage: From the Hallams to Edwin Booth* (Washington DC, 1976).

Smith, Steven Escar, '"The Eternal Verities Verified": Charlton Hinman and the Roots of Mechanical Collation', *Studies in Bibliography* 53 (2000), 129–61.

*Sturgess, Kim C., *Shakespeare and the American Nation* (Cambridge, 2004).

Teague, Frances, *Shakespeare and the American Popular Stage* (Cambridge, 2006).

Thorndike, Ashley Horace, *Shakespeare in America* (London, 1927).

*Vaughan, Alden T. and Virginia Mason Vaughan, *Shakespeare in America* (Oxford, 2012).

——, *Shakespeare in American Life* (Washington DC, 2007).

Willoughby, Edwin Eliott, 'The Reading of Shakespeare in Colonial America', *Papers of the Bibliographical Society of America* 31 (1937), 45–56.

Woods, Alan, 'Frederick B. Warde: America's Greatest Forgotten Tragedian', *Educational Theatre Journal* 29 (1977), 333–44.

FILMS AND TELEVISION SERIES

As You Like It, dir. Kenneth Branagh (UK/USA, 2006).

As You Like It, dir. Paul Czinner (UK, 1936).

House of Cards, written by Andrew Davies and Michael Dobbs, dir. Paul Seed (UK, 1990).

House of Cards, exec. prod. David Fincher, Kevin Spacey, Beau Willimon et al. (USA, 2013–).

The Life and Death of King Richard III, dir. André Calmettes and James Keane (USA, 1912).

Looking for Richard, dir. Al Pacino (USA/France, 1996).

Shakespearean Spinach, dir. Dave Fleischer and Roland Crandall (USA, 1940).

Ten Things I Hate About You, dir. Gil Junger (USA, 1999).

India

PRIMARY SOURCES

Dutt, Utpal, *Towards a Revolutionary Theatre* (Calcutta, 1982).

Hansen, Kathryn (ed.), *Stages of Life: Indian Theatre Autobiographies* (London, 2011).

Kendal, Geoffrey with Clare Colvin, *The Shakespeare Wallah* (London, 1986).

Littledale, Harold 'Cymbeline in a Hindoo Playhouse', *Macmillan's Magazine* 42 (May–Oct, 1880), 65–68.

The Mahabharata, trans. and abridged J. D. Smith (London, 2009).

Ramanathan, Ramu, *Shakespeare and She*, unpublished play (2008).

The Ramayana: A Modern Translation, trans. Ramesh Menon (New Delhi, 2003).

'Report of the Select Committee of the House of Lords on Colonisation from Ireland, Together with the Minutes of Evidence, 1847', *The Edinburgh Review* 91 (January, 1850), 1–62.

Tagore, Rabindranath, *Selected Writings on Literature and Language*, ed. Sukanta Chaudhuri, Sankha Ghosha and Sisir Kumar Das (New Delhi, 2001).

SECONDARY SOURCES

Banerji, Arnab, 'Rehearsals for a Revolution: The Political Theatre of Utpal Dutt', *Southeast Review of Asian Studies* 34 (2012), 222–30.

Bharucha, Rustom, *Theatre and the World: Performance and the Politics of Culture* (London, 1993).

Bhatia, Nandi, 'Different Othello(s) and Contentious Spectators: Changing Responses in India', *Gramma* 15 (2007), 155–74.

——, 'Shakespeare and the Codes of Empire in India', *Alif: Journal of Comparative Poetics* 18 (1998), 96–126.

*Bishop, Tom and Alexander C. Y. Huang (eds), *Shakespeare International Yearbook 12: Special Section, Shakespeare in India* (Burlington, VT, 2012).

Bose, Mihir, *Bollywood: A History* (Stroud, 2006).

Burnett, Mark Thornton, *Shakespeare and World Cinema* (Cambridge, 2013).

Chatterjee, Sudipto and Jyotsna Singh, 'Moor or Less? The Surveillance of *Othello*, Calcutta 1848', in Christy Desmet and Robert Sawyer (eds), *Shakespeare and Appropriation* (London, 1999), 65–84.

Dionne, Craig and Parmita Kapadia (eds), *Bollywood Shakespeares* (New York, 2014).

De, Esha Niyogi, 'Modern Shakespeares in Popular Bombay Cinema: Translation, Subjectivity and Community', *Screen* 43 (2002), 19–40.

Gandhi, L., 'Unmasking Shakespeare: the Uses of English in Colonial and Postcolonial India', in Philip Mead and Marion Campbell (eds), *Shakespeare's Books: Contemporary Cultural Politics and the Persistence of Empire* (Melbourne, 1993), 81–97.

Gunawardana, A. J., 'Theatre as a Weapon: An Interview with Utpal Dutt', *The Drama Review* 15 (1971), 224–37.

*Gupt, Somnath, *The Parsi Theatre: Its Origins and Development*, trans. Kathryn Hansen (Calcutta, 2005).

Hansen, Kathryn, 'Parsi Theatre and the City: Location, Patrons, Audiences', *Sarai Reader 2002: The Cities of Everyday Life* [www.sarai.net/journal/02PDF/04spectacle/02parsi–theatre.pdf].

*Lal, Ananda (ed.), *The Oxford Companion to Indian Theatre* (Oxford, 2004).

Lal, Ananda and Sukanta Chaudhuri (eds), *Shakespeare on the Calcutta Stage: A Checklist* (Calcutta, 2001).

Loomba, Ania, 'Shakespearian Transformations', in John J. Joughin (ed.), *Shakespeare and National Culture* (Manchester, 1997), 109–41.

Menon, Madhavi, *Unhistorical Shakespeare: Queer Theory in Shakespearean Literature and Film* (London, 2008).

Miola, Robert S., *Shakespeare's Reading* (Oxford, 2000).

Pande, Mrinal, '"Moving beyond themselves": Women in Hindustani Parsi Theatre and Early Hindi Films', *Economic and Political Weekly* 41/17 (April, 2006), 1646–53.

Shah, C. R., 'Shakespearean Plays in Indian Languages', 2 parts, *The Aryan Path* (November and December 1955), 483–88, 541–44.

Singh, Jyotsna, 'Different Shakespeares: The Bard in Colonial/Postcolonial India', *Theatre Journal* 41 (1989), 445–58.

*Sisson, C. J., *Shakespeare in India: Popular Adaptations on the Bombay Stage* (London, 1926).

Tejaswini, Ganti, *Bollywood: A Guidebook to Popular Hindi Cinema*, 2nd edn (London, 2012).

Trivedi, Poonam, '"Filmi" Shakespeare', *Literature/Film Quarterly* 35 (2007), 148–58.

*Trivedi, Poonam and Dennis Bartholomeusz (eds), *India's Shakespeare: Translation, Interpretation and Performance* (Newark, DE, 2005).

Venning, Dan, 'Cultural Imperialism and Intercultural Encounter in Merchant Ivory's *Shakespeare Wallah*', *Asian Theatre Journal* 28 (2011), 149–67.

Verma, Rajiva, '*Hamlet* on the Hindi screen', *Hamlet Studies* 24 (2002), 81–93.

Viswanathan, Gauri, *Masks of Conquest: Literary Study and British Rule in India* (New York, 1989).

Wells, Henry W. and H. H. Anniah Gowda, *Shakespeare Turned East: A Study in Comparison of Shakespeare's Last Plays with some Classical Plays of India* (Mysore, 1976).

*Yajnik, R. K., *The Indian Theatre* (London, 1933).

FILMS

10 ml Love, dir. Sharat Katariya (India, 2010).

36 Chowringhee Lane, dir. Aparna Sen (India, 1981).

Angoor, dir. Gulzar (India, 1982).

Bhranti Bilas, dir. Manu Sen (India, 1963).

Bobby, dir. Raj Kapoor (India, 1973).

Bodyguard, dir Siddique (India, 2011).

Dil Chahta Hai, dir. Farhan Akhtar (India, 2001).

Do Dooni Char, dir. Debu Sen (India, 1968).

Haider, dir. Vishal Bhardwaj (India, 2014).

Hamlet: A Free Adaptation, dir. Kishore Sahu (India, 1954).

Ishaqzaade, dir. Habib Faisal (India, 2012).

Kaliyattam, dir. Jayaraaj Rajasekharan Nair (India, 1997).

Kannaki, dir. Jayaraaj Rajasekharan Nair (India, 2002).

The Last Lear, dir. Rituparno Ghosh (India, 2007).

Life Goes On, dir. Sangeeta Datta (India, 2009).

Main Nashe Mein Hoon, dir. Naresh Saigal (India, 1959).

Maqbool, dir. Vishal Bhardwaj (India, 2003).

Omkara, dir. Vishal Bhardwaj (India, 2006).

Shakespeare Wallah, dir. James Ivory (USA, 1965).

South Africa

PRIMARY SOURCES

Donne, John, *The Complete English Poems*, ed. C. A. Patrides (London, 1985).

Goldblatt, David, *Photographs* (Rome, 2006).

Gollancz, Israel (ed.), *A Book of Homage to Shakespeare* (Oxford, 1916).

Mandela, Nelson, *Long Walk to Freedom* (Boston, 1994).

Okri, Ben, *A Way of Being Free* (London, 1997).

Plaatje, Solomon, *Dintshontsho tsa bo-Juliuse Kesara* [*Julius Caesar*] (Johannesburg, 1937).

——, *Diphosho-phosho* [*The Comedy of Errors*] (Morija, 1930).

——, *Mhudi*, ed. Stephen Gray (London, 1978).

——, *Native Life in South Africa*, ed. Brian Willan (Harlow, 1987).

——, *Selected Writings*, ed. Brian Willan (Johannesburg, 1997).

Quarshie, Hugh, *Second Thoughts about Othello* (Chipping Campden, 1999).

SECONDARY SOURCES

Bartels, Emily, 'Making More of the Moor: Aaron, Othello, and Renaissance Refashionings of Race', *Shakespeare Quarterly* 41 (1990), 433–54.

——, 'Too many Blackamoors: Deportation, Discrimination, and Elizabeth I', *Studies in English Literature 1500–1900* 46 (2006), 305–22.

*Bohannan, Laura, 'Shakespeare in the Bush', *Natural History* 75/7 (1966), 28–33.

Brockbank, Philip, 'Shakespeare's Stratford and South Africa', *Shakespeare Quarterly* 38 (1987), 479–81.

Buntman, Fran Lisa, *Robben Island and Prisoner Resistance to Apartheid* (Cambridge, 2003).

Couzens, Tim, 'A Moment in the Past: William Tsikinya-Chaka', *Shakespeare in Southern Africa* 2 (1988), 60–66.

Couzens, Tim and Brian Willan, 'Solomon T. Plaatje, 1876–1932' [Plaatje centenary issue], *English in Africa*, 4 (1977).

Desai, Ashwin, *Reading Revolution: Shakespeare on Robben Island* (Pretoria, 2012).

*Distiller, Natasha, 'Authentic Protest, Authentic Shakespeare, Authentic Africans: Performing *Othello* in South Africa', *Comparative Drama* 46 (2012), 339–54.

——, *Shakespeare and the Coconuts* (Johannesburg, 2012).

——, *South Africa, Shakespeare, and Post-Colonial Culture* (Lewinston, NY, 2005).

Gray, Stephen, *Sources of the First Black South African Novel in English: Solomon Plaatje's Use of Shakespeare and Bunyan in 'Mhudi'* (Pasadena, CA, 1976).

*Holmes, Jonathan, '"A world elsewhere": Shakespeare in South Africa', *Shakespeare Survey* 55 (2002), 271–84.

Hutton, Barbara, *Robben Island: Symbol of Resistance* (Johannesburg, 1994).

Johnson, David, *Shakespeare and South Africa* (Oxford, 1996).

Johnson, Lemuel A., *Shakespeare in Africa (and other venues): Import and the Appropriation of Culture* (Trenton, NJ, 1998).

Kahn, Coppélia, 'Remembering Shakespeare Imperially: the 1916 Tercentenary', *Shakespeare Quarterly* 52 (2001), 456–78.

Lindfors, Bernth, *Ira Aldridge*, 2 vols (Rochester, NY, 2011).

Marshall, Herbert and Mildred Stock, *Ira Aldridge: The Negro Tragedian* (Carbondale, IL, 1958).

Molema, Seetsele Modiri, *Lover of his People: A Biography of Sol Plaatje*, trans. and ed. D. S. Matjila and Karen Haire (Johannesburg, 2012).

Orkin, Martin, *Shakespeare Against Apartheid* (Craighall, 1987).

Peterson, Bhekizizwe, 'Apartheid and the Political Imagination in Black South African Theatre', *Journal of Southern African Studies* 16 (1990) 229–45.

*Quince, Rohan, *Shakespeare in South Africa: Stage Productions During the Apartheid Era* (New York, 2000).

Rosenthal, Eric, 'Early Shakespearean Productions in South Africa', *English Studies in Africa* 7 (1964), 202–16.

Roux, Daniel, 'Hybridity, Othello and the Postcolonial Critics', *Shakespeare in Southern Africa* 21 (2009), 23–31.

*Schalkwyk, David, *Hamlet's Dreams: The Robben Island Shakespeare* (London, 2013).

——, 'Portrait and Proxy: Representing Plaatje and Plaatje Represented', *Scrutiny2* 4 (1999), 14–29.

——, 'Shakespeare's Untranslatability', *Shakespeare in Southern Africa* 18 (2006), 37–48.

Schalkwyk, David and Lerothodi Lapula, 'Solomon Plaatje, William Shakespeare, and the Translations of Culture', *Pretexts: Literary and Cultural Studies* 9 (2000), 9–26.

Seddon, Deborah, 'Shakespeare's Orality: Solomon Plaatje's Setswana Translations', *English Studies in Africa* 47 (2004), 77–95.

Seeff, Adele, '*Othello* at the Market Theatre', *Shakespeare Bulletin* 27 (2009), 377–98.

Shole, Shole J., 'Shakespeare in Setswana: An Evaluation of Raditladi's *Macbeth* and Plaatje's *Diphosophoso*', *Shakespeare in Southern Africa* 4 (1990), 51–64.

Suzman, Janet, '*Othello*: A Belated Reply', *Shakespeare in Southern Africa* 2 (1988), 90–6.

——, 'South Africa in *Othello*', in Jonathan Bate et al. (eds), *Shakespeare and the Twentieth Century* (Newark, DE, 1998,) 23–40.

*Thurman, Chris (ed.), *South African Essays on 'Universal' Shakespeare* (Farnham, 2014).

*Willan, Brian, *Sol Plaatje: South African Nationalist, 1876–1932* (Berkeley, CA, 1984).

Willan, Brian, 'Whose Shakespeare? Early Black Engagements with Shakespeare', *Shakespeare in Southern Africa* 24 (2012), 3–24.

Wright, Laurence, 'Cultivating Grahamstown: Nathaniel Merriman, Shakespeare and Books', *Shakespeare in Southern Africa* 20 (2008), 25–38.

——, 'Shakespeare in South Africa: Alpha and "Omega"', *Postcolonial Studies* 7 (2006), 63–81.

*—— (ed.), *The Shakespearean International Yearbook, Volume 9: Special Section, South African Shakespeare in the Twentieth Century* (Ashgate, 2009).

China

PRIMARY SOURCES

Lamb, Charles and Mary Lamb, *Tales from Shakespeare*, ed. Marina Warner (London, 2007).

Li, Zhisui, *The Private Life of Chairman Mao: The Memoirs of Mao's Personal Physician*, ed. Anne F. Thurston (London, 1994).

SECONDARY SOURCES

Barber, C. L., *Shakespeare's Festive Comedy* (Princeton, NJ, 1959).

Berry, Edward, 'Teaching Shakespeare in China', *Shakespeare Quarterly* 39 (1988), 212–16.

Boorman, Howard L., 'The Literary World of Mao Tse-tung', *The China Quarterly* 13 (1963), 15–38.

Brockbank, Philip, 'Shakespeare Renaissance in China', *Shakespeare Quarterly* 39 (1988), 195–204.

Brooks, Douglas A. and Lingui Yang (eds), *Shakespeare and Asia* (Lewiston, NY, 2010).

Dusinberre, Juliet, *Shakespeare and the Nature of Women* (London, 1975).

Empson, William, *The Structure of Complex Words*, 3rd edn (London, 1995).

Fan, Shen, 'Shakespeare in China: *The Merchant of Venice*', *Asian Theatre Journal* 5 (1988), 23–37.

He, Qixin, 'China's Shakespeare', *Shakespeare Quarterly* 37 (1986), 149–59.

Howard, Jean E. and Scott Cutler Shershow (eds), *Marxist Shakespeares* (London, 2000).

Hsu, Tao-Ching, *The Chinese Conception of the Theatre* (Seattle, 1985).

*Huang, Alexander C. Y., *Chinese Shakespeares: Two Centuries of Cultural Exchange* (New York, 2009).

Huang, Alexander C. Y. and Charles S. Ross (eds), *Shakespeare in Hollywood, Asia and Cyberspace* (West Lafayette, IN, 2009).

Irish, Tracy, *Shakespeare: A Worldwide Classroom* (London: RSC Education/British Council report, 2012).

Jardine, Lisa, *Still Harping on Daughters: Women and Drama in the Age of Shakespeare* (London, 1983).

Kennedy, Dennis and Yong Li Lan (eds), *Shakespeare in Asia: Contemporary Performance* (Cambridge, 2010).

*Lanier, Douglas M., 'Shakespearean Rhizomatics: Adaptation, Ethics, Value', in Alexander C. Y. Huang and Elizabeth Rivlin (eds), *Shakespeare and the Ethics of Appropriation* (New York, 2014), 21–40.

Lee, Adele, '"Chop-socky Shakespeare"?!: The Bard Onscreen in Hong Kong', *Shakespeare Bulletin* 28 (2010), 459–80.

*Levith, Murray J., *Shakespeare in China* (London, 2004).

Li, Jun, 'Popular Shakespeare in China: 1993–2008', unpublished PhD thesis, Chinese University of Hong Kong (2013).

Li, Ruru, 'The Bard in the Middle Kingdom', *Asian Theatre Journal* 12 (1995), 50–84.

*——, *Shashibiya: Staging Shakespeare in China* (Hong Kong, 2003).

Lu, Tonglin, 'Zhu Shenghao: Shakespeare Translator and a Shakespearean Tragic Hero in Wartime China', *Comparative Literature Studies* 49 (2012), 521–36.

Makaryk, Irena R. and Joseph G. Price (eds), *Shakespeare in the Worlds of Communism and Socialism* (Toronto, 2006).

Ng, Yong-sang, 'The Poetry of Mao Tse-tung', *The China Quarterly* 13 (1963), 60–73.

Spurgeon, Caroline F. E., *Shakespeare's Imagery, and What it Tells Us* (Cambridge, 1935).

Sun, Yanna, 'General Problems in Chinese Translations of Shakespeare', *Asian Culture and History* 2 (2010), 232–35.

——, 'Shakespeare Reception in China', *Theory and Practice in Language Studies* 2 (2012), 1931–38.

Tam, Kwok-kan, Andrew Parkin and Terry Siu-han Yip (eds), *Shakespeare Global/Local: The Hong Kong Imaginary in Transcultural Production* (New York, 2002).

Terrill, Ross, *Madame Mao: The White-Boned Demon, a Biography*, 3rd edn (Stanford, CA, 1999).

Wong, Dorothy, '"Domination by consent": A study of Shakespeare in Hong Kong' in Theo D'haen and Patricia Krüs (eds), *Colonizer and Colonized* (Amsterdam, 2000), 43–56.

Yu, Weijie, 'Topicality and Typicality: The Acceptance of Shakespeare in China', in Erika Fischer-Lichte (ed.), *The Dramatic Touch of Difference: Theatre, Own and Foreign* (Tübingen, 1990).

Zha, Peide and Tian Jia, 'Shakespeare in Traditional Chinese Operas', *Shakespeare Quarterly* 39 (1988), 204–11.

Zhang, Xiao Yang, *Shakespeare in China: A Comparative Study of Two Traditions and Cultures* (Newark, DE, 1996).

Zhang, Chong, 'Translating Shakespeare across Language and Culture: a Chinese Perspective', in Douglas A. Brooks and Lingui Yang (eds), *Shakespeare and Asia* (Lewiston, NY, 2010), 281–96.

FILMS

The Bad Sleep Well [*Warui Yatsu Hodo Yoku Nemuru*], dir. Akira Kurosawa (Japan, 1960).

Censor Must Die, dir. Ing Kanjanavanit (Thailand, 2014).

Shakespeare Must Die, dir. Ing Kanjanavanit (Thailand, 2012).

Throne of Blood [*Kumonosu-Jō*], dir. Akira Kurosawa (Japan, 1957).

Yi jian mei [*A Spray of Plum Blossom*], dir. Bu Wancang (China, 1931).

General reference

Boose, Lynda E. and Richard Burt (eds), *Shakespeare, the Movie: Popularising the plays on Film, TV and Video* (London, 1997).

——, *Shakespeare, the Movie II: Popularising the Plays on Film, TV, Video and DVD* (London, 2003).

Bullough, Geoffrey, *Narrative and Dramatic Sources of Shakespeare*, 8 vols (London, 1957–75).

De Grazia, Margreta and Stanley Wells (eds), *The New Cambridge Companion to Shakespeare* (2010).

Dickson, Andrew, *The Rough Guide to Shakespeare*, 2nd edn (London, 2009).

Dobson, Michael and Stanley Wells (eds), *The Oxford Companion to Shakespeare* (Oxford, 2003).

Honan, Park, *Shakespeare: A Life* (Oxford, 1998).

Nicholl, Charles, *The Lodger: Shakespeare in Silver Street* (London, 2008).

Rothwell, Kenneth S. and Annabelle H. Melzer, *Shakespeare on Screen: An International Filmography and Videography* (New York, 1990).

Shakespeare, William, *The Complete Works*, ed. Stanley Wells and Gary Taylor, 2nd edn (Oxford, 2005).

Wells, Stanley and Sarah Stanton (eds), *The Cambridge Companion to Shakespeare on Stage* (Cambridge, 2002).

Wells, Stanley, Russell Jackson and Jonathan Bate (eds), *The Oxford Illustrated History of Shakespeare on Stage* (Oxford, 2001).

Acknowledgements

Five years of travelling, reading, watching and interviewing have left me with countless debts scattered across the world. Many of the people who helped me plot a route, or assisted me along the way, appear in these pages. Many more do not. To all, my thanks.

To the folk at the Wylie Agency, particularly Alba Ziegler-Bailey; and most of all to my agent, Sarah Chalfant, who believed in this book when many people – including its author – did not.

To the superb team at Bodley Head: Will Hammond for imaginative and thoughtful editing; Stuart Williams for commissioning the book and cheering me on; and Mary Chamberlain for gimlet-eyed copy-editing; and John Garrett for meticulous proofing.

I owe a huge debt of gratitude to Jonathan Buckley, Paul Prescott and Stanley Wells, who valiantly read the entire manuscript and contributed numerous thoughts and pointers. Thanks also to Laura Barnett and Emma Draper, both of whom read specific sections. My specialist readers, Alexa Huang, Emily Oliver, Kim C. Sturgess, Preti Taneja and Chris Thurman, generously set aside large amounts of time to read and comment on individual chapters, and have spared me multiple blushes. (Any errors and blushes that remain are my own.)

Thanks to the Society of Authors, for their generous gift of a Michael Meyer award, which helped considerably with research expenses. To Anna Cochemé, Matthew Fox, Varsha Panjwani, Robin Powell and Ashley Shen, who offered expertise with translation and transliteration from a great feast of languages. To Shonali Gajwani, who cheerfully (and accurately) transcribed many hours of tape. To Bob Dylan, who generously allowed use of lines from 'Stuck Inside of Mobile with the Memphis Blues Again'.

Aoife Monks and Louise Owen invited me to join the Centre for Contemporary Theatre at Birkbeck as an honorary fellow, which made the research process several million times easier and infinitely more enjoyable. Paul Prescott and Paul Edmondson kindly asked me to join them on a visiting fellowship at the University of Warwick, which provided valuable thinking time and enabled me to deliver some early material in lecture form.

Scholars and Shakespearians have let me bother them with damn-fool questions, or shared work in progress: Thea Buckley, Christie Carson, Koel Chatterjee, Natasha Distiller, Michael Dobson, Rachel Dwyer, Peter Holland, Tony Howard, Christa Jansohn, Adele Lee, Sonia Massai, David Schalkwyk, Ben Schofield, Emma Smith, Poonam Trivedi, René Weis and Stanley Wells.

Guardian colleagues have indulged my Shakespearian obsessions, or fed the addiction, by commissioning me to write about them: notably Lisa Allardice, Michael Billington, Melissa Denes, Lyn Gardner, Charlotte Higgins, Paul Laity, Caspar Llewellyn-Smith, Alex Needham, Alan Rusbridger, Catherine Shoard, Liese Spencer and Chris Wiegand.

Tom Bird at Shakespeare's Globe courteously allowed me to rummage through his contacts book and offered assistance at numerous points. Brian Willan responded to a fusillade of queries about Solomon Plaatje, and kindly sent me unpublished chapters of his updated biography. Matthew Hahn generously shared his play about the Robben Island Bible and transcripts of his interviews with surviving prisoners. Ruru Li went far beyond the call of duty and put me in touch with an army of Chinese Shakespearians. David Smith did similar in Johannesburg.

For kindnesses large and small: Jamie Andrews, Margaret Makepiece and Zoë Wilcox at the British Library; Rachel Aspden; Jenny Carpenter; Alisan Cole at the Shakespeare Birthplace Trust; Christopher Cook; Yaël Farber; Ben Fowler; Cathy Gomez, Rebecca Simor and Paul Smith at the British Council; Roger Granville and Corinne Jaber; Donald Howarth; Tracy Irish; Patrick Spottiswoode; Janet Suzman; Becky Vincent at the BBC.

A sizeable cast of people helped behind the scenes during my travels, either making time to speak to me or pinning down people who would.

In Poland and Germany: Jerzy Limon, Robert Florczak and everyone at the Teatr Szekspirowski, Gdańsk; Tobias Döring, Werner Habicht, Dieter Mehl and Sabine Schülting at the Deutsche Shakespeare-Gesellschaft; Manfred Koltes, Susann Leine and Ulrike Müller-Harang in Weimar; Anke Hoffsten at the NS-Dokumentationszentrum in Munich; Lars Eidinger, Annika Frahm, Thomas Ostermeier, Volker Lösch and Marius von Mayenburg at the Schaubühne, Berlin; Stephan Dörschel and Maren Horn at the Heiner Müller archive, Akademie der Künste, Berlin; Mark Espiner, Maik Hamburger, Norbert Kentrup, Ramona Mosse and Philip Oltermann in Berlin.

In the US: Juliette Swenson at Anne Hathaway's Cottage, Staunton; Ralph Cohen and Sarah Enloe at the American Shakespeare Center; Garland Scott and Georgianna Ziegler at the Folger; Michael Kahn at the Shakespeare Theatre Company, Washington DC; Marilyn Langbehn at Cal Shakes; Bill Eddelman in San Francisco; Daniel Ketcham at the Nevada County Historical Society; Pat Chesnut at the Searls Historical Library, Nevada City; Mike Hausberg and Darlene Gould Davies at the Old Globe; Mairi McLaughlin and Stewart Maclennan in LA.

In India: Nasreen Munni Kabir; Ramu Ramanathan; Tigmanshu Dhulia; Punam Sawhney at VB Pictures; Coomi Vevaina and students at Elphinstone College, Mumbai; Kunal Kapoor and Ankita at Prithvi Theatre; Shanta Gokhale, Sharat Katariya, Atul Kumar, Leo Mirani and Sunil Shanbag in Mumbai; staff at the National Film Archive of India, Pune; Anshuman Bhowick, Chandan Sen and Koushik Sen in Kolkata; Sukanta Chaudhuri and Ananda Lal at Jadavpur University, Kolkata; Samarjit Guha and Sujata Sen at the British Council in Kolkata; Amitava Roy and members of the Shakespeare Society, Eastern India; Bishnupriya Dutt and Sanjna Kapoor in Delhi; Neel Chaudhuri and Anirudh Nair at Tadpole Theatre; Poonam Trivedi and everyone at the Shakespeare Society of India.

In South Africa: Andrea Harris and David Smith; Chris Thurman; Colette Gordon; Annabell Lebethe and Malcom Purkey at the Market Theatre, Johannesburg; Marcus Mabusela and the members of Johannesburg Awakening Minds; participants in *The Julius Caesar Project* at Wits University, Johannesburg; staff and students at Mondeor High, Johannesburg; Lali Dangazele and Craig Higginson; Johan Cronje and the Sol Plaatje Educational Trust in Kimberley; Teneille Pillay and the family of Sonny Venkatrathnam; staff and students at Danville Park Girls' School, Durban; Margie Coppen in Durban; Marthinus Basson, Roy Sargeant, Pieter-Dirk Uys and Laurence Wright in Cape Town; Nolubabalo Tongo-Cetywayo at the Robben Island Museum; staff and students at Vista Nova High School, Cape Town; staff and students at Chris Hani Secondary School in Khayelitsha.

In China, Taiwan and Hong Kong: Ashley Shen; Tania Branigan and Cecily Huang; Krista Wang at the Lin Zhaohua Theatre Studio; Qiuyun Wang; Guo Qi, Huang Ying, Xie Yuti and Emily Zeng in Beijing; Xiaoying Wang at the National Theatre of China; David Li and students at UIBE in Beijing; Gary Yang, Julia Zhou and staff at Donghua University, Shanghai; Lisa Xie and Nick Yu at the Shanghai Dramatic Arts Centre; Emilie Wang at the Shanghai Grand Theatre; Stan Lai and Vanessa Yeo at the Stan Lai Performance Workshop; Wu Hsing-Kuo and Ruei Yen at Contemporary Legend Theatre, Taipei; Beatrice Lei and everyone at the Asian Shakespeare Association; Jason Gleckman and the team at the Chinese Universities Shakespeare Festival; Rupert Chan, Matthew Gregory, Tang Shu-Wing and Hardy Tsoi in Hong Kong; Ceri Sherlock and students at the Hong Kong APA.

Most of all, deep and lasting thanks to friends, for allowing me to dematerialise for months at a stretch, then putting me back together when I returned: Kirstie Beaven and Luke Youngman; Rachel and Gregg Ellman; Susanne Hillen and Jonathan Buckley; Alice Ladenburg; Sara Mohr-Pietsch; Francesca Panetta; Elizabeth Prochaska and Duncan Clark; Rana Refahi and Robin Powell; Jane Wilkinson and Joe Staines; Lyndsey Winship. And to my family, who have done the usual plus a great deal more: Jen, Dave and Gemma (and brood); my grandmother, Joan Mays; and my parents, Sue and Peter, to whom this book is dedicated, with love.

Index